THE INTERNATIONAL TRUST

THE INTERNATIONAL TRUST

Edited by John Glasson, MA, LLM
Solicitor, Consultant to Eversheds and Stuart Smalley & Co LLC,
and Editor of *International Trust Laws*

JORDANS

2002

Published by
Jordan Publishing Ltd
21 St Thomas Street
Bristol BS1 6JS

British Library Cataloguing-in-Publication Data
A catalogue record for this book is available from the British Library.

ISBN 0 85308 598 6

This book is produced in-house by Jordans
Printed in Great Britain by MPG Books Ltd, Bodmin, Cornwall

Preface

The aim of this book is to provide, in convenient single-volume form, guidance to international trust practitioners and litigators on a wide range of specialist topics.[1]

The material in this book (except for the Introduction and the final chapter) is derived from contributions to the loose-leaf encyclopaedia *International Trust Laws*.

The majority of the material has been revised over recent months. New cases discussed or referred to include:

(1) the House of Lords appeal in *Twinsectra v Yardley* [2002] UKHL 12;[2]
(2) the Jersey decision on the Pauline Action (and other issues) in the long-running *Grupo Torras* litigation;[3]
(3) the Court of Appeal's decision in *IRC v Hashmi*;[4]
(4) Lawrence Collins J's decisions in *Tod v Barton* [2002] EWHC 506 (Ch),[5] and *Chellaram (No 2)* [2002] EWHC 632.[6]

There was just time for a brief editorial note in Chapter 10 on the Guernsey appeal decision in *Stuart-Hutcheson v Spread Trustee Company Ltd*.[7]

Amendments take into account recent European developments in the field of jurisdiction and enforcement, tax recovery, and insolvency.

My thanks go to all those contributors who have revised their work for the purposes of this publication, and to the publishers, Jordans, for their continuing support.

Although this book was produced mainly with practitioners in mind, I hope that university law departments will also find the book of value.

John Glasson
Great Sutton Farm, Stanton Lacy, Ludlow, England, SY8 2AJ
glasson@harvey.sonnet.co.uk

3 September 2002

---

1 See 'Editor's Introduction' for a fuller description of this book's evolution, scheme and content.
2 [2002] 2 WLR 802.
3 Judgment of the Royal Court of Jersey of 17 January 2002: 2002/15A.
4 [2002] All ER (D) 71.
5 [2002] WTLR 469.
6 *Chellaram v Chellaram (No 2)* [2002] 3 All ER 17.
7 15 July 2002, unreported at the time of going to press.

Contents

PART 3 THE CIVIL LAW PERSPECTIVE

PART 4

APPENDIX

Table of Cases

References are to paragraph numbers.

Table of National Legislation

References are to paragraph numbers.

Bahamas *cont*

Barbados

Belize

Bermuda

Bermuda *cont*

British Virgin Islands

British Virgin Islands *cont*

Canada

Cayman Islands

Cook Islands *cont*

Cyprus

France

Germany

Gibraltar

Isle of Man *cont*

Italy

Italy *cont*

Japan

Jersey

Labuan

Liechtenstein

Mauritius

Mexico

Nauru

Netherlands

Nevis

New Zealand

Seychelles

Seychelles *cont*

International Trusts Act 1994 *cont*
s 10(2) 11.1
s 29 10.7.16
s 31 10.7.16
s 42 10.7.16

South Africa

Trust Property Control Act 1988, Act 57 of 1988 14.6
Trust Property Control Act 1998
ss 15–19 10.7.17

Spain

Civil Code 4.2.1

Sri Lanka, *see* Ceylon

Switzerland

Code civil suisse (CCS) RS 210
Arts 80–89*bis* 12.4.1
Art 335, 2 12.4.1
Art 488 12.4.1
Art 875 12.4
Code des obligations (CO) RS 220
Art 401, 3 12.4.2, 12.4.3
Arts 404, 405 12.4.2
Arts 1157–1186 12.4

Federal Statute of 18 March 1994 (RS 951.31) 12.4

Geneva Administration, Instruction No 103 (May 1977) 12.5

Loi fédérale concernant la lutte contre le blanchiment d'argent dans le secteur financier RS 955.0 (1998) 12.2
Loi fédérale sur les banques et les caisses d'épargne RS 952.0 12.4.3
art 16 12.4.3
1–3 12.4.3
art 37b 12.4.3
1–3 12.4.3
Loi fédérale sur l'harmonisation des impôts directs des cantons et des communes RS 642.14 12.5

Penal Code
Art 305 *bis*, *ter* 12.2
Private International Law Act 1987
Art 90, 2 12.2
Art 150 3.3.1, 12.2
(1) 12.2
Arts 150–165 12.2
Art 154(1) 12.2

Turks and Caicos Islands

Trusts Ordinance 1990 (No 25 of 1990) 4.6.2
s 13 4.6.2, 11.1
s 14(2) 11.1
s 20(5) 10.7.18
s 28 10.7.18
s 61 7.3.12

Voluntary Disposition Ordinance 1998 (No 14 of 1998) 7.3.12
ss 1, 2 7.3.12
s 3(1),(2) 7.3.12
s 4(1)–(5) 7.3.12
s 5 7.3.12
(2), (3) 7.3.12
(a)–(c) 7.3.12
(4)–(6) 7.3.12
(7)(1), (2) 7.3.12
s 6 7.3.12
ss 9–12 7.3.12
Sch 7.3.12

United Kingdom

Act Against Fraudulent Deeds, Gifts, Alienations etc 13 Eliz I, c 5, 1571 4.5.6, 7.2.1, 7.2.2, 7.2.3, 7.2.4, 7.3.1, 7.3.2, 7.3.4, 7.3.6, 7.3.8, 7.3.9, 7.3.10, 7.3.11, 7.3.12

United Kingdom *cont*

United Kingdom *cont*

United Kingdom *cont*

United Kingdom *cont*

United Kingdom *cont*

United States

Venezuela

Table of Conventions and EC Materials

References are to paragraph numbers.

Table of Abbreviations

References are to paragraph numbers.

2001 Revision	Trusts Law (2001 Revision) (Cayman Islands)
AA 1996	Arbitration Act 1996 (England and Wales)
AJA 1920	Administration of Justice Act 1920 (England and Wales)
Brussels Convention	Brussels Convention on Jurisdiction and the Enforcement of Judgments in Civil and Commercial Matters 1968
Brussels Regulation	Regulation on Jurisdiction and Enforcement of Judgments in Civil and Commercial Matters 2000
BTA 1992	Belize Trusts Act 1992
CA 1983	Conveyancing Act 1983 (Bermuda)
CAA 1994	Conveyancing Amendment Act 1994 (Bermuda)
CJJA 1982	Civil Jurisdiction and Judgments Act 1982 (England and Wales)
CLA 1977	Criminal Law Act 1977 (England and Wales)
CPR	Civil Procedure Rules 1998 (England and Wales)
ECJ	European Court of Justice
FDA 1991	Fraudulent Dispositions Act 1991 (Bahamas)
Hague Trusts Convention	Hague Convention on the Law Applicable to Trusts and on their Recognition 1985
IA 1986	Insolvency Act 1986 (England and Wales)
IMTA 1995	Isle of Man's Trust Act 1995
ITA 1984	International Trusts Act 1984 (Cook Islands)
ITL 1992	International Trusts Law 1992 (Cyprus)
LOTA 1996	Labuan Offshore Trusts Act 1996

Lugano Convention	Lugano Convention on Jurisdiction and Enforcement of Judgments in Civil and Commercial Matters 1998
RHC	Rules of the High Court 1952 (Isle of Man)
STAR legislation	Special Trusts (Alternative Regime) Law 1997 (Cayman Islands)
STEP	Society of Trusts and Estate Planners
TA 1992	Trusts Act 1992 (Belize)
TAA 1993	Trustee (Amendment) Act 1993 (No 7 of 1993) (British Virgin Islands)
TCGLA 1989	Trusts (Choice of Governing Law) Act 1989 (Bahamas)
TFEL 1987	Trusts (Foreign Element) Law 1987 (Cayman Islands)
TGL 1989	Trusts (Guernsey) Law 1989
TJL 1984	Trusts (Jersey) Law 1984
TO 1990	Trusts Ordinance 1990 (Turks and Caicos Islands)
TSPA 1989	Trusts (Special Provisions) Act 1989 (Bermuda)
TSPAA 1998	Trusts (Special Provisions) Amendment Act 1998 (Bermuda)
Worldwide Judgments Convention	Hague Convention on Jurisdiction and the Recognition and Enforcement of Judgments in Civil and Commercial Matters

Editor's Introduction

THE PHENOMENON OF THE INTERNATIONAL TRUST

John Glasson

INTERNATIONAL TRUSTS

The expression 'international trust' has no settled definition, although it is in common use.[1] Generally speaking, the term is applied to a trust that has a connection of legal significance with two or more countries, typically where:

- a settlor from country A creates a trust governed by the law of country B (the 'offshore' trust being a prime example);
- a trust governed by the law of country A holds or claims property in country B (or in countries B and C);
- a trust governed by the law of country A has a trustee resident in country B.

Until the 1960s, international trusts were rarely encountered. They are now commonplace – partly because of the increased mobility of people and property, but mostly because of the growth of the offshore trust industry.

THE OFFSHORE TRUST INDUSTRY

'Offshore' conventionally describes any jurisdiction whose trust services are promoted abroad. Although the typical offshore centre is a small island, geographical description has become immaterial. Thus, Panama, Liechtenstein,

1 'Practitioners and now writers are using the term with confidence' – Donovan Waters QC, Chapter 14, p 598.

and, nowadays, New Zealand[1] can all be termed 'offshore'. Offshore jurisdictions currently number about 30.[2]

In the offshore centres, trust legislation is generally seen as a marketing aid, and it appears with great regularity. In some cases, the aim of offshore legislation is simply to modernise or clarify trust law. Often, however, it offers a particular facility thought to be attractive to foreign settlors, eg the ability to use a trust to help protect assets against claims from heirs[3] or (more controversially) from creditors,[4] or to establish a trust to further non-charitable purposes.[5]

The offshore trust world sometimes faces criticism for bad or sloppy practices – especially failing to pay due attention to basic legal requirements when a trust is being created or administered.[6] However, these shortcomings are far from universal and, where they exist, seem likely to be addressed by the industry's increasing commitment to training.[7]

More historically significant is the way in which the offshore industry has sought to adapt the private trust for use in today's international and commercial environment, generating in the process unprecedented academic and practitioner attention.[8]

CONFLICT OF LAWS

By their nature, international trusts give rise to questions that need to be decided by the application of rules of conflict of laws – questions such as:

- which law or laws determine whether a valid trust has been created?
- which law or laws govern the interpretation and the administration of the trust?
- the courts of which countries can exercise jurisdiction over the trust?
- when will a court of one country recognise a trust governed by the law of another country?
- when will a court of one country give effect to a trust judgment delivered in another country?

---

1 Listed among offshore financial centres in the *OFC Report 2002* (Campden Publishing, 2002).

2 For digests of trust law in a wide range of offshore jurisdictions, and statutory texts, see Glasson (ed) *International Trust Laws* (Jordans, loose-leaf).

3 See Chapter 4.

4 See Chapter 7.

5 See Chapter 6, which includes discussion of the conceptually innovative Special Trusts (Alternative Regime) Law 1997 (the STAR legislation).

6 See, particularly, Wadham *Willoughby's Misplaced Trust* (Gostick Hall Publications, 2nd ed, 2002).

7 As evidenced by the initiatives of the Society of Trust and Estate Planners (STEP) and its overseas branches.

8 In this work, see the discussion of specific offshore statutes in various chapters, and the more general consideration in Chapter 14.

As will be seen from Part 1 of this book, identifying the conflict-of-laws rule to apply in a particular case is not always straightforward, although sometimes the process is helped by the existence of an international Convention[1] or regulation,[2] or a statute on conflict of laws specific to a jurisdiction.

In the offshore jurisdictions, legislation on conflict-of-laws issues resulting from trusts has become routine.[3]

LOOKING AHEAD

The future of international trust practice is far from certain. An immediate concern is the pressure for more offshore regulation.[4] A more fundamental problem is the risk of trusts, or their consequences, not being fully recognised in places that do not have a trust law, particularly in parts of the civil law and Moslem worlds.[5]

Recent offshore initiatives[6] have triggered debate over where the limits of the trust concept lie. The debate is certain to continue as practitioners devise new uses for the trust to meet contemporary requirements. A century ago Frederick Maitland famously spoke of the elasticity of the trust;[7] today's concern is to discover the point at which the elastic snaps.

During the formative years of the trust (then the 'use') the Lord Chancellor was prepared to uphold any directions to trustees that, in the words of the historian Sir William Holdsworth,[8] 'were not positively illegal'. Arguing from this, it could be said that theoretical concepts of what a trust is, and is not, should not be allowed to hold back its development. However, there are dangers of having a trust concept with no discernible shape – particularly in the context of recognition of the trust in civil law and Moslem jurisdictions. As Professor Waters warns in the final chapter of this book,[9] the trust 'will seem to other legal systems to be but a jumble of ideas without focus'.

---

1 Particularly the Hague Convention on the Law Applicable to Trusts and on their Recognition 1985 (the Hague Trusts Convention), discussed in Chapter 3, and the Brussels and Lugano Conventions on Jurisdiction and the Enforcement of Commercial Matters (respectively 1968 and 1988), discussed in Chapter 1.

2 For example, the new 'Brussels Regulation' on jurisdiction and enforcement, discussed in Chapter 1.

3 Stimulated and influenced in large measure by the Cayman Islands 1987 legislation in this field drafted by Antony Duckworth.

4 Pressure which, to date, shows a lack of complete understanding of the trust concept.

5 See Chapter 14. See also Chapters 12 and 13 as to recognition of the trust in Switzerland and Italy.

6 Especially the STAR legislation, discussed in Chapter 6.

7 See collected lectures in *Equity and Forms of Action* (Cambridge University Press, 1913), p 23.

8 Holdsworth *An Historical Introduction to the Land Law* (Oxford University Press, 1935), p 149.

9 See p 614. Concern over the width of the definition of 'trust' in the Hague Trusts Convention, on an arguable construction, is discussed in Chapter 3, at **3.2.4**, 'The "shapeless" trust'.

THE EVOLUTION OF THIS BOOK

In 1991 the loose-leaf encyclopaedia *International Trust Laws*[1] was published. The work has been updated and expanded twice yearly since then.

The main purpose of *International Trust Laws* was to provide digests of the trust laws of a wide range of jurisdictions (including offshore centres) together with statutory source material. However, an important supplementary purpose was to build up over a period of years a series of studies of international trust topics – topics that had received relatively little attention in the legal press.

On its first appearance *International Trust Laws* covered four topics. By 2001 the number had risen to 12. The work also now contained contributions on trusts from the perspective of two civil law countries – Italy and Switzerland. It was felt by both editor and publishers of *International Trust Laws* that the time had come to make this material more widely and conveniently available by publishing it in this present volume.

Fortuitously, just before going to press, Professor Donovan Waters had completed a thought-provoking paper on the future of the trust from a worldwide perspective. This paper, with some revision, has been included as the book's final chapter.

SCHEME AND CONTENT

The book is divided into four parts.

Part 1 – Chapters 1 to 3 – is concerned with conflict of laws in relation to trusts.

In Chapter 1, Professor Jonathan Harris discusses issues of jurisdiction and enforcement; issues which in an ideal world should be taken into consideration both when a trust is created and during its administration.

In Chapter 2, the same author considers 'rocket launching' issues in relation to trusts, ie the preliminary issues which need to be satisfactorily dealt with before the trust 'rocket' gets off the ground.

Chapter 3, by Professor David Hayton, deals with international recognition of trusts (including issues of applicable law) both inside and outside the Hague Trusts Convention.

Part 2 – Chapters 4 to 11 – covers a variety of topics of practical importance to international trust practitioners. Further details are given in the Introduction to Part 2.

---

1 See n 2 on p 2.

Part 3 – Chapters 12 and 13 – looks at trusts from the civil law perspective, focusing on Switzerland (which has not ratified the Hague Trusts Convention) and Italy (which has). The authors are, for Switzerland, Professor Alfred von Overbeck, and, for Italy, Ferdinando Albisinni and Regina Gambino.

Part 4 – Chapter 14 – comprises the material already mentioned on the future of the trust by Professor Donovan Waters.

PART 1

Trusts and the Conflict of Laws

Chapter 1

JURISDICTION AND THE ENFORCEMENT OF FOREIGN JUDGMENTS IN TRANSNATIONAL TRUSTS LITIGATION

*Jonathan Harris**

1.1 INTRODUCTION

The jurisdiction of a court to determine a dispute of a transnational nature is a subject of critical importance. Choosing the appropriate forum in which to sue (often referred to as 'forum shopping') can have numerous advantages, aside from pure convenience. There may be substantial differences in the procedures used in courts of different countries and varying interim measures available; the law to be applied on the substance may differ; and the judgment may be more or less easily enforceable in other countries, depending upon where it was delivered. Indeed, a claimant who seeks to enforce a judgment in England might in some cases be better advised to sue overseas and claim enforcement in England rather than to subject himself to unfavourable laws which would be applied directly were the case to be heard in England.

Nor should it always be assumed that the party allegedly in breach is powerless to dictate the forum. There may be powerful remedies available to him to ensure that litigation occurs in his preferred forum, such as seeking a declaration of non-liability before he is sued, or an injunction restraining proceedings against him overseas.

The law in this field is highly complex and rapidly evolving. In England, two principal sets of jurisdictional rules exist: the harmonised rules contained in the relevant European Regulation (and Conventions) and the common law. It is indisputable that the European harmonised rules are now the first point

* Professor of International Commercial Law, University of Birmingham, Birmingham. The author would like to thank Philip C Dunkley of Higgs and Johnson, Christopher McKenzie of Harney Westwood & Riegels, Martine Fleming of Stuart Smalley & Co and Edward Davenport of Mourand de Feu & Jeune, who kindly provided primary materials relating to the offshore jurisdictions respectively of the Bahamas, the British Virgin Islands, the Isle of Man and Jersey.

of reference. The application of the common law rules is residual. Moreover, it is critical to appreciate that the European harmonised rules do not apply only to disputes between domiciliaries of Member States. In civil or commercial matters,[1] the European rules will apply if the defendant is domiciled in a Member State and even, in some cases, when neither party is domiciled in Europe. Hence, the following examples would be governed by the European harmonised rules and not the common law, were it sought to bring the claim in the English courts:

- an action for breach of contract brought by a US domiciliary against an English domiciliary;
- a dispute between a Brazilian and an Argentinian domiciliary relating to title to land in England.

Conversely, the following examples would be governed by the common law:

- a breach of trust claim brought by an English domiciliary against a US domiciliary in relation to assets held in Switzerland;
- a negligence action brought by an English domiciliary against a Brazilian domiciliary following an accident occurring in Paris.

Moreover, the rules on recognition and enforcement of a foreign judgment differ depending on whether the European rules, other statutory schemes or the common law rules apply. The difference can be critical; it is of little use to secure a judgment overseas against a defendant who holds all his assets in England, if the English courts will not enforce the judgment. Yet whilst the European harmonised rules on enforcement are extremely liberal, the common law rules are almost equally restrictive.

Once again, the scheme which should be applied is not necessarily that which one would instinctively think. The European rules will apply to all judgments delivered in a Member State in a civil or commercial matter, *however* the court took jurisdiction. Hence, an English judgment in relation to an alleged breach of trust will be subject to the European rules, even if the court took jurisdiction on the basis of its common law rules; conversely, a French judgment in divorce proceedings will not be entitled to recognition in England under the European rules.

The present concern is with litigation which might arise in relation to transnational trusts disputes. In this context, it is essential not to be lured into an obvious trap. It is tempting to look only for provisions which contain the word 'trusts' and to assume that these are the only bases of jurisdiction.

1 Falling within Art 1 of the Regulation on Jurisdiction and the Recognition and Enforcement of Judgments in Civil and Commercial Matters 2000 or the Lugano Convention on Jurisdiction and the Enforcement of Judgments in Civil and Commercial Matters 1998 (the Lugano Convention), as amended.

However, it is in the nature of transnational litigation that disputes which might not succeed by English domestic law can none the less be brought in an English court. Accordingly, there may sometimes need to be a special *private international law meaning* of certain terms. This point can be illustrated by a simple example. Suppose D (a Brazilian domiciliary) and C (an English domiciliary) entered into an agreement yesterday to be governed by Utopian law, whereby D agrees to pay C £50 for cutting his grass last week. By Utopian, but not by English, law there is a binding contract. It would be extraordinary if an English court did not include this claim within its definition of contractual obligations for jurisdictional purposes, if C sought to sue D in England for non-payment.

This applies to *a fortiori* to equitable obligations, which are largely unknown throughout the rest of Europe, but which it might be possible to equate to jurisdictional provisions which deal solely with matters relating to contract and tort in a *private international law* sense. The possibility that, for example, the liability of a fiduciary to account for profits might be classified for jurisdictional purposes as contractual, or that a claim for knowing receipt of trust property or knowing assistance in breach of trust should be seen as tortious, should not be ignored.

This chapter examines the rules relating to jurisdiction and the enforcement of foreign judgments as they may affect commercial[1] transnational *inter vivos* trust litigation and related equitable claims which might ensue.[2] It looks primarily at the law in England, but also at the position in certain offshore jurisdictions. It also considers the availability of interim relief, certain remedies to ensure the effectiveness of international litigation, such as the asset freezing order (formerly known as the *Mareva* injunction), and the law of international arbitration. Discussion is limited to claims brought *in personam*. The examination of the law in other jurisdictions is kept somewhat briefer. This can readily be justified: the European rules considered dominate the law of jurisdiction and enforcement throughout the major commercial European jurisdictions; and the common law rules are the inspiration behind the laws which continue to apply in many offshore jurisdictions.

---

1 An EC Regulation on jurisdiction and enforcement of foreign judgments in matters of divorce proceedings and parental responsibility for joint children has recently been adopted: see Regulation EC 1347/2000 (2000) OJ L 160/19. The UK has opted into the initiative. There is also a recently adopted Regulation on cross-border insolvency, which the UK also opted into: see Regulation EC 1346/2000 (2000) OJ L 160/1.

2 More detailed discussion can be found in certain standard works, such as A Briggs and P Rees *Civil Jurisdiction and Judgments* (LLY Limited, 2nd ed, 1997); Cheshire and North *Private International Law* (Butterworths, 13th ed, 1999); L Collins (ed) *Dicey and Morris on the Conflict of Laws* (Sweet & Maxwell, 13th ed, 2000); Hartley *Civil Jurisdiction and Judgments* (1984); Kaye *Law of the European Judgments Convention* (1999); S O'Malley and A Layton *European Civil Practice* (Sweet & Maxwell, 1989). All will always merit consultation for more detailed discussion; however, for ease of reference, this chapter will refer solely to the provisions in Briggs and Rees.

1.2 JURISDICTION UNDER THE EUROPEAN REGIME

1.2.1 Introduction

The Regulation on Jurisdiction and the Recognition and Enforcement of Judgments in Civil and Commercial Matters 2000 (the Brussels Regulation)[1] provides a set of uniform jurisdictional rules for European Member States.[2] It entered into force on 1 March 2002. The Regulation has largely superseded the rules previously contained in successive versions of the Brussels Convention on Jurisdiction and the Enforcement of Judgments in Civil and Commercial Matters (the Brussels Convention). The Regulation is directly effective in the Member States.

The Brussels Regulation has been made possible by the inclusion of private international law matters within the first pillar of European Community law by virtue of the Treaty of Amsterdam.[3] This inserted a new Art 65 into the EC Treaty, which applies to judicial co-operation in civil matters having cross-border implications, insofar as it is necessary for the completion of the internal market.[4] This means that other future European initiatives in the field of private international law can take the form of a Regulation (or Directive).[5] The United Kingdom and Ireland are permitted to opt out from initiatives made pursuant to Art 65; this clause is contained in Arts 1 and 2 of the Protocol on the position of the United Kingdom and Ireland.[6] However, the United Kingdom has opted into the Brussels Regulation.[7] Denmark also has an opt-out clause but has decided not to adopt the Regulation. Accordingly, it will continue to apply the Brussels Convention.

The Brussels Regulation does more than simply change the nature of the instrument in which the relevant rules are contained. It also contains a significant number of substantive changes to the rules of jurisdiction and enforcement of foreign judgments.

---

1 Regulation (EC) No 44/2001 of 22 December 2000 (2001) OJ L 12/1.

2 With the exception of Denmark, to which the Brussels Convention still applies.

3 It is also important to note that an EC Regulation on the service of judicial and extra-judicial documents overseas has recently been adopted; see Regulation EC 1348/2000 (2000) OJ L 160/37.

4 See P Beaumont 'Current Developments: EC Law' (1999) 48 ICLQ 225.

5 Substantial advances have already been made in this respect, such as Regulation EC 1348/2000 of 29 May 2000 on the Service in the Member States of Judicial and Extra-judicial Documents in Civil or Commercial Matters (2000) OJ L 160/37, Regulation EC 1347/2000 of 29 May 2000 on Jurisdiction and Recognition and Enforcement of Judgments in Matrimonial Matters and in Matters of Parental Responsibility for Children of Both Spouses (2000) OJ L 160/19 and Regulation (EC) No 1346/2000 of 29 May 2000 on Insolvency Proceedings (2000) OJ L 160/1.

6 Article 69 preserves the Protocol on the position of the United Kingdom and Ireland (for the text of which, see (1997) OJ C 340/99).

7 And has opted back into other initiatives such as the Regulations on: Service in the Member States of Judicial and Extra-Judicial Documents in Civil or Commercial Matters; the Jurisdiction and Recognition and Enforcement of Judgments in Matrimonial Matters and in Matters of Parental Responsibility for Children of Both Spouses; and Insolvency Proceedings.

The Regulation's ultimate aim is to secure the free and easy mutual recognition and enforcement of foreign judgments. It is thought that this can most easily be secured if each state recognises the same bases for taking jurisdiction, since the fear that a state will exercise jurisdiction in an inappropriate case will be alleviated.[1] Ultimately, the free flow of judgments may be seen as promoting the fundamental freedoms safeguarded by European law.

The jurisdictional rules of the Brussels Regulation are very detailed and, in contrast to the common law, provide very little scope for the exercise of discretion by the courts of a Member State with jurisdiction as to whether to exercise it. Being in origin a European text, it is unsafe to assume that terms with which an English lawyer might be familiar in a domestic context bear the same meaning for Convention purposes.

The European Court of Justice (ECJ) has jurisdiction to interpret the Brussels Regulation.[2] Member States' courts must reach their decisions in accordance with prior ECJ rulings and take judicial notice thereof.[3]

Prior to the entry into force of the Brussels Regulation on 1 March 2002, the European harmonised jurisdictional rules were contained in Conventions. Those Conventions have official commentaries, to which English courts are entitled to refer. The ECJ was guided, but not bound, by these commentaries. It is likely that these commentaries will still be of persuasive force in respect of substantive matters left unchanged in the Brussels Regulation.

1.2.2 The Brussels Regulation and the Brussels and Lugano Conventions: which scheme applies?

The Brussels Regulation will apply to questions of jurisdiction arising between European Member States in respect of proceedings instituted after 1 March 2002. In England, proceedings are 'instituted' for these purposes on the date on which process was issued, not the date on which the defendant was served with a claim form.[4]

The one exception is in the case of jurisdictional disputes between Denmark and one or more other European Member States. As the Brussels Regulation does not apply to Denmark, an English court must continue to

---

1 Although this is not quite true, since sometimes states are free to apply their national jurisdictional rules pursuant to Art 4 – see below.

2 Under the Brussels Convention, such authority is given to the ECJ by the Civil Jurisdiction and Judgments Act 1982 (CJJA 1982), Sch 2. However, under the Brussels Regulation, this Schedule will not be required, since the Regulation is directly effective in Member States and a court may request a reference pursuant to EC Treaty, Art 234.

3 This requirement (which is self-evident now under the Brussels Regulation) was stated in respect of the Brussels Convention in CJJA 1982, s 3.

4 *Canada Trust Co v Stolzenberg (No 2)* [2000] 3 WLR 1376.

apply the Brussels Convention to such jurisdictional disputes.[1] It must do likewise to the recognition and enforcement of Danish judgments in England. Of course, the Brussels Convention must also be applied to any proceedings instituted in England before 1 March 2002 involving any European Union Member State.

There exists also a parallel Convention to the Brussels Convention, concluded at Lugano on 16 April 1988 (the Lugano Convention).[2] The Lugano Convention applies between European Union Member States and certain European Union non-Member States.[3] Today, the Lugano Convention must still be applied in an English court to jurisdictional disputes between Member States and Iceland, Norway, Poland[4] and Switzerland.

1.2.3 Intra-United Kingdom jurisdiction disputes

The Brussels Regulation will often allocate jurisdiction specifically to the English courts, for example, where the parties submit to those courts, or a contractual obligation is to be performed in London. However, at other points jurisdiction is merely allocated to the courts of the United Kingdom. It is then a matter for UK law to determine the particular country within the United Kingdom in which the case may be heard. The relevant provisions are contained in the Civil Jurisdiction and Judgments Act 1982 (CJJA 1982) and in Sch 4 to the Act.[5] Since the Regulation's work is done once jurisdiction has been handed to the UK courts, it follows that the United Kingdom may apply its common law rules to permit a stay of proceedings, for example, in England in favour of the courts of Scotland.

Where a jurisdictional dispute is wholly intra-UK, for example, between a Scottish and English domiciliary, the Brussels Regulation will not apply at all and the ECJ will have no interpretative jurisdiction. In a civil or commercial matter,[6] Sch 4 to the CJJA 1982 will determine jurisdiction. However, the intra-UK jurisdiction rules are similar, although not identical, to the Brussels Regulation, and will generally be interpreted in accordance with the ECJ's interpretations of the latter.[7]

---

1 The most recent text of the Convention (which has been modified several times) can be found in the Civil Jurisdiction and Judgments Act 1982 (Amendment) Order 2000 (SI 2000/1824). This version of the Convention came into force on 1 January 2001. The version of the Convention which was in force at the time of the United Kingdom's accession to the Convention can be found in CJJA 1982, Sch 1.

2 See CJJA 1982, Sch 3C, inserted by CJJA 1991, Sch 1. The European Commission has adopted a recommendation for a Council Decision to adopt a new version of the Lugano Convention. This will bring the substantive provisions of the Lugano Convention into line with those of the Brussels Regulation.

3 The ECJ does not have jurisdictional competence to interpret the Lugano Convention.

4 Poland joined the Lugano scheme on 1 August 2000: see SI 2000/1824, n 1 above.

5 As amended by Civil Jurisdiction and Judgments Order 2001 (SI 2001/3929), Sch 2.

6 CJJA 1982, s 16.

7 See *Kleinwort Benson Ltd v City of Glasgow District Council* [1995] ECR I-615, ECJ; [1999] 1 AC 153, HL.

1.2.4 Scope of discussion

The following discussion in this chapter will speak solely of the Brussels Regulation. Readers should be aware of the possibility of differences should the Brussels or Lugano Convention apply.

Note that the relevant cases referred to in this discussion will have been decided on the basis of the Brussels Convention.

1.2.5 Interpretative methodology

It is vital to resist the temptation to construe the Brussels Regulation by English tools of construction. Almost all terms are to be given a uniform, European autonomous interpretation and are not to be interpreted in the light of idiosyncrasies of national law, except for matters of pure procedure and evidence, which are governed by the rules of the court in question and upon which the Brussels Regulation does not directly impact.[1]

1.2.6 A hierarchical system

The Brussels Regulation rules are not highly approachable. However, Briggs and Rees show that a series of hierarchical questions arise.[2] The correct approach is to continue along the chain until a head of jurisdiction is found. Although discussion will focus primarily on those bases which could conceivably relate to trusts litigation, it is vital to understand how these bases fit into the overall scheme.

It should be noted that the cornerstone of the Brussels Regulation is that jurisdiction should rest in the courts of the defendant's domicile. Questions 2 to 8 represent exceptions to that principle. As such, the ECJ has frequently reiterated that these exceptions should be construed narrowly.[3] The first question to be considered is (1) below.

(1) Is the dispute within the Regulation? (Art 1)

Article 1 determines the boundaries of the Brussels Regulation. Once a matter is within Art 1, it is *ex hypothesi* within the Regulation and jurisdiction is taken pursuant thereto, even if the Regulation ultimately determines that the English court should apply its common law rules on jurisdiction. The result is that a judgment delivered will fall within the Regulation recognition and enforcement rules.

Article 1 states that the Brussels Regulation applies to civil or commercial matters. In order to ensure the uniform application of the Regulation, these

---

1 *Kongress Agentur Hagen GmbH v Zeehaghe BV* [1990] ECR I-1845. However, there is now a definition of when a court is seised for the purposes of the Regulation, contained in Art 30.

2 Note 2 on p 11, pp 16–17.

3 See, eg, *Reichert v Dresdner Bank* [1990] ECR I-27; *Kalfelis v Bankhaus Schröder* [1988] ECR 5565; *Marinari v Lloyds Bank plc* [1995] ECR I-2719.

terms have a European autonomous meaning. However, no definition of the terms has been given, and their meaning can be discerned only by looking at decided cases. In *LTU Lufttransportunternehmen GmbH & Co KG v Eurocontrol*,[1] a body regulating civilian air traffic collected a compulsory levy from users of its services. It sued Lufthansa in Belgium for non-payment. The ECJ held that the matter was not civil or commercial, within the European autonomous meaning, since it sought to enforce public law rights. It matters not that the national court would see the matter as civil or commercial, if it does not fall within the Community definition.[2] In *Sonntag v Waidmann*,[3] due to a German schoolteacher's apparent negligence, a pupil was killed on a school trip. The parents sued for damages and the schoolteacher contended that as a state employee he did not owe ordinary private law duties. The ECJ held that although the insurance cover was provided under a public scheme, the damages claim was a civil or commercial one and the standards of care in German law were not special simply because the schoolteacher was a public employee. In other words, duties must be peculiarly public in nature, as well as in origin, to fall within Art 1.

As well as excluding 'revenue, customs or administrative matters', the following are also specifically excluded from the Brussels Regulation by Art 1.

(1) *The status or legal capacity of natural persons, rights in property arising out of a matrimonial relationship, wills and succession.* Hence, divorce proceedings and other family law matters would fall outside the Regulation. However, in *Van den Boogaard v Laumen*,[4] the ECJ held that whilst an order to divide property between spouses was one concerning the distribution of matrimonial property and excluded from the Brussels Regulation by Art 1, an order made to enable a spouse to provide for him or herself would be a matter concerned with maintenance, and hence a civil or commercial matter within the meaning of Art 1 of the Brussels Regulation.[5] The dividing line is a thin one, but the relevant question is to determine the primary concern of the proceedings.

(2) *Bankruptcy, proceedings relating to the winding up of insolvent companies or other legal person, judicial arrangements, compositions and analogous proceedings.* This is subject to an autonomous meaning.[6] It would seem that the claim must be peculiar to the law of bankruptcy. Hence, an action by a trustee in bankruptcy to recover property from a third party was held

---

1 [1976] ECR 1541.

2 *Netherlands v Rüffer* [1980] ECR 3807.

3 [1993] ECR I-1963.

4 [1997] ECR I-1147.

5 Indeed there is even a basis of special jurisdiction in relation to maintenance orders which is contained in Art 5(2).

6 *Gourdain v Nadler* [1979] ECR 733.

in *Re Hayward (Deceased)*[1] not to be covered by this exclusion, since the action for recovery depended not on the law of bankruptcy, but on ordinary principles of ownership.

(3) *Social security*. The public law nature of this area justifies its exclusion. The provision has proved unproblematic to date.

(4) *Arbitration*. This is examined below. All aspects of the arbitration process are excluded. The major point of controversy is where one party denies the existence or validity of an arbitration agreement. In such a case, can a court interpret the alleged agreement to determine whether it is valid? In *Marc Rich & Co AG v Società Italiana Impianti PA*,[2] the court answered this question in the negative. The result is counter-intuitive, in that a court may not examine the limits of its jurisdictional competence in this instance. It may safely be said that this issue has not been resolved beyond doubt.

If the dispute does not fall within the boundaries of the Brussels Regulation, the Regulation will be inapplicable. If the matter falls within the Regulation, then (2) below should be considered.

(2) Does any other Regulation exist to which the Member States are, or will be, parties and which governs jurisdiction and/or the enforcement of foreign judgments? (Art 71)

Article 71(1) provides that:

> 'this Regulation shall not affect any conventions to which the Member States are parties and which in relation to particular matters, govern jurisdiction or the recognition or enforcement of judgments'.[3]

However, the Regulation does not provide (as did Art 57(1) of the Brussels Convention) that states may enter into new Conventions after the entry into force of the Regulation. It appears that the European institutions will henceforth have an exclusive competence to act on behalf of their Member States in negotiation of international treaties concerning subject matter falling within the scope of the Brussels Regulation.[4]

The most important Conventions which might interact with the Brussels Regulation in this context are maritime Conventions, namely the Arrest

---

1 [1997] Ch 45; see J Harris 'Rights *in rem* and the Brussels Convention' (1997) 22 EL Rev 179.

2 [1991] ECR I-3855.

3 Note also that Art 67 states that the Regulation does not prejudice the application of Community instruments (or national legislation harmonised pursuant to such instruments) dealing with jurisdiction and the recognition and enforcement of foreign judgments in specific matters.

4 This will be especially significant in relation to the proposed Hague Convention on Jurisdiction and the Recognition and Enforcement of Judgments in Civil and Commercial Matters ('the Worldwide Judgments Convention'). See the discussion of this draft Convention below.

Convention 1952 and the Collision Convention 1952. Detailed examination of these is not required here.

If no other Regulation is applicable, then (3) below should be considered.

(3) Do the courts of any Member State have exclusive jurisdiction regardless of the defendant's domicile? (Art 22)

This is of critical importance in the trusts context. If a dispute relating to trusts is none the less caught by the exclusive jurisdiction provisions, jurisdiction rests solely in the courts identified. The relevant provisions are contained in Art 22, of which only one provision is of great importance in the present context. This is Art 22(1), which provides that jurisdiction shall rest in the following courts:

> 'in proceedings which have as their object rights *in rem* in immovable property or tenancies of immovable property, the court of the Member State in which the property is situated.'

This will apply even if neither party is domiciled in a Member State. No other court can take jurisdiction, even if the parties have designated it by a choice of court agreement or the defendant is willing to submit to it.

Rights in rem – trusts of land

Trusts of land are particularly problematic. The courts have had to determine whether, for the purposes of a European Regulation, a claim to beneficial entitlement concerns a right *in rem*. The conclusions are somewhat surprising.[1]

In *Webb v Webb*,[2] an English farmer bought land in France in the name of his son. Some 20 years later they fell out and the father sought to sue the son in England, claiming equitable ownership on the basis of a resulting trust. The son claimed that the case should be heard instead in France, where the land was situated, as it fell within Art 22(1)(a). The ECJ, in a wholly unconvincing judgment, disagreed. It found that the father did not seek to exercise rights *in rem* because: (a) he went to court saying he did not have legal ownership but that he should be made owner; and (b) an equitable interest was held not to be a right *in rem*. However, if the claim is to assert a property right, even if one is not yet vested in the claimant, it is difficult to see why (a) should be material. As to (b), whilst this might reflect the historical origins of equitable rights, given that they are enforceable against all but a *bona fide* purchaser for value without notice, it seems absurd to treat them as purely personal.

---

1 J Harris, n 7 on p 16.

2 [1994] ECR I-1717.

The decision sits especially uncomfortably with the English case of *Re Hayward (Deceased)*,[1] in which Rattee J held that a claim by a trustee in bankruptcy to a half-interest in immovable property in Minorca fell within the exclusive jurisdiction provisions, since the primary purpose of the action was to assert proprietary rights. *Webb* was distinguished on the basis that the trustee sought legal title to be transferred to him under Spanish law and this was a genuine property right. Yet it seems indefensible to distinguish legal and equitable title in this manner. The result is that one who claims absolute ownership may be able to evade Art 22(1)(a) by claiming only equitable entitlement and then subsequently invoking the right to terminate the trust under the *Saunders v Vautier*[2] principle.

Tenancies

Tenancies are of less importance in the present context. However, they will be of significance where a tenancy is itself held on trust. The cases indicate that Art 22(1)(a) covers only genuine landlord/tenant disputes and not all questions that may arise from an agreement to let.

In *Sanders v Van der Putte*,[3] a dispute arose as to a provision in a lease under which the tenant undertook to run the landlord's business from the premises. The ECJ held that this did not fall within Art 22(1)(a), as although it was a covenant in a lease, the obligation could have been found in any contract and was not peculiar to land law. Moreover, Art 22 was to be construed restrictively, as it deprived the defendant of the right to defend himself in his home courts.

In contrast, *Rösler v Rottwinkel*[4] concerned two Germans litigating in relation to a holiday letting in Italy. The dispute centred around possession, repair, rent and utility charges. It was held that this was a claim to enforce common covenants in a lease and hence a genuine landlord/tenant dispute falling within Art 22(1)(a).[5]

Rösler was a particularly unsatisfactory case, in that two Germans were forced to litigate a short-term letting overseas. To counter this problem, Art 22(1)(b) was introduced, which provides that where the tenancy is for temporary private use for a maximum period of six consecutive months, the claimant may choose between suing in the courts of the situs of the property and those of the defendant's domicile.[6]

---

1 Note 7 on p 16. See also *Ashurst v Pollard* [2001] Ch 595; J Harris 'Ordering the Sale of Land Situated Overseas' [2001] LMCLQ 205.

2 (1841) 4 Beav 115. This assumes that the trust is governed by English law.

3 [1977] ECR 2383.

4 [1985] ECR 99.

5 See also *Hacker v Euro-Relais GmbH* [1992] ECR I-1111; *Dansommer A/S v Götz* [2000] ECR I-393; *Gaillard v Chekili* [2001] ECR I-2771.

6 'Provided that the tenant is a natural persons and that the landlord and tenant are domiciled in the same Member State.'

Other bases of exclusive jurisdiction

The only other potentially relevant head of exclusive jurisdiction in the trusts context is Art 22(3), which grants exclusive jurisdiction where a dispute concerns entry in a public register to the courts of the place where the register is kept. *Re Hayward (Deceased)* (see above) was a case which also fell under this provision, since the claimant also sought to have the register overseas rectified.

If no other courts of a Member State have exclusive jurisdiction regardless of domicile, then (4) below should be considered.

(4) Will the defendant submit to the courts of a Member State? (Art 24)

If Art 22 is inapplicable, the courts of any state before which the defendant will appear may take jurisdiction, even if the parties have previously agreed to litigate elsewhere. The defendant will not be taken as submitting where his appearance is solely to contest jurisdiction.[1] Indeed, given that a Regulation judgment will generally be freely enforceable in other Member States, tactically a defendant is well advised to object to jurisdictional competence in the overseas forum when the Regulation applies and must be free to do so. In *Établissement Rohr Société anonyme v Ossberger*,[2] local procedure forced the defendant to make his defence on the merits at the same time as contesting jurisdiction. The ECJ ruled that a defendant who filed a defence on the merits at the same time as contesting jurisdiction had not submitted, as long as he objected to jurisdiction at the first available opportunity. Hence, in *Elefanten Schuh GmbH v Jacqmain*,[3] where the defendant entered a defence on the merits and a year later objected to jurisdiction, he was deemed to have submitted.

If the defendant will not submit to the courts of a Member State, then (5) below should be considered.

(5) Do the insurance contract provisions apply? (Arts 8–14)

An insurance holder is treated as a weaker party and worthy of special protection, so is given a wide choice of where to sue by Arts 8–14. By contrast, the insurer is given very little protection. These provisions need not detain us in the present context. Choice of court agreements is permitted by Art 13 only in restricted circumstances.

If the insurance contract provisions do not apply, then (6) below should be considered.

---

1 This is expressly stated in Art 24. In England, such a contest must be made pursuant to Civil Procedure Rules 1998 (CPR) Part 11.

2 [1981] ECR 2431.

3 [1981] ECR 1671.

(6) Do the consumer contract provisions apply? (Arts 15–17)

A consumer is also considered to be a weaker party and it is thought appropriate to protect him more extensively. Article 16(1) allows the consumer to sue in his own state's courts or those of the other party, if there is a contract of the type specified in Art 15. Article 17 limits the circumstances in which a jurisdiction clause can grant jurisdiction elsewhere, the concern being that otherwise the more powerful contracting party will be able to force the consumer into an agreement unfavourable to the latter. Once again, it is difficult to see these provisions applying in the trusts context.

If the consumer contract provisions do not apply, then (7) below should be considered.

(7) Do the employment contract provisions apply? (Arts 18–21)

These provide additional protection to employees. They apply to individual contracts of employment. Where applicable, they limit the effectiveness of jurisdiction clauses[1] and permit an employee to sue an employer either where the latter is domiciled, or where the employee habitually carries out his work.[2] In contrast, an employer may sue an employee only in the state of the employee's domicile.[3]

Presumably, these provisions could apply to professional trustees subject to an individual contract of employment if the litigation related to the contract of employment itself.

If the employment contract provisions do not apply, then (8) below should be considered.

(8) Is there a valid choice of court agreement for the courts of a Member State? (Art 23)

A choice of court agreement is the most effective way to ensure the jurisdictional competence of the preferred forum. Article 23 contains a special provision in relation to trusts in sub-paragraph (4). This states that where a trust instrument provides that the courts of a Member State shall have exclusive jurisdiction, those courts alone may entertain proceedings brought against a settlor, trustee or beneficiary, if relations between these parties or their rights or obligations under the trust are involved. This provision apparently applies irrespective of the domicile of the parties to the litigation and without any further formal requirements, although it is subordinate to the

1 Article 21 states that such clauses must either have been agreed after the dispute has arisen or confer on the employee the right to bring proceedings additionally in courts other than those competent elsewhere under the employment contract provisions.

2 Article19.

3 Article 20.

provisions of Arts 13, 17, 21 and 22.[1] Presumably, where there is no trust instrument, Art 23 jurisdiction can only be conferred if the conditions of Art 23(1) are satisfied. Article 23(1) has given rise to extensive case-law;[2] however, detailed discussion is unnecessary here, since it is unlikely that a trusts dispute will not be covered by Art 23(2), yet still satisfy Art 23(1). Suffice it to note that the latter lays down detailed formality requirements, namely that the clause was in writing or evidenced in writing,[3] in a form which accords with a practice previously adopted by the parties or in a form widely in use in international commerce of which the parties were, or should have been, aware. However, the ECJ has increasingly focused less on the technicalities of Art 23(1) and more on whether a party had what a common lawyer would describe as actual or constructive notice thereof.[4]

As well as ascertaining the formal validity of the clause, logically it should also have been agreed upon according to its governing law. Where one party denies agreeing to the term, logically a choice of law in contract issue should arise, since the issue is essentially one as to the validity of a contractual term. This would be highly inconvenient at the jurisdiction stage and has been rejected by the ECJ in *Benincasa v Dentalkit Srl*.[5] The decision is more pragmatic than principled.

Where a jurisdiction clause is concluded between two parties, neither of whom is domiciled in a Member State, the chosen court has exclusive jurisdiction. However, in this scenario, the chosen court may decide, in its discretion, not to take jurisdiction. Unless and until it elects not to take jurisdiction, no other state has jurisdiction.[6] In England, the discretion will be exercised by applying the common law principles on dealing with jurisdiction clauses.[7] Under the Brussels Convention, it was less clear what happened if the parties agreed that more than one state's courts had jurisdiction (for instance they provided that disputes may be heard in France or Germany).[8] The Regulation clarifies the matter, by providing that jurisdiction clauses 'shall be exclusive unless the parties have agreed otherwise'.[9] Whilst this is a rebuttable presumption against non-exclusive jurisdiction clauses, it indicates that they will be allowed in principle.

---

1 Article 23(5).

2 See Briggs and Rees, n 2 on p 11, pp 63–79.

3 Article 23(2) provides that 'any communication by electronic means which provides a durable record of the agreement shall be equivalent to "writing"'.

4 See *Powell Duffryn plc v Petereit* [1992] ECR I-1745.

5 [1997] ECR I-3767. Criticised in J Harris 'Jurisdiction Clauses and Void Contracts' (1998) 23 EL Rev 279. See also *Transporti Castelletti Spedizioni Internazionali SpA v Hugo Trumpy SpA* [1999] ECR I-1597.

6 Article 23(3).

7 Discussed in **1.3.3** below.

8 In *Anterist v Crédit Lyonnais* [1986] ECR 1951, the ECJ tentatively suggested that the parties' intentions should be respected and the clause treated as effective.

9 Article 23(1).

If there is no valid choice of court agreement for the courts of a Member State, then (9) below should be considered.

(9) Is the defendant domiciled in a Member State? (Art 2)

We are now at the core of the Brussels Regulation. If none of the above questions has been affirmatively answered, the defendant's domicile becomes central.

In the Brussels Convention, there was no definition of the word 'domicile', either for individual or corporate defendants. The Brussels Regulation introduces a new European autonomous definition of the domicile of companies. However, there remains no European definition of the domicile of individuals, which is a matter for each state to determine by applying its own rules.[1] However, in order to promote uniformity, the United Kingdom adopted a special definition of the domicile of individuals for Regulation purposes which is different to that used elsewhere in the conflict of laws and which is more in line with that prevailing on the continent. This is contained in the CJJA 1982.

In order to determine whether an individual is domiciled in the United Kingdom (and more particularly in England), an English court should apply these provisions.[2] However, Art 59(2) tells us that to determine whether he is domiciled in, for example, France or Germany, the English court must respectively apply the domicile rules of France and Germany. The result of this approach is that a defendant clearly based in Europe could be deemed to be domiciled in more than one Member State (in which case the claimant may choose between them) or in no Member State (in which case Art 4 should be applied).

The domicile provisions – individuals

An individual is domiciled in the United Kingdom if he resides there and the nature and circumstances of his residence indicate that he has a substantial connection with the United Kingdom, which is rebuttably presumed after three months or more continuous residence.[3] He is domiciled in England if the same criteria are satisfied in relation to that country.[4]

The domicile provisions – companies

Under the Brussels Convention, there was no European definition of the domicile of companies. The United Kingdom enacted provisions to the effect

1 In the United Kingdom, CJJA 1982, s 41 (re-enacted by Civil Jurisdiction and Judgments Order 2001 (SI 2001/3929), Sch 1, para 9).

2 Article 59(1).

3 CJJA 1982, s 41(2). CJJA 1982, s 41 has been re-enacted in Civil Jurisdiction and Judgments Order 2001 (SI 2001/3929), Sch 1, para 9.

4 CJJA 1982, s 41(3). It would suffice that he resides in England and has no particular connection with another part of the UK, according to CJJA 1982, s 41(5).

that a corporation is domiciled where it has its seat, which is stated to be in the United Kingdom if it was incorporated or formed under the law of a part of the United Kingdom and has its registered office or central management and control in the United Kingdom.[1] It is domiciled in England if these criteria apply thereto.[2] It is domiciled overseas if the same conditions apply, unless it is demonstrated that the overseas state would not regard the company as having its seat there.[3]

However, the Brussels Regulation introduces a European autonomous definition of domicile for companies, which replaces the definition in the CJJA 1982. Article 60(1) provides that:

> 'a company or other legal person or association of natural or legal persons is domiciled at the place where it has its: (a) statutory seat; or (b) central administration; or (c) principal place of business. The statutory seat means, for the purposes of the UK and Ireland, "the registered office or, where there is no such office anywhere, the place of incorporation, of where there is no such office anywhere, the place under the law of which the formation took place".'[4]

Whilst this definition replaces the United Kingdom's definition of corporate domicile contained in the CJJA 1982, it does not appear significantly to affect the substantive criteria.

If the defendant is not domiciled in a Member State, jurisdiction may be taken under the common law rules (Art 4).

Article 4 deems that a court should apply its own national jurisdictional rules. In other words, an English court would apply its common law rules. However, since it is the Brussels Regulation which tells the court to do so, the *lis alibi pendens* provisions of Arts 27–30 below will apply and the judgment will be a Regulation judgment for recognition and enforcement purposes.

If the defendant is domiciled in a Member State, the courts of the defendant's domicile have jurisdiction. However, even if the defendant is domiciled in another Member State, an English court might none the less have jurisdiction, since (10) below should be considered.

(10) Can a defendant who is domiciled in a Member State be sued in another Member State? (Arts 5 and 6)

Articles 5 and 6 open up other courts in which the claimant may sue. However, it is imperative to appreciate that this 'special' jurisdiction exists only when jurisdiction exists in a Member State pursuant to Art 2. It will not suffice

1 Ibid, s 42(3).
2 Ibid, s 42(4).
3 Ibid, s 42(6), (7).
4 Article 60(2).

that the defendant is domiciled in a Member State, if jurisdiction comes from one of questions (2) to (8) above.

The most obviously relevant provision for present purposes is Art 5(6), which provides that a person domiciled in a Member State may also be sued:

> 'as a settlor, trustee or beneficiary[1] of a trust created by the operation of statute, or by a written instrument, or created orally and evidenced in writing, in the courts of the Member State in which the trust is domiciled.'

It is not immediately obvious how the domicile of a trust is to be determined. Article 60(3) states that a court should apply its own rules of private international law in order to determine whether a trust is domiciled in that state. In England, it is to s 45(3) of the CJJA 1982[2] that we must look to find out whether the trust is domiciled in England. That subsection states that:

> 'A trust is domiciled in a part of the United Kingdom if and only if the system of law of that part is the system of law[3] with which the trust has its closest and most real connection.'

When applying this provision, one would expect that the rules of Art 7 of the Hague Convention on the Law Applicable to Trusts and on their Recognition 1985,[4] which determine the applicable law in the absence of choice, would be applied.[5] Hence, factors such as the place of administration of the trust, the *situs* of the assets, the residence or business address of the trustee and the place where the purposes of the trust are to be fulfilled will all be relevant in determining the trust's domicile.[6] If it transpires that the trust is domiciled in England and the defendant in a European Member State, the English court will have jurisdiction, providing that it is the court first seised[7] and that the matter in question is civil or commercial.[8] It would appear that the trust created by a contract for the sale of land is excluded from Art 5(6).[9]

---

1 The defendant must be a trustee or beneficiary at the time at which proceedings are instituted: *Chellaram v Chellaram (No 2)* [2002] EWHC 632 (Ch), [2002] 3 All ER 17.

2 This has been re-enacted in Civil Jurisdiction and Judgments Order 2001 (SI 2001/3929), Sch 1, para 12.

3 If different laws are applicable under the trust to questions of validity and administration, the relevant law for the purposes of CJJA 1982, s 45(3) is the law governing validity: *Chellaram v Chellaram (No 2)*, n 1 above.

4 Enacted by the Recognition of Trusts Act 1987. For detailed discussion, see J Harris *The Hague Trusts Convention* (Hart Publishing, 2002).

5 Lawrence Collins J did just that in *Chellaram v Chellaram (No 2)*, n 1 above.

6 In *Chellaram v Challaram (No 2)*, n 1 above, Lawrence Collins J said that if the settlor had chosen law A to govern a trust, this fact could be used to negate a claim that law B was the law of closest connection. However, it is not clear why this should be so, since CJJA 1982, s 45(3) clearly lays down an objective test to determine the domicile of a trust.

7 See Brussels Regulation, Arts 27–30, and question (11) below.

8 Wills or matrimonial property, for example, are not within the scope of the Brussels Regulation.

9 *Schlosser Report* (1979) OJ C 59/71, paras 117, 172. Briggs and Rees, n 2 on p 11, p 129, dispute this, pointing out that in English law the contract itself will be in writing and that it is difficult to see why this should not suffice.

Indeed, Lawrence Collins J stated in *Chellaram v Chellaram (No 2)* that 'Article 5(6) does not apply to constructive trusts'.[1] The law of closest connection is to be determined as of the date at which proceedings are instituted, not at the date at which the cause of action allegedly arose.

Equitable obligations – other heads of special jurisdiction

Whilst the above provision will deal with actions based on breach of trust, it is much less certain how other types of equitable obligations (for example, a claim for breach of confidence)[2] fit within Art 5, if at all. In this regard, the provisions of Arts 5(1) and (3) dealing respectively with matters relating to contract and tort merit consideration. To a common lawyer, it would seem very surprising that certain equitable claims could fall within provisions dealing with liability in contract and tort. However, given that these terms have a European autonomous meaning for Regulation purposes and that there are no separate provisions to deal with claims based on unjust enrichment or equitable wrongs, this is a possibility which cannot be ignored, since the law/equity dichotomy should not be relevant in a European Regulation. Briggs and Rees[3] argue that the classification should hinge upon whether the original obligation arises from an agreement.[4] Hence, the liability of agent to principal would fall within Art 5(1), as would that of, for example, a solicitor who receives confidential information through his fiduciary position. In contrast, the liability of a person who wrongfully acquires confidential information should fall within Art 5(3), as should that of the dishonest recipient of trust property. These provisions have given rise to a great body of case-law and only a brief outline is provided here.[5]

Matters relating to contract

Article 5(1) gives special jurisdiction in matters relating to contract to the courts for the place of performance of the obligation in question. 'Matters relating to contract' has an autonomous meaning. In *Martin Peters Bauunternehmung GmbH v Zuid Nedelandse Aannemers Vereniging*,[6] a dispute between members of a trade association and the association itself was held to fall within this autonomous definition, even though the Dutch court before which the claim was brought did not think this a contractual claim. In *Jakob Handte & Co GmbH v Traitements Mécano-chimiques des Surfaces SA*,[7] it was explained that an obligation freely entered into by one party in relation to

---

1 [2002] EWHC 632 (Ch), [2002] 3 All ER 17 at **[138]**.

2 This question arose, but was not resolved, in *Kitechnology BV v Unicor Plastmaschinen GmbH* [1994] IL Pr 568.

3 Note 2 on p 11, p 117.

4 In a factual sense; there clearly need not be a contractual agreement in the English domestic sense, supported by consideration.

5 See further Briggs and Rees, n 2 on p 11, pp 91–126.

6 [1983] ECR 987.

7 [1992] ECR I-3967.

another fell within Art 5(1). Accordingly, claims which would sound in tort in English domestic law may be contractual for jurisdictional purposes (for example, a negligent misstatement in a survey provided free of charge which induces economic loss). This definition could apparently cover the liability of willing fiduciaries (for example, in the solicitor/client or principal/agent relationship) to account for profits. Indeed, on one view, any obligation consensually incurred could fall within Art 5(1).[1]

The 'obligation in question' is that in respect of which the claimant sues.[2] If there is more than one, the court should identify what it considers to be the principal obligation.[3] However, if there are two obligations of equal importance, one to be performed in England and one overseas, the English court may hear only the claim relating to the former obligation. There is no provision allowing composite proceedings to be brought under Art 5(1) in such circumstances.[4] Furthermore, all obligations in respect of which the claimant claims must be contractual if they are all to be brought within Art 5(1).

The 'place for performance of the obligation' is determined by the law applicable on the substance, as identified by the court's choice of law rules.[5] The phrase does not have an autonomous meaning. This is because where an obligation is to be performed is determined by the contract itself and hence should be resolved by the applicable law of the contract.[6]

That said, the Brussels Regulation does provide an autonomous meaning of 'place of performance' for certain contracts. It states that, unless otherwise agreed, the place of performance in sale of goods contracts is the Member State where the goods were delivered or should have been delivered; in contracts of service, the relevant place is the state where under the contract the services were provided or should have been provided. But for all other contractual matters, the position remains unchanged.

Matters relating to tort, delict or quasi-delict

Article 5(3) grants jurisdiction in such matters to the place where the harmful event occurred.

---

1 Hence the liability, for example, of one who knowingly assists in a breach of trust would not be included, as the claimant and defendant have not agreed on a voluntary undertaking. See also *Agnew v Länsfösäkringsbolagens AB* [2000] 2 WLR 497.

2 *De Bloos v Bouyer* [1976] ECR 1497.

3 *Shenavai v Kreischer* [1987] ECR 239.

4 *Leathertex Divisione Sintetici SpA v Bodetex BVBA* [1999] ECR I-6747.

5 *Industrie Tessili Italiana Como v Dunlop AG* [1976] ECR 1473; *Custom Made Commercial Ltd v Stawa Metallbau GmbH* [1994] ECR I-2913; *GIE Groupe Concorde and Others v The Master of the Vessel Suhadiwarno Panjan* [1999] ECR I- 6307.

6 For a recent example of the determination of the place of performance, see *Viskase Ltd and Another v Paul Kiefel GmbH* [1999] 1 WLR 1305.

The interpretation of 'matters relating to tort' has been strikingly wide. In *Kalfelis v Bankhaus Schröder*,[1] the ECJ ruled that it covers all actions seeking to establish the defendant's liability which do not relate to contract. However, it is clear that Art 5(3) is in fact not the catch-all provision that this definition would suggest and that some forms of liability are to be treated as neither contractual nor tortious. So, in *Reichert v Dresdner Bank (No 2)*,[2] a creditor's claim to an order that a transfer from the debtor to another was ineffective against the creditor was held to fall outside Art 5(1) and (3). More recently, the House of Lords held that restitutionary obligations arising for payment under a void contract also fell under neither category.[3]

What then are the limits of Art 5(3)? Briggs and Rees convincingly argue that Art 5(3) should not extend to all civil and commercial claims against a defendant which do not relate to contract and should apply only where compensation is sought for wrongdoing.[4] The Briggs and Rees view would exclude, for example, the liability to account for profits, since such a claim is based on a restitutionary obligation and not on a duty to compensate. However, they concede that this line is very hard to draw, since *ex hypothesi* the fiduciary is doing wrong by keeping hold of the money. It is a particularly difficult distinction, they note, where a claim for return of chattels is brought in a conversion action.

Recently, English courts have held that claims against a third party to a trust based upon knowing assistance or knowing receipt claims may both be treated as 'matters relating to tort'.[5] It should be noted that it is essential to determine whether a particular claim is contractual, tortious or neither where more than one cause of action is alleged, since the ECJ in *Kalfelis v Bankhaus Schröder*[6] ruled that Art 5(3) only allows the court to take jurisdiction over those parts of a dispute falling within the provision. The result may be an untidy fragmentation of related claims; however, it must be recalled that the claimant can still bring a composite action in the courts of the defendant's domicile.

As to the 'harmful event', the ECJ in *Handelskwekerij GJ Bier BV v Mines de Potasse d'Alsace SA*[7] ruled that this phrase allows the claimant to sue either where the damage was sustained or where the act giving rise to it occurs. Where damage is purely economic or emotional, an ingenious claimant could argue that he invariably sustains damage in his place of domicile and hence seeks to sue in his home courts. To forestall this, the ECJ in *Dumez France SA*

1 [1988] ECR 5565.

2 [1992] ECR 2149.

3 *Kleinwort Benson Ltd v City of Glasgow District Council (No 2)* [1997] 4 All ER 641.

4 Note 2 on p 11, p 113.

5 *Casio Computer Co Ltd v Sayo and Others* [2001] EWCA Civ 661, [2001] IL Pr 43; *Dexter v Harley* (2001) *The Times*, April 2. Both cases are noted by T Yeo 'Constructive Trustees and the Brussels Convention' (2001) 117 LQR 560.

6 [1988] ECR 5565.

7 [1976] ECR 1735.

and Tracoba SARL v Hessische Landesbank[1] ruled that the damage must be immediate damage. In *Marinari v Lloyds Bank plc and Zubaidi Trading Company*,[2] the claimant, an Italian, went into an English bank with a great value of promissory notes issued by the Philippines Government. He was arrested, but subsequently acquitted. He wanted to sue in tort and claimed he could do so in Italy, where he sustained damage. The ECJ recognised the correctness of the *Bier* ruling, but held that it could not be construed so widely as to include any place where the adverse consequences of an event that had already caused actual damage elsewhere could be felt. It could not be construed to include the place where a victim claimed to have suffered financial damage consequential on initial damage arising from and suffered by him in another Member State. Once again, the need restrictively to construe an exception to the domiciliary principle was stressed. A similar view was taken by the ECJ in *Réunion Européenne SA v Spliethoff's Bevrachtingskantoor BV*.[3] In that case, a cargo of pears was to be transported from Melbourne to Rotterdam by sea, then on to France by land, where it was received by a French company. The cooling system on the ship was allegedly defective and the cargo was ruined. It was held that no action in tort for defective carriage by sea could be brought by the French company in France under Art 5(3), as although the company suffered loss there, it was too remote. Article 5(3) would grant jurisdiction only to the Dutch courts. It would also appear that whilst the courts of the place where the act giving rise to the damage occurred may award compensation for all loss incurred, those where damage was sustained may only rule in respect of harm occurring in that country.[4]

The Regulation accords jurisdiction to 'the courts for the place where the harmful event occurred *or there is a risk of it occurring*'. This is intended to make clear that the Article applies to claims brought before damage has occurred as a preventative step.

Claims arising from branch or agency

The only other potentially relevant provision for present purposes is Art 5(5), which allows a defendant to be sued in a dispute relating to the operation of a branch or agency in the courts of the place where the branch is situated. The branch must be sufficiently under the control of the defendant for it to be fair to sue him where it is situated and the claim must arise out of the operations of the branch itself. However, the branch's undertakings do not need to be performed in the state where it is established.[5]

---

1 [1990] ECR I-49.
2 [1995] ECR I-2719.
3 [1998] ECR I-6511.
4 *Shevill and Others v Presse Alliance SA* [1995] ECR I-415.
5 *Lloyd's Register of Shipping v Société Campenon Bernard* [1995] ECR I-961.

Multiple actions – Art 6

Article 6 seeks to avoid the fragmentation of claims involving multiple parties by allowing composite actions to be brought. Its provisions may only be applied to a person domiciled in a Member State.

Article 6(1) allows jurisdiction to be taken over co-defendants if one defendant is being sued where he is domiciled. It may not be used where the basis of jurisdiction over the first defendant is other than that he is being sued where he is domiciled.[1] Furthermore, there must be a necessary link between the claims against the defendants. In *Kalfelis v Bankhaus Schröder*,[2] the ECJ held that to apply there must be a connection between the actions against the various defendants of such a kind that it is expedient to determine the actions together to avoid the risk of irreconcilable judgments resulting from separate proceedings in different states.[3] Domicile is to be assessed at the time of issue of the claim form, not when it is served.[4]

Article 6(2) allows jurisdiction to be taken over third parties domiciled in a Member State where the court has jurisdiction over the original claim, provided that the initial proceedings are not instituted solely to ensure that the third party is not sued in the courts which would otherwise be competent. It will apply whenever there is a sufficient nexus between the claimant's claim against the defendant and the defendant's claim against a third party to justify overriding the basic right of the defendant to be sued in the courts of his domicile. Once again, the fear of irreconcilable judgments is prevalent. But the court may apply its national law to decide whether to exercise this jurisdiction in a given case. The phrase 'third party proceedings' does not have an autonomous meaning and Art 6(2) will generally apply whenever domestic procedural rules permit a third party to be joined in proceedings.[5]

Article 6(3) allows jurisdiction over counterclaims to be taken where the main proceedings are pending. It applies to claims by a defendant which may lead to a separate judgment.[6]

Article 6(4) allows the defendant to be sued in matters relating to contract, if the action may be combined with an action against the same party to assert rights *in rem* in immovable property, in the courts where the land is situated. So, for example, a mortgagee may combine an action for sale of the mortgaged land with one for breach of the covenant to repay.[7]

However, it should be noted that Art 6 does not provide a right to join additional claims against a defendant simply because they are related to a claim

---

1 *Réunion Européenne SA v Spliethoff's Bevrachtingskantoor BV* [1998] ECR I-6511; *Jordan Grand Prix Ltd v Baltic Insurance Group* [1999] 2 AC 127; *Hough v P&O Containers Ltd* [1999] QB 834.

2 [1988] ECR 5565.

3 This is now expressly stated in Art 6(1).

4 *Canada Trust Co v Stolzenberg (No 2)* [2000] 3 WLR 1376.

5 *Kinnear and Others v Falconfilms NV and Others; Hospital Rubber Internacional and Another* [1996] 1 WLR 920.

6 *Danvaern Production A/S v Schuhfabriken Otterbeck GmbH & Co* [1995] ECR I-2053.

7 The example given by Briggs and Rees, n 2 on p 11, p 137.

over which the court does have jurisdiction. To do this, the defendant must be sued in the courts of his domicile.[1]

If the courts of more than one Member State have jurisdiction by virtue of all the questions considered above, which state's courts may actually exercise it in practice?

(11) Can prima facie jurisdiction of the English courts be removed? (Arts 27 and 28)

Although we have seen that Arts 5 and 6 may grant jurisdiction to the courts of more than one Member State, this does not mean that the claimant may simultaneously launch proceedings in more than one country. Indeed, this would undermine the free movement of judgments, since it would greatly increase the chances of irreconcilable judgments being delivered. To prevent this, the Regulation provides that only the court first seised of the case may hear a dispute.

Under the Brussels Convention, determining when a court was seised was a matter of national, and not European autonomous, definition. English law had adopted a special definition for the purposes of the Brussels Convention, so as to bring it more into line with other Member States. It was decided in *Dresser UK Ltd v Falcongate Freight Management Ltd*,[2] that an English court was seised for Convention purposes when a claim form[3] was served and not when it was issued. The Regulation changes matters, as it lays down an autonomous definition of seisure. Article 30 states that a court will be deemed to be seised at the time when the document instituting the proceedings is lodged with the court, provided that the claimant has not subsequently failed to take the steps he was required to take to have service effected on the defendant. This is much closer to a time of issue rule than a time of service rule and materially affects the existing position in English law. Henceforth, an English court will be seised at the point of issue, not service. However, in any Member State where the document is served before being lodged with the court, the relevant time will be that when it is received by the authority responsible for service.

The situation where identical or related proceedings are already under way in a foreign court is termed *lis alibi pendens* and is dealt with by Arts 27 and 28.

Identical parties/actions

Article 27 states that:

---

1 *Canada Trust Co v Stolzenberg (No 2)* [2000] 3 WLR 1376.

2 [1992] QB 502.

3 This is the new name for a writ under the CPR. Other name changes include 'asset freezing order' for the old *Mareva* injunction; 'search order' for the former *Anton Piller* order; 'claimant' for 'plaintiff'; 'permission' for 'leave' (in the sense of leave to serve out of the jurisdiction) and 'application without notice' for 'ex parte'.

> 'Where proceedings involving the same cause of action and between the same parties are brought in the courts of different Member States, any court other than the court first seised shall of its own motion stay its proceedings until such time as the jurisdiction of the court first seised is established.'
>
> 'Where the jurisdiction of the court first seised is established, any court other than the court first seised shall decline jurisdiction in favour of that court.'

This provision is given a fairly broad construction, so as to minimise the risk of legally irreconcilable judgments. In *Gubisch Maschinenfabrik KG v Palumbo*,[1] a German vendor sought to enforce a contract in Germany; subsequently the Italian purchaser sought a declaration in Italy that the contract did not bind him. The ECJ ruled that Art 27 prevented the purchaser from so doing. Although the claims were not identical, the risk of irreconcilable judgments was clear. Hence, an action for damages for breach of trust by a beneficiary against a trustee and a declaration sought by a trustee against a beneficiary that the former was not in breach of trust could not be brought in the courts of different Member States.

Determining whether the parties are the same can be more complex. In *The Tatry*,[2] the ECJ ruled that where actions were brought in two jurisdictions, and the parties to both were not identical, Art 27 operated only to prevent the second action proceeding between those parties who had also been parties to the first. In *Drouot Assurances SA v Consolidated Metallurgical Industries*,[3] the ECJ held, in the context of simultaneous actions involving respectively an insurer and the insured, that only where the degree of identity between the interests of the two was such that a judgment against one would be *res judicata* against the other, should they be considered the same party for Art 27 purposes.

It should be noted that Art 27 (and Art 28) will apply to any jurisdictional disputes falling within Art 1 of the Regulation. In *Overseas Union Insurance Ltd and Others v New Hampshire Insurance Company*,[4] the defendant was a US corporation. The common law rules would determine the English court's jurisdiction. However, the same matter was to be litigated in France under its national rules. It was held that Art 27 none the less applied to prevent the court second seised from hearing the case. This must be correct, as each court was only applying its national rules because the Regulation so decreed under Art 4. The judgments would be Regulation ones and hence it was essential to avoid irreconcilable judgments.

Related actions

Article 28 states that:

---

1 [1987] ECR 4861.
2 [1994] ECR I-5439.
3 [1998] ECR I-3075.
4 [1991] ECR I-3317.

> 'Where related actions are pending in the courts of different Member States, any court other than the court first seised may stay its proceedings.
>
> Where these actions are pending at first instance, any court other than the court first seised may also, on the application of one of the parties, decline jurisdiction if the court first seised has jurisdiction over the actions in question and its law permits the consolidation thereof.
>
> For the purposes of this Article, actions are deemed to be related where they are so closely connected that it is expedient to hear and determine them together to avoid the risk of irreconcilable judgments resulting from separate proceedings.'

This is a broader and more discretionary provision, which recognises that whilst a court may technically have jurisdiction, it is not at present expedient for it to exercise it, given that a related action is pending overseas. The concern is not only that the two judgments will be mutually unenforceable,[1] but that the judicial process will function more smoothly. The ECJ has stated that a broad approach should be taken to the interpretation of the Article, to avoid the risk of conflicting reasoning, albeit not legally irreconcilable judgments.[2] In *Sarrio SA v Kuwait Investment Authority*,[3] the House of Lords called for a 'broad and common sense' approach, whereby the sole question would be whether it is expedient that the cases be heard together.

As between the powers to stay and to decline jurisdiction, it would seem that the former is the primary duty[4] of the court. Indeed, the overseas trial may make many matters *res judicata* in England, thereby ensuring a speedier trial in England, or even prompting a settlement. Only when *res judicata* cannot operate, because the parties are not identical, but the issues in question are, is the case for declining jurisdiction strong.

If prima facie jurisdiction is not removed by the Regulation, can an English court none the less decide not to hear the case?

(12) Does an English court with jurisdiction have a residual discretion not to exercise it?

The Regulation rules are intended to be mandatory and to remove the flexibility inherent in a discretionary doctrine such as *forum non conveniens*. (This doctrine is discussed later in this chapter.) But what if an English court feels that another state's courts are clearly more appropriate to hear the case? Where the jurisdictional dispute is solely intra-United Kingdom, it must be correct that *forum non conveniens* can be invoked. Beyond that, s 49 of the CJJA 1982 allows the doctrine to be invoked when not inconsistent with the Regulation.

---

1 Although this is the risk identified in the third paragraph of Art 28, the courts have not seen fit to limit its application thereto.

2 See, eg, *The Tatry* [1994] ECR I-5439.

3 [1999] AC 32. See J Harris 'Related Actions and the Brussels Convention' [1998] LMCLQ 145.

4 See *Jenard Report* (1979) OJ C 59/41.

However, the Brussels Regulation is silent on when a stay would be inconsistent. Four primary situations can be discerned.

Jurisdiction is taken under the Regulation rules and it is sought to stay in favour of a non-Member State

Given that the courts of a Member State have exclusive jurisdiction in relation to disputes concerning rights *in rem* in immovable property and choice of court agreements, it would seem odd if an English court were forced to entertain a claim in relation to title to land in Brazil simply because the defendant was domiciled in England, or permitted a claimant to sue here in breach of an agreement to litigate solely in Argentina.[1]

More generally, the Court of Appeal in *Re Harrods (Buenos Aires) Ltd*[2] said that an English court could stay in favour of a non-Member State, since the Regulation is not intended to apply to jurisdictional disputes between Member and non-Member States. The view has been confirmed by the Court of Appeal in *Ace Insurance SA-NV v Zurich Insurance Co.*[3] The reasoning is attractive, but erroneous, since a stay will necessarily affect other Member States for two reasons. First, if an English court stays its proceedings, it remains seised, thereby preventing other Member States' courts from taking jurisdiction (since Art 27 will be triggered). Secondly, this means that the claimant is denied his right to a judgment of a Member State, which can be enforced throughout Europe. The result is uncertainty. It cannot be assumed that the ECJ will agree if and when it gets an opportunity to consider the matter.

Jurisdiction is taken under the Regulation rules and it is sought to stay in favour of a Member State

Such a situation is manifestly incompatible with the workings of the Regulation and cannot be permitted.

Jurisdiction is taken under common law rules pursuant to Art 4 and it is sought to stay in favour of a non-Member State

In such a case, *forum non conveniens* must have a central role. The Brussels Regulation tells an English court to apply its national rules, of which the doctrine is a key part.

Jurisdiction is taken under common law rules pursuant to Art 4 and it is sought to stay in favour of a Member State

This is a complex situation, as although the Brussels Regulation tells the court to apply its common law rules, a stay will have the effect that the English court is still seised. Accordingly, Art 27 will apparently prevent the courts of another

---

1 This is sometimes described as giving 'reflexive effect' to the Regulation.

2 [1992] Ch 72.

3 [2001] 1 Lloyd's Rep 618. An appeal in this case is currently pending before the House of Lords.

Member State from hearing the case. The matter arose in the Court of Appeal in *Sarrio SA v Kuwait Investment Authority*,[1] where Evans LJ dismissed this as a technical argument and ruled that a stay could be granted.[2] Unfortunately, technical though it might be, it is no less logically watertight for it.

1.2.7 Tactical conclusion on the Regulation

The effect of the broad recognition and enforcement rules of the Brussels Regulation is that a defendant who believes that the overseas court in which he is being sued lacks jurisdiction will ignore its proceedings at his peril. However, it is possible for both sides to choose a forum in which to sue. One approach is to insert an arbitration clause, which will take the matter outside the Regulation. Another is to use a choice of court clause, although limitations to its effectiveness are highlighted in this chapter.

More generally, the 'court first seised rule' has important tactical implications. Where more than one jurisdiction is potentially available, it can be inadvisable for a person against whom a claim might be made to sit back and wait to be sued. If, for example, a trustee is alleged to have violated his duties, he might be wise to turn himself into a claimant by seeking a declaration against the beneficiary (who would now be the defendant) that he is not in breach of trust. The ECJ has confirmed that a negative declaration may be sought under the Brussels Regulation.[3] The manner in which an English court exercises its discretion to grant this remedy will be discussed later in this chapter. Another possibility might be for one who is being sued in a state whose courts he believes lacks jurisdiction to seek an anti-suit injunction in England restraining proceedings overseas. The Court of Appeal thought such a remedy available in *Continental Bank NA v Aeakos Compania Naviera SA and Others*[4] to restrain proceedings in another Member State. In *Turner v Grovit*[5] the Court of Appeal extended this principle and stated that an anti-suit injunction could be granted when proceedings in another state were brought purely to oppress the defendant and when the overseas claimant was abusing the process of the English court, even if the foreign court technically had jurisdiction under the Regulation. The House of Lords has now referred the case to the ECJ.[6] However, in this author's view, anti-suit injunctions should not be permitted to restrain proceedings in another Member State.

---

1 [1977] 1 Lloyd's Rep 113. See J Harris 'Staying Proceedings for a Contracting State to the Brussels Convention' (1979) 113 LQR 557. This point was not in issue in the House of Lords' proceedings. However, the Court of Appeal's view was endorsed in *Haji-Ioannou v Frangos* [1999] 2 Lloyd's Rep 337.

2 Although it was not on the facts.

3 See, eg *Gubisch Maschinenfabrik KG v Palumbo* [1987] ECR 4861, ECJ; *The Tatry* [1994] ECR I-5439.

4 [1994] 1 WLR 588.

5 [1999] 3 WLR 794, on which see J Harris 'Use and Abuse of the Brussels Convention' (1999) 115 LQR 576.

6 [2002] 1 WLR 107. But the views of the House of Lords appear sympathetic to the granting of an anti-suit injunction on the facts of the case.

Such injunctions fly in the face of the international harmony which is so important to the Regulation's workings and violate the principle that each state is equally competent to construe the Regulation's provisions.

1.2.8 Future developments: a worldwide jurisdiction and judgments Convention?

Discussions are currently in progress at the Hague Conference on Private International Law for a proposed Convention on Jurisdiction and the Enforcement of Foreign Judgments in Civil and Commercial Matters ('the Worldwide Judgments Convention'). This would create a degree of harmonisation of jurisdictional rules for contracting states from across the globe. Like the Brussels scheme, it would greatly facilitate the recognition and enforcement of foreign judgments. In particular, judgments from states outside the European Union would be far easier to enforce in England, and vice versa.

A preliminary draft of the Convention was agreed in October 1999 and modified in June 2001. It can be obtained from the Hague Conference's website.[1] There will be further important discussion on the Convention during 2002.

The draft Convention contains trusts specific bases of jurisdiction in Art 11. This draft Article provides that:[2]

> '1. In proceedings concerning the validity, construction, effects, administration or variation of a trust created voluntarily and evidenced in writing, the courts of a Contracting State designated in the trust instrument for this purpose shall have jurisdiction, and that jurisdiction shall be exclusive unless the instrument provides otherwise. Where the trust instrument designates a court or courts of a non-Contracting State, courts in Contracting States shall decline jurisdiction or suspend proceedings unless the court or courts chosen have themselves declined jurisdiction. [The validity of such a designation shall be governed by the law applicable to the validity of the trust.]
>
> 2. In the absence of such [valid] designation, proceedings may be brought before the courts of a State –
>
> (a) in which is situated the principal place of administration of the trust; or
> (b) whose law is applicable to the trust; or
> (c) with which the trust has the closest connection for the purpose of the proceedings, taking into account in particular the principal place where the trust is administered, the place of residence or business of the trustee, the situation of the assets of the trust, and the objects of the trust and the places where they are to be fulfilled; or

1 See *www.hcch.net/e/workprog/jdgm.html*.

2 Those words which are contained in square brackets are especially tentative and will certainly require further discussion at the Hague Conference.

(d) in which the settlor (if living) and all living beneficiaries are habitually resident, if all such persons are habitually resident in the same State.

[3. This Article shall only apply to disputes among the trustee, settlor and beneficiaries of the trust.]'

If this Convention is ultimately ratified and brought into force, it will be of potentially enormous significance. It would greatly restrict the scope of the common law jurisdiction rules. It would also limit the impact of the common law rules on recognition and enforcement of foreign judgments, which, as we shall see below, are very restrictive. The Convention would make it far easier to enforce English trusts judgments outside Europe and to ensure the recognition of foreign trusts judgments in England. Whether sufficient political consensus can be achieved to ensure the Convention's success remains to be seen.

1.3 JURISDICTION AT COMMON LAW

Whilst the common law rules now apply only in a residual manner, their role in English law is still considerable, both in civil and commercial matters where the defendant is domiciled in a non-Member State and matters fall outside Art 1 of the Brussels Regulation. Moreover, they continue to be the inspiration for the jurisdiction rules of many Commonwealth countries.

In contrast to the Regulation, the common law rules on jurisdiction *in personam* are highly discretionary and contain relatively little in the way of hard and fast rules. Much hinges upon whether the defendant can be served with a claim form within the jurisdiction.

1.3.1 Service as of right

An English court has jurisdiction as of right if the defendant can be validly served with a claim form. This will be permitted either where he is present in the jurisdiction or submits to the English courts.

Presence

In *Maharanee of Baroda v Wildenstein*,[1] the defendant, who was resident abroad, paid a very brief visit to England to attend a race meeting and was served with a claim form. The English court had jurisdiction.[2] As Edmund-Davies LJ remarked 'some may regard it as bad form; no one can condemn it as an abuse

1 [1972] 2 QB 283.

2 Today, the CPR regulate the manner in which a person can actually be served.

of process'. The only exception is where the defendant is fraudulently induced by the claimant to enter the jurisdiction.[1]

A company which is not domiciled in a Member State may be sued under the common law rules pursuant to the Companies Act 1985.[2] If the company is registered in England, even if its business is conducted abroad, service may be made at the registered office.[3] If the company is incorporated abroad but has a branch in England, it must file with the Registrar of Companies the name and address of those persons resident in Britain who are authorised to accept service on its behalf.[4] If it defaults in doing this, it can be served at its place of business.[5] If the company has no branch in England, but does have an established place of business, it may be served at the business address.[6]

Submission

In a civil or commercial matter, submission to an English court will be governed by Art 24 of the Brussels Regulation. Where the Regulation is inapplicable, the common law submission rules apply. Submission will occur if the defendant instructs his solicitor to accept service[7] or he contracts to submit to the English court's jurisdiction. If he pleads to the merits, he will be taken to have submitted. However, this will not be so if he appears solely to contest the court's jurisdiction.[8]

Evaluation

The above rules might appear striking, in that it is irrelevant whether the parties or the litigation have any connection with England. However, a defendant who has been served as of right will be able to apply to the court to stay its proceedings in favour of a more appropriate forum. Where the sole connection to England of the matter is the presence of the defendant, he is quite likely to succeed. It is to this doctrine that we now turn.

1.3.2 Staying proceedings commenced as of right

A doctrine evolved from Scottish law which recognised that injustice could result from hearing a case where jurisdiction was taken as of right if a more appropriate forum existed overseas. This doctrine is called *forum non conveniens*. The doctrine is now firmly established in English law and provides a defendant who can make out the plea with a means of escape from the clutches of the

---

1 *Watkins v North American Land and Timber Co Ltd* (1904) 20 TLR 534.

2 See also the procedures for serving a company detailed in CPR Part 6.

3 Companies Act 1985, s 725.

4 Ibid, s 690A(2).

5 Ibid, s 694(2).

6 Ibid, ss 691 and 695.

7 When a defendant is served with a claim form and believes that the English court lacks jurisdiction, it is incumbent upon him to apply to have service set aside pursuant to CPR Part 11.

8 *Williams and Glyn's Bank plc v Astro Dinamico Compania Naviera SA* [1984] 1 All ER 760.

English court. The doctrine has developed substantially in the last 25 years. However, for present purposes a historical account thereof is unnecessary. Suffice it to note that, initially, a stay would only be granted if the English proceedings were shown by the defendant to be vexatious or oppressive.[1] The result was an open incentive to forum shop in English courts. The law has liberalised considerably, although it would still be misleading to suggest that the plea is easy to make out.

Attention should today be focused on unquestionably the leading authority, namely the House of Lords decision in *Spiliada Maritime Corp v Cansulex Ltd*.[2] In that case, Lord Goff laid down a two-stage test. The defendant must first prove that there is another available forum which is clearly or distinctly more appropriate for resolution of the dispute.[3] If he succeeds, the burden of proof passes to the claimant, who may none the less resist a stay if he shows that it would be unjust to require him to sue overseas. It appears that the first limb should be concerned with objective questions about the dispute; the latter may deal with more subjective issues relating to the circumstances of the parties.

The first limb

The defendant must plead for a stay; a court will not grant one of its own motion. The decision to stay may be based on a large range of factors and an appellate court should be reluctant to intervene in the trial judge's exercise of discretion. The judge should assess the situation at the time of the stay hearing.[4]

In demonstrating that the overseas forum is available, it will not be necessary for the claimant to be able to bring exactly the same form; *a fortiori*, the forum is still available even if the claimant is very likely to lose overseas on the merits. It is not certain whether the defendant also must show that the forum is available to the claimant in practice. In *Mohammed v Bank of Kuwait and the Middle East KSC*,[5] Mohammed was an Iraqi national employed in Kuwait; after war broke out, he returned to Iraq and was prevented by Kuwaiti and Iraqi law from returning to Kuwait. He sued for money due in London. The bank argued that the natural forum was Kuwait and that by pointing to Kuwait it had established the first stage of the *Spiliada* test. The claimant responded that the bank must show that he could in practice sue there. The Court of Appeal agreed. The result was critical, since it placed the burden of proof on the defendant. However, the decision is very questionable, since the restriction did not change the fact that Kuwait was the natural forum; the claimant's

---

1 *St Pierre v South American Stores (Gath & Chaves) Ltd* [1936] 1 KB 382. Forum shopping in England was justified by Lord Denning MR in *The Atlantic Star* on the basis that England was a 'good place to find justice' ([1973] QB 364 at 382).

2 [1987] AC 460.

3 The application for a stay is made pursuant to CPR Part 11.

4 [1996] 1 WLR 1483.

5 Ibid.

problem was a subjective one and as such ought to have fallen within the second limb of *Spiliada*, thereby placing the burden of proof in this matter on the claimant.[1] In the case of *Lubbe and Others v Cape plc (No 2)*,[2] the court did not regard the practical availability of the foreign forum as a relevant factor under the first limb of *Spiliada* and it may now be assumed that this issue becomes relevant only under the second limb of the *Spiliada* test.

The defendant must show that the natural forum is overseas; it will not suffice to show that England is an inappropriate forum. Briggs and Rees helpfully identify five categories of potentially relevant factors.[3]

(1) *The places of residence of the parties.* Should both reside, for example, in Brazil, the case for resolution of the action in that country will be strong.

(2) *The factual connection of the litigation to a particular court.* If the relevant evidence is situated overseas, this will be highly material. *Spiliada* itself was the second of two related actions in London; hence there were lawyers versed in the matters and relevant evidence was situated in England. This led the trial judge to rule that England was the natural forum. It may also be that the language of the evidence will influence the court.

(3) *The law applicable on the merits.* It is assumed that if, for example, Brazilian law is to be applied, it would be more naturally applied in a Brazilian court. However, this reasoning is dangerous, since it assumes that the Brazilian judge will apply Brazilian law. Each country has its choice of law rules, so this cannot be taken for granted.[4]

(4) *The same matter is being or may be litigated overseas – lis alibi pendens.* This is likely to impact on the court's discretion, in order to facilitate judicial co-ordination and reduce the risk of irreconcilable judgments. It is likely to impact particularly where the foreign proceedings are well advanced.[5]

(5) *Other parties to the litigation.* Where a dispute involves more than one party, it may be necessary to determine whether all of the defendants may be sued overseas. It would be desirable that composite proceedings in one forum were brought.

---

1 It was expressly doubted by the Court of Appeal in *Askin v Absa Bank* [1999] IL Pr 471.

2 [2000] 1 WLR 1545.

3 Briggs and Rees, n 2 on p 11, p 197.

4 See *Trendtex Trading Corp v Credit Suisse* [1982] AC 679.

5 *The Varna (No 2)* [1994] 2 Lloyd's Rep 41.

The second limb

The burden of proof now switches to the claimant to demonstrate that he will not obtain justice overseas. It will not suffice to show simply that the overseas procedures are different to those in England.[1] However, if natural justice would be denied, this will be highly material. An unreasonable delay overseas, an unreasonably short limitation period, a repugnant law which might be applied overseas, an unfair costs structure, or a lack of opportunity to defend oneself would all be relevant.

An example of the operation of the second limb can be found in *Connelly v RTZ Corp plc*.[2] A claimant could not get legal aid in Namibia, which he accepted was the natural forum in which to bring his claim. He could accordingly afford to finance the litigation only in England, where legal aid was available. This was held by the Court of Appeal not to be a relevant factor, partly due to the provisions of s 31 of the Legal Aid Act 1988, but more generally because comity dictates that cases should be heard where they have the most real and substantial connection. The main concern was *forum conveniens* not *fiscus conveniens*. This is dubious reasoning, as the comity argument is rather unconvincing when a claim cannot practically be brought overseas. However, the claimant subsequently further appealed,[3] alleging that he had entered into a conditional fee arrangement with a solicitor in England, which would enable him to finance proceedings in England. The House of Lords played a rather different tune and thought this relevant. Their Lordships sensibly ruled that the interests of justice weigh in favour of the court where a claimant may vindicate his rights and that such a factor is relevant under the second limb of the *Spiliada* test.[4]

Advantages to the claimant from suing in England, which create a corresponding disadvantage to the defendant, ought generally not to be relevant. The availability of higher damages in England will accordingly generally not be persuasive.[5] The fact that a more favourable law will apply on the merits in England will only be material if the applicable law overseas is manifestly unsatisfactory.[6] Similarly, the fact that the claimant will lose overseas should not be relevant, since the court must be even-handed between the parties.

---

1 Less expansive discovery rules would not suffice, according to *Spiliada* itself.

2 [1996] QB 361.

3 [1998] AC 854.

4 See also *Lubbe and Others v Cape plc* [2001] 1 WLR 1545, where the House of Lords ruled that an English court could take jurisdiction in respect of claims by persons injured whilst working in mines in South Africa, it being highly doubtful whether the claimants could fund litigation in South Africa.

5 *Spiliada Maritime Corp v Cansulex Ltd* [1987] AC 460. However, if the measure offends public policy or an international Convention, this will exceptionally be material: *Caltex Singapore Pte Ltd v BP Shipping Ltd* [1996] 1 Lloyd's Rep 286.

6 *Banco Atlantico SA v British Bank of the Middle East* [1990] 2 Lloyd's Rep 504.

1.3.3 Staying proceedings where the parties have contractually agreed to litigate in a non-Member State to the Brussels Regulation

It might be questioned whether the defendant's job should be made easier when the claimant is suing in England in breach of an exclusive jurisdiction clause for a non-Member State to the Regulation[1] and whether a court should be willing to grant a stay. Both questions should be answered in the affirmative. In effect, once the defendant has demonstrated the existence and validity of the clause, the claimant will immediately have the burden of proof of showing why a stay should not be granted.[2]

However, it is not inevitable that the claimant will be unsuccessful. In *The El Amria*,[3] a cargo of rotten potatoes arrived in Liverpool. The cargo owner sued the carrier in England in breach of an agreement to refer all disputes to the courts of Alexandria. None the less, the court refused a stay, since the cargo had arrived in England, the expert examiner was in England, the relevant witnesses were English residents and the claim was part of collective litigation against the Mersey dockyards. England was so clearly the natural forum, and the risk of irreconcilable judgments so strong, that the clause should not be enforced. It seems that another relevant factor may be that the proceedings in the foreign court are time-barred, provided that the claimant was not at fault in failing to protect the limitation period overseas.[4] If the court does allow a claim to proceed in breach of a jurisdiction clause, a claimant may be able to counterclaim for the damages that an English court awards above the level of the foreign court, if he is able to prove this.

Clearly, it would be inappropriate to apply *Spiliada* principles where a breach of contract is in issue.[5] However, Briggs and Rees point out that the court still looks to identify the natural forum and that a better analogy may be with the exercise of discretion under CPR, r 6.20, whereby the claimant must show that England is the natural forum and only then should the defendant be required to show that it would be unjust for him to be sued in England.[6] This is an eminently sensible approach.

---

1 A choice of a Member State will fall within Art 23 of the Regulation, considered above.

2 See *The Eleftheria* [1970] P 92; *The El Amria* [1981] 2 Lloyd's Rep 119; *The Sennar (No 2)* [1985] 1 WLR 490.

3 Ibid. See also *Bouygues Offshore SA v Caspian Shipping Co (Nos 1, 3, 4 and 5)* [1998] 2 Lloyd's Rep 461.

4 *The Pioneer Container* [1994] 2 AC 324; *Citi-March Ltd v Neptune Orient Lines Ltd* [1996] 2 All ER 545.

5 The Royal Court of Jersey stated in *EMM Capricorn Trustees Ltd v Compass Trustees Ltd* [2001] 4 ITELR 34 that a foreign exclusive jurisdiction clause should be accorded less weight when contained in a trust instrument than in a contract, since successor trustees and beneficiaries will not expressly have agreed to the clause. The decision is considered in the discussion of Jersey at **1.8.5** below, where it will be seen that this author doubts the correctness of this view.

6 Note 2 on p 11, p 215.

1.3.4 Service out of the jurisdiction

CPR, r 6.20 – provisions relating to trusts

Where jurisdiction is not available as of right, the claimant must persuade the court to exercise its discretion to serve the claim form on the defendant outside the jurisdiction. The claimant will make an application without notice, stating the grounds for the application.[1] If permission is granted pursuant to CPR Part 6,[2] the defendant must acknowledge service and may then apply to have the service set aside under CPR, r 11(1). However, in substance the claimant must now prove that the defendant's application should not be granted. Several matters will affect the court's exercise of its discretion. In the first place, the claimant must show a good arguable case that his claim falls factually within one of the heads of CPR, r 6.20(1).[3]

He must identify a particular sub-rule which is applicable; however, the sub-rules are not necessarily mutually exclusive, so it is possible that he will be able to identify more than one. The most important provisions in the trusts context are considered below.

The provisions of CPR Part 6 entered into force on 2 May 2000.[4] They replace the provisions of the Rules of the Supreme Court 1965[5] (RSC) Ord 11. Although there are some changes of substance, many of the CPR sub-rules are identical or very similar to RSC sub-rules. However, the cases considered below were decided pursuant to RSC Ord 11 provisions.

(1) CPR, r 6.20(1)

> '[A] claim is made for a remedy against a person domiciled within the jurisdiction.'

Since in such cases the Brussels Regulation will ordinarily apply, this provision is only of importance when the matter is excluded from the Regulation by Art 1.

(2) CPR, r 6.20(2)

> '[A] claim is made for an injunction ordering the defendant to do or refrain from doing an act within the jurisdiction.'

---

1 CPR, r 6.21(1)(a).

2 Inserted into the CPR by the Civil Procedure (Amendment) Rules 2000 (SI 2000/221).

3 *Seaconsar Far East Ltd v Bank Markazi Jomhouri Islami Iran* [1994] 1 AC 438. However, the good arguable case test applies only to factual matters. Where satisfaction of a head of CPR, r 6.20 depends on a matter of law or construction, the court must authoritatively decide that issue, rather than applying the good arguable case test. So, in the case of CPR, r 6.20(11), the court must decide at the jurisdiction stage whether the trust is governed by English law. See *Chellaram v Chellaram (No 2)* [2002] EWHC 632, [2002] 3 All ER 17.

4 Civil Procedure (Amendment) Rules 2000 (SI 2000/221).

5 SI 1965/1776.

In *ISC Technologies Ltd v Radcliffe*,[1] an order that a defendant be made to account in England was held to fall outside this provision, as not essentially injunctive. The anti-suit injunction[2] might be seen as seeking to ensure that a defendant is not sued overseas and hence increasing the likelihood that he will be sued in England. However, it cannot be said to order the claimant to sue here[3] and thus falls outside this head. The asset freezing order will also be excluded, since the sub-rule applies only to claims instituted in connection with substantive rights.[4] However, the new provision of CPR, r 6.20(4) now provides a basis for service out in the case of interim relief.[5]

(3) CPR, r 6.20(3)

> '[A] claim is made against someone on whom the claim form has been or will be served and—
>
> (a) there is between the claimant and that person a real issue which it is reasonable for the court to try; and
> (b) the claimant wishes to serve the claim form on another person who is a necessary or proper party to that claim.'

There must be a genuine issue between the original two parties; the first defendant must not have been served simply so that jurisdiction could then be taken over another.[6] In *Barings v Coopers & Lybrand*,[7] the court said that the relevant test was whether it was desirable that composite proceedings be brought so as to avoid the possibility of conflicting decisions. It should also be asked whether there is a serious risk that the defendant will be sued in two different jurisdictions.

(4) CPR, r 6.20(10)

> '[T]he whole subject-matter of a claim relates to property located within the jurisdiction.'

It is suggested that where trusts of land are concerned, these provisions should apply to disputes which relate primarily to ownership at law or in equity, even if matters relating to the validity of the trust arise in determining this question. However, if the dispute relates purely to the personal liability of a trustee, the fact that the trust is of land situated in England should not suffice for the purposes of these subsections.

---

1 (Unreported) 7 December 1990.
2 See the discussion of reverse forum shopping below.
3 Indeed, no action might be possible in England.
4 *The Siskina* [1979] AC 210.
5 See the discussion of interim relief below.
6 CPR, r 6.21(2).
7 [1997] IL Pr 12.

In respect of movable property, this sub-rule will encompass disputes relating to legal or equitable title, or the authority of the settlor to dissipate the property, or of the beneficiary to claim the property absolutely. However, it should not extend to the personal rights and duties of the trust relationship merely because, for example, shares happen to be held on trusts in England.

(5) CPR, r 6.20(11)

> '[A] claim is made for any remedy which might be obtained in proceedings to execute the trusts of a written instrument where—
>
> (a) the trusts ought to be executed according to English law; and
> (b) the person on whom the claim form is to be served is a trustee of the trusts.'

It would appear that the Hague Convention[1] will be applied to determine whether the trust is governed by English law.[2] This should be determined at the time at which the claimant applies for permission to serve out.[3] If different laws govern the validity and the administration of a trust, it would suffice that either is governed by English law.[4]

(6) CPR, r 6.20(9)

> '[A] claim is made to enforce any judgment or arbitral award.'

Where common law enforcement is required, an action on the judgment must be brought in England by the enforcing party. Obviously, it is highly likely that the defendant will not be available to be served as of right and this provision relieves this difficulty. Presumably, the court must be satisfied that there is a *prima facie* case for enforcement under its common law rules before exercising its discretion to serve out.

(7) CPR, r 6.20(14)

> '[A] claim is made for a remedy against the defendant as constructive trustee where the defendant's alleged liability arises out of acts committed within the jurisdiction.'

Some aspects of the liability of a fiduciary may fall within this provision.[5]

In cases of alleged knowing receipt of trust property, the receipt itself must occur within the jurisdiction. It has been held that it is insufficient that a

---

1 Hague Convention on the Law Applicable to Trusts and on their Recognition 1985 (the Hague Convention).

2 See generally J Harris *The Hague Trusts Convention* (Hart Publishing, 2002).

3 Rather than at the time at which the cause of action allegedly accrued: *Chellaram v Chellaram (No 2)* [2002] EWHC 632 (Ch), [2002] 3 All ER 17.

4 Ibid.

5 Any broader jurisdictional basis for such claims could only be found if one or more of sub-rules (5), (6) and (8) are capable of covering fiduciary duties.

breach of fiduciary duty occurred in England, if the receipt was outside the jurisdiction.[1] However, in *ISC Technologies v Guerin*,[2] Hoffmann J remarked *obiter* that as long as some of the acts inducing liability occurred in England, that would suffice. This latter view seems correct.[3] As Briggs and Rees convincingly say, 'If the sub-rule is designed to apply to international fraud, it would be surprising if it could be defeated by the simple fact of the defendant arranging to receive the money outside England'.[4]

(8) CPR, r 6.20(15)

> '[A] claim is made for restitution where the defendant's alleged liability arises out of acts committed within the jurisdiction.'

This new provision reflects the evolution of the law of restitution in England. It is quite capable of applying to proprietary restitutionary claims (eg on the basis that a trustee has made an unauthorised profit). However, most instances where it is sought to impose a constructive trust on the defendant will also be caught by CPR, r 6.20(14). CPR, r 6.20(15) may prove particularly useful in claims based on the alleged existence of a resulting trust. It will also be essential where the restitutionary remedy sought against the trustee is purely personal, for example in the case of a personal claim for knowing receipt of trust property. It does, however, threaten to be a sub-rule overshadowed by very complex questions about where, in a restitutionary context, the trustee's 'alleged liability arises'.

Other potentially relevant provisions

As with the Brussels Regulation, it is not safe to assume for jurisdictional purposes that a term will bear the same meaning as it does in domestic law. Accordingly, it would be unwise wholly to ignore the jurisdictional headings dealing with contract and tort. However, it must be conceded that equitable obligations are less likely to fall within these provisions than under the Brussels Regulation, since the latter operates in an environment in which equitable claims other than breach of trust are largely unknown and in which no attempt was accordingly made to fit them into other parts of the Regulation. The following discussion will accordingly only be brief.

(1) CPR, r 6.20(5)–(7) (Contractual claims)

CPR, r 6.20(5):

> '[A] claim is made in respect of a contract where the contract—

---

1 *ISC Technologies Ltd v Radcliffe* (unreported) 7 December 1990.

2 [1992] 2 Lloyd's Rep 430.

3 A view followed in *Polly Peck International plc v Nadir* (1993) *The Times*, March 22.

4 Note 2 on p 11, p 237.

(a) was made within the jurisdiction;
(b) was made by or through an agent trading or residing within the jurisdiction;
(c) is governed by English law; or
(d) contains a term to the effect that the court shall have jurisdiction to determine any claim in respect of the contract.'

CPR, r 6.20(6):

'[A] claim is made in respect of a breach of contract committed within the jurisdiction.'

CPR, r 6.20(7):

'[A] claim is made for a declaration that no contract exists where, if the contract was found to exist, it would comply with the conditions set out in paragraph (5).'

CPR, r 6.20(5)–(7) may be used, for example, in the case of an agreement to transfer an equitable interest. Whether they may extend more generally to equitable obligations is unclear. Since these may well be treated in the Rome Convention on choice of law in contract[1] as contractual within the meaning of Art 1,[2] it is suggested that they could fall within these sub-rules. Briggs and Rees suggest that it would be going too far to adopt the definition of 'contract' used for a European Regulation on choice of law in the context of English common law jurisdiction rules.[3] However, it is difficult to see why the terms of CPR Part 6 should not have a special private international law meaning extending beyond the scope of domestic concepts, given that it is an inevitable aspect of transnational litigation that causes of action which are unknown to, or would not succeed by, English domestic law, can successfully be brought in an English court; in which case, the liability, for example, of a fiduciary who has profited from a position into which he willingly placed himself might fall within this sub-rule.

(2) CPR, r 6.20(8)

'[A] claim is made in tort where—

(a) damage was sustained within the jurisdiction; or
(b) the damage sustained resulted from an act committed within the jurisdiction.'

It had until recently appeared that there must be a tort according to English domestic law.[4] If this is still so, claims for breach of fiduciary duty or liability to account as constructive trustee are apparently excluded. However, the reason for such a view may have been that, prior to the enactment of the

---

1 Enacted by the Contracts (Applicable Law) Act 1990.
2 *Dicey and Morris*, n 2 on p 11, Chapter 32.
3 Note 2 on p 11, p 227.
4 *Metall und Rohstoff AG v Donaldson Lufkin & Jenrette Inc* [1990] 1 QB 391.

Private International Law Miscellaneous Provisions Act 1995, Part III,[1] which reformed the choice of law rules in tort, such claims could not succeed on the merits, since for liability to ensue, the alleged wrong had, inter alia, to be tortious according to English law.[2] Now that this is no longer the case,[3] there might now be a special private international law definition of 'tort' for common law jurisdictional purposes, which might extend to a broader range of non-contractual liability, including certain equitable obligations, such as the duty of confidentiality.[4] It is suggested that an action, for example, for breach of confidence should fall within this subhead.

According to Slade LJ in *Metall und Rohstoff AG v Donaldson Lufkin & Jenrette Inc*,[5] there must be either significant damage in England or the defendant must have committed substantial and efficacious acts in the jurisdiction. However, whilst either will suffice to bring the claim within the sub-rule, it is probable that if the tort itself is ultimately found to have occurred overseas, the court will not exercise its discretion to serve out, according to *dicta* in *The Albaforth*.[6]

1.3.5 The exercise of the court's discretion to serve out

Once the claimant has shown that his claim falls within a sub-rule of CPR, r 6.20, he must persuade the court to exercise its discretion to serve out. The constituent factors of this discretion were reviewed by the House of Lords in *Seaconsar (Far East) Ltd v Bank Markazi Jomhouri Islami Iran*.[7]

(1) *The claimant must show that England is clearly or distinctly the natural forum*.[8] This requirement, previously a matter of common law authority, is now stated in CPR, r 6.21(2)(a). The factors which would be relevant to establishing this are those considered in relation to the first limb of the stay test above; the only difference is the reversal of the burden of proof.[9]

(2) *Permission will none the less not be granted if it would be unjust for the defendant to be sued in England*. It is suggested that the burden of proof on this point should transfer to the defendant, though the matter is by no means clear. The relevant factors ought to be those which apply under the second limb of *Spiliada* in the stay context.

---

1 In force since 1 May 1996.

2 *Chaplin v Boys* [1971] AC 356.

3 The *prima facie* applicable law is now that of the place of the tort.

4 See further J Harris 'Choice of Law in Tort – Blending in with the Landscape of the Conflict of Laws?' (1998) 61 MLR 33.

5 [1990] 1 QB 391.

6 *Cordoba Shipping Co v National State Bank*, Elizabeth, New Jersey: *The Albaforth* [1984] 2 Lloyd's Rep 91.

7 [1994] 1 AC 438.

8 This comes from *Spiliada* itself: [1987] AC 460.

9 For a recent example of the application of the natural forum doctrine to trusts litigation, see *Chellaram v Chellaram (No 2)* [2002] EWHC 632 (Ch), [2002] 3 All ER 17.

(3) *There must be a serious issue to be tried on the merits.* At common law, it was established that the claimant's *prima facie* case must be a strong enough case that the defendant could not successfully have it struck out. CPR, r 6.21(1)(b) now states that the claimant must assert in his application that he believes that he has a reasonable prospect of success on the merits. However, it must be recalled that English law will not necessarily govern on the merits. It could be contended that whether there is a 'serious issue' should be determined by applying the applicable law on the merits of the dispute.[1] However, this would be extremely inconvenient at the jurisdiction stage and it appears that there need only be a serious issue according to English domestic law.

1.3.6 Non-justiciability

One final point on common law jurisdiction should be made. It is often said that where a dispute concerns any property rights in immovable property situated in a non-Member State, the claim is not justiciable in an English court.[2] However, there are limits to this rule. Section 30 of the CJJA 1982 allows claims for trespass or other torts relating to foreign land to be brought in England, if they do not primarily concern rights in the land. An English court will also have jurisdiction in relation to obligations arising from contracts for the sale of land and, most importantly for present purposes, from trusts of land, even if an order to transfer an interest in the land is sought.[3]

1.4 REVERSE FORUM SHOPPING

It is all too easy to assume that all litigation has a natural claimant and a natural defendant. However, this makes transnational litigation very one-sided. It allows the claimant to seek out the most convenient and advantageous forum. To combat this, it may be possible for the person against whom liability is alleged to launch his own proceedings, either for a declaration that he is not liable or an injunction to restrain proceedings in a foreign court where he is being sued. Such forum selection by the 'natural' defendant is known as 'reverse forum shopping'.

1.4.1 Anti-suit injunctions

An anti-suit injunction is an order directed to the overseas party not to pursue proceedings overseas, on pain of contempt of court. Although not directed at the overseas court itself, its detrimental effect on international harmony makes

---

1 There is a suggestion of this in *Metall and Rohstoff AG v Donaldson Lufkin & Jenrette Inc* [1990] 1 QB 391.

2 *British South Africa Co v Companhia de Mocambique* [1893] AC 602.

3 *Penn v Lord Baltimore* (1750) 1 Ves Sen 444.

it a weapon which an English court will not use lightly. Indeed, some cases have suggested that the aggrieved party should first appear overseas to argue that the foreign court should not hear the case.[1] However, this involves the very type of inconvenience which he will hope to avoid and has little to commend it as a general rule, especially since he risks being deemed to have submitted to the overseas court.

As with any other action, the English court must first have jurisdiction over the defendant (here, this will be the party sought to be restrained, i.e. the overseas claimant). This will be determined by the rules considered in this chapter. However, it is highly dubious whether an injunction should be permitted when the overseas claimant is suing in a Member State to the Regulation pursuant to the Regulation rules.[2]

Where proceedings may be brought overseas or in England

If proceedings may be brought overseas or in England, the question then becomes whether the court will, in its discretion, grant the remedy. The Privy Council in *Société Nationale Industrielle Aerospatiale (SNIA) v Lee Kui Jak*[3] laid down what is now taken as the law as regards the availability of anti-suit injunctions to restrain proceedings in a foreign court. Lord Goff said that where a remedy would be available both in an English and a foreign court:

> 'the English … court will, generally speaking, only restrain the plaintiff from pursuing proceedings in the foreign court if such pursuit would be oppressive or vexatious. This presupposes that, as a general rule, the English … court must conclude that it provides the natural forum for the trial of the action; and further, since the court is concerned with the ends of justice, that account must be taken not only of injustice to the defendant if the plaintiff is allowed to pursue the foreign proceedings, but also of injustice to the plaintiff if he is not allowed to do so. So the court will not grant an injunction if, by doing so, it will deprive the plaintiff of advantages in the foreign forum of which it would be unjust to deprive him.'[4]

Hence, it is not sufficient that England is the natural forum, if an overseas claimant would be unfairly deprived of a right available overseas. In the instant case, however, the fact that the overseas defendant could not claim an indemnity in Texas and that the natural forum lay elsewhere justified the injunction.

The English courts are not available

It is less certain whether this test should apply where no claim is possible in England. Two situations should be distinguished: where no other forum is obviously available, so that if the claimant does not sue overseas he cannot

---

1 *Pan American Airways v Andres* 1992 SLT 268.

2 See the discussion of tactical conclusions in relation to the Brussels Regulation above.

3 [1987] AC 871.

4 Ibid at 896.

successfully bring the claim; and where the claim can be brought elsewhere, but the natural forum is shown to be neither England nor the state where the claimant is currently litigating.

(1) No other courts are available

The House of Lords in *British Airways Board v Laker Airways Ltd*[1] apparently did think that different injunction rules applied for single forum cases. Lord Scarman said that:

> 'The power of the English court to grant the injunction exists, if the bringing of the suit in the foreign court is in the circumstances so unconscionable that in accordance with our principles of a "wide and flexible" equity it can be seen to be an infringement of an equitable right of the applicant.'[2]

In that case, an insolvent airway company (Laker Airways) sued other airways which it alleged had conspired to drive it out of the market. The liquidator wanted to sue in the United States on the basis of anti-trust legislation which permitted the court to award penal damages in support of US competition policy. British Airways sought an injunction in England, but failed. The House of Lords said that it had not been shown to be unconscionable for the liquidator to sue in the United States. It was particularly influenced by the fact that this cause of action could not be brought in England.

However, closer scrutiny reveals that there is no need for a separate test in this area. It may be inherently less probable that proceedings in the only available forum will be oppressive or vexatious, but that is a question of degree. There is no reason why the *Aerospatiale* test cannot apply. Nor is there an obvious distinction in reality between Lord Scarman's test and that in *Aerospatiale*. In *South Carolina Insurance Co v Assurantie Maatschappij De Zeven Provincien NV*,[3] the House of Lords said that unconscionability includes 'conduct which is oppressive or vexatious or interferes with the due process of the court'. 'It would be a brave man who sought to distinguish oppressive from unconscionable behaviour, and it may be realised that the test is the same one in each case.'[4] Nor does the *British Airways* case sit well with the Court of Appeal decision in *Midland Bank plc v Laker Airways Ltd (In Liquidation)*,[5] where an injunction to restrain an action against an English defendant in the United States under anti-trust legislation was granted because the claimant's dealings with the defendant were solely in England and the overseas defendant had no connection with the United States. In short, it is contended that the *Aerospatiale* test should continue to apply in a single forum case.

---

1 [1985] AC 58.

2 Ibid at 95.

3 [1987] AC 24.

4 A Briggs 'Restraint of Foreign Proceedings' [1987] LMCLQ 391 at 395.

5 [1986] QB 689.

(2) The natural forum lies in another overseas state

This situation arose in *Airbus Industries GIE v Patel*,[1] where Airbus sought an injunction in England to restrain parties from pursuing an action against it in Texas. The claim arose from an air accident in India. Clearly, neither Texas nor England was the natural forum. In these circumstances, Lord Goff felt unable to grant an injunction. Although he stressed that the remedy could be granted 'when the ends of justice require it', he stressed the need to respect comity. He distinguished *Midland Bank plc v Laker Airways Ltd (In Liquidation)*[2] as a case which was 'overwhelmingly English in character'. On the facts, Lord Goff accepted that the Texas proceedings were oppressive, but found that 'the basic principle is that only courts of an interested jurisdiction can act in the matter; and if they are powerless to do so, that will not of itself be enough to justify the courts of another jurisdiction to act in their place'.

(3) The overseas proceedings are in breach of an English jurisdiction clause

Unsurprisingly, the English court's reticence to grant an anti-suit injunction will disappear if the overseas proceedings are in breach of an English jurisdiction clause. In *Aggeliki Charis Compania Maritima SA v Pagnan SpA (The Angelic Grace)*,[3] in the context of an English arbitration clause, Millett LJ suggested that the availability of the injunction is still at the court's discretion, although 'good reason needs to be shown why it should not be exercised in any given case'. It is suggested that the *Aerospatiale* test should still be applied, but that suing overseas in breach of choice of court clause is *prima facie* oppressive. This is consistent with *Sohio Supply Co v Gatoil (USA) Inc*, where Staughton LJ stated that breach of an English choice of court clause 'may well in itself be vexatious or oppressive in any given case'.[4]

However, an English court might refuse to grant an anti-suit injunction if the claim brought overseas is part of a larger pattern of litigation. In *Donohue v Armco*,[5] the House of Lords recently refused to issue an anti-suit injunction to restrain proceedings brought in New York in breach of an English exclusive jurisdiction clause. Although the applicant had the benefit of the English jurisdiction clause, the proceedings in New York involved a range of parties, most of whom were not bound by the jurisdiction clause. If the House of Lords had issued the injunction, the result would have been fragmented litigation in England and in New York. In other words, the pattern of litigational convenience favoured not granting the injunction.[6]

---

1 [1999] AC 119.
2 [1986] QB 689.
3 [1995] 1 Lloyd's Rep 87 at 96.
4 [1989] 1 Lloyd's Rep 588 at 592.
5 [2002] 1 All ER 749
6 See also *Bouygues Offshore SA v Caspian Shipping Co (Nos 1, 3, 4 and 5)* [1998] 2 Lloyd's Rep 461.

1.4.2 The declaration of non-liability

A declaration of non-liability is a remedy which can be tactically devastating. By being first off the mark and launching such proceedings, a party may effectively nullify any overseas proceedings against it; for it provides a judgment on the merits and hence may make the matters in question *res judicata* overseas. It is particularly effective where jurisdiction is taken under the Brussels Regulation. Because jurisdiction rests in the court first seised, Art 27 will prevent the other party from litigating the same matter between the same parties in the courts of any other Member State. The declaration can also be immensely helpful for the applicant in helping to establish at an early stage liability for insurance purposes.

The court must first have jurisdiction against the defendant to the declaration action. If jurisdiction is sought under the main Regulation rules, there is little apparent difficulty.[1] Where jurisdiction must be sought pursuant to CPR Part 6, however, the court in *The Volvox Hollandia*[2] indicated that an application for service out would not be treated favourably, especially when proceedings were long since under way overseas and the English action represented blatant forum shopping. Once again, the 'sue first or risk being sued in an undesired forum' lesson of international litigation is apparent.

Historically, the attitude of English courts to the declaration of non-liability was one of scepticism. The Court of Appeal in *First National Bank of Boston v Union Bank of Switzerland*[3] stressed that a declaration should not be granted unless it had a clear purpose. In the instant case, proceedings were already under way in Switzerland and it was thought that the Swiss courts would ignore the declaration. However, this is unconvincing. Where the applicant has a valid reason in England for seeking the award (eg because his assets are located in the jurisdiction) it is difficult to see why the overseas court's reactions should be critical. In *Smyth v Behbehani*,[4] the Court of Appeal stated that the claimant may not use the negative declaration to obtain an illegitimate procedural advantage. However, in that case, three related claims for negative declaratory relief could all be heard in England, whereas the claims would otherwise be fragmented overseas. Nourse LJ viewed this as a legitimate procedural advantage and ruled that the declaration could, in principle, be granted.

The Court of Appeal has recently shown a much more benevolent attitude to the declaration of non-liability. In *Messier Dowty Ltd v Sabena SA*,[5] it held that a court should not be reluctant to grant a negative declaration if this would help to ensure that the aims of justice are achieved. In the instant case, Dowty

---

1 *The Tatry* [1994] ECR I-5439.
2 [1988] 2 Lloyd's Rep 361.
3 [1990] 1 Lloyd's Rep 32.
4 [1999] IL Pr 584.
5 [2001] 1 WLR 2040.

sought a declaration that it was not liable to Sabena or to the second and third defendants for losses incurred following an accident at Brussels Airport. Lord Woolf MR saw no reason to be adverse to negative declarations and treated with reservation adverse comments made about them in earlier cases. He said that a court with jurisdiction should only refuse to consider granting a negative declaration where it would serve no useful purpose. Although the declaration was not granted on the facts (because the likelihood of Sabena wanting to sue Dowty was thought to be very small), the case is of wider significance in suggesting that a court will no longer treat an application for a negative declaration with inherent suspicion. This is a development very much to be welcomed.

1.5 INTERIM RELIEF

1.5.1 Substantive proceedings are in England

Even where litigation is under way in a court of competent jurisdiction, a claimant in international litigation may feel the need to take action in England to ensure that any assets which the defendant has are safeguarded pending the outcome of the main dispute. Where the substantive litigation is in England, an English court may clearly assume jurisdiction to grant interim relief.[1] But a more complex problem arises either where the substantive litigation takes place overseas or where the defendant's assets are situated overseas and there is a risk that they will be dissipated before judgment on the merits is delivered. One must ask whether the court has jurisdiction to make the award; and if so whether, in the exercise of its discretion, it might choose to do so. The law in this area has been liberalised considerably since 1997.

1.5.2 Jurisdiction to grant interim relief in support of overseas proceedings

Prior to 1982, great problems obstructed the path of a claimant seeking interim relief in England when the English court had no jurisdiction on the substance. In *The Siskina*,[2] the House of Lords decided that an asset freezing order could not be granted where the court had no jurisdiction on the substance and that the predecessor to CPR, r 6.20(4), which presently permits service out of the jurisdiction where 'a claim is made for an interim remedy under section 25(1) of the 1982 [Civil Jurisdiction and Judgments] Act', could not apply. The key question was whether the English court could take

1 On the basis of the jurisdictional rules considered above.

2 [1979] AC 210.

jurisdiction on the merits; it mattered not that ultimately a foreign court heard the final case.[1]

The position was ameliorated for judgments of contracting states to the Brussels Convention by Art 24 thereof. The relevant provision is now contained in Brussels Regulation, Art 31, which provides that:

> 'Application may be made to the courts of a Member State for such provisional, including protective, measures as may be available under the law of that State, even if, under this Regulation the courts of another Member State have jurisdiction as to the substance of the matter.'

In *Van Uden Maritime BV v Kommanditgesellschaft in Firma Deco-Line*,[2] the ECJ stated that this definition should:

> 'be understood as referring to measures which … are intended to preserve a factual or legal situation so as to safeguard rights the recognition of which is otherwise sought from the court having jurisdiction as to the substance of the case.'

It also ruled that the granting of a provisional measure pursuant to (what is now) Art 31:

> 'is conditional, inter alia, on the existence of a real connecting link between the subject-matter of the measures sought and the territorial jurisdiction of the Member State of the court before which those measures are sought.'[3]

This connection would most readily be shown where the defendant's assets were within the jurisdiction.

However, the effect of *The Siskina*[4] was that an English court would still not grant such interim relief unless the English court was jurisdictionally competent on the merits. The position was remedied by s 25 of the CJJA 1982, which is the basis of jurisdictional competence to grant interim relief when the English court does not have jurisdiction over the substantive dispute.[5] The result was that an English court would be jurisdictionally competent to grant interim relief in support of overseas litigation where the foreign court had

---

1 *Channel Tunnel Group Ltd v Balfour Beatty Construction Ltd* [1993] AC 334.

2 [1998] ECR I-7091, at para 37. See also *Mietz v Intership Yachting Sneek BV* [1999] ECR I-2277.

3 *Van Uden Maritime BV v Kommanditgesellschaft in Firma Deco-Line* [1998] ECR I-7091 at para 40. Curiously, the ECJ also held that the predecessor to Art 31 could be used to grant such relief in support of substantive arbitration proceedings, even though arbitration falls outside the scope of the Convention by Art 1.

4 [1979] AC 210.

5 Article 31 applies only to substantive disputes occurring overseas; accordingly, its limitations do not apply to situations where an English court is jurisdictionally competent on the merits.

taken jurisdiction on the basis of the Brussels Regulation.[1] In any other case, *The Siskina* limitations would still hold sway.

Section 25(3) of the CJJA 1982 allowed for an extension of the English court's jurisdiction so as to allow it to grant interim relief in relation to a dispute in a non-Member State and in relation to matters which are not civil or commercial within the meaning of Art 1 of the Brussels Regulation. With effect from 1 April 1997, this power has been exercised.[2] An English court may now grant interim relief in relation to proceedings[3] commenced:

(a) in a Member State pursuant to the Brussels Regulation;
(b) in a Member State in a matter outside the scope of the Regulation; or
(c) in a non-Member State.

However, the court may still refuse to grant the relief if 'the fact that the court has no jurisdiction apart from this section in relation to the subject-matter of the proceedings makes it inexpedient for the court to grant it'.[4] If England is not the natural forum for the substantive litigation and it is not apparent either that an English court would enforce the overseas judgment or that the English interim order would be effective in the overseas jurisdiction, the case for intervening may be weak. In other words, the expansion of the jurisdictional competence to award interim relief may be accompanied by a greater willingness to invoke the discretion provided for in s 25(2).

Section 25(7) of the CJJA 1982 states that 'interim relief' includes all relief which a court has power to grant in proceedings relating to matters within the jurisdiction, except a warrant for the arrest of property or provision for the obtaining of evidence. On one view, this might seem to exclude search orders.[5] Moreover, whilst interlocutory anti-suit injunctions would clearly come within the provisions, it is less clear that final anti-suit injunctions would do so. Briggs and Rees suggest that such relief could be included, since it does not affect the substance of the dispute.[6] However, since the anti-suit injunction interferes directly in the jurisdictional competence of other states, comity would suggest that the provisions should not be taken to extend so far.

---

1 However, it seems that, despite s 25, interim relief (including the *Mareva*) could not be granted where it was necessary to serve the defendant out of the jurisdiction, since no head of RSC Ord 11 existed under which to serve out: see Briggs and Rees, n 2 on p 11, p 296.

2 Civil Jurisdiction and Judgments Act 1982 (Interim Relief) Order 1997 (SI 1997/302). CPR, r 6.20(4) (which replaced RSC Ord 11, r 8A) now provides that a claim form may be served out of the jurisdiction with the permission of the court if 'a claim is made for an interim remedy under section 25(1) of the 1982 Act'. Presumably, the English court will apply the same criteria as it uses in determining whether to serve out in a substantive dispute.

3 The word 'proceedings' may well include overseas arbitrations: see Briggs and Rees, n 2 on p 11, p 297.

4 CJJA 1982, s 25(2).

5 Although see Briggs and Rees, n 2 on p 11, pp 299–300.

6 Note 2 on p 11, p 300.

1.5.3 Enforcement of interim awards

An English award in a civil or commercial matter ought to be enforced in Europe under the Regulation rules for the enforcement of foreign judgments,[1] since it is a judgment within the meaning of Art 32. Conversely, a Member State's judgment in such a matter ought to be enforced in England. However, Briggs and Rees point out that such relief may have been obtained without notice and hence infringe Art 34(2).[2] This means that even if an English court were to grant an asset freezing order in relation to the defendant's assets in, for example, Italy, that order may be ineffective in Italy.

Where an interim order has been made in the courts of a non-Member State, recognition will only be given to it if the common law or statutory rules are satisfied.[3]

1.5.4 Interim orders

The fact that an English court has jurisdiction to grant an award does not mean that it will do so. Although not strictly a matter of the court's jurisdiction, it is worth considering briefly the remedies available to a court and its likely willingness to grant them. Pursuant to s 37(1) of the Supreme Court Act 1981, the court may make orders which are extraterritorial in nature.[4] Of these, two of the most important are the asset freezing order and the search order (formerly known as the *Anton Piller* order).

Asset freezing order

An asset freezing order[5] is issued against a defendant, normally to prevent him from removing assets[6] from the jurisdiction or dissipating assets outside the jurisdiction.[7] It is available if a good arguable case on the merits exists against him and there is a serious risk that he will remove or dissipate the assets. The sanction of contempt of court exists for breaching the injunction. The claimant's application will normally be without notice and he must undertake to pay damages for loss suffered should he fail on the merits.

For present purposes, interest centres on the 'worldwide' asset freezing order.[8] This is an order made against a person over whom the court has jurisdictional competence in relation to assets held overseas. Its impact overseas means that a court will not be too ready to grant this form of award

---

1 Provided that the relief does not contravene the natural justice provision of Art 34(2).
2 Note 2 on p 11, p 303.
3 See below for a discussion of the various schemes of enforcement of foreign judgments.
4 Since such remedies are made against the defendant and not directly against his assets, a court with *in personam* jurisdiction can in theory make orders which affect the defendant's overseas assets.
5 See *Mareva Companie Naviera SA of Panama v International Bulk Carriers SA* [1975] 2 Lloyd's Rep 509.
6 To the value of the claim made against him.
7 He can also be ordered to disclose the whereabouts of assets or to move them between jurisdictions.
8 See *Babanaft International Co SA v Bassatne* [1990] Ch 13.

and will not do so if sufficient assets exist within the jurisdiction to satisfy any potential judgment in the claimant's favour. It is likely to be especially cautious about intervening if the substantive dispute is not to be heard in England.[1] However, the court may be more willing to grant the relief post-judgment.[2]

Search order

A search order[3] requires a defendant to allow his property to be searched and to allow property to be removed so that it may be preserved for the main action. The applicant, who will apply without notice, must show a clear risk that the property will otherwise be destroyed. This may be made in relation to premises outside England,[4] although a court is likely to be cautious to permit this.

1.6 RECOGNITION AND ENFORCEMENT OF FOREIGN JUDGMENTS

1.6.1 Recognition or enforcement?

Enforcement of a judgment (which necessarily requires recognition) will be required by a creditor who has been awarded relief overseas and now wishes to secure access to the defendant's assets in England. Recognition alone will suffice where a defendant overseas faces the prospect of the same action being litigated against him overseas and he wishes to use the foreign judgment as a defence, ie he seeks no further remedy in England.

Four major schemes of recognition and enforcement of foreign judgments are applicable in England. The Brussels Regulation, common law, the Administration of Justice Act 1920 and the Foreign Judgments (Reciprocal Enforcement) Act 1933 all need consideration. The appropriate scheme depends upon the court which delivered judgment and/or the basis of its jurisdiction.

1.6.2 The Brussels Regulation rules

Having laid down complex, detailed, but uniform jurisdictional rules, the Brussels Regulation paves the way for an uncomplicated and liberal system of mutual enforcement. The Regulation rules apply if the judgment was delivered

1 *Rosseel NV v Oriental Commercial & Shipping Co (UK) Ltd* [1990] 3 All ER 545; but see *Republic of Haiti v Duvalier* [1990] 1 QB 202.

2 *Babanaft International Co SA v Bassatne* [1990] Ch 13.

3 See *Anton Piller KG v Manufacturing Processes Ltd* [1976] Ch 55.

4 *Altertext Inc v Advanced Communications Ltd* [1985] 1 WLR 457.

in the courts of a Member State[1] in a civil or commercial matter, even if jurisdiction was taken under national jurisdictional rules pursuant to Art 4.[2] It follows that only where a matter is excluded altogether from the Regulation by Art 1 will the common law rules apply to a Member State's judgment. However, the English court may be entitled to check for itself that the judgment is indeed within the Regulation when recognition is sought.[3]

Article 33(1) simply provides that 'a judgment given in a Member State shall be recognised in the other Member States without any special procedure being required'.

The word 'judgment' is defined in Art 32 to mean 'any judgment given by a court or tribunal of a Member State, whatever the judgment may be called, including a decree, order, decision or writ of execution, as well as the determination of costs or expenses by an officer of the court'. This broad definition none the less excludes purely procedural rulings[4] and may exclude without notice applications[5] (including an asset freezing order).

Given the assumed equal competence of the courts of each Member State to interpret the Regulation, a party cannot generally resist enforcement by arguing that the overseas court lacked jurisdiction. It follows that if a defendant wishes to challenge the jurisdiction of a Member State's courts, he would be wise to do so overseas and not wait until the enforcement stage. This is the very converse of the advice one might give to a defendant being sued in a state to which the common law enforcement regime applies in England, where widespread challenges can be made at the enforcement stage and the defendant might have more to lose by being deemed to have submitted to the overseas court.

Defences – lack of jurisdictional competence

Nevertheless, the debtor may in very limited circumstances object to the Member State's jurisdiction under Art 35. This provides three exceptions. A judgment should not be recognised if it conflicts with the exclusive jurisdiction provisions of Art 22 or the insurance or consumer contract provisions,[6] ie if those provisions gave jurisdiction to the courts of another Member State and not to those of the state where the judgment was delivered. Note that violation of a choice of court agreement is not a reason to refuse enforcement. Accordingly, a defendant who believes he is being sued in a Member State in

---

1 If the judgment was delivered in Denmark, the Brussels Convention will apply to its recognition and enforcement. The Brussels Convention will also apply to foreign judgments delivered before 1 March 2002.

2 The Lugano Convention will apply to a judgment delivered in Iceland, Norway, Poland or Switzerland.

3 See Briggs and Rees, n 2 on p 11, pp 312–313.

4 *Schlosser Report* (1979) OJ C 59/127 at para 187.

5 *Denilauler v SNC Couchet Frères* [1980] ECR 1553, ECJ. The problem is that such decisions are likely to fall foul of the natural justice defence in Art 34(2) (on which, see below).

6 Although in the case of the last two, enforcement will still be possible if the defendant had submitted to the overseas jurisdiction.

breach of an agreement for another state must make his challenge where he is being sued. In all cases, the court seised shall be bound by the findings of fact on which the court of the state of origin based its jurisdiction.[1] Hence, only legal errors in application of the Regulation will fall within these provisions.

Other defences

Article 34 provides four substantive defences to recognition.

Recognition would be manifestly contrary to English public policy

This provision should be construed narrowly, a fact emphasised by the word 'manifestly'.[2] Recognition of the judgment itself, not the underlying subject matter of the dispute in which judgment was given, must be contrary to public policy. The English court may not invoke this head where a foreign court has taken jurisdiction pursuant to Art 4 simply because it disapproves of its jurisdictional rules.

The fact that the judgment of the state of origin is allegedly illegal is not in itself enough to justify use of the public policy defence. In *Krombach v Bamberski*[3] the ECJ held that:

> 'In order for the prohibition of any review of the foreign judgment as to its substance to be observed, the infringement would have to constitute a manifest breach of a rule of law regarded as essential in the legal order of the State in which enforcement is sought or of a right recognised as being fundamental within that legal order.'[4]

The ECJ ruled in *Régie Nationale des Usines Renault SA v Maxicar SPA and Another*[5] that even an alleged breach of EC law is not in itself enough to justify invoking the defence. There is no separate Regulation defence that a foreign judgment was fraudulently procured. It appears that such an argument must fall within the public policy head. However, the correct courts to adjudicate on such an allegation are normally those of the state where judgment was delivered.[6] Certainly the common law fraud defence, which may allow an English court to re-examine if there has been fraud, even if this effectively means retrying the case, has been ruled inappropriate.[7] The High Court held that where remedies to complain of fraud existed in the state of origin, any objection should be made there and that the foreign court's findings thereon should be binding.

---

1 Article 35(2).

2 Which was added in the Regulation and which was not previously founded in the Brussels Convention.

3 [2000] ECR I-1935.

4 Ibid, at para 37 of the judgment.

5 [2000] ECR I-2973.

6 *Schlosser Report* (1979) OJ C 59/71, p 192.

7 *Interdesco SA v Nullifire* [1992] 1 Lloyd's Rep 180.

The judgment was given in default of appearance and the defendant was not duly served with the document which instituted the proceedings or with an equivalent document in sufficient time and in such a way as to enable him to arrange for his defence, unless the defendant failed to commence proceedings to challenge the judgment when it was possible for him to do so

Only default judgments are covered. Where the defendant seeks to have the default judgment set aside overseas, he may lose the protection of this provision, unless the very existence of the original order has adversely affected him in the sense of shifting the burden of proof onto him to get the order set aside.[1] It appears that the phrase 'default judgment' has a European autonomous meaning. In *Hendrikman v Magenta Druck & Verlag GmbH*,[2] the ECJ held that a judgment given against a person who had no knowledge that proceedings had been initiated against him was not entitled to recognition in other Member States, even where a lawyer had appeared on behalf of that person. This applied where a lawyer acted for a person without his knowledge, since that person was powerless to defend himself adequately in such a situation. This was so even though the court of origin had not given a judgment in default of appearance. As to what constituted 'due service', it must be shown that the defendant was duly served in a way which would reasonably allow him to ensure that a default judgment was not entered against him.[3] In this regard, the fact that he was properly served according to the national procedural rules of the state of origin is a necessary, but not sufficient, condition.[4] The state where recognition is sought may re-examine for itself whether the time was sufficient.[5]

The Regulation makes clear that if the defendant failed to commence proceedings overseas to challenge the judgment when it was possible for him to do so, he will be precluded from raising the defence at the recognition stage.

The judgment is irreconcilable with a judgment between the same parties in the court in which recognition is sought

Article 27 should prevent this occurring in civil or commercial matters. Where it does occur, however, the English court's judgment prevails in England, even if it is delivered subsequent to the foreign judgment. Article 34(3) is more likely to be relevant if the foreign court took jurisdiction within the Regulation and there is a related action in England which falls outside the Regulation. Such a case arose in *Hoffmann v Krieg*,[6] where the ECJ held that a Dutch court was entitled to deny recognition to a German order that a man give

1 *Minalmet GmbH v Brandeis Ltd* [1992] ECR I-5661, ECJ.
2 [1996] ECR I-4943, ECJ.
3 *Klomps v Michel* [1981] ECR 1593.
4 *Debaecker v Bouwman* [1985] ECR 1779.
5 *Pendy Plastic Products BV v Pluspunkt Handelsgesellschaft mbH* [1982] ECR 2723.
6 [1988] ECR 645.

maintenance to his wife (ie a Regulation judgment), when the Dutch court had issued a decree of divorce (a judgment falling outside the Regulation). The ECJ stated that judgments are 'irreconcilable' if they lead to consequences which are mutually exclusive.

> The judgment is irreconcilable with an earlier judgment given in another Member State or in a third state involving the same cause of action and between the same parties, provided that the earlier judgment fulfils the conditions necessary for recognition in the Member State addressed

Hence, if a judgment was given in a non-Member State, such as the United States, and is entitled to recognition by English common law rules, it would prevail if delivered prior to a German judgment.

There had been a lacuna in the Brussels Convention as to what should happen where two judgments delivered in overseas Member States (eg France and Germany) were irreconcilable with one another. It was unclear whether the first to be handed down, the first sought to be recognised or (where one judgment was a Brussels Convention judgment, eg on maintenance, and the other fell outside the Convention, eg a divorce petition) the Brussels Convention judgment prevailed. The Regulation clarifies matters by providing that a Regulation judgment may be refused recognition if irreconcilable with an earlier judgment given in another Member State qualifying for recognition. In other words, the first judgment to be handed down will prevail.

One further exception should be mentioned. Article 59 of the Brussels Convention allowed a contracting state to enter into a treaty with a non-contracting state, exempting certain persons from the Convention regime, where the courts of a Member State had taken jurisdiction under their national rules pursuant to Art 4. Article 72 of the Brussels Regulation provides that such treaties as were entered into when the Convention was in force will still be effective. The United Kingdom has two such treaties, which apply respectively to defendants domiciled or habitually resident in Australia[1] and Canada.[2] However, it should be noted that Brussels Regulation, Art 72 does not confer on Member States the power to enter into new treaties of this nature.

Aside from the grounds mentioned above, Art 36 states that 'under no circumstances may a foreign judgment be reviewed as to its substance'.

The enforcement procedure

The enforcement procedure is set out in detail in Arts 38–52. The provisions are not complex and it is not necessary to examine them at any length. A judgment shall be enforced in England when, on the application of any

---

1 Reciprocal Enforcement of Foreign Judgments (Australia) Order 1994 (SI 1994/1901), Sch 3, Art 3.

2 Reciprocal Enforcement of Foreign Judgments (Canada) Order (SI 1987/468).

interested party, it has been registered for enforcement in England.[1] The claimant seeking enforcement[2] should apply without notice for an order for registration before the High Court[3] and produce a copy of the judgment.[4] When a judgment is entitled to recognition under the Regulation, the applicant may seek such interim relief prior to obtaining a declaration of enforceability.[5]

Article 41 provides that 'the judgment shall be declared enforceable immediately on completion of the [requisite] formalities ... without any review under Articles 34 and 35'. In other words, the defendant to the enforcement proceedings will at this stage get no opportunity to argue that one of the defences to recognition is applicable. Instead, that person must launch an appeal on this basis pursuant to Art 43(1). This streamlines the enforcement procedure, but has the result of putting the judgment debtor firmly on the back foot.

However, if an appeal is pending overseas, the court may stay its proceedings on the question of enforcement.[6] Once registration is granted, the defendant may then appeal to the High Court against the registration.[7] If registration was refused, the claimant may appeal.[8] When the judgment is conclusively registered in whole or in part,[9] it is treated for the purposes of English law as equivalent to a High Court judgment.[10]

1.6.3 Common law

Where the Regulation rules are inapplicable, the common law, or one of the statutory schemes which modifies the rules in relation to judgments of certain states, will govern enforcement. Since the latter are largely a codification of the former, attention will focus primarily on the common law. Discussion of the statutes will consider any material differences from the common law.

In order to enforce at common law, a party cannot rely on a registration procedure. Instead, an action must be brought on the judgment itself seeking summary judgment.

In contrast to the Regulation, the common law rules are highly restrictive.

---

1 Article 38(2).

2 Pursuant to CJJA 1982, s 4.

3 Annex II to the Regulation.

4 Article 53.

5 Article 47(1).

6 Article 37.

7 Article 43. The court may also stay the appeal against registration if an appeal is pending overseas: Art 46 (cf the Brussels Convention position: *SISRO v Ampersand Software BV* [1995] ECR I-2269).

8 Article 43(5) states that: 'An appeal against the declaration of enforceability is to be lodged within one month of service thereof. If the party against whom enforcement is sought is domiciled in a Member State other than that in which the declaration of enforceability was given, the time for appealing shall be two months and shall run from the date of service, either on him in person or at his residence'.

9 Partial enforcement is permitted by Art 48(1).

10 Civil Jurisdiction and Judgments Order 2001 (SI 2001/3929), Sch 1, para 1(3).

The jurisdictional competence of a foreign court

A judgment will not be recognised if the foreign court was not jurisdictionally competent in the eyes of English law. In marked contrast to the Regulation, the English court will assess this question for itself. This means that it is often wise to keep clear of a foreign jurisdiction's courts which would not otherwise be considered to be jurisdictionally competent in an English court's eyes, for fear of being deemed to have submitted thereto.

The defendant was present and/or resident in the overseas jurisdiction

INDIVIDUALS

It is somewhat uncertain whether the defendant must be resident in the state of origin, or whether his presence at the time of instigation of proceedings will suffice. The classic judgment of Buckley LJ in *Emanuel v Symon*,[1] suggests that residence is required. However, the Court of Appeal in *Adams v Cape Industries*[2] reviewed the law and thought that presence was sufficient.[3] It left open the situation where the defendant was resident but not present in the jurisdiction at the time of commencement. However, it would be surprising[4] if this were not sufficient.

COMPANIES

Where there is a corporate defendant, it was decided in *Adams* that there must be a fixed place of business maintained at the company's own expense from which it has carried out its own business in the overseas jurisdiction. It will suffice that its business is transacted at that place through representatives of the company carrying out the corporation's business.[5] In *Adams*, an English company was held not to be caught by these provisions where it operated in the United States through a marketing organisation, since the US company was held to be engaged in its own business and not that of the defendant. Particularly relevant in this respect will be whether it may enter into contracts on the corporation's behalf. So in *Vogel v R & A Kohnstamm Ltd*,[6] an English defendant who sold goods in Israel through an agent resisted enforcement of an Israeli judgment on the grounds that the agent had merely acted as a channel of communication without any authority to bind the defendant.

THE PROBLEM OF FEDERAL JURISDICTIONS

Where any defendant is sued in a federal jurisdiction, it was suggested in *Adams* that it must be present in the particular state which gave judgment

---

1 [1908] 1 KB 302.

2 [1990] Ch 433.

3 It relied in part on *Carrick v Hancock* (1895) 12 TLR 59.

4 Although not inconceivable, since presence alone is sufficient in an English court to give it jurisdiction as of right. However, the enforcement rules are not intended exactly to mirror the jurisdiction rules.

5 See also *Littauer Glove Corp v FW Millington* (1928) 44 TLR 746.

6 [1973] QB 133.

(for example, Texas, not simply anywhere in the United States), unless the judgment is from a federal, rather than a state, court.

Submission

A court to which a defendant has submitted will also be seen as jurisdictionally competent in the eyes of English law. The most obvious means of submitting is by voluntarily pleading to the merits. However, he will be protected if he appears solely to challenge the jurisdiction of the foreign court by s 33 of the CJJA 1982, which states that an appearance solely to contest the jurisdiction of the court or to ask it to dismiss or stay proceedings for another country's courts or for arbitration, or to protect or obtain the release of property seized or threatened with seizure shall not constitute submission.[1] None the less, the scope of the provision is uncertain[2] and hence a defendant still needs to tread very carefully. However, it is tentatively suggested that appearing, for example, to have a default judgment set aside, or pleading to jurisdiction and to the merits because local procedure so requires should not constitute submission. In all cases, the key issue is whether the purpose was solely to challenge jurisdiction. Hence, an appeal on the merits to a higher court against a default judgment would constitute submission.

A defendant may also have contractually agreed[3] to submit litigation to the courts of a particular state. It is uncertain whether the contractual term must be express or can also be implied into a contract. It was suggested *obiter* in *Blohn v Desser*,[4] that a sleeping partner in a firm which had been conducting business in Austria could be treated as implicitly agreeing with all parties who contracted with the firm in Austria to submit all disputes to the Austrian courts. However, the court in *Vogel v R & A Kohnstamm Ltd*[5] thought that an agreement must be express. It is difficult to see any reason for this. As Briggs and Rees succinctly put it: 'as long as submission is not inferred too loosely, it is hard to see a convincing doctrinal objection to the implication of [the clause's] existence'.[6]

Finally, it is important, if not self-evident, to note that a claimant, by instigating proceedings, will be deemed to have submitted to the court. This can be very important, since he is then estopped at the enforcement stage from contesting a judgment against him in a counterclaim made by the defendant. Where there are a number of co-defendants, a submitting co-defendant will be deemed to have submitted to any claims which another co-defendant might properly bring arising from the action.[7]

1 Compare the pre-Act position in *Henry v Geoprosco International Ltd* [1976] QB 726.

2 See Briggs and Rees, n 2 on p 11, pp 337–340.

3 In a suitable case of reasonable detrimental reliance on a party's assurance that he will agree to litigation in a particular jurisdiction, submission might occur by estoppel.

4 [1962] 2 QB 116.

5 [1973] QB 133. The Court of Appeal in *Adams* thought that clear evidence of agreement was needed.

6 Note 2 on p 11, p 341.

7 *Murthy and Another v Sivajothi and Others* [1999] 1 WLR 467.

A mirror of common law jurisdiction rules?

It is tempting to think that the jurisdictional competence of a foreign court in English eyes is a mirror of the English common law rules on jurisdiction as of right. This, however, would be a fallacy. The rules are both broader and narrower than those of the common law. They are broader in the sense that no doctrine of *forum non conveniens* applies to foreign judgments. The courts of a foreign country in which the defendant was present will be jurisdictionally competent however manifestly that country might be an inappropriate forum. On the other hand, the English rules are far narrower, in that no equivalent jurisdictional basis to that which an English court may take pursuant to CPR Part 6 is recognised at common law. Indeed, the argument that a foreign judgment should be recognised if the foreign court took jurisdiction in circumstances where an English court would have served out had the facts arisen in England was expressly rejected in *Schibsby v Westenholz and Others*.[1] The position is somewhat anachronistic and the case for reform so as to recognise judgments delivered in the natural forum is a strong one.[2]

Further conditions for enforcement

No other bases of jurisdictional competence in a foreign court can be found at common law. Moreover, there are further conditions which the judgment must satisfy if it is to be enforced in England.[3]

The judgment must be final, and conclusive on the merits and for a fixed sum of money

The word 'final' means that the judgment is binding in the court which gave judgment and cannot be reopened therein, even if the same matter can be appealed to a higher court.[4] A default judgment may thus be final until the time for setting aside has expired.[5] The judgment will not be conclusive if further defences to its recognition are available in the overseas court. A judgment which is on a pure issue of procedure (eg an order for discovery) will not be entitled to enforcement, because not on the merits.[6]

---

1 (1870) LR 6 QB 155.

2 This is effectively what has happened in Canada: see *De Savoye v Morguard Investments* [1990] 3 SCR 1077. For arguments relating to reform of the English rules, see A Briggs 'Which Foreign Judgments Should We Recognise Today?' (1987) 36 ICLQ 240 and J Harris 'Recognition of Foreign Judgments at Common Law: the Anti-Suit Injunction Link' (1997) 17 OJLS 477.

3 These further conditions do not need to be satisfied if only recognition is sought. For a foreign judgment to be recognised at common law, the foreign court need only be jurisdictionally competent in the eyes of English law.

4 *Nouvion v Freeman* (1889) 15 App Cas 1.

5 Briggs and Rees, n 2 on p 11, p 354.

6 A decision that an action was time-barred would be on the merits, however: Foreign Limitation (Periods) Act 1984, s 3.

The judgment must be for a fixed sum; accordingly a judgment for specific performance or injunctive relief will not be enforced. Nor can a damages claim be enforced if the total sum to be awarded is variable.

The English court will not enforce a foreign penal, revenue or public law judgment

This is but a part of the general conflict of laws rule that such laws will not be enforced or applied in an English court. A tax liability[1] or an order for confiscation of property[2] in the name of the state would not be enforceable. An order to pay penal damages will certainly not be enforceable if payable to a state authority.[3] However, penal damages which are awarded to a private individual should not be caught by this exclusion.[4] In any event, if it is possible to sever the compensatory part of a judgment, that alone may be enforced.[5]

The judgment must not order the payment of multiple damages

Where a judgment is 'for an amount arrived at by ... multiplying' the sum assessed as compensation, it shall not be enforced.[6] This provision seeks largely to counteract US anti-trust legislation which purports to have extraterritorial effect. If the defendant has already paid the multiple, he may reclaim it in an English court.[7]

Where a judgment relates to rights in immovable property, that property must be situated in the country of origin

This is the corollary of the rule in *British South Africa Co v Companhia de Mocambique*,[8] that an English court will not entertain proceedings in relation to land situated overseas. The courts of the situs of land have sole control thereof and it is thought inappropriate for other courts to rule on title thereto.[9]

---

1 *United States of America v Inkley* [1989] QB 255.

2 *Attorney-General for New Zealand v Ortiz* [1984] AC 1.

3 *Huntington v Attrill* [1893] AC 150.

4 *SA Consortium General Textiles v Sun & Sand Agencies Ltd* [1978] QB 279.

5 *Raulin v Fischer* [1911] 2 KB 93.

6 Protection of Trading Interests Act 1980, s 5.

7 Ibid, s 6.

8 [1893] AC 602. See the discussion of non-justiciability in relation to common law jurisdiction above.

9 Technically, this is a rule affecting recognition and enforcement. However, if the land is situated in the state which gave judgment, nothing more is required than the recognition of its judgment. In this scenario, the judgment will obviously not fall foul of the *Mocambique* rule. It is only where the land is situated outside the state that gave judgment that enforcement of the judgment will be required. It is this which will be refused under the rule stated in this paragraph, Hence, in practice, the defence will be one to enforcement only. See further *Dicey and Morris*, n 2 on p 11, pp 508–511.

Defences to recognition and enforcement[1]

Assuming that the conditions thus far discussed are satisfied, a judgment is *prima facie* entitled to enforcement. We now turn to consider potential defences available to the defendant. However, it is instructive first to consider two claims which will not avail him.

(a) *Error of law*: the fact that a foreign court has allegedly misapplied the law, or applied a law which seems inappropriate, cannot be pleaded in defence.[2] This serves a strong public interest in ensuring that matters cannot readily be reopened in England.

(b) *The foreign court lacked jurisdiction by the procedural law of that state*: even if it is alleged that the particular court, which heard the case in the state of origin lacked jurisdiction, this will be irrelevant, unless the error made the judgment null and void in that state.[3] An English court should not seek to fathom the civil procedure of another country and should presume that state to be best placed to determine whether its procedures have properly been applied.

If properly made out, the following will provide valid defences to recognition and enforcement.

The judgment was procured by the claimant's fraud

In the face of such an allegation, English courts are, in contrast, prepared effectively to retry the case on its merits. In this regard, it matters not that the foreign court rejected this allegation on the basis of the same evidence. In *Abouloff v Oppenheimer & Co*,[4] the claimant was defeated in enforcement proceedings in relation to an action for late delivery of goods by evidence that he had untruthfully and fraudulently told the court that he did not possess them, even though the Russian court had rejected the defendant's allegation. Nor does it matter that the defendant had the opportunity to raise the defence overseas but did not do so; he may still raise it in enforcement proceedings.[5]

However, the Privy Council in *Owens Bank Ltd v Etoile Commerciale SA*,[6] suggested that the defence should be struck out where the defendant offers no particulars of the alleged fraud. More generally, the court should decide in each case if justice requires further investigation of fraud, bearing in mind whether it is reasonable to make the claimant wait any longer to have the judgment enforced.

---

1 The defences that we are about to consider would prevent recognition as well as enforcement.

2 *Godard v Gray* (1870) LR 6 QB 288.

3 *Vanqueilin v Brouard* (1863) 15 CBNS 341; *Pemberton v Hughes* [1899] 1 Ch 781.

4 (1882) 10 QBD 295.

5 *Syal v Heyward* [1948] 2 KB 443.

6 [1995] 1 WLR 44.

There is one exception to the availability of the defence. Where a separate judgment has been delivered on the fraud issue, the defendant will be estopped from raising it in England. In *House of Spring Gardens Ltd v Waite (No 2)*,[1] the claimant obtained a judgment in Ireland. The defendant started separate proceedings in Ireland to have the original judgment set aside, but was defeated. It was held to be an abuse of process for him to raise the matter again in English enforcement proceedings.

The judgment was in breach of natural justice

The defendant must have had the opportunity adequately to defend himself. It is apparently open to him to allege that standards of natural justice have been violated, even if such an allegation had been made overseas.[2] It does not appear that the defendant must take advantage of any procedures existing in the state of origin to make his complaint.[3]

The English courts have traditionally been reluctant to condemn foreign procedures. However, a more liberal view was taken in *Adams v Cape Industries*,[4] where it was suggested that even if there was strictly speaking no breach of natural justice, the court could refuse to enforce the judgment if the foreign proceedings amounted to a denial of substantial justice. In that case, the judge, with the assistance of counsel, awarded compensation to the claimants on a basis which did not obviously reflect the extent of the injuries each had suffered. The Court of Appeal held that compensation should be objectively and independently assessed. Unfortunately, no guidance on the concept of 'substantial justice' was forthcoming. It is a rather unhelpful term, since it is clear that an English court may not refuse to enforce simply because it finds the outcome on the merits of the foreign litigation unpalatable.[5]

Recognition would be contrary to public policy

This head is rarely used. However, it was applied in *Re Macartney*[6] to deny enforcement of a perpetual maintenance order made against a father for his illegitimate child. A more controversial case is *Israel Discount Bank of New York v Hadjipateras*,[7] where the defendant alleged that a New York judgment for the claimant was obtained because his father had exercised undue influence over him to make him enter into a contract of guarantee. The public policy defence to enforcement was rejected by the Court of Appeal,[8] on the grounds that the defendant failed to raise the issue overseas. It is doubtful if this is a fair view,

---

1 [1991] 1 QB 241.

2 An unlikely event if the alleged breach is a lack of opportunity to be heard.

3 *Adams v Cape Industries* [1990] Ch 433.

4 Ibid.

5 Whether the Human Rights Act 1998 will increase the scope of the natural justice defence remains to be seen.

6 [1921] 1 Ch 522.

7 [1983] 3 All ER 129.

8 CJJA 1982, s 32(3).

however, given that the defence is that English public policy, not that of the state of origin, has been infringed.

The mere fact that a foreign judgment was obtained on the basis of laws of which an English court disapproves should be irrelevant, as the defence relates to the judgment itself and not the underlying cause of action. None the less, the dividing line is thin. The temptation for a court to accept the defence, for example, where a judgment was delivered on the basis of very different rules of forced heirship would be very strong. However, it is thought that the interest in finality of foreign judgments should mean that the defence should not avail unless the rules were manifestly discriminatory on a basis which could not be objectively justified.

The judgment was in breach of a choice of court or arbitration agreement

If the judgment was in breach of a valid exclusive jurisdiction clause,[1] s 32(1) of the CJJA 1982 states that the judgment shall not be enforced. The only exception is where the defendant submitted to the court delivering judgment or counterclaimed therein. It should be noted that an English court is not bound by the foreign court's finding that the jurisdiction clause was invalid or did not apply to the facts and may decide this issue itself.

The judgment is inconsistent with another judgment

This is unsurprisingly a valid defence where an English judgment also exists.[2] Where there are two irreconcilable foreign judgments, the Privy Council has held that the first judgment to be delivered will prevail.[3]

1.6.4 The effect of foreign judgments

Both parties may seek to rely on the impact of a foreign judgment. Its impact may be much wider than one might initially believe.

Cause of action estoppel

A successful claimant overseas may none the less feel that he could have obtained higher damages in England and seek to sue afresh. He will be estopped from doing so by s 34 of the CJJA 1982, which provides that:

> 'no proceedings may be brought by a person in England and Wales or Northern Ireland on a cause of action in respect of which a judgment has been given in his favour in proceedings between the same parties, or their privies, in a court in another part of the United Kingdom or in a court in an overseas country, unless that judgment is not enforceable or entitled to recognition in England and Wales or, as the case may be, Northern Ireland.'

1 That is to say it is not illegal, void, unenforceable or incapable of performance: CJJA 1982, s 32(2).
2 *Vervaeke v Smith* [1983] 1 AC 145.
3 *Showlag v Mansour* [1995] 1 AC 431.

The phrase 'cause of action' is broadly construed. In *The Indian Grace*,[1] a claim in India for defective delivery and one in England for damage to cargo were held to arise from the same cause of action. The 'same parties' will cover a foreign action *in personam* and an English action *in rem* in the same matter.[2]

If the claimant was unsuccessful overseas, the defendant may argue that the matter is now *res judicata*, if the same cause of action between the same parties is in issue. Furthermore, if the dispute in question in England is not identical, but could have been raised in the foreign court, estoppel will not operate, but it may be deemed an abuse of process to allow the claimant now to litigate in England.[3]

Issue estoppel

This doctrine has important ramifications in international litigation. It may be that, whilst overseas litigation does not prevent a related action from being brought in England, an issue decided by the foreign court in the process of reaching its judgment will bind an English court in resolving its dispute. This may effectively make litigation in England futile.

It is clearly desirable that an issue effectively determined between two parties in a jurisdictionally competent state should not generally be reconsidered. However, English courts have urged caution in the application of the doctrine,[4] stressing that it may be very hard to determine whether a foreign court has decided a particular issue in reaching its judgment. A court must satisfy itself that the issue in question in the foreign and English courts is identical, that the parties are identical and that the foreign ruling was final and conclusive. This last requirement can be especially difficult to demonstrate when the court expresses a view on a matter which is none the less not a critical part of its reasoning process.

Logic would suggest that estoppel should only operate once a foreign court has been shown to be jurisdictionally competent in the eyes of English law. Accordingly, the foreign court's findings of jurisdictional competence should not bind an English court. But the controversial decision in *Desert Sun Loan Corp v Hill*[5] has complicated matters. In that case, the Court of Appeal indicated that it could be bound by the foreign court's finding that the defendant submitted thereto, even though he appeared merely to contest the jurisdiction of the court.[6] Although estoppel did not operate on the facts, the implications of the case are startling, since this would effectively empower a foreign court conclusively to determine its jurisdictional

1 [1993] AC 410.

2 *The Indian Grace (No 2)* [1997] 4 All ER 380.

3 *Henderson v Henderson* (1843) 3 Hare 100.

4 *Carl Zeiss Stiftung v Rayner & Keeler Ltd and Others* [1967] 1 AC 853.

5 [1996] 2 All ER 487.

6 The judgment of Evans LJ is flawed, in that it is difficult to see how an estoppel could have arisen consistent with CJJA 1982, s 33.

competence in the eyes of English law. It is difficult to believe that this will appeal to any English court when put in these terms.

1.6.5 The statutory schemes

Judgments of some states outside the European Union are enforced under one of two statutory schemes of registration, rather than by action on the judgment at common law. The criteria for enforcement and defences thereto differ little from the common law.

The Administration of Justice Act 1920

The Administration of Justice Act 1920 (AJA 1920) allows for the reciprocal enforcement of money judgments between the United Kingdom and certain Commonwealth and colonial countries.[1] Its provisions are not mandatory and the claimant may choose instead to rely on the common law rules.[2] The AJA 1920 applies to judgments of superior courts,[3] which may be registered if 'just and convenient' within 12 months. The court must have been jurisdictionally competent. In this regard, the rules are similar to the common law, save that an individual defendant must have resided or carried on business in the state of origin (or submitted thereto).[4] The available defences are much the same: fraud, lack of due service, affront to public policy, or that an appeal is pending in the court of origin.[5]

Registration is made without notice and notice of the registration is then served on the defendant. No permission is required to do so, even if he is outside the jurisdiction.[6] The defendant may apply to have service set aside if he shows due cause.[7]

The Foreign Judgments (Reciprocal Enforcement) Act 1933

The Foreign Judgments (Reciprocal Enforcement) Act 1933 applies to enforcement and recognition of money judgments of superior courts in countries to which an Order in Council has been made extending its provisions. Like the AJA 1920, the enforcement regime is reciprocal between

1 The list is lengthy, but includes eg Bahamas, Belize, Bermuda, Botswana, the British Virgin Islands, the Cayman Islands, Cyprus, the Falkland Islands, Fiji, Ghana, Gibraltar, Jamaica, Kenya, Malaysia, Malta, Mauritius, New Zealand, Nigeria, Papua New Guinea, Singapore, the Solomon Islands, Sri Lanka, Uganda, Zambia and Zimbabwe.

2 Although he will generally not recover costs if he chooses not to use the Act's provisions.

3 AJA 1920, s 9(1).

4 Ibid, s 9(2).

5 Although not expressly stated CJJA 1982, s 32 will also apply to preclude enforcement of a judgment in breach of a jurisdiction clause.

6 AJA 1920, s 9(4).

7 Ibid.

the two countries. It applies to judgments from a broad range of countries.[1] Unlike the AJA 1920, registration is mandatory where the requisite provisions are satisfied; nor can the claimant choose to rely on the common law rules in lieu.[2]

The jurisdictional competence of the foreign court is much the same as at common law,[3] except that presence of the defendant will not suffice; rather, an individual must be resident, or a company have its principal place of business,[4] in the state of origin. The judgment must be final, conclusive and for a fixed sum.[5]

The substantive defences are: fraud, failure to receive notice of proceedings in time to defend oneself and affront to public policy.[6] The court may set aside or stay registration pending an appeal in the state of origin.[7] Registration may also be set aside if the foreign judgment was given after a judgment of another jurisdictionally competent foreign court.[8]

Registration should be sought without notice within six years of judgment or any appeals against the judgment.[9] A notice of registration should be served on the defendant,[10] who may apply to have the registration set aside.

1.6.6 Intra-UK judgments

The CJJA 1982 provides for the free recognition and enforcement of a judgment of the courts of one part of the United Kingdom in any other part.[11] Enforcement may only be achieved by registration.[12] There are no requirements of jurisdictional competence. The provisions are not limited to monetary awards; hence, an order for specific performance, or injunctive relief, will fall within these provisions.

The 'standard' common law defences do not apply; nor, it seems, does s 32 of the CJJA 1982 dealing with judgments in breach of a jurisdiction clause. Hence, a jurisdictional objection must be made in the court of origin and not at the enforcement stage. However, enforcement may be refused where the

---

1 The list includes eg Austria, Australia, Belgium, some Canadian courts, France, some Indian courts, the Isle of Man, Israel, Italy, Jersey, the Netherlands and Norway. However, in the case of states which are now within the Brussels or Lugano Convention scheme, it is the Convention, not the Act, which will govern enforcement.

2 AJA 1920, s 6.

3 Ibid, s 4(2).

4 It will also suffice if the company had an office in the state, through whose transactions the claim arose.

5 AJA 1920, s 1(2).

6 Ibid, s 4(1). Presumably, breach of a jurisdiction clause would also be a defence pursuant to CJJA 1982, s 32.

7 AJA 1920, s 5. It is not obliged to do so.

8 Ibid.

9 Ibid, s 2(1).

10 Ibid, s 2(2).

11 Ibid, ss 18 and 19; Schs 6 and 7.

12 Ibid, s 18(8).

judgment conflicts with one previously given by another court of competent jurisdiction.[1]

1.7 ARBITRATION

Once a dispute has arisen, parties may resolve to settle their differences by reference to international arbitration. The private nature of the process, its efficiency, and the greater freedom given to the parties to select the governing procedures, arbitrator and applicable law on the merits may all make this an attractive solution. The law in this area has been extensively rationalised and modernised by the Arbitration Act 1996 (AA 1996).

This is a complex field and the following account is intended merely as an outline of the terrain.[2]

1.7.1 Law governing the arbitration agreement

Where the existence or validity of the agreement to refer to arbitration is itself in dispute, the question arises as to which law determines whether it was agreed upon. In other words, a choice of law question arises at the jurisdiction stage. Since arbitration is excluded from the Rome Convention on choice of law in contract, the answer must be determined applying common law contractual conflict of laws rules. Although an arbitration agreement is technically separate from the main contract[3] and could hence be governed by a different law to that main contract, the laws will generally coincide and either the expressly chosen law or the objective proper law will apply. Where there is no express choice, there will be a strong case for application of the law of the place of arbitration as the objective proper law.

1.7.2 Law governing the proceedings

The procedures used by the arbitrator and the powers of a court to supervise the arbitration will be governed by the AA 1996, if arbitration occurs in England. Provisions are divided into those which are mandatory[4] and those which are non-mandatory. Mandatory provisions override the wishes of the parties when applied (although the court none the less retains a discretion as to whether to apply them). Non-mandatory provisions will apply where the parties have not stipulated for a particular matter. In this respect, the fact that

---

1 Ibid, Sch 6, para 10(b); Sch 7, para 9(b).

2 A clear, succinct account can be found in Briggs and Rees, n 2 on p 11, Ch 9.

3 AA 1996, s 7.

4 Ibid, s 4 and Sch 1.

the arbitration agreement is governed by a foreign law suffices to oust the non-mandatory (but not mandatory) provisions.[1]

In relation to arbitration overseas, the jurisdictional rules of the AA 1996 are still relevant insofar as they deal with proceedings brought in breach of an arbitration clause.[2] Furthermore, the AA 1996 allows interim orders to be made in support of foreign proceedings.[3] However, it would be comparatively rare for an English court to intervene in matters which ought naturally to be resolved by the courts of the seat of arbitration.

1.7.3 Breach of the arbitration agreement

The AA 1996 requires a court to stay proceedings where an overseas arbitration agreement exists, if certain conditions are met. The arbitration agreement must be made or evidenced in writing[4] and must not be void or incapable of being performed by its proper law.[5] Moreover, the dispute must fall within the scope of the arbitration agreement according to the proper law of the agreement[6] and be capable of reference to arbitration.[7] However, if the defendant submits to the court (by filing a whole or partial defence on the merits), his right to a stay will be lost.[8]

1.7.4 Enforcement of foreign arbitral awards

Which scheme?

Three schemes exist for enforcing or recognising[9] arbitration awards in England. The principal regime is the AA 1996, which enacts the provisions of the New York Convention 1958.[10] The Arbitration Act 1950, Pt II applies only to countries which have ratified the Geneva Convention on the Execution of Foreign Arbitral Awards 1927, but not the New York Convention 1958,[11] and the common law provisions apply to countries which have ratified neither Convention.

---

1 Ibid, s 4(5).

2 Ibid, s 2(2).

3 Ibid, s 44.

4 Ibid, s 5. A written term accepted orally would suffice: *Zambia Steel & Building Supplies Ltd v James Clark & Eaton* [1986] 2 Lloyd's Rep 225.

5 Ibid, s 9(4).

6 Ibid, s 9(1).

7 Ibid, s 81(1)(a).

8 Ibid, s 9(3).

9 Recognition will suffice where a party seeks to rely on the award as a defence to a subsequent action by the same party in relation to the same matter. All New York Convention awards are *prima facie* to be recognised in England, unless one of the eight conditions specified below applies.

10 Which has been enacted by some 100 countries.

11 The practical importance of the provisions of the Arbitration Act 1950 is limited, as there are few countries to which it now applies.

The AA 1996 now dominates this area of law and it is upon its provisions that discussion will focus. It applies to awards made pursuant to a written arbitration agreement in a state which is party to the New York Convention at the time of enforcement.[1]

Grounds for refusing or postponing enforcement

An award must be enforced, unless at least one of the grounds specified in the AA 1996 applies.[2] Even then, the court retains a discretion as to whether to refuse to enforce the award.

(1) A party to the agreement lacked capacity to make that agreement.[3]
(2) The arbitration agreement was not valid according to the law which the parties chose to govern it.[4]
(3) The arbitration proceedings were in breach of natural justice.[5]
(4) The arbitrator exceeded its jurisdiction in making the award.[6]
(5) The arbitration was in breach of the procedures chosen by the parties to govern.[7]
(6) The award does not have binding legal effect between the parties.[8]
(7) The dispute was not one which could be resolved by arbitration.[9]
(8) Enforcement would infringe English public policy.[10]

The AA 1996 also provides that where an appeal against enforcement is pending in the state of origin, an English court may postpone its enforcement decision if it considers it appropriate to do so.[11] The court should have regard

---

1 AA 1996, s 100.

2 These are set out in AA 1996, s 103.

3 Ibid, s 103(2)(a). We are concerned here with the capacity to make the arbitration agreement. An English court may not refuse to enforce an award based on a finding of breach of trust simply because it believes that a party lacked capacity to create the trust by the choice of law rules that an English court would have applied had the dispute been litigated in an English court.

4 Ibid, s 103(2)(b). Or the law of the seat of arbitration, if the parties did not specify a law.

5 Ibid, s 103(2)(c). However, due regard must be given to the arbitrator's freedom to adopt what it considers to be the most appropriate procedure.

6 Ibid, s 103(2)(d). The part of the award which does not exceed the arbitrator's jurisdiction may be enforced, if it can properly be severed: AA 1996, s 103(4).

7 Ibid, s 103(2)(e). Or the law of the seat of arbitration, if no such agreement existed.

8 Ibid, s 103(2)(f). An appeal might make the award for the time being unenforceable in the overseas state.

9 Ibid, s 103(2)(g). C Clarkson and J Hill (eds) *Jaffey on the Conflict of Laws* (Butterworths, 2nd ed, 1997), p 292, suggest that the provision refers to arbitrability by the law of the enforcing court, not by the law of the seat of arbitration.

10 AA 1996, s 103(2)(h). Despite calls for the public policy provisions to be interpreted restrictively in the arbitration context, recent decisions have taken a broader view. See *Westacre Investments Inc v Jugoimport SDPR Holding Co Ltd and Others* [2000] 1 QB 288, and *Soleimany v Soleimany* [1999] QB 785. See also J Harris and F Meisel 'Public Policy and the Enforcement of International Arbitration Awards: Controlling the Unruly Horse' [1998] LMCLQ 568.

11 AA 1996, s 103(5).

to the likelihood that the award is invalid and to the potential damage to the enforcing party of a delay in enforcement.

1.8 JURISDICTION AND ENFORCEMENT OF FOREIGN JUDGMENTS IN OFFSHORE STATES

The rules of transnational litigation applicable in offshore jurisdictions are heavily influenced by the English common law. Reference should accordingly be made to the discussion above of the common law rules of jurisdiction and enforcement of foreign judgments. This section will look briefly at some of the similarities and differences in a selection of jurisdictions. No attempt will be made comprehensively to examine the legislation in each state considered.

1.8.1 The Bahamas

English common law is not binding in the Bahamas, but is of strong persuasive authority, as supplemented or amended by local laws.

The common law jurisdiction rules largely hold sway in the Bahamas. Interim relief, such as the asset freezing order, will be awarded where a real risk that assets will be dissipated exists. This risk may be significant where trust funds have already been moved between various jurisdictions.[1]

The United Kingdom has extended the AJA 1920 to the Bahamas, on the basis of a reciprocal enforcement arrangement between the countries.[2] Where the statute is inapplicable, common law enforcement rules will apply and an action on the judgment should be brought. It appears that these common law rules are identical to those of the English courts.[3]

However, one further important restriction on enforcement exists in the trust context. The Trusts (Choice of Governing Law) Act 1989, as amended by the Trusts (Choice of Governing Law) (Amendment) Act 1996, contains strict limitations. Section 8 of the Act provides that no trust governed by the law of the Bahamas or disposition of property on trust which is valid under the law of the Bahamas shall be void, voidable or liable to be set aside by reference to foreign law; nor may the settlor's capacity be questioned by reason that a foreign jurisdiction's laws do not recognise the trust concept or the trust defeats rights conferred upon any person by way of a personal relationship to

---

1 See eg *Archway Ltd v Grupo Torras SA*, Civil Appeal 38 of 1995, sub nom *The Private Trust Corporation and Others v Grupo Torras SA and Another* (1997/98) 1 OFLR 443. The court was prepared to lift the corporate veil of a trust effectively controlled by a settlor/beneficiary so as to freeze his assets: see further J Glasson (ed) *International Trust Laws* (Jordans, loose-leaf), Chapter A3, para 129.

2 The AJA 1920 is discussed above.

3 See *Vosko v Chase Manhattan Bank*, Civil Appeal 29 of 1991. This was a case where almost every conceivable defence to enforcement was raised. On each defence, the Court of Appeal applied the principles of English common law.

the settlor or by forced heirship rules of a foreign law. Section 9 states that an heirship right conferred by foreign law in relation to the property of a living person shall not affect the ownership of immovable property in the Bahamas or movable property wherever situate. Section 10 then states that 'a foreign judgment shall not be recognised or enforced or give rise to any estoppel insofar as it is inconsistent with sections 8 or 9'. This is a surprising and unattractive provision. Its purpose is to 'insulate' Bahamas trusts against foreign laws and has the merits of certainty and security. However, whilst one can understand how forced heirship rules might sometimes be said to offend Bahamas public policy and that this may sometimes need to be invoked as a defence where enforcement would be manifestly inappropriate,[1] this provision is much more far-reaching. It seems to mean that many foreign judgments delivered on a basis incompatible with the way that the Bahamas court would have decided the case if it had heard the substantive dispute and applied Bahamas law will not be enforced. The 'insulation' argument is unconvincing, in that it has no obvious limits. It could be applied to transnational litigation in any country concerning almost any subject matter. Yet most countries manage without any defences to enforcement of this nature. The Bahamas legislation is the very antithesis of the conflict of laws, in that it allows wholesale non-recognition on grounds relating not to the judgment itself, but to the underlying cause of action. Judgments as to the merits of a foreign law are inevitably made in a manner which hardly seems conducive to comity. Were judgments to be enforced only when consistent with the way the dispute would be handled in the state of enforcement, the law of enforcement of foreign judgments would be torn apart. The legislation is also potentially self-defeating, in that it risks reciprocal restrictive measures being taken in foreign jurisdictions, who may refuse to enforce Bahamas judgments and/or to grant any necessary interim relief in support of transnational trusts litigation in the Bahamas. As a result, a party suing overseas in a transnational trusts matter who will need to enforce the judgment in the Bahamas needs to look at these provisions with great care.

1.8.2 The British Virgin Islands

British Virgin Islands (BVI) law derives from English common law,[2] although it may be supplemented by local legislation. Hence the influence of *Spiliada*[3] will be great. RSC Ord, r 1 is closely modelled on the English equivalent for service out of the jurisdiction.

---

1 Although even this argument should be used with care: see the discussion of the public policy defence to the English common law enforcement above.

2 1705 Common Law (Declaration of Application) Act (c 310) and West Indies Associated States Supreme Court (Virgin Islands) Act (c 80).

3 *Spiliada Maritime Corp v Cansulex Ltd* [1987] AC 460.

One significant area of supplement by local statute is in the field of transnational trust litigation. Section 82 of the Trustee Act (c 303) states that the BVI courts will have jurisdiction if one of the following grounds is met:

(a) the proper law of the trust or a particular aspect of it is that of the Territory;
(b) the trustee of any trust is resident in the Territory;
(c) in the case of a corporate trustee of any trust, it is incorporated or registered to do business in the Territory;
(d) any trust property is situate in the Territory but only in respect of property so situate;
(e) the administration of any trust is carried on in the Territory;
(f) the court thinks it appropriate.

Apart from (f) which appears effectively to allow jurisdiction to be taken where BVI law is the natural forum, the other provisions will apply even if BVI law is clearly not the *forum conveniens* for the dispute. Where, for example, jurisdiction was taken solely on the basis that the governing law was that of the BVI, an English court would not enforce that judgment.

A foreign judgment may be enforced at common law by action on the judgment and the English common law rules will be applied. There is also a statutory scheme of reciprocal enforcement applicable to the judgments of some countries, akin to Part II of the (English) AJA 1920, which is to be found in the BVI Reciprocal Enforcement of Judgments Act (c 65). This allows judgments of the UK courts to be enforced on much the same basis as the English AJA 1920. An application for registration should be made within a year of judgment (although the court may allow this time to be extended). A judgment of a jurisdictionally competent court in the eyes of BVI law, which is final and conclusive and for a fixed sum, will none the less be refused enforcement if the debtor was not duly served, or the judgment was procured by fraud or infringes BVI public policy.[1] Even then, the court appears to have a residual discretion as to whether to enforce, if they feel that this would be 'just and convenient'.[2] A judgment should not be registered pending an appeal. Section 6(1) of the BVI Reciprocal Enforcement of Judgments Act (c 65) allows the scheme to be extended to other countries with which reciprocal arrangements have been agreed.[3] As with the UK version of the Act, the creditor may choose to proceed instead by action at common law, but is then unlikely to receive costs.

1 Reciprocal Enforcement of Judgments Act (c 65), s 3(2).
2 Ibid, s 3(1).
3 This has been acted upon to extend the Act's provisions to the Bahamas, Barbados, Bermuda, Belize, Grenada, Guyana, Jamaica, New South Wales, some Nigerian High Courts, St Lucia, St Vincent and Trinidad and Tobago.

The BVI Foreign Judgments (Reciprocal Enforcement) Act 1964 (c 27), which is modelled on the (English) Foreign Judgments (Reciprocal Enforcement) Act 1933, ought to provide a mandatory system of registration for the judgments of the superior courts of a range of specified countries. An Order pursuant to s 9(1) of the 1964 Act has been made stating that these provisions should be applied to those countries.[1] Unfortunately, no Order under s 3(1) of the 1964 Act has been made extending the 1964 Act to those jurisdictions.[2] Hence it seems that the 1964 Act is not effective in the BVI. This is more than unfortunate, as it also stifles the extension of the Reciprocal Enforcement of Judgments Act, since its provisions cannot be extended to those countries specified in the Order relating to the BVI Foreign Judgments (Reciprocal Enforcement) Act. As a result, the common law enforcement rules continue to play the major role in the BVI law on enforcement of foreign judgments.

1.8.3 The Cayman Islands[3]

The Grand Court of the Cayman Islands acts as a court of first instance in larger civil claims and as a court of appeal from summary courts.[4] The Grand Court Law 1975 expressly states the residual role to be played by English law in plugging gaps in the Cayman Islands law. Section 20(2) states:

> 'In any matter of practice or procedure for which no provision is made by this or any other Law or by any Rules the practice and procedure in similar matters in the High Court in England shall apply so far as local circumstances permit and subject to any directions which the Court may give in any particular case.'

The Grand Court's jurisdiction is stated to be equivalent to that of the English High Court and Divisional Courts, subject to any other laws of the Islands.[5] Hence, the principles of *Spiliada*[6] will generally hold sway. Jurisdiction may be taken as of right if the defendant is served[7] in the jurisdiction or submits thereto, and it is then incumbent on the defendant to seek a stay.[8] If service cannot be made as of right, the court's permission to serve out of the

---

1 The Foreign Judgments (Reciprocal Enforcement) (Commonwealth) Order 1983. The countries mentioned include some or all of the courts in the Bahamas, Barbados, Belize, Bermuda, Jamaica, Nigeria, St Lucia, St Vincent, Trinidad and Tobago and certain Australian States.

2 *Yukon Consolidated Gold Corp Ltd v Clark* [1938] 1 AC 366.

3 This account draws heavily on information which can be found in D Campbell (ed) *Enforcement of Foreign Judgments* (Informa Publishing Group Ltd, 1997), ch 6.

4 At a higher level, there is a Cayman Islands Court of Appeal and ultimately the Privy Council.

5 Grand Court Law 1975, s 13.

6 *Spiliada Maritime Corp v Cansulex Ltd* [1987] AC 460.

7 He should normally be served by delivering a sealed copy of the originating process: Grand Court (Civil Procedure) Rules, r 13(1).

8 The *Spiliada* principles will determine whether the stay is granted: *C Stewart v Ask Securities Ltd* [1986–87] Cayman Islands Law Reports 28.

jurisdiction will be required.[1] The *Spiliada* doctrine would require the claimant, inter alia, to show the Cayman Islands to be the natural forum. However, the Cayman Islands' courts are not restricted by the (English) CPR Part 6 criteria when it comes to service out of the jurisdiction and have refused to incorporate them directly into their law, preferring merely to be able to have regard to these criteria in exercising their discretion.[2]

Interim relief is available in the form, inter alia, of the asset freezing order or search order.[3] The former may be granted under an inherent power following an application made without notice. The grounds for issuing the asset freezing order[4] jurisdiction will be those applied in English law, but the relative importance of each factor may differ. One relevant factor will be the likelihood that the defendant will remove assets from the jurisdiction. It is thought that this factor should be given greater weight in the Cayman Islands as this scenario is inherently more likely,[5] but that the mere factor that the defendant resides overseas should not suffice for the granting of the injunction.[6] If the danger of removal of assets is thought to be greater in the Cayman Islands, it might be that the competence conferred in recent years on English courts to grant interim relief in support of proceedings overseas in the courts of a state not bound by the Brussels regime will provide a stimulus for the development of Cayman Islands law.[7]

Enforcement of foreign judgments may be governed either by a common law action on the judgment or registration under the Foreign Judgments Reciprocal Enforcement Law (Revised) 1976. The latter provides for reciprocal enforcement of foreign judgments under a scheme very closely modelled on the (English) Foreign Judgments (Reciprocal Enforcement) Act 1933. Where applicable, its provisions are mandatory and a claimant may not instead choose to enforce at common law.[8] However, it has not been extended to a great range of countries.[9] Where applicable, it allows for registration within six years of judgment in the Grand Court of a final and conclusive judgment.[10] Registration may be set aside on grounds of fraud, lack of

---

1 Grand Court (Civil Procedure) Rules, r 13(3).

2 *Lake v Cordoba Ltd*, discussed in Campbell, n 3 on p 80, pp 102–103.

3 The Cayman Islands does have laws which protect confidentiality. Hence, the rules of discovery and tracing of assets need to be looked at closely by a potential litigant. However, it seems that tracing in the event of an apparent breach of trust will normally be permitted: *Kilderkin Investment Ltd v Player and Others* [1980–83] Cayman Islands Law Reports 403. For a general account of the law in this area, see Campbell, n 3 on p 80, pp 107–110.

4 This includes the worldwide asset freezing order: Clause 230 of 1989 of the Grand Court of the Cayman Islands.

5 *Kilderkin Investments v Player* [1980–83] Cayman Islands Law Reports 403.

6 *Bank of Nova Scotia v Emerald Seas Ltd* [1984–85] Cayman Islands Law Reports 180.

7 See the discussion of interim relief above.

8 Foreign Judgments Reciprocal Enforcement Law (Revised) 1976, s 8.

9 This law will apply primarily to judgments of Australian states.

10 Foreign Judgments Reciprocal Enforcement Law (Revised) 1976, s 4(1). A pending appeal to a higher court does not make a judgment unenforceable (s 3(3)), but registration may be set aside or stayed pending the appeal (s 7). Registration should be made in Cayman Islands dollars.

opportunity to defend oneself properly, or infringement of Cayman Islands public policy.[1]

Common law enforcement will be the norm in the Cayman Islands. However, the rules do not require consideration, as they are those of the English common law on enforcement.[2] After serving the defendant, the judgment creditor may apply for a swift judgment under r 23 of the Grand Court (Civil Procedure) Rules, alleging that the debtor has no defence to enforcement.

The Cayman Islands also have a provision very similar to that of the Bahamas[3] in s 6B of the Trusts (Foreign Element) (Amendment) Law 1995[4] to deal with enforcement in the context of transnational trust litigation. The author's views (expressed above) as to the principled objections to such blanket legislation, which is aimed at preventing enforcement of foreign forced heirship, family property and capacity rules where a trust is governed by Cayman Islands law apply with equal force here.

In the arbitration context, the Foreign Arbitral Awards Enforcement Law[5] gives effect to the New York Convention 1958. A Cayman Islands court would normally stay its proceedings where an arbitration agreement existed between the parties. Section 5 of the Law states that an award made in an overseas state which is party to the New York Convention 1958 shall be enforced.[6] An arbitration agreement which is void or unenforceable by the law which the parties chose to govern it will not, however, be enforced; nor will an award made in proceedings of which the defendant did not have adequate notice.

1.8.4 The Isle of Man

The Isle of Man is a separate jurisdiction, for which the highest court of appeal is the Privy Council. Privy Council decisions in relation to other jurisdictions will strongly guide, but not technically bind, Manx law. The UK Parliament may legislate for the Isle of Man, although it is not clear that its authority to do so is either exclusive or applicable to all aspects of Manx law. The English common law is a key source of inspiration for the development of Manx law, in the absence of local authority on a particular issue.[7]

---

1 Ibid, s 6.

2 On which see above. Curiously, it is stated in Campbell, n 3 on p 80, p 113 that a judgment will also not be enforced if founded on a cause of action not recognised in the Cayman Islands. It would be surprising if this were so, since one cannot expect causes of action in transnational litigation to be the same in different states. Such a rule would drive a coach and horses through the law of enforcement of foreign judgments and it is submitted that it cannot be supported.

3 See **1.8.1**.

4 Incorporated into the Trusts Law (2001 Revision), s 93.

5 Law 30 of 1975.

6 As if it were a Cayman Islands award made under the Arbitration Law 1974, s 22.

7 Especially decisions of the House of Lords and Court of Appeal. See *Frankland v R* [1987–89] Manx Law Reports 65.

It follows that the influence of *Spiliada*[1] on the court's transnational jurisdiction will be strong. There are equivalent provisions for service out to those which exist in England. These are contained in Rules of the High Court 1952 (RHC), Ord 6, r 1. An example of their operation is *Manco Ltd v Institute of Chartered Accountants in England and Wales*.[2] This concerned sub-rule (e), which allows service out where the action is to enforce a contract or obtain relief in respect of its breach, and the contract was made directly or through agents in the Isle of Man or is governed by Manx law. The claimant was a Manx-registered company which developed computer software for accountants. It contracted with the defendant company, which was registered and conducting its business in England, to work on a program manual. The planning meetings occurred in England, but the work was largely done in the Isle of Man. No governing law of the contract was specified. The defendants applied for service out following a dispute between the parties. The court refused. It found that the contract was made in England. This was also a material factor in indicating that the contract was governed by English law, as was the fact that planning occurred in England, performance was largely to take place there and most of the relevant witnesses were in England. It stated that RHC Ord 6, r 1 operated in a very similar manner to the (English predecessor to) CPR Part 6, and that the claimant must satisfy the court that the case was a proper one for service out and that there was a good arguable case that there was a contract satisfying the conditions of a head of RHC Ord 6, r 1.

The Isle of Man has reciprocal enforcement arrangements with the United Kingdom, Guernsey, Jersey, Surinam, The Netherlands, Israel and Italy under the Judgments (Reciprocal Enforcement) (Isle of Man) Act 1968.[3] This allows for enforcement by registration of judgments delivered in superior courts of those countries, if final and conclusive and for a fixed sum and enforceable in the state of origin. Registration in the High Court must be within six years of judgment.[4] The defendant must be served with notice of the registration and may apply to have it set aside. The court may set the registration aside or stay proceedings if an appeal is pending, or if another enforceable judgment has been given on the same matter in a different state.[5]

The court is required to set aside registration if the court of origin was not jurisdictionally competent in the eyes of Manx law.[6] The rules in this respect resemble those of English law.[7] Hence, service on a defendant resident in the state of origin (in the case of a company, having its principal place of business there or served in respect of a transaction effected through an office or place

1 *Spiliada Maritime Corp v Cansulex Ltd* [1987] AC 460.

2 [1987–89] Manx Law Reports 352.

3 These provisions may be extended by Order in Council to courts giving reciprocal treatment to Manx judgments: s 1.

4 Judgments (Reciprocal Enforcement) (Isle of Man) Act 1968, s 2.

5 Ibid, s 5.

6 Ibid, s 4(1).

7 They are set out in ibid, s 4(2).

of business of the defendant established in the country of origin) or submission by him (either by pleading to the merits or agreeing to a jurisdiction clause, or if the action against him is a counterclaim) to those courts will suffice to make the judgment *prima facie* entitled to enforcement.[1] However, registration should be set aside if the defendant did receive sufficient notice to arrange his defence properly, the judgment was procured by fraud, enforcement would infringe Manx public policy, or the rights under the judgment are not vested in the applicant.[2]

Where the Act is inapplicable, common law will apply and an action on the judgment will be necessary. However, the substantive grounds for enforcement differ little as between common law and statute.

1.8.5 Jersey

As with other offshore jurisdictions, the influence of the English common law in Jersey is strong. The Privy Council is the highest court of appeal.

However, Jersey also has a broader provision which deals particularly with jurisdiction in relation to trusts. This is contained in the Trusts (Jersey) Law 1984. Article 5 provides that the court has jurisdiction where one or more of the following conditions is met:

(a) the trust is a Jersey trust;[3]
(b) a trustee of a foreign trust is resident in Jersey;
(c) any trust property of a foreign court is situated in Jersey; or
(d) administration of any trust property of a foreign trust is carried on in Jersey.

If the court has jurisdiction as of right, the defendant may apply for a stay of proceedings. Essentially, the *Spiliada* principles applicable in England at common law will be used to determine whether the application should succeed and the defendant will have the burden of proving that the natural forum for the litigation lies in an overseas state.[4] However, as in England, if proceedings are brought in breach of an exclusive jurisdiction clause contained in a contract, the court will *prima facie* grant a stay, unless the claimant can prove good reason why the stay should not be granted.[5]

One interesting point which arose in *EMM Capricorn Trustees Ltd v Compass Trustees Ltd*[6] regarded the principles which a Jersey court should apply to an application for a stay where proceedings were brought in breach of a foreign

---

1 Unless the judgment is in respect to immovable property situated outside the country of origin, or the action overseas was brought in breach of a choice of court clause: ibid, s 4(3).

2 Ibid, s 4(1).

3 That is to say the trust is governed by Jersey law.

4 See **1.3.2** above

5 See **1.3.3** above.

6 [2001] 4 ITELR 34.

exclusive jurisdiction clause contained not in a contract, but in a trust instrument. The Royal Court held that the clause bound not only the settlor and the original trustees, but also successor trustees and beneficiaries under the trust. It then ruled that the same principles should broadly apply to the stay application as would apply where a foreign exclusive jurisdiction clause was contained in a contract, so that the burden would rest with the claimant to show why the stay should not be granted. However, it went on to say that because successor trustees and beneficiaries under a trust would not normally have expressly agreed to the jurisdiction clause in a trust instrument, the weight to be accorded to the clause should be less than that contained in a contract and that it should accordingly be easier for a claimant in trusts litigation to show why litigation should proceed in Jersey notwithstanding a foreign exclusive jurisdiction clause.[1] The correctness of this view is not beyond doubt. Successor trustees agree to be bound by the terms of the trust instrument. Beneficiaries take the benefit of an interest under the trust and it is arguable that they should equally take the 'burden' of being bound by the terms of the trust, including an exclusive jurisdiction clause. That would tend to suggest that the weight to be given to a foreign exclusive jurisdiction clause should be as strong when contained in a trust instrument as it is when contained in a contract.

As to enforcement of foreign judgments, both statutory and common law schemes apply. The former is embodied in the Judgments (Reciprocal Enforcement) (Jersey) Law 1960, which may be extended to countries providing reciprocal treatment to Jersey judgments.[2] A final and conclusive judgment for a fixed sum may be registered without notice[3] in Jersey currency within six years from judgment or the conclusion of any appeals, providing that it is enforceable in the state of origin. However, a penal or revenue law will not be enforced.[4]

The foreign court must be jurisdictionally competent in the eyes of Jersey law. It will be so if the debtor submitted by voluntarily pleading on the merits, counterclaimed in the proceedings, agreed upon a jurisdiction clause for the state of origin, or resided in that state when proceedings were commenced (in the case of a company, it will suffice if its principal place of business was in that state or it had a place of business there and the proceedings were in

1 Indeed, the court did not grant a stay on the facts of the case. One key reason for this was that there was also a related claim for breach of contract which would clearly be heard in Jersey in any event and it was undesirable that the trusts litigation should be heard in a separate forum to the contract litigation.

2 Judgments (Reciprocal Enforcement) (Jersey) Law 1960, art 3(1). It applies to judgments delivered in the UK, Isle of Man and Guernsey.

3 Judgments (Reciprocal Enforcement) (Jersey) Rules 1961, s 3. This Order contains detailed procedural rules for the registration of judgments (and applications to set registration aside).

4 Judgments (Reciprocal Enforcement) (Jersey) Law 1960, art 3(2). See eg *Le Marquand v Hall* [1987–88] Jersey Law Reports 86.

respect of a transaction effected through that office).[1] The debtor may apply for judgment to be set aside if the courts of origin lacked jurisdiction, the defendant was not served in sufficient time to defend himself properly, the judgment was obtained by fraud or contravened Jersey public policy, the rights under the judgment were not vested in the enforcing party, or it was inconsistent with a previous judgment of a jurisdictionally competent court in another country.[2] Registration may also be set aside or stayed pending an appeal.[3] If a court in another country has also delivered a final and conclusive judgment in the same matter which is *prima facie* entitled to recognition, the Privy Council ruled that the judgment delivered first should be recognised and registration of the later judgment should be set aside, unless the first defendant is estopped from relying on the first judgment.[4]

1.8.6 Conclusion on offshore jurisdictions

On the whole, the jurisdiction rules of the offshore jurisdictions studied adopted the same approach as the English common law. The enforcement of foreign judgments rules are equally as narrow as those of the English common law. However, those of some jurisdictions (for example, the Bahamas and the Cayman Islands) are still more restrictive in the trusts context. The provisions in those countries come dangerously close in many areas to requiring foreign law to produce the same effects as local law before enforcement can occur. The unfortunate result is a need for caution amongst claimants who may need to enforce judgments in those jurisdictions. It is hoped that other offshore jurisdictions will not follow the inspiration of these provisions.

1.9 CONCLUSION

The findings of this article are too numerous to summarise here. However, if there are some key lessons which could be extracted, they would include the following:

(1) A person seeking to get at another's assets in a particular jurisdiction should consider whether suing in that jurisdiction is the best solution.

---

1 Judgments (Reciprocal Enforcement) (Jersey) Law 1960, art 6(2). The judgment will none the less not be enforced if it relates to rights in immovable property which was situated outside the state of origin or the foreign proceedings were brought in breach of a choice of court clause. However, it seems that an English Order directing a party to transfer an interest in immovable property overseas in fulfilment of an agreement to do so may be enforced: *Lane v Lane* [1985–86] Jersey Law Reports 48.

2 Ibid, art 6(1).

3 Ibid, art 7(1).

4 *Showlag v Mansour* [1995] 1 AC 431, construing art 6(1)(b). Estoppel might operate eg if the claimant had indicated that he would not seek to rely on the judgment he obtained in State X and for this reason the defendant submitted to subsequent proceedings in State Y.

He may find that a more favourable law will be applied in a foreign court and that he can then enforce the judgment in the state where the assets are situated.

(2) In making the decision where to sue, the availability and scope of interim relief in that and other jurisdictions to support the action should be closely examined.

(3) Very often, it is highly dangerous to wait to be sued. Taking the initiative in the form of an action for a declaration of non-liability or anti-suit injunction can ensure that a 'natural' defendant may choose his preferred forum. The declaration will be especially powerful where the Brussels Regulation applies, as it will prevent the same matter being heard in another Member State.

(4) A defendant to a Brussels Regulation action would be unwise to ignore foreign proceedings, since he will not normally be able to contest the foreign court's jurisdiction at the enforcement stage in England.

(5) In contrast, a defendant to an action in a non-Member State should be very careful about his actions in that country, as submissions to its court will make it jurisdictionally competent in the eyes of English law for recognition and enforcement purposes.

(6) Where a foreign court is clearly jurisdictionally competent, a defendant should normally make his defences on the merits in that court and not expect to wait to raise them in England at the recognition and enforcement stage.

(7) Choice of court clauses are a good way to ensure that litigation takes place in the desired forum. However, one must be aware that they will not be all powerful where the Brussels Regulation applies.

(8) If it is desired to circumvent the restrictions of the Brussels Regulation and to ensure that a more flexible resolution mechanism for resolution of the dispute exists, an arbitration agreement can be a powerful weapon.

The tactical game of transnational litigation is not an easy one to play but it is immensely important to persevere. The results can be extremely rewarding.

Chapter 2

LAUNCHING THE ROCKET – CAPACITY AND THE CREATION OF *INTER VIVOS* TRANSNATIONAL TRUSTS

*Jonathan Harris**

2.1 INTRODUCTION

The image has been formed in relation to transnational trusts of the rocket launcher and the rocket.[1] The former concerns those preliminary matters necessary for creation of the trust, such as the capacity of the settlor to dispose of his property on trust, the vesting of the property in the trustee on trust and the validity of the formal instrument creating the trust; the latter governs matters affecting the trust once it has come into existence, such as the role of the trustee, the administration of the trust and the relationship between the trustee and the beneficiary. Whilst the latter is largely the province of the Hague Convention on the Law Applicable to Trusts and on their Recognition 1985 (the Hague Convention), enacted into English law by the Recognition of Trusts Act 1987, it will not come into consideration unless the preconditions for the formation of a trust are satisfied. As von Overbeck states in the *Official Report on the Hague Trusts Convention* (the *Official Report*), 'the law designated by the Convention applies only to the establishment of the trust itself, and not to the validity of the act by which the transfer of assets is carried out'.[2] This chapter considers the preliminary steps to the creation of express *inter vivos* transnational trusts. Inconvenient though it might be that all issues that arise in

---

* Professor of International Commercial Law, University of Birmingham, Birmingham. The assistance of Mr John Glasson is acknowledged with gratitude.

1 See von Overbeck *Official Report on the Hague Trusts Convention*, at para 53; Hayton 'The Hague Convention on the Law Applicable to Trusts and on their Recognition' (1987) 36 ICLQ 260 at 268; Underhill and Hayton *Law of Trusts and Trustees* (Butterworths, 15th ed, 1995), p 946; Collins (ed) *Dicey and Morris on the Conflict of Laws* (Sweet & Maxwell, 13th ed, 2000), pp 1088–1089. For more detailed coverage of the issues discussed in this chapter, see J Harris *The Hague Trusts Convention* (Hart Publishing, 2002).

2 *Official Report*, para 54.

relation to a transnational trust are not governed by one law, the law applicable to most issues of the rocket-launcher process is relatively uncontroversial. There is one notable exception to this, on which there is a dearth of authority and on which the proffering of advice is notoriously difficult: namely the law which governs capacity to create a transnational trust. Accordingly, it is on this issue that this chapter will focus primarily. By necessity, the opinions proffered here are largely speculative and constructed on the basis of both general conflict of laws principles and the specific choice of law rules for other aspects of the creation of trusts.

A variety of issues will arise in the creation of an *inter vivos* trust. The most important ones are:

(a) does the would-be settlor have capacity to transfer property on trust; and
(b) has legal title passed from the would-be settlor to the would-be trustee and equitable title passed to the would-be beneficiary?

2.2 WHAT IS EXCLUDED FROM THE HAGUE CONVENTION?

The exact extent to which the matters listed above form part of the rocket-launching process must now be considered.

Article 4 of the Hague Convention states that:

> 'the Convention shall not apply to preliminary issues relating to the validity of wills or of other acts by virtue of which assets are transferred to the trustee.'

2.2.1 Capacity

Whose capacity?

The capacity of a settlor validly to transfer assets to the trustee seems to be an act 'by virtue of which assets are transferred'. Von Overbeck, in the *Official Report*, states that the views of civil law states and common law countries were largely opposed in the negotiation of the Convention, the former regarding capacity as requiring a distinct choice of law rule, the latter tending to subject capacity to the law governing essential validity. This view is highly suspect in relation to the English conflict of laws. In any event, it appears that the settlor's capacity is outside the Hague Convention:

> 'in the end the Commission did not expressly exclude general capacity, although a consensus emerged that this was not to be governed by the Convention, while the specific capacity to become a trustee was to be so governed.'[1]

The latter rule is expressly stated in Art 8(a) of the Hague Convention. It is difficult in principle to see why the trustee's capacity should be a part of the 'rocket' itself. The *Official Report* concedes that Art 8(a) is largely concerned with questions relating to a person's fitness to be a trustee and that capacity fits rather awkwardly within its ambit. Moreover, it points out that the applicable law of the trust may contain very protective capacity restrictions. Not only is this scarcely convincing, but it hardly seems to address the point.

Declarations of trust

More critically, it leaves the situation where the settlor declares himself to be trustee of property, rather than transferring it to another person on trust, in a profoundly complex position. For on one view, the settlor still must have capacity to create the trust; but on another view, there is no transfer of legal title. Accordingly, this might be said to be a question relating simply to his capacity to act as trustee. The *Official Report* states that declarations of trust raise issues which are excluded from the Hague Convention by Art 4.[2] This seems correct in principle, in that the key 'rocket-launcher' questions are not really focused on whether legal title has been transferred, but on whether the settlor may alienate *any property right at all.* Clearly, in the case of the declaration of trust, the equitable interest will be alienated. Indeed, were this not correct, a settlor who is forbidden from alienating property to X could evade that restriction simply by declaring a trust for X. X could then terminate the trust and claim the property absolutely, if the governing law of the trust so permitted.

2.2.2 Constitution of trusts

It is clear from the wording of Art 4 that the vesting of the property in the trustee on trust is also excluded from the Hague Convention. The *Official Report* states that:

> 'Article 4 is intended to exclude from the Convention's scope of application both the substantive validity and the formal validity of the transfers which are preliminary to the creation of the trust.'[3]

Again, this must include the passing of equitable title where a settlor simply declares himself trustee, for the reason outlined above.

---

1 Ibid, para 59.
2 Ibid, para 57.
3 Ibid, para 55.

2.3 WHAT IS CAPACITY?

2.3.1 Status and capacity

A person's 'status' refers to his connection with a particular country (such as his domicile, nationality or habitual residence) or to his membership of a particular class of persons (eg his race, marital status, minority, religion or bankruptcy). The law of the country from which the individual derives his status does not, however, necessarily determine whether he has capacity to enter into a transnational transaction.

2.3.2 Essential validity and capacity

General

The most critical distinction to be drawn is between essential validity and capacity. Capacity defines a particular class of persons who by a given law cannot enter into a transaction into which other people generally may enter, eg a provision that *no* person aged under 16 may enter into a contract to buy cigarettes. Essential validity, on the other hand, concerns provisions which state that no person may validly enter into the transaction in question. Yet this seemingly straightforward distinction can lead to great complexity.

Consider a provision of the law of State A that no person may enter into a given transaction. *Prima facie*, this looks like an issue of essential validity. Yet if this provision is intended only to apply to persons who are domiciled in State A, then it is arguably correctly to be considered as a rule relating to capacity, limited as it is to a particular class of persons. However, it is not unreasonable to assume that many countries have particular restrictions which are intended to apply either only to purely domestic transactions, or, if they also apply to transnational transactions, only to domiciliaries of that state; in which case the potential scope of capacity rules could be very wide.

The matter is complicated by the decision in *Bodley Head Ltd v Flegon*,[1] where Brightman J held that an alleged incapacity by Russian law to trade abroad was to be treated as a rule concerning essential validity, since it was a law applicable to all Russian citizens. Yet if, in a dispute governed by Russian law, a particular provision is not applicable to non-Russian citizens, it should arguably be treated as a question of capacity. In contrast, if the Russian law were that *no* person could enter into a given transaction, but Russian domestic law was not designed to apply to transnational matters and the Russians themselves would not apply it to such matters, but would instead apply a different country's law, the rule is better viewed as a matter of essential validity, since when Russian law does apply its effects are not confined to a particular class of persons.

---

1 [1972] 1 WLR 680 at 688.

Of course, this distinction is often acutely difficult to make. Were it the case that the same law applied to all questions of capacity and essential validity, the distinction would be relatively unimportant. However, given the uncertainty of the law on capacity, that cannot be taken for granted. Accordingly, it is vital to attempt to distinguish between the two.

Characterisation

Unfortunately, matters are still more complex. Imagine that, adopting the English classification, a matter of capacity is raised, to which we are minded to apply the law of State A. What if State A would classify this rule, which we would think of as relating to capacity, as one relating to essential validity? How then can an English court decide, when confronted with transnational trusts litigation, into which category an issue falls? This is the process of characterisation. It is a doctrine of famed complexity, the details of which are beyond the scope of this chapter.[1] Put very simply, however, three obvious methods of characterisation could be used.

Characterisation entirely by English domestic law categories[2]

If, for argument's sake, capacity were to be governed by the law of the settlor's domicile (*lex domicilii*), State A, one would simply ask if any rules existed in that legal system which restricted the class of persons who may enter into such a transaction, ignoring how State A would classify that rule. This is the approach most favoured in English law, but it has a distinct drawback: if State A would not regard this issue as a matter of capacity, it could lead to the application of State A's laws in a situation where the courts of State A would not apply that law if the dispute were litigated in their courts. Accordingly, it can lead to distortion of the foreign law.

Characterisation according to the categories of the governing law[3]

In other words, one would ask whether according to the *lex domicilii* a matter was regarded as an issue of capacity and, if so, apply that law. But this is circular reasoning. One would only consider the *lex domicilii* if one had already taken the view that the issue was one of capacity to be referred to that law; yet whether it is a capacity issue is precisely the point in question. Moreover, if the *lex domicilii* does not consider that, for example, its law prohibiting persons under the age of 16 from creating a trust is a capacity issue, the result could be that foreign restrictions are not applied in situations where an English court would feel it appropriate to apply them.

1 See *Dicey and Morris*, n 1 on p 89, Ch 2; Cheshire and North *Private International Law* (Butterworths, 13th ed, 1999), Ch 3.

2 See *Ogden v Ogden* [1908] P 46.

3 See *Re Maldonado's Estate* [1954] P 223; *In re Cohn* [1945] Ch 5.

Characterisation prima facie made according to English law, but regard given to how the matter is treated in the state whose law might stand to be applied

Whilst this has the attraction of avoiding logistical difficulties and at the same time introducing an element of discretion to produce what might be considered a 'fair' characterisation, it would be so uncertain as potentially to prove unworkable. For this reason, characterisation is still essentially done by English categories alone, and the fact that State A does not consider a particular rule to be one of capacity will largely be irrelevant if it is so treated by English law.

A meaningful distinction?

Sykes and Pryles argue that the distinction between capacity and essential validity is not meaningful in any event, since, they say, capacity is but an aspect of essential validity.[1] They argue that 'it is difficult to see why capacity should be different from say essential validity'.[2] It may indeed be that ultimately the same choice of law rule will be applied to both. Yet the distinction is still highly important. An example will illustrate the point.

The rule that a contract governed by English law must be made for consideration is, simply considered, an appropriate legal rule for contracts governed by English law; but it is not to be used when the contract is governed by a different law.[3] It is a rule of essential validity. By contrast, a rule that no person under 16 may buy cigarettes has a more mandatory characteristic, and it is reasonable to assume that the policy of that legislation requires that we at least treat with some reservation the view that an English domiciliary should be able to evade that rule by choosing another law to govern the contract, including his capacity to make that contract. Accordingly, it is suggested that the Sykes and Pryles view cannot be supported. It is arguable that the freedom given to a party to choose the law governing a contract or trust cannot be extended to his capacity to enter into that transaction.

As to capacity itself, Matthews and Sowden distinguish between two aspects thereof:

(a) qualities relating to the individual settlor which prevent him from passing property (eg a minor); and
(b) whether the particular transaction can be carried out by the settlor, eg because he may not alienate a particular piece of property.[4]

---

1 Sykes and Pryles *Australian Private International Law* (3rd ed, 1991), pp 614 and 715.

2 Ibid, at p 614.

3 See Rome Convention, Arts 8 and 10; note, however, the limited exceptions to be found in Arts 7(2) and 16.

4 Matthews and Sowden *The Jersey Law of Trusts* (3rd ed, 1994), p 53.

It is true that if the alleged reason for a restriction of the second type is that the settlor has, eg, entered into a marriage settlement, or there is community of property by the law of his domicile, this question must be answered by the relevant choice of law rules for these areas,[1] since without the alleged restriction on property disposition, the settlor would not lack capacity. But this is no different from, eg, the obvious point that a testamentary trust can not be created unless there is first a valid will according to the law governing essential validity of the will.[2] Generally, however, the two categories of capacity do not require separate treatment. Restrictions on distribution of property imposed upon a particular person of full age and sound mind who is the sole owner thereof are no less a question of capacity than alleged restrictions imposed on minors and should be governed by the same law.

2.4 THE CHOICE OF LAW RULE FOR CAPACITY QUESTIONS

At first sight, it might seem that, in terms of practical convenience, it would be desirable if capacity could be governed by the applicable law of the trust, as determined by the Hague Convention. Clearly, this would offer the most certain and easily applicable choice of law rule. However, a glance at other relevant areas of the conflict of laws where capacity is in question reveals a reluctance to adopt this approach.

2.4.1 Capacity and other branches of the conflict of laws

A detailed examination of the treatment of capacity throughout the conflict of laws would be inappropriate here. So, whilst in matters relating, eg, to wills of movable property or to marriage settlements, which are closely bound up with personal status, the *lex domicilii* has a strong claim to govern capacity questions, the principles applied in those areas are less obviously of use in relation to *inter vivos* trusts. Accordingly, this section is confined to an examination of the law of capacity in areas where commercial considerations might be thought to be broadly analogous to those of the law of trusts, from which there may be important lessons to be drawn. As Sykes and Pryles note: 'The topic of trust partakes of the character of contract … and of assignment'.[3] For this reason, the discussion here will focus upon contracts and property transfers.

---

1 On which see *Dicey and Morris*, n 1 on p 89, Ch 28; Cheshire and North, n 1 on p 93, Ch 34.

2 On which see *Dicey and Morris*, n 1 on p 89, Ch 27; Cheshire and North, n 1 on p 93, Ch 33.

3 Sykes and Pryles, n 1 on p 94, p 711.

Contracts

It is worth reflecting upon the approach taken to capacity when a transnational contract is purported to be made, since if freedom of choice is not permitted in this area, it is unlikely to be permitted in trusts law either.

Article 1(2)(a) of the Rome Convention[1] excludes from its ambit 'questions involving the status or legal capacity of natural persons, without prejudice to Article 11'. Article 11 provides that:

> 'in a contract concluded between persons who are in the same country, a natural person who would have capacity under the law of that country may invoke his incapacity resulting from another law only if the other party to the contract was aware of this incapacity at the time of the conclusion of the contract or was not aware thereof as a result of negligence.'

This is a limited application of the law of the place of conclusion of the contract (*lex loci contractus*), designed to protect a person who believes in good faith that he is contracting with a person of full capacity. But it does not support the general application of the place of conclusion of a contract, which may, particularly where the parties are in different countries, be wholly arbitrary; nor will it be relevant at all where the party already has capacity by the 'general' capacity choice of law rule for contracts. In England, this general rule will be determined by the common law.

Unfortunately, English common law is largely short of authority on this question.[2] Rule 181(1) in *Dicey and Morris* reads:[3]

> 'The capacity of an individual to enter into a contract is governed by the law of the country with which the contract is most closely connected or by the law of his domicile or residence:
>
> (a) If he has capacity to contract by the law with which the contract is most closely connected, the contract will (*semble*) be valid so far as capacity is concerned.
>
> (b) If he has capacity to contract by the law of his domicile and residence, the contract will (*semble*) be valid so far as capacity is concerned.'

Consistent with questions of status generally being intrinsically personal[4] and thus determined by domicile, it is tempting to argue that capacity should be determined by the *lex domicilii* of the individual alleged to lack capacity. Dicey and Morris point out that:

> 'An individual's capacity to contract can be looked at as an emanation of his status and therefore governed by the law of his domicile. Alternatively, it can be considered as a factor determining the validity of the contract and therefore determined by its governing law.'[5]

---

1 Enacted by the Contracts (Applicable Law) Act 1990.

2 See Fisher 'The Law Governing Capacity with Regard to Bills of Exchange' (1951) 14 MLR 144; Smith 'Capacity in the Conflict of Laws – a Comparative Study' (1952) 1 ICLQ 446.

3 Note 1 on p 89, pp 1271–1272.

4 Although it has been stated above that capacity and status are not conceptually the same, there is an obvious link between the two.

5 Note 1 on p 89, p 1272.

They do not go on to commit themselves as to which characterisation is correct and their rule contains aspects of both classifications. However, they rightly point out that in the modern commercial world it would be impractical for all questions of capacity to be governed by the *lex domicilii*. If X, domiciled in Brazil, enters into a contract with an English domiciliary, governed by English law, it would be very inconvenient if X could escape liability for an alleged breach on the grounds that he lacked capacity by the law of his domicile.

It is true that there is some judicial authority for the application of the *lex domicilii*,[1] but this is largely in the context of cases concerned with matrimonial capacity or marriage settlements. Yet it is self-evident that in commercial matters, the convenience of applying the applicable law of the contract is far greater and, presumably, that the state of the contracting party's domicile will have less interest in its law being applied to a commercial contract than to matters such as matrimonial status. More importantly for present purposes, the lesser interest of the *lex domicilii* is likely also to extend to capacity to create trusts.

In *Male v Roberts*[2] Lord Eldon, in an unconvincing judgment, appeared to suggest that the relevant governing law is the *lex loci contractus*. Yet there appears to be no reason for that law's application. The place of contracting may be entirely fortuitous, and, in the trust context, so equally may the place of creation of a trust, and capable of manipulation in order to avoid the clutches of any potentially applicable incapacity. Moreover, the *lex loci contractus* was at the time of the *Male* decision presumed to be the proper law, so is consistent with the argument that the proper law governs capacity.

The law chosen by the parties is favoured by some Australian writers. Nygh argues that:

> 'In principle the capacity to enter into a settlement inter vivos should, by analogy with contracts, be regarded as part of the question of validity and thus governed by the proper law of the trust determined in accordance with Article 6 or 7 [of the Hague Convention].'[3]

Sykes and Pryles, who view capacity as an aspect of essential validity, argue that parties should be able deliberately to:

> 'choose the laws of a state which upholds the validity of the transaction as opposed to the law of a state which does not … The problems of scope of party autonomy in cases of essential validity and capacity are analogous and it is not immediately apparent why a different rule should be employed for each issue.'[4]

---

1 See *Sottomayor v De Barros (No 1)* (1877) 3 PD 1, 5; *Re Cooke's Trusts* (1877) 56 LJ Ch 637 at 639; *Cooper v Cooper* (1888) 14 App Cas 88 at 99–100.

2 (1800) 3 Esp 163.

3 Nygh *Conflict of Laws in Australia* (6th ed, 1995), p 518.

4 Note 1 on p 94, p 614.

Yet there is an obvious retort to that. Many rules of English law are really designed with the purely domestic factual situation in mind, and are not necessarily designed to apply automatically to transnational matters.[1] Rules which are restricted to a particular class of person are likely to take on more of a mandatory character, in the sense that they are specifically directed at certain parties, and should not be freely avoidable by those parties, at least not if the transaction in question has no material connection with another state.

The objectively applicable law has some support from the Canadian case of *Charron v Montreal Trusts Co*, in which the Court of Appeal of Ontario accepted that capacity is governed by the proper law of the contract, 'that is the law of the country with which the contract is most substantially connected'.[2] However, it has been pointed out that the case is weak authority, since it was primarily concerned with an initial question of essential validity, not capacity.[3] Brightman J also stated *obiter* in *Bodley Head Ltd v Flegon*[4] that the proper law of the contract governs capacity, by which he is thought to have meant the proper law objectively ascertained.[5] As seen above, the application of this law is supported by *Dicey and Morris*, on the at least partly persuasive grounds that, for example, a 14-year-old boy could confer capacity on himself to buy cigarettes in England simply by choosing a law under which he had no incapacity. Of course, this assumes that some legal system's rules of capacity ought to be applied on a mandatory basis to the contracting party and that freedom of choice is unacceptable; however, it is not hard to see the force in the argument that capacity rules are not supposed to be 'voluntary'. The objective proper law approach attempts to reconcile the undesirability of a potential lifelong burden being imposed on a person by the law of his domicile, with the need to prevent free evasion of capacity rules.

However, the *Dicey and Morris* fear of giving autonomy of choice free rein does not mean that the objectively applicable law must be used instead. Whilst their rule tends to mitigate in favour of capacity, in that capacity can be obtained under either of two laws, it lacks the very commercial convenience which the authors purport to instil. To apply the rule one must look at the law of the domicile of the allegedly incapacitated party; then, if he has no capacity according to that law, one must work out with which legal system the alleged contract as a whole is most closely connected. This will be a very uncertain process, not least because the common law rules on the objectively applicable law will have to be used, rather than those found under Art 4 of the Rome Convention for determining the applicable law in the absence of choice. Such matters as choice of court clauses, the place of conclusion of the contract, the

1 Although there are some 'overriding' rules which are intended to be applied in an English court whatever the governing law of the contract. An example is Unfair Contract Terms Act 1977, s 27(2).

2 (1958) DLR (2d) 240 at 244–245.

3 Clarkson and Hill *Jaffey on the Conflict of Laws* (Butterworths, 2nd ed, 1997), p 234.

4 [1972] 1 WLR 680.

5 Cheshire and North, n 1 on p 93, pp 593–594.

place of performance and the currency in which payment is to be made may all need consideration. Nor is it reasonable to expect the objectively applicable law to be any easier to determine in relation to transnational trusts. It would not be far-fetched to imagine a case where a settlor in State A purports to transfer assets which he has in State B to a trustee in State C to hold for a beneficiary in State D. The proffering of advice in such situations would be immensely difficult and fraught with danger.

Uncertain though the authorities are, it is tolerably clear that in English law unfettered freedom of choice is not permitted in relation to contractual capacity. Indeed, Cheshire and North state that the choice lies between the law of the domicile, the place of contracting and the proper law objectively ascertained, not even considering the law chosen by the parties as a viable option.[1] This is particularly material in formulating a choice of law rule for trusts. For if the chosen law will not be allowed to govern contractual capacity, one cannot expect that it will be allowed to govern all issues relating to the capacity to dispose of property on trust. The entire premise of the conflict of laws property rules is that property rights are sufficiently powerful and connected to the particular state in which assets are situated that freedom of choice should not generally be allowed, even on questions of essential validity. *A fortiori*, then, with the rules on capacity.

Capacity to transfer property

Land

Capacity to convey land is governed, unsurprisingly, by the law of the place where the property is situated (*lex situs*). In *Bank of Africa Ltd v Cohen*,[2] a married woman domiciled in England, by deed executed in England, purported to agree to mortgage to a bank in England her land in South Africa to secure debts of her husband. Under South African law she had no legal capacity to do so. The South African rule was one intended to protect married women. It was not clearly designed to protect non-South African domiciliaries. None the less, the *lex situs* was applied and the woman was held to lack capacity.

Tangible movables

The case for the application of the *lex situs* is greater for immovable property than for other species of property, since the *situs* can not be manipulated so as to confer capacity on the settlor. Yet property rights are so powerful that for conflict of laws purposes the *lex situs* is generally regarded as having the strongest interest in being applied to the essential validity of transfers of

---

1 Note 1 on p 93, p 592.

2 [1909] 2 Ch 129.

movables, especially in relation to tangibles.[1] Given the 'mandatory' characteristics of capacity rules, one might expect that the *lex situs* has an even stronger claim to be applied in relation to capacity to transfer tangible movables.

Intangible movables

The Rome Convention does not address the capacity of a natural person to assign, or to receive an assignment of, an intangible. Unfortunately, the common law authorities are of limited use. *Lee v Abdy*[2] and *Republica de Guatemala v Nunez*[3] support the application of the proper law, which is thought to be either the law of the place of the transferor's domicile or of the conclusion of the transaction. Both are rightly criticised by Cheshire and North.[4] The former is commercially inconvenient; the latter is capable of easy manipulation. Given that the *situs* of an intangible is actually likely to be more enduring than that of a tangible movable,[5] and that the *lex situs* can sensibly be applied to capacity to transfer the latter, it is difficult to see in principle why the *lex situs* ought not also to be applied to the transfer of intangibles.

2.4.2 Trusts and capacity

Very little authority is to be found on the choice of law rule for capacity to create a trust. Sykes and Pryles lend express support to the proper law, which, where the settlor has made a choice, will be the law chosen by the parties.[6] This is largely based on their view that capacity should be treated as an aspect of essential validity, a view which has been criticised above. Nor is it easy to believe, on the basis of the above analysis of other commercial areas, that unfettered freedom will be given here when it is not permitted in those fields.

One question or two?

It is contended that most of the problems in this area have arisen from a failure, common to both English writers and offshore legislators, to appreciate that there are in fact two distinct aspects to the capacity to create a trust. Matthews and Sowden hint at this when they state that whilst the use of the proper law is unsuitable in relation to the capacity to transfer property, it might be used in relation to capacity to create the trust structure rather than some other.[7]

---

1 See paras 2.5.3 and 2.5.4 below.
2 (1886) 17 QBD 309.
3 [1927] 1 KB 669.
4 Note 1 on p 93, pp 959–960.
5 See para 2.5.4 below
6 Note 1 on p 94, pp 614 and 715.
7 Note 4 on p 94, p 45.

The transfer of property

This dichotomy is critical. A settlor who wishes to transfer property to a trustee is disposing of his property no less than an owner who simply gives away or sells his property to another person absolutely. He needs capacity to alienate that property every bit as much as the outright donor and should not be able to avoid the otherwise applicable law for property transfers by creating a trust structure, especially as the beneficiary may have the right to terminate the trust and have the property vested in him absolutely. Therefore, the rules which determine whether he may alienate his property *must* logically be the same as those advocated in relation to capacity to transfer property above. It is suggested that, whatever the form of property involved, the *lex situs* should be applied to that question.

Support for this view is also to be found in Underhill and Hayton,[1] though their comments are not wholly clear and, on one view, appear to be confined to cases where the *situs* is England.

> 'Inter vivos trusts of English movables and immovables transferred validly under the *lex situs* to trustees of an English or other trust by a settlor of foreign domicile, habitual residence or nationality are valid and unimpeachable …'

Earlier, they had stated that:

> 'It is clear that questions of capacity, form and essential validity affecting English land are governed by the English *lex situs* irrespective of the settlor's domicile, habitual residence or nationality … The position seems to be the same for gratuitous transfers to trustees by foreign settlors of English movables, whether tangible or intangible.'[2]

An application of the *lex situs* at the time of transfer might be thought to secure the optimal compromise between certainty and convenience, on the one hand, and the application of the law which might legitimately be said to have the strongest interest in its law being applied to questions of capacity, on the other. It might be objected that this will mean that capacity to transfer property will be governed by one law, but that the trust itself will be governed by another, and that this is inconvenient. However, it should be remembered that another aspect of the rocket-launching process is the actual vesting of the property in the trustee. That will be determined by the *lex situs*.[3] An advantage of the approach advocated here is that both questions relating to the initial

---

1 Note 1 on p 89, p 241.

2 Note 1 on p 89, p 203, citing *Pouey v Hordern* [1900] 1 Ch 492. Note that the 14th edition (1987) simply states that 'for trust of movables questions of capacity and validity are governed by the proper law of the contract or trust, subject to the possible disapplication of that law on public policy grounds', although there is no real analysis of the matter and the (now amended) views of *Dicey and Morris* (Sweet & Maxwell, 10th ed), r 120 are relied upon.

3 See para 2.5.

transfer of the property to be held on trust to the trustee will be governed by the same, easily ascertainable, law.

The creation of the trust structure

There will then be a second question as to whether the settlor, who has capacity to alienate property according to the *lex situs*, has capacity to create the trust structure with that property. On this issue, it is suggested that there is a much stronger case for party autonomy, since the interest of the *lex situs* can sensibly be confined to the question whether the settlor can dispose of his property *at all*. Once he is able to do so, it should not be that law's concern whether he makes an outright transfer of the property or transfers on trust.

Nor does the *lex domicilii* seem an appropriate choice.[1]

> 'It would amount to allowing the itinerant domiciliary to carry around the disabling incapacity in his baggage and use it to escape liability for it in other jurisdictions, even those which do not recognise the status at all.'[2]

Alternatively, an English court might apply the law with which the trust has its closest connection, However, such an approach would give rise to grave uncertainty and impracticality. Nor does it seem necessary to apply that law to the second question.

There is no obvious policy reason for not applying the law chosen by the settlor to this issue. The restrictions upon a settlor seem legitimately targeted at the question whether he may dispose of property at all, not whether he may dispose thereof on trust. On the second question at least, this would accord with the views of Sykes and Pryles, and also with those of Nygh.[3]

Declarations of trust

This leaves one residual and complex question. What if the settlor simply declares himself trustee of his property? Arguably, he has not alienated his legal title, so the first question above does not apply; he has merely created the trust structure with the property, which, on the view advocated here, would be a second question issue, to be resolved by the chosen law. But, the effect would be the equitable alienation of property of which the settlor may not dispose at all according to the *lex situs*. That cannot be right in principle, not least because the beneficiary might be able to call for the property to be vested in him absolutely and to terminate the trust altogether, thereby by-passing the *lex situs* rule. Since it has been suggested that the *lex situs* is likely to have an interest in whether *any* interest in the property can be disposed of by the

---

1 Although, in relation to movables, it is favoured by Matthews and Sowden, n 4 on p 94, p 44. Theirs seems to be something of a lone voice in advocating this rule.

2 Sykes and Pryles, n 1 on p 94, p 344.

3 Note 3 on p 97, p 518.

settlor, it is suggested that, in the case of the declaration of trust, one should ask:

(a) does the settlor have power to alienate *any* interest in his property by the *lex situs*? and, if so
(b) does he have power to create a trust according to the proper law of the trust?

Corporate settlors
Finally, it is sometimes suggested that a different choice of law rule might apply to the capacity of a corporation to create a trust. So, for example, the capacity of corporations to contract is excluded altogether from the Rome Convention.[1] Certainly, a company may not enter into a transaction which is prohibited by the rules of its constitution. But in addition to being within its constitution, the company must also have capacity according to the relevant choice of law rule.[2] On one view, which seems to have an effect on some of the offshore legislators,[3] capacity should be governed by the law of the place of incorporation.[4] However, that cannot be correct in principle, at least in relation to trusts, because it is, in substance, an application of the *lex domicilii* to companies. Yet a company is likely to have a much weaker connection with the state of incorporation than an individual has with his state of domicile, because companies are set up entirely by law and can choose where to incorporate. And we have already seen that the *lex domicilii* cannot be accepted in relation to individuals. Since there is no reason why the *lex situs* should have any less interest in the capacity of a corporation than an individual, it is suggested that exactly the same choice of law rules should be applied.

2.4.3 Conclusion

In sum then, the following choice of law rule is suggested.

(a) The capacity of any party to dispose of any property right is governed by the *lex situs* at the time of the purported transfer.
(b) The capacity of any party to create a trust of any property of which he may, according to rule (a), dispose is governed by the proper law of the trust.

---

1 Article 1(2)(e).
2 See *Dicey and Morris*, n 1 on p 89, pp 1109–1111, r 156.
3 See para 2.6.
4 See *Janred Properties Ltd v ENIT (No 2)* [1989] 2 All ER 444.

2.5 THE VESTING OF PROPERTY IN THE TRUSTEE

2.5.1 Introduction

Once it has been established that the settlor has capacity to dispose of his property on trust, the next question concerns the constitution of the trust. This involves consideration of the law that determines whether property may be, and has successfully been, vested in the trustees. In principle, there is no reason why this should not be governed by the general conflict of laws rules for the transfer of property, which are outlined below. Put very simply, *inter vivos* property transfers are generally governed by the *lex situs*, at least if the transfer is of immovable or tangible movable property.

One question or two?

Technically, one could argue that two questions arise as to the passing of property:

(a) the transfer of legal title to the trustee; and
(b) the transfer of equitable title to the beneficiary.

The latter question arises because, in the words of Sykes and Pryles, 'the trust document may therefore be viewed as a type of *equitable* conveyance'.[1] Thus, if A purports to transfer property to B to hold on trust for C, the *lex situs* might permit the transfer of property to B, but not accept the validity of the equitable transfer. Accordingly, one could argue that the *lex situs* should apply to both questions. Yet this cannot be correct in principle. Otherwise, it would seem to preclude, for example, the creation in England of a trust of land situated in any country where the passing of equitable ownership is not permitted or recognised, even if English law is stated to be the governing law of the trust. Indeed, it would seem to prevent the creation of a trust, the assets of which are held in a country which does not have any analogous concept to that of equitable ownership. Rather, it is suggested that once legal title has validly been transferred to B, the rocket-launching process is at an end.

The Australian decision in *Augustus v Permanent Trustee Co (Canberra) Ltd*[2] seems to support this. In that case the application of the rule against perpetuities, which would obviously affect the creation of an equitable interest in a would-be beneficiary, was held to be governed by the proper law of the trust. The particular interest of the beneficiary should be considered as an aspect of the relationship between trustee and beneficiary,[3] and hence governed by the law determined by the rules of the Hague Convention. Accordingly, this section is concerned solely with the principles which will

1 Note 1 on p 94, at p 712.
2 (1971) 124 CLR 245.
3 Which Art 8(g) states to be within the Convention's scope.

govern the vesting of property rights in the trustee, not the vesting of equitable title in the beneficiary.

Declarations of trust

Once again, the case of the declaration of trust creates problems. Whilst there will be no transfer of legal title, there will still be the passing of a property right from the would-be settlor. Consistent with the argument made above in relation to capacity,[1] the question whether *any* property right has passed from the settlor should be governed by the *lex situs*, so as not to evade the application of that law to property transfers; but the question whether the title which the would-be beneficiary has received is *equitable* ownership should be determined by the proper law of the trust; otherwise, no valid trust could be made whenever assets were situated in a country in which the concept of equitable ownership was unknown.

2.5.2 Immovable property

The general rule

The *lex situs* clearly holds sway in relation to the essential validity and formalities[2] necessary for transfers of immovable property. In *Nelson v Bridport*,[3] Lord Nelson had sought to devise his Sicilian estate in a way which infringed Sicilian law. It was held that he could not do so. The rationale of the decision, the correctness of which is beyond doubt, is that:

> 'At the end of the day, only the law of the situs can control the way in which land, which constitutes part of the situs itself, is transferred.'[4]

Renvoi

For this reason, the doctrine of *renvoi* will also be applied here.[5] This is a doctrine of enormous complexity, the details of which are outside the scope of this chapter.[6] However, in the property context, it essentially entails the English court trying to decide a case using the substantive law that a judge in the courts of the *situs* would use. So, to take a very simplified example, if land was situated in Brazil, but a Brazilian judge, when applying *Brazilian* conflict of laws rules, would apply Argentinean law, then this is the law which an English court will apply, if *renvoi* is applied. In other words, when we refer to the *lex situs*, this refers not just to its domestic law, but all of its law, including any

---

1 See *Official Report*, para 57; see also the discussion of declarations of trust in para 2.4.2 above.

2 However, a contract to transfer an interest in land need not satisfy the formal requirements of the *lex situs*: *In re Smith, Lawrence v Kitson* [1916] 2 Ch 206.

3 (1846) Beav 547.

4 Cheshire and North, n 1 on p 93, p 929.

5 See *Re Ross* [1930] 1 Ch 377; *Re Duke of Wellington* [1947] Ch 506.

6 For an overview, see *Dicey and Morris*, n 1 on p 87, Ch 4; Cheshire and North, n 1 on p 93, Ch 5.

conflict of laws rules it has which may lead to the application of a different law. Given that the *situs* has total control over land within its jurisdiction, it would be futile to decide the case in a manner inconsistent with how it would be resolved in that legal system.

2.5.3 Tangible movable property

What does 'lex situs' mean?

One obvious problem in relation to movable property is that its *situs* can change. Potentially, this could mean that if A purports to transfer property to B in State X, by whose law the transfer is valid, but B moves the property to State Y, by whose law the transfer is invalid, ownership of the property would change. This would clearly be a most unsatisfactory and uncertain state of affairs. However, the conflict of laws rule is that title is governed by the law of the place where the most recent purported transfer took place. So, in our example, the fact that property was subsequently taken to State Y would not affect title, and the law of State Y would be irrelevant, unless a purported transaction took place in that state. If such a transaction did occur, the law of State Y would determine ownership, even if its findings would be inconsistent with those of State X. In *Cammell v Sewell*,[1] Cammell owned timber, title having been acquired by Russian law when in Russia. The timber was shipped from Russia to England on a Prussian ship which was wrecked off the coast of Norway. The ship master sold the timber to Sewell in Norway, which gave Sewell title under Norwegian, but not English, law. Sewell brought the timber to England and Cammell sued him. It was held that Sewell's title prevailed. Whilst this might seem harsh on the previous owner, who could lose title without knowing that his goods were being dealt with in another country, the case shows just how much power the *lex situs* exerts in this area.

In the converse case of *Winkworth v Christie Manson and Woods Ltd*,[2] pictures were stolen from England and taken to Italy, where they were bought by D2 and were later returned to England to be put up for auction by D1; but since no transaction in them had taken place in England, Italian law still determined title. So D2 acquired good title against the world. The effect was that the original owner found goods validly on sale by D1 in England which he had previously owned. Slade J said that the rule is necessary for commercial certainty and because the innocent purchaser overseas is just as worthy of protection as the original owner.[3] Moreover, as North notes,[4] to apply the *lex situs* will generally accord with the expectations of parties to a transfer and,

---

1 (1858) H&N 617.

2 [1980] Ch 496.

3 It may be that an exception will operate where the subsequent purchaser did not act *bona fides*. Slade J suggested this as a possible exception in *Winkworth*, but its existence is dubious, and rejected by Cheshire and North, n 1 on p 93, at pp 944–945.

4 North *Private International Law Problems in Common Law Jurisdiction* (Martinus Nijhoff, 1993), p 192.

even with movables, a party may need to invoke the authorities of the *situs* to ensure transfer of title is completed. In multiple assignment cases, buyers would otherwise have to investigate title of the vendor not just by the current *lex situs* but also to trace the entire history of the goods.

Exceptions

There are a limited number of exceptions to the *lex situs* rule, most of which are stated by Slade J in *Winkworth v Christie Manson and Woods Ltd*.[1] These include:

(a) where goods are in transit, with a casual or unknown presence;[2]
(b) where the application of the *lex situs* is contrary to English public policy;
(c) where an English statute prescribes the mandatory application of English law;
(d) general assignments of movables on bankruptcy or succession are governed by the law of the domicile of the bankrupt or the deceased.

Renvoi

There is some support for the application of this doctrine in relation to movable property in *Winkworth*, where Slade J stated that he 'supposes' it would be open to the plaintiff to plead *renvoi*.[3] Although the need to decide a case in exactly the same manner as would the courts of the *situs* is obviously not as great where property can be removed from that jurisdiction, none the less, if the *lex situs* is considered to be the most appropriate law to be applied to tangible movables, there is a strong argument for applying the same substantive law as would be applied in that jurisdiction, and hence for applying *renvoi*.

2.5.4 Intangible movable property

The situs

The law still purports to ascribe a *situs* to intangible property.[4] Shares have their *situs* in the country where they may be dealt with between shareholder and company. So, if shares are only transferable by entry on the register, they are situated in the country where the register is kept.[5] If the company has a

---

1 Note 2 on p 106.

2 Ibid, at 501. For the applicable law in such a case, see Cheshire and North, n 1 on p 93, pp 951–952.

3 Ibid, at 514.

4 For criticism, see Rogerson 'The *Situs* of Debts in the Conflict of Laws – Illogical, Artificial and Misleading' [1990] CL J 441. See also Moshinsky 'The Assignment of Debts in the Conflict of Laws' (1992) 108 LQR 591.

5 See eg *Brassard v Smith* [1925] AC 371; *Erie Beach Co Ltd v Attorney-General for Ontario* [1930] AC 161; *R v Williams* [1942] AC 541; *Macmillan Inc v Bishopsgate Trust plc (No 3)* [1996] 1 WLR 387, CA.

register in two countries, and the transfer may be registered in either, the *situs* is the place where in the ordinary course of business the transfer would be registered.[1] A debt due under a contract generally has its *situs* where the debtor resides,[2] because that is where it generally needs to be enforced. If he has more than one residence, it is where the creditor stipulates for the debt to be paid[3] and in the absence of such a stipulation, where it is payable in the normal course of business.[4]

Assignment

Suppose that A owes B £50 under a contract governed by English law and B purports to assign the right to that £50 to C to hold on trust for D. Which law determines: (i) whether the right can be assigned at all; and if so, (ii) whether a fully constituted trust exists?

Assignability

For matters within the scope of the Rome Convention, an apparently straightforward answer is given. Article 12(2) states that questions relating to the assignability of a right and to the relationship between that debtor and assignee are to be governed by the law governing the right to which the assignment relates. In the example above, that would be the law of the original contract, ie English law.

However, Art 1(2)(g) excludes from the scope of the Convention the constitution of trusts. Accordingly, it is necessary to have regard to common law principles. It appears that the assignability of an intangible will still, however, be governed by the law from which the right originates, which will, of course, in the case of a debt, be the original law of the contract. In *Trendtex Trading Corp v Crédit Suisse*,[5] a Swiss company sued a Nigerian bank in England. The Swiss company then assigned this right of action in the English court to a Swiss bank in Geneva. The Swiss company alleged that the assignment was void as contrary to English law. The Court of Appeal agreed, since the assignability of the English cause of action was governed by English law, not by the proper law of the assignment itself. The characteristics of a cause of action could only sensibly be answered by the law of its origin.

The assignment of the debt

Whether a debt which *can* be assigned actually *has* been assigned is a matter for the law applicable to the contract of assignment.[6]

---

1 *Treasurer of Ontario v Blonde and Others; Treasurer of Ontario v Aberdein and Others* [1947] AC 24; *Standard Chartered Bank Ltd v Inland Revenue Commissioners* [1978] 3 All ER 644.

2 *New York Life Insurance Co v Public Trustee* [1924] 2 Ch 101.

3 *Kwok Chi Leung Karl v Commissioner of Estate Duty* [1988] 1 WLR 1035.

4 *Power Curber International Ltd v National Bank of Kuwait SAK* [1981] 3 All ER 607.

5 [1980] QB 629.

6 See Rome Convention, Art 12(1); *Trendtex Trading Corp v Crédit Suisse*, n 5 above.

Title to the property

More complex is the question whether the assignee has legal title to the debt purported to be transferred. The assignee may not seek to claim a contractual right thereto, but rather may assert that he is already the owner of the chose in action. This might be particularly important if the debtor were to be declared bankrupt.

Jaffey states that:

> 'from a policy point of view what is required is a choice of law rule which promotes stability in proprietary relations ... Essentially there are two options: the *lex situs* or the law under which the interest was created.'[1]

Since the *lex situs* holds sway in relation to proprietary questions in relation to tangible movables and immovables, there is an obvious attraction in applying that law here as well. In our earlier example, this would point to Ruritanian law, the residence of the debtor.

This argument has, however, recently been rejected by the Court of Appeal in *Raiffeisen Zentralbank Osterreich AG v Five Star General Trading LLC*.[2] Mance LJ ruled that the assignment of the benefit of a marine insurance policy must be resolved by application of contractual, and not proprietary, choice of law rules. A similar rule should apply to assignment of debts. The debt is a form of property whose existence cannot easily be divorced from the contract which creates it. For matters within the scope of the Hague Convention, Art 12(1) and (2) exclusively determine the validity and effects of an assignment. Even for matters outside the Convention's scope, the view that the debt and its contractual origin are inextricably intertwined should today lead to rejection of the *lex situs* with respect to assertions of 'title' to the chose in action.

Nevertheless, the law of the contract of assignment cannot be used where the assignment is by gift. In that scenario, the assignability of the debt may be governed by the law under which it was created; but whether it *has* been assigned should be a matter for the *lex situs*.[3]

2.5.5 Conclusion

The following choice of law rules are suggested for the transfer of property on trust.

(1) Whether any proprietary interest has been transferred *inter vivos* from a would-be settlor to a would-be trustee is determined by the *lex situs* at the time of transfer. However, in the case of debts, the assignability of the debt will be determined by the law

---

1 *Jaffey on the Conflict of Laws*, n 3 on p 98, p 453.

2 [2001] 2 WLR 1344; on which, see R Stevens and T Struycken 'Assignment and the Rome Convention' (2002) 118 LQR 15.

3 A view shared by D Hayton 'Trusts and Forced Heirship Problems' (1993) 2 J Int Corp P 3, at 7.

under which the debt arose; and the question whether the debt has been assigned to the trustee will be determined by the law governing the assignment itself.

(2) Whether the transfer is effective to transfer *equitable* title to the would-be beneficiary, and thus to form a completely constituted trust, is determined by the proper law of the trust.

2.6 CAPACITY AND THE TRANSFER OF PROPERTY IN OFFSHORE JURISDICTIONS

Until relatively recently, the rocket-launching aspects of trusts were governed in most offshore jurisdictions by common law conflict of laws principles. More recently, statutory intervention has sought to bring greater clarity to these issues. Whether it has been fully successful in so doing is often highly dubious. This section focuses on the legislation of the Cayman Islands, Bermuda, Jersey and the Isle of Man.

2.6.1 The Cayman Islands

The Trusts (Foreign Element) Law 1987 was the first major statute in its field and has been used as a model in other jurisdictions. The statute's provisions (as amended) are now incorporated into the Cayman Islands Trusts Law (2001 Revision), Part VII.[1]

The statute states that all questions relating to a trust shall be determined by the law of the Cayman Islands *if Cayman Islands law is the governing law*. In other words, if Cayman Islands law governs the rocket itself, it will generally govern the rocket-launching process too. Section 89 of the 2001 Revision provides thus:

> '(1) In determining the governing law of a trust, regard is first to be had to the terms of the trust and to any evidence therein as to the intention of the parties; and the other circumstances of the trust are to be taken into account only if the terms of the trust fail to provide such evidence.
>
> (2) A term of the trust expressly selecting the laws of the Islands to govern the trust is valid, effective and conclusive regardless of any other circumstances.'

In other words, the parties can expressly choose Cayman Islands law to govern the trust, including questions of the settlor's capacity to create the trust, thereby avoiding any incapacity that the settlor might have by his *lex domicilii* or by the *lex situs*. Section 90 states that:

---

1 Hereafter 'the 2001 Revision'.

> 'All questions arising in regard to a trust which is for the time being governed by the laws of the Islands or in regard to any disposition of property upon the trusts thereof including questions as to—
>
> (a) the capacity of any settlor;
>
> (b) any aspect of the validity of the trust or disposition or the interpretation or effect thereof: …
>
> are to be determined according to the laws of the Islands without reference to the laws of any other jurisdictions with which the trust or disposition may be connected.'

Section 91 overcomes the problems that the laws of a foreign jurisdiction might prohibit or not recognise the trust concept, or, more importantly for present purposes, that the trust might avoid rights or claims of parties which exist according to any foreign law by providing that 'no trust governed by the laws of the Islands and no disposition of property to be held upon the trusts thereof is void, voidable, liable to be set aside or defective in any fashion, nor is the capacity of the settlor to be questioned, nor is the trustee, any beneficiary or any other person to be subjected to any liability or deprived of any right on such grounds'.

Section 89(3) states that if the trust contains a term to the effect that Cayman Islands law is to apply to a particular aspect of the trust, or that the Cayman Islands courts are the forum for the administration of the trust or any like provision, this is to be treated as conclusive evidence that Cayman Islands law is intended to govern the entire trust, subject to any express provision to the contrary. This also suggests that a settlor could choose a different law to govern different parts of the trust. Arguably, he could even provide that the issue of capacity alone was to be governed by Cayman Islands law and this choice would be treated as valid in the Cayman Islands courts. Moreover, a settlor may change the governing law to that of the Islands, if the change is recognised by the governing law of the trust previously in effect, or change from the Islands' laws, if the new governing law recognises the validity of the trust and the beneficiaries' interests (s 89(4)).

The whole effect of the Act is, *prima facie* at least, to give great freedom to a settlor to confer capacity on himself to dispose of property. In so doing, it might be said to value pragmatism more than consistency with conflict of laws principles on capacity and the transfer of property.

However, there are certain restrictions to the scope of the applicable law. These are set out in s 90. Three are of particular interest for present purposes. First, the section does not validate any disposition of property not owned by the settlor or subject to a power vested in the settlor. Secondly, as regards a corporation's capacity, it is provided that Cayman Islands law 'does not affect the recognition of the laws of its place of incorporation'. The word 'recognition' is open to different interpretations. On one view, it might suggest that the capacity to create a trust is governed solely by the law of the place of a company's incorporation; on another view, that a corporation must have capacity both by Cayman Islands law *and* the law of the place of incorporation; and on a third view, Cayman Islands law still determines capacity, subject to a discretion to apply the law of the place of incorporation where it is thought appropriate. Unfortunately, no further guidance is provided as to which meaning is correct. Thirdly, Cayman Islands law does not validate any trust or disposition of immovable property situated in a jurisdiction other than the Islands which is invalid according to the laws of such jurisdiction. This means that the vesting of property in the trustee will be determined by the *lex situs*; presumably it also refers capacity to the *lex situs*, since a disposition will not be valid according to the law of the place of the immovable property if the settlor lacked capacity to dispose of his property. Nor does the statute state whether a transaction which is valid by the *lex situs* can be invalidated by Cayman Islands law. In principle, it seems that it should be, since, with the exception of the s 90 criteria, the scope of Cayman Islands law when applicable is almost unlimited. On the other hand, it would mean that the rocket would have to be launched by both the *lex situs* and Cayman Islands law in relation to land, which would tend to mitigate against the validity of trusts of land. Moreover, since the whole point of the reference to the *lex situs* in relation to land is that it is futile to decide a case in a manner different from the courts of the *situs* for immovable property, it makes little sense to refer other than exclusively to that state's law, at least on the question of whether the settlor may alienate *any* property right.

Furthermore, the statute makes no reference to the capacity of the trustee to hold on trust as being governed by Cayman Islands law when that is the applicable law. Presumably, however, this is to be governed by the applicable law, since it is regarded as part of the rocket itself even under the Hague Convention,[1] and this statute provides considerably more party autonomy than does that Convention.

Nor does the Convention tell us which law is to govern capacity and the vesting of property in the trustee when Cayman Islands law is not the governing law. In principle, one might expect this also to be governed by the applicable law of the trust. On the other hand, the decision not to legislate at all in relation to such trusts suggests that the omission is material and that these issues should continue to be governed by the common law principles considered above; in which case the unbounded application of the applicable law will be hard to defend.

Finally, it is unclear whether *renvoi* is included when Cayman Islands law is chosen. It might be assumed that it is not, since s 90 states that the matters which it has previously mentioned 'are to be determined according to the laws of the Islands, without reference to the laws of any other jurisdiction with which the trust or disposition may be connected'. However, to adopt *renvoi* is

1 Although the Act was not framed with the Convention provisions in mind, as the Cayman Islands has not adopted the Convention.

to employ the *Cayman Islands' own* private international law rules, which might state that a foreign law is applicable. Accordingly, the provision is not obviously conclusive. However, a more principled argument against *renvoi* is that once party autonomy is allowed, one must respect the intentions of the parties. If a settlor states that Cayman Islands law is to govern, he almost certainly means Cayman Islands domestic law alone; in which case there is no role here for the *renvoi* doctrine.

2.6.2 Bermuda

The principal statute in Bermuda addressing conflict of laws questions in relation to trusts is the Trusts (Special Provisions) Act 1989, Part I. Many aspects of the Act are similar to the Cayman Islands legislation, but Part I is not limited to trusts governed by the law of Bermuda.[1]

The general rule is that the settlor may choose the governing law of the trust (which choice can be implied from the terms of the trust instrument, interpreted, if necessary, in the light of the circumstances of the case),[2] or the law with which the trust is most closely connected.[3] A list of matters which this law will govern is found in s 7, but does not include either capacity (for which there is separate provision) or the vesting of the property in the trustee by the settlor (for which there is no provision). One might assume from this that the transfer to the trustee will be governed by the *lex situs*. On the other hand, the Act does not contain an express provision excluding rocket-launching aspects of the trust and does expressly deal with capacity; in which case one might assume that the constitution of the trust will be governed by the governing law of the rocket aspects of the trust. Yet there is no express indication that this is the case in the Act, even where the governing law is that of Bermuda. Nor does anything other than the application of the *lex situs* have anything to commend it in principle, given that the transfer of property is an 'ordinary' incidence of the proprietary aspects of the conflict of laws.

As to capacity, there is express provision in s 10(1) that, subject to s 10(2), a person has capacity to create a trust as follows:

(a) where the trust property is movable –

---

1 Although this is not as clear as it might be. Section 3 of the Trusts (Special Provisions) Act 1989 provides that 'this Part applies to trusts created voluntarily and evidenced in writing and also to any other trusts of property arising under the law of Bermuda or by virtue of a judicial decision whether in Bermuda or elsewhere'. It is suggested that this must mean that all voluntary trusts evidenced in writing, no matter what the governing law, are included, and also trusts which do not fulfil these criteria, but which are none the less governed by the law of Bermuda. Since: (i) the wording of s 3 is taken from the UK Order in Council which extends to Bermuda the provisions of the Hague Trust Convention (with modifications); (ii) the Convention is clearly international in scope; and (iii) many of the provisions of Part I are taken directly from the Convention, the conclusion that the Act is not limited to trusts whose proper law is that of Bermuda appears overwhelming.

2 Trusts (Special Provisions) Act 1989, s 5.

3 Ibid, s 6.

(i) in the case of an *inter vivos* trust, if he has capacity to create a trust of movable property by the law of Bermuda;

(ii) in the case of a testamentary trust, if he has capacity to create a trust of movable property by the law of his domicile;

(b) where the trust property is immovable, if he has capacity to create a trust by the *lex situs* of the immovable.

Section 10(2) further provides that all questions relating to the capacity of the settlor arising in regard to a trust governed by the law of Bermuda are to be determined according to the law of Bermuda only, subject to exceptions, including that:

(a) the property must originally have been owned by the settlor;

(b) the provision takes effect subject to any express term to the contrary;

(c) in relation to the capacity of a corporation, the provision does not affect the recognition of the laws of the place of incorporation. This contains the same ambiguity as the Cayman Islands legislation discussed above;

(d) the recognition of foreign laws prescribing formalities for disposition of property remains unaffected;

(e) the provision does not validate any trust or disposition of immovable property situated outside Bermuda which is invalid according to the *lex situs*. This is another provision whose scope is uncertain in a manner similar to the Cayman Islands provision;

(f) a testamentary trust or disposition invalid according to the laws of the testator's domicile will not be validated.

Overall, this is a rather curious set of provisions. The basic capacity rule for *inter vivos* trusts of movables seems to be a blanket application of the law of Bermuda, whatever the governing law of the rocket itself. It appears that the law of Bermuda is simply applied as the law of the forum (*lex fori*). The application thereof is very hard to justify in principle. It is true that capacity rules have mandatory characteristics to them and this may lead the Bermuda court to feel that capacity restrictions by its law should never be avoided when litigation occurs in the jurisdiction. But, the settlor may have no real connection with Bermuda.[1] Indeed, by litigating in Bermuda, he may be able to avoid an incapacity which he possesses by his *lex domicilii* or by the *lex situs*. It can hardly be argued that Bermuda capacity rules merit application in all instances.

The rules look particularly curious when one notes that the *lex situs* holds complete sway in relation to immovables. Whilst this is understandable, one would have thought that if it were felt necessary to apply Bermuda law to all

1 Given the rules on jurisdiction to be found in s 9, it is not necessary that he has such a connection.

capacity questions in relation to movables, it ought also to have at least a role in relation to immovables.

2.6.3 Jersey

Whilst Jersey harmonised its rules with those of the Hague Convention in 1991, and became party thereto in 1992, the rocket-launching provisions of Jersey law are largely to be found in the Trusts (Jersey) Law 1984 (inserted by the Trusts (Amendment) (Jersey) Law 1989). The approach taken therein is striking. A person domiciled outside Jersey is deemed to have capacity to make a lifetime gift to a 'Jersey trust' if he is of full age and of sound mind by the law of his domicile.[1] A Jersey trust is defined in Art 1 as 'a trust whose proper law is the law of Jersey'. Article 8A(2)(b) provides that no rule relating to inheritance or succession of any system of law shall affect the transfer of property or the validity of the trust, although this provision is limited to *inter vivos* trusts. However, the *lex domicilii* rule will apply even in the case of *inter vivos* trusts of land. One might pause to reflect on the desirability of a settlor domiciled in State A, who owns land in State B, which he purports to transfer to trustees under a trust expressly stated to be governed by Jersey law, but who lacks capacity to dispose of the property by the law of State B and Jersey, being able validly to transfer legal title to the trustee, when according to the law of State B, the settlor still owns the property.

The statute does not deal with Jersey domiciliaries, although it would be highly surprising in the light of the above, and the general preference in offshore jurisdictions for the application of the law of the forum, if their capacity was not governed by Jersey law, at least when the governing law of the trust was that of Jersey. The result, however, is that overseas domiciliaries may be able to transfer on trust property in Jersey which a Jersey domiciliary does not have capacity to transfer.

Nor does the statute address capacity when the proper law is not that of Jersey. Regard will have to be had to common law principles in this regard. Matthews and Sowden argue that the general conflict of laws rule is that the settlor's capacity to dispose of the property is governed by the *lex domicilii* for movables and the *lex situs* for immovables.[2] They cite the case of *Attorney-General v Belilios*[3] in support of the proposition. Yet not only was that case not really about capacity, but they ignore all the rest of the English authorities on capacity, which, particularly in commercial subject areas, give domicile a very limited role. They are rightly concerned about the free evasion of capacity restrictions by application of an expressly chosen proper law; but that fear does not lead logically to the conclusion that the *lex domicilii*, as opposed to, for example, the *lex situs*, is the appropriate law.

---

1 Art 8(2)(a).

2 Note 4 on p 94, pp 44–45.

3 [1928] 1 KB 798 at 826.

It appears that Matthews and Sowden are amongst the very few writers who (rightly) distinguish between capacity to transfer property and capacity to create a trust. The rule that they suggest appears to apply to the former question. It seems that they might be prepared to accept that the proper law governs capacity to create the trust structure rather than some other.[1]

Finally, it should be noted that Art 8A(2) refers only to transfers or disposals to a trust; it does not appear to deal with the settlor's capacity to declare himself a trustee. Yet that, no less than a transfer on trust, involves the disposition of the settlor's beneficial interest and ought, accordingly, to be governed by the same principles.[2]

2.6.4 The Isle of Man

The Isle of Man's Trust Act 1995 (IMTA 1995), which came into operation on 17 January 1996, is largely inspired by the Cayman Islands legislation (the Trusts (Foreign Element) Law 1987). There are significant similarities, as detailed below.

(1) Generally all questions relating to the trust are to be determined by Manx law *if Manx law is the governing law of the trust.*[3]
(2) The provision for determining if Manx law governs and for allowing changes to and from that law are similar to those of the Trusts (Foreign Elements) Law 1987.[4]
(3) There are many similar exceptions to the general dominance of the governing law.[5]
(4) The Act prevents the capacity of the settlor from being questioned by reason of the fact that the laws of a foreign jurisdiction prohibit or do not recognise the trust.[6]
(5) Manx trusts are similarly 'insulated' from forced heirship claims arising under a foreign law. No trust governed by Manx law may be impugned by reason that rights are conferred by a foreign law *or foreign judicial or administrative order* upon a person 'by reason of a personal relationship to the settlor or by way of heirship ...'.[7] However, this provision is problematic, since the Isle of Man is bound by the scheme of the Judgments (Reciprocal Enforcement) (Isle of Man) Act 1968 to recognise on a reciprocal basis money judgments from states which are party to the scheme. That scheme includes several civilian

1 Note 4 on p 94, p 45.
2 Matthews and Sowden, n 4 on p 94, pp 45–46, agree.
3 IMTA 1995, s 4.
4 Ibid, ss 2 and 3.
5 Ibid, ss 1(1) and 4(3).
6 Ibid, s 5(a).
7 Ibid, ss 5(b)(i) and (ii). Emphasis added.

> states,[1] which might, of course, have forced heirship rules capable of impugning the trust. If all relevant conditions are met, a judgment delivered in one of these states should, in principle, be recognised in the Isle of Man, even if it orders the payment of a sum of money[2] from an Isle of Man trust, on the basis of heirship rights conferred by local law. The Act *requires* the Isle of Man to register judgments which comply with its requirements, and sets out[3] the (only) grounds on which registration may be set aside. The only possible argument would be that recognition of foreign judgments hinging on such matters as forced heirship infringes Manx public policy. However, this is to give an extremely broad meaning to the concept of public policy (and invites foreign courts asked to recognise Manx 'insular' trusts judgments to play a tit-for-tat game and refuse recognition).

There are, however, material differences between the two Acts. In the Trusts (Foreign Elements) Law 1987, the provisions for determining when Cayman Islands law governs are preceded by rules laying down the governing law for *any* trust, not just one governed by the *lex fori*. No such provision exists in the IMTA 1995, presumably because the general choice of law rule for trusts is dealt with in the Hague Convention, which was adopted in the Isle of Man by the Recognition of Trusts Act 1988.

Nor does the IMTA 1995 contain a clause to the effect that, where Manx law is stated to govern a particular aspect of the trust, it shall be presumed that Manx law was intended to apply to the whole trust – again, presumably, to avoid conflict with the Hague Convention rules, which defer to the law with which the trust is most closely connected in the absence of choice.

By s 4(1)(d) and (2)(a), questions including the capacity of the settlor and the validity of a disposition are to be determined by Manx law. Oddly, and importantly, the section does not state that this rule only applies if Manx law is the governing law of the trust. Since the Act only really deals with the choice of Manx law, one might assume that to be the case. If not, the result would be that Manx law would always be applied to the capacity question as the *lex fori*. Such a choice of law rule has already been criticised in relation to the Bermuda legislation.

As regards the transfer of property to constitute the trust, it appears that the Manx law will be used if it is the governing law, since Manx law applies to 'dispositions',[4] which are defined in s 6 to include every manner in which any legal or equitable interest in property is extinguished. Consistent with the

1 For a full list of states within the scheme, see A Briggs and P Rees, *Civil Jurisdiction and Judgments* (LLP, 2nd ed, 1997), 364 (footnotes 380–382).

2 It could be said that the order will relate to a liability to account, rather than the payment of a fixed debt. However, a civilian state may simply order the payment of a certain sum from the trust, if there are no other assets available to satisfy the forced heirship claim.

3 See Foreign Judgments (Reciprocal Enforcement) Act 1933, s 4.

4 IMTA 1995, s 4(1)(b).

general rule for the transfer of property at common law, it might be hoped that, where Manx law is not applicable, the *lex situs* will determine whether the settlor has alienated a proprietary interest.

Finally, it should be noted that s 1(1) provides that the Act does not apply unless, in the case of a testamentary trust or disposition, the trust or disposition is valid under the law of the testator's domicile at time of death, nor, and more significantly for present purposes, to trusts or dispositions of immovables, unless the trust or disposition is valid by the *lex situs*.[1] So, capacity to transfer on trust and the vesting of the property in the trustee, still require consideration of the *lex situs*. However, s 1(1) seems to require that the trust itself be valid by the law of the testator's domicile (in the case of testamentary trusts) or the *lex situs* (in the case of trusts of immovables). Yet, the Hague Convention clearly indicates that the trust itself should be subjected only to its governing law, and not to any other law.[2] Section 1(1) of the IMTA 1995 seems inconsistent with this requirement.

2.7 CONCLUSION AND TACTICAL OBSERVATION

It is suggested that neither the common law nor the offshore legislation has come up with a truly convincing answer to the complex problems raised by the rocket-launching aspects of transnational trusts, and especially to the problem of capacity. However, no attempt will be made to reiterate the conclusions expressed above as to the most principled and pragmatic choice of law rules. Instead, one final, very important observation should be made. The choice of law process is but one aspect of transnational litigation. At least as important is the question of which courts will have jurisdiction to resolve any disputes that might arise. For it is apparent that different rocket-launching choice of law rules are applied in different jurisdictions around the world. In any potential litigation, this may make the choice of jurisdiction in which to litigate especially important. Imagine a case of movable property situated in England, which a domiciliary of State A seeks to transfer to X in England. By English law, he lacks capacity to alienate the property; by the law of State A, he has capacity so to do. Suppose that according to the English conflict of laws, the choice of law rule is the *lex situs* and that by State A's law it is the *lex domicilii*. If the would-be trustee sued in England, it would be held that no trust had been created due to the settlor's incapacity; but if the action were brought in State A, it would be held that a trust had been created. It may well be that this judgment could be

1 Ibid, s 1(1).

2 Save in respect of the mandatory rule provisions identified in Arts 15 and 16, and the public provision of Art 18. It can hardly be argued that *all* rules of the *lex situs* or the law of the testator's domicile at death are mandatory rules.

enforced in other countries, including England.[1] This means that, whatever the choice of law rule in England transpires to be, one must be alert to the possibility that litigation in a transnational matter could take place first in an overseas forum, where quite different choice of law rules might be applicable, and that the effects of that litigation would be unlikely to be confined to the state in which it takes place. In the creation of any transnational trust, that is a possibility which cannot sensibly be ignored.

1 An English court will not refuse to recognise a judgment simply because it would have applied a different law had the case been heard in England. See generally, *Dicey and Morris*, n 1 on p 89, Ch 14; Cheshire and North, n 1 on p 93, Chs 15 and 16. See also Hague Trusts Convention, Art 11.

Chapter 3

INTERNATIONAL RECOGNITION OF TRUSTS

David Hayton[*]

3.1 THE BACKGROUND PROBLEMS

In common law jurisdictions, few problems arise because the trust concept is a well understood integral part of domestic law. In civil law jurisdictions, however, major problems arise because the Anglo-American trust concept is alien to their domestic law. Not only is there, therefore, no concept of equitable property rights, there is also no concept of the joint tenancy (enabling the surviving trustee or other co-owner to become sole legal owner of jointly owned property). Furthermore, a civil law jurisdiction will have succession laws (providing for forced indefeasible shares vesting directly on death in the heirs) and, often, matrimonial property regimes (providing for surviving spouses) capable of taking precedence over the law governing a settlor's trust.

As a matter of private international law, a civil law jurisdiction will, to some extent, recognise and give effect to a foreign trust through a domestic law analogue like contract or agency, although subject to safeguards concerning succession law, matrimonial property law and bankruptcy law, for example. However, the trust will be recognised as such, subject to similar safeguards, if the civil law jurisdiction (eg Italy, The Netherlands) has ratified the Hague Convention on the Law Applicable to Trusts and on their Recognition 1985 (the Hague Convention) (the text of which is fully set out in the Appendix to this work). This Convention was prepared under the auspices of the Hague Conference on Private International Law as a collaborative effort between common law and civil law countries. It reflects the common law rules for private international law matters concerning trusts.

---

* Barrister, 5 Stone Buildings, Lincoln's Inn, and Professor of Law, King's College, University of London. David Hayton headed the UK Delegation to the Fifteenth Session of The Hague Conference, which settled the terms of the draft Convention.

3.2 THE HAGUE CONVENTION

3.2.1 Signatories and ratifiers

The Hague Convention has been signed by the United Kingdom, Italy, Luxembourg, Malta, The Netherlands, the United States, Canada, Australia and France, while Italy, the United Kingdom, Hong Kong, The Netherlands, Malta, Australia and Canada (in respect of Alberta, New Brunswick, British Columbia, Newfoundland, Manitoba, Saskatchewan and Prince Edward Island) have so far gone on to ratify it, and so implement it, within their jurisdictions. Within the United Kingdom umbrella are included Bermuda, British Antarctic Territory, the Falkland Islands, the Turks and Caicos Islands, St Helena and Dependencies, South Georgia and the South Sandwich Islands, Sovereign Base areas of Akrotiri and Dhekelia, the British Virgin Islands, Montserrat, the Isle of Man, Jersey and Gibraltar. The (English) Recognition of Trusts Act 1987 has been in force in England and Wales, Scotland and Northern Ireland since 1 August 1987.

The French intended, once they had enacted a Bill concerning *La Fiducie* into their domestic law to introduce the concept of a fiduciary patrimony separate from one's own personal patrimony, to implement and so ratify the Convention. However, problems as to how to tax fiduciaries (and foreign trusts which would be taxed as if fiduciaries) led to the Bill being shelved.

The Hague Convention technically came into force on 1 January 1992 and courts of countries which have not yet implemented it will take it into account as reflecting common law countries' private international law rules and the essential characteristics of a trust when trying to resolve particular issues concerning trusts.[1] Such characteristics can also be ascertained from principles of European Trust Law developed by an International Working Group of Experts and based upon a trust as a special type of obligation owed by a trustee to beneficiaries in respect of a trust fund owned by the trustee as a separate fund immune from claims by the trustee's creditors or heirs.[2]

3.2.2 Purpose of the Hague Convention

The Convention *does not* introduce the Anglo-American trust concept into the domestic law of countries lacking the concept ('non-trust countries'). There is no question of such countries having to introduce new property concepts, like equitable interests, into their domestic law, and so having to recognise a beneficiary under a trust as having an equitable proprietary right in property

---

1 In respect of other Conventions, see Cour d'Appel de Paris *Banque Ottomane* 19 March 1965, 1966 Clunet 118; Trib gr inst de Paris 3 February 1982, 1982 Dalloz IR 143, 1986 Clunet 156; Netherlands Hague District Court *Compagnie Européenne des Pétroles v Sensor* 17 September 1982, (1983) 22 ILM 66.

2 DJ Hayton (ed) *Principles of European Trust Law* (with a General Commentary and National Commentaries revealing the extent to which the elements of a trust are already present in many civilian jurisdictions and are capable of further development) is published by Kluwer Law International (1999).

enabling him to claim such property or its traceable equivalent from all but a *bona fide* purchaser of the property. Moreover, the Hague Convention is concerned only with trusts of property and not with the imposition of constructive trusteeship upon a defendant as a formula for making him personally liable to account as a constructive trustee if he was involved in a breach of trust or other fiduciary duty.

The Hague Convention *does* make non-trust countries, like trust countries, recognise trusts of property as a matter of private international law (subject to significant safeguards). It sets out common private international law rules on the law applicable to trusts and then goes on pragmatically to emphasise the consequences of recognising a trust created under the applicable law. In implementing the Convention this should lead countries to provide expressly, as did The Netherlands, for the trustee of a foreign trust to own the trust fund as a separate fund immune from the claims of his creditors, spouse and heirs which relate only to his private patrimony.

Of course, the Hague Convention, being a private international law Convention, does not affect the domestic trust law of trust countries. Thus, the extent to which the applicable law can be expressly or impliedly changed and the distinction between matters of validity and matters of administration may vary according to the appropriate applicable law because one country's domestic trust rules may vary from such rules of another country.

3.2.3 Deliberately flexible 'grey' areas

In interpreting the Hague Convention, it is important to appreciate that near unanimity on clear 'black and white' provisions in a complex area was impossible, especially in view of time constraints. Often a problematic point was perceived and common lawyers would produce a proposal 'x', while civil lawyers would produce a proposal 'z'. After a 2-hour discussion the matter would be referred to the drafting committee to produce a compromise 'y' in the light of the discussion and in the light of the need to have the matter dealt with in French words comprehensible to civilian lawyers which would then have a parallel English text.

This led often to curiously expressed English provisions and to matters being 'fudged' by the use of 'grey' open-textured language capable of being interpreted narrowly or broadly, while some dangerous areas (eg the extent to which the creation of a trust created obligations that were more than merely personal obligations and affected property, rightly or wrongfully, substituted for original trust property) were skirted around, leaving it open for countries to develop these areas as they thought fit as they became more accustomed to, and became more relaxed in relation to, trusts.

Thus, the Hague Convention has much scope to become a very significant force for developing the use of trusts or trust-like concepts in civilian jurisdictions in Europe. However, to attain ratification of the Convention by such jurisdictions, most of those involved in developing the Convention emphasised the superficial narrow scope of the Convention.

3.2.4 The 'shapeless' trust

The momentum for the Hague Conference on Private International Law to deal with trusts came from civilian notaries who had difficulty with the increasing number of nationals in common law jurisdictions who held property in civilian jurisdictions and who purported to subject such property to testamentary trusts, and from civilian governments or large enterprises which sought to attract investment or lending from trustees. While it was the Anglo-American trust that was the catalyst for the Hague Convention, it was also necessary to take into account Scots, South African and Indian trusts, where no division existed between legal proprietary interests of trustees and equitable proprietary interests of beneficiaries, and any similar trust that might exist or arise in other countries. Finally, one had to consider the fact that trustees are commonly regarded as holding trust assets (eg stocks and shares) through a custodian-nominee rather than technically owning as a trust asset their rights against the custodian-nominee.

To deal with these matters, Art 2 states:

> 'The term "trust" refers to the legal relationships created – *inter vivos* or on death – by a person, the settlor, when assets have been placed under the control of a trustee for the benefit of a beneficiary or for a specified purpose. A trust has the following characteristics:
>
> (a) the assets constitute a separate fund and are not a part of the trustee's own estate;
> (b) title to the trust assets stands in the name of the trustee or in the name of another person on behalf of the trustee;
> (c) the trustee has the power and the duty, in respect of which he is accountable, to manage, employ or dispose of the assets in accordance with the terms of the trust and the special duties imposed upon him by law.'

Unfortunately, in covering the case where Custodian plc has title to 10,000 shares in 'A Company plc' on a bare trust for T on trust for the benefit of T's beneficiaries, Art 2 can be construed[1] as covering the case where O, the owner of the asset, remains owner thereof but gives control (and perhaps custody) of it to an agent, A, for the benefit of O and perhaps of P and Q, so creating an agency or mandate relationship (or bailment) rather than a trust relationship in the view of common law trust countries. That construction can probably be avoided on the basis that under Art 2(a) it is crucial that 'the assets constitute a separate fund' from the other assets of the owner thereof so as to be excluded from O's estate which is not the case where O has created an agency mandate or bailment.

---

1 M Lupoi, in Jackson and Wilde (eds) *The Reform of Property Law* (Dartmouth, 1997), p 222.

It is clear that if there is an Anstalt, Stiftung or Foundation that has legal personality and has legal beneficial ownership of assets, then in the absence of a separate fund of such assets separate from its own assets, there can be no trust within Art 2.

3.2.5 Scope of the Hague Convention

The Hague Convention is universal. It is not restricted to trusts created or administered in countries that have ratified the Convention but applies to all trusts irrespective of the date of creation (unless a country reserves[1] the right not to apply the Convention to trusts created before that country ratified the Convention). In the United Kingdom, s 1(5) of the Recognition of Trusts Act 1987, *ex abundante cautela*, prevents the Convention from affecting the law to be applied to anything done or omitted before 1 August 1987.

By Art 3, the Hague Convention applies only to trusts created voluntarily (whether gratuitously or for value) and evidenced in writing. This seems capable of extending to the situation where a settlor voluntarily creates a trust which operates for a period but then fails to provide effectively for how income or capital is to be used, so that a resulting trust in favour of the settlor (or his estate if he were dead) arises: to the extent that the settlor does not effectively dispose of his beneficial interest in the assets transferred to trustees, those assets are held on resulting trust for him.

Indeed, where a purchase money resulting trust arises (eg A provides half the money used to purchase a house in the name of B, who provides the other half of the purchase money so as to hold the house on trust for A and B equally) this seems to be the effect of a voluntary act, so that if evidence in writing subsequently materialises, Art 3 should apply. Presumably, such evidence in writing would consist of writing signed by B or a court order declaring that B holds on a resulting trust for himself and A equally.

In almost all trusts, the assets within the trust fund will change many times in the life of a trust, so that Art 3 must apply not only to the original trust assets but to the substituted trust assets making up the trust fund from time to time. Sometimes a trust instrument will make this clear by declaring expressly that subject to the trusts contained therein are the assets originally settled and any additions or accretions thereto and the assets from time to time representing such assets. In any event, the fruits of trust assets amount to trust assets, as do trust assets for which trust assets are exchanged. This is an institutional constructive trust arising by operation of law to vindicate the existence of the voluntarily created express trust: the function of the court is

---

1 See Art 22. Note also that under Art 21 'Any Contracting State may reserve the right to apply the [recognition] provisions of Chapter III only to trusts the validity of which is governed by the law of a Contracting State'.

simply to declare that the express trust's terms also apply to such fruits or exchanged assets from the date the fruits arose or the assets were exchanged.[1]

Where the relevant events occurred in England and the exchanged asset is then taken to a civil jurisdiction ('Civilopia') which has ratified the Convention, one expects Civilopian judges and notaries to accept that such asset is a trust asset and make the trustee (and his private creditors or his spouse or heirs) respect the trust. If the trustee then gives the trust asset in Civilopia to D or sells it in exchange for another asset, then difficulties arise. Civilopia may take a strict conservative line taking account of Civilopian property law or may try to circumvent or develop such law, eg by regarding T's transfer to D as a nullity due to his lack of power to make such a gift and by extending to the relevant asset real subrogation principles already applicable to partnership property and matrimonial regime property.

Just as the Hague Convention does not apply to the personal remedy of liability to account as a constructive trustee (for dishonest assistance in a breach of trust or dishonest dealing with trust property) so, too, it does not apply to the American or Canadian proprietary remedy of a remedial constructive trust imposed prospectively by a court at the date of a court order.[2]

A trust instrument executed in favour of one's children and soon-to-be-divorced wife so as to avoid a divorce court order is within the Convention but a trust created pursuant to a judicial adjudication of a matrimonial dispute is not, unless the trust aspect can be regarded as mere judicial confirmation of a voluntary agreement.[3] However, under Art 20, any country can extend the Convention to trusts declared by judicial decisions anywhere and the United Kingdom has done this.[4] Indeed, any EU or EFTA country should do likewise (at least in respect of EU and EFTA countries) to comply with its obligations under the Brussels and Lugano Conventions on Jurisdiction and the Enforcement of Judgments. The United Kingdom has further extended the Convention to 'any other trusts of property arising under the law of any part of the UK',[5] for example trusts arising by operation of law due to co-ownership or to intestacy.

The Hague Convention applies only to a trust once it has been successfully launched like a rocket by some valid will, instrument or act (the

---

1 See *Westdeutsche Landesbank Girozentrale v Islington LBC* [1996] AC 669 at 714.

2 This will not be imposed where the owner is insolvent and a statutory priority scheme applies: *Re Polly Peck International plc (In Administration)* [1998] 3 All ER 812, CA, where Nourse LJ considered that a remedial constructive trust could not be imposed even on a solvent owner because an Act of Parliament is needed to permit a variation of established proprietary rights.

3 See von Overbeck *Official Report on the Hague Trusts Convention* (the *Official Report*), para 49; and Gaillard and Trautman (1987) 35 Am J Comp L 318. Cf *Re Flint* [1993] Ch 319. The text of the *Official Report* (in English translation) is reproduced in J Glasson (ed) *International Trust Laws* (Jordans, looseleaf), Section C, Appendix 5.1.

4 Recognition of Trusts Act 1987, s 1(2).

5 Ibid.

'rocket-launcher'). In a nutshell, the Convention applies to the rocket but not the rocket-launcher. By Art 4, antecedent preliminary issues that may affect the validity of wills, deeds or other acts by which property is allegedly subjected to a trust fall outside the Convention. The settlor's capacity is thus outside the Convention.[1] The forum's private international choice of law rules will determine the law applicable to formal and substantive validity of testamentary dispositions or lifetime declarations of trust or transfers of property. The Convention will only apply if whatever is the applicable law governing capacity or formal or substantive validity has not operated to prevent the relevant property being available to be subjected to trusts.

By Art 13 a court in a non-trust country (or a trust country) has a discretionary power to refuse to recognise a trust if the significant elements of the trust (eg *situs* of assets, habitual residence of settlor and beneficiaries) are more closely connected with non-trust countries than with trust countries, except for the choice of the applicable law, the place of administration and the habitual residence of the trustees. It will be up to the court in a particular case to decide what are the significant elements which connect the trust more closely to a non-trust country. The relevant time for these significant elements to be so connected seems to be the time of the events occasioning the claim for recognition rather than the time of creation of the trust.[2] The Milan Commercial Court in its supervisory role has approved debenture trusts, where all the elements were Italian except for the choice of Jersey law in one case and Maltese law in another case: the Italian Bankers' Association has produced guidelines recommending such trusts to its members. The United Kingdom considered that its courts did not need to have the discretionary power conferred by Art 13 so the Recognition of Trusts Act 1987 omitted Art 13.

3.2.6 Law applicable to the trust

Express or implied choice by settlor

The settlor can choose the law[3] to govern his trust or any severable aspect of the trust,[4] eg validity, construction, administration or property situated in a different jurisdiction from the rest of the trust property. Article 6 provides:

---

1 *Official Report*, n 2 on p 126, para 54.

2 DJ Hayton (1987) 36 ICLQ 260 at 274. The Italian courts have not sought to invoke Art 13 against internal trusts with a foreign trust law: see M Lupoi 'The Development of Protected Trust Structures in Italy' in DJ Hayton (ed) *Extending the Boundaries of Trusts and Similar Ring-Fenced Funds* (Kluwer Law International, 2002).

3 Law means the rules of law in force in a country other than its private international law rules so *renvoi* is excluded: Art 17. An unambiguous, meaningful, express choice is conclusive: *Tod v Barton* (unreported) 20 February 2002, ChD, per Lawrence Collins J.

4 See Art 9.

> 'The choice must be express or be implied in the terms of the instrument creating or the writing evidencing the trust interpreted, if necessary, in the light of the circumstances of the case.'

Normally, in the trust instrument the settlor will expressly state which country's law is to govern his trust and, normally, this one law will be the applicable law for all aspects of the trust. If the settlor does wish to have one law governing validity and another law governing administration, whether at the outset or after some authorised replacement of the applicable law, he should expressly provide the means for distinguishing between matters of validity and matters of administration. This is advisable because the distinction between such matters may be uncertain, especially if a jurisdiction regards matters affecting the nature or quantum of a beneficiary's interest to be matters of validity. It may thus be helpful to specify that powers of maintenance and advancement are to be treated as matters of administration.

If authorised by the original trust law governing the trust, the law or laws chosen by the settlor can be replaced in specified fashion by another law or laws, eg where the trust instrument authorises the trustees, with the consent of a specified protector, to change the place of administration and the law governing administration. To prevent any derogation from the interests of the beneficiaries the replacement of the law governing validity or administration must be valid under the law applicable to the validity of the trust.[1]

Where there is no express choice of the law of a specified jurisdiction then one has recourse to the terms of the trust document interpreted, if necessary, in the light of the circumstances of the case. It is possible that the terms of the trust refer to statutes of a particular jurisdiction so as to enable the court to find an implied choice of the law of that jurisdiction without considering other circumstances. However, common law judges will normally wish to consider all the relevant circumstances such as the domicile or habitual residence of the settlor and the principal beneficiaries, the *situs* of assets, the place of administration of the trust. Logically, there is a clear difference between a subjective implied choice of law by the settlor and an objectively applicable law which the court chooses as the most closely connected law if there is no subjective express or implied choice: pragmatically, there may be little difference.

The objectively applicable law

In the absence of subjective choice, the applicable law is that with which the trust is most closely connected. In ascertaining such law under Art 7:

> 'reference shall be made in particular to:
>
> (a) the place of administration of the trust designated by the settlor;

[1] As recognised by Art 10.

(b) the situs of the assets of the trust;
(c) the place of residence or business of the trustee;
(d) the objects of the trust and the places where they are to be fulfilled.'

This does not prevent reference being made to other significant elements such as those taken into account for Art 13 purposes, eg domicile or habitual residence of the settlor or the beneficiaries.[1]

Article 7 is too short and ambiguous to be helpful in many cases but it was considered that some guidelines should be attempted rather than having none at all or a lengthy comprehensive list. Because the Article covers the applicable law for validity, for construction and for administration it has to be ambiguous and leave open the relevant time for ascertaining close connection: the date of executing a will (for construction of a testamentary trust), the date lifetime trusts take effect (for validity, construction and administration), and the date the applicable law is replaced by another one (for validity and administration). Moreover, the relevance and significance of particular factors depends upon whether one is concerned with ascertaining the law governing validity or the law governing administration and whether one is concerned with a testamentary trust, a lifetime trust, a marriage settlement or a charitable trust. The four criteria were specified as premised upon private lifetime trusts.

Trust-country lawyers and judges will continue to examine all the factors traditionally considered relevant for particular types of trust[2] (eg testator's domicile for testamentary trusts, matrimonial domicile for marriage settlements) and to take into account whether validity or administration or construction is the issue in question. Non-trust-country lawyers and judges are expected to leave matters relating to the internal trustee/beneficiary relationship (as opposed to the external relationship of the trustees with third parties) to the jurisdiction of the trust country court whose law governs such internal relationship. If, however, in an exceptional case, non-trust country notaries and judges do have to determine an objectively applicable law it is to be hoped that they will not be misled by the four enumerated factors in Art 7 (which are particularly relevant if the law governing administration of a lifetime trust is in issue) to ignore the significance of other factors. Of course, an express choice of law will prevent any such problems arising.

---

1 See *Official Report*, n 3 on p 126, para 122 on Art 13.

2 See DJ Hayton (1987) 36 ICLQ 260 at 271–272; Delaney (1961) 10 ICLQ 385; Wallace (1987) 36 ICLQ 454; *Dicey and Morris on the Conflict of Laws* (Sweet & Maxwell, 13th ed, 2000), Ch 29, Trusts; Honoré's *South African Law of Trusts*, Ch 14, Conflict of Laws; *Chellaram v Chellaram* [1985] Ch 409; *Re Lord Cable* [1977] 1 WLR 7; *Iveagh v Inland Revenue Commissioners* [1954] 1 Ch 364; *Duke of Marlborough v Attorney-General* [1945] Ch 78; *Re Hewitt's Settlements* [1915] 1 Ch 228; *Chellaram v Chellaram (No 2)* [2002] EWHC 632 (Civ), [2002] 3 All ER 17 (where Collins J doubted whether there was any significant difference between Art 7 and the likely approach of the common law (para 166)). In Scotland, *Re Betts Brown Trust* 1968 SC 170. In Australia, *Perpetual Executors & Trustees v Roberts* [1970] VR 732; *Londsay v Miller* [1949] VR 13. In South Africa, *Re Pollak's Estate* [1937] TPD 91.

3.2.7 Recognition of trusts and their characteristics

Article 8 (also dealt with at **3.3.2** under 'Distinction between matters of validity and of administration' below) provides for the applicable law or laws as determined under Art 6 or Art 7 to govern matters affecting the validity of a trust, its construction, its effects and its administration, and then particularises a variety of matters that may arise during the existence of a trust. The Convention makes no attempt to specify whether any of these particularised matters are matters of validity or construction or administration, leaving such issues to be determined by the law governing validity of the trust, the Convention not affecting substantive trust law.

If the applicable law is that of State X, a trust country, then the courts of State Y, a non-trust country which has ratified the Convention, are bound to recognise the characteristics of the State X trust without the need for express recognition provisions in the Convention. However, it was felt advisable to spell out the effects of recognition and clarify limitations thereon.

Article 11 expressly provides that a trust validly created in accordance with the applicable law shall be recognised as a trust. In its second and third paragraphs it states:

> 'Such recognition shall imply, as a minimum, that the trust property constitutes a separate fund, that the trustee may sue and be sued in his capacity as trustee, and that he may appear or act in this capacity before a notary or any person acting in an official capacity.
>
> In so far as the law applicable to the trust requires or provides, such recognition shall imply, in particular:
>
> (a) that personal creditors of the trustee shall have no recourse against the trust assets;
> (b) that the trust assets shall not form part of the trustee's estate upon his insolvency or bankruptcy;
> (c) that the trust assets shall not form part of the matrimonial property of the trustee or his spouse nor part of the trustee's estate upon his death;
> (d) that the trust assets may be recovered when the trustee, in breach of trust, has mingled trust assets with his own property or has alienated trust assets. However, the rights and obligations of any third party holder of the assets shall remain subject to the law determined by the choice of law rules of the forum.'

The second paragraph mandatorily requires certain minimum essential characteristics of a trust to be recognised, whilst the third paragraph mandatorily requires certain further characteristics to be recognised where such further characteristics arise under the law applicable to the trust, as will normally[1] be the case for the classic Anglo-American trust. These paragraphs are intended to ensure that the trustees as managers of the trust property will be able to look after it effectively and that the beneficiaries' interests will be

---

1 Exceptionally, where trusts have been created to defraud creditors the creditors will be able to have recourse to the trust assets whether or not the settlor is also a trustee.

properly safeguarded as interests in a fund separately owned by the trustee and immune from claims of his private creditors, his spouse or his heirs.

As the *Official Report* states[1] of the second paragraph:

> 'This paragraph determines first of all that the assets of the trust are separate from those of the trustee. This is an essential element of a trust, without which its recognition would have no meaning.'

However, it would still have a little meaning in allowing a trustee to sue and to be sued in his office as trustee and to appear in such capacity to represent the trust in dealings with notaries and other officials if antipathy to the trust led a foreign court to exploit Art 15 to undermine the apparent separateness of a trust fund from the trustee's private patrimony.

The better view is the broader view, accepted by The Netherlands,[2] that Art 11 requires the trust fund to be regarded as separate from the trustee's private patrimony. Thus, it should not be available to the trustee's private creditors on the insolvency of the trustee nor to the trustee's heirs on the death of the trustee. Of course, if the trustee has a life interest or an interest in capital after the death of the life tenant and then becomes insolvent, such life interest or interest in capital will be available to his creditors whose interests are safeguarded by Art 15(e). Moreover, if the settlor created the trust in order to defraud creditors then the trust assets in the hands of the trustees can be made available to satisfy creditors' claims also safeguarded by Art 15(e).

Other interests, however, also need proper safeguards. Thus, the last sentence of para 3(d) inserted due to great pressure from Swiss banks, restricts a beneficiary's fundamental right to trace property into the hands of third parties in receipt of trust property and to sue them. Under standard conflict of laws principles, the *lex situs* normally determines questions of transfer of title to property and whether or not a donee or a purchaser has obtained good title free from other claims. If the *lex situs* is the law of a trust state having tracing rules this will not matter very much except to the extent that registration of title statutes may confer a good title irrespective of notice. If the *lex situs* is the law of a non-trust state, which does not have the distinction between legal and equitable interests and has no tracing or constructive trusteeship rules, this will make meaningless the right to trace or the right to make someone personally accountable as a constructive trustee, except to the extent that a recipient's actual knowledge of a breach of trust may make it possible to take advantage of rules of the *lex situs* concerning fraud. Such rules may make the fraudster personally liable or, if he still has the property, may require him to return it.[3]

---

1 Note 2 on p 126, para 108.

2 Article 4 of the Dutch Law on Conflict Rules of Trusts excludes the application of Art 15(d) and (e) of the Convention.

3 Note that Art 14 provides: 'The Convention shall not prevent the application of rules of law more favourable to the recognition of trusts'. Further see Trib civ Le Mans (20 November 1934) *Milthorp v Fielding* 1935 Clunet 651 (where the beneficiary recovered French land from the mistress of the trustee

Further separate protection for purchasers or third parties in good faith is provided in Art 15(f).

Article 12 enables the trustees if they so desire to register their title to property as trustees or in such other way that the existence of the trust is disclosed insofar as this is not prohibited by or inconsistent with the *lex situs*.[1] Instead of taking advantage of this facility they may register ordinarily as co-owners (eg if marketability, and thus value, might otherwise be adversely affected) but registration should take place if necessary to protect beneficiaries against creditors of the trustee according to mandatory rules of the *lex situs* which treat a registered proprietor as absolute beneficial owner unless he is registered as holding property as trustee or nominee.

3.2.8 Limitations upon application of the trust law

Quite apart from the limiting effect of Arts 4 and 13 as already seen, Arts 15, 16 and 18 dramatically restrict the scope for the application of the law applicable to the trust. They represent hurdles that the trust must surmount.

Article 15 is designed to ensure the application of the domestic mandatory rules of a country whose law is applicable according to the private international law rules of the forum, irrespective of the law applicable to the trust. A forum will have choice of law rules in areas such as succession, transfer of title to property and bankruptcy, and these rules may lead to the *lex successionis*, *lex situs*, or *lex fori* being invoked so as wholly or partly to undo the effect of creating a trust. Mandatory rules (*droits impératifs*) are rules that cannot be derogated from by voluntary act.

Mandatory succession rules (eg French *réserve héréditaire*, Italian *legitima portio*, German *Pflichtteil*) are of particular significance. If, after the death of the settlor, trust assets are found situated in the civil law forum of the settlor's forced heir then the forum will enable the heir to claim his share out of such assets.[2] However, if a settlor domiciled in, habitually resident in, and a national of, a non-trust country had transferred English assets to English trustees of a trust governed by English law then the trust should be safe from forced heirs' claims while the assets remain in England or a common law country. English private international law choice of law rules should lead an English court to characterise the transfer of title to property merely as an *inter vivos* transfer governed by the *lex situs*[3] (and having nothing to do with succession law governed by the relevant foreign *lex successionis*), the supremacy of the *lex situs*

---

who was the beneficiary's husband) and Trib de Commerce Geneva (22 January 1874) *Pugh v Schlesinger* 1874 Clunet 324.

1 For example if the *lex situs* prohibits any reference to trusts in company share registers.

2 *Holzberg v Sasson* (1986) 75 Rev cr de dr int priv 685; *Caron v Odell* (1986) 75 Rev cr de dr int priv 66.

3 *Cf* Florida law in *Sanchez v Sanchez* 547 So 2d 945 (1989); New York law in *Hutchinson v Ross* 211 NE 2d 637 (1965); *Wyatt v Fulrath* 187 NE 65 (1933); P Matthews (2001) 5 *Chase Journal* 15. On the approach to identify the appropriate applicable law, see *Raiffeisen Zentralbank Osterreich AG v Five Star General Trading LLC* [2001] EWCA Civ 68, [2001] QB 825, CA.

being buttressed by Art 15(1)(d). Thus, the court should reject the claims of the forced heir against the trustee just as it would reject the claims of the heir of a deceased foreign joint tenant of English property against the surviving joint tenant.[1]

Articles 15 and 16 both commence 'The Convention does not prevent the application of provisions of the law' so that the question arises whether this is mandatory or merely permissive, ie whether such provisions must be applied or may or may not in the court's discretion be applied. The answer is that the provisions *must* be applied. How can the forum do otherwise than apply under Art 16 the 'provisions of the law of the forum which must be applied even to international situations, irrespective of rules of conflict of laws'? Thus, the *Official Report* states:[2]

> 'The first paragraph of Art 16 provides that the forum's laws of immediate application will *override* the other provisions of the Convention.'

It also states in respect of Art 15:[3]

> 'The first paragraph of this provision *preserves* the mandatory rules of the law designated by the conflicts rules of the forum for matters other than trusts,'

having earlier stated:[4]

> 'It may be that the law applicable to a trust will encroach on the area of another law designated by the forum's conflict rules. Under Art 15 it is then that other law which will prevail but only – and this is its difference from Art 4 – as concerns the mandatory rules of that other law. By virtue of Art 15 the law applicable to the trust *must* yield to the provisions for forced heirship of the law governing succession to property upon death as designated by the forum's conflict rules.'

The mandatory nature of Arts 15 and 16 thus led to s 1(3) of the Recognition of Trusts Act 1987 being worded:

> 'In accordance with Articles 15 and 16 such provisions of the law as are there mentioned *shall* [not may], to the extent there specified, apply to the exclusion of the other provisions of the Convention.'[5]

Article 16's first paragraph is an overriding provision which emphasises the obvious point that the court of the forum must apply 'those provisions of the

---

1 See further DJ Hayton *European Succession Laws* (Jordans, 3rd ed, 2002) Ch 1, paras **1.67–1.70**.

2 Note 3 on p 126, para 150. See also M Lupoi's note on *Cassani v Mattei* (Foro Italiano no 1, 2007 (1998)), in *Trusts and Trustees* (October 1998), Vol 4, p 24.

3 Note 3 on p 126, para 136 and *Tod v Barton* (unreported) 20 February 2002, ChD, per Lawrence Collins J.

4 Ibid, para 54.

5 Emphasis and words in square brackets added by author.

law of the forum which must be applied even to international situations, irrespective of rules of conflict of laws'. Such 'international' mandatory provisions are known in civil law countries as *lois de police* or *lois d'application immédiate* and involve measures specially designed to protect the interests of a country in, for example, preventing the export of currency or of cultural heritage objects or prohibiting the export of arms or technical equipment to certain countries.[1]

Article 16's second paragraph gives the court a discretion, to be exercised only in exceptional circumstances, to apply the 'international' mandatory provisions of some country whose law is neither the *lex fori* nor the applicable law of the trust, so long as this country has 'a sufficiently close connection with a case'. This will protect a trustee if sued for breach of trust by a beneficiary for not transferring to the beneficiary some asset the beneficiary would be entitled to but for the law of State X preventing the export of such asset.

Since a Court of Equity will do nothing in vain and will not require a person to do an act that is illegal where it is to be done,[2] so that sufficient defined protection exists, there seems no need for a common law country to adopt this paragraph of worryingly wide ambit.[3] The third paragraph of Art 16 thus allows a state to declare that it will not apply the second paragraph.[4] The United Kingdom made this declaration when it ratified the Convention so the Recognition of Trusts Act 1987 deliberately omits the second paragraph of Art 16.

If the forum cannot rely on Art 16 to oust the application of the law governing the trust then Art 18 falls to be considered.

It is a standard clause found in Hague Conventions. It provides for the provisions of the Convention to be disregarded if the forum considers that their application would be *manifestly* incompatible with its public policy.[5] Use of 'manifestly' indicates that public policy should only be resorted to in extreme cases. It should be rare, indeed, for the *lex fori* to deny effect to a foreign rule of law, declared applicable pursuant to the forum's choice of law rules, on the

---

1 English examples seem to include *Black v Yates* [1992] QB 526 (need to comply with English infancy law requiring court's approval of compromise or settlement of minor's claim); *Boissevain v Neil* [1950] AC 327 (defence regulations prohibiting British subjects from borrowing foreign currency); *Regazzoni v Sethia Ltd* [1958] AC 301 (contract made with object of breaking the law of a foreign friendly country); Unfair Contract Terms Act 1977, s 27(2).

2 *Re Lord Cable* [1976] 3 All ER 417 at 435; *Zivonestenska Bank v Freeman* [1950] AC 57 at 74; *Euro-Diam Ltd v Bathurst* [1987] 2 All ER 113.

3 No such paragraph appears in the Hague Convention on the Law Applicable to Contracts for the International Sales of Goods 1988.

4 A similar reservation is permitted in Art 7 of the European Community Rome Convention on Contractual Obligations, and the UK took advantage of this in its Contracts (Applicable Law) Act 1990.

5 On the problems of distinguishing between public policy, international mandatory rules and domestic mandatory rules, see Ch 1 for each country in M Rubino-Sammartano and CGJ Morse *Public Policy in Transnational Relationships* (Kluwer, 1991).

ground that the foreign law is repugnant to some fundamental policy of the forum.

However, an English court may well rely on Art 18 where there is English property held by English trustees on trust for English beneficiaries allegedly forever under a choice of a foreign law which has no rule against perpetuities, or English property is held by English trustees on trust for non-charitable purposes to be fulfilled in England indefinitely under a choice of foreign law which has a law abolishing the rule against inalienability and permitting valid non-charitable purpose trusts. Indeed, if English property is held on trust for English 'beneficiaries' under Cayman STAR law where beneficiaries have no rights (other than the right to retain any trust property transferred to them by the trustees) unless appointed an enforcer of the trust, and no beneficiary has been appointed an enforcer, then the Cayman trust for the 'beneficiaries' is likely to be regarded as a resulting trust for the settlor with a power to benefit the 'beneficiaries' as simply objects of a power. 'An irreducible core of obligations owed by the trustees to the beneficiaries and enforceable by them is fundamental to the concept of a trust', as Millett LJ has emphasised.[1] In a trust for beneficiaries the beneficial interest must be in the beneficiaries or, if not, must remain with the settlor, the legal and beneficial interest only necessarily being in the trustees where there is a purpose trust.[2]

3.2.9 The facilitative approach to the Convention

The Convention is a flexible, facilitative Convention enabling a foreign forum to go a long way towards recognising trusts as such or only a little way. As non-trust countries acquire greater experience and understanding of trusts they can be expected to go further and further towards recognising trusts as such, although, of course, one cannot expect settlors to be allowed to use trusts to evade their obligations towards their heirs, creditors or spouses.

3.2.10 Better prospects if Hague Succession Convention 1989 implemented

Problems involving a trust and the *lex successionis* governing the deceased settlor's estate may be minimised if the Hague Convention on Succession to Deceased Persons' Estates 1989 is implemented. It allows a person to choose as his *lex successionis* the law of his habitual residence or of his nationality at the date he makes his will. When habitually resident in, or a national of, a common law country a settlor could choose the law of such country to govern succession to his estate. Such country will normally have no forced heirship rules but only discretionary judicial provision available under an Act like the (English) Inheritance (Provision for Family and Dependants) Act 1975. The

---

1 *Armitage v Nurse* [1998] Ch 241 at 253.

2 See further DJ Hayton 'STAR Trusts' (1998) 8 *Offshore TR* 43, (2001) 117 LQR 96.

settlor's trust will be unimpeachable, unless created within six years of his death with intent to defeat claims under such Act, and in any claim against assets in the settlor's estate at his death the court will take account of any interest in the trust that the claimant might have.

3.3 WHERE TRUSTS CONVENTION INAPPLICABLE

3.3.1 Civil law jurisdictions

Introduction

In civil law jurisdictions, other than Liechtenstein which has its own Trust Code of 1926, there are a wide variety of concepts none of which is the same as the trust so that the problem of finding an adequate characterisation, adaptation or analogue of the trust[1] is a very difficult one, especially when there are various types of trust which also may either be testamentary or *inter vivos*, eg a *bare* trust for A or for A, B, C and D; a *fixed* trust for A for life, remainder to B; a *discretionary* trust for discretionary payment of income and capital to such of A, B, C and D, their spouses and issue as the trustees may see fit from time to time; a *charitable* trust for the Red Cross or such other charitable purpose or purposes as the trustees may see fit from time to time. There is little reported case-law and some cases are based on misconceptions of trust law. With greater understanding of trust law, liberal developments can be expected. Advice from a lawyer in the relevant jurisdiction will always be needed.

Increasingly, the courts or notaries in civil law countries pay close attention to the provisions of a particular trust instrument and its consequences under trust law to try to ascertain its true nature by reference to their own concepts.[2] A bare trust may be regarded as creating an agency or mandate. A fixed trust may be regarded as a type of contract or, if concerning local assets, may be regarded by the *lex situs* either as conferring ownership on the life tenant subject to an obligation to pass ownership on to the remainderman or as conferring ownership forthwith on the remainderman subject to personal obligations owed to the life tenant. A discretionary trust should normally be regarded as a contract. A charitable trust may be regarded as a contract or, possibly, as if it were a foundation or *stiftung* with separate personality. An *inter vivos* trust where the settlor in his lifetime retains extensive powers of

---

1 Civil law courts do not on *ordre public* grounds refuse recognition of a foreign trust simply because the trust has no complete equivalent in civil law: Austrian Supreme Court judgment (27 February 1952) (1952) 2 ICLQ 148–149 (Abel); Greek Aeropagus Judgment No 1286 of 1977, Tribune Jurid (1978), 1046, (1981) 94 *Journal du droit int* and other civil law cases cited below.

2 There are two very useful French books: J-P Béraudo *Les trusts anglo-saxons et le droit français* (LGDJ, 1992) and M Revillard *Droit International Priveé et Pratique Notariale* (Defrenois, 4th ed, 1998) paras 414–435.

appointment or revocation may be regarded as a testamentary trust with the trustees being *exécuteurs testamentaires*. In testamentary trusts, the trustees will normally be regarded as special *exécuteurs testamentaires* with more powers than those of such executors or of *mandataires*. Where the issue concerns powers of trustees the courts of the *lex situs* of the relevant assets favour facilitating matters by holding that the trustees have the necessary ownership powers to enable a transaction to be effected in the course of the trustees' management of the assets.[1]

Inter vivos trusts

Characterisation or transposition into civil law analogues

It is not surprising that the flexible contract concept is normally chosen to give effect to some extent to a trust. After all, a trust seems very like a contract to a civil lawyer ignorant of the distinction between legal and equitable ownership but accustomed to valid contracts for the benefit of third parties. Usually, a trustee has accepted the obligation to manage someone else's property and distribute income and capital to those entitled to it and has the right to have his expenses paid and to be paid for his services. He can thus easily be regarded by a civilian as a person contracting for payment to look after someone else's property.

Use of the contract concept usually produces a sensible solution giving effect to the settlor's intentions if later some disgruntled relative or legatee not having forced heirship rights seeks to upset an *inter vivos* family trust.

In *Courtois v De Ganay*[2] the settlor (of French nationality and habitual residence) transferred securities situate in America to an American insurance company and executed a trust deed before the American consul in Paris. The trust income was to be paid to the settlor during her life and then capital and income was to be paid to certain members of her family, the defendants, who resided in America. The plaintiffs, legatees under the settlor's will, claimed the trust was a gift forbidden under the French law of succession. The Paris Court of Appeal held that the trust 'does not depend on the law of succession but on the law of autonomy, ie the law under which the parties have intended to place themselves', such by implication being the law of an American state which treated the trust as valid. Thus the trust was upheld as a sort of synallagmatic

---

1 See Paris Court of Appeal 29 November 1952, 1953 Clunet 140; Cour de Cassation Crim 4 June 1941 Dalloz 1942, 1, 5; Cour de Cassation Civ (3 November 1983), 1984 Rev cr de dr int pr 336; Trib Seine (10 December 1880), 1880 Jo de dr int pr 435; Trib Seine (28 June 1901), 1901 Clunet 812; Court of Oristano (15 March 1956); *Piercy v Etfas* 79 Foro Italiano no 1, 1019, (1957) 6 ICLQ 169; Trib des Alpes-Maritimes (22 February 1928), 1929 Clunet 433; Trib grande instance de Bayonne (28 April 1975), 1976 Rev cr de dr int pr 330.

2 Paris Court of Appeal (10 January 1970), 1971 Rev cr de dr int pr 518, 1973 Clunet 201. It is considered that there is now no need in order to preserve the integrity of a complex *inter vivos* trust to fall back upon the concept of the trustee being a *mandataire* (Trib Seine (19 December 1916), 1917 Clunet 1069) or a special *exécuteur* (Trib Pau (3 July 1956), 1956 *Gazette du Palais* 339).

contract. The court indicated that the law governing succession might well have been concerned if heirs' indefeasible shares had been in issue.

This point was also made by the Swiss Federal Court in *Harrison v Crédit Suisse*[1] where no forced heirship claim arose. An American, Harrison, had made an irrevocable transfer of Swiss assets to Crédit Suisse in Zurich under a trust instrument choosing Zurich as the forum for any trust proceedings. This trust was in favour of his first wife and children. After he died domiciled in New York his second wife whom he had made sole legatee contested the validity of the trust in the Swiss courts but she did not have any claim to be a forced heir. The court held that since Swiss law does not have the trust concept 'it is necessary to examine to which legal institutions of Swiss law the legal relationship in dispute has the closest resemblance as far as its effects are concerned'. The court found that the trust was really a mixed contract depending on the law of obligations since it contained aspects of a contract of mandate, of an agreement to make a fiduciary transfer of property, of a gift and of a contract for the benefit of a third party. Swiss law was the applicable law since the characteristic performance of the trusteeship obligations had to take place in Switzerland. The court held that such a mixed contract involving the law of obligations was not incompatible with Swiss law, which could implement it so that the second wife's claim failed. It should be noted, however, that under the Swiss Private International Law Act (effective 1 January 1989), Art 150, most types of trusts will be characterised as companies subject to their governing law because 'company' is defined to 'include all organised associations of persons and all organised associations of property'.[2]

In other contexts the courts have been prepared to find that there is a mandate or agency contract enabling the court to look past the trustee, eg to enable judicial steps to be taken by a separated wife's creditors directly against her husband who had agreed to pay $6,000 a year to a trustee for payment to her, the court regarding the husband and not the trustee as the wife's debtor.[3] In *Faillité Four Seasons Overseas NV v SA Finimtrust*,[4] where a commercial trust deed for the issue of Eurobonds clearly purported to transfer title to the trustee, the Luxembourg court characterised the trust merely as a contract of

---

1 ATF 96, 1970, II 79. In *Zieseniss v Zieseniss* the Cour de Cassation on 20 February 1996 held where a forced heirship claim arose in respect of an *inter vivos* transfer to trustees that the transfer ranked as a *donation indirecte* and not as *un legs*.

2 See D Forbes-Jaeger and E Storman in [2000] JTCP 141.

3 Trib Seine (26 December 1894), 1895 Clunet 587; and see Paris Court of Appeal (18 April 1929), 1935 Rev cr de dr int pr 149 (where the settlor's assets settled on herself for life were held recoverable from the trustee by creditors).

4 Trib d'arrondissement de Luxembourg (21 January 1971), 1972 Rev cr de dr int pr 51; and see *Pyrénées Minerals Ltd* (Toulouse (18 July 1905, appeal 19 February 1908), 1906 Clunet 451, 1912 Clunet 243) and judgment of Swiss Federal Court (Lausanne) (26 May 1936) BGE 62 11 140 holding that, although the Bank for International Settlements (set up to implement the 1929 Young Plan for settling the German reparations question) was 'a trustee', it was essentially an intermediary agent between the principal debtor (Germany) and the bondholders.

mandate, the trustee simply being the bondholders' agent so that it was the bondholders and not the trustee who had *locus standi* to bring legal actions.

Nowadays, it is considered that if it can be shown that under the applicable law of the trust the trustee had independent discretionary control which he can exercise irrespective of the wishes of the beneficiaries then the trustee alone should be regarded as having the right to sue[1] and effect transactions concerning the trust assets.

Where the trustee is regarded as having ownership, subject to obligations of a contractual nature, major problems, however, arise if the trustee dies or becomes insolvent or wrongfully transfers the property in breach of trust. In civil law countries, a person's property belongs to him without any distinction between a private patrimony and a fiduciary patrimony and so will pass directly to his heirs on his death (civil law systems not having the joint tenancy concept for co-owners) or on bankruptcy to his bankruptcy liquidator. It may well be that nothing can be done upon bankruptcy but where trust property passes to the trustee's heirs it may be possible to bring an action to prevent the unjust enrichment of the heirs, especially if, for example, the only son and heir was aware that his father had agreed to be trustee of the property in question. Indeed, if the trustee in breach of trust had transferred trust assets to a third party who was not a *bona fide* purchaser (but, for example, a donee who knew of the trust) then there may well be civil law provisions against fraud that could be taken advantage of to recover the assets or the value thereof; indeed, it may be that the *lex situs* could regard the trustee as having had no power to transfer a valid title to the third party.

The root of the difficulty is that in civil law countries there is a limited catalogue of property interests, known as the *numerus clausus*, so that ownership has to be in either the trustee or the beneficiary or beneficiaries. However, in Germany a court might be persuaded to consider a particular trust as a *Treuhand*, especially if the settlor was also a beneficiary. The transferor, the *Treugeber*, is protected in respect of the original transferred property (and, perhaps, substitutions therefor)[2] against the creditors and transferees of the fiduciary transferee, the *Treuhänder*, although a third party beneficiary only has a personal claim against the *Treuhänder*.

It is crucial to appreciate that where transfer of title to third parties is concerned the *lex situs* will normally govern the matter. The civil law rule that, for a corporeal movable, possession amounts to title has considerable significance in protecting transferees in good faith, so trustees need to be very wary of letting a beneficiary have possession of assets like a valuable painting or jewellery.

---

1 An unreported 1996 Luxembourg case involving *Trustees of Alan Clore Foundation (A Charitable Trust) v ABN-Amro Bank (Luxembourg) SA* adopts a liberal approach entitling the trustees to sue and restricts *Faillité Four Seasons* to its special facts: see discussion of case by P Kinsch in [1996] JTCP 121–123.

2 See H Kötz, in *Principles of European Trust Law* (Kluwer, 1999).

Applicable law

Where a trust is characterised as a contract then the applicable law will be that chosen by the settlor and 'accepted' by the trustees, just as the parties to a contract can choose the applicable law of the contract, although it will be sensible to ensure that there is some significant connection with the chosen law. However, the characteristic performance rules laid down by the Rome Convention on Contractual Obligations 1980 for ascertaining the law objectively applicable to a contract will not apply because the Convention expressly excludes trusts.[1] In the absence of a subjectively chosen law, then the objectively applicable law should be the law that is most closely connected to the trust according to the common law rule reflected in the Hague Trusts Convention, it being presumed that the applicable law for a trust will be that of some common law jurisdiction. However, in an exceptional case[2] a civil law court may find that the law of no common law country applied to the original 'trust', so that the original concept has to be a civil law concept like a contract (there being no question of there being a trust originally which then has to be transposed into a civil law concept).

While, for example, English law might apply to a trust transposed into a contract for the benefit of third parties or a contract of mandate or agency, the ambit of such law will be restricted by mandatory rules of the *lex situs* or *lex successionis* concerning transfer of title to property, bankruptcy and forced heirship. These proprietary aspects have already been dealt with. Forced heirship provisions providing for minimum fixed indefeasible shares for close heirs will usually require bringing into hotchpot all lifetime gifts made within *x* years of death, whether outright or on trusts, and can lead to such gifts being upset *pro tanto*. Forced heirship rights under a civil *lex successionis* will be applied by civil law courts to assets in their jurisdiction irrespective of the laws applicable to the trust: *Holzberg v Sasson*.[3]

Testamentary trusts

Characterisation or transposition into civil law analogues

In English law it became clear relatively recently[4] that one law may govern the validity of a will (which may be likened to a 'rocket launcher'), and another law may govern the validity or administration of a trust (the 'rocket') contained in the will. Civil law courts traditionally have made no such distinction, viewing the trust provisions in a will as a way of organising one's estate just like any

---

1 See Art 1, para 2(g).

2 As in *Harrison v Crédit Suisse* ATF 96, 1970, II 79.

3 Cour de cassation (4 February 1986), 1986 Rev cr de dr int pr 685. See also *Zieseniss v Zieseniss* Cour de cassation (20 February 1996), 1996 Rev trim dr civ, 454 (J Patavin) where a gift to trustees of a revocable *inter vivos* trust was held to be a *donation indirect* and not *un legs* for determining the order of recourse for satisfying a forced heirship claim.

4 *Re Lord Cable* [1976] 3 All ER 417 at 431; *Chellaram v Chellaram* [1985] 1 All ER 1043 at 1056.

other testamentary provisions, so that the *lex successionis* governs everything. However, it is possible that such a distinction could be made in civil law systems,[1] eg where a will may create a foundation (*fondation or Familienstiftung*) it would seem that it ought to be possible to submit such foundation to a law other than the *lex successionis*, though subject to any forced heirship rights affecting the amount of property capable of being subjected to a foundation.

Civil law systems also have difficulties in recognising as effective *inter vivos* trusts, trusts where the settlor has in substance full control over whether any of the trust assets pass on his death to other persons, eg where the settlor in his lifetime has a unilateral power of revocation of the trusts and no investments can be bought or sold without his consent.[2] There will be good reason for this if the transfer of the trust assets occurred in a civil law country and contravened a mandatory rule thereof, *donner et retenir ne vaut*. However, civil law courts can, like common law courts, see through an apparent *inter vivos* trust where the settlor retains equitable ownership of *capital* and income for life and categorise it correctly as a testamentary trust, so that the trustee is in the position of an *exécuteur testamentaire*.[3] As Béraudo points out,[4] the modern French trend is to assimilate the trustee of a testamentary trust to an *exécuteur testamentaire* and with more powers than an *administrateur* or a *mandataire* so that he is treated as the owner of the property. In Germany the traditional tendency in simple cases has been to assimilate the trustee to a *Testamentsvollstrecker* who has no legal ownership, which vests directly in the beneficiaries, but who has wide administrative powers. However, the modern view is that the trustee should be assimilated to a *Treuhänder* who acquires legal ownership in order to administer it for the benefit of the beneficiaries.[5] In Italy where the beneficiaries were ascertained adults the court has held that the beneficiaries were the legal owners but that the trustees were administrators *sui generis* with very wide powers including power to sell immovables.[6] In Switzerland the trustee can manage matters by being regarded as an *exécuteur testamentaire avec administration prolongée* although a Swiss author[7] has suggested that in some circumstances transposition of the trust into a *fondation*, *usufruit* or *substitution fideicommissaire* may be more appropriate.

---

1 See A Dyer and H van Loon Report on Trusts and Analogous Institutions in *Actes et Documents of 15th Session of Hague Conference on Trusts*, Vol II; and DWM Waters 'Official Report on Hague 1989 Convention on Succession to Deceased Persons' Estates' in *Actes et Documents of 16th Session of the Hague Conference* (SDU Publishers, 1990), Vol II, para 109.

2 See unreported 1991 case noted in Béraudo *Les trusts anglo-saxons et le droit français* (LGDJ, 1992), p 213.

3 Trib Seine (22 March 1967), Paris Court of Appeal (6 November 1967), 1968 Rev crit de dr int pr 503; and, further, see DJ Hayton 'When is a trust not a trust?' (1992) 1 *Journal of International Planning* 3.

4 Note 2 on p 136, pp 197–198, Trib de Bayonne (28 April 1975), 1976 Rev crit de dr int pr 331.

5 See Dyer and van Loon, n 1 above, para 172.

6 See *Piercy v Etfas Oristano* (15 March 1956), 79 Foro Italiano no 1, 1019, (1957) 6 ICLQ; *Forbes* Trib Casale Monferrato (13 April 1984); and *Gatta v Gatta* (30 April 1955), 1958 Clunet 169.

7 See Dyer and van Loon, n 1 above, para 177.

Applicable law

Where the law of a common law country is the *lex successionis* then a civil law country will apply such *lex* to succession to movables including a testamentary trust implemented as already seen by a civil law analogue, and no question of civil law forced heirship rules will arise. Succession to immovables is governed by the *lex situs* so that a testamentary trust of immovables located in a civil law country will normally be subject to the forced heirship rules of such *lex situs*. Exceptionally, if in the case of an English domiciled British citizen the *lex situs* refers the matter back to English law and refuses to recognise any *renvoi* back to the *lex situs*[1] then the forced heirship rules of the *situs* will be avoided.[2]

Where the law of a civil law country is the *lex successionis* it will give effect to the trust by means of a civil law analogue as already seen, but the trust can only take effect upon what is left after the application of forced heirship rules.

Civil law courts are astute to prevent attempts to avoid the application of forced heirship rules. Thus, in *Caron v Odell*[3] a French national emigrated to America and became a naturalised American, taking up permanent residence there, so that succession to movables would be governed by common law rules. He wanted an apartment in France but did not want a French immovable which could be used to satisfy the forced heirship claim of his French daughter. Thus, he formed an American corporation, holding 10,000 shares himself with the other 5,000 shares being given to Mrs Odell. This company then purchased a French apartment. He transferred his 10,000 shares to a trustee for himself for life, remainder to Mrs Odell. By his will he left half his estate to Mrs Odell and half to charity, but nothing for his daughter, Leslie Caron. The Cour de Cassation held that it was a fraud on the law to manipulate rules of conflict of laws in an attempt to disinherit a child by making what ought to be an immovable (whose use and sale was under the settlor's control) into a movable. Thus the apartment was available to satisfy Leslie's heirship claim. However, French notaries consider that the case can be restricted to circumstances where there is a blatant scheme to defraud an heir and that the purchase of an immovable by a company should not be presumed fraudulent especially when a person is merely trying in a fair way to arrange estate planning for the benefit of his family.

3.3.2 Common law jurisdictions

Introduction

In the case of common law jurisdictions having the trust concept as part of internal domestic law there is no problem over recognising a foreign trust as a

1 Eg Spain, The Netherlands, Denmark and Greece.

2 See further DJ Hayton, *European Succession Laws* (Jordans, 3rd ed, 2002).

3 (2 March 1985), 1986 Rev crit de dr int pr 66; (23 January 1990), 1990 Clunet 996, 1991 Rev crit de dr int pr 92, with epilogue in Cour de Cassation (19 March 1991).

trust having effect inside the jurisdiction.[1] There is clearly no need for characterising the trust as some analogous local concept. It will be necessary to ascertain what particular law governs a particular trust or aspects thereof for those cases where differences in detail between various countries' substantive trust laws may be significant, eg as to which trusts may be charitable, as to what powers may be implied by statutes, whether or not the beneficiaries collectively can terminate the trust upon *Saunders v Vautier*[2] principles even though the settlor has tried to prohibit this until some purpose of his has been effected, or whether a trust is void at common law from the outset for infringing the perpetuity rules or is saved by some statutory 'wait and see' provisions for a statutory period.

However, there are limits upon the scope of the applicable trust law that will be set by the *lex fori* or *lex situs*, especially where upholding a foreign-law-governed trust would prejudice the claims of creditors or of a divorcing spouse or of dependants claiming under legislation like the (English) Inheritance (Provision for Family and Dependants) Act 1975.

Applicable law

Old cases emphasise distinctions that are increasingly being seen to be obsolete, the distinction between movables and immovables, and between testamentary trusts and *inter vivos* trusts (with a sub-distinction between marriage settlements and other settlements), while overlooking the distinction between wills or other instruments and the trusts created by them, and the distinction between matters of validity and matters of administration. The modern approach, influenced by private international law developments concerning contracts, is to lay emphasis upon the intentions of the settlor or testator and to treat a trust as one unit governed by one law, irrespective of the *situs* of movables or immovables (although subject to public policy rules of the *situs*), except to the extent that the settlor or testator has chosen different laws for different aspects of his trust.

Distinction between matters of validity and of administration

If a settlor wishes he can have one law govern construction of his trust (eg whether 'children' covers adopted or illegitimate children and rules as to closing of classes), another law govern validity, and another law govern administration, although such a choice of three different laws would need to be express. The distinction between matters of validity and matters of

---

1 In mixed jurisdictions such as South Africa, where a special trust concept exists without the distinction between legal and equitable proprietary interests, the effect of a foreign trust may be less than normal, eg as to tracing unauthorised transactions.

2 (1841) 4 Beav 115. This is part of trust law and so is applicable to an express English trust of a Texan domiciliary with a Texan *lex successionis*: *Tod v Barton* (unreported) 20 February 2002, ChD.

administration is not clear-cut[1] so that it will be wise to provide express guidance in the trust instrument. It may be that the distinction derives from an analogy with the separation of functions between the law of succession and of administration of estates. The distinction is concerned with the difference between matters of management and administration on the one hand and the nature and quantum of beneficial interests. Because dispositive powers of trustees effect the nature or quantum of beneficial interests it may be that guidance on the distinction can be obtained from *Pearson v Inland Revenue Commissioners*[2] which was concerned with 'dispositive' powers that prevent a beneficiary having an interest in possession under a trust. Statutory powers of maintenance and advancement can affect the nature and extent of beneficiaries' interests so that if they are intended to change if the law governing administration is replaced by another law then the trust instrument should make this clear.[3]

The Variation of Trusts Act position requires special consideration, especially since most jurisdictions have such an Act. If the application under the Act is to change the nature and extent of beneficial interests under the trust one might have expected the court's jurisdiction to be restricted to those trusts whose validity is governed by the *lex fori*, although if the application related only to enlargement of investment or other management powers then the court should have jurisdiction if matters of administration of the trust are governed by the *lex fori*. However, English, Albertan and Western Australian courts[4] have arrogated to themselves unlimited jurisdiction in the absence of restricting words in the relevant Act, although[5] 'where there are substantial foreign elements in the case the court must consider carefully whether it is proper to exercise the jurisdiction'. The court will need to bear in mind that all parties before it will be eager for the jurisdiction to be exercised for family or tax reasons (the jurisdiction is based on the consent of adults and the consent of the court on behalf of other beneficiaries), but that some other forum may take the point that the variation is ineffective except, perhaps, to the extent that adult beneficiaries who consented to the variation may be estopped from reverting to the pre-variation position. For countries, like England and Australia, which have implemented the Hague Trusts Convention it would seem in the light of Art 8(h) that courts therein should decline jurisdiction if

---

1 See further Hayton and Marshall *Commentary and Cases on Law of Trusts and Equitable Remedies* (Sweet & Maxwell, 11th ed, 2001), paras 12-11 to 12-14; Waters *Law of Trusts in Canada* (Carswell, 2nd ed, 1984), pp 1124-1128; *Scott on Trusts* (Little Brown, 4th ed, 1991), Vol VA, paras 576, 587, 604.

2 [1951] AC 753.

3 However, see *Re Nanton's Estate* [1948] 2 WWR 113, 56 Manitoba R 71; *Re Kehr* [1952] Ch 26; *Kalshoven v Kalshoven* 1966 (3) SA 466.

4 *Re Ker's Settlement* [1963] Ch 553; *Re Paget's Settlement* [1965] 1 WLR 1048; *Commercial Trust Co v Laing* (unreported, 1981) cited in Waters, n 1 on p 141, p 1134; *Faye v Faye* [1973] WAR 66.

5 *Re Paget's Settlement* [1965] 1 WLR 1046 at 1050. The English courts will not make *cy-près* schemes for charitable trusts of foreign property administered abroad: *Attorney-General v Lepine* (1818) 2 Swan 181; *Re De Noailles* (1916) 114 LT 1089.

the forum's law is applicable neither to validity nor administration of the trust, except where public policy considerations reflected in Arts 18 and 15(b) may justify the Divorce Court extending its jurisdiction so far as practical to foreign trusts.[1]

Express or implied choice of law

Just as contracting parties can expressly or impliedly choose the law to govern their contract so the settlor can expressly or impliedly choose the law to govern his trust or a particular aspect thereof.[2] However, if the chosen law has no significant connection with the contract or trust then it may be disregarded if its application (eg allowing full capacity at 16 years of age) would contravene fundamental public policy rules of the forum so that the trust then falls to be governed by the objectively applicable law. Even where the expressly chosen law has a significant connection with the trust, so that the choice is a valid one, the court of the forum in an extreme case can rely on public policy to deny the trust some of the effects it would otherwise have under its applicable governing law.

The objectively applicable law

If the form and contents of the trust instrument (eg limiting or extending specified statutes) are not themselves sufficient to evidence an implied subjective choice of law then one has to ascertain the objectively applicable law. This will be the law with which the trust has the closest and most real connection, an intention to have such law as the applicable law being imputed to the settlor.[3]

In ascertaining the country with which the trust is most closely connected, the courts consider not just the form and contents of the trust instrument but all other relevant factors (at the date of creation of the trust) such as the place where the trust instrument was prepared and executed, the domicile of the settlor (of particular significance for most testamentary trusts) and his habitual residence, the domiciles and habitual residences of the beneficiaries, the location of the trust assets and of the trustees.[4] Where these factors point to more than one country then the court has to weigh the relative importance of these factors taking account of the maxim *ut res magis valeat quam pereat* or *semper*

---

1 Cf *T v T* [1996] 2 FLR 357 at 363; and the broad purposive approach of Lord Nicholls to the Matrimonial Causes Act 1973, s 24 in *Brooks v Brooks* [1995] 3 All ER 257 at 263.

2 *Augustus v Permanent Trustee Co* (1971) 124 CLR 245; *Re Lord Cable* [1976] 3 All ER 417 at 731.

3 *Duke of Marlborough v Attorney-General* [1945] Ch 78; *Iveagh v IRC* [1954] Ch 364; *Chellaram v Chellaram* [1985] Ch 409; *Chellaram v Chellaram (No 2)* [2002] EWHC 632 (Civ), [2002] 3 All ER 17. See also *Dicey and Morris on the Conflict of Laws* (Sweet & Maxwell, 13th ed, 2000); and Cheshire and North *Private International Law* (Butterworths, 13th ed, 1999).

4 The relative weight to be given to the various factors will vary according to the circumstances of a particular case. In, for example, *Chellaram v Chellaram (No 2)* [2002] EWHC 632 (Civ), [2002] 3 All ER 17, Collins J attached little weight to the trustees' residence and the contemplated place of administration (see **[167]**).

in dubiis benigniora praeferenda sunt.[1] Thus, the court will strive to avoid finding that the applicable law is one that would invalidate the trust if it can reasonably find a law which upholds the trust.[2]

It is open to the court to conclude that one law governs validity but that another governs administration, it being presumed that if the settlor or testator appoints as trustee a trust company of another country then the trust is to be administered in that country whose law, therefore, should govern administration.[3]

For matters of construction and interpretation the court applies the law intended by the settlor or testator which, in the absence of any express or implied choice, will be the law of the country with which the trust has its closest and most real connection.[4] In the case of testamentary trusts this is presumed to be the law of the testator's domicile at the time he made his will.[5] In the case of matters pertaining to the administration of a trust it will be presumed that the settlor or testator intended that the rules of construction of the country in which he had fixed the administration of the trust should be applicable.[6]

Limits upon the law applicable to the trust

As a preliminary matter there cannot be a valid trust until property has been effectively transferred to the trustees by a valid will, deed or other act. Even if there is a valid will, capacity to dispose of property by will (whether outright or on trusts) is governed by the *lex successionis*[7] which may well have forced heirship provisions preventing the testator from having capacity to dispose of more than a fraction of his estate, eg one-half or one-third or one-quarter depending on the number of children he has.[8] However, capacity in one's lifetime to transfer property to persons and have those persons hold the property on trust is governed by the law governing *inter vivos* transfers of

1 For this facilitative approach (in a charitable trusts context), see Lord Hailsham in *IRC v McMullen* [1981] AC 1 at 14 and Lord Keith in *Guild v Inland Revenue Commissioners* [1992] 2 All ER 10 at 18.

2 The fact that the trusts are to be administered by trustees in State X can lead to such state's law governing administration, and since this presupposes a valid trust to be administered this may lead to such law governing validity, especially if under the competing law for governing validity the trust would be invalid, eg as perpetuitous or non-charitable and uncertain: *Augustus v Permanent Trustee Co Ltd* (1971) 124 CLR 245; *Hope v Brewer* (1892) 136 New York 126; *Re Chappell's Estate* (1923) 124 Washington 128; *Re Grant* (1950) 101 New York State 2d 423; but *cf* much criticised *Jewish National Fund Inc v Royal Trust Co* (1965) 53 DLR (2d) 577. See further ss 107 and 403 of the Uniform Trust Code (2000).

3 *Chellaram v Chellaram* [1985] 1 All ER 1043 at 1056.

4 *Perpetual Executors & Trustees Association of Australia v Roberts* [1970] VR 732.

5 *Re Adams* [1967] IR 424 at 458; *Re Levick's WT* [1963] 1 WLR 311 at 319; *Philipson-Stow v IRC* [1961] AC 727.

6 *Re Dow* (1977) 390 New York S(2d) 721.

7 *Re Annesley* [1926] Ch 692; *Re Groos* [1915] 1 Ch 572; *Re Adams* [1967] IR 424.

8 See DJ Hayton *European Succession Laws* (Jordans, 3rd ed, 2002).

property (usually the *lex situs*) and, most probably,[1] the law applicable to validity of the trust.[2]

The *lex situs* has paramount significance where trustees are to retain immovables upon trust because the validity of the trust is determined by the local law,[3] eg on perpetuities, or formalities or illegal conditions. Because the court of the *situs* will apply its local law and is the controlling main jurisdiction[4] for determining matters a court in another jurisdiction will apply the same law if the matter comes before it. The situation appears to be different where the trustees are directed to sell the immovables and remit the proceeds to another jurisdiction where the trustees are to administer the trust: the trust will be valid if valid under the law of this other jurisdiction.[5]

Finally, the *lex fori* may well have significant rules concerning trusts of property set up to avoid claims of creditors, divorcing spouses or dependants, eg ss 423–425 and 339–342 of the (English) Insolvency Act 1986, s 37 of the (English) Matrimonial Causes Act 1973 and s 10 of the (English) Inheritance (Provisions for Family and Dependants) Act 1975.[6] Clearly, simply choosing a foreign trust law to govern the trust, even if there are some connections with such law, will not oust the otherwise applicable provisions of English law.

---

1 *Dicey and Morris*, n 3 on p 145; Cheshire and North, n 3 on p 145; *Fattorini v Johannesburg Board of Executors Ltd* (1948) (4) SA 806 (capacity to revoke governed by trust law). On this complex area, see Jonathan Harris's preceding chapter.

2 It seems this will be the objectively applicable law if the expressly chosen law was deliberately chosen in order to confer capacity, eg if allowing majority at 16 years.

3 *Scott on Trusts*, n 1 on p 144, paras 651, 652.

4 However, there is a tendency (see Scott J in *Chellaram v Chellaram* [1985] Ch 409 and Scott LJ and Taylor LJ in *Webb v Webb* (1992) *Financial Times*, 11 March, CA, and [1994] QB 696, ECJ) to place more emphasis on the jurisdiction where the trustees reside, amenable to *in personam* orders made by the court of such jurisdiction. This may be mistaken: if the person entitled if the trust is void takes action in the *situs* the judgment of the court of the *situs* must prevail over the judgment of the court of the trustees' residence if there is any conflict.

5 *Scott on Trusts*, n 1 on p 144, paras 651, 652.

6 Note that the 1975 Act applies only if the deceased died domiciled in England and Wales and not if he died domiciled in a country which permits him expressly to choose the law of his English citizenship to govern succession to his estate (eg Switzerland, The Netherlands).

PART 2

Specific Issues

Editor's introduction to Part 2

Part 2, comprising Chapters 4 to 11, covers topics of practical importance to international trust practitioners.

In Chapter 4, Antony Duckworth discusses the issue of forced heirship, how trusts could be affected by forced heirship claims, and the impact of offshore legislation in this area.

In Chapter 5, Robert Ham QC, Emily Campbell and Michael Tennet consider the developing topic of protectors.

The much debated issue of asset protection trusts is considered by Professor Geraint Thomas in Chapter 6. The chapter includes commentary on the legislation in the Cook Islands and elsewhere.

The creation of non-charitable purpose trusts has been made possible by legislation in various offshore centres. In Chapter 7, Professor Thomas looks at the English law background, and comments on purpose trust laws in a variety of jurisdictions.

The subject of trading trusts, discussed by Professor David Hayton in Chapter 8, is as relevant to domestic as to international trusts, but the ever-growing importance of trustee liability issues in international trust practice gives the topic a place in this book.

A crucial issue for trustees is when, and when not, to pay foreign taxes. Chapter 9, by Christopher Sly and the editor, reviews case-law on this subject from a number of onshore and offshore jurisdictions and refers to recent European developments.

The topic of disclosure of information by trustees is currently receiving a good deal of attention from the courts. Emily Campbell in Chapter 10 considers the cases and possible principles in play. The chapter includes references to legislation on disclosure in various onshore and offshore jurisdictions.

Finally in Chapter 11, Wolfe Goodman QC discusses the topical issue of settlor control.

Chapter 4

FORCED HEIRSHIP AND THE TRUST[*]

Anthony Duckworth[**]

4.1 INTRODUCTION

Should an individual be free to dispose of his property as he pleases? To such a basic question one might expect the legal systems of the world to give much the same answers, but they do not. Some allow far greater freedom than others. That fact, so simple to state, has complicated consequences in a world where national frontiers do not limit the movement of people and property.

4.1.1 Reasons for restrictions

It appears that dispositive restrictions serve five main purposes:

(a) the interests of the state – for example gift and inheritance taxes exist in many parts of the world and constitute a real restriction on the freedom of the individual;
(b) the interests of the individual – all legal systems restrict the freedom of those who, through tenderness of age or for other reasons, are deemed incapable of looking after their own interests, and some restrict dispositions in favour of persons deemed to have undue influence over the donor;
(c) the interests of the family – most legal systems protect the family in one way or another and so restrict the freedom of the individual;

---

[*] **NB: This chapter was written in 1993 for publication in J Glasson (ed) *International Trust Laws* (Jordans, looseleaf) and has not been updated (save that footnote references to Underhill and Hayton *Law of Trusts and Trustees* (Butterworths, 1995) are now to the current 15th edition).**

[**] Attorney-at-law, Partner, Charles Adams, Ritchie & Duckworth, Zephyr House, Mary Street, PO Box 709, Grand Cayman, British West Indies; also of International Trust Protector Limited at the same address.

(d) the interests of creditors – most legal systems restrict the individual's ability to place his property beyond the reach of his creditors or to dispose of his property while remaining in apparent ownership;

(e) the public interest – this is the convenient explanation for restrictions which appear not to be in the interests of any particular person, group or institution, for example rules against perpetuity and the corresponding rules of civil law systems which prevent property being tied up for future generations.

These interests exist in all developed societies – as does the counter-balancing interest of society and the individual in freedom of disposition. Yet, although there are some similarities in the restrictions imposed by legal systems around the world, the differences are more striking.

Why, for example, does the law insist that the child should inherit a large share regardless of need in France, Colombia, Japan, Turkey and Scotland – but not in England, the United States of America, Costa Rica, China or Israel? Why can a trust be created for successive beneficiaries, including persons yet unborn, in New York or Kuala Lumpur but not in Buenos Aires or Jakarta?

Some differences can be attributed to religion[1] and some to political ideology.[2] One might suppose that social or economic conditions would account for much, but seemingly they do not – at least if one may judge by the fact that the same regime or concept flourishes in entirely different societies and economies.

History is largely to blame. Due to the influence of the European colonial powers most of the world fell under England's common law or Continental Europe's civil law – and some places had the dubious privilege of both. Varying degrees of sensitivity were shown for pre-existing laws and customs.[3] The world became polarised between England's freedom of disposition and the Continent's more restrictive approach.

To explain the divergence between England and the Continent one must delve more deeply into the past – for there is no explanation to be found in contemporary social, economic, religious or political differences. Far-fetched as it may sound, the explanation must go back at least as far as the Norman conquest of England, nearly a millennium ago, to the system of land tenure introduced by the Conqueror and the reaction of the English to it – to the revival of interest in Roman law in Mediaeval European universities and its blending with Germanic customs of family ownership of land – to Henry VIII's attempt to outlaw the trust in the interests of the fisc[4] – to the excesses

---

1 Islamic regimes, for example, derive forced heirship rules from the Koran and other holy texts.

2 In communist systems, for example, interests in collective undertakings are generally non-inheritable.

3 Not surprisingly, laws and customs based on religion, eg Islam and Hinduism, tend to be more enduring.

4 The Statute of Uses 1535, followed by the Statute of Wills 1540.

of the Ancien Regime and the social engineering by which Napoleon hoped to build a new and better society.

It is remarkable that the imprint of such events on the law should remain so deep; most aspects of human existence and society have since been transformed beyond recognition. It is especially remarkable that the imprint should remain deep in parts of the world where European history must seem utterly remote and irrelevant.

There have been some developments in recent times. The lot of the spouse and the illegitimate child has improved in civil law. The common law has swung back from complete dispositive freedom to give protection to a surviving spouse. But still the fundamental divergence remains.

This is a good demonstration of the momentum which a principle of law may acquire, keeping it on the same heading until some compelling reason, or a determined ruler, demands a change of course. But perhaps we are now seeing both systems, common and civil, face a crucial test – an open world society in which increasing numbers of people conduct their business and family lives in more than one country and are familiar with the different degrees of freedom permitted. In these conditions the peaceful co-existence of opposing principles seems improbable in the long run.[1] But will it be a case of restrictions being circumvented and ultimately changed? Or will there be demands for new or improved rights and restrictions by those who see merit in the rules which exist elsewhere? Perhaps some middle ground will be found. Or will freedom and restriction, the protagonists in this contest, be kept safely apart by a network of international agreements defusing every potential conflict? Can they be kept apart?

4.1.2 Succession rights

In every legal system marriage and parenthood give rise to financial obligations. In some legal systems marriage immediately alters the entitlements of the spouses to their property.[2] In many legal systems marriage and parenthood give rise to succession rights; these restrict the individual's freedom of testamentary disposition and usually his freedom of disposition *inter vivos* as well.

Succession rights can be grouped into three main categories:[3]

(1) *Strict forced heirship.* The individual has testamentary power over part only of his estate.

---

1 The United States demonstrate that differences in detail can co-exist; but the civil law principles inherited by Louisiana have been greatly modified. See n 2 on p 162.

2 Community of property, dotal and other marital regimes are outside the scope of this chapter, as are concepts of family ownership found, eg, in African customary laws.

3 Other forms of succession right include, eg, the rights of a surviving spouse in respect of the marital home.

(2) *Forced heirship by indefeasible shares.* The individual has testamentary power over his entire estate but the law confers on the protected family members, if they have not received the minimum shares prescribed by law, the right to make claims against the estate or the testamentary heirs.

(3) *Judicial adjustment.* The individual has full testamentary power but a protected family member may apply to the court which has a discretion to make provision for the applicant out of the estate without regard to the deceased individual's wishes. Compared with forced heirship by indefeasible shares the key feature is that there is no right to a fixed or definite share. The court exercises its discretion according to the circumstances of each case.

Examples are given in **4.2**.

An important feature of most but not all forced heirship regimes may be described as 'claw-back'.[1] On the individual's death account is taken of gifts made by him during his lifetime. If these are found to be excessive in the sense that the residual estate is insufficient to satisfy the forced heirs, the gifts are clawed back. The donees must return the gifts or compensate the forced heirs. Claw-back is problematic because at the time a gift is made no one can be sure whether it will prove to be excessive, and the recipient may not even be in a position to make an informed guess. The recipient may not even know that the donor is subject (prospectively) to a forced heirship regime.

4.1.3 The trust

From the point of view of the trust industry, onshore and offshore, forced heirship is a problem largely because of the claw-back feature. Trustees and beneficiaries may encounter unpleasant and expensive surprises after the settlor's death. At the same time the existence of forced heirship and other dispositive restrictions in some parts of the world creates an opportunity for the trust industry by adding to the list of reasons why an individual might wish to create a trust. Of all legal concepts the trust is probably the most attractive in terms of enabling individuals to make whatever arrangements they wish for the management, use and enjoyment of their property. Both problem and opportunity are discussed throughout **4.3**.

This leads to the question which lies at the heart of this chapter. What is the outcome of a confrontation between a trust and the settlor's heirs? Can the trust arrangements survive attack?

---

1 See also **4.2.4**.

4.1.4 Survivability

This question of survivability, like so many good questions, has no answer – or no single answer. It is not a single issue but a bundle of issues. There are several ways in which a trust may be attacked by the settlor's heirs.

For each issue a court must first decide which state's law should govern; the court will apply the conflict of laws rules of its own state in deciding this preliminary but vital point. Conflict of laws rules vary significantly from state to state. The courts of one state may refer a particular issue to the laws of State A (which is sympathetic to the trust) and the courts of another state may refer the same issue to the laws of State B (which is sympathetic to the forced heirs). In other words the answer to the question of survivability depends on where you ask it. Survivability and what that really entails is discussed at **4.4–4.4.1**.

Survivability in the chosen trust domicile is a necessity. If the trust cannot survive there, it can hardly be defended anywhere else. It would be convenient if survivability in the trust domicile were all that mattered. Regrettably offshore trusts nearly always have significant contacts or links with other states. These links may render the trust arrangements vulnerable to the settlor's heirs. For example, the trust beneficiaries usually reside elsewhere, so they are susceptible to foreign legal proceedings. The trust may have foreign investments, and they will probably be susceptible to judicial process wherever they are situate. So the question of survivability arises in relation to every state with which there are or may be significant links. The links which are significant for this purpose are discussed at **4.4.2**.

Until relatively recently survivability in the trust domicile tended to be taken for granted. Often little if anything was done to guard against the possibility of an attack by the settlor's heirs. However, English conflict of laws rules in relation to matters of trust and succession (rules inherited by most offshore trust centres) do not justify such confidence. There is remarkably little judicial authority on any of the questions involved. The English rules are discussed throughout **4.5**.

The legislative changes trade in offshore trust centres in recent years for the purpose of clarifying their conflict of laws rules are discussed throughout **4.3**. The discussion which follows is entitled 'Survivability in other states' but, apart from a brief discussion of the US position, it offers only some general observations on a subject which evidently is too big to be discussed in a single chapter or even a single book.

Finally, this chapter looks to the future and discusses whether wider ratification of the Hague Convention on the Law Applicable to Trusts and their Recognition 1985 would assist survivability. It also discusses the impact of the draft Convention on Succession.

4.1.5 Planning

Planning notes are contained in **4.9**.

4.1.6 Trustees

Forced heirship is discussed at **4.10** from the point of view of trustees and the protection of their own interests.

4.1.7 Definitions

Some of the expressions used in this chapter deserve explanation:

'*claw-back*' – see **4.1.2**;

'*constituent law*' – the system of law under which an item of intangible property has been constituted. For example, the constituent law of a debt arising from a contract is the proper law of the contract. The constituent law of the shares of a company is generally the law of the state in which the company was incorporated;

'*governing law*' – see '*proper law*' below;

'*home state*' – see '*succession law*' below;

'*lex situs*' – the system of law of the place where the property is situate. That is easy enough for land or tangible property. So far as intangible property is concerned the concept is somewhat artificial but, according to English conflict of laws rules, for example, a debt is generally deemed situate where the debtor resides, and the shares of a company unless they are in bearer form are deemed situate in the place where the register is kept upon which the shares may be transferred;

'*proper law*' – the system of law which governs the essential validity and certain other attributes of a contract, trust or other transaction. It does not follow that all aspects of the transaction are governed by the same law. 'Governing law' is a more general expression. One may talk of the governing law of a contract, trust or transaction – in which context 'governing law' is synonymous with 'proper law'. But one may also talk of governing law in relation to some particular issue, for example the legal capacity of a settlor – and in this context 'governing law' means simply the system of law which governs the issue;

'*state*' – a less cumbersome word than 'jurisdiction', it is used to mean any place with its own legal system. Some states (the United Kingdom and the United States of America, for example) have several states within them;

'*succession law*' – the system of law which governs the succession to an individual's movable property upon his death. The reference here is to movable property because many systems of law regard succession to immovable property as a separate matter governed by the *lex situs* of the property. For want of a better expression, 'home state' is sometimes used for the state whose law is, or foreseeably will be, the individual's succession law;

'*succession rights*' – as used in this chapter this expression is restricted to indefeasible rights conferred by law, not those which arise under a testator's will or those which arise only in the absence of an effective will;
'*trust domicile*' – the state whose law the settlor has chosen to be the governing or proper law of his trust. Whether the trust administration is conducted there is another matter.

4.1.8 Apology

Finally in this introduction an apology: this chapter addresses an enormous subject involving major portions of the domestic laws and conflict of laws rules of all states. Of necessity the aim is more to identify issues than to solve them.

Much of this chapter is devoted to discussion of legal systems in which the writer professes no competence.

4.2 SUCCESSION RIGHTS

This section gives examples of succession rights and related restrictions.

4.2.1 Strict forced heirship

France[1]

In France the individual's power of testamentary disposition is limited to a portion of his property, the disposable portion (*quotité disponible*). On his death the rest of his property, the reserved portion (*réserve héréditaire*) devolves without regard to his wishes upon the persons prescribed by law, the forced heirs. The size of the reserved portion depends on whether the individual is survived by descendants or ascendants. If there are none, there is no reserved portion. If there is one living child (or a deceased child with living issue), the reserved portion is one half of the estate. If there are two such children the reserved portion is two-thirds of the estate. If there are more, it is three-quarters of the estate. If there are no children or other descendants but there are surviving ascendants in both maternal and paternal lines, the reserved portion is one half of the estate. If there are ascendants in one line only, it is one quarter of the estate.

The same restriction applies during the lifetime of the individual. In principle lifetime gifts may be made only from the disposable portion. However, the calculation of the disposable and reserved portions cannot be

[1] Jean-Pierre Le Gall and Marion Barbier of Jeantet & Associes, avocats, assisted in reviewing and commenting upon this section. For further explanation see, eg, DJ Hayton *European Succession Law* (Jordans, 2nd ed, 1998); or Lawrence *International Personal Tax Planning Encyclopaedia*.

made until the donor's death and so lifetime gifts are valid for the time being, but may have to be reduced or returned on the donor's death. This is the claw-back feature mentioned already.

For the purpose of calculating the disposable and reserved portions, and the entitlements of the forced heirs, the actual estate left by the deceased individual is grossed up by the amount of all gifts made in his or her lifetime. This applies to all gifts, however long before the date of death they were made, and regardless of whether the motive of the gift was to avoid or adjust the entitlements of the forced heirs. The reserved portion is calculated by reference to this grossed-up amount, and hence the entitlement of each forced heir. If a forced heir has received lifetime gifts, these are charged against his share, and his entitlement is reduced accordingly.

If the actual estate exceeds the entitlements of the forced heirs, legacies granted by will may be paid from the excess and lifetime gifts are safe from claw-back. If the actual estate is less than the entitlements of the forced heirs, no legacies can be paid and lifetime gifts are subject to claw-back (reduction) in inverse order, ie the most recent first.

For example, if an individual died with an actual estate of 10 million francs but in his lifetime had made gifts totalling 6 million francs, the entitlements of the forced heirs would be calculated by reference to a fictitious estate of 16 million francs. For simplicity we assume there was no surviving spouse. If there was one surviving child, his forced share – the whole of the reserved portion – would be half this amount, ie 8 million francs. Of the actual estate this would leave 2 million francs to pay the legacies granted under the individual's will.[1] If the will purported to grant legacies of a greater amount, they would be abated rateably, subject to any contrary direction in the will.

If in the same example the individual had been survived by three children, instead of one, the reserved portion would be three-quarters of 16 million francs, ie 12 million francs (4 million francs per child), a figure in excess of the actual estate. As a result, legatees under the will would receive nothing. Further, the forced heirs could require reduction of the lifetime gifts in inverse order. Recipients of the more recent gifts would be obliged to compensate the forced heirs to the tune of 2 million francs, regardless of whether they still held the gifted property.

The recipient of a gift subject to claw-back is not excused by the fact that he has consumed or disposed of the gifted property. If the recipient did dispose of the property and is now impecunious, the forced heirs may go against the disponee whether he took by gift or by purchase for value, with or without notice, unless the heirs consented to the disposition.

---

1 This assumes that the child received none of the lifetime gifts. If the child did receive, say, 3 million of the 6 million francs gifted by his parent, the child's entitlement from the actual estate would be 5 million, and there would be 5 million left to pay legacies.

It should be said that the above is an oversimplified description of rules which in practice are quite complex.

The surviving spouse has no forced heirship rights in French law. Marital property rights are normally fixed by agreement between the spouses at the time of marriage. The parties may, if they wish, agree upon complete separation of property but, in the absence of agreement to the contrary, the law imposes a community of property regime, giving each spouse an equal interest in property acquired by either of them during the marriage. On death (or on divorce) the community is dissolved and the property is divided between the surviving spouse and the estate of the deceased spouse. The heirs and legatees of the deceased spouse participate in the net estate after accounting to the surviving spouse for his or her community share.

The surviving spouse does have one advantage in regard to succession. Subject to certain strict limits a testator may make provision for his or her spouse out of the reserved portion of the estate, thus reducing or postponing the interests of the forced heirs.

Apart from the forced heirship regime there are other restrictions of French law whose purpose or effect is to protect the existing family. Even as regards the disposable portion of his estate the individual is strictly limited in his ability to create successive interests or confer benefits on future generations. Before the French Revolution the law was more permissive, to such an extent that much of the land was tied up for future generations by means of 'substitution', a concept of Roman law with resemblances to the strict settlement of English law. As a general rule, substitution is now prohibited although there are exceptions. For present purposes the most important exception is that a parent may give property to a child on terms that ownership will pass on the child's death to the child's children; but this concession applies only if it is a gift to all of the child's children in equal shares regardless of age, sex or other circumstances.

A restriction which relates only to lifetime dispositions is the rule *donner et retenir ne vaut* ('to give and keep back is invalid'). In general, a gift is ineffective so long as the donor retains possession of, or any freedom of disposition over, the property. Revocable interests or dispositions are generally impossible, but there are exceptions to this rule.

There are restrictions upon donations or bequests in favour of charitable and other institutions – or, to be exact, there are restrictions upon the capacity of institutions to accept gifts.[1]

There are strict formalities for gifts, even of movable property. For most types of property there must be a notarial *acte*; the donee's acceptance of the gift must be recorded in the *acte*; a full inventory with values must be prepared; and in the case of real property the *acte* must be registered at the *Bureau des Hypothèques*.

---

1 Recalling English Statutes of Mortmain.

France's succession rules apply:

(a) to the movable estate of a person who at the time of death was habitually resident in France; and
(b) to the immovable estate located in France of a person wherever resident.

A rule which has been much criticised in France and elsewhere gives heirs of French nationality special rights. Even if the deceased was not an habitual resident of France and had no immovable property in France, French law will intervene on behalf of any heirs of French nationality, conferring upon them the same forced heirship entitlements as they would have enjoyed if the succession had been governed by French law, and permitting the French heirs to effect recovery of their entitlements against any French property.

Spain[1]

In Spain the rules vary from one part of the country to another. The constitution permits individual provinces (Autonomous Communities) to establish their own civil laws modifying or replacing the national Civil Code. Some provinces have done so, while others apply the Civil Code. The reserved portion (*legitima*) under the Civil Code is two-thirds of the estate if there are any surviving descendants; but in provincial legislation it varies from four-fifths of the estate to a merely symbolic amount.

Perhaps the greatest difference, compared with France, is that under the Civil Code the surviving spouse is a forced heir, enjoying the usufruct in a portion of the estate. Another interesting difference is that under the Civil Code the reserved portion for descendants is divided into two equal parts. In one part the shares of the descendants are fixed by law but in the other part (*mejora*) the shares may be fixed by the testator. In other words, the *mejora* may be allocated among the descendants as the testator pleases, although no part of it may be given to any third party.

In contrast to France, Spanish conflict of laws rules refer matters of succession to the deceased's national law, not that of his habitual residence. This applies in relation to immovable property as well as movable property.

Scotland[2]

Scotland is another example of a forced heirship jurisdiction in this category. The share of the surviving spouse (*ius relictae*) is one half of the movable estate or, if there are surviving descendants, one-third. The share of descendants (*legitim*) is one half or, if there is a surviving spouse, one-third. There is no claw-back of lifetime gifts except in certain particular cases, for example if the

---

1 For further explanation see, eg, DJ Hayton, n 1 on p 157; or Lawrence, n 1 on p 157.

2 For further explanation see, eg, DJ Hayton, n 1 on p 157; or Lawrence, n 1 on p 157.

donor retained the benefit of the property or the right to require its reconveyance.

Islamic law[1]

Islamic systems of law also impose forced heirship of a strict sort. Regardless of circumstances,[2] the disposable portion is one-third of the estate, the reserved portion two-thirds. The forced heirs include not only descendants and surviving spouses but also parents and other relatives. The devolution rules for the reserved portion are complex and there are variations between the different schools of Islamic law. A notable feature of the Islamic regimes is that no account is taken of lifetime dispositions and there is no claw-back except in the case of gifts made during the individual's 'death illness'. Another interesting feature is that in general the individual may not use the disposable portion to prefer some heirs over others. He may give it to outsiders as he pleases; otherwise it must pass to the heirs under the intestacy rules.

Other states

Strict forced heirship is found in a number of other states – in Europe, Latin America, and elsewhere.

4.2.2 Forced heirship by indefeasible shares

Germany[3]

German law does not, strictly speaking, restrict the individual's testamentary powers, but it confers succession rights on those who, for want of a better expression, may be referred to as forced heirs.

The individual may by will appoint whomever he pleases to be his heir or heirs. However, each of the protected family members (being the individual's descendants, surviving spouse and parents[4]) is entitled to a minimum statutory share (*gesetzlicher Pflichtteil*) being one half of the value of his or her intestate share – the amount to which he or she would have been entitled if the individual had died without leaving a will. Unless the forced heir has received this amount under the individual's will or *inter vivos* dispositions, the forced heir may make a monetary claim for the shortfall against the testamentary heirs.

It is up to the forced heir whether to pursue his claim against the testamentary heirs but he must make up his mind within 3 years after learning of the testator's death. After that period the forced heir's claim is statute-barred.

---

1 Michael Chalhoub of Naji Beidoun and Associates, Dubai assisted in reviewing and commenting upon this section. For further explanation see, eg, Nasir *The Islamic Law of Personal Status*.

2 Except that forced heirs may agree to dispositions out of the reserved portion.

3 For a more detailed explanation see, eg, DJ Hayton, n 1 on p 157; or Lawrence, n 1 on p 157.

4 Parents may not claim in competition with descendants. So, eg, a parent may not claim if a descendant is the testamentary heir.

The testamentary heirs can limit their payments to the amount of the actual estate but, if that is insufficient, the forced heirs may in general effect recovery from the recipients of lifetime gifts.

For the purpose of calculating their entitlements, forced heirs may require the inclusion of gifts made to third parties within the period of ten years before death.

In general and subject to a number of exceptions, lifetime gifts to forced heirs must be brought into hotchpot only if the individual so stipulated when making the gift. This hotchpot requirement applies however long before the death the gift was made.

German conflict of laws rules refer questions of succession to the deceased's national law.

The United States[1]

The United States offer several examples of forced heirship by indefeasible shares in favour of the surviving spouse. In some states the surviving spouse is protected by a community of property regime, in a few by a modification of the ancient rights of dower and in many by statutory rights to an 'elective share'. The extent of the spouse's rights varies considerably from state to state, from a life interest in one-third of the estate to an outright entitlement to one half. There is also much variation as regards claw-back. No state except Louisiana[2] gives indefeasible succession rights to children.

Other states

Forced heirship by indefeasible shares exists in many other states, in Europe and elsewhere.

4.2.3 Judicial adjustment

England[3]

Under English law the individual may by will dispose of his estate as he pleases, but the Inheritance (Provision for Family and Dependants) Act 1975 enables a surviving spouse, former spouse, child or other dependant of the deceased to apply to the court for relief if the deceased has failed to make 'reasonable financial provision' for the applicant. In the case of children and other dependants this expression contemplates the applicant's maintenance, nothing more. So, for example, an adult child who is able to support himself

---

1 M Glenn Vinson Jr of Coudert Brothers, San Francisco, assisted in reviewing and commenting upon this section. See, eg, Schoenblum, *Multistate and Multi-National Estate Planning*; see also *Martindale-Hubbell Law Directory*, Vol VIII, Law Digest.

2 Louisiana's rules have been much modified over the years. A child can now claim forced heirship rights only if under the age of 23 or incapable. The constitutionality of recent modifications is now under attack, the principle of forced heirship being enshrined in Louisiana's constitution.

3 See, eg, Mellows *The Law of Succession* (Butterworths, 5th ed). References to England include Wales.

can expect little or nothing under the Act. In the case of the surviving spouse the court is directed to have regard to the provision which the surviving spouse might have expected if the marriage had ended by divorce rather than death. Naturally the court's view of what is reasonable depends on the circumstances of the case. An application under the Act must generally be made within six months after the grant of probate.

The Act does not restrict the individual's freedom of disposition *inter vivos* except that there is an anti-avoidance rule which may apply if within six years before his or her death the individual disposed of property for less than full consideration with the intention of defeating applications under the Act. In the case of a disposition in trust the Act limits the liability of the trustees to the property in their hands when the court makes its order. In any case the court has a discretion and must have regard to the circumstances of the disposition.

The Act applies only in the case of an individual dying domiciled in England.

Ireland[1]

Ireland is a hybrid jurisdiction providing judicial adjustment for children but forced heirship for the surviving spouse. The spouse's share is one half of the estate or, if there are children, one-third. Applications to the court by children may only be made on the basis that the deceased 'failed in his moral duty to make proper provision for the child in accordance with his means'. Anti-avoidance rules enable the court to set aside a lifetime disposition if (a) beneficial ownership vested in possession in the donee within three years before the death of the donor, and (b) the disposition was made for the purpose of defeating or substantially diminishing the spouse's rights or of leaving any of the children insufficiently provided for.

Other states

Judicial adjustment regimes are found in many former British colonies.[2] This is not a case of England leading; the genesis of judicial adjustment was New Zealand's Testators Family Maintenance Act 1900. Judicial adjustment is also found outside the Commonwealth, for example in China where the court may make an award in favour of heirs 'devoid of labour ability or without source of income'.[3]

4.2.4 Notable features of succession rights

From the superficial and selective outline of succession rights given in this chapter it will be apparent that there is not much uniformity. The one point on

---

1 For further explanation see, eg, DJ Hayton, n 1 on p 157; or Lawrence, n 1 on p 157.

2 Not including the United States.

3 Article 19 of China's Law of Succession. See also Tome II, Proceedings of the 16th Session of the Hague Conference on Private International Law – Succession to Estates, p 170.

which most legal systems agree is that a spouse should have some sort of protection, and in many systems the protection includes succession rights. But beyond this point of general agreement legal systems vary widely.

The extent of the spouse's protection varies – from a large indefeasible share of the estate to nothing more than a presumption, in the absence of agreement to the contrary, that spouses are to hold in common property acquired during the marriage.

In some systems children (or descendants) are the only forced heirs and take the lion's share of the estate; in others the succession rights of children are limited to their needs; in others children have no succession rights at all. In some systems parents and ascendants have succession rights regardless of who else survives; in some they take only in default of descendants; and in some they have no rights at all. In some systems other relations have succession rights; in some they do not.

In some systems the rights and restrictions apply regardless of the age, means and conduct of the heirs, regardless of the length of the marriage, regardless of whether the individual is rich or poor, regardless of whether the principal asset is a farm which the family has worked or a business in which the workers are outside the scope of family protection. In some systems the rules take some account of such factors.[1] In some the court is given a discretion to decide what is reasonable in the circumstances.

There is considerable variation in the claw-back rules of different legal systems. In some claw-back is unlimited in time and unconditional. That is to say every lifetime gift is susceptible to claw-back (if the actual estate proves insufficient to satisfy the forced heirs) regardless of when it was made and regardless of whether it was intended to avoid or adjust forced heirship rights. In some legal systems claw-back is limited to particular types of disposition, for example those which were revocable by the disponer. In some there is a time limit; dispositions made more than a certain period before death are safe. The period varies. In Japan, for example, it is one year, in Switzerland five years, in Germany ten years. In many of these systems in which there is a time limit, earlier gifts may be clawed back if made with intent to defeat heirs. In some there is no claw-back at all unless the gift was made with intent to defeat heirs. In some claw-back is a matter for the court's discretion. In some there is no claw-back at all.

In some systems claw-back is not a mere appendage to the law of succession, an anti-avoidance device. It reflects a principle which applies to *inter vivos* dispositions as much as testamentary. In life or on death an individual should not be able to give away more than the prescribed portion of his property.

Many but not all forced heirship regimes prohibit or restrict agreements between an individual and his prospective heirs affecting their succession

---

1 For example, the US *Uniform Probate Code* Chap 2 (1990 version).

rights. For example, France and Spain (with the exception of some provinces) are restrictive, Germany and Switzerland are permissive.

4.2.5 Conflict-of-laws rules

Conflict-of-laws rules also vary significantly.[1] In some legal systems succession and forced heirship are regarded as matters for the national law of the deceased individual; in others they are referred to the law of his last domicile; in others the reference is to the law of his habitual residence. In some legal systems succession to immovable property is a matter for the *lex situs*, regardless of the deceased individual's nationality, domicile or residence. Different approaches are taken with regard to *renvoi* – the question that arises when an issue is referred to a system of law whose conflict of laws rules would refer it to yet another system of law or back to the referring jurisdiction.

The Hague Convention on Succession,[2] if ratified by a sufficient number of countries, would help in this respect by harmonising the conflict of laws rules of contracting states in relation to matters of succession. However, it is important to note that the Convention seems to require recognition and enforcement of claw-back rules, apparently regarding it as a matter of succession on death notwithstanding the seemingly incontrovertible fact that claw-back affects lifetime dispositions.

4.3 THE TRUST

No book on trust in an international context would be complete without quotations extolling the virtues of the trust concept, especially the remark of FW Maitland that the trust 'perhaps forms the most distinctive achievement of English lawyers. It seems to us almost essential to civilisation, and yet there is nothing quite like it in foreign law'.[3]

It is equally *de rigueur* to include remarks, more or less tongue-in-cheek, from civil lawyers expressing their admiration for the concept. A favourite is the remark attributed to P Lepaulle comparing the trust to 'those extraordinary drugs curing at the same time toothache, sprained ankles, and baldness sold by peddlers on the Paris boulevards …'.[4]

The enlightened commentator must also allude to the fact that civil laws are not completely bankrupt in comparison.[5] In the proceedings of the Hague Conference on Trusts, Adair Dyer and Hans Van Loon took issue with one of

---

1 See generally Tome II Proceedings of the 16th Session of the Hague Conference on Private International Law – Succession to Estates.

2 See **4.8.2**.

3 FW Maitland *Equity, A Course of Lectures* (Cambridge University Press, 1916), p 23.

4 P Lepaulle 'Civil Law Substitutes for Trusts' (1927) 36 *Yale Law Journal* 1126.

5 See, eg, WA Wilson *Trusts and Trust-Like Devices.*

FW Maitland's less gracious comments (to the effect that the absence of anything like the trust concept in civil law is 'a big hole') saying:

> 'In all humbleness, a civil lawyer will submit that instead of a big hole, civil law offers a bouquet of institutions which either alone or in combination fulfil most if not all of the functions of a trust.'[1]

In this debate France's decision (tax difficulties aside) to adopt a trust concept (*la fiducie*), despite evident difficulty, may be regarded as an action speaking louder than words.[2]

Having attended to the proprieties, we may now turn to discussion of the relationship between forced heirship and the trust. From the point of view of the trust industry, onshore and offshore, the existence of forced heirship regimes in some parts of the world is a problem and at the same time an opportunity.

4.3.1 The problem

Forced heirship is a problem because the trust, the trustees and the trust beneficiaries may be attacked after the settlor's death by persons claiming to have forced heirship entitlements. Evidently this is not likely to be a problem so far as testamentary trusts are concerned; all claims to succession rights should be identified and sorted out before the trust takes effect. But a trust *inter vivos* may exist for years before the trustee or anyone else involved becomes aware that there might be a forced heirship attack.

At the time an *inter vivos* trust is created it is not possible to say:

- what will be the settlor's nationality, domicile or place of residence at the time of his death and, hence, what will be his succession law;[3]
- what the settlor's succession law will say in 10, 20 or 50 years' time, when the settlor dies, about lifetime dispositions in general;
- what will be the effect of the succession law in the particular circumstances of the settlor, his family and his estate at the time of his death.

At the time the trust is created one can talk only in terms of possibilities, or at best probabilities. Even if the settlor has no links whatever with a forced heirship regime, it is possible that circumstances will change. If it is recognised as a probability that the settlor will die in circumstances subjecting his estate to a forced heirship regime, the trustee can form no view of the likelihood of an

1 Tome II Proceedings of the 15th Session of the Hague Conference on Private International Law – Trusts, p 40.

2 See J Glasson (ed) *International Trust Laws* (Jordans, looseleaf), Chap A10.

3 Or what states will assert that theirs is the succession law.

attack by forced heirs except by investigating the foreign law and the settlor's financial and family affairs in sufficient detail to determine whether, as matters stand, the trust would encroach upon the entitlements of the forced heirs. Even if that investigation were carried out, the situation would assuredly change – unless the settlor met his fate with convenient swiftness. The settlor might marry, remarry or have further children. His financial condition might decline or suffer sudden setbacks; and, just as problematic under some regimes, the trust property might grow in value in the years before the settlor's death.

It is important to recognise that these uncertainties are of concern only because of claw-back. If forced heirship regimes did restrict themselves to matters of succession – succession to the actual estates of deceased persons – the situation would be straightforward.

Of course one reason for having some form of claw-back in a forced heirship regime is apparent; it would otherwise be too easy for people to circumvent the forced heirship rules. But the extent of the claw-back is a different matter. To extend the claw-back to all lifetime dispositions, however long before death and regardless of motive, does appear to be an extreme solution. Restricting claw-back to dispositions made within a certain period before death seems a more reasonable approach, especially if intent to defeat the heirs must be proved. Perhaps the fairest approach gives the court a discretion to weigh the circumstances before deciding to deprive the trust beneficiaries in favour of the settlor's heirs – although this approach does impose on claimants the cost and uncertainty of litigation.[1]

However, as has been noted earlier, the claw-back rules in some systems, France's for example, are not merely anti-avoidance devices. They reflect a principle that the individual should not be able to give away more than the prescribed portion of his property, whether he does so during his life or on his death.

From the point of view of the trustee the problem of forced heirship is given an extra edge by the possibility of ending up out of pocket. If for one reason or another the trustee is obliged to succumb to the claw-back process, the trustee's obligation to compensate the forced heirs may not be limited to the trust assets remaining in the trustee's hands. The rules vary from one forced heirship regime to another but in some regimes lifetime dispositions are valued at the time of disposition. If since the creation of the trust the trust assets have been reduced by distributions to beneficiaries, investment losses, the trustee's own fees and the other costs of administration, the trustee could find itself obliged to make up the deficit out of its own pocket.[2] In all probability the trustee would also have incurred significant expenses in

---

1 See, eg, England's Inheritance (Provision for Family and Dependants) Act 1975, s 10(6).

2 This is unlikely to be a problem in relation to judicial adjustment regimes. See, eg, England's Inheritance (Provision for Family and Dependants) Act 1975, s 13.

defending the trust from the heirs and, even if there were no suggestion that the trustee had defended with undue zeal, the trustee could find itself unable to recover these costs.

4.3.2 The opportunity

For the trust industry the existence of forced heirship regimes constitutes an opportunity as well as a problem, because it adds to the list of reasons for having a trust. The trust is one method by which an individual who is dissatisfied with the rules and restrictions that will probably or possibly apply to his estate may endeavour to make more satisfactory property arrangements. In historical terms it is entirely appropriate that the trust should be used for this purpose. Above all else the trust has always been the champion and instrument of freedom. The trust, or its precursor the 'use', was the means by which the English threw off the yoke of primogeniture and acquired testamentary freedom.[1] Those days are long past but the trust has continued to be a vital element of dispositive freedom, enabling practically any conceivable arrangement for the management, use and enjoyment of property by the living and the not-yet-born. It is no coincidence that the states in which the trust concept is established (roughly speaking the common law jurisdictions) lie at the freer end of the spectrum while the non-trust states (roughly speaking the civil law jurisdictions) tend to the more restrictive end.

The trust is also useful in dealing with those international situations in which identification of the individual's succession law might foreseeably be a matter for dispute. For example, there might be room for argument about which state was the individual's domicile. Disputes might also arise if, for example, the individual was a national of a state such as Japan,[2] which regards succession as a matter for the national law, but was an habitual resident of a state such as France, which regards succession as a matter for the law of habitual residence.

4.3.3 Confrontation

It is inevitable that confrontations sometimes occur between an individual's trust arrangements and his heirs. The confrontation may be a matter of the settlor's design or it may be a matter of accident and unforeseen circumstances. Whichever it is, the question which lies at the heart of this chapter is whether the trust arrangements can survive attack by the settlor's heirs.

Whether the trust arrangements *can* survive is the subject of the next few sections of this chapter; whether they *will* survive is another matter altogether,

---

1 See, eg, SFC Milsom *Historical Foundations of the Common Law*.

2 See Lawrence, n 1 on p 157.

one in which other factors come into play – the skill and ingenuity of the protagonists and the depth of their pockets, to name but some.

4.4 SURVIVABILITY IN GENERAL

As was noted in the introduction to this chapter the survivability of a trust against attack by the settlor's heirs is not a single issue but a bundle of issues. To each issue different answers may be given by the courts of different states – because domestic laws differ and because different conflict of laws rules lead to different conclusions on the vital preliminary question of which state's law should govern the substantive issue.

The purpose of this section is to consider in more detail what is involved in survivability, and to break it down into its constituent issues. Later sections of this chapter suggest what conclusions the courts of particular states might reach on these issues.

It is important to remember that attacking heirs are not restricted to attacks based on their forced heirship rights. They can be expected to make an assortment of claims, some invoking the domestic law of the forum,[1] some invoking foreign law, some asserting forced heirship, some on other grounds. Any claim which undermines the trust and throws the property back into the settlor's estate will serve the heirs' purposes. So a forum which refuses to recognise foreign forced heirship rights in any way must still be rated badly in terms of survivability if, for example, it refers questions of legal capacity to the individual's domiciliary law – badly, that is, for trusts whose settlors are domiciled in states which deny capacity to create trusts, or trusts of that description.

4.4.1 Survivability issues

Survivability may be broken down as follows.[2]

(1) *Validity of the trust ('the rocket').*[3] Suppose that the heirs bring proceedings in the forum asserting that the trust is invalid – from the

---

1 The word 'forum' is used in this analysis to denote the state or legal system in which the trust's survivability is under scrutiny.

2 This analysis is made from an English point of view and is likely to be relevant in most common law states. An analysis of survivability in a civil law state may differ in some respects.

3 The best explanation of the distinction between the validity of the trust and, on the other hand, the validity of the disposition is that of DJ Hayton who in the context of the Hague Convention on Trusts draws an analogy with a rocket and its launcher: 'Just as a rocket launcher is needed to launch a rocket so some instrument or act is necessary to get a trust off the ground. Only when the trust has been launched does the Convention apply: it does not apply to antecedent issues of form, capacity or validity which may vitiate the instrument or act which purports to subject assets to a trust.' See Underhill and Hayton *Law of Trusts and Trustees* (Butterworths, 15th ed), p 947. See also **4.5.1** and **4.5.3**.

outset or from the settlor's death. They assert that according to applicable law there is some fatal defect – perhaps that the trust is invalid because it is inconsistent with their rights – or that the concept of a trust is simply an impossibility under the applicable law.

(2) *The settlor's title to the settled property.* Suppose the heirs assert that according to applicable law the settlor was not the owner of the property which he purportedly placed in trust or, at least, his ownership was qualified by the existence of proprietary interests already held by the prospective heirs at the time the trust was created. The heirs assert that the trustee must now recognise these proprietary interests which, so they say, have come to fruition following the settlor's death and have priority over the rights or interests of the trustee and the trust beneficiaries.

(3) *Validity of the disposition ('the rocket-launcher').*[1] Suppose the heirs assert that the creation of the trust, or the property transfer or other transaction by which the settlor placed property in the trust, were invalid. They assert that according to applicable law there was some fatal defect – perhaps in the capacity of the settlor, or in the observance of required formalities, or in the lawfulness of the transactions or in other matters of essential validity.

(4) *Direct enforcement of the heirs' rights.* Suppose the heirs refer to the succession rights which they enjoy under the succession law and (assuming these include the right to recover property or receive compensation from the recipients of excessive gifts) the heirs simply commence proceedings in the forum against the trustee or the trust beneficiaries to enforce their rights.

(5) *Claims in tort.* Suppose the heirs maintain that the trustee and, perhaps, the settlor's advisers interfered with the heirs' rights. They assert that under applicable law the actions complained of amount to a civil wrong entitling them to compensation or damages.

(6) *Claims for restitution.* Suppose the heirs assert that, even if they have no proprietary interest (item 2) and are unable to proceed with their direct claim (item 4) and have no claim in tort (item 5), they are none the less entitled under applicable law to restitution – perhaps on the basis that the trust beneficiaries have been unjustly enriched at the expense of the heirs, perhaps on the basis that the settlor had fiduciary responsibilities to his heirs, perhaps on the basis that the heirs should be treated in a manner akin to defrauded creditors.

(7) *Enforcement of foreign judgments.* Suppose the heirs have obtained a favourable judgment from the courts of another state and now bring it to the forum for enforcement there. The foreign judgment may be in respect of any of the foregoing issues – by way of a declaration or an

---

[1] See n 3 on p 169.

order for payment or otherwise. This is an issue of some importance. However sympathetic to the trust the forum may be in other respects, if the forum will enforce a foreign judgment in favour of the heirs, the forum cannot be rated well in terms of survivability. One should presume that the heirs could obtain some sort of judgment in their favour, in the settlor's home state if nowhere else.

(8) *Succession law.* Unlike the foregoing items, this is an issue which might be raised in defence of the trust. Would the heirs be recognised as such in the forum? Would the forum agree with the heirs on the identification of the settlor's succession law? If not, the forum might not even acknowledge that the heirs had claims in respect of the settlor's estate, let alone claims in respect of the trust.

(9) *Assumption of jurisdiction.* In what circumstances would the forum assume jurisdiction over the heirs' claims? If the heirs cannot get into court, all other questions are academic.

(10) *Bars to the heirs' claim.* Would the heirs' claims be barred by any procedural or substantive rule of the forum. Is there, for example, a statute of limitations?

Consideration of these survivability issues will indicate whether the forum in question is sympathetic to the trust or unsympathetic.

No state is invariably sympathetic to all trusts; and, probably, no state is invariably unsympathetic. To take an extreme example, suppose an individual were to die in circumstances which left no room for argument about the applicable succession law (in other words he was clearly a national, domiciliary and resident of a single state and he owned no foreign property) but he left a will establishing an offshore trust in respect of a part of his property. Such a trust, if inconsistent with the heirs' entitlements, would probably find little sympathy anywhere. Most states would be constrained by their conflict of laws rules to refer the validity of the testamentary trust to the individual's succession law. At the other extreme, suppose that a socialist state constituted itself the obligatory heir of all its citizens in respect of their foreign property, with a claw-back rule purporting to undo all lifetime gifts of foreign property. If a national of that state, domiciled and resident elsewhere, created during his lifetime an offshore trust of immovable property outside the socialist state, that trust would probably receive sympathetic treatment, although not necessarily the same treatment as in the trust domicile, everywhere except in the socialist state itself.

4.4.2 Significant links

The existence of unsympathetic states or legal systems is not in itself serious. What matters is the existence of significant links between the trust and an unsympathetic state. Without such a link the state is unlikely to assume jurisdiction over the heirs' claims and, even if it does, and even if its decision is unfavourable to the trust, there will be no means of enforcing the judgment there, and scant prospect of enforcing it anywhere else. But if, for example, there is trust property situate in the state, that may be a sufficient link to induce the court to assume jurisdiction; and a judgment might be enforced against the property there.

That leads to the question of what links should be regarded as significant for these purposes, another question to which there is no short and complete answer. There are three sorts of 'significance':[1]

(a) significance in terms of the forum's decision whether to assume jurisdiction over the heirs' claims;
(b) significance because the link provides a means by which an unfavourable judgment (of the forum or of a foreign court) might be enforced in the forum – generally a matter of whether persons or property can be seized or subjected to other judicial process there;
(c) significance because states outside the forum might regard the link as giving the forum jurisdiction over the issue. This may be crucial to whether other states would enforce unfavourable judgments of the forum.

Although a comprehensive list of significant links cannot be given except by reference to particular legal systems and particular circumstances, one can identify a number of links which are generally significant:

- the place or places in or from which the trust is administered;
- the places of residence and domicile of a trustee and, in the case of a corporate trustee, its place of incorporation and its places of business;
- the locations[2] of the trust investments and other property;
- if the trust owns or controls an investment company or similar vehicle, its place of incorporation and places of business;
- the places of residence and domicile of trust beneficiaries.

Other links which may very well be significant include, for example:

- the place or places in which the documents and actions creating and funding the trust were executed;
- the locations of investments or property of an investment company owned or controlled by the trust, especially if the corporate veil might be lifted there;

---

1 We are here considering links which are significant in a harmful sense. Beneficial links are considered elsewhere – see, eg, **4.9.3**(a) and **4.9.4**(b).

2 As regards the location of intangible property, see the explanation of *lex situs* at **4.1.7**.

- places in which a trustee has property of his or its own;
- places in which trust beneficiaries have property;
- the places of residence and domicile of a protector.

There are of course two states, at least, with which the trust will definitely have significant links – the settlor's home state(s) and also the trust domicile. By hypothesis the home state is unsympathetic. So far as the trust domicile is concerned, it has already been noted that survivability is essential. If the trust cannot survive in the trust domicile, it can hardly be defended anywhere else.

4.5 SURVIVABILITY IN ENGLAND

This section discusses the survivability of trusts in the English courts – whether the chosen trust domicile is England or some other state. England is considered before other places because English conflict of laws rules are applicable or influential in many common law systems, including most of the offshore trust centres. Of necessity conclusions are tentative, there being no judicial authority directly bearing on this topic.

4.5.1 Validity of the trust ('the rocket')[1]

The Recognition of Trusts Act 1987 incorporated into English law the Hague Convention on Trusts.[2] Before the Act, there was, in the words of the most influential commentary on this subject, 'a remarkable dearth of English and Commonwealth authority on what law governs the validity of a trust; the literature is almost equally sparse'.[3] Now, however, the basic rule can be stated as follows:

> 'The validity, construction, effects and administration of a trust are governed by the law chosen by the settlor or, in the absence of any such choice, by the law with which the trust is most closely connected.'[4]

This formulation summarises Arts 6, 7 and 8 of the Convention.

Regrettably this commendably simple rule is of limited application. Article 4 of the Convention provides:

> 'The Convention does not apply to preliminary issues relating to the validity of wills or other acts by virtue of which assets are transferred to the trustee.'

---

1 See **4.4.1**.

2 With exceptions, notably of Art 13 and the second part of Art 16. The Convention is discussed further at **4.8.1**.

3 *Dicey and Morris on the Conflict of Laws* (11th ed), p 1072.

4 Ibid (fourth cumulative supplement to the 11th ed), r 157.

The scope of this exclusion is wider than it might at first appear. Professor Hayton has written:

> 'Just as a rocket launcher is needed to launch a rocket so some instrument or act is necessary to get a trust off the ground. Only when the trust has been launched does the Convention apply: it does not apply to antecedent issues of form, capacity or validity which may vitiate the instrument or act which purports to subject assets to a trust.'[1]

Forced heirs may question the validity of the trust (the rocket) – and in that respect the Convention is applicable. But the heirs are just as likely, perhaps more likely, to question the launch of the trust – and in that respect the Convention is inapplicable. The launch elements are discussed at **4.5.3**.

As regards the validity of the trust (the rocket) the Convention applies (and hence the Recognition of Trusts Act 1987) but it is not conclusive in relation to the forced heirship issue. This is because of Art 15 which provides in pertinent part:

> 'The Convention does not prevent the application of provisions of the law designated by the conflicts rules of the forum, insofar as those provisions cannot be derogated from by voluntary act, relating in particular to the following matters:
>
> ...
>
> (c) succession rights, testate and intestate, especially the indefeasible shares of spouses and relatives.'

This throws open the door to a pre-Convention doubt about evasive choices of law. It has been written:

> 'But if there is a strong public policy in the system of law with which the trust has its closest and most real connection, it seems doubtful whether the settlor would be allowed to evade it by selecting some other law.'[2]

Presumably the forced heirship regime of a foreign state might well be regarded as a matter of 'strong public policy'. Suppose a person domiciled and resident in Ruritania declared himself a trustee of Ruritanian property for the benefit of persons also domiciled and resident in Ruritania; and suppose the declaration of trust executed in Ruritania contained an express selection of English law to govern the trust. If the purpose was to evade Ruritanian forced

---

1 Underhill and Hayton, n 3 on p 169, p 946. See also von Overbeck *Official Report on the Hague Trusts Convention* (the *Official Report*) at paras 53–60.

2 *Dicey and Morris on the Conflict of Laws* (10th ed), pp 679, 680. In the next edition the sentence was changed to read 'The settlor's freedom of choice might be subject to the requirements of English public policy' but no explanation was given for this significant change. Indeed no authority was cited for the original sentence which may have been influenced by American ideas.

heirship rules, would an English court none the less give effect to the choice of English law in these circumstances? It seems improbable.[1]

Evidently the example just given is an extreme one in the sense that the only English connection is the choice of law, and all other connections are with Ruritania. But where is the line to be drawn? The common law rules are most unclear,[2] and neither the Convention nor the Recognition of Trusts Act 1987 is of any assistance in this respect. No criticism is intended so far as the Convention is concerned. Its purpose was to secure from non-trust states a measure of recognition of foreign trusts, not to provide England with a comprehensive set of conflict of laws rules.

4.5.2 The settlor's title to the settled property[3]

For immovable property the basic rule is that all rights over, or in relation to, the property are governed by the *lex situs*.[4]

For tangible movables the general rule again points to the *lex situs*.[5] However, if title has been obtained according to the *lex situs* of the moment, that title will still be recognised even although the property is moved to another state. The old title remains effective until displaced by a new title acquired under the new *lex situs*.[6] So in order to assess the settlor's title to tangible movables, one should look first to the laws of the state where the property was situate at the time the settlor acquired title to it.

For intangible movables the English conflict of laws rules are less clear. This is discussed in a little more detail at **4.5.3**. Seemingly, however, the main contenders for dominance in so far as the settlor's title is concerned are (a) the constituent law of the intangible thing, (b) the *lex situs* of the intangible thing, and (c) if the settlor acquired the movable by assignment, the proper law of the assignment.

A determination that property is English property (in the sense that application of the foregoing rules points to English law as the governing law) does not exclude foreign laws altogether. For example, succession to movable English property is in general governed by the law of the deceased's last domicile.[7] The effect of marriage in relation to movable English property is in general a matter for the law of the matrimonial domicile.[8] Apart from death and marriage, it seems that foreign rights arising from status, for example the relationship of parent and child, may be recognised and enforced in respect of

---

1 Alternatively or additionally the court would in these circumstances be able to rest its decision on the failure of the launcher – see **4.5.3**.

2 *Dicey and Morris*, n 3 on p 173, pp 1073, 1074.

3 See **4.4.1**(2).

4 *Dicey and Morris*, n 3 on p 173, p 936.

5 Ibid, p 942.

6 Ibid, p 948.

7 Ibid, Ch 27.

8 Ibid, Ch 28.

movable English property, the reference in that case being to the law of the parent's domicile.[1] A foreign contract may create rights in respect of English property, movable and immovable; and seemingly this is so even although the contractual terms are not express terms but are implied by foreign law.[2] The beneficiaries of a foreign trust may be recognised as having rights in respect of English trust property.

However, it is one thing to recognise foreign rights *in personam* against the owner of English property, quite another to recognise such rights as proprietary interests enforceable against third parties. Whether that proprietary question is exclusively a matter of English law, so far as English property is concerned, is open to some doubt, but at the least English law determines what kinds of proprietary interest are capable of existing in English property. In English law successive interests in property, real or personal, can only exist in equity behind a trust.

If, therefore, the heirs of a person who has settled English property upon trusts *inter vivos* wish to question the settlor's title to the settled property on the footing that, as forced heirs, they already at the time of settlement possessed proprietary interests, their argument necessarily entails the proposition that the settlor held his property as a trustee for them.

Such an argument seems never to have been considered by an English or Commonwealth court but in the Florida case of *Sanchez v Sanchez de Davila*[3] the court at first instance accepted the heirs' claim to a remainder interest in Florida property arising from Venezuelan forced heirship rules.

It seems probable that an English court would approach the issue in two stages. First, it would consider the foreign law and its forced heirship rules, seeking to identify the respective rights and obligations of the settlor and his prospective forced heirs at the time of settlement in order to decide whether under the foreign law there was at that time a trust in the English sense. If the answer were affirmative the court would in the second stage apply English conflict of laws principles to decide whether the foreign trust should be recognised and enforced in relation to English property.

The first stage: questions of foreign law

If the foreign law has concepts of trust and property similar to England's, it may be relatively easy to determine whether the forced heirship rules give rise to a trust in the English sense – and, if so, whether it is the kind of trust under which beneficiaries are regarded as having proprietary interests in the trust

1 *Phrantzes v Argenti* [1960] 1 All ER 778.

2 *De Nicols v Curlier (No 1)* [1900] AC 21 and *(No 2)* [1900] 2 Ch 410.

3 See **4.8.1**.

property.[1] Otherwise, if no direct comparison is possible, the court must consider the effect of the foreign law and its forced heirship rules.

Plainly the first question is whether under the foreign law prospective forced heirs have any rights at all in relation to a living individual's property, or merely a hope of succeeding to it, a *spes successionis*, arising from the restricted nature of the individual's dispositive powers.

This question is not answered by the existence of claw-back rules. Such rules do not necessarily or probably signify the existence of rights before the individual's death. There is a world of difference between, on the one hand, a present right in relation to the property of a living individual and, on the other hand, a right arising on the individual's death in relation to property previously given away by him.

This distinction between present and future rights, although clear and important for our purposes, will not necessarily be clear or important in the foreign law. It may be necessary to consider a number of indicative questions, for example, whether prospective heirs can require the individual to give them information about his property and his dealings with it; whether the individual has any obligation in dealing with his property to take into consideration the interests of his heirs; whether the foreign court might in any circumstances intervene on behalf of prospective heirs to prevent the individual from dealing with his property to their detriment.

In some forced heirship regimes it seems the individual has no legal obligations to his prospective heirs and may deal with his property entirely as he pleases. He may, if he wishes, consume or dissipate his estate by riotous living, poor investments or disastrous ventures. He may incur debts and obligations without regard to his heirs. He may make whatever gifts he wants and during his lifetime the gifts are unassailable by his heirs. Prospective heirs have no legal remedy in the individual's lifetime, however much he is acting to their detriment. This would seem to negate any suggestion that the individual had fiduciary obligations to his heirs. In such regimes it seems that, although the forced heir may acquire formidable rights on the individual's death, he has in the meantime nothing but hope.

In other regimes the position may be less clear. In Spain, for example, it appears that the court may intervene on behalf of prospective forced heirs to prevent excessive gifts and other irresponsible behaviour on the individual's part. The court may even appoint an administrator or co-administrator of the individual's property to protect the interests of the heirs.

The next question, if it has been proved that under the foreign law prospective forced heirs do have rights in the individual's lifetime, is whether those foreign rights have the characteristics of equitable proprietary interests

---

1 In *Archer-Shee v Garland* [1931] AC 212, for example, the House of Lords compared English and New York law on the question of whether a beneficiary with a life interest is regarded as having a proprietary interest in the trust property.

under English law – a question which would be easier to analyse if English law had a clearer conception of the essential characteristics of a proprietary interest.

In *National Provincial Bank Ltd v Ainsworth*[1] the House of Lords demolished the theory of the 'deserted wife's equity' in the matrimonial home. It was said by Wilberforce LJ:

> 'On any division, then, which is to be made between property rights on the one hand, and personal rights on the other hand, however broad or penumbral the separating band between those two kinds of rights may be, there can be little doubt where the wife's rights fall. Before a right or an interest can be admitted into the category of property, or of a right affecting property, it must be definable, identifiable by third parties, capable in its nature of assumption by third parties, and have some degree of permanence or stability.'

In the case of forced heirship it seems doubtful whether the rights of prospective forced heirs could pass this test during the individual's lifetime. A third party acquiring property from the individual would be unable to identify the rights of the heirs except in terms of an unquantifiable risk of attack on the individual's death by a class of persons unascertainable until the individual's death. The third party could not even obtain an effective release or assignment of these rights during the individual's lifetime.

At least in the case of the deserted wife's equity there was not much doubt about the property allegedly subject to the wife's proprietary interest – the matrimonial home. In the case of forced heirship it seems there must in all regimes be a fatal uncertainty as to the subject matter of the prospective heirs' rights. A significant analogy can be drawn with the position of residuary legatees during the period of administration of the estate of a deceased person.

It is well established by several House of Lords and Privy Council decisions[2] that during the period of administration, while the deceased's debts remain unsettled, residuary legatees have no proprietary interests, legal or equitable, in the property comprising the estate. It is noteworthy that this is so even although the personal representatives are plainly fiduciaries and may not use the estate property for their own benefit. Residuary legatees have nothing more than an enforceable right to have the estate properly administered. In the words of Viscount Radcliffe in *Commissioner of Stamp Duties (Queensland) v Livingstone*:[3]

> 'What equity did not do was to recognise or create for residuary legatees a beneficial interest in the assets in the executor's hands during the course of administration. Conceivably, this could have been done, in the sense that the assets, whatever they might be from time to time, could have been treated as a present, although fluctuating, trust fund held for the

---

1 [1965] 2 All ER 472.

2 [1965] AC 694; *Sudeley (Lord) v Attorney-General* [1897] AC 11; *Dr Barnardo's Homes v Special Income Tax Commissioners* [1921] 2 AC 1.

3 [1965] AC 694.

> benefit of all those interested in the estate according to the measure of their respective interests. But it never was done. It would have been a clumsy and unsatisfactory device from a practical point of view; and, indeed, it would have been in plain conflict with the basic conception of equity that to impose the fetters of a trust upon property, with the resulting creation of equitable interests in that property, there had to be specific subjects identifiable as the trust fund. An unadministered estate was incapable of satisfying this requirement. The assets as a whole were in the hands of the executor, his property; and until administration was complete no one was in a position to say what items of property would need to be realised for the purposes of that administration or of what the residue, when ascertained, would consist or what its value would be.'

Later Viscount Radcliffe added:

> 'Therefore, while it may well be said in a general way that a residuary legatee has an interest in the totality of the assets ... it is in their Lordships' opinion inadmissible to proceed from that to the statement that such a person has an equitable interest in any particular one of those assets ....'

It seems unlikely that an English court would regard the prospective heir of a living individual as being in a better position than a residuary legatee of an unadministered estate.[1] The position of the prospective heir is far more precarious and uncertain. Both are subject to the individual's debts, but the prospective heir is subject to any further debts which the individual may incur in his lifetime, subject also to the individual's freedom to consume or dissipate, subject indeed to the risk of dying before the individual and thus inheriting nothing.

The subject matter of the alleged trust would be uncertain in another vital respect. Forced heirship regimes restrict part only of the individual's estate, leaving him free to dispose of a portion by *inter vivos* disposition or by will. It seems that no forced heirship regime requires the individual to keep the reserved portion of his estate separate from the disposable portion. The two are mixed, legitimately and unavoidably. This appears to add a final and conclusive element to the fatal uncertainty of the alleged trust its relation to any specific property of a living individual.

However, before the heirs' claim is dismissed altogether on the ground of uncertainty, it must be noted that equity seems to have developed a concept of 'floating trust' which can exist despite uncertainty of subject matter in circumstances not dissimilar to those of prospective forced heirs. This floating trust is imposed by equity to prevent fraud in respect of mutual wills.[2] Much simplified the mutual wills doctrine is that, if A dies leaving property to B pursuant to an agreement that the survivor should make and not revoke a will in favour of C, equity will intervene to ensure that B honours the agreement. Intervention is necessary because otherwise lack of privity would prevent C

---

1 Although heirs might point out that one reason for Equity's refusal to impose a trust in favour of residuary legatees is that legatees have other effective remedies – which perhaps heirs do not.

2 And in comparable secret trust situations: *Ottaway v Norman* [1971] 3 All ER 1325.

from enforcing the agreement. Equity does not prevent B from exercising his legal right to make and revoke wills but imposes a constructive trust in favour of C which binds B, his personal representatives and all those interested in B's will or intestacy.[1]

The constructive trust which arises in the case of mutual wills is full of uncertainties and anomalies, much debated but beyond the scope of this chapter.

English courts have not shed much light on it but the following extract from the judgment of Dixon J in the High Court of Australia in a case[2] on mutual wills has been referred to with approval by English judges on more than one occasion,[3] and indicates the parallels which forced heirs might seek to draw:

> 'The purpose of an arrangement for corresponding wills must often be, as in this case, to enable the survivor during his life to deal as absolute owner with the property passing under the will of the party first dying. That is to say, the object of the transaction is to put the survivor in a position to enjoy for his own benefit the full ownership so that, for instance, he may convert it and expend the proceeds if he choose. But when he dies he is to bequeath what is left in the manner agreed upon. It is only by the special doctrines of equity that such a floating obligation, suspended, so to speak, during the lifetime of the survivor can descend upon the assets at his death and crystallise into a trust. No doubt gifts and settlements, *inter vivos*, if calculated to defeat the intention of the compact, could not be made by the survivor and his right of disposition, *inter vivos* is, therefore, not unqualified. But, substantially, the purpose of the arrangement will often be to allow full enjoyment for the survivor's own benefit and advantage upon condition that at his death the residue shall pass as arranged. … But I do not see any difficulty in modern equity in attaching to the assets a constructive trust which allows the survivor to enjoy the property subject to a fiduciary duty which, so to speak, crystallised on his death and disabled him only from voluntary disposition *inter vivos*.'

With respect to Dixon J there do seem to be difficulties in the doctrine expounded, and one may prefer the remark of one commentator that 'perhaps the only answer is to regard the trust imposed to give effect to mutual wills as an entrenched anomaly'.[4]

Be that as it may, it has been suggested[5] that the fiduciary obligation (not to make gifts *inter vivos* calculated to defeat the mutual wills agreement) gives C the right to trace property given away in breach of the obligation. If that is correct, it seems that in a forced heirship situation the English court might find nothing inherently impossible in the notion that the foreign law gives rise to a kind of floating trust crystallising on the individual's death and, although not until then conferring any proprietary interests as such, giving the forced

---

1 For further explanation see Underhill and Hayton, n 3 on p 169, p 390 *et seq*.

2 *Birmingham v Renfrew* (1937) 57 CLR 666.

3 For example, *Re Cleaver* [1981] 2 All ER 1018.

4 AJ Oakley *Constructive Trusts* (2nd ed), p 138.

5 Hayton and Manstall *Cases and Commentary on the Law of Trusts* (8th ed), p 109.

heirs a right to trace property given away by the individual in his lifetime with intent to avoid forced heirship.

The second stage: English conflict-of-laws rules

If the heirs have been successful in the first stage and the court is satisfied as a matter of fact that the foreign law gave rise to a trust or floating trust, the court must also be persuaded that, applying English conflict-of-laws rules, the foreign trust should be recognised and enforced in relation to English property.

The Hague Convention on Trusts does not apply to trusts which arise automatically by operation of law. Article 3 provides:

> 'The Convention applies only to trusts created voluntarily and evidenced in writing.'

The Recognition of Trusts Act 1987, s 1(2) extends the Convention rules in England to 'any other trusts of property arising under the law of any part of the United Kingdom', thus suggesting that forced heirs from Scotland or Ireland might have an advantage. But, as has already been noted, the Convention does not address preliminary questions of validity.[1]

Reverting to general principles, it seems that there are three main questions determining whether the foreign trust will be recognised and enforced. At the time of settlement did the necessary connecting factor exist pointing to this foreign law as being the applicable law to govern the prospective heirs' rights in respect of the settlor's English property? Would recognition and enforcement of the foreign trust be inconsistent with English public policy?[2] Would enforcement by an English court constitute a remedy so different to that available under the foreign law as to have the effect of changing the substance of the foreign rights?[3]

Both technical and policy considerations suggest rather strongly that an English court would not recognise foreign succession rights in relation to the property of a living person, especially if the rights would constitute proprietary interests, or give rise to proprietary remedies, affecting third parties. That would be a return to the law and practice of the twelfth century when the parties to a transfer of property would seek the concurrence of as many of the transferor's potential heirs as they could manage, in the hope that the transferee would enjoy peaceable possession.[4] Since 1200 the rule in domestic English law has been *nemo est heres viventis*; a living person has no heir. This is reflected in English conflict of laws rules which identify an individual's succession law by reference to his circumstances at death – his domicile at death, as regards his movable estate, and the *situs* at death of his immovable

---

1 See **4.5.1**.

2 *Dicey and Morris*, n 3 on p 173, p 92 *et seq.*

3 Ibid, pp 175–176.

4 Pollock and Maitland *The History of English Law* Vol 2, pp 306–311.

estate. There is no basis upon which recognition could be given to a foreign law as the prospective succession law of a living person.

The heirs would have to argue that for conflict-of-laws purposes the issue should not be characterised as one of succession, that the essence of their case was that they possessed rights in respect of the settlor's property during his lifetime. Heirs who were children of the settlor might argue that the issue should be treated as one of rights and obligations arising by reason of status, therefore governed by the law of the settlor's domicile for the time being.[1] A surviving spouse might argue that the issue should be treated as one of matrimonial property, governed by the law of the matrimonial domicile. In relation to a community of property regime this would generally be correct.[2] But in a forced heirship regime which put the spouse on the same precarious footing as the other prospective heirs, the spouse's claim would naturally receive the same treatment as theirs under English conflict-of-laws rules.

The characterisation of issues for conflict-of-laws purposes is a subject of notorious difficulty on which there has been much academic debate but little guidance from the courts. In this case, however, it does seem likely that a court looking at the substance and overall effect of the foreign law would prefer to characterise the issue as one of succession. Any rights and obligations which the court was persuaded did exist in the settlor's lifetime might reasonably be regarded as merely incidental to the succession rights.

From a policy viewpoint, the court would presumably find most unpalatable the prospect of English property being subject to proprietary interests of an uncertain nature dictated by the owner's domiciliary law, interests which vanish, appear or are transformed whenever, unbeknownst to third parties (and perhaps to himself), the individual changes his domicile. Even if the owner's domicile remains unchanged, the interests of his heirs vary according to family and financial circumstances of which third parties could not be aware. Moreover, it would be impossible to clear off the encumbrance by discharge or by obtaining a release or assignment. Titles would remain blighted until the individual's death and the elapse of the applicable limitation period. Even the bona fide purchaser for value of the legal estate might be in difficulty; for how could he assert ignorance of the inchoate rights of the seller's heirs?

To put it at its lowest, the English court would have ample grounds for treating the issue as one of succession. On that footing the heirs would fail for the reasons outlined above.

---

1 *Phrantzes v Argenti* [1960] 1 All ER 778.

2 *De Nicols v Curlier (No 1)* [1900] AC 21 and *(No 2)* [1900] 2 Ch 410.

4.5.3 Validity of the disposition ('the rocket-launcher')[1]

In order to launch a trust, two steps are generally needed, although sometimes achieved by a single document:

(a) the assets in question must be transferred to the trustee – unless the trustee already has them. This is referred to below as 'the asset transfer'; and
(b) there must be an appropriate instrument or act to subject the assets to the trust. This is referred to below as 'subjection to the trust'.

It has been noted already under 'Validity of the trust' (see **4.5.1**) that neither the Hague Convention nor the Recognition of Trusts Act 1987 applies to the launch of a trust.[2] The common law rules are uncertain in some important respects.

So far as immovable property is concerned the rules appear to be relatively straightforward. In general, the *lex situs* governs all aspects of the launch. This is so whether the trust is testamentary or *inter vivos.* As regards testamentary trusts of movable property, the law of the testator's last domicile governs most aspects. Greater uncertainty exists in relation to the third category, trusts *inter vivos* of movable property, and unfortunately this is the category of greatest practical importance in the offshore trust field.

Considering first the asset transfer aspect in relation to tangible movables, the general rule is that the proprietary effects of a disposition *inter vivos* are governed by the *lex situs* at the time of the disposition. For intangible movables the position is more difficult. A recent article on the subject starts with the following discouraging remarks:

> 'The assignment of intangible things, such as debts, has long been one of the most intractable topics in English conflict of laws. The writers on the subject are fundamentally divided and the little case law that exists is old, confused and inconclusive.'[3]

Dicey and Morris suggest that assignability is a matter for the constituent law and that other issues affecting validity are to be analysed as although the assignment were a contract – a method of analysis which points largely, although not entirely, to the chosen proper law of the assignment.[4] One ground for criticism is that in the case of a gift there is no contract, and it seems artificial to analyse the transaction as although there was one. This is not the place in which to embark on a detailed discussion, but for planning purposes it may suffice to note that the main contenders for dominance

---

1 See **4.4.1**.
2 See also Cheshire and North *Private International Law* (Butterworths, 12th ed, 1992), pp 883, 884.
3 M Moshinsky 'The Assignment of Debts in the Conflict of Laws' [1992] 108 LQR 591.
4 *Dicey and Morris*, n 3 on p 173, p 957 *et seq.*

appear to be (a) the constituent law of the intangible thing, (b) the *lex situs* of the intangible thing and (c) the proper law of the assignment. If all three are one and the same, there should be nothing left to argue about.

There remains the question of which system of law governs the other main element of the launching process, subjection to the trust. If, for example, this step is achieved, or allegedly achieved, by a declaration of trust, which system of law governs the validity and effect of the declaration for this purpose? It would be most convenient if it were the same system of law as governed the trust,[1] but it is not clear that this is so. For example, it appears that the question of the settlor's capacity to create a trust of movables *inter vivos* is probably governed by the system of law with which the trust is (or would be) most closely connected – not necessarily the system of law chosen by the settlor to govern the trust.[2] In the context of a marriage settlement contract it was said by Lord McNaghten in *Cooper v Cooper*:[3]

> 'It is difficult to suppose that [the settlor] could confer capacity upon herself by contemplating a different country as the place where the contract was to be fulfilled.'

The common law rules give no clear guidance on how to identify or evaluate the closeness of connection for this purpose,[4] but it does seem that the settlor's domicile may be a major factor.[5] Indeed it used to be said that capacity was entirely a matter for the settlor's domiciliary law; but the maxim *mobilia sequuntur personam* has been discredited by most commentators save in relation to matters of succession.[6]

Note also, under 'Validity of the trust' at **4.5.1**, the doubt concerning evasive choices of law, a doubt which exists equally in the present context.[7]

In some cases, if for example the settlor of a trust of movables reserved a life interest and a power of revocation, the heirs might argue that for conflict of laws purposes the disposition should be regarded as being essentially testamentary in nature – a will-substitute – hence governed by the settlor's succession law. It is hard to see how the argument could succeed. Until his death the settlor's succession law cannot be identified; the validity of the disposition cannot stay in limbo until the settlor dies. Of course the heirs will have an argument of a very different and more effective sort if, applying ordinary domestic principles of English law, the disposition appears to have been a sham or not intended to take effect until the settlor's death.

---

1 See 'Validity of the Trust' at **4.5.1**.

2 *Dicey and Morris*, n 3 on p 173, pp 1075 and 1061–1063.

3 (1888) 14 App Cas 88 at 108.

4 The Convention rules in Art 7 are also inapplicable.

5 *Dicey and Morris*, n 3 on p 173, pp 1073, 1074.

6 Ibid, p 943; Cheshire and North, n 1 on p 183, p 795 *et seq.*

7 In this context the meaning of 'strong public policy' is not limited in scope by Art 15 of the Convention.

4.5.4 Direct enforcement of the heirs' rights[1]

As the heirs would be pursuing claims unknown to English domestic law, one might suppose that they would have an insuperable difficulty in bringing English proceedings to enforce them directly. The case of *Phrantzes v Argenti*[2] demonstrates the error of that reasoning.

In that case the daughter of a Greek national sued him in England for enforcement of her right under Greek law to a dowry. Both were resident in England and it was alleged by the daughter, although denied by the father, that he was domiciled in Greece. Leaving that question of fact to one side, and assuming that the father was domiciled in Greece, the court decided the preliminary issue of whether the daughter's right was of a kind that the English court would enforce. It was contended on behalf of the father that the daughter's claim was based on a cause of action unknown to and not recognised in English law, and therefore it would not be enforced in an English court. On this point, the court found against the father.

The court referred with approval to remarks of Cardozo J in the New York case of *Loucks v Standard Oil Co of New York*:[3]

> 'If aid is to be withheld here, it must be because the cause of action in its nature offends our sense of justice or menaces the public welfare … Our own scheme of legislation may be different. We may even have no legislation on the subject. That is not enough to show that public policy forbids us to enforce the foreign right. A right of action is property. If a foreign statute gives the right, the mere fact that we do not give a like right is no reason for refusing to help the plaintiff in getting what belongs to him. We are not so provincial as to say that every solution of a problem is wrong because we deal with it otherwise at home …'[4]

The daughter failed for quite different reasons having to do with the particular nature of the Greek right of dowry and the relief afforded by Greek law for non-provision of dowry.

So it appears that the settlor's heirs would not be stopped simply because their rights were unknown to English law. However, they would encounter a problem of a different sort. In *Phrantzes v Argenti* the court characterised the daughter's right as one arising from her family relationship with her father and, as such, governed by the law of her father's domicile. That was the essential connection with Greece. Although not enunciated as such, the rule accepted by the court appears to have been that English courts will in general recognise and enforce the rights of a child against a parent arising from the parent/child relationship under the law of the parent's domicile. This rule can be of no assistance to a forced heir (whether a child or other relative of the deceased)

---

1 See **4.4.1**(4).

2 [1960] 1 All ER 778.

3 (1978) 224 NY 99.

4 By the time of *Phrantzes v Argenti* in 1960 it seems that the 'vested rights' approach to the conflict of laws, epitomised by the remarks of Cardozo J had passed from fashion in the US: see Scoles and Hay *Conflict of Laws*, Ch 2.

who seeks to enforce rights against a trustee or against trust beneficiaries – for the heir has no relationship with them, or, if by coincidence he does, the rights he asserts do not arise from the relationship.

The forced heir would have to show why the existence of the alleged rights against the trustee or beneficiaries should be regarded as a matter for the settlor's succession law. No doubt the heir would argue that his rights were a matter of succession and hence should be referred to the settlor's succession law, but it seems unlikely that an English court would accept that characterisation.[1] The rights asserted by the heir might have arisen in consequence of the settlor's death and in that respect have the characteristic of succession rights, but they could hardly be described as rights in respect of the settlor's property – unless, perhaps, the settlor had reserved substantially all of the beneficial interest in the trust property to himself during his lifetime.

It seems that the heirs might have a better argument in the case of a trust in which the settlor had reserved a power of revocation. The heirs might argue that the resolution of conflicting claims in respect of property over which the settlor at his death had a general power (such as a power of revocation) was a matter of succession and should be referred to the settlor's succession law – deriving some support from the Inheritance (Provision for Family and Dependants) Act 1975, s 25(1) and its definition of 'net estate' which includes 'any property in respect of which the deceased held a general power of appointment (not being a power exercisable by will) which has not been exercised'.

4.5.5 Claims in tort[2]

Unless the actions complained of took place in England, the heirs would first have to deal with the conflict of laws question. The general rule is that an act done in a foreign country is a tort and actionable as such in England only if it is both:

(a) actionable as a tort according to English law, or in other words is an act which, if done in England, would be a tort; and
(b) actionable according to the law of the foreign country where it was done.[3]

Interference with the rights of prospective heirs does not appear to be an acknowledged tort in English law. However, the lists are not closed and the heirs might argue by analogy with the acknowledged economic torts, particularly that of inducing a breach of contract. Despite its accepted name,

---

1 However, if England became party to the Hague Convention on Succession, the court's view might be quite different: see **4.8.2**.

2 See **4.4.1**(5).

3 *Dicey and Morris*, n 3 on p 173, pp 1365–1366.

that tort already extends beyond purely contractual obligations to the violation of other rights where such violation is an actionable wrong. This is not the place for a detailed discussion of economic torts[1] but it does seem improbable that the English courts would see fit to acknowledge this new category or sub-category of tort.

Even if the settlor's home state viewed the creation of the trust as an immediate and unconditional violation of the heir's rights, an English court would presumably see several objections. To allow the heir's claim would permit an 'end-run' around established conflict of laws rules. There would in effect be a return to the discredited maxim *mobilia sequuntur personam*. The court would also presumably take note of the consequences of upholding the claims of heirs. It would be unsafe for any financial institution or adviser to assist any individual with estate planning in his or her lifetime.

4.5.6 Claims for restitution[2]

The English law of restitution seems to be in a state of uncertain development, and one supposes that the related conflict of laws rules are equally uncertain.

According to Dicey and Morris,[3] the general conflict of laws rule in England is that the obligation to restore the benefit of an enrichment obtained at another person's expense is governed by the law of the place where the enrichment occurred.[4]

That leads to the question of where the alleged enrichment occurs when the transaction in question is the creation of an offshore trust. Insofar as it is alleged that the trustee has been enriched, it is presumably the trust domicile or, if different, the *situs* of the property at the time of settlement. Insofar as it is alleged that the trust beneficiaries have been unjustly enriched, the place of enrichment is presumably the *situs* of the beneficiaries' interest in the trust. If it is a trust in which the beneficiaries are regarded as having proprietary interests in the trust property, their interests are situate where the property is situate; but if the beneficiaries have only a right of action against the trustee, their interests are situate wherever the trustee resides.[5]

If the circumstances of the case did point to English law, the heirs' claim could not be brought within any of the acknowledged grounds for restitution except, conceivably, the statutory provisions for the avoidance of transactions at an undervalue under the Insolvency Act 1986. Section 423 enables the court to set aside a transaction at an undervalue if satisfied that it was entered into for the purpose of:

---

1 See, generally, *Clerk and Lindsell on Torts*.

2 See **4.4.1**(5).

3 *Dicey and Morris*, n 3 on p 173, p 1350.

4 This does not apply when the alleged obligation arises in connection with a contract or a transaction concerning immovable property.

5 *Dicey and Morris*, n 3 on p 173, p 913.

> 'putting assets beyond the reach of a person who is making, or may at some time make, a claim against [the maker of the transaction] or of otherwise prejudicing the interests of such a person in relation to the claim which he is making or may make.'

Is 'claim' wide enough to encompass the claims of forced heirs? The Act does not answer the question but it seems probable that s 423 is limited to claims against a person rather than claims to a person's estate. As support for that view it is noteworthy that the Inheritance (Provision for Family and Dependants) Act 1975 provides its own anti-avoidance rules enabling the court to set aside evasive dispositions.[1] It seems improbable that the subsequent insolvency legislation was intended to provide additional and different anti-avoidance rules for the protection of succession rights.

There is authority[2] for the existence of a common law rule against transactions in fraud of creditors, independent of the Statute of Elizabeth, the Law of Property Act and the Insolvency Acts, but there appear to be no grounds for suggesting that the scope of the common law rule is wider than that of the statutory rule.

Forced heirship survived in English law until the eighteenth century in the customs of the City of London. The custom applied only to personal property and there was no claw-back rule even as regards lifetime gifts intended to defeat forced heirs. But equity did intervene to set aside dispositions deemed to be in fraud of the custom. It seems to have been regarded as fraudulent if, for example, the individual failed to divest himself fully of the property or retained power over it or possession of it. In *Tomkins v Ladbroke*[3] the Lord Chancellor commented:

> 'It is said that a freeman may by act in his life, and *in extremis*, give away any part of his personal estate, provided he devests himself of all property in it: although if he reserves to himself a power over it, that is considered as void. Indeed in general those propositions are right; but then where there is any case of such an act by a father upon his death-bed, and no evidence of actual possession or effect of possession or enjoyment during the life of the father … then the consideration is, what construction ought to be made upon the nature and intent of the act done? It appears to me that this act of the father was in nature of a testamentary act, done at the same time as he made his will; and therefore must be judged to be an act in fraud of the custom, although not an actual fraud.'

The report of *Turner v Jennings*[4] reads as follows:

> 'A freeman of the City of London, by deed executed in his lifetime, grants and assigns over the greatest part of his personal estate, in trust for himself for life, and then for the benefit of his grandchildren (the children of his son then deceased, R.L.); his son dying in his

---

1 Sections 10 and 11.

2 *Cadogan v Kennett* 2 Cowp 433.

3 2 Ves Sen 591.

4 2 Vern 612.

> lifetime; the plaintiff, who married the freeman's daughter, brought his bill to set aside the deed, and to have his wife's orphanage part in her right, according to the custom of the City of London. And although it was admitted that if the father had made an actual gift of any part of his personal estate to his grandchildren in his lifetime, or had actually given all to one child in his lifetime, that would have held good against the custom; or if he had turned all his personal estate into a purchase of lands, he might have disposed of it as he although fit; yet it was decreed for the plaintiff, and the deed set aside; for that the freeman had not entirely dismist [sic] himself of the estate in his lifetime; and the deed being made when he was languishing, and but a little before his death, it ought to be looked upon as a *donatio causa mortis*: Lord Chancellor declaring that either the custom must be entirely given up, or this deed must be looked upon, as made in fraud of the custom; but will stand good as to a moiety, which he, having no wife, might dispose of.'

The question is whether in modern times equity might intervene to set aside a settlement as being in fraud of foreign forced heirship laws – if the settlor reserved such powers and interests as to make the disposition illusory in his lifetime or, in other words, a will-substitute. It may be doubted whether equity would lend support to foreign laws in the same way as domestic laws, but none the less there may be some additional reason for the misgivings expressed elsewhere in this chapter concerning the survivability in England of trusts in which the settlor has reserved substantial powers and interests.

Apart from the Insolvency Act 1986 it appears that the only acknowledged form of restitutionary claim which the heirs might conceivably make would entail the premise that the settlor had during his lifetime held his property in a fiduciary capacity for the benefit of the prospective heirs. On that premise equity might intervene in the event of a breach of fiduciary duty, making available to the heirs the remedies of tracing and constructive trust.

This has already been discussed under 'The settlor's title to the settled property' at **4.5.2**.

4.5.7 Enforcement of foreign judgments[1]

English common law rules for the recognition and enforcement of foreign judgments are now heavily overlaid with statutory provisions, notably those of the Civil Jurisdiction and Judgments Act 1982 (as amended in 1991) arising from the Brussels and Lugano Conventions. However, the Conventions and the Act are stated not to apply to matters of succession[2] and so presumably could not be enlisted by a forced heir.

It appears that under the common law rules[3] or, where applicable, the statutory rules[4] a foreign judgment *in personam* will generally be recognised and

---

1 See **4.4.1**(7).

2 Article 1 in both Conventions excludes 'the status or legal capacity of natural persons, rights in property arising out of a matrimonial relationship, wills and succession'.

3 *Dicey and Morris*, n 3 on p 173, pp 425–426.

4 The Administration of Justice Act 1920 and the Foreign Judgments (Reciprocal Enforcement) Act 1933.

enforced if (a) for a debt or definite sum of money (not being in respect of taxes or other charges of a like nature or in respect of a fine or other penalty) and (b) final and conclusive – but only if (c) the foreign court is regarded according to the English conflict of laws rules as having jurisdiction over the issue. Under statute and common law the jurisdictional rules are essentially the same, providing the following grounds for the jurisdiction of a foreign court:

(a) residence (or, perhaps, presence) of the judgment debtor in the foreign jurisdiction at the time the foreign proceedings were instituted;
(b) the judgment debtor being plaintiff in, or counterclaiming in, the foreign proceedings;
(c) the judgment debtor submitting to the foreign jurisdiction by voluntarily appearing in the proceedings;
(d) the judgment debtor having agreed in respect to the subject matter of the proceedings to submit to the jurisdiction of the courts of the foreign country.[1]

There are significant differences between the statutory and common law rules in relation to the residence of a corporation. Under the Foreign Judgments (Reciprocal Enforcement) Act 1933 there is jurisdiction only if (a) the corporation has its principal place of business in the foreign country, or (b) it has an office or place of business there which is not its principal place of business but the cause of action arose from a transaction effected through that office. At common law any place of business in the foreign country is sufficient to constitute residence.

There are different rules as regards foreign judgments *in rem*.[2] In general, the courts of a foreign state have jurisdiction to give a judgment *in rem* capable of enforcement or recognition in England if the subject matter is immovable or movable property situate in the foreign state.

If the forced heir had obtained a foreign judgment *in personam* or *in rem* complying with the requirements so far indicated, the only defences to enforcement would be on the basis of fraud, natural justice or public policy. There is no reason to suppose that either of the first two heads would apply.

In the absence of judicial authority one should hesitate to express a view on the question of public policy but it seems that English courts have taken a fairly restrictive view of this defence.[3] Presumably the argument against enforcement would focus upon the public interest in the individual's freedom of disposition, the undesirability of subjecting persons in England to claims in respect of transactions entered into in good faith years previously and the undesirability of placing trustees and advisers at such risk as to deter people

1 *Dicey and Morris*, n 3 on p 173, pp 436, 437, 479, 485 and 486.
2 Ibid, pp 455 and 456.
3 Ibid, pp 472–474.

from acting as such.[1] Presumably the defence would be weaker in relation to a foreign judgment *in rem* relating, as it would have to do, to property abroad.

England's adherence to the Hague Convention on Trusts and the enactment of the Recognition of Trusts Act 1987 presumably make the public policy argument more difficult, acknowledging as they do that foreign jurisdictions may withhold recognition of trusts which are inconsistent with forced heirship laws.[2] England's adherence to the Hague Convention on Succession would presumably make the public policy argument untenable.

4.5.8 Succession law[3]

Under English conflict of laws rules succession is not a single issue but several. In relation to immovable property, succession issues are in general governed by the *lex situs*.[4] In relation to movable property, succession issues are generally governed by the law of the deceased's last domicile.[5]

If the Hague Convention on Succession became effective and were ratified by England, the conflict of laws rules in matters of succession would change radically.[6]

4.5.9 Assumption of jurisdiction[7]

The High Court has jurisdiction to entertain an action *in personam* if and only if the defendant is served with a writ in England or abroad in the circumstances authorised by, and in the manner prescribed by, statute or statutory order. The statutory jurisdiction under the Brussels and Lugano Conventions and the Civil Jurisdiction and Judgments Act 1982 (as amended in 1991) appears not to be relevant in relation to matters of succession.[8]

The circumstances in which leave may be given to serve a writ abroad are numerous. Though undoubtedly important, they are outside the scope of this chapter, as is the jurisdiction of English courts to stay or strike out an action or other proceeding by reason of the existence of a more convenient forum.

4.5.10 Bars to the heirs' claim[9]

As a result of the Foreign Limitation Periods Act 1984, English courts will now generally apply the limitation rules of the *lex causae*, the system of law which governs the substantive issue.

---

1 DJ Hayton, n 1 on p 157, pp 1–17.
2 See **4.8.1**.
3 See **4.4.1**(8).
4 *Dicey and Morris*, n 3 on p 173, p 1007.
5 Ibid, p 1005
6 See **4.8.2**.
7 See **4.4.1**(9).
8 See **4.5.7**.
9 See **4.4.1**(9).

4.5.11 Summary

The survivability of trusts in England is subject to a real measure of uncertainty. The uncertainty has not been significantly diminished by the Recognition of Trusts Act 1987. It is to be hoped that the courts will have an opportunity to clarify the law. Meanwhile, although the uncertainties may be avoided to some extent by careful planning, England cannot be given a perfect score as an offshore trust centre or as a place for investment by trusts established elsewhere. For reasons discussed at **4.8.2**, England's adherence to the Hague Convention on Succession would make it positively unsuitable, unless the enabling legislation excised the objectionable elements of the Convention.

4.6 SURVIVABILITY IN OFFSHORE CENTRES

In recent years there has been a spate of trust legislation in offshore centres, much of it aimed at improving or clarifying conflict of laws rules. This section discusses in relation to each offshore centre how the new legislation has affected the survivability there of trusts which are domiciled there.[1]

The reader should be warned that this section does not delve into pre-existing conflict of laws rules, although in many offshore centres they remain of prime importance. The reader should also be warned that the legislation is new and largely untested. Time will tell whether the legislators have achieved the results they desired – and whether the comments in this section are correct.

This section divides offshore centres into the following groups.

Group 1 – Gibraltar, Hong Kong and the Isle of Man. These centres have incorporated into their laws the Hague Convention on Trusts but have to date taken no other legislative action to clarify their conflict of laws rules.

Group 2 – The Cayman Islands, the Cook Islands, the Bahamas and the Turks and Caicos Islands. Although there are important variations, each of these centres has adopted basically the same legislation to clarify its conflict of laws rules. None of these centres is presently a party to the Hague Convention on Trusts.

Group 3 – Jersey and Guernsey. These two centres deserve separate treatment because their trust legislation is substantially the same, both have mixed common law and civil law origins, both are themselves forced heirship jurisdictions and both are, or intend to become, parties to the Hague Convention on Trusts.

---

1 See **4.1.7** for the concept of 'trust domicile'.

Group 4 – Belize, Bermuda, Cyprus [the British Virgin Islands and Labuan]. This is not a homogeneous group but it contains all the other offshore centres covered in this book which have common law origins. Some are party to the Hague Convention on Trusts. Some are forced heirship jurisdictions.

Group 5 – Liechtenstein. As the only civil law trust centre covered in this book, Liechtenstein deserves its own category. It is not a party to the Hague Convention on Trusts.

4.6.1 Group 1 – Gibraltar, Hong Kong and the Isle of Man

These three centres have followed England's lead and have enacted legislation to incorporate the Hague Convention on Trusts:

Gibraltar – Trusts (Recognition) Ordinance 1989;
Hong Kong – Recognition of Trusts Ordinance 1989;
Isle of Man – Recognition of Trusts Act 1988.

As was noted in relation to England, this legislation makes little difference to pre-existing conflict of laws rules and uncertainties, and does not affect the survivability of trusts.

4.6.2 Group 2 – The Cayman Islands, the Cook Islands, the Bahamas and the Turks and Caicos Islands

The Cayman Islands
With the Trusts (Foreign Element) Law 1987 (TFEL 1987) the Cayman Islands was the first offshore centre to clarify its conflict of laws rules in relation to the survivability of trusts. The TFEL 1987 provides a fairly comprehensive system of rules governing the recognition/exclusion of foreign laws in trust-related matters.

Validity of the trust ('the rocket')

An express choice of Cayman Islands law to govern the trust is effective regardless of circumstances; and no special form of words is needed to make a valid choice. If Cayman Islands law is chosen, it governs all questions arising in regard to the trust and the validity and effect of the trust provisions. Subject to certain stated exceptions, foreign laws are excluded. The exceptions deserve careful attention. For example, TFEL 1987, s 5 does not validate a testamentary trust which is invalid according to the laws of the testator's domicile. Nor does it validate a trust of real property if the trust is invalid under the *lex situs*.

The settlor's title to the settled property

TFEL 1987, s 5(a) provides: '… nor does this section affect the recognition of foreign laws in determining whether the settlor is the owner of such property …'. Whether TFEL 1987, s 6 affects the recognition of foreign laws for this purpose is open to argument.

Validity of the transfer ('the rocket-launcher')

TFEL 1987, s 5 applies Cayman Islands law not only to the trust itself but also to dispositions of property to the trustee, including questions of the settlor's capacity and the validity and effect of the disposition. Again foreign laws are excluded, subject to stated exceptions. As well as exceptions concerning testamentary dispositions and dispositions of foreign real property, TFEL 1987, s 5(d) provides:

> 'This section does not affect the recognition of foreign laws prescribing generally (without reference to the existence or terms of the trust) the formalities for the disposition of property.'

It should be noted that 'formalities' is specially defined in TFEL 1987, s 2(1).

Direct enforcement of the heirs' rights

The TFEL 1987 (s 6 in particular) has probably eliminated any prospect of the heir enforcing succession rights against the trustee or the trust beneficiaries by action in the Cayman Islands.

Claims in tort

Again, the TFEL 1987 (s 6 in particular) has probably eliminated any prospect of the heir making a successful claim in tort for interference with his succession rights.

Claims for restitution

The TFEL 1987 (s 6 in particular) has probably eliminated any prospect of the heir making a successful restitutionary claim to trust property or compensatory payment by the trustee. The same presumably applies as regards a restitutionary claim against trust beneficiaries. Section 8 of the Fraudulent Dispositions Law 1989 dispels any notion that aggrieved heirs should be equated with defrauded creditors.

Enforcement of foreign judgments

TFEL 1987, s 6 restricts the recognition or enforcement of a foreign judgment if it recognises, protects, enforces or gives effect to forced heirship rights. It is not clear how much effect TFEL 1987, s 6 would have in relation to a foreign judgment whose effect upon the trust was indirect – if, for example, the foreign judgment ordered compensatory payments to be made by the trust beneficiaries to the heirs, but it seems that TFEL 1987, s 6 would provide powerful support for the argument that enforcement would be contrary to public policy.

Succession law

The TFEL 1987 does not affect pre-existing conflict of laws rules in this respect.

Assumption of jurisdiction and bars to the heirs' claim

These are not affected by the TFEL 1987.

The Cook Islands

The new conflict of laws rules were introduced in 1989 and 1991 by amendments to the International Trusts Act 1984 (ITA 1984).

ITA 1984, ss 13G, 13H and 13I follow very closely equivalent provisions of the Cayman Islands' TFEL 1987; the effect upon the survivability of trusts appears to be identical. However, there are some additional features of the ITA 1984, which are not derived from the Cayman Islands' TFEL 1987 and which could materially affect survivability.

ITA 1984, s 13D contains more detailed rules concerning the recognition and enforcement of foreign judgments. The essential criterion is whether the judgment (a) 'is based upon the application of any law inconsistent with the provisions of this Act', and[1] (b) 'relates to a matter or particular aspect that is governed by the law of the Cook Islands'. The second limb may lead to some uncertainty, but clearly ITA 1984, s 13D enhances the survivability of trusts in the Cook Islands.

ITA 1984, s 13K provides a short limitation period of two years for an action in the Cook Islands to 'set aside the settlement of an international trust' or to 'set aside any disposition to any international trust'. The same two-year limitation period is imposed in relation to any action in the Cook Islands in which any person claims 'to have had an interest in property before that property was settled upon or disposed to an international trust'. The scope of these provisions may be narrower than it might appear. For example, if the creation of a trust were fatally flawed such that it was void from the outset, would the settlor (and those claiming through him) be barred after two years from recovering the property? If so, the trustee would become absolutely entitled.

It appears that the new conflict of laws rules apply only to 'international trusts', not to Cook Islands trusts in general. Care, therefore, needs to be taken in establishing and maintaining international trust status. The rules in this respect leave some questions unanswered. For example, does a trust lose international trust status if it ceases to have a qualifying trustee (ITA 1984,

---

1 It is not entirely clear whether this is 'and' or 'or', but 'and' seems more likely.

s 2(1) 'international trust') or if there is default in the annual renewal of registration (ITA 1984, s 16)? The cautious view is that all conditions and requirements must be observed on a continuing basis.

The Bahamas

The Trusts (Choice of Governing Law) Act 1989 is in very similar form to the Cayman Islands' TFEL 1987. On the survivability issues it appears to have the same effect.

The Turks and Caicos Islands

The Trusts Ordinance 1990 (TO 1990) is modelled closely on the Jersey legislation in most respects. However, TO 1990, s 13 introduces provisions derived from the Cayman Islands' TFEL 1987, (ss 5 and 6). The result in terms of the survivability of trusts appears to be the same as that of the Cayman Islands legislation.

4.6.3 Group 3 – Jersey and Guernsey

Jersey[1]

The Trusts (Jersey) Law 1984 (TJL 1984) in its original form contained some conflict of laws rules but was not designed to meet the special problems of forced heirship. The 1989 Amendment dealt directly with the forced heirship question, at the same time dealing with the important issue of the settlor's capacity. The 1991 Amendment was made to facilitate the extension of the Hague Convention on Trusts. The Convention has now been extended to Jersey. Interestingly, the Convention provisions have not been specifically incorporated into the law of Jersey and so, assuming that Jersey follows the English approach and not the French approach to treaties and their effect upon domestic law, the significance of the Convention provisions in Jersey law is presumably subject to some doubt.

Validity of the trust ('the rocket')

An express choice of Jersey law as the proper law of the trust appears to be effective regardless of the circumstances. Presumably questions concerning the validity and effect of a Jersey trust *inter vivos* are in general governed by Jersey law, but it should not be assumed that foreign laws are totally excluded. For example, if a Jersey trust were purportedly constituted of foreign immovable property, its validity and effect in the eyes of the Jersey court would presumably be affected by the *lex situs*. With regard to forced heirship, the TJL 1984 now contains a specific exclusionary rule. TJL 1984, s 8A(2) is in the following terms:

---

1 See DJ Hayton, n 1 on p 157, for details of Jersey's forced heirship regime.

'(2) If a person domiciled outside Jersey transfers or disposes of property during his lifetime to a trust:

(a) he shall be deemed to have had capacity to do so if he is at the time of such transfer or disposition of full age and of sound mind under the law of his domicile; and

(b) no rule relating to inheritance or succession (including, but without prejudice to the generality of the foregoing, forced heirship, legitime or similar rights) of the law of his domicile or any other system of law shall affect any such transfer or disposition or otherwise affect the validity of such trust.'

Evidently the specific exclusionary rule of TJL 1984, s 8A(2)(b) has limited scope. It only excludes foreign rules relating to inheritance or succession. If the heir based his complaint on some other foreign law – perhaps a rule of the settlor's domicile or of the *situs* of the trust property invalidating all trusts, or trusts in which the settlor reserves an interest – the defenders of the trust would have to rely upon general principles.

The settlor's title to the settled property

The TJL 1984 does not appear to affect this issue. It is beyond the scope of this chapter to discuss Jersey's law of property or related conflict of laws rules.

Validity of the disposition ('the rocket-launcher')

TJL 1984, s 8A(2) contains provisions, quoted above, prescribing the test for capacity to transfer property to a trust. The reference is to the settlor's law of domicile – but only to determine whether he is of full age and sound mind. If he is, he is deemed to have full capacity to make a disposition in trust; but presumably this is subject to any Jersey laws of specific application, for example, the Bankruptcy (Désastre) (Jersey) Law 1990. TJL 1984, s 8A(2) also confirms that no transfer or disposition of property is affected by rules relating to inheritance or succession (including forced heirship etc). Plainly TJL 1984, s 8A(2)(b) applies in relation to a transfer or disposition governed in all respects by Jersey law; it is less clear whether it has any effect in relation to a transfer or disposition which, according to Jersey's conflict of laws rules, is governed in whole or part by the laws of other states, perhaps for the reason that the property is situate outside Jersey. A further uncertainty has already been noted, that TJL 1984, s 8A(2)(b) has limited scope and would not impede an heir whose complaint was not based on a foreign rule of inheritance or succession.

Other survivability issues

Presumably TJL 1984, s 8A(2) would be of assistance in the protection of the trust as regards the direct enforcement of heirs' rights, claims in tort and claims for restitution.

Guernsey[1]

The Trusts (Guernsey) Law 1989 (TGL 1989) was modelled on the Jersey legislation. The TGL 1989, like Jersey's TJL 1984, does not set out to provide a comprehensive system of rules concerning the exclusion/recognition of foreign law in trust-related matters. However, some of the major forced heirship questions have been addressed in the 1990 Amendment. These provisions do not follow the Jersey model. TGL 1989, s 11A(1) provides:

> 'Where a person (the "settlor") creates a Guernsey trust, or during his lifetime makes any transfer or disposition of property or any interest therein to a Guernsey trust –
>
> (a) neither the trust nor the transfer or disposition is invalidated by any foreign rule of forced heirship or by reason of the fact that the concept of trusts is unknown to or not admitted by the law of a jurisdiction other than Guernsey;
>
> (b) the settlor shall be deemed to have had capacity to create the trust or to make the transfer or disposition if he had capacity to do so under –
>
> (i) Guernsey law;
>
> (ii) the law of his domicile or nationality; or
>
> (iii) the proper law of the transfer or disposition.'

The settlor is deemed to have capacity to create the trust and to make the disposition of property if he has that capacity under Guernsey law, his domiciliary law, his national law or the proper law of the disposition. That provides plenty of validating choices and in many cases the settlor's capacity will, therefore, be beyond doubt. However, it seems that questions could none the less arise in some situations.

First, does 'the proper law of the transfer or disposition' mean that which the parties have selected to govern it or, alternatively, the system of law with which the transfer is most closely connected on an objective basis? If it is the former, does this mean that the settlor can confer capacity upon himself by choosing an appropriate proper law to govern the transfer and the trust? If so, what was the legislative purpose behind this rather complex rule? It seems that the 'proper law' alternative may have to be given the more restrictive interpretation.

Secondly, what is meant by the reference in TGL 1989, s 11A(1)(b) to 'Guernsey law'? Presumably this is a reference to Guernsey's domestic law, not including its conflict of laws rules; but are we to test for capacity under Guernsey's domestic law on the footing that there are no forced heirs or that the settlor's family enjoy the succession rights conferred by Guernsey's own forced heirship laws? – probably the latter. So what freedom of disposition do Guernseymen have under domestic Guernsey law?

In other respects the comments made above on Jersey apply to Guernsey, although it is noteworthy that TGL 1989, s 11A(1) does address directly the

---

1 See Pugh *The Administration of Foreign Estates* for details of Guernsey's forced heirship regime.

possibility that a foreign law governing some aspect of a property transfer does not know or admit the trust concept.

4.6.4 Group 4 – Belize, Bermuda and Cyprus

Belize

With the Trusts Act 1992 (TA 1992) Belize joins the group of offshore centres which have borrowed heavily from Jersey's landmark legislation, but it has not adopted Jersey's conflict-of-laws rules. Belize has not yet become a party to the Hague Convention on Trusts.

The TA 1992 does not set out to provide a comprehensive system of rules concerning the exclusion/recognition of foreign law in trust-related matters. However, the TA 1992 does deal with some of the major forced heirship questions.

Validity of the trust ('the rocket')

By virtue of TA 1992, s 4(1) an express choice of Belize law as the proper law of the trust appears to be effective regardless of the circumstances. Presumably questions concerning the validity and effect of a Belize trust are in general governed by Belize law, but it should not be assumed that foreign laws are totally excluded. For example, if a Belize trust were purportedly constituted of foreign immovable property, its validity and effect in the eyes of the Belize court would presumably be affected by the *lex situs*.

The settlor's title to the settled property

The TA 1992 does not appear to affect this issue. It is beyond the scope of this chapter to discuss Belize's law of property or related conflict of laws rules.

Validity of the disposition ('the rocket-launcher')

TA 1992, s 7(2)(b)(iv) implies that the settlor's capacity to create a trust is governed at least in part by the law of Belize. However, this provision raises several questions. Does it apply to all trusts, even testamentary trusts? On a strict reading it seems even to apply to a trust of which Belize law is not the proper law. More significantly, it is not clear that foreign law is entirely excluded in determining whether the settlor has capacity. With one possible exception (s 7(6) discussed below) the TA 1992 appears to provide no other rules concerning the exclusion/recognition of foreign law in relation to the validity of the disposition.

Other survivability issues

TA 1992, s 7(6) provides:

'Where a trust is created under the law of Belize, the court shall not vary it or set it aside or recognise the validity of any claim against the trust property pursuant to the law of another jurisdiction or the order of the court of another jurisdiction in respect of –

(a) the personal or proprietary consequences of marriage or the termination of marriage;
(b) succession rights (whether testate or intestate) including the fixed shares of spouses or relatives; or
(c) the claims of creditors in an insolvency.'

A number of points should be noted in relation to TA 1992, s 7(6):

(1) Presumably it applies to a trust of which the proper law is that of Belize pursuant to TA 1992, s 4. Possibly it applies only if that was the original proper law, not in a case in which a non-Belize trust has 'moved' to Belize.
(2) It seems probable that TA 1992, s 7(6) is concerned only with Belize trusts which have been validly created. If so, it would not be of assistance in relation to an heir complaining that the trust had never been validly created or that trust property had never been validly transferred into the trust. There are two reasons for this view. First, the terminology of TA 1992, s 7(6) appears to contemplate an existing trust. Secondly, if TA 1992, s 7(6) were concerned with the validity of the trust and the transfer of property to it, there would presumably be some exceptions, at least in the case of a testamentary trust or a trust in respect of foreign immovables.
(3) It appears that the main purpose and effect of TA 1992, s 7(6) is to deal with restitutionary claims by the settlor's heirs (as well as spouses and creditors), and also attempts by the heirs to enforce foreign judgments in Belize. It is not clear to what extent TA 1992, s 7(6) would impede enforcement of a foreign judgment whose effect upon the trust was indirect, for example a judgment requiring trust beneficiaries to compensate the settlor's heirs. Presumably TA 1992, s 7(6) eliminates any prospect of the heirs bringing an action in Belize to enforce their succession rights or, indeed, making a successful claim in tort.

Bermuda

The Trusts (Special Provisions) Act 1989 (TSPA 1989) appears to have derived some inspiration from the Hague Convention on Trusts and some from the Cayman Islands' TFEL 1987. Bermuda is a party to the Hague Convention and England's Recognition of Trusts Act 1987 has been extended to Bermuda by the Recognition of Trusts Act 1987 (Overseas Territories) Order 1989. Accordingly Bermuda has two pieces of legislation covering the same topics. Although in general terms the TSPA 1989 seems consistent with the mandatory provisions of the Convention, this duality may perhaps cause some confusion.[1]

Validity of the trust ('the rocket')

From TSPA 1989, s 5 it appears that an express choice of Bermuda law to govern the trust is effective regardless of circumstances. TSPA 1989, s 7 establishes that Bermuda law will then govern the validity of the trust. Surprisingly there seem to be no exceptions to this rule but, as noted below, it may be that the exceptions in TSPA 1989, s 10(2) apply for this purpose.

The settlor's title to the settled property

The TSPA 1989 appears not to affect this issue. TSPA 1989, s 10(2)(a) seems to confirm that pre-existing conflict of laws rules are to be applied.

Validity of the transfer ('the rocket-launcher')

The question of the settlor's capacity is dealt with by TSPA 1989, s 10 in which there appears to be a degree of inconsistency between subs (1) and subs (2). However, as the former is said to be subject to the latter, it appears that subs (1) is of little or no effect. The upshot is that capacity is governed by the law of Bermuda without reference to the law of any other jurisdiction, subject to stated exceptions. The list of exceptions is in one sense predictable[2] – referring, for example, to the *lex situs* in regard to immovable property, the testator's domiciliary law in the case of a testamentary trust and to the constituent law of a corporate settlor. In another sense, however, the list of exceptions is puzzling – it goes beyond what would normally be regarded as matters of 'capacity'. In the interests of survivability it is to be hoped that s 10(2) will be regarded by the Bermuda court as applying not merely to the question of capacity but also to other aspects of the validity of the disposition. The TSPA 1989 appears to have no other rules concerning the exclusion/recognition of foreign law in relation to the validity of the disposition.

Other survivability issues

TSPA 1989, s 11 is similar in most respects to the TA 1992, s 7(6) of Belize discussed above; and the same comments apply. However, TSPA 1989, s 11 has the additional closing words:

---

1 Note that TSPA 1989, s 2 incorporates Art 2 of the Convention. Read out of their Convention context these provisions could on a literal interpretation have a significant impact on Bermuda's domestic trust law. One suspects that the Bermudian court would recognise the origin of TSPA 1989, s 2 and treat it as a matter of conflict of laws only.

2 It is derived from the Cayman Islands' TFEL 1987, s 5.

'... unless the law of Bermuda has corresponding laws or public policy rules.'

In relation to succession rights Bermuda has a judicial adjustment regime in the Succession Act 1974 comparable to that of England. So what is the effect of the closing words of TSPA 1989, s 11? Will the judicial adjustment regimes of other states be enforced – directly or by enforcement of foreign judgments? If so, what would be regarded as the crucial link with the foreign judicial adjustment regime – domicile at death, perhaps, or at the time of settlement, or perhaps any link which the foreign regime treated as sufficient? What of forced heirship regimes? Might the forced heir's claim be recognised, or a foreign judgment enforced, if it seemed comparable in amount to the award that a Bermuda court might have made under the domestic regime? The Succession Act 1974, s 12(1) defines 'net estate' to include property over which the individual had a general power, presumably including property held in a revocable trust; so will foreign forced heirship rights be recognised in relation to revocable Bermuda trusts?

Since the enactment of the TSPA 1989 one forced heirship case has come before the Bermuda courts. *Garner v Bermuda Trust Company Ltd*[1] concerned a trust set up in 1979 by a settlor who allegedly was domiciled in Mexico at all times from then until her death in 1989. The settlor's nephew asserted succession rights under Mexican law and argued that since the TSPA 1989 did not come into operation until 1990 the case should be decided without reference to the TSPA 1989. At the trial it was agreed to deal first with a preliminary question – whether the TSPA 1989 governed the trust. The Chief Justice decided that it did – not because the TSPA 1989 was retroactive but because it was merely declaratory of existing law. The nephew appealed. The Court of Appeal upheld the decision of the Chief Justice although, seemingly, for different reasons. From a juristic point of view it is a pity that the case was then settled out of court.

The two key passages in the judgment of the Court of Appeal were:

'The parties agreed to the trial of two preliminary issues and the matter came before the Chief Justice. After hearing some of the argument he althought that there was another issue which could more conveniently be tried as a preliminary point, and he asked counsel to confine their arguments to that issue, namely whether the Trusts (Special Provisions) Act 1989, governed the trust, for, if it did, that statute clearly provided (a) that this trust would be governed by Bermuda law and (b) that the trust could not be varied or set aside pursuant to the law of Mexico in respect of succession rights. The Chief Justice decided that the statute was as to this merely declaratory of the existing law and that the trust was governed by Bermuda law. It is against his decision on this point alone that the appeal comes to us.'

And later, as the reasons for its decision:

1 (Unreported) 3 March 1992 and 10 July 1992, but noted in [1992] 1 JIP 51 and [1992] 2 JIP 133.

> 'Counsel for the appellant was unable to point out to us in what respects the material part of the Act changed the law. Indeed, as regards section 10 we understood him to agree with Henry J.A. that his case was that the section did not so much change the law as states [sic] it only in part. As regards section 11 he said that there was previously no rule of law which prevented the Bermuda Courts from setting aside trusts in order to enforce succession rights under a foreign law. However, he did not show that either here or in England a court had ever set aside a trust in such circumstances, and we are not persuaded that there would have been power so to do.'

The judgment is perplexing in several respects, as follows.

(1) The lack of Bermudian or English cases in which trusts had been set aside was surely no basis for decision. There was an equal lack of cases in which trusts had been upheld in similar circumstances.

(2) There being no legislative or judicial statement of the pre-TSPA 1989 rules, how did the Court of Appeal compare the law before and after TSPA 1989 and decide that there had been no change? There is no indication in the judgments of the Chief Justice or the Court of Appeal that they undertook their own analysis of pre-TSPA 1989 authorities and principles.

(3) Why did the Chief Justice regard this preliminary point as an appropriate one? There seems to have been no doubt about the TSPA 1989's non-retroactivity, so why then embark on the large and difficult question of whether the TSPA 1989 changed the law? Why not simply apply the relevant pre-TSPA 1989 rules so as to dispose of this particular case? One suspects the problem was the difficulty of identifying the relevant pre-TSPA 1989 rules. But that takes us back to question (2) above. If the court could not identify the pre-TSPA 1989 rules, how could it decide that the TSPA 1989 was merely declaratory of them?

(4) The closing words of TSPA 1989, s 11 seem to have been ignored. If, as the Court of Appeal apparently believed, there was before TSPA no power to set aside trusts in order to give effect to foreign succession rights, TSPA 1989, s 11 changed the law by creating such a power – wherever 'the law of Bermuda has corresponding laws or public policy rules'. Bermuda's Succession Act 1974 establishes a judicial adjustment regime on English lines and at s 21 gives the court power to set aside lifetime disposition made within three years before death with the intent of defeating claims under the Act. Indeed, if the settlor reserves a general power of appointment over the trust property (as the settlor did in the *Garner* case) the Succession Act 1974[1] enables it to be set aside regardless of how long before the settlor's death it was made and regardless of the settlor's motive.

---

1 Section 12(1): definition of 'net estate'.

(5) Why was it the nephew who argued against the application of TSPA 1989, s 11? The Mexican regime under which he made his claim is comparable in several respects to Bermuda's judicial adjustment regime. Perhaps the nephew's advisers althought there were even better prospects of success in exploiting the uncertainty of the pre-TSPA 1989 rules.

In criticising the *Garner* judgments it is only fair to note that the courts were wrestling with a problem which the Bermuda legislature could have avoided or resolved. In borrowing from the Cayman Islands' TFEL 1987, the legislature for some reason elected to omit the section giving the new legislation retroactive effect. Existing trusts were left unprotected – if anything, worse off than before the TSPA 1989. It must be a source of some relief to Bermuda's trust industry and the beneficiaries of pre-1990 trusts that the judiciary grasped the nettle.

Cyprus

The International Trusts Law 1992 (ITL 1992), although a latecomer to the field of offshore trust legislation, ploughs its own furrow. Cyprus is not at present a party to the Hague Convention on Trusts. Cyprus is a forced heirship jurisdiction but with the unusual feature that the applicable legislation exempts 'any person who is born or whose father was born in the United Kingdom or any of the self-governing Dominions'.[1]

The ITL 1992 does not set out to provide a comprehensive system of rules concerning the exclusion/recognition of foreign law in trust-related matters.

In terms of survivability the only significant provision is ITL 1992, s 3(1):

> 'A settlor who transfers or who in whatever manner disposes of assets to an International Trust shall be deemed to have the capacity to do so, if at the time of such transfer such person is of full age and of sound mind under the law of the country of which he is a permanent resident. The law relating to inheritance or succession in force in the Republic or in any other country shall not affect in any way the transfer or disposition referred to above or the validity of the International Trust.'

Validity of the trust ('the rocket')

The ITL 1992 is silent as to the choice or identification of the proper law of a trust. Assuming that Cyprus would look to English conflict-of-laws rules (pre-Recognition of Trusts Act 1987), that leads to a situation of some uncertainty. Presumably questions concerning the validity and effect of a Cyprus International Trust are in general governed by Cyprus law, but it should not be assumed that foreign laws are totally excluded – except as specifically provided by the latter part of ITL 1992, s 3(1). The validity of an International Trust is not affected by the inheritance or succession laws of any

---

1 The Wills and Succession Law (c 195), s 42.

country, including Cyprus itself. One supposes that there must be a few exceptions to ITL 1992, s 3(1). For example, in the case of a testamentary trust it would be strange to exclude all inheritance and succession laws. Evidently ITL 1992, s 3(1) has limited scope. It applies only if the heir's complaint is based on a law relating to inheritance or succession – not, for example, if the heir based his complaint on a rule of the settlor's domicile invalidating all trusts, or a rule of the *lex situs* of property restricting the creation of successive interests.

The settlor's title to the settled property

The ITL 1992 appears not to affect this issue. It is beyond the scope of this chapter to discuss Cyprus' law of property or related conflict-of-laws rules.

Validity of the disposition ('the rocket-launcher')

ITL 1992, s 3(1) establishes that capacity to make the transfer is referred to the law of the country[1] of which the settlor is a permanent resident – but only to determine whether he is of full age and of sound mind. It is also provided that the validity of the disposition is not affected by inheritance or succession laws of any country, Cyprus included. Plainly this applies in relation to a transfer or disposition governed in all respects by Cyprus law; it is less clear whether it has any effect in relation to a transfer or disposition which, according to Cyprus' conflict-of-laws rules, is governed in whole or part by the laws of other states – perhaps for the reason that the property is situated outside Cyprus. Another uncertainty, already noted, is that ITL 1992, s 3(1) has limited scope and would not impede an heir whose complaint was not based on a rule of inheritance or succession.

Other survivability issues

Presumably ITL 1992, s 3(1) would be of assistance in the protection of the trust as regards the direct enforcement of heirs' rights, claims in tort and claims for restitution.

The protection afforded by the ITL 1992 is restricted to 'international trusts'. The conditions for that status are described in ITL 1992, s 2 and include the requirement that 'at least one of the trustees for the time being is, during the whole duration of the trust, a permanent resident in the Republic'. The consequences of breaching this or other conditions is unstated. The cautious view would appear to be that all the conditions must be maintained, failing which international trust status will be lost automatically.

---

1 It is unusual in this context to refer to a 'country' because of the existence of multiple jurisdictions within one country, the United States, for example.

4.6.5 Group 5 – Liechtenstein

It is noted in *International Trust Laws*,[1] in relation to Liechtenstein, that heirs who have protected succession rights may challenge an *inter vivos* voluntary trust. According to Liechtenstein conflict of laws rules it is the settlor's national law which determines his capacity to create a trust and also governs his succession on death. It seems that the Liechtenstein court, whether applying its own forced heirship laws or those of another country, would not set aside the trust upon the application of the heir but would rather recognise that the heir had a pecuniary claim against the trustee. That distinction is not likely to be of much comfort to those seeking to protect their trusts from the risk of attack by heirs. Evidently Liechtenstein could not be regarded as a suitable trust centre from that point of view.

4.7 SURVIVABILITY IN OTHER STATES

This section contains observations on a subject which evidently is too big to be discussed in a single chapter or even a single book.

4.7.1 In general

The conflict of laws rules of various states in relation to matters of succession are mentioned throughout **4.2**. The Hague Convention on Trusts and the draft Hague Convention on Succession are discussed throughout **4.8**. Numerous bilateral treaties exist between individual states concerning matters of succession.

As a very general rule of thumb it seems reasonable to suppose that the survivability of a trust in a common law state will be comparable to its survivability in England. There may well be some differences but the general picture is likely to be similar. However, that likelihood is reduced in the case of a state such as Scotland or South Africa which has mixed civil and common law origins.

On the other hand, it would seem reasonable to expect unsympathetic treatment from states which (a) have forced heirship regimes and claw-back rules comparable to those of the settlor's succession law, and (b) agree with the heirs' identification of the settlor's succession law. The second element is important since there is so much division in the world over whether it is the settlor's national law, domiciliary law or law of habitual residence that governs succession to movables.

---

1 Note 2 on p 166, paras A17.27 and A17.85.

Evidently the foregoing categories will not exhaust the world and there will be a large residual group in which the trust's survivability must be regarded as uncertain pending investigation.

4.7.2 The United States[1]

The United States deserve particular mention in this context partly because of their importance in relation to trustee investments and partly because they are trust jurisdictions whose conflict-of-laws rules have, by comparison with England's, received much more attention from legislators, judges and commentators.

More attention does not necessarily mean more clarity and, to the English eye at least, the situation is confusing in some respects. The States[2] do not all have the same conflict-of-laws rules. There are important statutory differences and, so far as the judiciary is concerned, there may well be different policy considerations from State to State.

Another potential cause of misunderstanding by the English observer is that the American approach to conflict of laws is different. The English approach, at least so far as the commentators are concerned, is to seek definite non-discretionary rules. The aim is that a court, having identified the issues at stake, need only apply the rules in a mechanical way to find out which system of law should govern each issue. Of course that is only an ideal; and it is not always entirely clear that the ideal is shared by the judiciary. Be that as it may, it is exceptional for the English court to deliberate openly upon the policy considerations of a choice of law and, in theory at least, the court's choice is not affected by its view of which choice would produce the better result.

By contrast, the American courts and commentators appear to eschew non-discretionary rules. The choice of law is made by reference to general principles, policy considerations and, it seems, the appropriateness of the consequences. There are, to be sure, some general rules, but courts feel at liberty to depart from them if the circumstances of the case appear to warrant a departure. Furthermore, it is a recurrent theme in relation to a wide variety of conflict-of-laws issues that the court looks for the system of law which has the 'most significant relationship' to the transaction or property in question. That gives the court considerable leeway to justify whatever result seems most appropriate in the circumstances of the case.

Although the Restatement of the Law (Second) Conflict of Laws is not an authoritative statement of the law in any part of the United States, it is

---

1 M Glenn Vinson Jr of Coudert Brothers, San Francisco, assisted in reviewing and commenting upon this section.

2 In this section 'State' with a capital 'S' means a state of the United States.

influential as a secondary source of law. Rule 6 of the Restatement describes general conflict-of-laws principles in the following terms:

> '6. *Choice of Law Principles*
>
> (1) A court, subject to constitutional restrictions, will follow a statutory directive of its own state on choice of law.
>
> (2) When there is no such directive, the factors relevant to the choice of the applicable rule of law include
>
> (a) the needs of the interstate and international systems,
> (b) the relevant policies of the forum,
> (c) the relevant policies of other interested states and the relative interests of those states in the determination of the particular issue,
> (d) the protection of justified expectations,
> (e) the basic policies underlying the particular field of law,
> (f) certainty, predictability and uniformity of result, and
> (g) ease in the determination and application of the law to be applied.'

In matters of succession to movables the general rule[1] is that the testator's law of domicile[2] governs, but in many States the testator is allowed some freedom of choice; and it seems that the choice may be upheld even although the result is to avoid the claims of forced heirs. In New York, for example, the Estates, Powers and Trusts Law provides:

> '*3-5.1 Formal validity, intrinsic validity, effect, interpretation, revocation or alteration of testamentary dispositions of, and exercise of testamentary powers of appointment over property by wills having relation to another jurisdiction.*
>
> ...
>
> (h) Whenever a testator, not domiciled in this state at the time of death, provides in his will that he elects to have the disposition of his property situated in this state governed by the laws of this state, the intrinsic validity, including the testator's general capacity, effect, interpretation, revocation or alteration of any such disposition is determined by the local law of this state. The formal validity of the will, in such case, is determined in accordance with paragraph (c).'

This legislation has been tested in court. The best known cases are *In re Estate of Clark*[3] and *In re Estate of Renard*.[4] In *Clark* a choice of New York law failed against the testator's surviving spouse claiming her elective rights under the law of Virginia (where the testator had been domiciled) to movable property in New York (securities on deposit with a New York bank). In *Renard* a choice of New York law succeeded against the testator's son claiming forced heirship rights conferred by the law of France (where the testator had been domiciled) to movable property in New York (bank and brokerage accounts in New York). It should be noted that in *Renard* the testator did have substantial

---

1 For example, Restatement, para 260. The general rule for succession to land is that the *lex situs* governs.
2 This section does not concern itself with *renvoi*.
3 (1968) 21 NY 2d 478, 236 NE 2d 152, 288 NYS 2d 933.
4 (1982) 56 NY 2d 973, 439 NE 2d 341, 453 NYS 2d 625.

connections with New York. She had lived and worked there for 30 years before returning to the land of her birth, and had acquired and retained US citizenship. Moreover, her son was a resident of California rather than France. None the less the court's decision appears to have been a matter of statutory interpretation rather than an assessment of the respective interests of France and New York. The court distinguished *Clark* because of a change in the New York legislation which at first instance and on appeal was regarded as crucial.[1] It may well be that the amended New York legislation would also enable the rights of a surviving spouse to be avoided.[2]

Four[3] other States have similar legislation, and another group of 15 States has adopted the Uniform Probate Code 2-602:

> '2-602. *[Choice of Law as to Meaning and Effect of Wills.]*
> The meaning and legal effect of a disposition in a will shall be determined by the local law of a particular state selected by the testator in his instrument unless the application of that law is contrary to the provisions relating to the elective share described in Part 2 of this Article, the provisions relating to exempt property and allowances described in Part 4 of this Article, or any other public policy of this State otherwise applicable to the disposition.'

According to a survey[4] conducted in 1981, shortly after the *Renard* decision, a large number of States might have reached the same decision without the benefit of statute. It does appear that there may be a significant difference in judicial attitude depending on whether the claim is by a surviving spouse or, alternatively, a child or other relative.

From the above, one might guess that in relation to trusts and other dispositions *inter vivos* the American courts would be even less inclined to countenance interference by forced heirs. It is not clear that this is so. The cases[5] seem to show no clear trend although it again appears that the courts may look more favourably on the interests of surviving spouses than children or other relatives.

The Restatement[6] suggests at §270 that:

---

1 *Clark* turned on Decedent Estate Law §47, re-enacted with the crucial modification in EPTL §3-5.1(h).

2 Although the spouse would then have the benefit of New York's own elective rights regime: EPTL §5-1.1(d)(7).

3 Connecticut, New Jersey, Florida and Illinois.

4 Robert A Hendrickson 'Choice of Law Directions for Disposing of Assets Situated Elsewhere than the Domicile of their Owner – The Refractions of Renard' (1983) 18(2) *Real Property Probate and Trust Journal* 407.

5 For the cases and analysis of them see, eg, *Scott on Trusts* (4th ed), paras 587–603 or Schoenblum *Multistate and Multi National Estate Planning*, Chs 10 and 12.

6 It seems the Restatement may reflect a position towards the less sympathetic end of the American spectrum, so far as the survivability of trusts is concerned.

'An *inter vivos* trust of interests in movables is valid if valid –

> (a) under the local law of the state designated by the settlor to govern the validity of the trust, provided that this state has a substantial relation to the trust and that the application of its law does not violate a strong public policy of the state with which, as to the matter at issue, the trust has its most significant relationship under the principles stated in §6, or
> (b) if there is no such effective designation, under the local law of the state with which, as to the matter at issue, the trust has its most significant relationship under the principles stated in §6.'

The Restatement comments in relation to §270 that 'where the settlor creates a revocable trust in a state other than that of his domicile, in order to avoid the application of the local law of his domicile giving his surviving spouse a forced share of his estate, it may be held that the local law of his domicile is applicable, even although he has designated as controlling the local law of the state in which the trust is created and administered'. No mention is made of children or other relatives as forced heirs. Indeed it is noteworthy that the comment refers to a revocable trust; would the compilers of the Restatement take the same view of an irrevocable trust?

Again some States have enacted legislation to clarify their conflict of laws rules in relation to trusts and other *inter vivos* transactions. For example, New York's Estates, Powers and Trusts Law provides:

> '7-1.10 *Provision by non-domiciliary creator as to law to govern trust*
>
> (a) Whenever a person, not domiciled in this state, creates a trust which provides that it shall be governed by the laws of this state, such provision shall be given effect in determining the validity, effect and interpretation of the disposition in such trust of:
> (1) Any trust property situated in this state at the time the trust is created.
> (2) Personal property, wherever situated, if the trustee of the trust is a person residing, incorporated or authorised to do business in this state or a national bank having an office in this state.'

A significant body of legislation has developed in relation to 'Totten trusts' – a concept which to English eyes appears to be a cross between a trust and a joint bank account. Florida amended its legislation on this subject as a result of a decision at first instance in favour of forced heirs. In *Sanchez v Sanchez de Davila*[1] children claimed forced heirship rights under Venezuelan law in respect of a Totten trust constituted at a Miami bank by their father in his lifetime for the benefit of some but not all of his children. The father had died. At first instance the court delivered a number of trenchant remarks which are interesting for their analysis of forced heirship:

> 'The decedent lacked the ability to create a valid Totten trust in Florida if the laws of Venezuela are applied. The decedent brought the property from his domicile, Venezuela. He

[1] (1989) 547 So 2d 943.

> was not only in fact but in law a trustee under Venezuelan law of all his property for the benefit of all his children. The laws of his domicile prohibited him from fraudulently dispossessing any of his heirs. The vested remainder in fee simple was in all fourteen children, in equal shares. The vested remainder is indestructible under the provisions of the Venezuelan Civil Code, section 1435.
>
> Of course, the decedent could have spent the money. He could have gambled it away and as long as he lived, could have used it in any manner, except that he could not give his money away by selecting two of his fourteen heirs. At the time of his death, under Venezuelan law, the vested remainder was in all of his heirs. Every one of the children of the decedent had a right to possession of his or her full ownership of their respective shares. See Venezuelan Civil Code, section 883.
>
> Through some magic, not clearly explained, the two children of the decedent seemed to think that the passage of the money from Venezuela to an ITF account in an American bank would cleanse the money of any right to distribution under the Venezuelan law.'

The Florida Legislature reacted with speed and clarified retroactively the relevant provision, section 655.55, Florida Statutes (Supp 1988). On appeal the decision at first instance was overturned on the footing that it was well settled law, confirmed by statute, that the disposition of a joint bank account is governed by the law of the *situs* of the account regardless of the domicile of the parties. Unfortunately the Appeal Court did not comment on the analysis of Venezuelan forced heirship but it appears to be a necessary implication that the Appeal Court rejected the view of the lower court that the decedent was by operation of Venezuelan law a trustee of all his property for the benefit of all his children.

4.8 SURVIVABILITY IN FUTURE – THE CONVENTIONS

4.8.1 Hague Convention on the Law Applicable to Trusts and on Their Recognition 1985

The Hague Convention on Trusts has become effective and has to date[1] been ratified by Australia, Canada (as to certain Provinces only), Italy and the United Kingdom. The United Kingdom has ratified on behalf of itself and some, but not all, of its dependent territories.[2] A number of other states have signed but not ratified the Convention; these are France, Luxembourg, The Netherlands and the United States.

Whether or not the Convention is widely ratified by trust states or non-trust states, it will not assist the survivability of trusts against forced heirship attacks. Some believe that the Convention is neutral in this respect; there are

---

1 1 May 1993.

2 The Isle of Man, Bermuda, British Antarctic Territory, the British Virgin Islands, the Falkland Islands, Gibraltar, St Helena, St Helena Dependencies, South Georgia and the South Sandwich Islands, United Kingdom Sovereign Base Areas of Akrotiri and Dhekelia in the Island of Cyprus, Hong Kong, Montserrat and Jersey.

those, the writer included, who consider it may have a prejudicial effect on survivability.

The most important features of the Convention from this point of view are:

(1) Article 15 permits contracting states to apply their own laws or those of other states against the trust in so far as they relate to certain matters. The list includes succession rights ('succession rights, testate and intestate, especially the indefeasible shares of spouses and relatives'). This feature by itself largely puts an end to any notion that the Convention might assist survivability.

(2) Article 4 stipulates that the Convention does not apply to 'preliminary issues relating to the validity of wills or of other acts by virtue of which assets are transferred to the trustee'. This is explained most succinctly in Underhill and Hayton *Law of Trusts and Trustees*:[1]

> 'Just as a rocket launcher is needed to launch a rocket so some instrument or act is necessary to get a trust off the ground. Only when the trust has been launched does the Convention apply: it does not apply to antecedent issues of form, capacity or validity which may vitiate the instrument or act which purports to subject assets to a trust.'

Contracting states can, and presumably will, apply their pre-existing conflict of laws rules in deciding whether the rocket was successfully launched into space – or whether it merely fizzled like a damp squib.

Whether the Convention is harmful to survivability is more debatable. If an otherwise sympathetic forum were considering the enforcement of a foreign judgment giving effect to the claims of a forced heir, it appears to this writer that the public policy argument against enforcement would be weakened by the Convention – assuming the forum had become a party to the Convention. The argument would be that there was an inconsistency between (a) the forum being party to an international agreement which expressly gives liberty to the courts of other states to apply forced heirship rules against trusts (even trusts constituted under the laws of the forum), and (b) the forum regarding as contrary to its public policy the enforcement of a judgment given by a foreign court exercising that liberty. That not everyone agrees with the writer's views on this matter is evident from the fact that several offshore centres have become party to the Convention.[2] Perhaps the counter-argument is that contracting states are not agreeing that foreign courts may apply forced heirship rules against trusts, merely acknowledging that there are limits to the commitments of other states to recognise trusts.

---

1 Note 3 on p 169, p 830.

2 See DJ Hayton, n 1 on p 157, pp 1–17.

4.8.2 The draft Hague Convention on the Law Applicable to Succession to the Estates of Deceased Persons

This draft Convention is not yet effective. It has not been ratified by any state.

In relation to the survivability of trusts, testamentary or *inter vivos*, this Convention could not possibly be regarded as neutral. There are three main features which are important in this respect, two are beneficial and one is seriously prejudicial:

(a) greater harmony in the conflict of laws rules of different states concerning matters of succession;
(b) limited freedom for the individual to choose his succession law;
(c) application of the claw-back rules of the succession law.

The first of these three features needs little further explanation. The Convention provides rules for identifying the succession law of a deceased individual.[1] Estates and trusts would be saved from the kinds of dispute which arise when more than one state asserts governance over an individual's succession. The example given earlier in this chapter was that of the individual who is a national of Japan (which regards succession as a matter for the national law), but is habitually resident in France (which regards succession as a matter of the law of habitual residence). The Convention rules would point to France if the individual had been resident there for a period of no less than five years immediately preceding his death[2] – and otherwise to Japan. Of course the Convention would not serve this beneficial purpose unless the forum or fora in which the heirs might seek to assert their claims were parties to the Convention.

The second feature, freedom of choice, may have benefits for individuals wishing to create trusts, testamentary or *inter vivos*. By making a choice the settlor/testator may be able to remove or reduce the risk of an attack by his heirs. However, the choice is limited. The individual must choose between his national law and the law of his habitual residence. The choice must be made using will-formalities. It seems that a choice is not invalidated by the individual subsequently changing his nationality or place of residence. This does suggest that whenever a trust is created *inter vivos*, and whenever a will is executed including provision for a testamentary trust, the individual should consider a formal choice of succession law – whichever of the alternatives seems at the time more favourable in terms of the trust's validity and survivability. If circumstances changed, the individual could make a new choice.

The third and most difficult feature of the Convention is its effect in relation to claw-back. It appears that contracting states would be required by

---

1 Article 3 contains the principal provisions. Depending upon the circumstances Art 3 points either to the deceased's national law or alternatively the law of his habitual residence.

2 Unless he was manifestly more closely connected with Japan.

the Convention to give effect to the claw-back rules of the succession law. The crucial Article reads as follows:

> 'Article 7
>
> (1) Subject to Article 6, the applicable law under Articles 3 and 5, paragraph 1, governs the whole of the estate of the deceased wherever the assets are located.
>
> (2) This law governs –
>
> (a) the determination of the heirs, devisees and legatees, the respective shares of those persons and the obligations imposed upon them by the deceased, as well as other succession rights arising by reason of death including provision by a court or other authority out of the estate of the deceased in favour of persons close to the deceased;
> (b) disinheritance and disqualification by conduct;
> (c) any obligation to restore or account for gifts, advancements or legacies when determining the shares of heirs, devisees or legatees;
> (d) the disposable part of the estate, indefeasible interests and other restrictions on dispositions of property upon death;
> (e) the material validity of testamentary dispositions.
>
> (3) Paragraph 2 does not preclude the application in a contracting state of the law applicable under this Convention to other matters which are considered by that state to be governed by the law of succession.'

If that language leaves any room for doubt, the *Official Report* at para 79 states that Art 7(2)(d) of the Convention:

> '... does cover issues as to what part of the estate the deceased is free to distribute to whom he will, and attempts by the deceased – in his lifetime or by his will or agreements as to succession – to avoid reserve, legitime, forced shares or judicial discretionary allocation of assets to immediate family members. This would include a situation where the deceased in his lifetime responds to an advertisement from a tax haven (a non-contracting state) that he deposit assets in an investment device in the haven, and thereby avoid family protection legislation in his home jurisdiction.'

That seems to put the point beyond doubt. Indeed, it follows from other provisions than Art 7(2)(d). For example, Art 7(2)(a) refers to 'other succession rights arising by reason of death'. Those words seem sufficiently wide to encompass all the rights which upon an individual's death are conferred upon his heirs – including claw-back rights. Article 7(2)(c) appears also to contemplate claw-back, although it could be restrictively interpreted to apply only to claw-back from heirs, devisees or legatees.

The only provision of the Convention which casts any doubt on the conclusion is Art 1(2)(d):

'The Convention does not apply to –

...

(d) property rights, interests or assets created or transferred otherwise than by succession, such as in joint ownership with right of survival, pension plans, insurance contracts, or arrangements of similar nature.'

The meaning of Art 1(2)(d) obviously turns on the phrase 'otherwise than by succession' and this begs the question – what is 'succession'? To the common lawyer the expression may have a restricted connotation, being concerned solely with the fate of the property owned by the individual at the moment of his death;[1] but to the civil lawyer it encompasses everything which passes to the heirs by reason of death, including claw-back rights if the deceased has made excessive lifetime dispositions. It is not through mere oversight that the Convention fails to define 'succession'. As the *Official Report* acknowledges (at paras 39 and 74), Art 7 must be treated as providing the functional definition of the word. One must conclude that claw-back is brought within the Convention by Art 7 and is not excluded by Art 1(2)(d). The function of Art 1(2)(d) seems to be quite simply to exclude from the Convention a lifetime disposition as to which the question or complaint is that it is in effect a will-substitute. But if the question or complaint is that the lifetime disposition has encroached on the entitlements of forced heirs, that is a different matter; Art 7(2) applies and Art 1(2)(d) has no effect.

Given the Convention's objectives, as described in the *Official Report*, it is no surprise that the draft Convention affects lifetime dispositions retrospectively in the manner suggested. At para 26 of the *Report* it is described as 'a central aim' of the Convention 'that family protection laws against disinheritance of the surviving spouse or children be honoured'. In para 29 it is said:

'In summary then this Convention is concerned with harmonising the choice of law rules of succession, to protect the inheritance expectations of the deceased's immediate family, to simplify and render less costly the distribution of the deceased's assets when they are in several jurisdictions and, where possible, to assist the testator's orderly distribution of his assets upon death (i.e. estate planning).'

Those stated aims might be regarded as completely uncontroversial viewed in relation to the property owned by an individual at the time of his death. Viewed in relation to the property dispositions made by him during his entire lifetime, they take on a different and much less agreeable aspect.

Presumably a state deciding whether to sign or ratify the Convention will consider whether its interest in protecting inheritance expectations (under its

---

1 But note the anti-avoidance features of common law judicial adjustment regimes constituting a form of discretionary claw-back; also extended concepts of 'estate', see, eg, England's Inheritance (Provision for Family and Dependants) Act 1975, s 25(1).

own law or that of foreign states) outweighs the other interests at stake. In particular a state has an interest in minimising retrospective interference with property transactions. This is especially the case when the retrospective interference is by a foreign law – one with which the transaction may have had no link whatever at the time it was effected. It is especially the case when the retrospective interference is unmitigated by judicial discretion. The risk of claw-back would be a blot on many titles. The state also has an interest in enabling charitable and other donations to be made and used without the recipient running a risk of claims for compensation from the donor's heirs.

It is not even clear that 'equity's darling', the *bona fide* purchaser for value without notice, would be safe from claw-back by the heirs of prior owners for he would presumably be taken to know of their inchoate rights,[1] but at this point, if not before, it is possible that a common law court might invoke Art 18 which provides:

> 'The application of any of the laws determined by the Convention may be refused only where such application would be manifestly incompatible with public policy (*ordre public*).'

Presumably a court would only feel free to invoke Art 18 in extreme situations. To apply it generally whenever a claw-back claim was made by an heir would undermine a major element of the Convention.

For the trust industry, offshore and onshore, the Convention would be a major setback. A contracting state would have to be regarded as equally unsuitable both as a trust domicile and as a place for investement by trusts.

4.9 PLANNING NOTES

The planning requirements for a proposed trust will vary from case to case, depending on the circumstances and the legal systems involved. The purpose of this section is to indicate features which commonly deserve consideration – whether the risk of forced heirship attack is seen as a high probability or a slim possibility. No doubt more care will be taken if it is the former.

The planner's first step will normally be to identify the settlor's home state and consider what rights the settlor's heirs might seek to assert under its law. If there are alternative or conflicting possibilities for the home state, due regard should be given to each.

Planning considerations may then be grouped under the following headings:

- Planning to avoid giving the settlor's heirs any cause for complaint;

---

1 Although he might hope that under the applicable succession law the heirs' rights would shift entirely and unconditionally from the property to the purchase price paid.

- Planning to discourage the settlor's heirs from making a complaint;
- Planning to ensure survivability in the trust domicile;
- Planning to encourage sympathetic treatment in other states;
- Planning to minimise exposure to unsympathetic states;
- Tactical considerations.

4.9.1 Planning to avoid giving the settlor's heirs any cause for complaint

(a) Permitted adjustments

Most forced heirship regimes do allow some freedom of action even as regards the reserved portion. For example, it may be legitimate to make dispositions in favour of the settlor's spouse. It may be legitimate to defer the forced heirs' receipt or enjoyment of the reserved portion. Thus it may be possible to construct a trust which meets the settlor's requirements and is substantially consistent with the rules of the home state.

(b) Immovables

If the home state acknowledges that succession to foreign immovables (including questions of forced heirship) is governed by the *lex situs*, the settlor might consider placing his foreign immovables in trust – alalthough this might have the effect of enlarging the forced heirs' claim to his other property. Whether the acquisition of foreign immovables for the purpose of gaining security from forced heirship attack would be recognised in the home state may be another matter. Another question answerable only by reference to a particular succession law is whether the trust would become exposed to attack if the immovable property were sold before the settlor's death. Immovables are worth consideration for another reason, that in some forced heirship regimes the heirs have different rights according to whether the property in question is movable or immovable.

(c) Agreement with the heirs

Consider obtaining the prospective heirs' agreement to the proposed trust, if such agreement would be recognised in the home state. Regimes which permit succession agreements generally impose special conditions and formalities which need to be observed with care. If there are alternative or conflicting home states, it may be as well to observe the requirements of both regimes.

(d) Claw-back conditions

As many claw-back rules have effect for a limited period (only affecting lifetime dispositions made within a certain period before the individual's death) it may be possible to construct a trust which after a period of time will become safe from attack. Care needs to be taken, however, that there are no other snags in the claw-back rule. For example, if there is an unlimited claw-back for dispositions in which the individual has reserved an interest, the settlor may be well advised to create two separate trusts – one in which he reserves an interest and one in which he has no interest. At least the latter may become safe from attack if the settlor survives long enough.

(e) Hague Convention on Succession

The draft Hague Convention on Succession contemplates that the individual will have a limited choice of succession law. The choice is between his national law and the law of his habitual residence. Evidently the settlor should consider exercising that choice if one law is more favourable than the other. If the less favoured state ratifies the Convention, the heirs will presumably be prevented from claiming under that state's law.

4.9.2 Planning to discourage the settlor's heirs from making a complaint

(a) Agreement with the heirs

Even if an agreement. with the heirs would not be valid according to the succession law, it may serve to discourage heirs from making a complaint.

(b) Heirs as beneficiaries

If, as is usual, the prospective heirs are also to be beneficiaries of the trust, the terms of the trust may be constructed to discourage attack. At its simplest, a term may be included which terminates the interest of a beneficiary who attacks the trust – although the settlor may well feel that this is going too far. Under English law on the basis of rather old judicial authority[1] such clauses may be valid and effective, but care is needed in the drafting. It is not generally a good plan to give the trustee a discretion to decide whether or not the clause should take effect. In self-protection a trustee would probably need to apply to the court for directions and it is not clear what directions a court might give.

4.9.3 Planning to ensure survivability in the trust domicile

Evidently the first planning requirement under this heading is to choose a suitable trust domicile. There are likely to be other factors but survivability does vary from one offshore centre to another – as discussed throughout **4.6**.

Thereafter the planning considerations will depend on which offshore centre has been chosen, but they are likely to include the following.

1 *Cooke v Turner* (1846) 15 M&W 727; *Adams v Adams* [1892] 1 Ch 369.

(a) Situs of property

Desirably the trust property will be situate in the trust domicile at the time the trust is created. If the trust domicile does not have clear exclusionary rules (excluding the application of foreign law in relation to property transfers), it is particularly important to arrange and document the transfer so as to remove all grounds for referring to unsympathetic (or doubtfully sympathetic) foreign laws; but no trust domicile completely excludes foreign law. As regards movables, foreign formalities (at least) will probably have to be observed. As regards immovables, the trust domicile is likely to refer all issues to the *lex situs*. Consider placing foreign property in a company incorporated in the trust domicile; the settlor then transfers to the trustee the shares and debt (if any) of the company, not the foreign property. The trust property should remain situate in the trust domicile or in some other reliably sympathetic jurisdiction.

(b) Trustee's foreign links

Ensure that the trustee has no significant links with another state which is unsympathetic or whose sympathy is uncertain. Otherwise the trust domicile might enforce a foreign judgment against the trustee. The same consideration may apply to the protector, if any, especially if the protector has extensive powers.

(c) Care in the case of will-substitutes

If the trust is in the nature of a will-substitute take care to avoid any suggestion that it is a disguised testamentary disposition.

4.9.4 Planning to encourage sympathetic treatment in other states

(a) Agreement with the heirs

Again the agreement of the prospective heirs, even if technically invalid under the succession law, may be highly significant as regards a state whose sympathy for the trust might otherwise be in doubt.

(b) Maximise the links with the trust domicile

This is a most important consideration. It is liable to improve survivability in a variety of respects. For example, close links with the trust domicile will improve survivability in all states which seek the 'closest connection' or which, like the United States, may undertake a balancing of interests between those of the trust domicile and those of the home state. Close links with the trust domicile will also reduce the risk of Art 13 of the Hague Convention on Trusts being invoked by contracting states.

(c) Minimise reservations

The settlor's reserved powers and interests should be kept to a minimum. If the settlor insists on reservations, consider establishing two trusts, one with reservations and one without. Reserved powers and interests may encourage the forum to regard the arrangement as testamentary or evasive. If the reserved powers are extensive, they may affect the forum's view of where the trust administration is conducted.

(d) Immovable possibilities

Immovable property may be of significance in this context – see **4.9**.

(e) Hague Convention on Succession

It may be worthwhile for the settlor to exercise his choice under the Convention even if neither of the states concerned is a party to the Convention. The choice could affect the sympathy of other states, especially those which do ratify the Convention.

4.9.5 Planning to minimise exposure to unsympathetic states

(a) Avoid all significant links

All significant links with unsympathetic states should be avoided if possible.

(b) Trustee links

It is particularly important that no trustee should have any significant link with unsympathetic states. For large trusts the incorporation of a private trust company may be worth consideration from this point of view.

(c) Discretionary trusts

If a link is unavoidable, minimise the resulting vulnerability. For example, offshore trusts are often linked to the home state by the fact that trust beneficiaries reside there. A discretionary trust may be preferable to a fixed interest trust for the reason that the heirs should then have difficulty in asserting that the beneficiaries had received a benefit (beyond distributions actually made to them) for which they should be required to provide compensation.

(d) Holding companies

If investments must be made in a state which is unsympathetic or whose sympathy is uncertain, they should normally be made by a company owned or controlled by the trust. Consider, however, the feasibility of heirs lifting the corporate veil in the investment state or the incorporation state. This is one reason why care should always be taken that holding companies operate properly as entities distinct from the trustee.

(e) Removal at death
Consider removing all property and investments, directly or indirectly held, from unsympathetic states on the settlor's death or if he suffers a serious accident or illness.

4.9.6 Tactical considerations

(a) Information and documents
Substantial information about the trust in a form which is admissible in evidence will probably be needed by any heir wishing to bring proceedings in respect of the trust. This is especially true of proceedings in civil law jurisdictions where in general the discovery process is unknown, the court will order production of documents only in limited circumstances, and the use of oral evidence tends to be restricted.[1]

Trust information may also be of importance in enabling heirs to locate investments or property with a view to bringing proceedings at the *situs* or enforcing an existing judgment there. Consider limiting the dissemination of trust information, especially in documentary form; and consider the inclusion of an appropriate provision in the trust instrument enabling the trustee to refuse demands for information and documents. The restriction should not apply only to those beneficiaries who are prospective heirs. Heirs may be able to obtain information and documents from other beneficiaries, and they may be able to enlist the aid of the settlor's personal representatives to obtain whatever was in the settlor's possession or control. Restrictive provisions of this sort require careful drafting in terms of their effectiveness and in relation to any argument that the transaction is a disguised testamentary disposition. A complete exclusion of the trustee's duty to account would probably be regarded as inconsistent with the trust concept.

(b) Trustee indemnity
Consideration should be given to the trustee's indemnity (express or implied) and that of any protector involved. If the indemnity is unqualified, the trustee may be more inclined to submit to the jurisdiction of a foreign court or to compromise with the forced heirs – on the basis that the trustee will be covered by its indemnity out of the trust assets.

(c) Settlement
If it appeared that a forced heirship attack stood a sufficient prospect of success, or was liable to cause substantial and irrecoverable legal expense, the trustee and the trust beneficiaries might be inclined to settle with the heirs. Unless the terms of the trust include an enabling power, a settlement involving the application of trust funds would generally be feasible only with the

---

1 See, eg, Platto *Trial and Court Procedures Worldwide.*

approval of adult beneficiaries and the sanction of the court. Consider inclusion of an enabling power, presumably with safeguards.

4.10 THE TRUSTEE

This section discusses the situation of a trustee in relation to forced heirship. The three main questions are as follows.

(1) May the trustee have liability to the heirs?
(2) What are the trustee's duties to the beneficiaries?
(3) What are the trustee's rights in terms of remuneration and reimbursement?

4.10.1 Liability to the heirs

This question has already been considered in terms of the survival of the trust. Earlier comments concerning survivability and the significance of links with unsympathetic states are equally applicable when considering the trustee's own interests. Much the same planning considerations apply for avoiding or reducing the risk.

4.10.2 Duties to the beneficiaries

The trustee has a duty to defend the trust property from adverse claims – presumably those of the settlor's heirs just as much as any others. It makes no difference whether the trustee considers the adverse claims are good or bad,[1] alalthough it appears that a trustee may apply to the court for relief. Plainly it would be an impossible situation for trustees, and counterproductive in terms of the interests of beneficiaries, if trustees were obliged to defend all adverse claims to the last ditch regardless of the odds.

More difficult is the question of what duties, if any, are implied on the part of trustees to avoid difficulties with the settlor's heirs. To give an extreme example, one presumes that a trustee would be liable who made an investment in the settlor's state knowing that the settlor had died and that the heirs were claiming that the trust encroached upon their entitlements. On the other hand, trustees are not insurers[2] and a trustee who made investments in an unsympathetic state, but with no reason to suppose that there would be a dispute with the settlor's heirs, would presumably not be liable for that decision – although there might be some question of whether the trustee should have disposed of the investments when it became aware that there

1 See Art 59, Underhill and Hayton, n 3 on p 169.
2 Article 55, Underhill and Hayton, n 3 on p 169.

would be a dispute with the settlor's heirs and that the investment state might be unsympathetic.

It seems probable that under English law and that of most offshore centres a trustee has a duty to preserve trust property from known risks of attack, just as much as it has a duty to defend trust property from an actual attack. The required standard of care is presumably the usual one – requiring the trustee to use such diligence and care in the management of the estate as men of ordinary prudence and vigilance would use in the management of their own affairs, a higher standard of diligence and knowledge being expected from paid trustees.[1]

Such a duty of care is all very well on paper but what does it really mean in practice? Should a trustee make efforts to assess the risk of forced heirship attack? Should it review the situation as the years go by, given that changes in the settlor's circumstances will assuredly affect the level of risk? On the settlor's demise should the trustee inform itself about the rights of the settlor's heirs? What action should the trustee take to ensure or enhance survivability? Survivability planning is a complex businees, certainly beyond the unassisted capabilities of most non-professional trustees. It involves expense and it may involve other trade-offs, such as selling or foregoing investments in otherwise desirable areas.

Pending judicial guidance one can only speculate. It appears to this writer that courts are likely to be lenient to trustees in this respect unless there is evidence that the trustee was in fact aware of the risk and the solution, and simply failed without good reason to act accordingly. Perhaps the court would be less lenient as regards losses suffered as a result of the trustee's own method of operations – if, for example, the trustee elected to conduct the trust administration in or from a probably unsympathetic state rather than the trust domicile. Perhaps the court's attitude would also depend on what representations, if any, were made by the trustee to the settlor at the time of the trust's creation concerning the safety of the trust from attack.

If the settlor's heirs or prospective heirs are beneficiaries of the trust, the trustee may encounter difficulties in terms of its duty to act impartially between the beneficiaries. To discriminate against a beneficiary on the grounds that he might make an adverse claim would presumably be reprehensible, but on the other hand a trustee presumably may, perhaps must, recognise realities. It would be unfortunate, to put it mildly, if the trustee gave an heir detailed information and substantial funds only to find that both were used to mount an attack against the trust and the interests of the other beneficiaries. Preferably with express sanction in the terms of the trust, the trustee should consider putting the beneficiary to his election, whether to take the benefits of the trust and relinquish adverse claims, or to attack the trust.

---

1 Article 54, Underhill and Hayton, n 3 on p 169.

Doubts about the trustee's duties may be reduced by appropriate provision in the terms of the trust.

4.10.3 Right to remuneration and reimbursement

It appears that normal considerations would apply. In England and most offshore centres a trustee would be well advised to seek a Beddoe order[1] from the court before appearing in or defending any proceedings in the trust domicile or elsewhere.

Reference has been made already to the significance of the trustee's indemnity in terms of vulnerability to unsympathetic states.

A prospective trustee who perceives a risk of forced heirship attack may wish to ensure that the charging provisions of the trust would enable fees to be charged for time spent in connection with the defence of the trust. If there seems to be a risk not only of attack but also of the trustee ending up out of pocket, the trustee may wish to think twice about accepting the trusteeship.

---

1 Article 86, Underhill and Hayton, n 3 on p 169, p 705.

Chapter 5

PROTECTORS

*Robert Ham QC**
*Emily Campbell**
*Michael Tennet**

5.1 INTRODUCTION

Historically, the term 'protector' in the context of settled property was used in the Fines and Recoveries Act 1833 to describe the owner of certain types of estate taking effect prior to an estate in tail. The provisions of the Act required the protector's consent to certain dispositions of the entailed land. The protector's discretion was very wide and the Act made it quite clear that the protector was not a fiduciary.[1]

In modern times, the term 'protector' has assumed a much wider meaning.[2] It is not a term of art and may have different meanings in different contexts. The term is usually used to describe a person, who is not one of the trustees of a trust, but upon whom the trust deed confers a 'watchdog' role in respect of the administration of the trust by the trustees. This watchdog role may be achieved in many ways. Often, the protector's consent is required to the exercise of administrative[3] or dispositive[4] powers by the trustees.[5] Occasionally, the protector is able to give directions to the trustees as to the exercise of their powers. At the other end of the scale, the trustees may simply be directed to consult with the protector prior to any exercise of their powers. Usually, the protector's watchdog role will be supplemented or enhanced by

---

* Wilberforce Chambers, Lincoln's Inn, London.

1 Fines and Recoveries Act 1833, s 36.

2 Other expressions are used from time to time, eg the 'Appointor', 'the appointed person', the 'guardian' or the 'specified person'.

3 Eg a power to insure or invest trust property.

4 Eg a power to appoint all or part of the trust fund to a beneficiary, or a power to accumulate income. For the distinction between a trustee's administrative and dispositive powers, see *Pearson v IRC* [1981] AC 753.

5 Or any other person in whom powers are vested pursuant to the terms of the trust deed.

incidental functions, of which the following serve as examples: the power to appoint and remove trustees,[1] which is almost always conferred upon the protector; the power to approve trustees' remuneration; and the power to require the production of trust accounts and to nominate the auditor.

Protectors are seldom found in onshore trusts, at any rate in the United Kingdom. In the context of such trusts, the settlor is usually able to retain some control over the exercise of the trustees' powers by acting as trustee himself, or by arranging for a trusted member of his family or adviser to do so. This simple solution is rarely available in the case of offshore trusts, although the settlor (or indeed his advisers) may be concerned about putting property into the hands of offshore trustees, far away, often in a different time zone, whom he does not personally know, without some mechanism to control them. Offshore trusts are generally established owing to the tax advantages associated with them. If the settlor and his family are resident in the United Kingdom, it is unlikely that any of them will be able to serve as trustee without prejudicing the tax status of the trust.[2] However, it may (although advice on this point must be taken in each case) be possible for the settlor[3] or a member of his family to act as protector of a trust without prejudicing its offshore tax status. Where this is not the case, the settlor may choose a friend, family member or adviser who is not resident in the United Kingdom to fulfil the role as protector, or may well wish an experienced offshore trust company to act as trustee.

The aim of the appointment of a protector is, therefore, to monitor the trustees in the administration of the trust, on one level to prevent those trustees from abusing their powers or breaching their duties, but also to ensure as far as possible that the trust is administered in accordance with the wishes of the settlor, at any rate in the case of the more important decisions and often on a day-to-day basis. Where, as is usual, the protector is given power to hire and fire trustees and to veto decisions, it is not unrealistic to regard the ultimate power as lying with the protector. If the protector is a member of the settlor's family or a close personal friend of his, he will have a far greater knowledge and understanding of the settlor's family (and therefore, in almost all cases, the beneficiaries of the trust) than even the most diligent of offshore

---

1 In ordinary parlance, it would not be usual for the vesting of the power to appoint or remove trustees in a named individual (as contemplated by the Trustee Act 1925, s 36(1)) alone to constitute that person a protector of the trust. In the widest sense, however, such person is a protector: he enjoys a watchdog role over the trustees and he is often the settlor. Further, the power is a fiduciary power: see *In re Skeats' Settlement* (1889) 42 Ch D 522; *Mettoy Pension Trustees v Evans* [1990] 1 WLR 1587 at 1620; *Simpson Curtis Pension Trustees Ltd v Readson Ltd* [1994] OPLR 231.

2 See eg Finance Act 1989, s 110, which sets out the circumstances where the presence of at least one UK resident trustee has the effect of bringing the non-resident trustees onshore for all the purposes of the Income Tax Acts.

3 There is no legal objection to making the settlor a protector, and unless there is some tax or other consideration making this undesirable, this is often the best way of giving a settlor the comfort he desires of being able to continue to exercise a degree of control.

trust corporations. However, there are such things as professional protectors, and there is something to commend the use of such protectors rather than friends or family with whom emotions run high, and with whom there may be a real danger that the settlor will fall out. On the other hand, they may be subject to exactly the same objections as offshore trustees in the sense of being remote strangers, unfamiliar to the settlor or his family. A trust may have more than one protector.

For trust lawyers one of the most difficult questions relating to protectors concerns the duties owed by the protector in a particular trust. This question will often arise when one or more of the settlors, the beneficiaries or the trustees have become discontented with the behaviour of the protector, and are considering mounting a legal challenge to his actions (or inactions). Ideally, however, the question will be addressed at the time when the trust is being drafted. It is desirable at this point to clarify the ambit of the protector's duties, and in particular whether he is intended to have a fiduciary role. *Prima facie*, there is no reason why the trust should not curtail or exclude any fiduciary duty, since the powers and duties of the protector depend on the trust instrument.

The answer to the question concerning a protector's duties is in the first instance a matter of construction of the particular trust instrument. This primarily depends upon the language of the trust instrument, although the surrounding circumstances may of course be taken into account as an aid to construction as in the case of any other instruments. However, the position of the protector may be modified or regulated by statute,[1] or by overriding public policy considerations.[2] Different legal systems may provide different answers to the question. As a matter of English private international law, the question of the protector's duties is answered by reference to the governing law of the trust.[3] The position under English domestic law is considered in detail in the following section. The position under the domestic law of other jurisdictions is considered at **5.3**.

Finally, it is fair at this juncture to refer to the existence of what might be regarded as a different approach to the role of protectors from that favoured above. The cornerstone proposition of the approach favoured above ('the wide view') is that although a protector may be in a fiduciary position, this is not necessarily the case: it all depends upon the circumstances. The alternative

---

1 See eg the Belize Trusts Act 1992, the British Virgin Islands Trustee Ordinance 1994, and the Cook Islands International Trusts Amendment Act 1989.

2 Eg if a protector clause is drafted so as to attempt to oust the jurisdiction of the court, the offending part of the clause may be struck down on the basis that it is contrary to public policy: see eg *Re Wynn* [1952] Ch 271; *Re Raven* [1915] 1 Ch 673.

3 The identity and role of the governing law of the trust is, we submit, covered by the Recognition of Trusts Act 1987 (implementing the Hague Convention). Although protectors are not mentioned in that Act, their role and duties are properly described as part of the construction, effects and administration of the trust within Art 8 of the Hague Convention.

school of thought[1] ('the narrow view') views the protector as the holder of a fiduciary office. By definition classified as a fiduciary, the protector, according to the narrow view, has an irreducible core of duties imposed upon him. It is submitted that the distinction between the wide and narrow views is largely semantic. For it cannot, surely, be disputed that it is possible to nominate a person with a non-fiduciary watchdog role under the express terms of a trust deed. If this is not the case, the expectations of many settlors and their advisers will be disappointed. To say that a person is a fiduciary is (as Frankfurter J once observed[2]) the beginning, not the end, of analysis to which we would add that to say that a person is *not* a fiduciary is not the end of the analysis. It should not, in our view, be supposed that the courts will be powerless to review the actions of a protector simply because he is not in a fiduciary position. The court's general jurisdiction to secure the good administration of trusts should, in principle, enable the court to intervene even if, for example, the trust instrument in terms lays down that the protector is to owe no fiduciary duties.[3]

5.2 DUTIES OF PROTECTOR UNDER ENGLISH LAW

Whereas there is a dearth of English authorities on the duties of the protector,[4] there is ample authority relating to the duties owed by the holders (or, as they are traditionally called, the 'donees') of powers. The duties of the protector must be considered in relation to each power which he has been given (although each power will obviously be construed in the context of the settlement as a whole). The fact that a protector is a fiduciary for the purposes of one power may not constitute him a fiduciary for the purposes of a different power.[5]

---

1 See eg Underhill and Hayton *Law of Trusts and Trustees* (Butterworths, 15th ed, 1995), pp 23–25.

2 *SEC v Chenery Corporation* 318 US 80, 85–6 (1943).

3 Compare the development of the employer's implied duty of good faith, which has been held to limit the ways in which a sponsoring employer may validly exercise non-fiduciary powers reserved under an occupational pension scheme: *Imperial Group Pension Trust v Imperial Tobacco Ltd* [1991] ICR 524. Similarly, it is axiomatic that powers should be exercised only for the purposes for which they are given, not for some collateral or improper purpose, whether or not they are classified as fiduciary: *Re Courage Pension Schemes* [1987] 1 WLR 498; *Hillsdown Holdings v Pensions Ombudsman* [1997] 1 All ER 862.

4 See, however, *IRC v Schroder* [1983] STC 480, a case in which Vinelott J held that the UK resident protector of a Bahamian settlement did not have power to enjoy the income accruing to trustees within the meaning of Income and Corporation Taxes Act 1970, s 478(5). See also *Lord Vestey's Executors v IRC* [1949] 1 All ER 1108, HL.

5 It is clear, for example, that in the context of a settlement where the settlor is given: (i) a special power of appointment over the capital of the trust fund; and (ii) the power to appoint new trustees, the former is rarely a fiduciary power, whilst the latter is a fiduciary power. See *In re Skeats' Settlement* (1889) 42 Ch D 522.

A starting point is the classification of powers adopted in *Mettoy Pension Trustees v Evans*.[1] In that case, the judge considered the duties owed by an employer in relation to an occupational pension scheme in the exercise of the employer's power to augment members' benefits upon a winding up of the scheme. He propounded a four-fold classification of powers as follows:

(1) a power given to a person to determine the destination of trust property without that person being under any obligation to exercise the power or to preserve it, for example, a special power of appointment given to an individual where there is a trust in default of appointment. Here, the donee owes duties to the beneficiaries of the trust not to misuse the power, but owes no duty to the objects of the power. The donee may thus release the power, but not commit a fraud on it;
(2) any power conferred on the trustees of property or on any other person as a trustee of the power itself. Such a power is a fiduciary power in the full sense. A power in this category cannot be released; the donee of it owes a duty to the objects of the power to consider, as and when it may be appropriate, whether and if so how he ought to exercise it; and he is to some extent subject to the control of the courts in relation to its exercise. See, for example, *In re Abrahams Will Trusts*,[2] *In re Manisty's Settlement*,[3] *In re Hay's Settlement Trusts*;[4]
(3) any discretion which is really a duty to form a judgment as to the existence or otherwise of particular circumstances giving rise to particular consequences. See, for example, *Weller v Ker*,[5] *Dundee General Hospitals Board of Management v Walker*;[6] and
(4) discretionary trusts, ie cases where someone, usually but not necessarily the trustees, is under a duty to select from among a class of beneficiaries those who are to receive, and the proportions in which they are to receive, income or capital of the trust property.

As the judge made clear in *Mettoy*, whether a power falls into one category or another is a matter of construction of the trust deed in light of the surrounding circumstances. He held that the employer's power in the case before him fell within category (2).

In relation to the powers of a protector, the issue is likely to be whether a particular power falls within category (1) or category (2) above. Irrespective of the category into which the relevant power falls, the protector will owe a duty

---

1 [1990] 1 WLR 1586 at 1613.
2 [1969] 1 Ch 463 at 474.
3 [1974] Ch 17 at 24.
4 [1982] 1 WLR 202 at 210.
5 (1866) LR 1 SC & Div 11.
6 [1952] 1 All ER 896.

to abide by the terms of the settlement, and not to commit a fraud on the power.[1] However, the classification of a power as falling within category (2) rather than category (1) will have wide-ranging consequences. Examples are as follows:

(a) the power generally cannot be released, other than pursuant to the exercise of a power to release the former power, which latter power is also likely to be fiduciary;
(b) the objects of the power in addition to the beneficiaries of the settlement will have standing to enforce the donee's duties;[2]
(c) the donees will be obliged to consider periodically whether or not to exercise the power;[3]
(d) in the exercise of the power, the donee must have regard to all relevant considerations, and disregard all irrelevant considerations;[4]
(e) if the power is of an administrative nature, for example, a power of investment, the donee may have a duty, when exercising the power, to use reasonable care.[5]

As the power will, *ex hypothesi*, be of a fiduciary nature, the donee must not place himself in a position where his personal interest conflicts with his duty (other than as permitted by the settlement), and he must not derive an unauthorised profit from the settlement.[6] Contrary to the views of some commentators,[7] we suggest that this consideration is not the touchstone for whether the donee of a power can charge for his services, or recover costs and expenses from the trust fund. It is difficult to see how the donee of a power in either category (1) or (2), above, would have a cause of action against the trustees in order to charge for services, or recover costs and expenses, irrespective of the equitable rules applying to fiduciaries. This point is discussed further at **5.5**.

Whether or not a particular power falls within category (1) or category (2), the donee is not a 'trustee' within the meaning of the Trustee Act 1925.[8] The provisions of this Act will apply to settlements governed by English law, although some of the provisions (for example, Part IV dealing with the powers

---

1 See *Duke of Portland v Topham* (1864) 11 HL Cas 32.

2 See *Re Manisty's Settlement* [1973] 2 All ER 1203 at 1210.

3 Ibid at 1210.

4 See *Re Hastings-Bass* [1975] Ch 25 at 41, CA; *Dundee General Hospitals Board of Management v Walker* [1952] 1 All ER 896, HL(Sc); *Mettoy Pension Trustees Limited v Evans* [1990] WLR 1587 at 1622 et seq.

5 See *Bartlett v Barclays Bank* [1980] 1 Ch 515; *Nestle v National Westminster Bank* [1993] 1 WLR 1260, CA.

6 See eg *Phipps v Boardman* [1967] 2 AC 46; *Regal (Hastings) Limited v Gulliver* [1967] 2 AC 134n.

7 See eg *Hartnett and Norris* [1995] PCB 109.

8 See Trustee Act 1925, s 68(17). The reason for this is that, save where the settlement is approaching a sham, and the trustees are nothing more than nominees for the protector, the protector has no trust property.

of the court) will apply to all settlements before an English court, irrespective of the governing law. This is discussed further at **5.4**.

5.3 DUTIES OF PROTECTOR: CASE-LAW FROM OTHER JURISDICTIONS

5.3.1 Bermuda: *Von Knierem v Bermuda Trust Co Ltd*[1]

Bermuda Trust Co Limited ('BTC') was the sole trustee of two Bermudian settlements which owned 29.3 per cent of the shares in an international holding company based in Bermuda ('the company'). The settlor of one settlement, Mr Engelhorn, was managing partner of the family partnership which settled the other settlement. He was also a director of the company. The protector of both settlements was the lawyer and personal friend of Mr Engelhorn.

A power struggle on the board of the company led to the proposal that Mr Engelhorn should be removed as director by the company in general meeting. Such a resolution could effectively be blocked by BTC as trustees of the settlements, but BTC declined to give confirmation to the protector that it would block the resolution. Accordingly, the protector, who had the power to appoint and remove trustees, purported to remove BTC as trustee and appoint another trustee, Grosvenor Trust Company Limited ('Grosvenor') as trustee in its place.

Two legal actions were brought, the first brought by the protector (who sought orders from the court requiring BTC to vest the trust property in Grosvenor) and Grosvenor (seeking a declaration that it had been properly appointed), and the second brought by BTC (who sought the court's directions, in particular as to whether it had been properly removed as trustee). The two actions were consolidated.

Meerabux J held, relying upon *Skeats'* case and the wording of the settlements, that the protector's power to appoint and remove trustees was a fiduciary power. Accordingly, the protector could not exercise the power to benefit himself (there was no question of this having happened on the facts). As to whether the protector had exercised the power capriciously or irrationally, he held (without giving any reason) that the pension cases cited (including *Mettoy*) were not relevant and that they applied only to pension schemes. The judge held that a person could only avoid an appointment if he could prove a corrupt purpose on the part of the appointor. The mere possibility of an improper motive was insufficient. Accordingly, he held that

---

1 (1994) *Butterworths Offshore Cases and Materials*, Vol 1, pp 116–125, Supreme Court of Bermuda.

the protector had validly exercised the power to remove BTC and appoint Grosvenor. The case has been subject to some criticism[1] in the legal press.

5.3.2 Isle of Man: *Steele v Paz Limited*[2]

A number of issues arose in this case, only one of which is relevant in the context of protectors. A declaration of trust, whereby the only current member of the class of beneficiaries was the Red Cross in the Republic of Ireland, made provision for certain of the powers of the trustees (including the power to nominate beneficiaries) to be exercisable only with the consent of the protector. The protector was also given various powers, such as the power to appoint trustees. However, the declaration of trust failed to nominate a protector.

In the first instance the judge, acting Deemster John Hall QC, held that the declaration of trust was invalid on the basis that without a protector, the class of beneficiaries failed for uncertainty.

On appeal, the Staff of Government Division of the Isle of Man High Court of Justice allowed the appeal. The two judges who heard the appeal (Hegarty JA and Smith JA) disagreed with the previous judge's reasoning that the trust could be void for uncertainty. The most that could be said was that the trusts failed because they were ineffectual. This was not the case, however, as the protector's powers were fiduciary powers, and by analogy with the case of trustees, the court had inherent jurisdiction to appoint a person to exercise those powers.

5.3.3 The Bahamas: *Rawson Trust v Perlman*[3]

Certain powers of the trustees of a settlement were not exercisable without the consent of the protector. It was proposed that the protector would consent to the trustees resettling the trust fund upon trusts which did not include a protector. An application was made to the court to determine whether the protector's power to consent to the proposed resettlement was a fiduciary power. Smith J held that the power was not a fiduciary power as the settlement gave the protector the power to further his own interests. Accordingly, the protector could properly consent to the resettlement.

---

1 See eg Matthews (1995) 9 *Trust Law International* 108; Penney [1995] J Int P 31; Conder [1995] PCB 288.

2 (10 October 1995) Butterworths *Offshore Cases and Materials*, vol 1, pp 338–418, CA of Isle of Man.

3 (Unreported) 25 April 1995, Supreme Court of the Bahamas, Smith J.

5.3.4 Jersey: *Re the settlements made between X and Charles Richard Blamfield and Abacus (C) Limited*[1]

This case concerned three Jersey settlements created by US citizens. One of the settlors died, and the Jersey trustees sought the directions of the court to permit them to disclose the existence of the settlements to the deceased settlor's personal representative in the United States, a step which would facilitate the winding up of the settlor's estate. The protector of the settlements cross-applied to the court for orders in the case of two of the settlements allowing the trustees to distribute the trust fund, and in relation to the third for an injunction to restrain the trustees from disclosing the existence of the settlement to the US personal representative.

The court held that the trustees were entitled to disclose the existence of the settlements to the deceased settlor's personal representatives, and dismissed the protector's cross-applications. The court did not, however, suggest that the protector had no *locus standi* to bring the cross-application.

The court awarded the protector his costs out of the trust fund on an indemnity basis, but declined to make an order in respect of future expenses. Further, the court made an order preventing the protector from attempting to remove trustees without the order of the court.

5.4 CONTROL OF PROTECTOR

This section is concerned with the control of protectors by the English courts. The position must be considered separately with respect to each of the relevant powers of the protector. In relation to powers of the kind described in category (1) at **5.2**, there can be no doubt that the court's power of control extends to ensuring that the protector complies with the terms of the settlement and does not commit a fraud on the power. But, as indicated above, it should not in our view be supposed that the court's powers stop there. In our view, the court's general jurisdiction to secure the good administration of trusts should, in principle, enable it to intervene even if, for example, the trust instrument in terms lays down that the protector is to owe no fiduciary duties.[2] Suppose, for instance, the case of a discretionary trust containing such a provision where all distributions of income or capital require the consent of the protector who perversely refuses to consider whether or not to give his consent. Can it be seriously doubted that the court would intervene to appoint a new protector, rather than allowing the trust property to be sterilised indefinitely to the detriment of the beneficiaries? Protectors are a relatively new development and just as the courts have developed new principles to

---

[1] (Unreported) 28 January 1994, Royal Court of Jersey (Samedi Division).

[2] See n 3 on p 228.

control power-holders in other contexts, we suggest that they will do so in relation to protectors as and when cases arise which call for judicial intervention.[1]

The problem of the control of the court over donees of fiduciary powers was considered in *Mettoy Pension Trustees* (referred to above),[2] where the donee of the relevant fiduciary power (the employer company, with respect to a pension scheme, which company had gone into liquidation) was unable to exercise that power. Warner J posed the question as to who should exercise the relevant power.[3] He cited a passage from the speech of Lord Wilberforce in *Re Baden's Deed Trusts*[4] in the following terms:

> 'As to powers, I agree with my noble and learned friend Lord Upjohn in *In re Gulbenkian's Settlements* [1970] AC 508 that although the trustees may, and normally will, be under a fiduciary duty to consider whether or in what way they should exercise their power, the court will not normally compel its exercise. It will intervene if the trustees exceed their powers, and possibly if they are proved to have exercised it capriciously. But in the case of a trust power, if the trustees do not exercise it, the court will … I would venture to amplify this by saying that the court, if called upon to execute the trust power, will do so in the manner best calculated to give effect to the settlor's or testator's intentions. It may do so by appointing new trustees, or by authorising or directing representative persons of the classes of beneficiaries to prepare a scheme of distribution, or even, should the proper basis for distribution appear, by itself directing the trustees so to distribute. The books give many instances where this has been done, and I see no reason in principle why they should not do so in the modern field of discretionary trusts.'

Warner J held that the latter part of this passage applied equally to powers in category (2) as to powers in category (4) at **5.2**. The parties in that case did not suggest that the court should appoint a new person to exercise the relevant power. One of the other methods was chosen (the report does not indicate which).

It seems, therefore, that in appropriate circumstances the court could control protectors in one or other of the following ways:

(a) by declaring that particular exercises of particular powers are invalid;[5]
(b) by appointing, removing or replacing the protector as donee of the power pursuant to its inherent jurisdiction.[6] This will be particularly appropriate where the protector is guilty of recurrent breaches of fiduciary duty;

---

1 See *Imperial Group Trust v Imperial Tobacco Ltd* [1991] ICR 524.
2 *Mettoy Pension Trustees v Evans* [1990] 1 WLR 1587.
3 Ibid at 1617.
4 [1971] AC 424.
5 See *Cloutte v Storey* [1911] 1 Ch 18; *Turner v Turner* [1984] Ch 100.
6 In the context of trustees, see eg *Re Harrison's Settlement Trusts* [1965] 3 All ER 795 at 799; *Clarke v Heathfield (No 2)* [1985] ICR 606; *Re Chetwynd's Settlement* [1902] 1 Ch 692. Part IV of the Trustee Act 1925 does not apply to non-trustees. In the context of protectors who are fiduciaries, see the Isle of Man case of *Steele v Paz*, discussed at **5.3.2**.

(c) by directing the protector as to the manner in which he should exercise his powers on a particular occasion, or by nominating a person to prepare a scheme as to the manner in which those powers ought to be exercised.

A final point is that if the trustees of the settlement act in breach of trust, there is a possibility that the protector may incur liability for wrongfully assisting in that breach of trust under the principles described in *Royal Brunei Airlines v Tan.*[1]

5.5 PROTECTORS' INDEMNITIES AND EXONERATION

This topic may be divided into two subsections: (a) ability of the protector to recover remuneration, legal costs and other out-of-pocket expenses from the trust fund; and (b) limitation on liability for breach of fiduciary duty by indemnity or exoneration clause.

As to (a), the general rule regarding remuneration will be the same whether or not the protector is described as a fiduciary. He has no right to recover remuneration from the trustees, save as expressly provided in the trust instrument. In the case of protectors who are fiduciaries, however, the court has an inherent jurisdiction to award them remuneration,[2] and we see no reason why it should not be extended to non-fiduciaries. An example of a case where it may be appropriate for the court to exercise this jurisdiction is where the court wishes to appoint a new protector. This jurisdiction is useful, having regard to the growing trend in the use of professional protector companies, although ideally the settlement will make provision for the remuneration of the protector.

Further as to (a), in relation to the protector's legal costs of litigation concerning the settlement to which the protector is party, whether or not the protector is classified as a fiduciary, the court has power, pursuant to its general discretion as to costs, to order that the protector's costs be paid out of the trust fund.[3] There may be an argument for saying that a protector who is a fiduciary is *prima facie* entitled to those costs by analogy with the principles described in *Re Beddoe.*[4] Connected with this question is the question of

---

1 [1995] 2 AC 378.

2 See *Re Berkeley Applegate Limited* [1989] 1 Ch 31; *Re Duke of Norfolk's Settlement Trusts* [1982] Ch 61, CA. In the context of protectors, see the Jersey case of *Blamfield and Abacus*, discussed at **5.3.4**.

3 See *Lloyds Bank International (Cayman) Ltd v Bylever Co SA* (20 October 1995) Grand Court of the Cayman Islands, where the protectors of two settlements, which were arguably in a non-fiduciary position, were held to be entitled to their legal costs out of the trust funds. The court also held that the protectors were entitled to charge for the professional services. See also *Re the Lemos Trust Settlement* (1992–3) CILR 26.

4 [1893] 1 Ch 547.

whether the protector is a proper party to litigation concerning the settlement at all. We suggest that he may be a proper party to litigation where it concerns the exercise of powers vested in him[1] whether or not he is a fiduciary.

Finally as to (a), in relation to the protector's out-of-pocket expenses, we suggest that in so far as he is a fiduciary, he will be entitled to a lien from those costs at common law by analogy with the case of trustees.[2] If he is not a fiduciary, the position will be less clear-cut. At first sight, it might appear difficult to find examples of when it would be reasonable for him to incur those out-of-pocket expenses. Examples might be the cost of obtaining legal advice on the duties pertaining to the exercise of the power, and the cost of preparing deeds in order to execute the powers. In practice, such costs are not infrequently paid by the trustees or by the settlor, and in an appropriate case we suggest that the court should be able to direct that they are paid out of the trust property.

As to (b), this is primarily a matter for the settlor when drafting the settlement, and we have already suggested that there is in general no reason why the responsibilities of a protector should not be limited by the trust instrument. It is important to test the validity of an exoneration or indemnity by reference to the governing law of the settlement.[3] The English courts do not have jurisdiction to exonerate a protector in respect of liability for breach of fiduciary duty.[4]

---

1 See the Bermudian *Von Knierem* case at **5.3.1**, and the Jersey *Blamfield and Abacus* case discussed at **5.3.4**.

2 See *Re Earl of Winchilsea's Policy Trusts* (1888) 39 Ch D 168. Section 30(2) of the Trustee Act 1925 does not apply to non-trustees.

3 See the Recognition of Trusts Act 1987.

4 Trustee Act 1925, s 61 does not apply to non-trustees.

Chapter 6

PURPOSE TRUSTS

Geraint Thomas[*]

6.1 INTRODUCTION

This chapter is concerned principally with non-charitable purpose trusts. For a number of reasons (not all of which are clear or consistent) such trusts cannot readily be created in England and Wales. Certain jurisdictions[1] have, however, enacted legislation authorising the creation of non-charitable purpose trusts, in some cases coupled with modifications to the law of charities.

---

[*] Professor of Equity and Property Law in the Queen Mary Law School, University of London, and Barrister of 10 Old Square, Lincoln's Inn, London.

[1] These include Belize, Bermuda, the British Virgin Islands, the Cayman Islands, the Cook Islands, Cyprus, the Isle of Man, Jersey, Labuan, Liechtenstein and Nauru. A discussion of the legislation in these jurisdictions (other than Liechtenstein and Nauru) may be found at **6.4** et seq. Alberta, British Columbia and Ontario have legislated to convert non-charitable purpose trusts into powers.

6.2 ENGLAND AND WALES[1]

6.2.1 The general rule

The generally accepted rule in English law is that, in order to be valid, a trust must have an ascertainable beneficiary (individual or corporate) in whose favour performance of the trust may be decreed.[2] A trust is obligatory and there cannot be an obligation unless there is a corresponding right. On this principle, trusts for purposes or objects are invalid, for a purpose or object cannot sue. Trusts for charitable purposes, however, are valid because they are enforceable by the Attorney-General.[3] As Lord Parker stated in *Bowman v Secular Society Ltd*:[4]

> 'A trust to be valid must be for the benefit of individuals ... or must be in that class of gifts for the benefit of the public which the courts in this country recognise as charitable in the legal as opposed to the popular sense of that term.'

On this basis, the courts have, for example, declared invalid trusts for 'objects of benevolence and liberality',[5] for 'the purpose of providing some useful memorial to myself',[6] for 'the maintenance ... of good understanding

---

1 Underhill and Hayton *Law of Trusts and Trustees* (Butterworths, 15th ed, 1995), pp 91–108; P Baxendale-Walker *Purpose Trusts for Commercial and Private Use* (Butterworths Tolley, 1999); Morris and Leach *The Rule Against Perpetuities* (Sweet & Maxwell, 2nd ed, 1962), Ch 12; Maudsley *The Modern Law of Perpetuities* (Butterworths, 1979), pp 166–178; Gray *The Rule Against Perpetuities* (Sweet & Maxwell, 4th ed, 1942), App H, pp 894–909; Scott *The Law of Trusts* (Little Brown & Co, 4th ed, 1987), pp 119, 123, 124; Jarman *A Treatise on Wills* (Sweet & Maxwell, 8th ed, 1951), pp 284–290, 898–899; JB Ames (1892) 5 Harv LR 389; JC Gray (1902) 15 Harv LR 509; C Sweet (1917) 33 LQR 342; WO Hart (1937) 53 LQR 24 at 33; DC Potter (1949) 13 Conv (NS) 418; AKR Kiralfy (1950) 14 Conv (NS) 374; RE Megarry (1952) 68 LQR 449; LA Sheridan (1953) Conv (NS) 46; OR Marshall (1953) 6 CLP 151; L Leigh (1955) 18 MLR 120; LA Sheridan (1958) 4 Univ of West Aus LR 235; PA Lovell (1970) 34 Conv (NS) 77; JW Harris (1971) 87 LQR 31; L McKay (1973) 37 Conv (NS) 420; N Gravells (1977) 40 MLR 397; K Widdows (1977) 41 Conv (NS) 179; A Duckworth *STAR Trusts: the Special Trusts (Alternative Regime) Law 1997* (Gostick Hall Publications, 1997); HAJ Ford 'Dispositions for Purposes' in PD Finn (ed) *Essays on Equity* (1985), pp 159–178; RBM Cotterrell 'Some Sociological Aspects of the Controversy Around the Legal Validity of Private Purpose Trusts' in Stephen Goldstein (ed) *Equity and Contemporary Legal Developments* (papers presented at the First International Conference on Equity, The Faculty of Law, The Hebrew University of Jerusalem, June 1990) at pp 302–334; P Matthews 'The New Trust: Obligations Without Rights?' in AJ Oakley (ed) *Trends in Contemporary Trust Law* (Clarendon Press, 1997), pp 1–31; [2000] JTCP 237, (2001) 117 LQR 96. No recommendation is made in the Law Commission's Report on *The Rules Against Perpetuities and Excessive Accumulations* (Law Com No 251) as to purpose trusts: see paras 1.14, 8.35–8.36.

2 *Morice v Bishop of Durham* (1804) 9 Ves 399 at 404; *Bowman v Secular Society Ltd* [1917] AC 406 at 441; *Re Chardon* [1928] Ch 464; *Re Diplock* [1941] Ch 253 at 259; *Re Wood* [1949] Ch 498; *Re Astor's Settlement Trusts* [1952] Ch 534; *Leahy v Attorney-General* (NSW) [1959] AC 457 at 478; *Re Denley's Trust Deed* [1969] 1 Ch 373; *Re Vandervell's Trusts (No 2)* [1974] Ch 269 at 319.

3 *Leahy v Attorney-General (NSW)* [1959] AC 457 at 478, 479.

4 [1917] AC 406 at 441. There is no shortage of statements to the same effect: see, eg, *Re Endacott* [1960] Ch 232 at 246; *Re Recher's Will Trusts* [1972] Ch 526 at 538.

5 *Morice v Bishop of Durham* (1804) 9 Ves 399.

6 *Re Endacott* [1960] Ch 232.

between nations … and … the preservation of the independence and integrity of newspapers'[1] or for the purpose of bricking up a house for 20 years after a testatrix's death.[2]

However, there are several examples of non-charitable purpose trusts being held valid by the courts. These have been judicially described as 'concessions to human weakness or sentiment',[3] as 'troublesome, anomalous and aberrant',[4] and as 'occasions when Homer has nodded'.[5] Nevertheless, their existence clearly indicates that some non-charitable purpose trusts may be valid, and in turn raises the question whether such instances 'are to be regarded as exceptional and anomalous or whether they are destructive of the supposed principle'.[6] Roxburgh J's conclusion, in *Re Astor's Settlement Trusts*,[7] was that the principle was well founded, both in theory and practical considerations:

> 'The typical case of a trust is one in which the legal owner of the property is constrained by a court of equity so to deal with it as to give effect to the equitable rights of another. These equitable rights have been hammered out in the process of litigation in which a claimant on equitable grounds has successfully asserted rights against a legal owner or other person in control of property. Prima facie, therefore, a trustee would not be expected to be subject to an equitable obligation unless there was somebody who could enforce a correlative right, and the nature and right of that obligation would be worked out in proceedings for enforcement … At an early stage, however, the courts were confronted with attempts to create trusts for charitable purposes which there was no equitable owner to enforce. … But if the purposes are not charitable, great difficulties arise both in theory and in practice. In theory, because having regard to the historical origins of equity it is difficult to visualize the growth of equitable obligations which nobody can enforce, and in practice, because it is not possible to contemplate with equanimity the creation of large funds devoted to non-charitable purposes which no court and no department of state can control, or in the case of maladministration reform. Therefore, Lord Parker's … proposition would prima facie appear to be well founded. Moreover, it gains no little support from the practical considerations that no officer has ever been constituted to take, in the case of non-charitable purposes, the position held by the Attorney-General in connexion with charitable purposes, and no case has been found in the reports in which the court has ever directly enforced a non-charitable purpose against a trustee.'

Thus, the emphasis here is on the unenforceability of non-charitable purpose trusts, which is itself seen as an inevitable consequence of the absence of any beneficiary – or, to be precise, of anyone who can claim 'equitable rights' in or to the trust property – to whom the trustees could owe any equitable duties. However, well established though this view has become, it does not provide a comprehensive analysis of the position in English law. On the one hand, it

---

1 *Re Astor's Settlement Trusts* [1952] Ch 534.

2 *Brown v Burdett* (1882) 21 Ch D 667. See also *M'Caig's Trustees v Kirk Session of United Free Church of Lismore* 1915 SC 426; and *Aitken's Trustees v Aitken* 1927 SC 374.

3 *Re Astor's Settlement Trusts* [1952] Ch 534 at 541.

4 *Re Endacott* [1960] Ch 232 at 251.

5 Ibid at 250.

6 *Re Astor's Settlement Trusts* [1952] Ch 534 at 541, per Roxburgh J.

7 Ibid at 541–542.

seems clear that the lack of a beneficiary with enforceable equitable rights in the trust property is not the sole reason why English courts have generally refused to uphold purpose trusts: indeed, the few reported cases suggest that such trusts might also be held invalid on one or more of many other grounds. On the other hand, it is not at all clear that the lack of such a beneficiary was always or consistently regarded as a fundamental obstacle to the validity of purpose trusts: indeed, the older decisions suggest that English law may originally have accorded greater significance to the intentions of the settlor or testator (provided they are lawful and clear) and to the need to enforce a moral obligation of conscience, which the trustees had recognised and accepted, rather than to questions of equitable proprietary rights or issues of practical difficulty in enforcement. Certainly, this seems to be the case for most of those purpose trusts which have been recognised in England.[1]

6.2.2 Valid non-charitable purpose trusts

Those trusts for non-charitable purposes which have been held valid were classified by Morris and Leach[2] into the following categories:

(a) trusts for the erection or maintenance of monuments or graves;
(b) trusts for the saying of masses (where such trusts are not regarded as charitable);
(c) trusts for the maintenance of particular animals;
(d) trusts for the benefit of unincorporated associations (although this group is more doubtful);
(e) miscellaneous cases.

Monuments and graves
Reasonable provision for the erection of a gravestone or the building of a tomb for a testator is apparently regarded as a funeral expense, and as valid independently of any principle or concession relating to private purpose trusts.[3] However, a trust to erect a monument to some member of the testator's family, or to erect headstones on specified graves, or to maintain a grave or keep it in repair, is valid, provided it does not infringe the rule against

---

1 This broad view was also put forward in an earlier version of this chapter. Since then, P Baxendale-Walker, n 1 on p 238, has argued for a more extreme proposition, namely that there is actually no rule against non-charitable purpose trusts in English law; or, alternatively, that, if there is such a rule, it is erroneous, being based on what he alleges is a misunderstanding of early equity jurisprudence and a misreading of early authorities by judges and lawyers over several centuries. See further at **6.2.6** below.

2 Morris and Leach, n 1 on p 238, p 310. This classification was adopted by Lord Evershed MR in *Re Endacott* [1960] Ch 232 at 246.

3 *Mellick v President and Guardians of the Asylum* (1821) Jac 180; *Trimmer v Danby* (1856) 25 LJ Ch 424. *Cf* Gray in Morris and Leach, n 1 on p 238, p 311.

perpetuities.[1] As Lindley LJ stated in *Re Tyler*,[2] 'There is nothing illegal in keeping up a tomb; on the contrary, it is a very laudable thing to do.' (If such a trust involves maintenance or repair of the fabric of the church, or the upkeep of the churchyard as a whole, it may be charitable.[3])

Masses

Trusts for the saying of masses may be charitable if the masses are said in public and the gifted property is used for the provision of stipends for the priests who are to say the masses (thereby relieving church funds).[4] If these requirements are not satisfied, the trust may possibly be valid as a non-charitable purpose trust, provided the rule against perpetuities is not infringed.[5]

Specific animals

Trusts for the care or maintenance of specific animals have also been upheld, eg an annuity to be applied in maintaining the testator's favourite black mare,[6] or a gift for the maintenance of the testator's horses and hounds.[7] The trust must again not be perpetuitous.

Unincorporated associations

An unincorporated association, unlike the individuals of which it is composed or a corporation, is not a legal person (unless made so by statute) and therefore cannot be an entity capable of holding property. It has been defined as 'two or more persons bound together for one or more common purposes, not being business purposes, by mutual undertakings each having mutual duties and obligations, in an organisation which has rules which identify in whom control of it and its funds rests and on what terms and which can be joined or left at will'.[8]

---

1 *Masters v Masters* (1718) 1 P Wms 421; *Trimmer v Danby* (1856) 25 LJ Ch 424; *Mussett v Bingle* [1876] WN 170; *Pirbright v Salwey* [1896] WN 86; *Re Hooper* [1932] 1 Ch 38. See also the Parish Councils and Burial Authorities (Miscellaneous Provisions) Act 1970.

2 [1891] 3 Ch 252 at 258–259.

3 *Re Vaughan* (1886) 33 Ch D 187; *Re Eighmie* [1935] Ch 524.

4 *Re Hetherington* [1990] Ch 1; *Re Caus* [1934] Ch 162.

5 *Bourne v Keane* [1919] AC 815 at 874–875; *Re Gibbons* [1917] 1 Ir R 448; *Re Will of Ryan* (1925) 60 Ir LTR 57; *Re Khoo Cheng Teow* [1932] Straits Setts LR 226.

6 *Pettingall v Pettingall* (1842) 11 LJ Ch 176.

7 *Re Dean* (1889) 41 Ch D 552.

8 *Conservative and Unionist Central Office v Burrell* [1982] 1 WLR 522 at 525, per Lawton LJ. Although the case concerned the meaning of 'unincorporated association' for the purposes of the Income and Corporation Taxes Act 1970, s 238(1), this definition is considered to be of general application. See also *Re Koeppler's Will Trusts* [1986] Ch 423 at 431, per Slade LJ.

The property of an unincorporated association may be held on its behalf in different ways.[1] In *Neville Estates Ltd v Madden*[2] Cross J laid down the often-cited principles which govern the validity of a gift to an unincorporated association:

> 'Such a gift may take effect in one or other of three quite different ways. In the first place, it may, on its true construction, be a gift to the members of the association at the relevant date as joint tenants, so that any member can sever his share and claim it whether or not he continues to be a member of the association. Secondly, it may be a gift to the existing members not as joint tenants, but subject to their respective contractual rights and liabilities towards one another as members of the association. In such a case a member cannot sever his share. It would accrue to the other members on his death or resignation, even though such members include persons who become members after the gift took effect. If this is the effect of the gift, it will not be open to objection on the score of perpetuity or uncertainty unless there is something in its terms or circumstances or in the rules of the association which precludes the members at any given time from dividing the subject of the gift between them on the footing that they are solely entitled to it in equity. Thirdly, the terms or circumstances of the gift or the rules of the association may show that the property in question is not to be at the disposal of the members for the time being, but is to be held in trust for or applied for the purposes of the association as a quasi-corporate entity. In this case the gift will fail unless the association is a charitable body. If the gift is of the second class, ie one which the members of the association for the time being are entitled to divide among themselves, then, even if the objects of the association are in themselves charitable, the gift would not, I think, be a charitable gift.'

Similarly, in *Re Recher's Will Trusts*[3] Brightman J stated:

> 'A trust for non-charitable purposes, as distinct from a trust for individuals, is clearly void because there is no beneficiary. It does not, however, follow that persons cannot band themselves together as an association or society, pay subscriptions and validly devote their funds in pursuit of some lawful non-charitable purpose. An obvious example is a members' social club. But it is not essential that the members should only intend to secure direct personal advantages to themselves. The association may be one in which personal advantages to members are combined with the pursuit of some outside purpose. Or the association may be one which offers no personal benefit at all to the members, the funds of the association being applied exclusively to the pursuit of some outside purpose. Such an association of persons is bound, I would think, to have some sort of constitution; that is to say, the rights and liabilities of the members of the association would inevitably depend on some form of contract *inter se*, usually evidenced by a set of rules.
>
> ...
>
> In the case of a donation which is not accompanied by any words which purport to impose a trust, it seems to me that the gift takes effect in favour of the existing members of the association as an accretion to the funds which are the subject matter of the contract which such members have made *inter se*, and falls to be dealt with in precisely the same way

---

1 See *Neville Estates Ltd v Madden* [1962] Ch 832 at 849; *Re Recher's Will Trusts* [1972] Ch 526 at 538; *Re Bucks Constabulary Fund (No 2)* [1979] 1 WLR 937; *Re Grant's Will Trusts* [1980] 1 WLR 360; *News Group Newspapers Ltd v SOGAT 82* [1986] ICR 716; J Warburton [1985] Conv 318; J Warburton *Unincorporated Associations, Law and Practice* (1986).

2 [1962] Ch 832 at 849. See also *Leahy v Attorney-General* (NSW) [1959] AC 457 at 478.

3 [1972] Ch 526 at 538.

> as the funds which the members themselves have subscribed. So in the case of a legacy. In the absence of words which purport to impose a trust, the legacy is a gift to the members beneficially, not as joint tenants or as tenants in common so as to entitle each member to an immediate distributive share, but as an accretion to the funds which are the subject-matter of the contract which the members have made *inter se*.'

The traditional view, therefore, is that a trust for the purposes of an association (as opposed to its members) will fail unless those purposes are charitable or fall within one of the exceptional categories of valid non-charitable purposes.

Miscellaneous cases

Amongst the miscellaneous cases are to be found a valid trust for 'the promotion of fox-hunting',[1] (in Ireland) a valid trust to dispose of property to the testator's 'best spiritual advantage',[2] and a trust to provide a maintenance fund for a historic building[3] or a sinking fund for the repair of a block of flats.

Trusts to provide an annual cup for yacht racing,[4] to keep a portrait in repair,[5] and (in Australia) to found a Catholic newspaper,[6] have all been held void, but on the ground of perpetuity and not for lack of a beneficiary.

6.2.3 Reasons assigned for invalidity of non-charitable purpose trusts

It is clear from the authorities that the courts have given several different reasons for holding non-charitable purpose trusts void. More than one reason may apply in any particular case. Very often, however, these reasons are not kept distinct.

The beneficiary principle

Lord Parker pointed out in *Bowman v Secular Society Ltd*[7] that there must be someone who can enforce a trust, other than a charitable trust, somebody in whose favour the court can decree performance. A trust creates an obligation, so there must be a correlative right in somebody to enforce it. In the case of a private trust, there is clearly no such difficulty; and, in the case of charitable trusts, the Attorney-General is charged with the duty of enforcement. A trust

---

1 *Re Thompson* [1934] Ch 342.

2 *Re Gibbons* [1917] 1 IR 448. Such a trust would be void for uncertainty in England and Wales, quite apart from the beneficiary principle.

3 Inheritance Tax Act 1984, s 77; *Glasgow Trades House v IRC* 1970 SC 101 at 108, 113. *Quaere* whether this is charitable.

4 *Re Nottage* [1895] 2 Ch 649.

5 *Re Gassiot* (1901) 70 LJ Ch 242.

6 *Re Lawlor* [1934] VLR 22.

7 [1917] AC 406 at 441. Sir William Grant MR is said to have expressed the same view in *Morice v Bishop of Durham* (1804) 9 Ves 399 at 405. However, his observations seem to have been directed at the need for certainty of objects rather than the beneficiary principle.

for a non-charitable purpose, however, lacks a beneficiary. On this basis, trusts for purposes have been declared void in *Re Wood*,[1] *Re Astor's Settlement*,[2] *Re Shaw*[3] and *Re Endacott*.[4] This is clearly not an absolute principle, however, because, as we have seen, there are several instances in which non-charitable purpose trusts have been upheld.

The beneficiary principle is closely related to the so-called rule in *Saunders v Vautier*,[5] but they are, none the less, separate principles. The beneficiary principle is concerned with enforceability and, as such, it requires that, at all times during the existence of a trust, there is some person who has a sufficient interest under the terms of that trust to be able to enforce it. Such a person may be a beneficiary with a fixed interest, someone (perhaps the settlor himself) entitled under a resulting trust, or an object of a discretionary trust: in other words, someone who has an equitable proprietary interest or right in the trust fund. The rule in *Saunders*, on the other hand, enables a trust to be terminated when, and only when, all the beneficiaries (and objects) of the trust are adults, *sui juris* and between themselves absolutely entitled to the trust fund: when all of these conditions are met, the beneficiaries can direct the distribution of the trust fund to themselves. Indeed, these conditions must always be satisfied at some point (but obviously not at every point) during the existence, or more likely at the natural termination, of any express private trust (and no later than the end of the perpetuity period applicable to that trust). It is immediately obvious that these are distinct principles and, in particular, that the beneficiary principle must be satisfied even when the rule in *Saunders* cannot apply. Given the strict requirements of the rule against perpetuities, it is difficult, if not impossible, to envisage any terms of any valid private trust which do not ensure that *someone* will have a sufficient direct proprietary interest or right in the trust fund to be able to ask the court for protection and enforcement of the trust. This is the case irrespective of the fact that the interest may be vested, contingent or defeasible in some way, that it may arise under some provision in default or under a resulting trust, that the beneficiaries may be infants or even unborn, that there may be a trust or power to accumulate income, or, indeed, that it is the proprietary right of a discretionary object (who, of course, has no interest properly so-called).[6] At the risk of labouring the point, this is precisely what the beneficiary principle requires and why it is the absence of such a 'proprietary' basis that is so fatal to the purpose trust.

---

1 [1949] Ch 498, especially at 501.

2 [1952] Ch 534, especially at 547.

3 [1957] 1 WLR 729.

4 [1960] Ch 232.

5 (1841) 4 Beav 115.

6 Although an object of a discretionary trust has no 'interest' in the technical sense, he does possess a 'proprietary' right (with several of the characteristics of 'property') and, as such, he has a sufficient interest to require protection and to enable him to enforce the trust: see generally G Thomas *Powers* (Sweet & Maxwell, 1998), pp 377–387.

It has been argued[1] that, in the nineteenth century, English courts upheld purpose trusts without any indication that they were inherently problematic: they were neither condemned nor approved.[2] Judicial tolerance of such trusts in the older cases depended primarily on the very limited scope of what settlors and testators sought to achieve by their use and the beneficiary principle was not considered a major obstacle. The purposes at issue in the older cases:

> 'appeared as a limited, narrowly circumscribed and … very insignificant category. … Although they did not benefit living family members, they allowed homage to the family dead or sentimental provision for domestic animals, or (in the old American cases) for faithful slaves. They could be seen as promoting sentimental purposes within "the private community of the family" … perhaps fostering its solidarity, reinforcing its traditions or emotional foundations, or merely allowing its living members to pay homage to deceased relatives by indulging the eccentricities or understandable sentiments of these relatives even after their death. At least where comparatively small amounts of property were involved, such trusts would not appear as seriously inimical to a policy of maintaining and promoting the general alienability of property and the facilitation of market activity.
>
> As long as purpose trusts remained within these kinds of category (or else could easily be invalidated for uncertainty or perpetuity) they could, thus, be accepted without need for an explicit beneficiary principle.'[3]

It was only when more ambitious projects were sought to be achieved in the twentieth century that an explicitly hostile judicial view was instituted, and that the beneficiary principle came to be regarded as one of the fundamental characteristics of a private trust, the requirements of which had to be satisfied or there could be no trust at all. In essence, the basic conception of a trust is said to have changed fundamentally from the position where a trust is regarded primarily as a moral obligation of conscience which is capable of fulfilment if the trustee himself recognises and accepts it to the situation where enforceability depends on the existence of someone who can claim some equitable interest or right in the trust property, ie a change from a 'moralistic' to a 'property-receptacle' conception of the trust.[4] Whether this view is actually supported by the authorities themselves is debatable. It is equally possible to argue that, until the second half of the nineteenth century, English courts were prone to regard as a *trust* what would now be more readily viewed as a fiduciary *power*; and it is clear that there is no obstacle, even in English law, to the conferring on trustees of a *power* to carry out or pursue non-charitable purposes. In any event, it is difficult to avoid the conclusion that, irrespective of the changes that may have occurred in the law's conception of a trust, English law today is wedded to the beneficiary principle and that it is this principle that poses the main obstacle to the creation of non-charitable

1 See RBM Cotterrell, n 1 on p 238, pp 302–334.
2 Ibid, pp 303–304.
3 Ibid, p 328.
4 Ibid, pp 303, 323–332.

purpose trusts in England. Recently, however, a much more comprehensive and sustained attack has been made on the very idea that English law does not permit the existence of non-charitable purpose trusts.[1] According to this view, it is erroneous to say that a trust cannot be enforced if there is no beneficiary, as is evidenced by a series of reported decisions extending back over several centuries; and, in those cases where an attempt to create a non-charitable purpose trust failed, the reason for failure was not the beneficiary principle but a breach of the rule against perpetuities or the absence of conceptual certainty. This provocative analysis is discussed at greater length below.[2]

In two decisions – *Re Denley*[3] and *Re Lipinski*[4] – the court has once again, arguably, exhibited a more liberal approach to the beneficiary principle. In *Re Denley*, trustees for sale were directed to maintain land as a sports ground 'primarily for the benefit of the employees of the company and secondarily for the benefit of such other person or persons (if any) as the trustees may allow to use the same'. Goff J held the gift valid. He distinguished between different kinds of purpose trusts:[5]

> 'I think there may be a purpose or object trust, the carrying out of which would benefit an individual or individuals, where that benefit is so indirect or intangible or which is otherwise so framed as not to give those persons any *locus standi* to apply to the court to enforce the trust, in which case the beneficiary principle would, as it seems to me, apply to invalidate the trust, quite apart from any question of uncertainty or perpetuity. Such cases can be considered if and when they arise. The present is not … of that character … Apart from this possible exception, in my judgment the beneficiary principle of *In Re Astor's Settlement Trusts*, which was approved of in *In Re Endacott decd*, … is confined to purpose or object trusts which are abstract or impersonal. The objection is not that the trust is for a purpose or object *per se*, but that there is no beneficiary or *cestui que trust* …
>
> Where, then, the trust, though expressed as a purpose, is directly or indirectly for the benefit of an individual or individuals, it seems to me that it is in general outside the mischief of the beneficiary principle.'

The trust in question did not infringe the rule against perpetuities; and its beneficiaries were ascertained or ascertainable at any given time.

It is not entirely clear how the trust in *Re Denley* was classified. Goff J clearly accepted that a trust expressed as a purpose, but indirectly for the benefit of an individual, was outside the mischief of the beneficiary principle.[6] Moreover, the purpose of extracting the relevant distinction from the authorities seems clearly to have been to justify the conclusion that the trust in question was valid, notwithstanding the fact that it was expressed to be for a non-charitable purpose. On the other hand, his concern that the employees to

---

1 P Baxendale-Walker, n 1 on p 238.
2 See **6.2.6** below.
3 [1969] 1 Ch 373.
4 [1976] Ch 235.
5 [1969] 1 Ch 373 at 380–382.
6 Ibid at 383–384.

be benefited should be ascertained or ascertainable at any given time suggests that it was a trust for individuals, and not a purpose trust at all. It is clear, however, that he equated the beneficiary principle simply with the question of enforceability and not with the issue of equitable ownership: the question of whether the employees of the company, together with those others who might be permitted to use the sportsground, could terminate the trust was clearly not regarded as material.

Re Denley leaves many questions unanswered. It does not, for example, identify the nature of the 'benefit' and, in particular, whether there has to be some legal or equitable interest or right (other than a right simply to enforce the trust) or whether a *de facto* advantage is sufficient. Nor does it suggest how 'indirect' a benefit may be before it falls within the beneficiary principle. The employing company presumably derived an indirect benefit from the provision of a fringe benefit to its employees,[1] but it is doubtful whether it would have had standing to enforce the trust, any more than a schoolteacher has standing to enforce a trust for the education of a schoolchild.[2]

Re Denley was subsequently approved by Oliver J in *Re Lipinski*. In that case, the testator bequeathed his residuary estate to trustees on trust as to one-half for the Hull Judeans (Maccabi) Association in memory of his late wife, to be used solely in constructing and improving new buildings for the Association. The Hull Judeans were not a charitable body. Oliver J held that, whether the gift was treated as a purpose trust or an absolute gift to an unincorporated non-charitable body with a superadded direction, the gift was valid if the beneficiaries were ascertainable; that the specified purpose of the gift to the Hull Judeans was within the power of that association and its members were the ascertained or ascertainable beneficiaries; and, accordingly, the association's members were the persons who were entitled to enforce that purpose. A gift to an unincorporated non-charitable association for objects upon which the association is at liberty to spend both capital and income will not fail for perpetuity.[3] Oliver J adopted the reasoning of Goff J which, he concluded, accorded both with authority and with common sense. He also pointed out that, although the distinction made by Goff J had not appeared in earlier cases, nevertheless they are consistent with it. For example, in *Re Clarke*[4] (a gift to the Corps of Commissionaires), *Re Drummond*[5] (a gift to the Old Bradfordians Club), *Re Taylor*[6] (a gift to the Midland Bank Staff Association) and *Re Turkington*[7] (a gift to a masonic lodge to build a suitable temple), in each of which the testator had prescribed the purpose for which

---

1 *Cf Oppenheim v Tobacco Securities Co Ltd* [1951] AC 297.
2 *Shaw v Lawless* (1838) 5 Cl&Fin 129 at 156. See also D Davies (1968) *Annual Survey of Commonwealth Law* 439 on a trust for the education of one's relations.
3 [1976] Ch 235 at 245G; *Re Price* [1943] Ch 422.
4 [1901] 2 Ch 110.
5 [1914] 2 Ch 90.
6 [1940] Ch 481.
7 [1937] 4 All ER 501.

the gift was to be used, and in each of which the gift was upheld, there were ascertainable beneficiaries. The same can be said of *Re Price*[1] (a gift to the Anthroposophical Society). In contrast, in *Re Wood*[2] (a gift for 'The Week's Good Cause' on the BBC) and *Leahy v Attorney-General (NSW)*[3] (a gift for an order of nuns or the Christian Brothers) the gifts failed because there were none.

More recently, however, Vinelott J in *Re Grant's Will Trusts*[4] refused to follow the more flexible approach established by *Re Denley* and *Re Lipinski*. In *Re Grant*, a testator had left his estate 'to the Labour Party property committee for the benefit of the Chertsey headquarters of the Chertsey and Walton Constituency Labour Party'. Vinelott J held that the gift failed and devolved as on intestacy. He considered that in *Re Lipinski* Oliver J had construed the gift, not as one on trust for a purpose, but as one under which the members of the association could have resolved to use the property for some other purpose, or indeed to divide it amongst themselves.[5] Moreover, he considered that *Re Denley*, on a proper analysis, fell outside the categories of gifts to unincorporated associations and purpose trusts. In his judgment, there was no distinction in principle between a trust to permit a class defined by reference to employment to use and enjoy land in accordance with rules to be made at the discretion of trustees, on the one hand, and, on the other hand, a trust to distribute income at the discretion of trustees amongst a class defined by reference to, for example, relationship to the settlor. In both cases, the benefit to be taken by any member of the class is at the discretion of the trustees.[6] Thus in effect the trust in *Re Denley* was reinterpreted as a trust for the benefit of individuals, thereby satisfying the requirements of the beneficiary principle. In reaching this result Vinelott J concluded that the reasons given for the decisions (if not the decisions themselves) in two cases, namely *Re Drummond*[7] and *Re Price*,[8] were not well founded.

Although the simple logic of *Re Grant* is appealing, it does not deal effectively with the discussion of purpose trusts in *Re Denley*. It does not take into account the fact that both Oliver J (in *Re Lipinski*) and Megarry V-C (in *Re Northern Developments (Holdings) Ltd*[9]) accepted the distinction drawn by Goff J. It also ignores several purpose trusts whose validity seems to have been accepted without question. In *Re Abbott's Fund Trusts*,[10] for example, a fund

1 [1943] Ch 422.
2 [1949] Ch 498.
3 [1959] AC 457.
4 [1980] 1 WLR 360.
5 Ibid at 368.
6 Ibid at 368.
7 [1914] 2 Ch 90.
8 [1943] Ch 422.
9 (Unreported) 6 October 1978; referred to in *Carreras Rothmans Ltd v Freeman Mathews Treasure Ltd* [1985] 1 All ER 155; see also P Millett (1985) 101 LQR 280; and **6.2.5** below.
10 [1900] 2 Ch 326.

constituted for the maintenance and support of two ladies was held, after their deaths, on resulting trust for the subscribers, apparently on the basis that it was a purpose trust. In *Re Harpur's Will Trusts*,[1] Lord Evershed MR thought that a gift upon trust to apply income during a limited period (of, say, 10 years) for certain named purposes, some of which are charitable and some not, as the trustees think fit, is by the ordinary law valid. Maintenance funds for historic buildings are often non-charitable purpose trusts.[2] It may also be the case that a trust created with the primary purpose of paying creditors is a type of purpose trust.[3] In any event, the status of Goff J's classification is now, following *Re Grant*, doubtful.

It would seem to be the case that a purpose trust which incidentally benefits persons (as in *Re Denley*) cannot be terminated by those persons who indirectly benefit from the purpose, and they have no right to call for distribution of the trust property. If this is indeed the case, then it seems clear that the distinction in *Re Denley* does not satisfy the requirements of one view (probably the prevailing view) of the beneficiary principle, namely that it is not just concerned with enforceability, with finding an ascertainable person who is sufficiently benefited by the trust to have *locus standi* to enforce it, but that it is in fact a manifestation of and based on equitable ownership, so that it is only those persons who have actual equitable proprietary interests or rights in the trust property who can enforce that trust: on this view, if there is no such person, there can be no valid trust. Instead, *Re Denley* arguably recognised a hybrid trust, one which is for the benefit of ascertained persons, but under which such persons have no equitable interests or rights in the trust property itself. In contrast, a trust for persons who are to be benefited by the carrying out of a stipulated purpose, eg the education and maintenance of the settlor's children, can be terminated by those persons (assuming they are adult, of full legal capacity, and between them absolutely entitled to the settled property). In the latter case, the purpose is merely the motive for the gift, and the beneficiaries may make the trust property their own.[4]

Uncertainty and impossibility

In view of the fact that English law has traditionally not recognised the validity of non-charitable purpose trusts, other than a few anomalous cases, it has never had to work out the implications of such trusts. The test of certainty of objects of a non-charitable purpose trust has never been determined. If a non-charitable purpose trust can exist at all, the definition or description of the

---

1 [1962] Ch 78 at 91; and also per Harman LJ at 96. See also *Re Aberconway's Settlement Trusts* [1953] Ch 647 at 665, per Evershed MR, and per Denning LJ at 669 (and per Danckwerts J at first instance: [1952] 2 All ER 981 at 986).

2 Inheritance Tax Act 1984, s 77.

3 *Carreras Rothmans Ltd v Freeman Mathews Treasure Ltd* [1985] 1 All ER 155; applying *Re Northern Developments (Holdings) Ltd* (unreported). See also **6.2.5**.

4 *Re Andrew's Trusts* [1905] 2 Ch 48; *Re Osoba* [1979] 1 WLR 247; *Re Compton* [1945] Ch 123; *Oppenheim v Tobacco Securities Trust Co* [1951] AC 297.

purpose must be sufficiently certain. Conceptual certainty would seem to be essential.[1] In *Morice v Bishop of Durham*,[2] for example, the gift was of personal estate upon trust 'to dispose of the ultimate residue to such objects of benevolence and liberality as the Bishop of Durham in his own discretion shall most approve of …'. It was held that such language did not confine the objects which the Bishop might choose to charitable objects. The gift can be said to have failed, in this instance, on the ground that the objects had not been described with sufficient certainty to enable the court to determine whether the trustee was properly carrying out his trust. Other similar examples include gifts for 'undertakings of general utility',[3] for 'deserving objects',[4] and 'for such purposes as they should think fit'.[5] The same could be said of *Re Endacott*[6] and *Re Astor's Settlement Trusts*.[7] This reasoning would explain why trusts for the maintenance of specific animals, or for the erection and maintenance of a specific tombstone, have been upheld. The requirement of certainty can be satisfied by the provision of a sufficiently precise description of the purpose intended to be provided for. However, certainty of object does not avoid the application of the beneficiary principle: even a specific purpose cannot ask the court to enforce a trust.

Similarly, administrative workability is essential. *Re Denley* could not save the trust in *R v District Auditor ex parte West Yorkshire Metropolitan County Council*,[8] where a local authority, purporting to exercise statutory powers, attempted to create a trust 'for the benefit of any or all or some of the inhabitants of the County of West Yorkshire'. The capital and income of the trust were to be applied in any of four expressed methods. The class of potential beneficiaries numbered around 2,500,000. It was held that the class was so large that the trust was administratively unworkable.

Delegation of power of testamentary disposition

It has been said that testamentary[9] non-charitable purpose trusts are void on the grounds that, as there is no one who can enforce the trust, the trustees are left to determine the destination of the subject matter of the trust: 'The testator has imperfectly exercised his testamentary power; he has delegated it, for the disposal of his property lies with them, not with him'.[10] However, it

1 *McPhail v Doulton* [1971] AC 424. See generally G Thomas *Powers* (Sweet & Maxwell, 1998), Ch 3.
2 (1804) 9 Ves 339.
3 *Kendall v Granger* (1842) 5 Beav 300.
4 *Harris v Du Pasquier* (1872) 26 LT 689.
5 *Fowler v Garlike* (1830) 1 Russ & M 232.
6 [1960] Ch 232.
7 [1952] Ch 534.
8 [1986] RVR 24; and see Thomas, n 1 above, pp 285–287.
9 The objection does not apply to *inter vivos* trusts.
10 *Leahy v Attorney-General (NSW)* [1959] AC 457 at 484, per Viscount Simonds. See also *Re Wood* [1949] Ch 498 at 501, per Harman J, and *Re Denley's Trust Deed* [1969] 1 Ch 373 at 387, per Goff J; *Buckle v Bristow* (1864) 11 LT 265; *Fowler v Garlike* (1830) 1 Russ & M 232.

appears that no such trust has ever been struck down for this reason. Indeed, it seems more apt as a description of one of the consequences of a failure caused by other factors, rather than a cause in itself. Indeed, in *Re Beatty's Will Trusts*,[1] in the context of powers of appointment, Hoffmann J stated that 'a common law rule against testamentary delegation, in the sense of a restriction on the scope of testamentary powers, is a chimera, a shadow cast by the rule of certainty, having no independent existence.' Whether it differs from the ancient principle that a testator must make an effective disposition of his property if he were to disinherit his heir is unclear.[2] In any event, neither principle seems to have much significance in the context of non-charitable purpose trusts.

Public policy

If the purpose of the trust is capricious, useless, wasteful, harmful, illegal or otherwise contrary to public policy, it will fail. Thus a direction to trustees to brick up a house for 20 years has been held void.[3] A similar fate befell a trust for the purpose of building statues of the testator and of his whole family and the building of 'artistic towers' at prominent points on his estates;[4] a trust to erect a massive bronze equestrian statue of the testator;[5] and a trust to provide a weekly supply of fresh flowers on the graves of the testatrix and her mother.[6] Such trusts are considered to have 'objects of no utility, private or public, objects which benefit nobody, and which have no other purpose or use than that of perpetuating at great cost, and in an absurd manner, the idiosyncrasies of an eccentric testator'.[7]

Perpetuity[8]

The rule against perpetuities is generally concerned with the commencement of interests – with the limit of time to which the vesting of future interests may be postponed – and not with the duration of interests. It is a rule directed against remoteness of vesting. In the context of non-charitable purpose trusts, however, it is the duration of the trust that matters: the period for which the

---

1 [1990] 1 WLR 1503; and see J Davies (1991) 107 LQR 211; J Martin [1991] Conv 138.

2 *Houston v Burns* [1918] AC 337, esp at 342–343; *Attorney-General v National Provincial and Union Bank of England* [1924] AC 262 at 268; *Fell v Fell* (1922) 31 CLR 268 at 284; *Batson v Morgan* (1894) 13 NZLR 525 at 528.

3 *Brown v Burdett* (1882) 21 ChD 667.

4 *M'Caig v University of Glasgow* 1907 SC 231; and *M'Caig's Trustees v Kirk Session of United Free Church of Lismore* 1915 SC 426. In the latter case, Lord Salvesen said (at 434): 'The prospect of Scotland being dotted with monuments to obscure persons who happened to have amassed a sufficiency of means, and cumbered with trusts for the purposes of maintaining these monuments in all time coming, appears to me to be little less than appalling'.

5 *Aitken's Trustee v Aitken* 1927 SC 374.

6 *Lindsay's Executor v Forsyth* 1940 SC 458.

7 *M'Caig v University of Glasgow* 1907 SC 231 at 242.

8 Morris and Leach, n 1 on p 238, pp 321–327; Maudsley, n 1 on p 238, pp 166–178.

trustees may apply the property vested in them for or towards the purpose or object of the trust must be confined to the perpetuity period.

The perpetuity period for this purpose is apparently the same as for any other trust, namely a period of lives in being plus 21 years. In *Re Howard*,[1] for example, a gift for the feeding of a parrot during the life of the survivor of two servants was upheld. In *Re Moore*[2] a trust for maintaining a tomb and keeping it in repair until the expiry of 21 years from the death of the last survivor of all persons living at the testator's death failed because of uncertainty (ie the impossibility of ascertaining when the last life would be extinguished) and not because of the use of lives in being. A royal lives clause was not challenged in *Re Astor*;[3] and in *Re Khoo Cheng Teow*[4] the Supreme Court of the Straits Settlements upheld a non-charitable purpose trust for a period of royal lives plus 21 years.

There is no doubt that the 'lives' in question must be human lives, and cannot be the lives of animals, fish, or trees in California.[5] Whether the option of using a perpetuity period of a fixed term of years, not exceeding 80, provided by s 1(1) of the Perpetuities and Accumulations Act 1964 is available in the case of purpose trusts is undecided, although it is difficult to see why not.[6]

If the stipulated perpetuity period is excessive, or if the trust is capable of being indefinite in its duration (eg because no perpetuity period has been stipulated), it will be void. The court will not read into the trust an implied limitation to 21 years or 'for so long as the law allows'.[7] Moreover, the 'wait and see' rules introduced by the Perpetuities and Accumulations Act 1964 do not apply to purpose trusts.[8] Nevertheless, the courts have often shown considerable reluctance to strike down purpose trusts on the ground of perpetuity. A direction to maintain a grave 'for so long as the law allows', or for as long as the trustees 'can legally do so', has been held valid for a period of 21 years.[9] On some occasions, judicial notice has been taken of the fact that the lifespan of an animal is not likely to exceed 21 years, so that a trust for the

---

1 (1908) *The Times*, October 30.

2 [1901] 1 Ch 936.

3 [1952] Ch 534.

4 [1932] Straits Setts LR 226.

5 *Re Kelly* [1932] IR 255, esp at 260–261.

6 Morris and Leach suggest that the Perpetuities and Accumulations Act 1964, s 1(1) does not apply to purpose trusts: Supp, 21. The contrary has been argued by Maudsley, n 1 on p 238, pp 177–178. See also P Matthews, n 1 on p 238, p 12. No recommendation is made by the Law Commission's recent Report on 'The Rules Against Perpetuities and Excessive Accumulations' (Law Com No 251) as to the removal of the uncertainty caused by s 15 in relation to the availability of the 80-year period to non-charitable purpose trusts: see paras 8.35–8.36 of the Report.

7 Morris and Leach, n 1 on p 238, p 322; *Re Kelly* [1932] IR 255; *Re Compton* [1946] 1 All ER 117. *Cf Re Budge* [1942] NZLR 350.

8 Perpetuities and Accumulations Act 1964, s 15(4).

9 *Pirbright v Salwey* [1896] WN 86; *Re Hooper* [1932] 1 Ch 38.

support of that animal could not exceed the perpetuity period.[1] Indeed, in *Re Dean*[2] North J upheld a gift of an annuity, for a period of up to 50 years, for the upkeep of the testator's horses and hounds, if they should live so long.

6.2.4 Alternative means of effectuating non-charitable purposes

There are various methods by which a non-charitable purpose may be carried into effect without resorting to a trust as the medium. It seems clear[3] that a gift to the members of an association which exists for the advancement of a non-charitable purpose, eg anti-vivisection, as joint tenants or subject to their contract *inter se*, and not for the association's purposes as such, is valid (subject to the rule against perpetuities). A gift to a corporation created to advance non-charitable purposes would not be received by it on trust[4] and would therefore be free from many of the difficulties facing a trust. Also, a gift of income to a company for as long (within the perpetuity period) as it carries out the expressed purpose would be valid.[5] A gift to a charitable body, subject to a request (but not an obligation) to carry out a particular purpose, such as the maintenance of a tomb or monument, with a gift over to another charitable body if the request is not complied with, has also been held valid.[6]

There seems to be no reason, in principle, why a non-charitable purpose should not be achieved by means of a mere power (as opposed to a trust power), rather than a trust (subject, of course, to satisfying the law's requirements as to certainty and perpetuity).[7] However, a purpose trust will not be construed as a power simply in order to save it from invalidity.[8]

Most, if not all, of these alternative methods suffer from some disadvantage or other. For example, an unincorporated association can alter its objects or be dissolved by its members, who could then distribute the gifted property amongst themselves. A gift to a non-charitable corporation will be applicable for its purposes whilst it is a going concern, but its objects may be altered or it may be wound up and its property distributed amongst its

---

1 *Re Haines* (1952) *The Times*, November 7. This contrasts with Meredith J's statement in *Re Kelly* [1932] IR 255 that the court does not enter into the question of a dog's expectation of life.

2 (1889) 41 Ch D 552. It is clear from North J's judgment that the need to satisfy the rule against perpetuities was present in his mind, but there is no indication why he thought it was satisfied in this particular instance.

3 From eg *Re Lipinski* [1976] Ch 235; *Re Recher* [1972] Ch 526.

4 *Bowman v Secular Society Ltd* [1917] AC 406 at 440–441.

5 *Re Chardon* [1928] Ch 464. The possibility of reverter in such a case was not subject to the rule against perpetuities until the enactment of the Perpetuities and Accumulations Act 1964, s 12.

6 *Re Tyler* [1891] 3 Ch 252; Re *Dalziel* [1943] Ch 277. However, if the second charity assigns its contingent interest to the first charity, the latter may presumably ignore its promise to carry out the purpose: *Re Emery* (1928) 34 ALR 167.

7 *Re Douglas* (1887) 35 Ch D 472, esp at 486; *Re Wootton* [1968] 1 WLR 681 at 688. See also *Re Harpur's Will Trusts* [1962] Ch 78 at 91, 96, and *Re Aberconway's Settlement Trusts* [1953] Ch 647 at 665, 669 (and at first instance [1952] 2 All ER 981 at 986).

8 *Re Shaw* [1957] 1 WLR 729 at 746; *IRC v Broadway Cottages Trust* [1955] Ch 20 at 36; *Re Endacott* [1960] Ch 232 at 246.

members, in accordance with its memorandum and articles, which are capable of alteration in accordance with statutory provisions. There may also be considerable practical difficulty in enforcing a promise or undertaking given by a corporation or charity. And a mere power need not be exercised by the donee.

6.2.5 *Quistclose* trusts

Quistclose trusts deserve special mention because of their increasing use and importance in modern commercial transactions. However, they will be dealt with relatively briefly because it is this author's view that they are not properly (or, indeed, widely) categorised as non-charitable purpose trusts – a view that has recently been endorsed by the House of Lords in *Twinsectra Ltd v Yardley*.[1] A detailed treatment of such trusts would therefore be out of place here.

The *Quistclose* trust takes its name from the case of *Barclays Bank Ltd v Quistclose Investments Ltd*,[2] the facts of which were as follows. R Ltd was a company in serious financial difficulties: it had an overdraft with Barclays Bank (in excess of the permitted limit). In order to pay a dividend (of roughly £210,000) which it had already declared, R Ltd borrowed money from Quistclose Investments. The loan was made on the agreed condition that it would be used to pay the dividend. It was paid into a separate account, opened especially for the purpose, with Barclays, who knew that the money was borrowed and who agreed with R Ltd that it would be used only for the purpose of paying the dividend. Before the dividend was paid, however, R Ltd went into voluntary liquidation. Quistclose brought an action against R Ltd and Barclays claiming that the money had been held by R Ltd on trust to pay the dividend; that, as the trust had failed, it was held on resulting trust for Quistclose; and that Barclays had had notice of the trusts and were, accordingly, constructive trustees of the money for Quistclose.

The House of Lords, affirming the decision of the Court of Appeal, held that first, arrangements of this character for the payment of a person's creditors by a third person gave rise to a relationship of a fiduciary character or trust in favour, as a primary trust, of the creditors, and, secondly, if the primary trust failed, of the third person. This had been recognised in a series of cases over some 150 years.[3] The fact that the transaction was one of a loan, giving rise to a legal action of debt, did not exclude the implication of a trust enforceable in equity. There was no difficulty in recognising the co-existence in one transaction of legal and equitable rights and remedies: when the money was advanced, *the lender acquired an equitable right* to see that it was applied for the primary designated purpose; when the purpose had been carried out (ie the

---

1 [2002] 2 WLR 802.

2 [1970] AC 567.

3 Ibid at 580. These cases included *Toovey v Milne* (1819) 2 B & A 683; *Edwards v Glynn* (1859) 2 E & E 29; *Re Rogers* (1891) 8 Morr 243; *Re Drucker (No 1)* [1902] 2 KB 237; *Re Hooley* [1915] HBR 181.

debt paid) the lender had his remedy against the borrower in debt; if the primary purpose could not be carried out, the question arose as to whether a secondary purpose (ie repayment to the lender) had been agreed, expressly or by implication; if it had, the remedies of equity might be invoked to give effect to it, and, if not (and the money was intended to fall into the general assets of the debtor), there was the appropriate remedy of a loan. Here, there was a clear intention to create a secondary trust for the benefit of the lender, Quistclose, to arise if the primary trust could not be carried out. Barclays had, on the facts, accepted the money with knowledge of the circumstances which made it trust money and could not retain it against Quistclose.

Lord Wilberforce, delivering the decision of the House of Lords, clearly thought[1] that it was the 'mutual intention' of the lender and borrower – indeed 'the essence of the bargain' – that the sum advanced should not become part of the assets of R Ltd, but should be used exclusively for the payment of a particular class of creditors, the shareholders entitled to the dividend:

> 'A necessary consequence from this, by process simply of interpretation, must be that if, for any reason, the dividend could not be paid, the money was to be returned to the respondents: the word "only" or "exclusively" can have no other meaning or effect.'[2]

It had been argued that a loan (giving rise to a legal action for debt) excluded the implication of any trust (enforceable in equity). He found this argument 'unattractive'.[3]

> 'It means that the law does not permit an arrangement to be made by which one person agrees to advance money to another, on terms that the money is to be used exclusively to pay debts of the latter, and if, so far as not so used, rather than becoming a general asset of the latter available to his creditors at large, is to be returned to the lender. The lender is obliged, in such a case, because he is a lender, to accept, whatever the mutual wishes of lender and borrower may be, that the money he was willing to make available for one purpose shall be freely available for others of *the borrower's creditors for whom he has not the slightest desire to provide*.'[4]

He added:[5]

---

1 [1970] AC 567 at 580.

2 The word 'only' appears in the letter from R Ltd to the Manager of Barclays. However, why should this necessarily point to a trust relationship between Quistclose and R Ltd, as opposed to a statement of an acknowledgement by Barclays (which it would presumably be estopped from denying) that it would not seek to apply that sum towards reducing R Ltd's unauthorised overdraft? In other words, it could simply be an indication of an agreed restriction on Barclays' rights as against R Ltd's money and nothing more.

3 [1970] AC 567 at 581.

4 Ibid at 581: emphasis added – indicating that he saw some of the borrower's creditors as those who were intended to benefit. In fact, he adds that the earlier cases had permitted such arrangements to be enforced 'and have approved them *as being for the benefit of creditors* and all concerned'.

5 Ibid at 581–582.

> 'There is surely no difficulty in recognising the co-existence in one transaction of legal and equitable rights and remedies: when the money is advanced, the lender acquires an equitable right to see that it is applied for the primary designated purpose:[1] when the purpose has been carried out (ie, the debt paid) the lender has his remedy against the borrower in debt: if the primary purpose cannot be carried out, the question arises if a secondary purpose (ie repayment to the lender) has been agreed, expressly or by implication: if it has, the remedies of equity may be invoked to give effect to it: if it has not (and the money is intended to fall within the general fund of the debtor's assets) then there is the appropriate remedy for recovery of a loan.'

The decision in *Quistclose* itself left unanswered a range of difficult questions, such as the location of the beneficial interest pending the application of the monies for the stipulated purpose, the respective rights (if any) of the lender, the borrower and the third party ultimately intended to benefit – all of which have subsequently given rise to an extensive literature.[2] However, for present purposes, it is relevant to highlight two points in particular. First, it is clear that the case was *not* argued before the House of Lords in terms of a non-charitable purpose trust. The appellants clearly contended that there was no trust at all. The respondents clearly thought in terms of a 'persons trust', for their counsel, in summarising their argument,[3] and having referred to a payment by A to B 'to be applied for a specific purpose' as creating a trust, stated:

> 'If the specified purpose is for the benefit of identified persons or for charity (subject to exceptions not here material) the court in the exercise of its equitable jurisdiction in the execution of trusts will enforce the equitable obligation of B.'

The House of Lords was not asked to consider and determine the possible existence or validity of a non-charitable purpose trust and it did not do so.

---

1 Referring to *In re Rogers* (1891) 9 Morr 243 where both Lindley LJ and Kay LJ recognised this.

2 See, eg, R Chambers *Resulting Trusts* (Clarendon Press, 1997), Ch 3; S Worthington *Proprietary Interests in Commercial Transactions* (Clarendon Press, 1996), Ch 3; RM Goode *Principles of Corporate Insolvency Law* (Sweet & Maxwell, 1990); LJ Priestley 'The Romalpa Clause and the Quistclose Trust' in PD Finn (ed) *Equity and Commercial Relationships* (Law Book Co Ltd, 1987), p 217; PJ Millett (1985) 101 LQR 269; RP Austin (1988) 11 UNSWLJ 66; CEF Ricketts (1991) 107 LQR 608; FR Burns (1992) 18 Mon LR 147; M Bridge (1992) 12 OJLS 333; J Payne 'Quistclose and Resulting Trusts' in P Birks and F Rose (eds) *Restitution and Equity – Volume One: Resulting Trusts and Equitable Compensation* (Mansfield Press, 2000), pp 77–95; L Ho and P St J Smart (2001) 21 OJLS 267. See also *Re EVTR Ltd* [1987] BCLC 646; *Twinsectra Ltd v Yardley* [1999] Lloyd's Rep Bank 438; *Re Branston & Gothard Ltd* [1999] 1 All ER (Comm) 289; *Burton v FX Music Ltd* (1999) *The Times*, July 8; *Re Australian Elizabethan Theatre Trust* (1991) 102 ALR 681; *Re McKeown* [1974] NILR 226; *General Communications Ltd v Development Finance Corporation of New Zealand Ltd* [1990] 3 NZLR 406; *Re Associated Securities Ltd* [1981] 1 NSWLR 742; *Guardian Ocean Cargoes Ltd v Banco da Brasil SA* [1991] 2 Lloyd's Rep 68. There are also some recent unreported decisions: *Hurst-Bannister v New Capital Reinsurance Corp Ltd* [2000] Lloyd's Rep IR 166; *Re Griffin Trading Co* [2000] BPIR 256; R *v Common Professional Examination Board ex parte Sally Mewling-McLeod* (2000) *The Times*, May 2; and *Shanshal v Al-Kishtaini* [1999] TLR 448. See now *Twinsectra Ltd v Yardley*, [2002] 2 WLR 802, discussed at pp 263–268 below.

3 [1970] AC 567 at 576.

Secondly, it is clear that Lord Wilberforce attached considerable importance to the intentions of the parties – not just whether there was an intention to create a trust of any kind, as opposed to a mere loan or a charge or an assignment, but also in whose favour, or for whose benefit, such a trust was intended. There does not seem to be any compelling reason why the parties to a *Quistclose*-type transaction should always have the same intentions: the fact that the third-party creditors were intended to have a beneficial interest in one case surely does not make it a requirement of a *Quistclose* trust that they must always have such an interest.

Nevertheless, subsequent English cases have confused, rather than clarified, these issues, and the nature and operation of a *Quistclose* trust became matters of considerable debate and uncertainty. The crucial point, for present purposes, however, is that some (albeit slight) support emerged for the proposition that a *Quistclose* trust is essentially another kind of non-charitable purpose trust. However, following the recent decision of the House of Lords in *Twinsectra Ltd v Yardley*,[1] any such proposition now seems untenable.

In *Carreras Rothmans Ltd v Freeman Mathews Treasure Ltd*,[2] the plaintiff (a manufacturer of tobacco products) advertised its products extensively in newspapers and periodicals, using the services of the defendant, an advertising agency. Such services included buying advertising space in publications and on billboards; and, in doing its work, the defendant negotiated favourable discounts and incurred debts *as a principal* to third parties for the space bought and for certain technical services. The plaintiff paid the defendant an annual fee in monthly instalments for the placement work, and each month the plaintiff would pay the defendant a sum equivalent to the amount of the invoices received by the defendant from third parties for liabilities incurred the previous month. The plaintiff paid the money in time for the defendant to pay the third parties when the debts became due for payment. When the defendant fell into financial difficulties, it was agreed that a special account should be opened into which the plaintiff would pay a sum equivalent to the monies due to third parties. The defendant then went into voluntary liquidation and its liquidator arranged for the special account to be frozen before cheques were cleared. The third-party publishers reacted to non-payment by threatening that, unless the plaintiff met the defendant's liabilities to them, they would not publish any advertisement of the plaintiff's products. The plaintiff paid the debts incurred by the defendant to the third parties and took an assignment of those debts. The plaintiff then brought an action against the defendant and its liquidator for a declaration that the monies in the special

1 [2002] 2 WLR 802 – see pp 263–268 below.

2 [1985] Ch 207.

account were held on trust for the sole purpose of paying the third-party creditors and for an order for those monies to be repaid to the plaintiff.[1]

Peter Gibson J (unfortunately in an unreserved judgment) held that the monies paid into the special account were never held by the defendant beneficially; that, since the monies had been paid in for a specific purpose, equity required that the monies be used only for that purpose; that, accordingly, the agreement created a trust and the plaintiff had a right to enforce the payment over of the monies to the third parties and the third parties had an interest in the orderly administration of those trust funds.

His conclusion on the first question, namely whether or not the loaned monies were subjected to a trust, is relatively unproblematic. This was a question of ascertaining the mutual intentions of the parties,[2] and the circumstances of this case pointed clearly to a trust:

> 'The moneys payable by the plaintiff were to be paid not to the defendant beneficially but directly into that account so that the defendant was never free to deal as it pleased with the money so paid. The moneys were to be used only for the specific purpose of paying the third parties … The account was intended to be little more than a conduit pipe, but the intention was plain that whilst in the conduit pipe the moneys should be protected. There was even a provision covering the possibility … that there might be a balance left after payment and in that event the balance was to be paid to the plaintiff and not kept by the defendant. It was thus clearly intended that the moneys once paid would never become the property of the defendant. That was the last thing the plaintiff wanted in view of its concern about the defendant's financial position.'[3]

Later in the judgment he added:[4]

> 'In my judgment the principle in all these cases is that equity fastens on the conscience of the person who receives from another property transferred for a specific purpose only and not therefore for the recipient's own purposes, so that such person will not be permitted to treat the property as his own or to use it for other than the stated purpose. … if the common intention is that property is transferred for a specific purpose and not so as to become the property of the transferee, the transferee cannot keep the property if for any reason that purpose cannot be fulfilled.'

On the facts and circumstances of this particular case, a *Quistclose*-type trust was found to have come into existence in accordance with what was perceived to be the common intention of the parties.

However, none of this indicates the capacity in which, or the mechanism by which, the plaintiff recovered the money: was it as the original lender and

---

1 The defendant and its liquidator claimed that the agreement was unenforceable being contrary to public policy (as an attempt to make a preferential payment) or void because it had created a charge on book debts that had not been registered as required by statute.

2 [1985] Ch 207 at 221, where the judge referred explicitly to Lord Wilberforce's remarks in *Quistclose* about the mutual intentions of the parties.

3 Ibid at 220.

4 Ibid at 222.

under a resulting trust? Or was it as assignee of the third-party creditors and under an express trust? A strict application of the decision of the House of Lords in *Quistclose* would seem to point clearly to the first of these two alternatives. Indeed, it is clear that, in *Carreras* itself, counsel for both plaintiff and defendant had submitted that the third-party creditors had no enforceable rights; and it seems equally clear that the plaintiff claimed that, in default of the stipulated purpose being fulfilled, there was a resulting trust in favour of the plaintiff.[1] However, Peter Gibson J (despite the fact that his judgment was unreserved) refused to accept *the joint submission* of counsel that the third-party creditors for the payment of whose debts the plaintiff had paid the monies into the special account had no enforceable rights. Instead, he preferred to base his conclusions on an earlier, unreported decision of Megarry V-C in *Re Northern Developments (Holdings) Ltd*.[2]

In none of the earlier cases, other than *Re Northern Developments Holdings Ltd*, had any consideration been given to the question of whether the person intended to benefit from the carrying out of the specific purpose (ie, the third-party creditor) had any enforceable rights. In *Quistclose* itself and earlier cases, either the primary purpose had been carried out, and the contest was between the borrower's trustee in bankruptcy or liquidator and the person to whom the money had been paid, or the purpose was treated as having failed, and the contest was between the trustee in bankruptcy or liquidator and the lender. Prior to *Re Northern Developments (Holdings) Ltd*, the position where the primary purpose was still capable of being carried out had not been considered.[3] In *Re Northern Developments (Holdings) Ltd*, a group of banks paid money into an account in Northern's name for the express purpose of paying the unsecured creditors of a subsidiary company (Kelly) in financial difficulties and for no other purpose. Over half the fund remained unexpended when Kelly was put into receivership. Megarry V-C held that there was a *Quistclose*-type trust here and that the trust was a *purpose trust enforceable by identifiable individuals*, namely the banks as lenders, Kelly itself and Kelly's creditors. He said:

> 'The fund was established not with the object of vesting the beneficial interest in them, but in order to confer a benefit on Kelly (and so, consequently, on the rest of the group and the bankers) by ensuring that Kelly's creditors would be paid in an orderly manner. There is perhaps some parallel in the position of a beneficiary entitled to a share of residue under a will. What he has is not a beneficial interest in any asset forming part of residue, but a right to compel the executor to administer the assets of the deceased properly. It seems to me that it is that sort of right which the creditors of Kelly had.'

---

1 Ibid at 219, 222 and 223.

2 (Unreported) 6 October 1978, per Megarry V-C.

3 *Twinsectra Ltd v Yardley* [2002] 2 WLR 802, at [**85**], per Lord Millett.

On this analysis, the third-party creditors do not have a beneficial interest as such under a *Quistclose* trust: instead, they have 'a right' to compel performance of the trust in their favour. In the words of Peter Gibson J in *Carreras*:[1]

> 'In the light of that authority I cannot accept *the joint submission* that the third-party creditors for the payment of whose debts the plaintiff had paid the moneys into the special account had no enforceable rights. In any event I do not comprehend how a trust, which on no footing could the plaintiff revoke unilaterally, and which was expressed as a trust to pay third parties and was still capable of performance, could nevertheless leave the beneficial interest in the plaintiff which had parted with the moneys. On Sir Robert Megarry V-C's analysis the beneficial interest is in suspense until the payment is made.'

This novel approach to the problem – one for which there is no trace of support in *Quistclose* itself – gives rise to several difficult questions. First, the nature of this 'right' is ambiguous. The analogy with the position of a beneficiary interested in unadministered residue seems completely inappropriate. Such a beneficiary has no proprietary interest at all – only a mere *spes* or hope of benefit – unless and until the estate is fully administered (or there is an earlier appropriation) and he may never actually receive such an interest at all. On the other hand, once a *Quistclose* trust is completely constituted (when monies are transferred to the borrower), there is no obvious reason why the purpose cannot be fulfilled, ie why the third-party creditors should not be able to demand its immediate performance. Why should the beneficial interest need to be in suspense at any stage and why should the purpose of the trust fail simply because the borrower had become insolvent? Indeed, in *Carreras* itself, the order made was that the liquidator should forthwith apply the money in the special account in carrying out the purpose of the trust.[2] If this was the case in *Carreras*, then why could it not equally be the case with other *Quistclose* trusts (including *Quistclose* itself), in which case how could a resulting trust arise in favour of the lender? One possible explanation is that the parties' intentions differ (and, in particular, the settlor/lender's intention differs) in each case. In most cases, the intention would seem to be to benefit the borrower (by saving him from becoming insolvent) and not to benefit the third-party creditor, so that, if the borrower becomes insolvent before the purpose is fulfilled, the primary trust automatically comes to an end and the creditor then has no right (if he ever had one) to compel the performance of the trust. On the other hand, *Carreras* could be said to have been a different kind of case in that the intention was that the creditor was intended to benefit (although this is difficult to justify

---

1 *Carreras Rothmans Ltd v Freeman Mathews Treasure Ltd* [1985] Ch 207 at 223.

2 Ibid at 232.

from the facts of the case) and to have a right to enforce the trust.[1] However, even if this distinction might explain why the third-party creditors have an enforceable right in one case, but not in another, it still does not provide a satisfactory explanation of why a *Quistclose* trust should be regarded as analogous to an unadministered estate. Under a *Quistclose* trust, the borrower trustee has the option of carrying out the purpose of the loan (according to the terms of the loan agreement) or returning the money to the lender: he has no other duties to perform; and, by definition, the trust fund cannot be diminished by any prior claims. This is the language of powers and not simply of trust.[2] A personal representative, on the other hand, takes absolute ownership of the assets in an unadministered estate, has a range of duties to perform which take priority over distribution to beneficiaries, and may, in fact, have no property left to give to any of them. But, in this latter case, non-payment is the result of the inadequacy of the assets and not a change in the status of the 'trustee'.

A second difficulty is that the *Carreras* analysis says nothing about the rights of the lender. It is well recognised that the lender in a *Quistclose* transaction acquires an equitable right to ensure that the monies that he has lent are applied for the primary designated purpose[3] (or, at least, a right to prevent their misapplication).[4] However, it is trite law that a settlor who retains no beneficial interest, and no express power of control over trustees, cannot enforce a trust which he has created.[5] Consequently, the settlor/lender must have some right which an ordinary settlor would not have, and the most likely explanation is that he has such a right because he has a beneficial interest under the trust.[6] Moreover, in several cases – including *Twinsectra Ltd v Yardley*[7] – the primary trust, if it said to have been a purpose trust at all, must have been for an abstract purpose, with no one but the lender to enforce

1 As Lord Millett has recently pointed out (with considerable justification) in *Twinsectra Ltd v Yardley* [2002] 2 WLR 802 at [**87**], the purpose of the loan in *Re Northern Ireland Developments (Holdings) Ltd* was to enable the subsidiary to continue trading, which necessarily involved incurring further liabilities to trade creditors. Therefore, the money was not solely applicable to existing creditors at the date the fund was established: it was not to enable the debtor to avoid bankruptcy by paying off existing creditors, but to provide it with working capital. On this basis, 'there is a powerful argument for saying that the result of the arrangements was to vest a beneficial interest in the subsidiary from the start. If so, then this was not a *Quistclose* trust at all'.

2 See pp 262–263.

3 [1970] AC 567 at 581, per Lord Wilberforce.

4 *Edwards Glyn* (1859) 2 El & El 29, at 50–51; *Re Rogers* (1891) 8 Morr 243 at 248, per Lindley LJ, *Twinsectra Ltd v Yardley* (above) at [**87**], per Lord Millett.

5 See Millett (1985) 101 LQR 269 at 287; *Twinsectra Ltd v Yardley* (above) at [**87**], per Lord Millett.

6 As argued, eg, by Millett, ibid – save that he went on to argue that the trust is actually an 'illusory trust', which seems unlikely. The 'settlor' presumably has a contractual right, arising from his contract with the borrower, to prevent (by injunction) the misapplication of the monies (*Palmer v Carey* [1926] AC 703 at 706; *Swiss Bank Corporation v Lloyds Bank Ltd* [1982] AC 584 at 613), but generally has no right to compel its application in a particular way (by specific performance).

7 [2002] 2 WLR 802 at [**89**], per Lord Millett.

performance or restrain misapplication.[1] However, as we have seen,[2] abstract purpose trusts are not recognised in English law: even *Re Denley* was not prepared to contemplate the possibility that they might be valid. In the context of *Quistclose* trusts, there is simply no reason to make an arbitrary distinction between money paid for an abstract purpose and money paid for a purpose which can be said to benefit an ascertained class of beneficiaries, and the cases rightly draw no such distinction. As Lord Millett emphasised in *Twinsectra*, any analysis of the *Quistclose* trust must be able to accomodate gifts and loans for an abstract purpose.[3]

Indeed, even before *Twinsectra*, the *Quistclose* trust was sometimes analysed in the simple terms of a straightforward express trust. In Australia, for example, in *Re Elizabethan Theatre Trust*,[4] Gummow J provided a persuasive analysis of the *Quistclose* trust and concluded:

> 'To speak of a *Quistclose* trust as if it were a new legal institution, rather than an example of the particular operation of principle upon the facts as found, is to set the listener or reader off on a false path.'

He pointed out that the *Quistclose* trust could be analysed easily in terms of existing principles and norms and that there was 'scarcely a need' for another kind of trust. It was an express trust with two limbs, rather than an express trust in favour of the shareholders and a resulting trust in favour of Quistclose.[5] In either case, however, there is clearly an express trust operating in accordance with well-recognised principles.

There is much to be said for this analysis. Under a *Quistclose* trust, the borrower holds the money on trust for the lender, but with a power to apply the money for (and only for) the stipulated purpose. If and when the borrower exercises that power, the purpose of the loan is fulfilled and the lender's beneficial interest is extinguished. It is a power exercisable for the 'benefit' of the borrower, but it is not a general power, for it can be exercised only in particular circumstances and in favour of a particular object or class of objects. It is also then largely immaterial whether one views the objects of the power as a 'purpose' or a class of persons.[6] Moreover, it is clearly not the case that, if the settlor/lender is regarded as the beneficiary under such a trust, he could then revoke the trust prior to the carrying out of the stipulated purpose.[7] The settlor would have no such right either under the contract or in equity. If S

---

1 See *Edwards v Glyn* (1859) 2 E & E 29; *Re EVTR* [1987] BCLC 646; *General Communications Ltd v Development Finance Corporation of New Zealand Ltd* [1990] 3 NZLR 406.

2 See pp 246–247 above.

3 [2002] 2 WLR 802 at [**89**].

4 (1991) 102 ALR 681.

5 Ibid at 691.

6 The class of objects of the power must, of course, be 'certain': see G Thomas, n 1 on p 250, Ch 3; *Twinsectra Ltd v Yardley* (above) at [**16**] and [**101**].

7 The same point is made by Chambers, n 2 on p 256, p 74.

directs T to hold property on trust for S, but T has a power to distribute the property to X (or a class comprised of A to F), then, for as long as that power subsists, S alone is not absolutely and indefeasibly entitled to that property. The question that would then arise is: what happens to the power when the borrower becomes insolvent, assuming it has not by then been exercised? The obvious answer is that it then ceases to exist, or at least to be exercisable. If the intention is to save the borrower from insolvency, the power – whether it be classified as a mere power or a fiduciary power – can be exercised only when, and for as long as, the borrower is solvent. There would then be no question of the power vesting in the borrower's trustee in bankruptcy, receiver or liquidator and being exercisable by any one of them (as the case may be).[1] It is conceivable, but highly unlikely, that the power conferred on the borrower is a trust power (in the sense that it must be exercised by the borrower). In that case, the creditors would have a right to compel its execution and the lender would then not have a beneficial interest. However, such an analysis would not be consistent with *Quistclose* itself or any of the subsequent *Quistclose*-type cases.

These issues were addressed directly and seemingly resolved in *Twinsectra Ltd v Yardley*.[2] Twinsectra loaned £1 million on the terms of a solicitors' undertaking to the effect that the money would 'be utilised solely for the acquisition of property' on behalf of the latter's client 'and for no other purpose', and would be retained by the solicitors until such time as it was so applied. In the event, and contrary to the terms of this undertaking, not all the money was used for this purpose but was simply paid over upon the client's instructions. The loan was not repaid. The first question at issue was whether the loan monies were subject to any form of trust in the solicitors' hands. All five Law Lords concluded that the money was held on trust – a *Quistclose* trust.

In his speech, Lord Millet provided a lengthy and detailed analysis of the *Quistclose* trust and addressed, in particular, the location of the beneficial interest under such a trust. He favoured the view that, pending the carrying out of the stated purpose, the beneficial interest under a *Quistclose* trust rests with the lender:

> 'the *Quistclose* trust is a simple commercial arrangement … akin to a retention of title clause (though with a different object) which enables the borrower to have recourse to the lender's money for a particular purpose without entrenching on the lender's property rights more than necessary to enable the purpose to be achieved. The money remains the property of the lender unless and until it is applied in accordance with his directions, and insofar as it is not so applied it must be returned to him. I am disposed, perhaps pre-disposed, to think that this is the only analysis which is consistent both with the orthodox trust law and with commercial reality.'[3]

---

1 See Thomas, n 1 on p 250, pp 194–210, on the exercise of powers on bankruptcy, receivership or liquidation.

2 [2002] 2 WLR 802.

3 Ibid at [**81**].

Lord Millett then went on to consider the alternative analyses. First, it was plain that 'the beneficial interest is not vested unconditionally in the borrower so as to leave the money at free disposal':

> 'The borrower's interest pending the application of the money for the stated purpose or its return to the lender is minimal. He must keep the money separate; he cannot apply it except for the stated purpose; unless the terms of the loan otherwise provide he must return it to the lender if demanded; he cannot refuse to return it if the stated purpose cannot be achieved; and if he becomes bankrupt it does not vest in his trustee in bankruptcy.'[1]

Secondly, the beneficial interest was clearly not vested in the contemplated beneficiary. Lord Millett pointed out that the position where the primary purpose was still capable of being carried out was not considered until *Re Northern Developments (Holdings) Ltd*,[2] where the contest was between the lender and the creditors (the borrower not being in liquidation and not making any claim on the money) and where it was held that the primary trust was a purpose trust enforceable by the subsidiary's creditors. He then proceeded to set out the difficulties with such an analysis. It is clear from Lord Wilberforce's references in *Quistclose* to *Re Rogers*[3] that the equitable right he had in mind was a negative injunction to restrain improper application of the money and not a mandatory order to compel performance. The purpose of the loan in *Re Northern Developments (Holdings) Ltd* was to enable the subsidiary to continue trading, which necessarily involved further liabilities to trade creditors. The money was not solely applicable to existing creditors at the date the fund was established: it was not to enable the debtor to avoid bankruptcy by paying off existing creditors, but to provide it with working capital. Moreover, the lenders' object was not to benefit the creditors, but to protect their own interests.

Thirdly, the 'purpose trust' analysis was neither workable nor necessary. In several cases, including *Twinsectra* itself, the primary trust was for an abstract purpose with no one but the lender to enforce performance or restrain misapplication. There was no reason to make an arbitrary distinction between money paid for an abstract purpose and money paid for a purpose which can be said to benefit an ascertained class of beneficiaries, and the cases rightly draw no such distinction: 'Any analysis of the *Quistclose* trust must be able to accommodate gifts and loans for an abstract purpose'.

Fourthly, the argument that the beneficial interest remained in suspense until the stated purpose was carried out was also defective: 'The difficulty with this (apart from its unorthodoxy) is that it fails to have regard to the role which the resulting trust plays in equity's scheme of things, or to explain why the money is not simply held on a resulting trust for the lender'.

---

1 Ibid at [**83**].

2 (Unreported) 6 October 1978.

3 (1891) 9 Morr 243.

Lord Millett concluded his analysis by saying that all the alternative analyses have their difficulties, but that there are two problems, in particular, which they fail to solve – problems which are easily solved if the beneficial interest remains throughout in the lender. The first is the fact, well established by the authorities, that the primary trust is enforceable by the lender. On what basis can he do so? Clearly not as beneficiary of the secondary trust and not as settlor. The second problem relates to the basis on which the primary trust is said to have failed. Given that the money does not belong to the borrower, his/its insolvency should not prevent the original purpose being fulfilled, unless the purpose is said to have been to avoid insolvency or collapse. However, one must not confuse the purpose of the trust with the settlor's motive: the frustration of the latter does not necessarily mean that the purpose of the trust has failed, '[b]ut if the borrower is treated as holding the money on a resulting trust for the lender but with power (or in some cases a duty) to carry out the lender's revocable mandate, and the lender's object in giving the mandate is frustrated, he is entitled to revoke the mandate and demand the return of money which never ceased to be his beneficially'.[1] His conclusion, therefore, is as follows:

> 'I ... hold the Quistclose trust to be an entirely orthodox example of the kind of default trust known as a resulting trust. The lender pays the money to the borrower by way of loan but he does not part with the entire beneficial interest in the money, and insofar as he does not it is held on a resulting trust for the lender from the outset. Contrary to the opinion of the Court of Appeal, it is the borrower who has a very limited use of the money, being obliged to apply it for the stated purpose or return it. He has no beneficial interest in the money, which remains throughout in the lender subject only to the borrower's power or duty to apply the money in accordance with the lender's instructions. When the purpose fails, the money is returnable to the lender, not under some new trust in his favour which only comes into being on the failure of the purpose, but because the resulting trust in his favour is no longer subject to any power on the part of the borrower to make use of the money. Whether the borrower is obliged to apply the money for the stated purpose or merely at liberty to do so, and whether the lender can countermand the borrower's mandate while it is still capable of being carried out, must depend on the circumstances of the particular case.'[2]

Thus, according to Lord Millett, the *Quistclose* trust, far from being *sui generis*, is in essence an entirely orthodox trust based on existing and well-understood principles and norms.

Whether the other four Law Lords agreed with the details of Lord Millett's analysis is unclear, however. Lord Hoffmann alone dealt directly with the nature of the trust created by the solicitors' undertaking. However, he did not expressly endorse Lord Millett's analysis, nor did he attempt to analyse a *Quistclose* trust himself – indeed, nowhere in his speech is *Quistclose* mentioned.

---

1 *Twinsectra Ltd v Yardley* [2002] 2 WLR 802 at **[98]**.

2 Ibid at **[100]**.

According to Lord Hoffmann, the undertaking made it clear that the money 'was not to be at the free disposal' of the client and that the solicitors 'were not to part with the money to [the client] or anyone else except for the purpose of enabling him to acquire property': '… the effect of the undertaking was to provide that the money … should remain Twinsectra's money until such a time as it was applied for the acquisition of property in accordance with the undertaking'.[1] His analysis of the trust in question was that the solicitors 'held the money in *trust* for Twinsectra, but subject to a *power* to apply it by way of loan' to the borrower in accordance with the undertaking. Lord Slynn agreed with Lord Hoffmann and made no reference to Lord Millett's speech. Lord Steyn agreed with the judgments of Lord Hoffmann and Lord Hutton, and did not refer to Lord Millett. Lord Hutton, for his part, indicated that he had read the draft speeches of both Lord Hoffmann and Lord Millett and, for the reasons they had given, agreed that the solicitors' undertaking 'created a trust', despite the fact that their reasons may not have been entirely in accord. Thus, even if it can be said that Lord Steyn and Lord Hutton agreed, directly or indirectly, with Lord Millett, it is not clear whether their agreement extended to the detailed analysis of a *Quistclose* trust put forward by Lord Millett or was simply confined to the conclusion that the solicitors' undertaking had created a trust – even a *Quistclose* trust – which is all that needed to be established in order for the second point in the case (the 'dishonest assistance' point) to be raised. In other words, once a trust (even a *Quistclose* trust) had been found to exist, there was no need to analyse the nature of that trust and the majority of the House of Lords did not attempt to do so.

Indeed, the analysis put forward by Lord Millett may not only have differed slightly from that suggested by Lord Hoffmann, but may also raise uncertainties of its own. It is clear that, for Lord Hoffmann, the solicitors held Twinsectra's money on trust, 'but subject to a *power* to apply it by way of loan'. Although he acknowledged that the solicitors owed 'fiduciary obligations … in respect of the exercise of the power', there is no hint that he considered that they were actually under a duty to exercise it. Lord Millett seems to have reached the same conclusion in that he too held that he money belonged to Twinsectra subject only to a 'right to apply it' for the stated purpose. Moreover, he clearly acknowledged that the lender's right may simply be a right to prevent misapplication for an unauthorised purpose and not to compel application for an authorised one. For example, he stated that, in *Quistclose*, Lord Wilberforce's reference to *Re Rogers* made it plain that 'the equitable right he had in mind was not a mandatory order to compel performance, but a negative injunction to restrain improper application of the money'. All of this clearly supports the analysis of a *Quistclose* trust in favour of the lender but with a mere *power* for the borrower to use the money for the stated purpose. However, at various points in his judgment, he also referred to the borrower

---

1 Ibid at [13].

being under a *duty* to apply the money. For example, he cited North J in *Gilbert v Gonard*:[1]

> 'It is very well known that if one person makes a payment to another for a certain purpose, and that person takes the money knowing that it is for that purpose, he must apply it to the purpose for which it was given. He may decline to take it if he likes; but if he chooses to accept the money tendered for a particular purpose, *it is his duty, and there is a legal obligation on him, to apply it for that purpose*.'

Similarly, when dealing with the question of certainty of objects, he says: 'the borrower is authorised (*or directed*) to apply the money for a stated purpose, but this is a mere power and does not constitute a purpose trust'. In other words, Lord Millett contemplated the possibility that the idea of a *Quistclose* trust encompassed a range of different arrangements, including not just cases where the borrower-trustee had a *power* to apply the loan for the specific purpose, but also where the borrower-trustee was under a *duty* to do so. 'Whether the borrower is obliged to apply the money for the stated purpose or merely at liberty to do so, and whether the lender can countermand the borrower's mandate while it is still capable of being carried out, must depend on the circumstances of the particular case.' Of course, there is no reason, in principle why a lender could not impose such an obligation on the borrower. However, once this point is reached and he is held to have done so, then the implications and consequences must surely be different from those outlined by Lord Millett.

First, if the borrower is *obliged* to apply the money for the stated purpose, and does not merely have a right or power to do so, then it is difficult to see how the beneficial interest can then be said to be vested in the lender. The borrower will hold the money on trust for the intended ultimate beneficiary (the unpaid creditors in the typical case). Even if the borrower is said to have a 'trust power' – in the sense of a power which he must exercise, as opposed to a mere power – it is surely the intended ultimate beneficiary who is the beneficiary and not the lender. The problematic question as to whether the 'beneficiary' of the trust or trust power was a human being (such as the creditors) or a purpose, and whether in the latter case there could be a valid trust at all, would need to be addressed all over again. Secondly, where such an arrangement has been created, can the primary trust ever fail? If not, how could a resulting trust ever arise in favour of the lender? Thirdly, how and why would the lender have any interest in enforcing the trust under such an arrangement? If the primary trust can be and is enforced and carried into effect, as it surely ought to be, there can be no secondary trust in favour of the lender. These are the very difficulties that were discussed at length by Lord Millett and which would not arise if the *Quistclose* trust were analysed simply as a trust for the lender, coupled with a *power* for the borrower to apply the

---

1 (1884) 54 LJ Ch 439.

money for the stated purpose, but which, it is suggested, would be as alive as ever once the borrower is held to be under an *obligation* to do so.

Some uncertainties as to the nature of a *Quistclose* trust therefore remain. In the past, this author has expressed the firm view that a *Quistclose* trust is an *express* trust, under which the settlor-lender retains the beneficial interest and the borrower possesses a *power* to pay the funds to a creditor. *Twinsectra*, and especially the judgment of Lord Millett, concludes that (in general) it is indeed a trust in favour of the lender, coupled with a power in the borrower, but that it is a resulting and not an express trust. It is not entirely clear why this should be the case. If A lends money to B for the specific purpose of paying debts, Lord Millett would say that the beneficial interest is not wholly disposed of (pending exercise of the power) and it therefore results back to A. This makes his analysis consistent with the decision in *Quistclose* itself. However, it could also be argued that this is an *express* trust. Indeed, it is difficult to imagine that any adviser acting for a lender, when asked by his client to ensure that money loaned to a borrower for a specific purpose was used solely for that purpose and would be returned to the lender in the event of the borrower becoming insolvent before that purpose could be implemented, would not seek to avoid the uncertainties of the law in this area. Surely such an adviser would seek to ensure that the difficult issues outlined above would never arise and the simple and obvious way to do so would be to create an *express* trust (coupled with a power) in terms which made it abundantly clear that, pending application of the money, the beneficial interest was vested in the lender and no one else, and also that the borrower had a mere power and no more. The form of such an *express* trust would be identical to Lord Millett's resulting trust. In any event, there is surely very little scope after *Twinsectra* to argue in favour of an analysis of a *Quistclose* trust as a non-charitable purpose trust – even one falling under the *Re Denley* principle[1] – or as a trust under which the beneficial interest remains in suspense until the creditor is paid. There is simply no need to do so. And if and insofar as a case is sought to be made out in favour of the validity of non-charitable purpose trusts in English law, support for that case can no longer be found in the *Quistclose* trust.

6.2.6 An alternative analysis of non-charitable purpose trusts

It has recently been argued[2] that the generally accepted view that English law does not permit the existence of non-charitable purpose trusts is simply wrong. According to this view, it is erroneous to say that a trust cannot be enforced if there is no beneficiary: indeed, it is argued that the exact opposite is evidenced by a series of reported decisions, dealing with a wide range of different subjects and extending back over several centuries. In those cases

---

1 [1969] 1 Ch 373; see pp 246–249 above.

2 Baxendale-Walker, n 1 on p 238.

where an attempt to create a non-charitable purpose trust failed, the reason for failure, it is said, was not the beneficiary principle, but a breach of the rule against perpetuities or the absence of conceptual certainty. This alternative analysis certainly raises some important questions about the very nature of the English trust and addresses, directly, some of the fundamental weaknesses and inconsistencies manifested in the cases dealing with non-charitable purpose trusts. However, it encompasses such a wide range of topics, subjects and arguments – many of which are of only marginal, if any, relevance, in this author's view – that not all the points in the argument can be dealt with in this chapter, either by way of agreement or refutation. Nevertheless, a few brief comments are clearly called for.[1]

Baxendale-Walker ascribes to the term 'purpose trust' the 'meaning customarily assigned to it in English law'. He defines 'purpose trusts' negatively: he excludes charitable trusts; and he states that 'any trust which conforms to the beneficiary principle[2] [is] a "beneficiary trust"' in order to distinguish it from a 'purpose trust'. A 'beneficiary trust' is a trust 'having fixed beneficiaries or a class of discretionary beneficiaries, or a combination of these'. There is nothing with which to take issue here. Nor, at first sight, is there any objection to his statement that 'any trust constituted by a fiduciary obligation to dispose of property to (and not merely for the benefit of) another or others, is a beneficiary trust'.[3] However, what might be objectionable here is the apparent implication that trusts which are 'merely for the benefit of' another or others are not also 'beneficiary trusts' (an implication which, if made, requires considerable qualification in order to be generally acceptable). In any event, the two main points of attack centre on the question of enforceability of a purpose trust and on the proposition that all trusts (other than charitable trusts) must have a beneficiary or beneficiaries who is or are the equitable owners of the trust property.

Baxendale-Walker invokes both history and logic in support of his case. His appeal to history is somewhat laborious, often inaccurate and (at best) ultimately inconclusive. There is insufficient space here to deal with all the examples of what are alleged to be valid and recognised non-charitable purpose trusts, but a specific comment on at least a few of them is warranted. First, he argues that the device of inserting a trustee for the preservation of contingent remainders into the classical strict settlement is one such example: such a trustee 'is not holding any power or property for any person. He is

1 Although this author agrees with very little that is said by Baxendale-Walker, there is insufficient space here to take issue with every point that he makes. Readers can acquire a clear and complete idea of his provocative argument, and can form their own view of it, only by consulting his book. This author has chosen to highlight only some of his points in this chapter and has necessarily provided only a partial glimpse of his argument. His views clearly require and deserve a more detailed discussion than is possible here.

2 He is content to accept that the beneficiary principle can be summarised as 'a gift on trust must have a *cestui que trust*': n 1 on p 238, p 8, quoting Harman J in *Re Wood* [1949] Ch 498 at 501.

3 See Baxendale-Walker, n 1 on p 238, pp 6 and 8, for these definitions.

holding powers over property in trust to [*sic*] a pure purpose'.[1] This, with respect, is an absurd conclusion. The background to the creation of this conveyancing device was the fact that *contingent* remainders under settlements could be destroyed relatively easily by artificial devices.[2] The essential feature of the new device was that such artificial destruction was prevented by introducing a *vested* remainder to take the place of an estate which was prematurely destroyed. Thus, where land was settled on 'A for life, remainder to his first-born son and the heirs of his body, remainder to B and his heirs', the entail given to A's son was clearly contingent until his birth and therefore liable to artificial destruction. By inserting a vested remainder in trustees between A's life interest and the entail, the settlor ensured that, if A's life estate should determine artificially in his lifetime, the land passed to those trustees on trust for A during his lifetime and to preserve the contingent remainders. In other words, the trustees took the land for an estate *pur autre vie* on trust for A until his death, when the entail took effect if it had then become vested. On the other hand, if A's life estate determined naturally on his death, the remainder to the trustees never took effect.[3] The whole point of the device was to ensure that the settlement intended by the settlor for the benefit of a human beneficiary or beneficiaries – ie a clear 'persons trust' – was not defeated artificially or prematurely: the trustee is clearly holding the legal estate on trust for a person or persons.

Another example dealt with at great length is the trust to pay creditors, in which category Baxendale-Walker includes not just a trust to pay funeral costs,[4] but also trusts to pay mortgages, trade debts and so forth.[5] He does not seem to distinguish between trusts to pay debts created *inter vivos* (such as *Quistclose* trusts)[6] and those created on death: he simply states that 'the life tenant'[7] is not a beneficiary of a purpose trust to pay debts; that a testator is obviously not a beneficiary; and that the creditors are also not beneficiaries. However, one must surely distinguish between a direction in a will to pay the testator's own debts (which may impose on an executor a fiduciary obligation to discharge such debts, but which obligations would, in any event, have to be

---

1 Ibid, pp 34–35. The lengthy quotation from Lord Hardwicke LC's judgment in *Garth v Cotton* (1753) 21 ER 239 does not seem in point at all: the claim in that case was actually made by a beneficiary under the settlement.

2 Contingent remainders might also be destroyed naturally because the common law abhorred an abeyance of seisin, so there could not be any gap between the determination of one estate and the vesting of the remainder, under the operation of the so-called rule in *Purefoy v Rogers* (1671) 2 Wm Saund 380. In time, such a fatal gap could be created artificially by a variety of means.

3 For the clearest account of the ancient law relating to future interests generally, see Megarry and Wade *The Law of Real Property* (4th ed, 1975), pp 173–199, and esp at pp 194–195, from where the above example is taken. See also AWB Simpson *An Introduction to the History of the Land Law* (1961), pp 213–215.

4 See p 240.

5 See n 1 on p 238, p 42.

6 See **6.2.5**.

7 Where he has come from is not made clear.

met out of the testator's estate irrespective of any such direction and without the need for any trust at all) and debts created by the will itself and charged on or payable out of assets comprised in the estate (which are effectively analogous to legacies and where it is difficult not to say that there are human beneficiaries). Moreover, in the case of *inter vivos* trusts to pay debts, it is not at all clear that there is no beneficiary: indeed, it has been argued above that there is always such a beneficiary.[1]

In support of his argument that trusts to pay debts are purpose trusts, Baxendale-Walker refers to a large number of cases, but it is difficult to see how any such conclusion could be drawn from any of them. One of these cases, for example, is *Bateman v Hotchkin*,[2] where a testator had directed that his debts be paid out of his personal estate and that, if that should not be sufficient, the balance was to be raised by trustees out of his realty (by sale, mortgage or other disposition). The trustees were also to apply the income of devised estates towards paying interest on mortgages and, until the mortgages were paid off and in order to do so, to raise £500 each year to form a sinking fund (with additional directions as to the investment of this annual sum). Such income of the estates as was not required for these purposes was to be paid to the person for the time being entitled to the estates. In effect, the testator's son was tenant for life of the estates subject to a term of 2000 years given to the trustees for the above purposes. The debts in question were either:

(a) mortgages existing at the testator's death; or
(b) debts created by his will, being charges on the estates in favour of others.

The main point in the case was whether or not these directions were void for remoteness. Lord Langdale MR held that they were valid: the first tenant *in tail* upon attaining the age of 21 could acquire absolute dominion over the estates, subject to the mortgages; and, without his consent, the trust for accumulation could not continue.

Baxendale-Walker concludes from these facts that this was a purpose trust for the payment of debts and asks: who could be argued to be the beneficiaries of such a trust? With respect, the answers seem perfectly clear. As for the debts created by the will and charged on the estates (ie (b) above), those entitled to the sums to be so raised and charged are clearly beneficiaries. Such debts are the equivalent of legacies; and the fact that such a legacy is to be raised out of a trust fund (as is usually the case, in fact, since debts and legacies are invariably directed to be paid out of the residuary estate after conversion) does not alter the fact that the person to whom the legacy is payable, as well as the person for whom the trust fund itself is held (subject to that debt), are

---

1 See pp 258–268.
2 (1847) 50 ER 646.

both beneficiaries. As for the debts that existed at the testator's death (ie (a) above), these are clearly payable out of his estate immediately following his death (subject, of course, to any express provision in the loan agreement to the contrary). The creditors can clearly seek repayment without resort to any trust of any kind and irrespective of any directions given by the testator. As Lord Langdale pointed out in *Bateman* itself, the mortgagees in question could 'enforce payment of their mortgages or foreclose the estate, without regard to the trust for accumulation'. The mortgages in question were charges on the devised estates and the 'trust fund' was, therefore, comprised of those estates subject to existing encumbrances and liabilities (it was effectively the equity of redemption). In the absence of any provision in the will for raising money to pay the debts, the estates in question would have to be sold (in fact, in certain circumstances they could be sold anyway). The accumulated income was to be applied in relieving the beneficiaries (the eldest son in the first instance) from a liability which they would otherwise have to discharge themselves and any unused surplus was payable to them in any event. The testator's directions in relation to this class of debts did not, therefore, constitute a separate, free-standing purpose trust with no beneficiary: they amounted to no more than administrative directions to trustees which were supplementary to the trusts of the estates and other gifts made by the will and intended as a mechanism for the implementation of those trusts for the benefit of very human beneficiaries.[1]

Other cases relied on seem to add nothing to the argument. In *Briggs v Earl of Oxford*,[2] for example, the trustees had power to fell timber on the estates and to apply the proceeds of its sale towards the discharge of mortgages on the estates. This power was held to have priority over the life tenant's rights as long as any mortgages remained. Leaving aside the point that this may have been a power and not a trust, it is clear that the intention was not to preserve the estate in some abstract sense, but to preserve it (or its value) for future beneficiaries: if the life tenant were allowed to cut timber for his own purposes, the value of the estates would clearly be diminished without reducing the mortgage burden, to the obvious detriment of future beneficiaries; it is a direction explicitly intended to protect and preserve the interests of human beneficiaries. Similarly, in *Bacon v Beauchamp*,[3] where the testator directed that a fund be raised by accumulation to pay certain debts and

---

1 In fact, Baxendale-Walker does not deal adequately, or at all, with what might be called 'administrative trusts': it is not at all clear whether he does not acknowledge their existence or whether he is implying that they, too, are separate purpose trusts. On his view of a 'purpose', it seems arguable that any direction to a trustee (say, to sell, build, repair or insure property, to establish a sinking fund, and so forth) is capable of being a purpose trust, whereas, in reality, such directions are merely ancillary to, and intended for the better implementation of, the beneficial trusts and interests.

2 (1852) ER 592.

3 (1822) 37 ER 1005.

charges, the sums in question were payable to sons and daughters and were charged on the estates. As Graham B stated:[1]

> '... the testator's intention was simply to provide a fund for some specific debts and charges, and then that the persons entitled should take. He had no intention of suspending the beneficial interest in the meantime till the debts and charges should be paid. All the authorities shew that where an estate is given to trustees to pay debts, and then to a person designated, the person designated takes at once, subject to the debts.'

Baxendale-Walker draws the conclusion that this case demonstrates the interaction of a purpose trust to pay debts and a beneficiary trust, whereas it is clearly a set of co-existing trusts for human beneficiaries.

Another approach adopted by Baxendale-Walker is to focus on cases in which the beneficiaries of a 'beneficiary trust' were all entitled to vested absolute interests, which would normally have entitled them to call for the immediate distribution of the trust fund to themselves under the rule in *Saunders v Vautier*,[2] but where (he alleges) an overriding purpose trust was not only recognised but held to have priority. One such case is said to be *Hilton v Hilton*,[3] where the capital of the estate was to be divided equally amongst all of the testator's children who attained the age of 21 or, being daughters, married under that age. The testator was engaged in trade in partnership. One of his objects was that the business should be carried on until his youngest child attained the age of 21, at which time it and his real and personal property were to be sold. He also directed the trustees to apply the whole or any part of the income 'as a common fund' for the maintenance, education and upbringing or otherwise for the benefit of the children until the youngest attained 21, accumulating any surplus income 'in aid of the said common fund', and so that any unapplied income and accumulations should go with the capital that produced them. There were also various directions relating to hotchpot. Both the testator and, after his death, the trustees, had advanced various sums to some of the children. There were substantial accumulations of income. The application before the court was made by the trustees, asking whether this fund could be distributed and whether the advancements made were to be brought into hotchpot.

It appears that, at his death, six of the testator's children had already attained their majority, although the youngest child did not attain that age until some five years later. Nevertheless, each child would have been entitled to at least a one-eighth share and, the property being personalty, the six adult children would immediately have taken a vested absolute interest at death and

---

1 Ibid at 1008: this is quoted by Baxendale-Walker, n 1 on p 238, p 45.

2 (1841) 4 Beav 115. See also p 244.

3 (1872) LR 14 Eq 468.

would normally have been entitled to call for immediate payment of their shares. As Malins V-C stated:[1]

> 'Nothing can be more plain than that each of the six children who were of age at the testator's death would, but for the fact of the business having to be carried on, have been entitled, as a matter of absolute right, to one-eighth of the property.'

He added:[2]

> 'It is a settled rule of this Court that when property is once absolutely vested in a person who is *sui juris*, he is entitled to receive it, although it may be directed to be accumulated for a period beyond the time of vesting, even though it has been directed to be paid at a future period … The rule of this Court is, that where a party has an absolute vested interest in property, and can give a discharge for it, he is entitled to an immediate transfer notwithstanding any restriction on the right to possession. But I agree that, under the peculiar circumstances of this case, a transfer could not have been enforced on account of the carrying on of the business.'[3]

Baxendale-Walker concludes from this[4] not only that a purpose trust for the maintenance of the business was clearly recognised, but also that it took precedence over all the beneficial gifts.

However, there is no reference in the case to a purpose trust of any kind. The reason why the general principle (for immediate distribution) was not applied was not because a purpose trust had been created and given priority, but because the beneficial interests of the infant children had to be protected and their value preserved. As Malins V-C made clear:[5]

> 'The reason why the testator postponed the division till the youngest child attained twenty-one is plain because during the whole of that period the business, which no doubt was a very profitable one, must have been exposed to some of the risks of business, and therefore, as he authorised it to be carried on at the expense of his estate, the whole estate might have been required for it, and consequently no division of the capital under this particular will could have taken place till the period arrived …'

The period did not arrive until the youngest child acquired a vested interest upon attaining the age of 21. In other words, the value of the shares or interests in the estate (and not, strictly speaking, in the business) of the two children who had not attained the age of 21 at the testator's death (and who, therefore, obviously could not call for their shares to be handed over) might have been seriously diminished if the six adult children had been allowed to

---

1 Ibid at 474–475.

2 Ibid at 475.

3 No point seems to have been taken on the fact that the accumulations were intended to form 'a common fund', which suggests that the income of one share might have been applicable for the maintenance etc of a beneficiary of another share.

4 Note 1 on p 238, p 50.

5 (1872) LR 14 Eq 468 at 474.

insist on their shares being paid over to them. This seems to be the same exception to the general rule that applies in relation to co-owned land, and even, in exceptional cases, to some forms of personalty (such as shares in a private company) and mortgage debts, namely that an absolute vested interest does not necessarily give the owner of that interest a right to direct the trustees to transfer to him an aliquot share of each and every asset of the trust fund.[1] In any event, a direction given to trustees to retain a trust asset in its existing state (for any period that is consistent with the rule against perpetuities) clearly does not convert what would otherwise be a trust for beneficiaries into a purpose trust: it remains a 'beneficiary trust' throughout. When all the beneficiaries acquire vested, absolute and indefeasible interests in the trust fund, they can indeed join together to override such a direction – a right they enjoy by virtue of their status as beneficiaries.[2] On the other hand, if they do not all have such interests (because, as in *Hilton*, some contingency has not yet been satisfied by some of them) they do not yet have that correlative right; there are still some beneficiaries (with contingent interests) of a 'beneficiary trust' and the direction to the trustees does not create an overriding and prior purpose trust.

Baxendale-Walker deploys a vast array of other cases, drawn from a number of different areas of trusts law, in support of his argument that, historically, non-charitable purpose trusts have frequently been recognised and upheld by English courts. It is this author's view that the case is simply not made out: at best, it remains inconclusive; at worst, it is a complete misreading of the cases and just wrong. As we have seen,[3] there *are* cases in English law – even if they are regarded as anomalous exceptions – where non-charitable purpose trusts have been upheld. However, the catalogue of authorities referred to by Baxendale-Walker are not of the same character: it is suggested that his examples can actually be analysed as trusts for human beneficiaries and not as purpose trusts at all. In any event, there is a limit to the authority and influence of history. It is a trite proposition that English law has not only evolved over centuries and continues to evolve, but also that it has changed and refined its principles and approaches as it does so: the law does not stand still. Virtually every element in the definition of 'equity's darling', for example, had to be established gradually and in a piecemeal fashion over centuries. Many instances of what would have been regarded as 'trusts' prior to the mid-nineteenth century would now be considered merely as fiduciary duties of a lesser kind. The present-day rules relating to certainty of objects of trusts are different in many respects from those that were laid down in the eighteenth century. The examples could obviously be multiplied. The basic point,

---

1 See, eg, *Stephenson v Barclays Bank Trust Co Ltd* [1975] 1 WLR 882 at 889–890; *Re Horsnaill* [1909] 1 Ch 631; *Re Kipping* [1914] 1 Ch 62; *Re Marshall* [1914] 1 Ch 192 at 199; *Re Sandeman* [1937] 1 All ER 368; *Re Weiner* [1956] 2 All ER 482.

2 See p 244.

3 See **6.2.2**.

however, is that, even if it could be shown that English courts did not at one time possess or apply a strict beneficiary principle (which, despite Baxendale-Walker's best efforts, remains unproven), this in itself does not provide a conclusive argument as to why it should not by now have come to be accorded a central and defining importance.

Even if Baxendale-Walker's historical survey is faulty and his analysis of ancient cases unconvincing, it would be quite wrong to dismiss his argument on those grounds alone, for he invokes not just history but also logic. Specifically, on the question of enforceability, Baxendale-Walker emphasises what is an elementary, but often forgotten, point, namely that it is not correct to say – either historically or at the present day – that charitable trusts can be enforced only by the Attorney-General.[1] Section 33 of the Charities Act 1993 provides expressly that:

> 'charity proceedings may be taken with reference to a charity either by the charity, or by any of the charity trustees, or by any person interested in the charity, or by any two or more inhabitants of the area of the charity if it is a local charity, but not by any other person.'

Although the Charity Commissioners should be asked to authorise charity proceedings, a 'person interested' may, in the event of a refusal, apply for leave directly to the High Court.[2] *Baldry v Feintuck*,[3] one of the 'students' union' cases, for example, provides a good example of this (and, incidentally, raises interesting questions as to who actually has standing to bring such proceedings: Any member of the student body? The fee-paying parent? The parent university or college? Local authorities or other funding bodies?). In any event, Baxendale-Walker deduces two further conclusions from this basic fact: first, it cannot be correct to state that charitable trusts are accepted as exceptions to the rule against purpose trusts simply because they are enforceable by the Attorney-General; and, secondly, if charitable trusts can be enforced by any 'person interested', then there is no reason why non-charitable purpose trusts could not be enforced in the same way. 'There is no obvious logical reason why not.'[4]

However, matters are not as simple as this. There are other important dissimilarities. At one point, Baxendale-Walker adopts the extreme view that it is 'another canard' to suggest that the charitable trust is 'an exception to the general trust model'.[5] However, an exception it clearly is, and not just on the basis that it is enforceable by the Attorney-General. If the established rules of private trusts were applied to the charitable trust, the purpose or object of the latter would have to be described or defined with sufficient conceptual

---

1 Note 1 on p 238, p 27.

2 Charities Act 1993, s 33(2), (5).

3 *Baldry v Feintuck* [1972] 2 All ER 81. See also pp 277–281 on the difficulties of establishing who is a 'person interested'.

4 Note 1 on p 238, p 27.

5 Ibid, pp 27–28, where he takes issue with P Matthews (1998) 12 *Trust Law Int* 98 at 100.

certainty, whereas, in reality, all that the law requires is that the purpose or object be exclusively charitable: if necessary, wide, vaguely described purposes objects can be rendered certain (in the sense of 'workable') by a *cy-près* scheme. Charitable trusts also enjoy other advantages, such as freedom from the full rigours of the application of the rule against perpetuities. The position of charitable trusts is altogether more complicated than a question of enforceability.

In any event, it is clearly not sufficient simply to focus on the possibility that some 'person interested' might have standing to enforce a charitable trust, for this tells us nothing about what is meant by the expression 'a person interested'. There are two important issues here: first, there is a need to define, with sufficient certainty, who qualifies as a 'person interested'; and, secondly, there is a question as to whether there are any legal requirements for the existence of a 'person interested' and, if so, what they might be. Even in the context of charity law, this is by no means clear. After some initial doubts, it has been held, for example, that the executors of a donor are not 'persons interested'.[1] It remains unclear whether a settlor,[2] or someone who claims to have a binding contract with a charity,[3] can be regarded as one. It must be someone who has 'some good reason for seeking to enforce the trusts of a charity or secure its due administration'.[4] Or, as Nicholls LJ stated in *Re Hampton Fuel Allotment Charity*:[5] 'If a person has an interest in securing the due administration of a trust materially greater than, or different from, that possessed by ordinary members of the public ..., that interest may, depending on the circumstances, qualify him as a "person interested"'. However, phrases such as 'some good reason' and 'materially greater', as found in these particular propositions, clearly do not provide much assistance in the process of identifying who such a person might be.

There is also a broader question as to whether a 'person interested' in relation to a charity can include anyone named or specified as such in the trust instrument (a matter which rests solely on the use of appropriate terminology) or whether such a person must possess certain attributes required by law. Specifically, must a 'person interested' be someone who is actually personally 'benefited'[6] by that particular charity, as opposed to someone who is simply named as a 'person interested' in the trust instrument, for example, a protector who is assigned the task of enforcement? Charitable trusts clearly have beneficiaries: they cannot be valid unless they are in favour of the public at large or an appreciable section of the public. A purpose which is not seen to

1 *Bradshaw v University College of Wales, Aberystwyth* [1988] 1 WLR 190.

2 Ibid (where Hoffmann J seems to have thought not); and *Re Hampton Fuel Allotment Charity* [1989] Ch 484 at 493 (where Nicholls LJ left the question open).

3 *Haslemere Estates Ltd v Baker* [1982] 1 WLR 1109, especially at 1122, per Megarry V-C; but *cf Gunning v Buckfast Abbey Trustees Registered* (1994) *The Times*, June 9.

4 *Haslemere Estates Ltd v Baker* [1982] 1 WLR 1109 at 1122.

5 [1989] Ch 484 at 494.

6 Itself a slippery word.

confer some tangible benefit on the public is not charitable. Indeed, even trusts whose purpose is to protect and promote the welfare of animals are admitted as charitable trusts only if they can be seen to provide some benefit to mankind.[1] In many cases, it may be relatively easy to identify, with sufficient certainty, who is a person interested in a particular charity, for example, the resident of an almshouse, a patient in a hospital, and so on. As noted above, in many other cases there may be no such certainty: it may not be possible, at least not without testing the matter in expensive litigation, to determine whether or not a particular person is indeed qualified as someone 'interested' in a particular charitable purpose. In order to avoid such difficulties, the Attorney-General is accorded the task of representing the public – an amorphous, changing, undefined mass of persons – in charity proceedings in the same way that he acts for the public in public law generally (for example, cases of public nuisance). Therefore, it is arguable that, when the statute refers to any 'person interested' in a charity, it intends to include only those who are directly benefited by that charity. In this sense, the commonly held view of charitable trusts should itself be turned on its head: perhaps we should analyse and describe them, not as acceptable purpose trusts, but as trusts for (generally) large groups of people which, but for the relaxation of the rules relating to perpetuities and certainty, would otherwise be invalid.

Any view of the matter tends to emphasise, rather than eliminate, the exceptional nature of charitable trusts: after all, there is no obvious reason why non-charitable purpose trusts, if allowed at all, should enjoy the same relaxation from the requirement of certainty of objects.[2] It would not be enough (essential although it undoubtedly is) simply to ensure that there existed a sufficiently precise description or definition of the particular non-charitable purpose. This alone is no more adequate for a non-charitable purpose trust than it is for a charitable one. We are again left with the fundamental question of what the law means by, and requires of, a 'person interested', and this seems to bring us back to the original starting point. The requirement of a 'person interested' seems to rule out the possibility of any trust for abstract or impersonal purposes, unless it can be established that such a person does not have to be someone who is benefited (directly or indirectly) under the trust – in other words, that such a trust can be enforced by a named person or officer (such as a protector) in the same way that the Attorney-General can enforce a charity. However, if we assume or accept this possibility, the argument for validity would be taken too far. A valid charitable trust can obviously have a protector, but that protector derives his authority from a valid trust instrument under which he was appointed and not because he is a 'person interested' in the charity. Similarly, there is no doubt that

---

1 *Re Grove-Grady* [1929] 1 Ch 557; *National Anti-Vivisection Society v IRC* [1948] AC 31.

2 Baxendale-Walker does not claim that a relaxed requirement of certainty should, or was ever applied historically, to non-charitable purpose trusts.

various powers (eg to appoint or remove trustees) can be conferred by any trust instrument (be it a private or a charitable trust) on a person who is not a beneficiary or a 'person interested' under that trust. However, here again there is a valid trust, ie a trust that satisfies the traditional rules. It does not follow from this, by analogy or otherwise, that a non-charitable purpose trust can be rendered valid because the trust instrument which purports to create it includes a provision appointing a protector as enforcer. In one case, the enforcer derives his authority from what is, in any event, a valid trust; in the other, the hope and intent is that the appointment of an enforcer will confer validity on what would otherwise be an invalid trust. They are not analogous cases at all. Indeed, from the viewpoint of initial validity, the appointment of a protector (or other person) is no better than the appointment of a 'trustee' of an invalid trust: neither can, by itself, confer validity on the particular trust.[1]

The perennial problem of finding a satisfactory working mechanism for ensuring enforceability of a non-charitable purpose trust therefore remains. It is not an answer to the problem to say that the settlor may reserve to himself powers of enforcement, or that a protector (or some other nominated officer) could be appointed by the trust instrument and expressly given the task – indeed the duty – of enforcing the trust.[2] The original difficulty remains: what happens when the settlor dies, or there is a flaw or lack of continuity in the operation of the enforcement mechanism (whatever it might be) set up by the trust instrument, or if the protector fails or refuses to carry out his duty? Who can then invoke the supervisory jurisdiction of the court in order to compel him to do so or to cure the defect? In the case of a charitable trust, the answer is clear: the Attorney-General and, indeed, any 'person interested' may do so. In the case of a pure non-charitable purpose trust, there is no one. It should also be mentioned that it is completely irrelevant that, in the event of a breach of trust, the court is not obliged to make an equal distribution of the trust property but can, instead, resort to a range of possible remedies, such as the replacement of the trustees or the exercise of a discretion by the court itself.[3] Why should it matter whether the court has available to it even a limitless number and range of remedies if there is no one who can claim any of them?

Ultimately, it is doubtful whether the case for non-charitable purpose trusts has been, or can be, taken any further than it was taken by Goff J in *Re Denley*.[4] There, it will be recalled, the judge expressed the view that the beneficiary principle was 'confined to purpose or object trusts which are abstract or impersonal'; and he concluded that the employees of the company who were

---

1 Cf DJ Hayton (2001) 117 LQR 96. See also *Shaw v Lawless* (1838) 5 Ce & Fin 129 at 155–156; *Gandy v Gandy* (1885) 30 Ch D 57; *Von Knierem v Bermuda Trust Co Ltd* (1994) *Butterworths Offshore Cases and Materials*, Vol 1, pp 116–125.

2 This is the solution suggested by Baxendale-Walker, n 1 on p 238, p 13. It is also the solution adopted by the STAR Trust legislation: see **6.7**.

3 See *McPhail v Doulton* [1971] AC 424 at 457. This is another point which Baxendale-Walker invokes in support of his argument.

4 [1969] 1 Ch 373.

'entitled to the use and enjoyment of the land' could apply to the court to have the trust enforced, if necessary.[1] In other words, there were clearly identified 'persons interested' in the trust (to use the language of charitable trusts). However, as we have seen, this gives rise to two serious problems. First, the trust in *Re Denley* is capable of being interpreted, and has been interpreted,[2] as a trust for persons, and not for a purpose at all: it is difficult to disagree with the interpretation subsequently put forward by Vinelott J in *Re Grant*[3] to the effect that the *Denley* trust was a trust for a class of persons defined by reference to employment, and therefore no different from a trust for a class of persons defined by reference to a blood relationship (coupled in each case with a discretion in the trustees to determine who could benefit). Secondly, even if it is regarded as a purpose trust, it is clear that the employees had a sufficiently direct and substantial 'interest' in the purpose to enable them to qualify as 'persons interested'. This is reinforced by the fact that Goff J referred to the employees as having an *entitlement* to use the land. Such a requirement would exclude not just abstract or impersonal purposes, but also a large number of more substantial commercial purposes. Thirdly, there was no protector (or other similar enforcer) in *Re Denley*, so it is no authority at all on the question of whether a non-charitable purpose trust might be enforceable by means of such an expressly appointed officer. It has been suggested above that such a strategy cannot have this effect: at the very least, it remains an open and uncertain question.[4]

As a postscript to this section, it is worth pointing out that it is difficult to avoid the conclusion that what is at stake here is no more than a reluctance to acknowledge that a trust is a human construct, designed for specific purposes. The defenders of the 'purpose trust' almost seem to assume that there exists some Platonic form of a 'trust', some entity which has all the characteristics (and only those characteristics) which they say it should have. In reality, a trust may have local variations and may evolve in different ways and directions: one has but to consider the different ways in which the constructive trust has developed in England, Australia, Canada and New Zealand, for example. Whether or not an English trust must satisfy the beneficiary principle is ultimately not a question of logic but of policy. Moreover, if an English trust must satisfy the beneficiary principle in order to be a trust at all, this does not mean that a Cayman Islands trust which does not satisfy the principle cannot therefore be a trust. The requirements of a contract in French and German law

---

1 Ibid at 383 and 388: he does not state explicitly that it was the employees who had standing to enforce the trust in the event of default or failure on the part of the trustees, but the discussion at 387–388 makes little sense if this is not what he had in mind.

2 *Re Grant's Will Trusts* [1980] 1 WLR 360; and see pp 248–249 above.

3 [1980] 1 WLR 360.

4 There was also no perpetuity problem in *Re Denley*, for the trust instrument contained an express perpetuity clause.

differ from those in English law, but the former are still valid and will generally be enforced in English courts.[1]

6.2.7 Summary of the position in English law

The status of non-charitable purpose trusts in English law is clearly an ambivalent one. Despite the obvious judicial hostility towards such trusts, various exceptional instances have been held valid. Moreover, the precise basis upon which purpose trusts are generally considered invalid is far from clear. In broad terms, the cases seem to fall into three distinct, although overlapping, categories (leaving aside the unincorporated association cases). First, there are those in which the purposes were minor, indeed trivial, but also specific, such as the tombs, monuments, and animal cases. The second group includes cases in which the purposes were expressed generally, indeed vaguely, as ones which might have been philanthropic or 'public' in nature, but which did not qualify as charitable purposes and therefore failed for conceptual uncertainty. The third category includes those instances which have failed on grounds of 'perpetuity'. All this suggests that, provided the purposes are specific and certain and are confined to the perpetuity period, a non-charitable purpose trust could be held valid.

However, this ignores the existence and primacy of the beneficiary principle and the need for enforceability. The crucial question seems to be whether non-charitable purpose trusts are simply not capable of being trusts at all in English law, ie *because* they have no identifiable beneficiaries, they are not enforceable or controllable and must therefore fail (and cannot even take effect as a power), or whether they are a legitimate form of trust but, because they are unenforceable and uncontrollable by the court, they can have no effect. For many, the beneficiary principle is generally identified as one of the fundamental characteristics of a private trust, without which there can be no trust at all.[2] A private trust requires that identifiable beneficiaries have entitlements to trust property in the form of equitable estates and interests, or other enforceable equitable proprietary rights. In English law, there must exist 'an irreducible core of obligations owed by the trustees to the beneficiaries and enforceable by them which is fundamental to the concept of a trust. If the beneficiaries have no rights enforceable against the trustees there are no trusts'.[3]

Others, however, would deny to the principle its central defining role. Instead, they emphasise a need to respect and give some effect to the settlor's or testator's intentions (provided they are lawful and clear). The trust is essentially a moral obligation of conscience, which is capable of fulfilment if

1 For example, in civil law systems, where there are no requirements relating to consideration or privity, a contract may be enforced by a third party benefited by it.

2 C Sweet (1917) 33 LQR 342 at 357–358.

3 *Armitage v Nurse* [1997] 2 All ER 705 at 713, per Millett LJ.

the trustee himself recognises and accepts it: 'the defect in the obligatory nature of the trust is not a contradiction in terms, for it is not the obligation but its enforcement which is at fault'.[1] The lack of means of enforcement presents merely practical difficulties.[2] After all, it is said to be doubtful whether anyone can claim an equitable interest or proprietary right in the trust fund of a charitable trust, but this never seems to have been considered an obstacle to the validity of such a trust. One of the things that distinguishes a charitable trust from a non-charitable purpose trust is precisely the availability of an ever-present enforcer (the Attorney-General). Thus, it can be argued that the fundamental problem of non-charitable purpose trusts is not one of essential validity but of enforceability, and, if the problem of enforceability could be resolved (as in the case of charitable trusts), such trusts would only have to satisfy the law's requirements as to certainty and perpetuity. In practical terms, this distinction might seem to have no significance, for the fact remains that, under English law, there is no recognised enforcer of any such trust. Nevertheless, it may be a material consideration which might affect the response of an English court if, and when, it is called upon to recognise or deal with a non-charitable purpose trust created in a different jurisdiction and in respect of which an enforcer has been appointed.

However, whether this is indeed an accurate assessment of a charitable trust may itself be debatable. It is arguable that the beneficiaries of a charitable trust (who constitute an appreciable section of the public) are indeed the equitable 'owners' of the trust property and that a charitable trust is saved from invalidity, not by the disapplication of the beneficiary principle, but by the disapplication of the rules relating to certainty of objects and/or the rule against perpetuity. In other words, it could be said that the beneficiaries of a charitable trust, which is usually a continuing trust with an open class of beneficiaries,[3] are effectively in the same position as the objects of a private discretionary trust. However, the law's requirements as to certainty of objects and perpetuity have been eliminated; and difficulties of enforcement (which, without certainty of objects, would otherwise be considerable) are resolved by the appointment of the Attorney-General, who performs a duty similar to that allotted to him in public law for the protection of amorphous public rights.

In any event, the uncertainties of English law in relation to non-charitable purpose trusts – even after the decision in *Re Denley* – have operated as a restricting influence on the creation of such trusts. They have also inspired other ('offshore') jurisdictions to attempt, through legislation, to remove the uncertainties and restrictions which are found in English law (which usually forms the basis of their own legal systems), thereby encouraging and enabling

---

1 L Leigh (1955) 18 MLR 120 at 137.

2 Cotterrell, n 1 on p 238, p 312. See also DC Potter (1949) 13 Conv (NS) 418 at 424; WO Hart (1937) 53 LQR 24 at 33; JW Harris (1971) 87 LQR 31 at 56–57; AKR Kiralfy (1950) 14 Conv (NS) 374 at 374–375; RE Megarry (1952) 68 LQR 449 at 451.

3 The rule in *Saunders v Vautier* (1841) 4 Beav 115 could not apply to such a class.

the creation of non-charitable purpose trusts within their own jurisdictions.[1] In doing so, they have been forced, as we shall see, to deal directly with those vitiating factors – primarily questions relating to enforcement, uncertainty of objects and perpetuity – which have proved to be such formidable obstacles under English law.

6.3 THE BAHAMAS

The Bahamas produced a draft Purpose Trusts Bill in 2000, but as yet, it has not been enacted. The Bill borrows several similar provisions from the legislation of other offshore jurisdicions (see **6.4–6.12** below), and seeks to address the same concerns, such as questions of uncertainty and duration. It is not as adventurous in its aims or scope as the Cayman Islands' STAR legislation (see **6.7** below) but it does allow Bahamian land to be held in a purpose trust and expressly declares that simply holding an investment (eg shares in a company) is permissible. However, until the Bill becomes law, any detailed analysis of its provisions is premature.

6.4 BELIZE

The Belize Trusts Act 1992 (BTA 1992) came into force on 18 May 1992.[2] It contains provisions relating to the definition of a trust (s 2), the validity of trusts (ss 2 and 7), the proper law of trusts (s 4), the creation of a trust (s 5), the maximum duration of a trust (other than one established exclusively for a charitable purpose or purposes) and of accumulation of income (s 6), the property which may be held on trust (s 8), who may be a settlor (s 9), the beneficiaries (s 10), the nature of a beneficial interest (s 11), protective or spendthrift trusts (s 12), precatory letters or memoranda of wishes (s 13), charitable purposes (s 14), trusts for non-charitable purposes (s 15), protectors and trustees (Part 3), duties and powers of trustees (Part 4), the termination or failure of trusts (Part 5), the variation of trusts (Part 6), breach of trust (Part 7),

---

1 It is not suggested, of course, that this is the primary or even a significant factor in the development of 'offshore' jurisdictions and novel legislation. 'Offshore' centres have in the past offered a wide range of advantages, including low taxation, transactional secrecy and more relaxed financial regulation. These, in turn, led to a seriers of attacks on certain 'offshore' jurisdictions: see The Financial Stability Forum's *Report of the Working Group on Offshore Centres* (2000) (available at *www.fsforum.org.uk*); the Financial Action Task Force's *Review to Identify Non-Cooperative Countries or Territories* (2000) (available at *www.oecd.org/fatf*); the OECD's Reports titled *Harmful Tax Competition* (1998) and *Towards Global Tax Cooperation* (2000) (both available at *www.oecd.org*); Andrew Edwards *Review of Financial Regulation in the Crown Dependencies* (Cmnd 4109); Powell (1999) 3 Jersey LR 22; Hay [1999] *Private Client Business* 345.

2 The day appointed by Order of the Attorney-General of Belize published in the *Belize Government Gazette*. See Trusts Act 1992, s 70.

powers of the court (Part 8), variant types of trust (Part 9), optional registration of trusts and exempt trusts (Part 10).

The law of non-charitable purpose trusts in Belize involves consideration of five sections of the BTA 1992:

(a) s 14 containing the statutory definition of charitable purposes;
(b) s 15 relating to non-charitable purpose trusts;
(c) s 16 relating to protectors of trusts;
(d) s 6 relating to the maximum duration of trusts and accumulation of income;
(e) s 7 governing the validity of trusts.

Section 14 provides that the following purposes shall be regarded as charitable:

(a) the relief of poverty;
(b) the advancement of education;
(c) the advancement of religion;
(d) the protection of the environment;
(e) the advancement of human rights and fundamental freedoms;
(f) any other purposes which are beneficial to the community.

Categories (a), (b), (c) and (f) correspond precisely with Lord Macnaghten's classification in *Commissioners for Special Purposes of Income Tax v Pemsel*.[1] In England, categories (d) and (e) may be charitable, although particular cases within category (e) (and possibly category (d) as well) may fall foul of the prohibition on political purposes qualifying as charitable. Even in Belize, the scope of category (e) is not defined: it is not clear how 'human rights' or 'fundamental freedoms' will be construed (the two terms presumably intended to convey different meanings) nor whether a trust intended to advance these objectives by changing the law of Belize or of another country would be regarded as charitable (despite ss 14(3) and 15(1)(b) discussed below).[2] Perhaps surprisingly, the BTA 1992 does not deal expressly with recreational charities, which in England have caused some difficulty.

Section 14(2) provides that a purpose shall not be regarded as charitable unless the fulfilment of that purpose is for the benefit of the community or a substantial section of the community, having regard to the type and nature of the purpose. This reproduces the requirement of public benefit which applies to all charitable trusts in England other than trusts for the relief of poverty. It may be that trusts for poor relations, which are, anomalously, valid charitable trusts in England, are not so in Belize, although they may be covered by the

---

1 [1891] AC 531 at 583.

2 *Cf National Anti-Vivisection Society v IRC* [1948] AC 31; *McGovern v Attorney-General* [1982] Ch 321.

final words of s 14(2) ('having regard to the type and nature of the purpose'); or, alternatively, they may be valid private trusts either as being trusts for the benefit of individuals or as being non-charitable purpose trusts.

Section 14(3) provides that a purpose may be regarded as charitable whether it is to be carried out in Belize or elsewhere and whether it is beneficial to the community in Belize or elsewhere.

The combined effect of s 15(1) and s 7(2) is that trusts for non-charitable purposes are valid in Belize provided that:

(a) the purpose is specific, reasonable and capable of fulfilment;[1]
(b) the purpose is not immoral, unlawful or contrary to public policy;[2]
(c) the terms of the trust are not so uncertain that its performance is rendered impossible;[3]
(d) the terms of the trust provide for the appointment of a protector who is capable of enforcing the trust and for the appointment of a successor to any protector.[4]

Section 7(3) makes provision for trusts which are created for two or more purposes, of which some are lawful and others are not, or where some of the terms of the trust are invalid and others are not. If the trust purposes or terms can be 'separated', the court may declare that the trust is valid as to the terms which are valid and the purposes which are lawful,[5] the invalid terms or the unlawful purposes being, in effect, struck out of the trust instrument. If no such separation is possible, the trust is invalid.[6]

The enforcement of non-charitable purpose trusts in Belize is dealt with by ss 16(2), 15(1)(c) and (2). Section 16(2) provides that a protector of a trust shall have the following powers:

(a) (unless the terms of the trust otherwise provide) power to remove a trustee and to appoint a new or additional trustee;
(b) such further powers as are conferred on the protector by the terms of the trust or the BTA 1992.

---

1 BTA 1992, s 15(1)(a) .

2 Ibid, s 15(1)(b).

3 Ibid, s 7(2)(b)(iii). To the extent that the court declares that the terms of the trust are so uncertain that its performance is rendered impossible the trust is invalid and unenforceable. A charitable trust, on the other hand, is deemed always to be capable of performance (ibid), with the result that questions of initial impossibility and general charitable intention appear to play no part in the law of charity in Belize.

4 Ibid, s 15(1)(c).

5 Ibid, s 7(3)(b). Where a trust is partially invalid the court may declare what property is to be held subject to the trust (s 7(4)), ie subject to so much of the trust as the court declares to be valid. Property as to which a trust is invalid is, subject to any order of the court, to be held on a resulting trust for the settlor or his estate (s 7(5)).

6 Ibid, s 7(3)(a).

Section 15(1)(c) requires a trust for non-charitable purposes to appoint a protector and to confer on him power to enforce the trust. Section 15(2) empowers the Attorney-General to appoint a protector, where he has reason to believe that there is no protector of a trust for non-charitable purposes or the protector is unwilling or incapable of acting. A protector appointed by the Attorney-General is empowered from the date of his appointment to exercise the functions of protector of the trust.

The protector may be the settlor or a trustee.[1] Where there is more than one protector then, subject to the terms of the trust, any functions conferred on the protectors may be exercised if more than one-half of the protectors for the time being agree on its exercise.[2]

In the exercise of his office, a protector is not to be accounted or regarded as a trustee[3] but, subject to the terms of the trust, 'shall owe a fiduciary duty … to the purpose for which the trust is created'.[4] Given that a purpose cannot sue for breach of duty and, indeed, that no duty can sensibly be said to be owed to any 'purpose', and given that the role of the Attorney-General is apparently confined to the appointment of a protector where none is acting or the protector is unwilling or incapable, the effect of the imposition of this fiduciary duty is unclear.

Section 6 of the BTA 1992 confines the duration of all trusts (other than trusts established exclusively for a charitable purpose or purposes) to a period of 120 years from the date of their creation and provides that a trust shall terminate on the 120th anniversary of its creation unless terminated sooner. Trusts for non-charitable purposes are accordingly subject to a maximum duration of 120 years. The BTA 1992 provides that, subject to the terms of the trust and to any order of the court, undistributed income or capital at the compulsory termination of the trust (not being a trust established for a charitable purpose) is to be held on a resulting trust for the settlor or his estate.[5] If the terms of the trust provide (as they may) for the trust property to vest in a particular person or persons, then it must be distributed to him or them within a reasonable time[6] subject to any retention by the trustee of sufficient assets to meet existing, future, contingent or other liabilities.[7]

Section 6(3) provides that 'the rule of law known as the rule against perpetuities shall not apply to any trust to which this section applies'. However, although s 6(2) expressly disapplies s 6(1) in the case of trusts established exclusively for a charitable purpose or purposes, the BTA 1992

---

1 Ibid, s 16(3).
2 Ibid, s 16(6).
3 Ibid, s 16(4).
4 Ibid, s 16(5).
5 Ibid, s 44(1). The words 'subject to any order of the court' in s 44(1) (which are also found in s 7(5)) suggest that a resulting trust is not an automatic or necessary consequence of the termination (or invalidity) of a trust, though the scope of the court's powers is unclear.
6 Ibid, s 46(1).
7 Ibid, s 46(2).

does not expressly apply s 6 to any trust. The intention appears to be that the rule against perpetuities should not apply to any trust the proper law of which is the law of Belize.[1] In other words, s 6(1) is intended to provide for a maximum duration of 120 years; s 6(2) then removes that restriction from charitable trusts; and s 6(3) is intended to abolish the rule with respect to all trusts governed by the law of Belize. However, all this is expressed in such a way that s 6 seems to have the somewhat surprising result that the rule against perpetuities continues to apply in the case of exclusively charitable trusts with regard to the vesting of interests (the position under English law), but does not apply to any other trusts, whether as regards the vesting of interests or the duration of the trust, subject only to the statutory maximum duration of 120 years.

The terms of a non-charitable purpose trust may direct or authorise the accumulation of all or part of the income of the trust for a period not exceeding the maximum duration of the trust,[2] ie for a period which may endure for 120 years.

Although the BTA 1992 contains provisions for the variation of trusts,[3] they do not authorise the court to approve a variation in respect of a trust for non-charitable purposes. A settlor who wishes to create a Belize trust for one or more non-charitable purposes, with or without an ultimate trust for ascertainable human beneficiaries, should consider the desirability of conferring on the trustees or protector an express power of variation.

6.5 BERMUDA

The general non-statutory law of Bermuda follows English law. Until the enactment of the Trusts (Special Provisions) Act 1989 (TSPA 1989)[4] a trust for a purpose could exist only if its purposes were exclusively charitable within one of the four recognised heads of charity (the relief of poverty, the advancement of education, the advancement of religion, or other purposes beneficial to the community)[5] and it was for public benefit. As in England, a charitable trust established under the law of Bermuda may exist in perpetuity.

Part II of the TSPA 1989 contained special provisions governing the creation, validity, administration and enforcement of purpose trusts, provisions

---

1 See also s 66(3) which applies certain sections of the BTA 1992 (including s 6) to trusts the proper law of which is the law of Belize.

2 Ibid, s 6(4).

3 Ibid, ss 45(2) (charitable trusts) and 48 (non-charitable trusts).

4 The Trusts (Special Provisions) Act 1989 came into force on 31 January 1990, the day appointed by the Premier of Bermuda pursuant to s 1.

5 A purpose which falls within the first three categories is charitable regardless of the place where the purpose is pursued or effected. A purpose may be charitable within the fourth category only if it is of benefit to the community of Bermuda.

which were subsequently adopted, in substantially the same form, by other jurisdictions. However, the original Part II of the TSPA 1989 has now been replaced in its entirety by a new Part II substituted by the Trusts (Special Provisions) Amendment Act 1998 (TSPAA 1998), which came into force on 1 September 1998.

6.5.1 Meaning of a 'purpose trust'

In the original legislation,[1] a 'trust for a purpose or purposes' was defined as any trust other than a trust for the benefit of particular persons (whether or not immediately ascertainable), or of some aggregate of persons ascertained by reference to some personal relationship. This rather odd definition raised numerous points of construction and sometimes proved difficult to satisfy. However, the TSPAA 1998 has now substituted a new s 12A, which provides that a trust may be created for a non-charitable purpose or purposes, provided that the conditions set out in s 12A(2) are satisfied. Such a trust is now referred to as a 'purpose trust' and the conditions laid down are that the purpose or purposes are:

(a) sufficiently certain to allow the trust to be carried out;
(b) lawful; and
(c) not contrary to public policy.

Under the original legislation (s 13(1)(a) and (b)), the purpose or purposes had to be 'specific, reasonable and possible' and not be 'immoral, contrary to public policy or unlawful'. Whether there is any change of substance here is doubtful: a trust which is 'sufficiently certain' for the purposes of limb (a) of the new definition is likely to be one which would also have been 'specific, reasonable and possible', and an 'immoral' purpose would seem to be against public policy in any event. Consequently, trusts for 'philanthropic purposes', for 'the promotion of democratic values' and the like are likely to be insufficiently certain to be valid. Similarly, trusts 'for artistic purposes'[2] or 'to present artistic dramatic works'[3] or 'for good works'[4] might be considered too vague, and a trust to block up a house for a lengthy period might be considered unreasonable.[5] And schools for prostitutes or pickpockets would presumably be against public policy and be void.[6] The applicable test of 'certainty of objects' of a purpose trust – and particularly a discretionary purpose trust – is not laid down in the TSPAA 1998, but, presumably, the

1 TSPA 1989, s 12(1).
2 *Re Ogden* (1909) 25 TLR 382.
3 *Associated Artists Ltd v IRC* [1956] 2 All ER 583.
4 *Re How* [1930] 1 Ch 66.
5 *Brown v Burdett* (1882) 21 Ch D 667.
6 *Re Pinion* [1965] Ch 85 at 105.

principles established in English law in relation to trusts for beneficiaries will apply, ie the 'complete list' test in the case of a purpose trust where there is no discretion as to the application of income or capital[1] and the 'any given postulant test' in the case of a discretionary trust for purposes.[2] It is also likely that a discretionary trust for purposes will fail for 'administrative unworkability'[3] in Bermuda, as in England.

A purpose trust may only be created in writing.[4] A purpose trust which does not comply with s 12A is invalid.[5]

6.5.2 Enforcement

The absence of any beneficiary who can claim a beneficial interest – at least, so as to enforce the primary trusts, as opposed to preventing misapplication – clearly presents a fundamental problem of enforcement for any purpose trust, whether or not it is created by statute (the TSPAA 1998 says nothing about the location of the beneficial interest under a purpose trust). Whereas the TSPA 1989 declared that the instrument creating a trust for purposes had to appoint a person to enforce the trust, and also had to make provision for the appointment of his successor,[6] the new legislation imposes no such requirement. Instead, s 12B(1) of the TSPAA 1998 simply provides that the Supreme Court may make such order as it considers expedient for the enforcement of a purpose trust on the application of any of the following persons:

(a) any person appointed by or under the trust for the purposes of the subsection;
(b) the settlor, unless the trust instrument provides otherwise;
(c) a trustee of the trust;
(d) any other person whom the court considers has sufficient interest in the enforcement of the trust.

In addition, where the Attorney-General satisfies the court that there is no such person who is able and willing to make an application under s 12B(1), the Attorney-General himself may make an application for enforcement of the trust (which he could not do under the TSPA 1989).

As an enforcement mechanism, this provision seems rather feeble – it is certainly weaker than that provided in the TSPA 1989. The court cannot act unless, and until, some authorised person makes an application to it. However,

1 *IRC v Broadway Cottages Trust* [1955] Ch 20.
2 *McPhail v Doulton* [1971] AC 424.
3 *R v District Auditor ex parte West Yorkshire Metropolitan County Council* (1986) 26 RVR 202.
4 TSPAA 1998, s 12A(3).
5 Ibid, s 12C.
6 TSPA 1989, s 13(1)(e).

there may not be any such person. For example, the trust instrument may not have appointed anyone; the settlor may be dead, or ruled out by the trust instrument (eg for tax reasons); the trustees may have taken an erroneous view of their duties or wilfully be refusing to act; and there may not be any person who has a sufficient interest to complain (especially where the purpose trust is perpetual). It is not at all clear how, in such a case, the Attorney-General (any more than the court) will have notice of any breach of trust or of the need to make an application to the court in respect of any matter connected with the enforcement of the trust. The TSPA 1989 contained detailed provisions requiring one of the trustees to be a 'designated person', whose duties, the performance of which was backed by criminal sanctions, included the supervision of the (compulsorily appointed) enforcer and the reporting to the Attorney-General of any refusal or failure to act on the part of the enforcer. Perhaps none of these provisions would have prevented a trustee and enforcer from committing a breach of trust if they were intent on doing so. Nevertheless, the TSPAA 1998 has removed one layer of protection entirely while weakening another. It is also rather bizarre to find a trustee of a purpose trust listed as one of the persons who may apply to the court for enforcement of the trust: if he is a sole trustee, he is hardly likely to bring proceedings against himself; and if he is one of several trustees complaining against his co-trustees, he would presumably have a right to bring proceedings in any event. It remains to be seen who will be regarded as having a 'sufficient interest' for the purposes of s 12B(1)(d). It seems clear that any such person need not have a proprietary 'interest' under the trust, although he may perhaps do so (say, as an ultimate remainderman), but exactly what kind of 'interest' it must be, and when it will be regarded as 'sufficient', are matters which remain ambiguous (probably deliberately so). It seems likely that such a person must be someone who, either expressly or by necessary implication, derives, or may derive, some benefit or advantage, whether directly or indirectly, from the purposes of the trust. Thus, employees of a company such as that under scrutiny in *Re Denley*,[1] and members of an unincorporated association such as that involved in *Re Lipinski*,[2] would probably qualify as persons with a 'sufficient interest'. However, the court will clearly have to look at the specific purposes of each trust and the particular circumstances of each case.

The new provisions do not make clear whether an enforcer owes any positive obligations at all, and, if so, what they might be. If a trust instrument appoints an enforcer, presumably it may expressly impose a duty on him to ensure that the purpose trust is executed properly, but there is no indication that it must do so: it may simply confer authority on the enforcer to apply to the court in the event that he becomes aware of a breach of trust, without requiring him to do so. Certainly, it is very unlikely that anyone within

---

1 [1969] 1 Ch 373.

2 [1976] Ch 235.

s 12B(1)(b) (ie a settlor) or (d) (ie a person with a sufficient interest) is intended, without more, to be under a duty to supervise the carrying out of the purpose trust, or to make application to the court. It is not even clear whether the Attorney-General, once apprised of the absence of any other qualifying complainant, is under such a duty. Nor is there any indication that the enforcer (whoever he might be) has a right to compel the trustees to disclose information concerning the trust, without which he might well find it impossible to determine whether or not the purpose trust is in need of being enforced.

These uncertainties are compounded by the absence of any guidance as to the duties of the trustees themselves. Are they subject to the same laws governing the investment of trust funds that apply to trustees of private trusts? If, for example, the purpose of the trust is to retain shares in a private family company, could the appointed person apply to the court for an order that such shares be sold or otherwise dealt with in cases of emergency (say, when the value of the shares is in danger of falling drastically)? Suppose, for example, that the purpose is to provide and maintain a sportsground for employees of a particular company. The value of the land increases greatly (as a result of development potential) or some dramatic change occurs to the company (because its workforce is reduced considerably, or it is relocated to another part of the country). Are the trustees failing to carry out their trust if they refuse to sell the land and acquire a new sportsground elsewhere? Is the appointed person under a duty to apply to the court in such circumstances? Are the trustees obliged to maintain an even balance between the non-charitable purposes and the ultimate human remaindermen (if any)? In short, there may be considerable ambiguity as to what the duties of the trustees ought to be in relation to the carrying out of the purpose trust and a corresponding uncertainty as to the need for enforcement or the existence of any ground upon which a complaint to the court could be founded.

It has already been indicated that the TSPAA 1998, unlike its predecessor, no longer requires the appointment of a 'designated person'. One of the trustees of a trust for purposes formerly had to be such a person (who had to be a Bermudan lawyer, chartered accountant, trust corporation or person designated by the Minister of Finance). The 'designated person' was required, inter alia, to keep at his office a copy of the trust instrument, a register of certain details appertaining to the trust, and such documents as were sufficient to show the true financial position of each trust in each financial year.[1] A number of criminal sanctions applied in the event that such duties were not performed. All such requirements have now been swept away. There is no longer any requirement to appoint a 'designated person' (or a similar officer) and all such duties and sanctions have therefore ceased to be relevant.

---

1 TSPA 1989, s 14.

6.5.3 Perpetuity

Whereas under the original legislation[1] a trust for purposes could not be created for a term exceeding 100 years, and the trust instrument had to specify the event upon the happening of which the trust terminated, s 12A(4) and (5) of the TSPAA 1998 now provides that the rule of law (known as the rule against excessive duration or the rule against perpetual trusts), which limits the time during which the capital of the trust may remain unexpendable to the perpetuity period under the rule against perpetuities, shall not apply to a purpose trust; but the rule against perpetuities (also known as the rule against remoteness of vesting), as modified by the Perpetuities and Accumulations Act 1989,[2] shall apply to a purpose trust. Thus, a purpose trust of indefinite duration can now be created in Bermuda: it will continue until all its capital has been distributed or expended. However, if the purpose trust is not of indefinite duration, the date of its termination and the vesting of interests at that time must all occur within a perpetuity period not exceeding 100 years (as under the TSPA 1989).[3]

6.5.4 Variation of a purpose trust

There was no provision in the TSPA 1989 for the variation of a trust for purposes. Section 12B(2) of the TSPAA 1998 now provides that the court may, upon the application of certain persons and if it thinks fit, approve a scheme to vary any of the purposes of the trust, or to enlarge or otherwise vary any of the powers of the trustees of the trust.[4] The persons who may make such an application are:

(a) any person appointed by or under the trust for these purposes;
(b) the settlor, unless the trust instrument provides otherwise;
(c) a trustee of the trust.

This is yet another provision in the TSPAA 1998 which has yielded simplicity at the expense of certainty and clarity. It may be reasonable to seek the enlargement or variation of the powers of trustees, but it is not at all clear how the purposes of a non-charitable purpose trust can or ought to be varied. Whereas, in the case of a trust for beneficiaries, the court would be expected

---

1 Ibid, s 13(1).

2 The Bermuda Act is in identical terms to the English Perpetuities and Accumulations Act 1964.

3 The doubt whether English Perpetuities and Accumulations Act 1964, s 1(1) applies to purpose trusts (see text and n 6 on p 252) did not, however, arise, for the 100-year trust period in the case of purpose trusts in Bermuda was authorised by TSPA 1989, s 13(1). Section 13(1) has now been repealed by the TSPAA 1998. However, TSPAA 1998, s 12A(5) seems to have the same effect.

4 TSPAA 1998, s 12B(3) provides that, where any costs are incurred in connection with any application under s 12B (ie both applications for enforcement and applications for variation), the court may make such order as it considers just as to payment of those costs (including payment out of the trust property).

to protect the interests of those beneficiaries, on behalf of whom it approves a scheme varying the trusts, by ensuring that the scheme is for their benefit,[1] there is no such requirement in s 12B(2) of the TSPAA 1998. Indeed, there is no guidance at all as to the manner in which the court is expected to exercise its jurisdiction. The intention may be to confer authority on the court to make a kind of *cy-près* scheme in respect of a purpose trust, in the same way that such a scheme can be made in relation to a charitable trust. However, whereas, in the latter case, the charitable purpose in question must have become impossible or impracticable (assuming Bermudan law is the same in this respect as English law), no such precondition is laid down in the TSPAA 1998 for a (non-charitable) purpose trust. There is not even a requirement that the court must have regard to the intentions of the settlor or to the spirit of the gift. Suppose, for example, that the purpose of the trust is to retain shares in a private family company, but the value of those shares is suddenly in danger of falling drastically. Could the court vary the purpose in such a case? If so, by reference to what criteria would it be able to do so?

6.5.5 Land

No interest in land in Bermuda shall be held, directly or indirectly, in a purpose trust.[2] The word 'indirectly' raises a doubt as to whether ownership by the trustees of shares in a company possessing land in Bermuda would amount to a breach of this prohibition (a doubt also raised under the TSPA 1989). There is no sanction for a breach of the prohibition: it does not appear to affect the validity of the trust (unlike a failure to comply with s 12A).

6.5.6 Purpose trusts pre-September 1998

The substitution by the TSPAA 1998 of a new Part II for the TSPA 1989 applies in relation to:

(a) trusts created after the coming into force of the TSPAA 1998 (on 1 September 1998); and
(b) in relation to trusts for non-charitable purposes validly subsisting immediately before that date.[3]

Special provision is made in order to bring existing purpose trusts within the new regime. Existing purpose trusts are *deemed* to satisfy the conditions set out in s 12A(2) of the TSPAA 1998 (ie the conditions which a purpose trust must satisfy in order to be valid). There does not seem to be a material difference between these new conditions and the requirement in the TSPA 1989 that

1 See, eg, the English Variation of Trusts Act 1958, s 1.
2 TSPAA 1998, s 12D.
3 Ibid, s 4(1)(a) and (b).

purposes had to be 'specific, reasonable and possible', so this provision probably serves only to remove any lingering doubt as to validity. The person appointed (and required to be appointed under s 13(1) and (2) of the TSPA 1989) as an enforcer by the trust instrument of a pre-September 1998 trust for purposes is deemed to have been appointed as a person who, for the purposes of s 12B(1) of the TSPAA 1998, may apply to the court for the enforcement of a purpose trust.[1] Moreover, a pre-September 1998 trust instrument is *deemed* to have provided that the settlor shall not make an application to the court for either the enforcement or the variation of a purpose trust.[2]

Other than the above-mentioned provisions, the TSPAA 1998 is silent about several aspects of pre-September 1998 trusts for purposes. Nothing is said about the role or status of any 'designated person' appointed by the trust instrument of an existing purpose trust. It seems clear that the statutory duties imposed on a 'designated person' by the TSPA 1989 no longer apply, but it is not clear whether any such duties expressly imposed by the trust instrument itself remain in force or have also been annulled, by implication, by the TSPAA 1998. Indeed, does any such creature as a 'designated person' continue in existence, or has the TSPAA 1998 provided, again by implication, for enforced retirement or removal?

6.6 THE BRITISH VIRGIN ISLANDS

The general trusts law of the British Virgin Islands is largely derived from English law, but supplemented by statute.[3] The main governing statute is the Trustee Ordinance (c 303), as amended by the Trustee (Amendment) Act 1993 (No 7 of 1993) (TAA 1993),[4] most of which came into force on 1 November 1993. The TAA 1993 includes special provisions governing the creation and validity of purpose trusts. These provisions are similar to, and evidently modelled on, those in Part II of the Bermudian Trusts (Special Provisions) Act 1989 (although with some differences). As we have seen,[5] the Bermudian provisions have now been replaced in their entirety by a new Part II substituted by the Trusts (Special Provisions) Amendment Act 1998, which came into force on 1 September 1998. However, the same provisions remain in force in the British Virgin Islands.

---

1 Ibid, s 4(2)(b).

2 Ibid, s 4(2)(c).

3 The Common Law (Declaration of Application) Act 1705 (c 13); and the West Indies Associated States Supreme Court (Virgin Islands) Act (c 80).

4 All references in this section are to the provisions of the unofficial consolidated Trustee Ordinance (which includes the 1993 amendments).

5 See **6.5**.

6.6.1 Statutory requirements for the creation of a valid purpose trust

Section 84(2) of the TAA 1993 authorises the creation of a 'trust for any purpose', whether charitable or not, provided it satisfies the following conditions.

(1) *Certainty etc.* The purpose must be 'specific, reasonable and possible' and must not be immoral, contrary to public policy or unlawful.[1] Thus, a trust for 'philanthropic purposes', for 'the promotion of democratic values' and the like might be insufficiently certain to be valid. Similarly, trusts for 'artistic purposes'[2] or 'to present artistic dramatic works'[3] or 'for good works'[4] might be considered too vague, and a trust to block up a house for a lengthy period might be considered unreasonable.[5] And schools for prostitutes or pickpockets would be void on grounds of immorality or public policy.[6]

(2) *Trustees.* At least one of the trustees must be a 'designated person',[7] ie a barrister or solicitor practising in the Territory of the British Virgin Islands, an accountant practising in the Territory who qualifies as an auditor for the purposes of the Banks and Trust Companies Act 1990, a licensee under the Banks and Trust Companies Act 1990, or such other person as may be designated by order of the Minister of Finance.[8]

(3) *Enforcement.* The trust instrument must appoint a person, who may be a protector, to enforce the trust and must provide for the appointment of his successor.[9] The person so appointed must be a party to the trust instrument or consent in writing, addressed to the trustee who is a 'designated person', to enforce the trust.[10] Although the TAA 1993 does not say so in terms, it seems likely from the scheme of s 84(2) that the enforcer cannot also be a trustee who is a designated person, and may not be able to be a trustee at all. There would seem to be no reason why the settlor should not reserve power to enforce the trust to himself as the named enforcer and/or power to appoint a successor/enforcer.

---

1 Trustee Ordinance (c 303), s 84(2)(a) and (b). For discussion of the corresponding requirements under English law, see pp 249–251.
2 *Re Ogden* (1909) 25 TLR 382.
3 *Associated Artists Ltd v IRC* [1956] 2 All ER 583.
4 *Re How* [1930] 1 Ch 66.
5 *Brown v Burdett* (1882) 21 ChD 667.
6 *Re Pinion* [1965] Ch 85 at 105.
7 Trustee Ordinance (c 303), s 84(2)(c).
8 Ibid, s 84(1)(a).
9 Ibid, s 84(2)(d).
10 Ibid, s 84(2)(e).

(4) *Termination and disposal of surplus assets.* The trust instrument must specify the event upon the happening of which the trust terminates and must provide for the disposition of surplus assets of the trust upon its termination.[1] This requirement seems confined, however, to cases where the trust is terminable. The TAA 1993 makes no express provision for the disposal of the trust property in the event that a perpetual non-charitable purpose trust fails by reason of a failure of objects or purposes. There is nothing corresponding to the *cy-près* jurisdiction applicable to charitable trusts.

6.6.2 Effect of satisfying the statutory conditions

A 'trust for any purpose' to which s 84 applies is not subject to the rule against perpetuities and remoteness of vesting.[2] The effect is to authorise perpetual non-charitable purpose trusts.

The exemption of a 'trust for any purpose' from the rule against remoteness of vesting is puzzling. It appears to enable such a trust to take effect at a remote future time, eg after a prior trust creating a series of life interests in favour of specified persons born during a 100-year trust period.[3] In English law, even charitable trusts are subject to the rule against remoteness of vesting, save as regards a passing from one charitable trust to another.[4] It is arguable that the point does not in fact arise, for the TAA 1993 seems to proceed on the basis that the trust will take effect at the moment of its creation: see, for example, s 84(2)(e), requiring the enforcer to be a party to the trust instrument or to consent in writing to act as the enforcer. However, the more obvious meaning of these provisions is that a 'trust for any purpose' may include both existing non-charitable purposes and those which may come into being at any time thereafter.

The TAA 1993 does not invalidate non-charitable purpose trusts which do not comply with the requirements of s 84(2): to the extent that such trusts may be valid under the general law they remain valid notwithstanding the TAA 1993.

Nothing in s 84 affects the existing law with respect to trusts established for charitable purposes.[5]

---

1 Ibid, s 84(2)(f).

2 Ibid, s 84(3).

3 The maximum perpetuity period under the Act is 100 years: ibid, s 68(1). It seems a strange policy (which is certainly not confined to the British Virgin Islands) to insist upon a limited perpetuity period for trusts for humans but to have none at all for trusts for non-charitable purposes.

4 See Picarda *The Law and Practice relating to Charities* (Butterworths, 2nd ed, 1995), pp 265–274.

5 Trustee Ordinance (c 303), s 84(4).

6.6.3 Meaning of 'trust for any purpose'

The central concept in s 84 of the TAA 1993 is a 'trust for any purpose'. The Act defines it as follows.[1]

> 'Trust for any purpose means a trust other than a trust –
>
> (a) that is for the benefit of particular persons whether or not immediately ascertainable; or
>
> (b) that is for the benefit of some aggregate of persons ascertained by reference to some personal relationship.'

The effect of the definition is that every trust which is not for the benefit of particular persons whether or not immediately ascertainable or for the benefit of some aggregate of persons ascertained by reference to some personal relationship is a trust for a purpose or purposes, the validity of which (unless charitable) depends entirely[2] on the conditions for validity laid down in s 84 of the TAA 1993.

The definition raises several questions of construction. The phrase 'particular persons' clearly is not confined to *named* persons, for it includes those who may not be immediately ascertainable. It is less clear, however, whether the word 'particular' is intended only to signify a particular individual differentiated from all other persons, such as the settlor's eldest son, or whether the expression 'particular persons' also includes the members of a class of individuals, such as the settlor's children or grandchildren.

It is yet more difficult to see what is meant by 'some aggregate of persons ascertained by reference to some personal relationship'. It may be that a class of persons related by blood to a common *propositus* – for example the settlor's issue – falls within these words, although the word 'aggregate' seems inappropriate to describe a class of persons. Indeed, an 'aggregate of persons' suggests a quasi-corporate body, not composed of individuals. But limb (b) of the definition cannot refer to members of an unincorporated association, for their relationship *inter se* is contractual, and not personal.

The definition clearly seems to result in a trust for the maintenance or education or advancement of a class of related persons (eg the *Re Compton* type of case of a trust for the education of descendants of a common ancestor) not being a 'trust for a purpose or purposes': the descendants of a common ancestor are either 'particular persons' within limb (a) of the definition or 'an aggregate of persons ascertained by reference to some personal relationship' within limb (b); and a trust for maintenance or education is presumably a trust for the benefit of the persons who are to be maintained or educated and therefore not a trust for a purpose or purposes. All such trusts fall outside the

---

1 Ibid, s 84(1)(b).

2 This is subject to the possibility that some non-charitable purpose trusts may be valid under the general law.

definition of a 'trust for a purpose or purposes' and their validity (or invalidity) is unaffected by the requirements of the TAA 1993.

But the definition leaves a case such as *Oppenheim*[1] (a perpetual trust for the education of children of employees of a particular company) uncertain: limb (b) seems to be inapplicable, for although the beneficiaries are in part ascertained by reference to their personal relationship to their parents, they can only be ascertained in the first place by ascertaining the relationship between their parents and the company employing them, and it seems at least doubtful whether such a relationship is a 'personal relationship' within the meaning of the definition; on the other hand, if a class comprising the children of present and future employees of a particular employer is a class of 'particular persons' within limb (a), it is difficult to conceive of a case to which limb (b) was intended to apply.

The word 'benefit' in the definition clearly leaves open the question whether the benefit which takes the trust outside the scope of s 13(1) must be a direct and tangible benefit (in the sense of conferring some legal or equitable interest on some person) or whether such benefit may be indirect (which might then mean that the *Re Denley*[2] type of trust would not be a 'trust for a purpose or purposes').

In any event, the definition clearly includes trusts for specific animals, tombs and monuments. The purposes of unincorporated associations may also be included, insofar as the trust is construed as one for purposes and not one for the members.

Examples of other non-charitable purposes which would qualify would seem to include: (a) furthering a particular profession, industry, trade union, trade association, or other group where the primary objective is the promotion of its/their purposes and not to make a gift to the members;[3] (b) maintaining a particular building; (c) purposes which are not exclusively charitable; (d) holding shares in a family trading or investment company where the primary intention is to retain the shares and not necessarily to benefit any individuals; (e) providing fringe benefits (eg education) for the employees, or children of employees, of a particular company or for any other group which does not constitute a section of the public (and which does not fall within paras (a) or (b) in the definition of 'trust for a purpose or purposes' in s 12(1)); (f) supporting yacht racing[4] or any other sport or recreation; (g) promoting political propaganda (whether masquerading as education or not).[5] Indeed, subject to the requirement of certainty, gifts to promote any non-charitable

---

1 *Oppenheim v Tobacco Securities Trust Co Ltd* [1951] AC 297.

2 [1969] 1 Ch 373.

3 *Re Mead* [1961] 1 WLR 1244; *General Medical Council v IRC* (1928) 97 LJKB 578; *Geologists' Association v IRC* (1928) 14 TC 271; *R v IRC ex parte Headmasters' Conference* (1925) 41 TLR 651; *Re Barnett* (1908) 24 TLR 788.

4 *Re Nottage* [1895] 2 Ch 649.

5 *Bonar Law Memorial Trust v IRC* (1933) 17 TC 508; *Re Hopkinson* [1949] 1 All ER 346; *Re Bushnell* [1975] 1 All ER 721.

purpose, such as anti-vivisection,[1] or the promotion of political parties, political dogma, changes in the law of a country[2] (presumably other than the British Virgin Islands), the promotion of temperance by political means,[3] the improvement of international relations,[4] or a trust to provide pensions for and donations to present and past employees and the education and benefit of their dependants[5] would seem to qualify under the TAA 1993.

6.6.4 Enforcement of a trust for any purpose or purposes

As mentioned above, it is a requirement of a valid 'trust for any purpose' that the instrument creating the trust appoints a person to enforce the trust and provides for the appointment of his successor. The primary mechanism by which the trust is enforced is the enforcer. The Attorney-General has no standing to enforce a 'trust for any purpose' which is not exclusively charitable.

A trustee who is a designated person is in the same position as any other trustee as regards observing and enforcing the terms of the trust, save that where he has reason to believe that a person appointed to enforce the trust is dead, is unwilling, refuses or is unfit to act or is incapable of acting, a trustee who is a designated person must as soon as practicable inform the Attorney-General in writing of the fact and send him a copy of the instrument creating the trust.[6] No such duty is imposed on any other trustee. The Attorney-General on being informed in this way, must, within 90 days, apply to the court for the appointment of a person to enforce the trust.[7] The procedure seems to be that a person, or perhaps a choice of persons, is nominated or recommended to the court, which then approves that choice. The court does not have power, apparently, to make provision for the appointment of a successor to such person. An order of the court declaring a person to be the person to enforce the trust is conclusive evidence of the appointment and the appointment takes effect from the date of the order.[8] Costs incurred by the Attorney-General in applying to the court may be ordered to be paid out of the assets of the trust.[9]

The TAA 1993 makes no provision as to the qualifications of the person so appointed or as to the manner in which he is to enforce the trust, nor does it impose any sanction on him in the event that he fails to enforce it. The circumstances in which the enforcer should intervene to enforce the trust are

---

1 *National Anti-Vivisection Society v IRC* [1948] AC 31.
2 *McGovern v Attorney-General* [1982] Ch 321.
3 *IRC v Temperance Council of Christian Churches of England and Wales* (1926) 136 LT 27.
4 *Re Strakosch* [1949] Ch 529; *Buxton v Public Trustee* (1962) 41 TC 235.
5 *Re Saxone Shoe Co Ltd's Trust Deed* [1962] 1 WLR 943.
6 Trustee Ordinance (c 303), s 84(5). A failure to inform the Attorney-General is a criminal offence: s 84(9).
7 Ibid, s 84(6).
8 Ibid, s 84(7).
9 Ibid, s 84(8).

not made clear. The prevention of the misapplication of funds by the trustees, and the recovery of misapplied funds, must obviously be one of the enforcer's tasks (although this role could already be undertaken by the ultimate remaindermen). Compelling the trustees to apply or distribute income or capital, or to consider the exercise of their dispositive powers and discretions, must be another function. Beyond this, however, matters become rather uncertain. Are the trustees obliged to maintain an even balance between the non-charitable purpose and the ultimate human remaindermen?

Are they subject to the same laws governing the investment of trust funds that apply to trustees of private trusts? If, for example, the purpose of the trust is to retain shares in a private family company, could the enforcer ask for those shares to be sold or otherwise dealt with in cases of emergency (ie when the value of the shares is in danger of falling drastically)? If the purpose is to provide and maintain a sportsground for employees of a particular company, could the enforcer ask for the sale of the land if its value increases greatly (as a result of development) or if some dramatic change happens to the company (ie because its workforce is reduced considerably, or it is relocated to another part of the country)? Indeed, what power, statutory or otherwise, does the court have to vary the trusts of a 'trust for any purpose'? Is the 'salvage' jurisdiction alone available?[1] Do the ultimate remaindermen themselves have any standing at all, or is the 'policing' role of the enforcer entirely exclusive? These and many other questions may be answered by the terms of the relevant trust instrument or may in due course have to be considered by the court in the British Virgin Islands.

As to the liabilities incurred by an enforcer who fails in performing his functions without refusing to act, it may be that, if he permits or acquiesces in a misapplication of trust assets or income (eg for a purpose not authorised by the trust instrument), he, together with the trustees, will be liable for breach of fiduciary duty to the person who is entitled to the trust assets on the termination of the trust. There would seem, however, to be no liability, civil or criminal, if the trustees and the enforcer acquiesce in the retention of trust assets or the accumulation of trust income, to the benefit of the person ultimately entitled to the trust assets, thereby wholly or partially defeating the intentions of the settlor. In particular, the TAA 1993 understandably imposes no obligation on a trustee who is a designated person (and who may be the sole trustee) to report breaches of trust to the Attorney-General, but neither is he under any obligation to report any failure to enforce the trust by a fit and capable enforcer who cannot be described as refusing to act.

---

1 The draftsman of a 'trust for any purpose' would be well advised to consider the incorporation of an express power of termination or variation.

6.6.5 Obligations of the 'designated person'

As mentioned, the sole trustee or at least one of the trustees of a trust for a purpose or purposes must be a 'designated person' as defined. Where a trustee who is a designated person has reason to believe that a person appointed to enforce the trust is dead, is unwilling, refuses or is unfit to act or is incapable of acting, he must as soon as practicable inform the Attorney-General in writing of the fact and send him a copy of the instrument creating the trust.[1]

6.6.6 Offences by 'designated persons'

Where a designated person fails to inform the Attorney-General that the person appointed to enforce the trust is dead, is unwilling, refuses or is unfit to act or is incapable of acting he is guilty of an offence and is liable on summary conviction to a fine of not more than $5,000.[2]

6.6.7 Relationship to charitable trusts

As mentioned, nothing in the TAA 1993 affects the existing law with respect to trusts established for charitable purposes.[3] It follows that a trust for charitable purposes is valid in the British Virgin Islands notwithstanding that (a) its purposes are not specific, (b) its trustees do not include a 'designated person', and (c) it makes no provision for the appointment of a person to enforce the trust. Apart from s 84, charitable trusts in the British Virgin Islands are enforceable by the Attorney-General.

On the other hand, the definition of a 'trust for any purpose' is wide enough to include charitable purpose trusts. It appears, therefore, that a trust for purposes which are exclusively charitable could comply with the statutory requirements for the creation of a 'trust for any purpose', including the appointment of a person to enforce the trust. By reason of the exemption of trusts to which s 84(1) applies from the rule against remoteness of vesting such a trust could possibly be created to take effect at a remote future time. It is unclear what powers of enforcement the enforcer of such a trust would have, and whether they would affect the powers of enforcement normally vested in the Attorney-General.

In order for a trust to be a valid charitable trust in the British Virgin Islands, apart from s 84 of the TAA 1993, its purposes must be exclusively charitable. A trust for purposes which include both charitable and non-charitable purposes can be valid under s 84. It is, therefore, possible in the

---

1 Trustee Ordinance (c 303), s 84(5). The TAA 1993 imposes no obligations on a 'designated person' comparable to those imposed by the Bermuda Trusts (Special Provisions) Act 1989, s 14(1) and (2) (now repealed) on which the TAA 1993 itself was based.

2 Trustee Ordinance (c 303), s 84(9). It is a defence to prove that the designated person took all reasonable steps and exercised all due diligence to avoid committing the offence: s 84(10).

3 Ibid, s 84(4).

British Virgin Islands to create a perpetual trust, for example, for philanthropic purposes but which, by reason of the inclusion of one or more non-charitable purposes, would be void under English law.

6.7 THE CAYMAN ISLANDS[1]

The most ambitious and sophisticated legislation dealing with purpose trusts is currently to be found in the form of the Cayman Islands' Special Trusts – Alternative Regime (STAR). STAR was introduced by the Special Trusts (Alternative Regime) Law 1997, now substantially incorporated into Part VIII of the Trusts Law (2001 Revision). Although one objective of STAR is clearly to cater for non-charitable purpose trusts (and will undoubtedly figure prominently in this area), it is certainly not confined to that purpose. Trusts of all kinds may be established under STAR, ie trusts for people as well as trusts for charitable and non-charitable purposes, or, indeed, all or any combination of these. It is said[2] that this will enable disputes as to whether a particular trust is a purpose trust or trust for persons to be avoided.[3] This may be so, but it is a solution which creates its own peculiar and potentially intractable problems. Specific provision is also made for the administration and enforcement of those trusts that are subject to STAR.

6.7.1 Trusts subject to STAR

STAR applies only to a 'special trust'. A 'trust' is said to include 'a trust of a power, as well as a trust of property' (and 'trustee' has a correspondingly extended meaning);[4] and 'a power is said to be held in trust if granted or reserved subject to any duty, expressed or implied, qualified or unqualified, to exercise the power or to consider its exercise'.[5] In addition, a 'power' includes an administrative power as well as a dispositive power. Consequently, for the purposes of STAR, the expression 'trust' is intended to include not just 'fixed' and discretionary trusts (which trustees are obliged to carry into effect),[6] but also all powers (whether dispositive or administrative) conferred on trustees

---

1 Duckworth, n 1 on p 238; P Matthews 'Shooting STAR: The New Special Trusts Regime from the Cayman Islands' (1998) 11 *Trust Law Int* 67; A Duckworth 'STAR WARS: The Colony Strikes Back' (1998) 12 *Trust Law Int* 16; P Matthews 'STAR: Big Bang or Red Dwarf' (1999) 12 *Trust Law Int* 98; A Duckworth 'STAR WARS: Smiting the Bull' (1999) 13 *Trust Law Int* 158; DJ Hayton (1998) 8 *Offshore Taxation Review* 43; Huxley 'Rhodes, Arakan, Grand Cayman: Three Versions of Offshore', in Edge (ed) *Comparative Law in Global Perspective* (Transnational Publishers, Inc, 2001).

2 Duckworth, n 1 on p 238, p 54.

3 See *Re Denley's Trust Deed* [1969] Ch 373 and *Re Grant's Will Trusts* [1980] 1 WLR 360 (and pp 246–249).

4 Trusts Law (2001 Revision), s 95(1).

5 Ibid, s 95(2).

6 *IRC v Broadway Cottages Trust* [1955] Ch 20; *McPhail v Doulton* [1971] AC 424. See Thomas, n 1 on p 250, pp 273–296.

qua trustees (the exercise of which such trustees are under a duty to consider from time to time, although not obliged actually to exercise them).[1] Thus, on this wide definition, any power conferred on any fiduciary (such as a protector or a management committee, and not just on a trustee) would be included. However, only 'special', as opposed to 'ordinary', trusts and powers are covered: the word 'special', in reference to a trust or a power, signifies that it is a trust or power which is subject to STAR.[2] Nothing in STAR affects an 'ordinary' trust or power, directly or by inference.[3] Indeed, even 'special' trusts and powers are subject to the same general law in every respect as 'ordinary' trusts and powers, save as provided in STAR itself.[4]

In order to be subject to STAR (and therefore regarded as 'special'):

(a) a trust or power must be created by or on the terms of a written instrument (testamentary or *inter vivos*); and
(b) the instrument must contain a declaration to the effect that STAR is to apply.[5]

Where a trust or power is created by written instrument in exercise of a special power (within the meaning of STAR, and therefore not necessarily a 'special' power in the 'ordinary' sense) and the instrument contains no declaration as to the application of STAR, then, subject to evidence of a contrary intention, STAR shall be *deemed* to be intended to apply (and the instrument shall be deemed to contain a declaration to that effect).[6] What this seems to mean is that, where a particular power is subject to STAR, then any trust or other power which is created by its exercise will itself be subject to STAR, unless the contrary is expressed. A trust or power created by the exercise of an 'ordinary' power may also be subject to STAR, but this clearly requires an express declaration within s 96(1)(b). Any trust or power which does not meet the requirements of s 96(1), or is not deemed to do so under s 96(2), is an 'ordinary' trust or power and is not subject to STAR.[7]

6.7.2 Objects of special trusts

STAR provides that the objects of a special trust or power may be persons or purposes or both[8] (as was always the case for ordinary powers). The persons

---

1 *Re Gestetner Settlement* [1953] Ch 672; *Re Gulbenkian's Settlements* [1970] AC 508. See Thomas, n 1 on p 250, pp 263–273.

2 Trusts Law (2001 Revision), s 95(1).

3 Ibid, s 97.

4 Ibid, s 98. Apart from the provisions of s 95(1), (2), terms and expressions defined in s 2 of the Trusts Law (2001 Revision) have the same meanings in STAR.

5 Ibid, s 96(1).

6 Ibid, s 96(2).

7 Ibid, s 96(3).

8 Ibid, s 99(1).

may be of any number[1] (and presumably may be corporations as well as human beings); and the purposes may be of any number or kind, charitable or non-charitable, provided they are 'lawful and not contrary to public policy'.[2] In broad terms, this expression is likely to be interpreted in the same way as under English law. In addition, it is expressly provided that no land nor any interest in land in the Cayman Islands shall be subject, directly or indirectly, to a special trust; but a special trust may hold an interest in a company, partnership or other entity which holds such land, or an interest in such land, for the purposes of its business.[3] It has been suggested[4] that, because a STAR trust must have an 'object', a 'self-serving' purpose, such as a trust simply to hold the shares in X Co Ltd, would not be an object in itself but a means to attaining an object. The *form* of the assets held by the trust is not a purpose at all: a purpose is what you *apply* the assets to.[5] This must be the safe view to adopt. However, it is not at all clear that this is a proper interpretation of the STAR legislation (or, indeed, of some of the anomalous exceptions found in English case-law). A purpose may be passive as well as active; and a trust simply to retain and preserve a particular asset (eg a tomb or monument) or simply to accumulate income (which, without more, would be an unusual trust in any event) may be just as capable of being a valid trust, with a well-defined obligation and object, as any other kind of trust. It depends on the way in which the trust is analysed and the manner in which it is said to be capable of enforcement. (By its very nature, it will not have a beneficiary as such.) If the trust is a non-charitable purpose trust of the *Re Denley* type,[6] then there will be (indeed, must be) someone with a sufficient interest in the purpose (in the sense of being directly benefited by it) to be able to enforce it, even if that person is not a beneficiary as such – such as the class of employees in *Re Denley* itself. On this analysis, a 'self-serving' purpose would indeed not be a valid purpose at all. On the other hand, if it is said that a non-charitable purpose trust does not need someone with such a direct interest, but can be enforced by someone (such as a protector) nominated in the trust instrument and who is effectively a stranger to the purpose, then it is not clear why a 'self-serving' purpose would not be valid (subject, of course, to any public policy objection). Of course, if any such purpose can be valid only if it leads ultimately to a distribution of income or capital, or to an active application in furtherance of some objective or cause, there is a danger that purpose trusts will be held to require some benefit, albeit indirectly, to some human beneficiary.

---

1 Ibid, s 99(2).

2 Ibid, s 99(3).

3 Ibid, s 16.

4 Eg, by DJ Hayton (1998) 8 *Offshore Taxation Review* 43 at 46; and also, in relation to purpose trusts generally, by Matthews, n 1 on p 238, pp 25–26.

5 Matthews, n 1 on p 238, p 25.

6 *Re Denley's Trust Deed* [1969] 1 Ch 373.

A special trust is not rendered void by uncertainty as to its objects or mode of execution.[1] The terms of a special trust may give the trustee or any other person power to resolve an uncertainty as to its objects or mode of execution.[2] It is not clear whether 'uncertainty' refers only to evidential uncertainty, in which case the trustee or other person can merely determine whether or not any given object falls within the description of the clearly defined class of objects as a whole, or extends to include conceptual uncertainty as well, so that the trustee or other person can determine the meaning of the words used by the settlor to describe or define the class of objects itself. It is likely to cover both kinds of uncertainty, however. If a special trust has multiple objects and there is no allocation of the trust property between them, the trustee, subject to evidence of contrary intention, has discretion to allocate the trust property.[3] It is not made clear, however, whether, in any such case, a trust for several objects which is not a fixed trust will effectively become a discretionary trust, ie one where the trustee must exercise his discretion, or whether the statute simply confers on the trustee a power to select which he is not obliged to exercise.

If an uncertainty as to the objects or mode of execution of a special trust cannot be resolved, or has not been resolved pursuant to the terms of the trust, the court:

(a) may resolve the uncertainty:
  (i) by reforming the trust,
  (ii) by settling a plan for its administration, or
  (iii) in any other way which the court deems appropriate; or
(b) insofar as the objects of the trust are uncertain and the general intent of the trust cannot be found from the admissible evidence as a matter of probability, may declare the trust void.[4]

6.7.3 *Cy-près* application

A STAR trust may be a perpetual trust. STAR clearly contemplates that a trust may be reformed in accordance with the express terms of the trust itself. In addition, it creates a mechanism for the court to reform the trust *cy-près*. Section 104(1) provides that, if the execution of a special trust in accordance with its terms is or becomes in whole or in part:

(a) impossible or impracticable,
(b) unlawful or contrary to public policy, or

---

1 STAR, s 103(1) (but this is subject to s 103(4)).
2 Ibid, s 103(2).
3 Ibid, s 103(3).
4 Ibid, s 103(4).

(c) obsolete in that, by reason of changed circumstances, it fails to achieve the general intent of the special trust,

then the trustee shall [*sic*], unless the trust is reformed pursuant to its own terms, apply to the court to reform the trust *cy-près* or, if or insofar as the court is of the opinion that it cannot be reformed consistently with the general intent of the trust, the trustees shall dispose of the trust property as though the trust or the relevant part of it has failed.[1]

6.7.4 Enforcement

It might have been thought that, where a STAR trust has a person as a beneficiary, it would be enforceable by that beneficiary, and only in the case of a STAR trust partly or exclusively in favour of a purpose would it be necessary to provide some mechanism for enforcement. However, this is not the approach adopted by STAR. The *only* persons who have standing to enforce a special trust are such persons, whether or not beneficiaries, as are appointed to be enforcers:

(a) by or pursuant to the terms of the trust; or
(b) by order of the court.[2]

In other words, a beneficiary of a STAR trust does not have any right, simply by virtue of his status as a beneficiary, to enforce that trust, although such a right may be conferred upon him expressly by the trust instrument or by the court. Nor does he have an enforceable right, as beneficiary, against a trustee or against an enforcer, or an enforceable right to the trust property.[3] A 'beneficiary' means 'a person who will or may derive a benefit or advantage, directly or indirectly, from the execution of a special trust'.[4] An 'enforcer' is 'a person who has standing to enforce a special trust'; and 'standing to enforce' means 'the right or duty to bring an action for the enforcement of a special trust'.[5] The expression 'right or duty' in this context seems to be intended to distinguish between an enforcer who is under a duty to enforce, and an enforcer who has authority or power to do so, but is under no such duty.[6] A right or duty to enforce a trust is presumed, subject to evidence of a contrary

---

1 Ibid, s 104(1). Section 72 (jurisdiction of the court to vary trusts) does not apply to special trusts (s 104(2)).

2 Ibid, s 100(2).

3 Ibid, s 100(1).

4 Ibid, s 95(1). STAR distinguishes (rightly) between an 'object' and a 'beneficiary' of a trust. An 'object' which is a purpose could not enforce a trust, in any event, so the provisions of s 100 could (and are expressed to) apply only to 'beneficiaries'.

5 Ibid, s 95(1).

6 Ibid, s 101(1), which declares that standing to enforce a special trust may be granted or reserved as a right or as a duty.

intention, to extend to every trust which is created by, or on the terms of the same instrument, or pursuant to a power so created.[1]

If an enforcer with a duty to enforce is unable, unwilling or unfit to do so, the court may, on the application of a trustee (or another enforcer), appoint an enforcer (or another enforcer).[2] In such a case, the enforcer himself may be guilty of, and liable for, a breach of duty, but it is not clear whether a trustee is obliged to make an application to the court in such circumstances and would be liable for breach of duty if he failed to do so. The court may also intervene, again on the application of a trustee (or enforcer), if the terms of the trust require the appointment of an enforcer but:

(a) it is impossible to make the appointment without the court's assistance or;
(b) it is difficult or inexpedient to make the appointment without the court's assistance.[3]

The trust instrument may impose an obligation to appoint an enforcer on a trustee and, in circumstances where the court's assistance is required, the trustee would presumably be under a duty to seek such assistance. However, if the trustee is not under a duty to appoint an enforcer, is he none the less under an implied duty to make an application to the court in these circumstances? Common sense would suggest that the provisions of s 100(4)(a) and (b) could be given comprehensive (as opposed to partial) effect only by construing them as imposing, by implication, a duty on a trustee to make the requisite application to the court. However, the provisions of s 100(5) (which are expressed to apply only to the circumstances described in s 100(4)(c)) seem to suggest otherwise. Limb (i) of s 100(4)(c) and s 100(5), taken together, have the effect that, in the event that there is no enforcer who is of full capacity and who is also a beneficiary, the trustee *shall* within 30 days apply to the court for the appointment of an enforcer, or for the administration of the special trust under the direction of the court, or for such other order as the court shall think fit. If the trustee knowingly fails to do so, he shall be guilty of an offence and shall be liable on summary conviction to a fine not exceeding $10,000. The same applies to limb (ii) of s 100(4)(c), which applies to the case where there is no enforcer 'of full capacity' who 'has a duty to enforce and is fit and willing to do so'. Although this provision, too, is not clearly expressed, the intention, it seems, is to ensure that a trustee must apply to the court if there is no effective enforcer; and there will be an effective enforcer only where there is either:

1 Ibid, s 100(3).
2 Ibid, s 100(4)(b).
3 Ibid, s 100(4)(a).

(a) a person who benefits under the terms of the trust and who is of full age and sound mind; or
(b) a person who has undertaken a duty to enforce the trust who is also of full age and sound mind.

Subject to evidence of a contrary intention, an enforcer is deemed to have a fiduciary duty to act responsibly with a view to the proper execution of the trust.[1] To whom this fiduciary duty is owed is unclear. In the case of a pure purpose trust, it cannot sensibly be said to be owed to the trust's purposes; nor does it make sense to say that an enforcer owes such a duty to himself; and there is no indication that the duty is owed to the settlor. Presumably what is meant is that an enforcer is subject to a statutory duty to act and to conduct himself with the same degree of responsibility *as if* he had been appointed an enforcer of a trust for persons (and see the provisions of s 102, referred to below). A trustee (or another enforcer), or any person expressly authorised by the terms of the special trust, has standing to bring an action for the enforcement of the duty (if any) of an enforcer.[2] Thus, an enforcer who fails to carry out his duty (if any) to enforce the trust can be brought to book by the appropriate authorised person and, in determining whether the enforcer should be held liable, as well as the extent of his liability, he will be judged as one deemed to owe fiduciary duties (eg to address his mind from time to time to the question of proper enforcement of the trust) and not as an ordinary individual owing no fiduciary obligations at all (which would enable him to ignore the trust and its enforcement entirely). Whether this enforcement mechanism will work or not remains to be seen: it certainly appears to be capable of operating in a circular (and possibly self-defeating) manner, in that the enforcer is supposed to ensure that the trustee carries out the trust, whilst it may be the trustee who has the task of ensuring that the enforcer fulfils his obligation to enforce.

Section 102 of the Trusts Law (2001 Revision) provides that, subject to the terms of his appointment, an enforcer has the same rights as a beneficiary of an ordinary trust:

(a) to bring administrative and other actions, and make applications to the court, concerning the trust; and
(b) to be informed of the terms of the trust, to receive information concerning the trust and its administration from the trustee, and to inspect and take copies of trust documents.

It also provides that, in the performance of his duties (if any), an enforcer has the rights of a trustee of an ordinary trust to protection and indemnity and to

1 Ibid, s 101(2).
2 Ibid, s 101(3).

make applications to the court for an opinion, advice or direction or for relief from personal liability. And also, in the event of a breach of trust, an enforcer has, on behalf of the trust, the same personal and proprietary remedies against the trustee and against third parties as a beneficiary of an ordinary trust. The enforcer clearly does not have a proprietary interest under the trust: he is simply given statutory remedies which are equivalent to the remedies that would be available to a beneficiary who had such an interest. In the exercise of any and all of these functions, an enforcer is deemed to have a fiduciary duty to act responsibly (subject to evidence of a contrary intention).[1]

Section 100 does not affect:

(a) the enforcement by a trustee, enforcer or any other person involved in the administration of a trust of a right to remuneration or indemnity; or

(b) the enforcement of a trustee's duties by a co-trustee or a successor trustee.[2]

6.7.5 Nature of a STAR trust

The unusual, indeed unique, form and structure of a STAR trust raises interesting and difficult questions as to the nature of the trust – indeed, whether it is a trust at all – and also as to ownership of the beneficial interest in the trust property.[3] In English law, there must exist:

> 'an irreducible core of obligations owed by the trustees to the beneficiaries and enforceable by them which is fundamental to the concept of a trust. If the beneficiaries have no rights enforceable against the trustees there are no trusts.'[4]

In the case of a STAR trust, however, those fundamental defining features or characteristics are expressly excluded. For example, a 'beneficiary' is simply someone who will or may derive a benefit or advantage, directly or indirectly, from the execution of a special trust. Such a 'beneficiary' may well have a full proprietary interest in the trust fund, but he may equally be no more than an object of a mere power (and therefore not a beneficiary in the English trust law sense at all). Moreover, a beneficiary of a STAR trust has no right to enforce the trust, no enforceable right against a trustee or an enforcer, and no enforceable right to the trust property itself[5] (which effectively excludes the rule in *Saunders v Vautier*[6]). Consequently, it has been argued[7] that, in the case

---

1 Ibid, s 101(2).

2 Ibid, s 100(6). Section 83 does not apply to special trusts: s 100(7).

3 See also pp 244–246, 256–268.

4 *Armitage v Nurse* [1997] 2 All ER 705 at 713, per Millett LJ.

5 Trusts Law (2001 Revision), s 100(1).

6 (1841) 4 Beav 115.

7 DJ Hayton in (1998) 8 *Offshore Taxation Review* 43 at 45. See also DJ Hayton (2001) 117 LQR 96.

of a STAR trust under which no person is both a beneficiary and an enforcer, the trustee holds the legal title on resulting trust for the settlor, but with a power to benefit 'beneficiaries' who are, in reality, no more than the objects of that power. The settlor's beneficial interest under such a resulting trust would form part of his estate (for the purposes of succession, insolvency, and so forth). Alternatively, the trustee of such a STAR trust may be held to have vested in him both the legal and beneficial ownership of the trust property, to the exclusion of both the 'beneficiaries' and the settlor, but to be subject, like the executor of an unadministered estate, to fiduciary obligations (towards whom is not entirely clear). Such analyses might well be appropriate in terms of English law: certainly, it is possible that a STAR trust may not be regarded as a trust at all (other than a resulting trust perhaps) in England.[1] However, English law is itself uncertain on many of these points. In any event, in view of the fact that the characteristics of a STAR trust are laid down by statute, it is difficult to see why such questions need to be raised at all within the Cayman Islands themselves. The duties, powers, rights and remedies imposed or conferred on various parties are statutory in origin and nature and, as such, they are enforceable in the domestic forum without any need to fit them into a traditional analysis. Section 90 of the Trusts Law (2001 Revision)[2] provides that all questions arising in regard to a trust which is for the time being governed by the laws of the Islands, or in regard to any disposition of property upon the trusts thereof, including questions as to any aspect of the validity of the trust or disposition or the interpretation or effect thereof, are to be determined by the laws of the Islands. Specific features of the STAR legislation may need to be interpreted and worked out in due course, but it is most improbable that the STAR trust itself will be considered unworkable or unenforceable. Nevertheless, the fact that STAR trusts are unique to the Cayman Islands and not duplicated or mirrored in any other jurisdiction may itself prove to be one restriction too many for settlors and their advisers.

It may be a different matter, of course, when the same issues have to be addressed in the context of a conflict of laws. Article 2 of the Hague Convention on Trusts refers to trusts 'for the benefit of a beneficiary or for a specified purpose', which might suggest that signatories to the Convention will recognise non-charitable purpose trusts as well as charitable ones, provided that they are created in accordance with the law specified in Chapter II of the

1 See **6.2.7** above.

2 Trusts Law (2001 Revision), Part VI (sic) applies to special trusts, but as though s 89(4)(b) were repealed and the following substituted: '(b) in the case of a change from the law of the Islands, the new governing law would recognise the validity of the trust (without any material effect on its objects) and the standing of the enforcers to enforce the trust'. The reference to Part VI is in error because s 89 is in Part VII. It is understood that, because the 2001 Revision is a consolidation under legislation that does not permit substantive amendments, the reference should be treated as though it were to Part VII.

Convention.[1] However, this must be doubtful. In 1982–83, when the Convention was being negotiated, only Liechtenstein and Nauru, neither of whom was represented at the negotiations, recognised non-charitable purpose trusts, and it has been observed that the reference in the Convention to 'a specified purpose' may have been intended to include only charitable and public purpose trusts.[2] In any event, Art 18 declares that the provisions of the Convention may be disregarded when their application would be manifestly incompatible with public policy. Thus, it may well be the case that a perpetual STAR trust of English land would not be recognised by an English court (although a similar effect could be engineered by conveying such land into the beneficial ownership of a holding company, the shares in which are owned by the trustees of the trust).[3] Similarly, it is conceivable that, where the arrangement created by a particular STAR trust would be regarded, if it had been created in England, as no more than a contractual relationship or as a resulting trust for the settlor, an English court might treat the trust as a sham or, at least, as not involving any effective disposition of property, with consequent adverse tax implications. However, it is suggested that any such outcome is unlikely, given that the trustees (and indeed the enforcer) of a STAR trust will be subject to specific and stringent statutory duties (some of which carry criminal penalties) in relation to the property subject to the trust. As previously discussed,[4] it is not at all clear, under English law, whether a non-charitable purpose trust is simply not a trust at all, because of the beneficiary principle, or whether it is a valid form of trust, but one which is simply unenforceable. If the latter view is the correct one, the existence of the all-important enforcer would resolve any practical difficulties with which an English court would otherwise be faced. Even if the former view is correct, it is difficult to see why an English court would refuse to recognise and assist in the enforcement of trust-like obligations, which are valid and effective in another jurisdiction, unless there are compelling domestic public policy reasons for not doing so.

6.7.6 Unlawful acceptance

Section 107 of the Trusts Law (2001 Revision) provides that a person who, as trustee, accepts a settlement of property upon a special trust without taking

---

1 See J Glasson (ed) *International Trust Laws* (Jordans, looseleaf), Section C, Appendix 51. Many 'trust-law jurisdictions' have *not* ratified the Convention (eg the USA, Ontario, New Zealand, South Africa) and very few 'non-trust law jurisdictions' have done so (eg Italy, the Netherlands).

2 Von Overbeck *Explanatory Report on the Convention*, para 39. See also DJ Hayton (1987) 36 ICLQ 260; Gaillard and Troutman (1987) 35 Am Jo Comp Law 307; Dyer (1999) 32 Vanderbilt Jo Transnat Law 999; *Fothergill v Monarch Airlines Ltd* [1981] AC 251 at 278, 283, 287, 294–295.

3 It is noteworthy that, even in the Cayman Islands and other 'offshore' jurisdictions, there is usually a prohibition on 'offshore' trusts owning land within the governing jurisdiction and that prohibition may even extend to owning an interest in a company, partnership or other entity which owns such land *unless* it is owned for the (active) purposes of its business.

4 See **6.2.7** above.

steps to ensure that the settlor, or the person making the settlement on his behalf, understands who will have standing to enforce the trust, is guilty of an offence and liable on summary conviction to a fine not exceeding $10,000, or to imprisonment for a period not exceeding one year, or to both, or on conviction on indictment to a fine not exceeding $100,000 or to imprisonment for a period not exceeding five years or both.

6.7.7 Trusteeship

Section 105(1) declares that, except as authorised by an order of the court or permitted by or pursuant to s 105:

(a) the trustee of a special trust shall be or include a trust corporation; and
(b) the trustee shall keep in the Islands at the office of the trust corporation a documentary record of:
   (i) the terms of the special trust,
   (ii) the identity of the trustee and the enforcers,
   (iii) all settlements of the property upon the special trust and the identity of the settlors,
   (iv) the property subject to the special trust at the end of each of its accounting years, and
   (v) all distributions or applications of the trust property.[1]

A 'trust corporation' for these purposes means a body corporate licensed to conduct trust business, with or without restriction, under the Banks and Trust Companies Law (2000 Second Revision).[2] Section 105(3) provides that the court may authorise non-compliance with s 105(1) on such terms as it thinks fit if it is satisfied that the execution of the trust will not be prejudiced.

6.7.8 Land

No land nor any interest in land in the Islands shall be subject, directly or indirectly, to a special trust, but a special trust may hold an interest in a company, partnership or other entity which holds land in the Islands, or an interest in such land for the purposes of its business.

6.8 THE COOK ISLANDS

The Cook Islands have a separate legislative regime for offshore entities. The governing legislation for international trusts is the International Trusts Act

1 Trusts Law (2001 Revision), s 105(1); s 105(4)–(8) contains criminal sanctions for breaches of s 105(1).
2 Ibid, s 105(2).

1984 (ITA 1984) (as amended by the International Trusts Amendment Acts 1985, 1989, 1991 and 1995–96, the International Trusts Amendment (No 2) Acts 1989 and 1995–96) and the International Trusts Amendment Act 1999.[1]

A trust registered under the ITA 1984 is a valid trust notwithstanding that it may be invalid according to the law of the settlor's domicile or residence or place of current incorporation.[2]

Section 12 contains provisions affecting (1) an 'international trust' which is a charitable trust and (2) purpose trusts (whether charitable or non-charitable).

6.8.1 Meaning of 'international trust'

An 'international trust' is a trust or disposition:

(1) which is registered under the ITA 1984; and
(2) in respect of which:
   (a) at least one of the trustees, donors or holders of the power of appointment or power of maintenance or power of advancement is either:
      (i) a registered foreign company; or
      (ii) an international company;[3] or
      (iii) a trustee company;[4] and
   (b) the beneficiaries are at all times non-resident.[5]

The expression 'international trust' shall also include, where the context so permits, a trust which is established or settled under the laws of another jurisdiction but which, subject to paras (a) and (b) of the above definition, is subsequently registered as an international trust under the ITA 1984.

6.8.2 Perpetuity period

Under s 6(1), both the rule against perpetuities or remoteness of vesting and the rule against perpetual trusts or against inalienability have no application to an 'international trust'.[6] However, notwithstanding this general disapplication, a trust instrument may make provision for vesting of all or any part of the

---

1 An unofficial consolidation of the amended Act is J Glasson (ed), n 3 on p 310, section D8.

2 ITA 1984, s 5(2).

3 The expression is not defined by the ITA 1984 but a 'foreign company' means a foreign company under the International Companies Act 1981–82.

4 The expression 'trustee company' is defined (in s 2) as 'a company registered as a trustee company under the provisions of the Trustee Companies Act 1981–82 and except in relation to s 15 [registration] includes a wholly owned subsidiary of a trustee company nominated pursuant to s 4A of the Trustee Companies Act 1981–82'.

5 Section 2. The expressions 'disposition', 'foreign company', 'non-resident', 'power of appointment' and 'trust' are all defined in s 2.

6 The rule against excessive accumulations also does not apply. Income of settled property may or shall be validly accumulated if the disposition of the accumulated income is itself valid: ITA 1984, s 9(1).

property of the trust upon such terms as are prescribed by the trust instrument, including, but not limited to, provision for:

(a) a period within which the property of a trust shall vest in any beneficiary of the trust; or
(b) the happening of an event upon which the property of the trust shall vest in any beneficiary of the trust; or
(c) the property of the trust not to vest in any beneficiary of the trust or the trust not to terminate.[1]

Section 6(3) provides that, where a trust would otherwise be held by the court to be void for uncertainty, because of its terms relating to termination of the trust or vesting of the property of the trust, and such uncertainty would be removed by imposing a date for termination of that trust, then the trust shall terminate on the date 100 years from the date of creation of the trust; and the property of the trust shall vest in the beneficiaries on that date, unless termination or vesting occurs earlier in accordance with the trust instrument.[2] Just what this ambiguous provision is aimed at is not at all clear. It seems to be intended to deal with some form of uncertainty, which can be cured by the imposition of a date for the termination of the trust and not with any form of uncertainty (such as uncertainty of objects) which might be fatal to the trust, but which cannot be cured simply by the adoption of a termination date. Since a trust may be perpetual, there is actually no need to stipulate any termination date (or vesting date) in the trust instrument, so, presumably, what is intended to be covered is the case where an attempt has been made to specify a termination date (or vesting date). However, it is one which is too uncertain to be workable – which may be due, for example, to the conceptual uncertainty of the words used or to difficulty in determining whether some specified precondition or triggering event has actually occurred. If the trust instrument provides that the trust shall be perpetual unless, say, the trustees decide to terminate it at some point in the exercise of a power or discretion conferred on them, but the terms in which their power or discretion are couched are uncertain, will it be the case that the trust remains a perpetual trust, but with no effective power to terminate, or will it be converted into a 100-year trust by s 6(3)?[3] It is also not clear whether the words 'would … be held by the court' actually require an application to, and a determination by, the court or whether, in a plain case or where the powers of 'variation' conferred by s 6(5) might be available (see below), it is sufficient to treat the trust as a 100-year trust without any such formal determination.

---

1 Ibid, s 6(2).
2 Ibid, s 6(3).
3 The provisions of ibid, s 6(4) (see below) do not seem to be relevant to this question.

Where a period or an event is specified within, or at the end of, or upon which the property of a trust shall vest in a beneficiary (or where s 6(3) applies), the property of the trust then remaining shall vest in the beneficiary in accordance with the provision, which specifies that period or event (or in accordance with s 6(3)) and such vesting shall apply in relation to all property then remaining of that trust and every general or special power of appointment under that trust shall be exercised in a manner consistent therewith.[1]

Without limiting any other rights conferred on trustees to vary a trust instrument, the trustees of an international trust may, with the prior consent of 'the interested parties', or if permitted by the trust instrument, vary the terms of the trust instrument to make provision:

(a) for a period being not less than the existing period provided for in the trust instrument within which the property of the trust shall vest in any beneficiary of the trust; or
(b) for the happening of an event being an event that will occur beyond the period within which the property of the trust would otherwise vest in the beneficiaries and upon the happening of which the property of the trust shall vest in any beneficiary of the trust; or
(c) to remove the period within which the property of the trust shall vest in any beneficiary.[2]

An 'interested party' means, in relation to any trust, any settlor, donor, trustee, protector, beneficiary and any person claiming through any one of such persons.[3] It is not specified whether 'the interested parties' whose consent is required means *all* such interested parties or a majority or just some of them (eg only those who may be directly affected by any proposed change), nor indeed whether they must all be adult and *sui juris*.

The inter-relationship of s 6(3) and (5) is not at all clear. If the termination date (or vesting date) of the trust is 'uncertain' (in the sense contemplated by s 6(3), whatever that might be), will this preclude the trustees (even with the consent of all 'interested parties') from exercising the powers conferred on them under s 6(5) to remove or extend such period? Presumably, this will be the case: otherwise s 6(3) would seem to be otiose. Even so, if a 100-year time-limit is imposed under s 6(3), will such limit then be extendable or removable by the trustees in accordance with s 6(5)?[4]

---

1 Ibid, s 6(4).
2 Ibid, s 6(5).
3 Ibid, s 2(1).
4 Ibid, s 6(4) is of no assistance, it seems, for (as we have seen) it provides only that 'every general or special power of appointment under the trust' shall be exercised in a manner consistent with the original or imposed termination date.

Finally, it is provided[1] that, except where there is express provision to the contrary contained in the trust instrument, where the proper law of an international trust is to be changed from that of the Cook Islands to that of another jurisdiction, the trustees may with the consent of the interested parties, or if permitted by the trust instrument, vary the terms of the trust instrument to provide for a lesser period in which the then remaining property of the trust shall vest in any beneficiary so as not to infringe the law of that other jurisdiction.

6.8.3 International charitable trusts

Section 12(1) provides that, notwithstanding any rule of law to the contrary, an international trust shall be deemed to be charitable or for charitable purposes where it is a trust *substantially* for one or more of the following objects or purposes:

(a) the relief of poverty;
(b) the advancement of education;
(c) the advancement of religion;
(d) other purposes beneficial to the community,

notwithstanding that the object or purpose may not be of a public nature or for the benefit of the public, but may be for the benefit of a section of the public or members of the public, or that it may also benefit privately one or more persons or objects or persons within a class of persons or is liable to be defeated whether by the exercise of a power of appointment or disposition or that the trustee has the power to defer the enjoyment of any charity or other beneficiary of the trust for any period not exceeding the term of the trust, and notwithstanding further that the trust may be discretionary or contingent upon the happening of any event.

In relation to 'international trusts', s 12(1) radically alters the law relating to the validity of charitable trusts. First, and most obviously, it dispenses with the requirement that a trust, in order to be a valid charitable trust, must have exclusively charitable objects or purposes: it is enough that the trust is 'substantially' for one or more of the objects comprised in the traditional four heads of charity. The meaning of the word 'substantially' which has been judicially described as being chameleon-like,[2] is capable of giving rise to difficult questions of fact and degree.

Secondly, it may be that s 12(1) was intended to dilute or remove the requirement in English law that a trust to be charitable must be for the benefit of the public or of a sufficient section thereof. However, the language of

---

1 Ibid, s 6(6).

2 See *R v Monopolies and Mergers Commission ex parte South Yorkshire Transport Ltd* [1992] 1 WLR 291 at 299, 302; and *Re Baden's Deed Trusts (No 2)* [1973] Ch 9 at 24.

s 12(1) arguably does not remove altogether the need for some public benefit: the phrase 'notwithstanding that the object or purpose may not be of a public nature or for the benefit of the public, but, may be for the benefit of a section of the public or members of the public' suggests that, while an international trust may remain charitable notwithstanding that its object or purpose is not of a public nature or for the benefit of the public, it must nevertheless be for the benefit of 'a section of the public or members of the public'.

The extent of the dilution of the English requirement of public benefit is left unclear: in England a trust may be charitable if it is for the benefit of a sufficient section of the public; and it is unclear:

(a) whether the expression 'a section of the public or members of the public' can mean anything different from a sufficient section of the public;
(b) how 'members of the public' differ from 'a section of the public', and
(c) how an object or purpose can at the same time be for the benefit of a section of the public or members of the public while not being of a public nature.

The uncertainty whether there is any continuing requirement for any public benefit makes it difficult to say whether trusts which failed in England for want of a public benefit, such as *Williams' Trustees v IRC*,[1] *IRC v Baddeley*,[2] *Re Compton*[3] and *Oppenheim v Tobacco Securities Trust Co Ltd*,[4] would be charitable under the laws of the Cook Islands if created as international trusts.

6.8.4 Purpose trusts

Section 12(2) provides that, notwithstanding any rule of law or equity to the contrary, a trust settled or established by a non-resident of the Cook Islands shall not be void or voidable by virtue of the fact that the trust fund shall be held for a purpose or purposes, whether charitable or not. And any trust so created shall be enforceable on the terms set out in the trust instrument or by the person or persons named in the instrument establishing the trust as the person or persons appointed to enforce the trust and the trust shall be enforceable at the instance of the person or persons so named notwithstanding that such person or persons are not beneficiaries under the trust.[5]

---

1 [1947] AC 447.
2 [1955] AC 572.
3 [1945] Ch 123.
4 [1951] AC 297.
5 The word 'trust' is defined in ITA 1984, s 2(1). Section 12 is not expressly confined to an international trust. However, apart from the title of the Act, s 5(1) declares that the Act applies, unless the context otherwise requires and subject to s 15, to (a) international trusts, (b) all registered instruments (whether they take effect on, before or after the commencement of the Act), (c) any disposition to or

There is no requirement, however, that an enforcer be appointed by the trust instrument; and there is no stipulation (as in certain other jurisdictions, such as the British Virgin Islands) that one of the trustees must be a 'designated person' for enforcement purposes. However, recent amendments to the legislation now make provision for replacement of enforcers. Section 12(3) provides that a person appointed to enforce the trust may resign or be removed or replaced in accordance with the trust instrument. Section 12(4) then provides further that, if the person appointed to enforce the trust resigns, or is removed, or is unwilling, refusing, unfit or unable to act, and if no successor can be appointed in accordance with the trust instrument, the trustees shall forthwith apply to the court for directions or for another person or persons to be appointed by the court to enforce the trust. The court shall be empowered to make an order appointing a person or persons to enforce the trust on such terms it sees fit, and pending appointment by the court the Attorney-General shall be entitled, on such terms as he may require, to enforce the trust with the same rights and powers as the person appointed under the trust instrument to enforce the trust.

For a discussion of some problems concerning enforcement generally, see the section dealing with Bermuda and the British Virgin Islands.

6.9 CYPRUS

Cyprus has enacted legislation similar to, but not identical with, that of the Cook Islands, providing for 'international trusts' and authorising the creation of certain non-charitable purpose trusts. The provisions are to be found in the International Trusts Law 1992 (ITL 1992) which came into force on 24 July 1992.[1]

The principal differences from the law of the Cook Islands are (a) that the ITL 1992 only validates purpose trusts (as defined) which are also international trusts, and (b) that they are not required to be registered.[2]

6.9.1 Meaning of 'international trust'

An 'international trust' is a trust in respect of which:

(a) the settlor is not a permanent resident in the Republic of Cyprus;
(b) at least one of the trustees for the time being is, during the whole duration of the trust, a permanent resident in the Republic;

---

by an international trust, and (d) all questions and matters relating to or concerning an international trust.

1 Date of publication in the *Official Gazette*.

2 ITL 1992, s 15.

(c) no beneficiary other than a charitable institution is a permanent resident in the Republic;
(d) the trust property does not include any immovable property situated in the Republic.[1]

A trust still qualifies as an international trust notwithstanding that the settlor or the trustee or a beneficiary is a partnership or company qualifying under s 8Y and s 28A of the Cyprus Income Tax Laws.[2]

6.9.2 International charitable trusts

Section 7(1) provides that, subject to the Constitution of the Republic of Cyprus and notwithstanding the existence of any contrary legal provision of the law of Cyprus or any other law, an international trust shall be deemed to be charitable where the trust has as its 'main purpose' the achievement of one or more of the following:

(a) the relief of poverty;
(b) the advancement of education;
(c) the advancement of religion;
(d) other purposes beneficial to the community.

The 'main purpose' requirement corresponds to the requirement under the law of the Cook Islands that the trust be 'substantially' for one or more of the stipulated objects or purposes. It is not clear that the difference in language has avoided (indeed, it may have increased) the difficulties in identifying those multi-purpose trusts which qualify as charitable trusts and those which do not.

By s 7(2) an international trust established for one or more of the above-mentioned objects or purposes is deemed to be charitable notwithstanding that the object or purpose may not be of a public nature or for the benefit of the public, but may benefit a section of the public, or that it may benefit particularly one or more persons or objects or persons within a class of persons or is liable to be modified or terminated whether by the exercise of a power of appointment or the disposition of assets, or that the trustee has the power to defer the distribution of benefits to any charity of the trust for a period not exceeding the period of the trust, and notwithstanding that the trust 'is or is considered to be in the category of discretionary trusts'. This provision is in very similar, though not identical, terms to the corresponding provision of the law of the Cook Islands.[3]

---

1 Ibid, s 2.
2 Ibid.
3 For a discussion of the effect of the Cook Islands provision on the law of charity, see **6.8**.

6.9.3 International purpose trusts

Section 7(3) of the Act provides that, notwithstanding the existence of any contrary legal provision of the law of Cyprus or of any other country, an international trust shall not be void or voidable by reason only that it is a 'purpose trust' provided that, where it is a non-perpetual or terminable trust the instrument creating the trust specifies the event or events upon the happening of which the trust terminates, and provides for the disposition of its net assets upon its termination.[1] The expression 'purpose trust' is defined to mean a trust other than 'a trust with beneficiaries being particular natural or legal persons whether or not immediately ascertainable' and other than 'a trust with beneficiaries being an aggregate of particular natural or legal persons ascertainable by reference to some personal attribute or relationship'.[2] This definition closely follows the definition of the expression 'a trust for a purpose or purposes' in the original Bermuda legislation of 1989.[3] Similar problems are likely to arise.[4]

An international trust which is a purpose trust is enforceable by the settlor or his personal representatives or by the person or persons named in the instrument establishing the trust as the person or persons appointed to enforce the trust and the trust is enforceable at the instance of the person or persons so named notwithstanding that such person or persons are not beneficiaries under the trust.[5]

As with the legislation of the Cook Islands there is no requirement that one of the trustees be a 'designated person'. Although there may be a nominated enforcer, there is no requirement to this effect; there is no involvement by the Attorney-General in ensuring that there is someone who is able and willing to act as the enforcer; there is no provision for a substitute enforcer; and there are no criminal sanctions.

For a discussion of some problems concerning enforcement generally, see the sections dealing with Bermuda and the British Virgin Islands.[6]

6.9.4 Perpetuity and accumulation periods

As already mentioned the duration of an international trust which is a purpose trust is not subject to any perpetuity period.[1] Additionally, s 6 of the Act

---

1 The Act seems to make no provision for the disposal of the trust property in the event that a perpetual non-charitable international purpose trust fails by reason of a failure of objects or purposes. There is nothing corresponding to the *cy-près* jurisdiction applicable to charitable trusts; and the requirement in s 7(3) that the trust instrument must provide for the disposition of its net assets upon its termination seems to be confined to cases where the trust is terminable.

2 International Trusts Law 1992, s 2.

3 See **6.5.1**. See also the British Virgin Islands legislation discussed at **6.6**.

4 Ibid.

5 The word 'trust' is defined in the International Trusts Law 1992, s 2 by reference to the Cyprus Trustee Law and includes trusts created by will.

6 At **6.5** and **6.6** above.

provides that in an instrument creating an international trust, a 'direction' for the accumulation of income is valid 'for any period within the period of the duration of the trust'. The expression 'direction' connotes a trust to accumulate as opposed to a mere power to do so.[2]

Section 6 would appear to authorise a perpetual trust to accumulate income in a perpetual international non-charitable purpose trust, but not a similar power to accumulate. It may, however, be doubtful whether a perpetual trust for non-charitable purposes, with a trust to accumulate the income in perpetuity, could indeed qualify as a purpose trust at all. On the other hand, an international trust for non-charitable purposes to terminate at the end of a period of, for example, 250 years, with a trust in remainder for the issue of the settlor living at the end of the trust period and containing a trust to accumulate the income for 50 years would apparently be a valid trust in Cyprus;[3] and if that is so it is difficult to see on what basis a similar trust with a direction to accumulate the income for, say, 200 years would not be likewise a valid trust. The possibility of the creation of such trusts principally for the benefit of human ultimate beneficiaries might be of considerable interest to a modern-day Thellusson.[4]

6.9.5 Confidentiality

The Act contains provisions for confidentiality in relation to international trusts, including purpose trusts.[5]

6.10 THE ISLE OF MAN

6.10.1 Requirements of a 'purpose trust'

The Purpose Trusts Act 1996 provides that a person may create a valid purpose trust, for a period not exceeding 80 years, provided the conditions laid down in the Act are complied with.[6] A 'purpose trust' is defined[1] as:

---

1 International Trusts Law 1992, s 5(2).

2 The decision in the English case of *Re Robb* [1953] Ch 459 that the prohibition on excessive accumulation contained in Law of Property Act 1925, s 164 (which refers to a 'direction' to accumulate) applies to powers as well as trusts does not appear to be inconsistent with the view expressed in the text.

3 However long the trust period, the trust in remainder for issue would not, it seems, be void for perpetuity, given the opening words of International Trusts Law 1992, s 7(3): 'Notwithstanding the existence of any contrary legal provision of the law of the Republic or of any other country ...', coupled with the requirement that the trust instrument provide for the disposition of the net assets of the trust on its termination.

4 *Cf Thellusson v Woodford* (1799) 4 Ves 227; (1805) 11 Ves 112.

5 See International Trusts Law 1992, s 11.

6 Purpose Trusts Act 1996, s 1(1). The provisions of the 1996 Act are similar to, and evidently modelled on, those in Part II of the Bermudan Trusts (Special Provisions) Act 1989, which has now been repealed, and also those of the British Virgin Islands' Trustee Ordinance (c 303), as amended by the

'a trust for a purpose or purposes other than a trust:

(a) that is for the benefit of particular persons whether or not immediately ascertainable; or
(b) that is for the benefit of some aggregate of persons ascertained by reference to some personal relationship; or
(c) that is for charitable purposes.'

A trust shall not be treated as being for charitable purposes by reason only of the fact that the instrument creating the trust contains a gift or bequest of any part of the trust assets to a charity.

The conditions with which the purposes must comply are as follows. They must be 'certain, reasonable and possible'; and they must not be 'unlawful, contrary to public policy or immoral'.[2] The trust must be created: (a) by deed; or (b) by a will which is capable of being and is admitted to probate in the Isle of Man, or in respect of which letters of administration in the Island are capable of being and are granted.[3] There must be two or more trustees, at least one of whom is a 'designated person'.[4] The instrument creating the trust must appoint a person who is independent of the trustees to enforce the trust (referred to in the Act as 'the enforcer'); and it must also provide for the appointment, as soon as is practicable, of such a person as enforcer in the event of a vacancy in the office of enforcer or in the event of an enforcer ceasing to be independent of the trustees, or if for any reason the enforcer is incapable, unable or unwilling to act as enforcer.[5] The instrument creating the trust must provide for the enforcer to have an absolute right of access to any information or document relating to the trust, the assets of the trust or to the administration of the trust.[6] Finally, the instrument creating the trust must specify the event upon the happening of which the trust terminates and provide for the disposition of surplus assets of the trust upon its termination.[7] Trusts for a non-charitable purpose or purposes which do not comply with these conditions are invalid.[8] No land or any interest in land in the Isle of Man shall be held, directly or indirectly, in a purpose trust.[9]

Trustee (Amendment) Act 1993 (No 7 of 1993), which remains in force (although with some differences). See **6.6.1** for further discussion of common terms.

1 Purpose Trusts Act 1996, s 9.
2 Ibid, s 1(1)(a).
3 Ibid, s 1(1)(b).
4 Ibid, s 1(1)(c).
5 Ibid, s 1(1)(d).
6 Ibid, s 1(1)(e).
7 Ibid, s 1(1)(f).
8 Ibid, s 1(3). Section 4 of the Act provides that neither the creation, variation, termination or validity of any trust created under or in accordance with any statutory provision or any other law nor any trust for charitable purposes or the law relating to such trusts is affected.
9 Ibid, s 5.

6.10.2 Designated person

A 'designated person' is defined as a person in the Isle of Man who is:

(a) an advocate;
(b) a legal practitioner registered under the Legal Practitioners Registration Act 1986;
(c) a person qualified under s 14(1)(a) of the Companies Act 1982 for appointment as auditor of a public company;
(d) a member of the Chartered Institute of Management Accountants;
(e) a member of the Institute of Chartered Secretaries and Administrators;
(f) a fellow or associate member of the Institute of Bankers; or
(g) a trust corporation (as defined in s 65A of the Trustee Act 1961).[1]

Section 2(1) of the Act provides that every designated person shall keep in the Island:

(a) a copy of the instrument which created or evidenced each purpose trust of which he is a trustee and also copies of amending and supplemental instruments;
(b) a register of each such trust specifying in respect of each such trust the name of the person who created the trust, a summary of the purpose or purposes of the trust and the name and address of the enforcer of the trust; and
(c) such documents as are sufficient to show the true financial position of each such trust at the end of the trust's last financial year together with details of all applications of principal and income during the financial year.

A designated person shall permit the Attorney-General or a person authorised by him to inspect the instruments, registers and documents referred to above.[2] However, these provisions do not create an obligation to make such instruments, registers and documents available for public inspection.[3]

Under s 6 of the Act, a designated person is guilty of an offence and is liable on summary conviction to a fine not exceeding £5000 where he:

(a) fails to comply with the above obligations;[4]
(b) makes, or authorises the making of, an untrue statement in an instrument, register or document referred to in s 2(1) of the Act;[1]

---

1 Ibid, s 9.
2 Ibid, s 2(2).
3 Ibid, s 2(3).
4 Ibid, s 6(1).

(c) refuses to permit the Attorney-General or a person authorised by him to inspect such an instrument, register or document (in which case he is also liable to a further fine of £500 for every day on which his refusal continues);[2] and
(d) fails to comply with the provisions of s 3(1) relating to the appointment of a replacement enforcer.[3]

In proceedings against a designated person for an offence under s 6(1), (2) or (4),[4] it shall be a defence for him to satisfy the court that he took all reasonable steps and exercised all due diligence to avoid committing the offence.[5] However, he is not entitled to rely on such a defence if he relied on information given by another, unless he shows that it is reasonable in all the circumstances for him to have relied on the information, having regard, in particular, to:

(a) the steps which he took, and those which might reasonably have been taken, for the purpose of verifying the information; and
(b) whether he had any reason to disbelieve the information.[6]

Where an offence under the Act is committed by a body corporate and is proved to have been committed with the consent or connivance of, or to be attributable to neglect on the part of, a director, manager, secretary or other similar officer of the body corporate or a person who was purporting to act in such capacity, he, as well as the body corporate, is guilty of the offence and liable to be proceeded against and punished accordingly.[7] Where the affairs of a body corporate are managed by its members, the last-mentioned provision applies in relation to the acts and defaults of a member in connection with his functions of management as if he were a director of the body corporate.[8]

6.10.3 Enforcer

The High Court may on the application of the enforcer of a trust make such orders as it considers necessary or expedient to enable or assist an enforcer:

(a) to enforce a trust; or

---

1 Ibid, s 6(2).
2 Ibid, s 6(3).
3 Ibid, s 6(4). See also **6.10.3**.
4 Ie a refusal to permit inspection of an instrument, register or document (see s 6(3)) is excluded from the scope of the defences referred to in s 7.
5 Ibid, s 7(1).
6 Ibid, s 7(2).
7 Ibid, s 8(1).
8 Ibid, s 8(2).

(b) to gain access to any information or document which relates to a trust, the assets of a trust or the administration of a trust.[1]

As discussed previously, the trust instrument itself ought to make provision for the appointment of an enforcer in the event of a vacancy or in the event of the enforcer ceasing to be independent of the trustees or for any reason being incapable, unable or unwilling to act.[2] Subject to such express provisions, s 3(1) of the Act provides that, where a trustee who is a designated person has reason to believe that:

(a) there is a vacancy in the office of enforcer; or
(b) the enforcer has ceased to be independent of the trustees; or
(c) the enforcer is for any reason incapable, unable or unwilling to act as enforcer, then that trustee 'shall' (ie it is a duty) as soon as practicable:
  (i) give written notice of, and the grounds for, his belief to the Attorney-General, and
  (ii) provide the Attorney-General with a copy of the instrument by which the trust was created.

On receipt of such a notice, the Attorney-General 'may' apply to the High Court for the appointment of a person as the enforcer of the trust and the High Court may by order declare that person to be the enforcer.[3] Such an order of the High Court is conclusive evidence of the appointment of an enforcer of a trust.[4] The High Court may also order that the costs and expenses of the Attorney-General shall be paid out of the assets of the trust.[5]

6.11 JERSEY

6.11.1 Trusts and purpose trusts

Jersey trusts are governed by the Trusts (Jersey) Law 1984 (TJL 1984) which came into force on 23 March 1984, and by three subsequent amending statutes.[6] Article 2 of the TJL 1984 declares that a trust exists where a person (known as a trustee) holds or has vested in him or is deemed to hold or have vested in him property (of which he is not the owner in his own right):

---

1 Ibid, s 1(2).
2 Ibid, s 1(1)(d)(ii).
3 Ibid, s 3(2). Presumably, this is in place of (and not in addition to) any previous enforcer who was/is not independent of the trustees.
4 Ibid, s 3(3).
5 Ibid, s 3(4).
6 The Trusts (Amendment) (Jersey) Law 1989, which came into force on 21 July 1989; the Trusts (Amendment No 2) (Jersey) Law 1991, which came into force on 9 October 1991; and the Trusts (Amendment) (Jersey) Law 1996, which came into force on 24 May 1996.

(a) for the benefit of any person (known as a beneficiary) whether or not yet ascertained or in existence; or
(b) for any purpose which is not for the benefit only of the trustee; or
(c) for a combination of (a) and (b) above.

The proper law of a trust shall be the law of the jurisdiction expressed by the terms of the trust as the proper law, or, failing that, be implied from the terms of the trust, and, failing either of these, the law with which the trust at the time it was created had the closest connection.[1] The court[2] has jurisdiction where the trust is a Jersey trust (meaning a trust whose proper law is the law of Jersey),[3] or where a trustee of a foreign trust (meaning a trust whose proper law is the law of some jurisdiction other than Jersey) is resident in Jersey, or where any trust property of a foreign trust is situated in Jersey, or the administration of any trust property of a foreign trust is carried out in Jersey.[4]

Article 9(1) of the TJL 1984 (which applies only to a Jersey trust) declares that a beneficiary shall be:

(a) identifiable by name; or
(b) ascertainable by reference to:
  (i) a class, or
  (ii) a relationship to some person,

whether or not living at the time of the creation of the trust or at the time which under the terms of the trust is the time by reference to which members of a class are to be determined.[5] Article 10(2)(a)(iv) declares that a Jersey trust shall be invalid if it is created for a purpose in relation to which there is no beneficiary, not being a charitable purpose. Thus, non-charitable purpose trusts *per se* are not valid in Jersey. Moreover, those few anomalous non-charitable purpose trusts recognised in English law would also not be valid in Jersey.

However, the Trusts (Amendment No 3) (Jersey) Law 1996 (the 1996 Law), which came into force on 24 May 1996, has modified the position by inserting in the TJL 1984 a new Art 10A which provides that non-charitable purpose trusts may now be created in Jersey, provided they satisfy the relevant statutory provisions. Article 10A declares that a trust shall not be invalid to any extent by reason of Art 10(2)(a)(iv) (see preceding paragraph) if the terms of

---

1 TJL 1984, Art 4. See also Trusts (Amendment No 2) (Jersey) Law 1991, Art 1.

2 Defined in ibid, Art 1(1) as the Inferior Number of the Royal Court.

3 A Jersey trust, which is not a trust for charitable purposes, may continue until the one hundredth anniversary of the date on which it came into existence, and if not sooner terminated shall then terminate: ibid, Art 11.

4 Ibid, Art 5.

5 Beneficiaries may be added or excluded (Art 9(2)); obligations may be imposed as a condition of benefit (Art 9(3)); a beneficiary may irrevocably disclaim his whole interest (or, subject to the terms of the trust, part thereof) in writing (Art 9(4)–(9)).

the trust provide for the appointment of an enforcer in relation to its non-charitable purposes, and for the appointment of a new enforcer at any time when there is none. Article 10B(1) then declares that it shall be the duty of an 'enforcer' to enforce the trust in relation to its non-charitable purposes; but a trustee of that trust cannot be appointed as an enforcer of it.[1] Article 17(4) of the TJL 1984 applies to an enforcer as it applies to a trustee, ie except with the approval of the court or as permitted by the TJL 1984 or expressly provided by the terms of the trust, he shall not directly or indirectly profit from his appointment or cause or permit any other person to profit directly or indirectly from such appointment or on his own account enter into any transaction with the trustees or relating to the trust property which may result in such profit.[2] Beyond this, there is very little indication as to the duties of an enforcer. Although he may not be a trustee, it seems clear that the intention is that he should occupy a fiduciary position and must act in good faith (although it is unclear as to whom he owes such duties).

Where there is more than one purpose, or at least one beneficiary and one purpose, then, subject to the terms of the trust, a trustee shall be impartial and shall not execute the trust for the advantage of one at the expense of another. The meaning of this vaguely worded provision is unclear. It is consistent with the view that the trustees must ensure equal distribution amongst the purposes and beneficiaries (an unequal distribution inevitably being an advantage to one at the expense of another), but it seems unlikely that this was intended. Does it mean that the trustees may not make illusory or exclusive appointments (both of which have been permitted in England since the early nineteenth century and now by s 158 of the Law of Property Act 1925)? Does it mean that the trustees must maintain an 'even hand' as between objects and beneficiaries?

A trustee of a trust for non-charitable purposes shall, at any time when there is no enforcer in relation to them, take such steps as may be necessary to secure the appointment of a new enforcer.[3] Where the trustee of a trust for non-charitable purposes has reason to believe that the enforcer in relation to them is unwilling or refuses to act, or is unfit to act or incapable of acting, he shall apply to the court for the removal of the enforcer and the appointment of a replacement.[4]

In order to assist an enforcer in fulfilling his duty to enforce the non-charitable purposes of a trust, he is given the same rights as a beneficiary to compel a trustee to disclose any document which 'relates to or forms part of the accounts of the trust'.[5] This provision, expressed in narrow terms, has

---

1 TJL 1984, Art 10B(1) and (2) (inserted by Trusts (Amendment No 3) (Jersey) Law 1996, Art 3). An action by the enforcer alleging breach of trust must be brought within three years of delivery of final accounts or of first having knowledge of the breach: ibid, Art 53(2) (as amended by Trusts (Amendment No 3) (Jersey) Law 1996, Art 9).

2 TJL 1984, Art 10B(3).

3 Ibid, Art 17(7) (inserted by Trusts (Amendment No 3) (Jersey) Law 1996, Art 4).

4 TJL 1984, Art 17(8) (inserted by Trusts (Amendment No 3) (Jersey) Law 1996, Art 4).

5 Ibid, Art 25 (as amended by Trusts (Amendment No 3) (Jersey) Law 1996, Art 6).

been construed widely by the Jersey court and it has been held[1] to include all documents and correspondence relating to the administration of the trust property or to the execution of the trust (as in *Re Londonderry's Settlement*).[2] However, an enforcer, like a beneficiary, has no right (subject to an order of the court) to compel a trustee to disclose any document which discloses the trustee's deliberations as to the manner in which he has exercised a power or discretion or performed a duty conferred or imposed upon him; or discloses the reason for any particular exercise of such power or discretion or performance of duty or the material upon which such reason shall or might have been based; or relates to the exercise or proposed exercise of such power or discretion or the performance or proposed performance of such duty.[3]

6.11.2 Failure or termination of trusts

Where property is held by trustees for a purpose (which may be a charitable or non-charitable purpose) which has ceased to exist or is no longer applicable, that property shall be held for such other purpose (charitable or non-charitable) as the court may declare to be consistent with the original intention of the settlor (meaning the person who provided that property).[4]

6.11.3 Resignation and removal of enforcer

An enforcer may resign his office by notice in writing delivered to the trustee; and his resignation takes effect on the delivery of such notice.[5] An enforcer shall cease to be the enforcer of the trust in relation to its non-charitable purposes immediately upon:

(a) his removal from office by the court;
(b) his resignation becoming effective;
(c) the coming into effect of a provision in the terms of a trust under which he is removed from office or otherwise ceases to hold office; or
(d) his appointment as a trustee of the trust.[6]

The 1996 Law provides no assistance on the question of what kind of non-charitable purpose is valid and acceptable in Jersey, the implication being that there are very few restrictions at all. Article 10(2) of the TJL 1984 declares that a trust shall be invalid if it purports to do anything, the doing of which is contrary to the law of Jersey; or it purports to confer any right or power or

1 *West v Lazard Brothers & Company (Jersey) Ltd* [1987–88] JLR 414.
2 [1965] Ch 918.
3 TJL 1984, Art 25(a)–(c).
4 Ibid, Art 38(2) (as amended by Trusts (Amendment No 3) (Jersey) Law 1996, Art 7). An application to the court *may* (but apparently need not) be made by the Attorney-General.
5 TJL 1984, Art 10C(1), (2).
6 Ibid, Art 10C(4).

impose any obligation the exercise or carrying out of which is contrary to the law of Jersey; or it purports to apply directly to immovable property situated in Jersey; or it is created for a purpose in relation to which there is no beneficiary, not being a charitable purpose and not being a trust which satisfies the requirements of the 1996 Law. In addition, a trust shall be invalid to the extent that the court declares that it is immoral or contrary to public policy or the terms of the trust are so uncertain that its performance is rendered impossible.[1] Thus, trusts for conceptually uncertain objects, such as 'objects of benevolence and liberality',[2] or 'some useful memorial'[3] or 'the maintenance of good understanding between nations',[4] may be declared invalid in Jersey, as they have been in England, but this is not entirely clear. Similarly, Jersey public policy, like that of England and Scotland, is likely to prohibit trusts which are capricious, useless, wasteful, or harmful.[5] However, this remains to be seen. Beyond these general restrictions, which are applicable to all Jersey trusts, there is no indication of any limit on the nature of the non-charitable purposes that may be created.

Where a Jersey trust is created for two or more purposes, of which some are lawful and others are unlawful, then, if those purposes cannot be separated, the trust shall be invalid.[6] However, where those purposes can be separated, the court may declare that the trust is valid as to the purposes which are lawful; and, in the case of such partial validity, the court may also declare what property is trust property and what property is not trust property.[7] Property as to which a trust is wholly or partially invalid shall, subject to any order of the court, be held by the trustees in trust for the settlor absolutely (the settlor being the person who provided that property) or, if he is dead, for his personal representative.[8]

6.11.4 Registration and filing

Jersey has no requirements for the registration or filing of trust instruments.

6.12 LABUAN

Labuan is a capital territory of Malaysia. Malaysian trust law is based on English law, but, in its application to Labuan, it has been modified extensively

---

1 Ibid, Art 10(2)(b)(ii) and (iii).

2 *Morice v Bishop of Durham* (1804) 9 Ves 399.

3 *Re Endacott* [1960] Ch 232.

4 *Re Astor's Settlement Trusts* [1952] Ch 534.

5 See *Brown v Burdett* (1882) 21 ChD 667; *M'Caig v University of Glasgow* 1907 SC 231; *M'Caig's Trustees v Kirk Session of United Free Church of Lismore* 1915 SC 426; *Aitken's Trustee v Aitken* 1927 SC 374.

6 TJL 1984, Art 10(3)(a).

7 Ibid, Art 10(3)(b), (4).

8 Ibid, Art 10(6), (7). See also Art 10(5).

by statute. The main statute is the Labuan Offshore Trusts Act 1996 (LOTA 1996) which deals with the creation, recognition and administration of Labuan 'offshore trusts'. The Trustee Act 1949 and the Trustee (Incorporation) Act 1952, which are the main statutes governing Malaysian domestic trusts, do not apply.

In many respects, the provisions of the LOTA 1996 are similar to, if not identical with, those enacted for similar purposes in other jurisdictions, eg Belize and Bermuda. Following a lengthy series of elaborate and often convoluted definitions (s 2), the LOTA 1996 deals with the existence of a trust (s 3), charitable and purpose trusts (s 4), spendthrift or protective trusts (s 5) and then the proper law of a trust (s 6). Part II (ss 7–21) of the LOTA 1996 deals with the creation and recognition of offshore trusts; Part III (ss 22–25) with the beneficiaries of offshore trusts; Part IV (ss 26–46) with the trustees of offshore trusts; and Part V (ss 47–62) with miscellaneous matters, such as the variation of trusts, the general powers of the courts, limitation of actions, and so forth.

6.12.1 Existence of a 'trust' and an 'offshore trust'

Section 3 of the LOTA 1996[1] (which is virtually identical with s 2 of the Belize Trusts Act 1992) declares that a trust exists where a person holds or has vested in him[2] property of which he is not the owner in his own right and is under an obligation as a trustee to deal with that property:

(a) for the benefit of any beneficiary, whether or not ascertained or in existence;
(b) for any purpose which is not for the benefit of the trustee;[3] or
(c) for both such benefit and purpose mentioned in paras (a) and (b).

Section 7(1) then provides that a trust is an 'offshore trust' where:

(a) the settlor is a qualified person at the time the trust is created;[4]

---

1 LOTA 1996, s 2(1) provides, in addition, that 'trust' includes 'the trust property and the rights, powers, duties, interests, relationships and other obligations under a trust'.

2 Belize Trusts Act 1992, s 2 also extends to the case where a trustee 'is deemed' to hold property or have it vested in him.

3 Belize Trusts Act 1992, s 2(b) refers to a purpose which is 'not for the benefit only' of the trustee. Thus, where a trustee is one of several persons who benefit from a purpose trust of the kind at issue in *Re Denley* [1969] 1 Ch 373 (sportsground for employees of a company), such a trust would fall within this provision, but not, it seems, within LOTA 1996, s 3(b).

4 Where the trust is created by will, this is the time at which the will takes effect: LOTA 1996, s 7(4), ie on death.

(b) the trust property[1] does not include any immovable property[2] situated in Malaysia, unless otherwise allowed by the relevant authorities[3] and laws for the time being in force;
(c) subject to s 7(2) and (3), all the beneficiaries[4] under the trust are qualified persons at the time the trust is created or at the time any one or more of them otherwise become entitled to be beneficiaries under the trust; and
(d) at least one of the trustees is a trust company.[5]

The key concept in this definition is 'a qualified person' (a requirement which applies to both the settlor and the beneficiaries of an offshore trust). This means 'a person who is not a resident of Malaysia'. A 'resident' is someone:

(a) who is a citizen or permanent resident of Malaysia; or
(b) who has established a place of business and is operating in Malaysia (other than an offshore company or a foreign offshore company incorporated or registered under the Offshore Companies Act 1953).

There is even an extended definition of 'Malaysia'.[6]

A trust shall remain as an offshore trust notwithstanding that one or more of the beneficiaries who are qualified persons at the time the trust is created subsequently become resident in Malaysia at the time they otherwise become entitled to be beneficiaries.[7] Moreover, a trust shall be an offshore trust notwithstanding that a person who is not a qualified person benefits together with any other persons as members of a class of persons who are beneficiaries under a trust for a charitable purpose.[8]

Subject to s 4(3) (see below), a beneficiary must be:

---

1 The expression 'trust property' is defined (somewhat unnecessarily) as 'the property for the time being held on trust': ibid, s 2(1).

2 'Immovable property situated in Malaysia' includes shares, stocks or debentures in or of a company whose assets include immovable property situated in Malaysia, other than a public company quoted on the official list of a stock exchange of any country or jurisdiction therein: ibid.

3 Which are not defined, which presumably include, but are not synonymous with 'the Authority' and the 'Minister', both of which terms are defined in LOTA 1996, s 2(1).

4 A 'beneficiary' means 'a person entitled to benefit under a trust or in whose favour a discretion to distribute property held in trust may be exercised': ibid.

5 A 'trust company' means 'a company registered under s 4 of the Labuan Trust Companies Act 1990 to carry on business as a trust company': ibid.

6 It means the territories of the Federation of Malaysia, the territorial waters of Malaysia and the seabed and subsoil of the territorial waters, and includes any area extending beyond the limits of the territorial waters of Malaysia, and the seabed and subsoil of any such area, which has been or may hereafter be designated under the laws of Malaysia and in accordance with international law as an area over which Malaysia has sovereign rights for the purposes of exploring and exploiting the natural resources, whether living or non-living. Why such an elaborate definition was considered necessary in a statute such as the LOTA 1996 is impossible to fathom.

7 Ibid, s 7(3).

8 Ibid, s 7(2).

(a) identifiable by name; or
(b) ascertainable by reference to a class or to a relationship to some persons, whether or not living at the time, which under the terms of the offshore trust is the time by reference to which members of a class are to be determined.[1]

Where there are no beneficiaries thus identifiable or ascertainable, the trust is not valid unless the purpose is a charitable purpose.[2] A settlor or trustee of an offshore trust may also be a beneficiary of the trust but, if he is the sole trustee, he shall not also be a beneficiary thereunder.[3]

6.12.2 Creation of an offshore trust

An offshore trust must be created by will or other instrument in writing, including a unilateral declaration of trust.[4] For this purpose, a unilateral declaration of trust is a declaration in writing by a trust company stating:

(a) that it is the trustee of an offshore trust;
(b) the name of the trust;
(c) the terms of the trust; and
(d) the names, or information enabling the identification, of all the beneficiaries.[5]

Given the definition of 'beneficiary' in s 2(1), the identification of any purpose, whether charitable or non-charitable, would not seem to be necessary (unless this is regarded as being required by 'the terms of the trust'). A unilateral declaration of trust need not contain the name of the settlor, but in such a case the declaration shall contain a statement by the trust company that the settlor is 'a qualified person' on the date of the making of the declaration.[6]

6.12.3 Charitable and non-charitable purpose trusts

A trust is regarded as a trust for charitable purposes under the LOTA 1996 where:

(a) the trust is made for any one or more of the purposes specified in s 4(1); and

---

1 Labuan Trust Companies Act 1990, s 22(1).
2 Ibid, s 22(2).
3 Ibid, s 22(3).
4 LOTA 1996, s 8(1).
5 Ibid, s 8(2). The rather odd requirement that the unilateral declaration of trust be made by a trust company, and not the settlor himself, seems merely to provide for evidence of the trusts.
6 Ibid, s 8(3).

(b) the fulfilment of such purpose or purposes is for the benefit of the community or a substantial section of the community, having regard to the type and nature of the purpose or purposes.

The specified charitable purposes are:

(a) the relief or eradication of poverty;
(b) the advancement of education;
(c) the promotion of art, science and religion;
(d) the protection of the environment;
(e) the advancement of human rights and fundamental freedom; and
(f) any other purposes which are beneficial to the community.

This list is based firmly on the fourfold classification of charities found in English law,[1] under which five of the six listed categories are clearly charitable. Whether a particular purpose is 'beneficial to the community', and therefore falls within category (f), will probably give rise to the same uncertainties and difficulties as are encountered in English law in relation to the fourth category of the *Pemsel* classification. As in the case of the Belize Trusts Act 1992, s 14 of the LOTA 1996 surprisingly does not deal expressly with recreational charities, which have caused some difficulty in England and which, presumably, remain non-charitable in Labuan. Category (e) would be regarded as a political purpose and not charitable under English law[2] and therefore represents a new departure. A purpose may be regarded as charitable whether it is to be carried out in Malaysia or elsewhere and whether it is beneficial to the community in Malaysia or elsewhere.[3] As in the case of Belize, regard must be given to the type and nature of the purpose, so that, for example, trusts for the relief of poor relations (which are valid charitable trusts in England, although anomalous) are presumably also charitable in Labuan.

Notwithstanding any law to the contrary (and s 22(1) in particular), a trust (which apparently need not be an offshore trust) may be created or established for a particular purpose or purposes, *whether charitable or not*. There is no express restriction on the kind of non-charitable purpose which is permissible: unlike other jurisdictions (eg Belize and Bermuda), the LOTA 1996 does not specify that such purposes must be specific, reasonable or capable of fulfilment, or even not against public policy. Section 9(2)(d) provides that an offshore trust shall be invalid and unenforceable where the court declares that the object for which it was created has failed or that the terms of the trust are such that its performance is not possible, but there is little guidance (beyond that which is an actual offence) as to the kind of purpose or object that might cause such

1 *Commissioners for Special Purposes of Income Tax v Pemsel* [1891] AC 531 at 583; *Scottish Burial Reform and Cremation Society Ltd v Glasgow Corporation* [1968] AC 138.

2 *McGovern v Attorney-General* [1982] Ch 321.

3 LOTA 1996, s 4(2).

failure or impossibility. There is a requirement that the trust property must vest in natural persons within the perpetuity period applying or expressed to apply to the trust.[1] Section 16 of the LOTA 1996 provides that an offshore trust shall, unless otherwise stated in and subject to the terms of the trust, continue to exist for a period not exceeding 100 years (but it may be terminated at any time in accordance with the provisions of the LOTA 1996). (The wording suggests that a period in excess of 100 years could be created expressly. However, this is clearly not what is intended.)

The settlor of a trust may give to the trustee a letter of his wishes (or the trustee may prepare a memorandum of the wishes of the settlor) with regard to the exercise of any functions conferred on the trustee by the terms of the trust.[2] The trustee may then have regard to such letter (or memorandum) in exercising any such functions, but shall not be accountable for his failure or refusal to do so. No fiduciary duty or obligation shall be imposed on the trustee merely by the giving to him of a letter of wishes (or preparation of a memorandum).[3]

6.12.4 Enforcement

Insofar as enforcement of a trust created or established for a purpose is concerned, s 4(3) provides that it shall be enforceable by the settlor or his personal representatives, or by the person or persons named in the instrument creating or establishing the trust as the person or persons appointed to enforce the trust; and the trust shall be enforceable at the instance of the person or persons so named, notwithstanding that such person or persons are not beneficiaries under the trust. The role of enforcer in relation to a purpose trust would seem to require some form of supervision or monitoring of the trustees' activities, but this is not made clear. Indeed, the LOTA 1996 is silent on a number of matters. Are the enforcer's duties fiduciary in nature (akin to those of a protector)? Must he be entirely independent of, and have no connection with, the purposes of the trust? What are his duties and powers in the event that he concludes that the trustees are failing to carry out their trusts? Can he remove the trustees or must he apply to the court for directions and assistance?

An offshore trust, validly created in accordance with or as provided by the LOTA 1996, shall be recognised and be enforceable in accordance with its terms by the courts in Malaysia situated at Labuan, or at such other place as may be designated by the Chief Justice of the Federal Court notwithstanding the provisions of any other law.[4] An offshore trust is not valid and is unenforceable in Labuan where:

1 Ibid, s 4(3).
2 Ibid, s 34(1).
3 Ibid, s 34(4), (5).
4 Ibid, s 9(1).

(a) it requires, purports or encourages the doing of any act, which is an offence under the laws of Malaysia or which, if carried out in Malaysia, would be such an offence (provided that such act is also punishable as a criminal offence in the other country or jurisdiction where the act takes place);
(b) it has income accruing or derived or originating from an operation, transaction or other activity which is or would be an offence of the kind referred to in (a) above;
(c) it comprises property the receipt, ownership or control of which is or would be such an offence; or
(d) the Court declares that the object for which it was created has failed or that the terms of the trust are such that its performance is not possible.[1]

There is no indication that the failure of the trust's object or the impossibility of performance must be established *ab initio*, so that the question of invalidity or unenforceability may arise (probably unexpectedly) during the lifetime of the trust.

Where an offshore trust is created for two or more purposes, of which some are lawful and others are unlawful, then the whole trust is invalid if the unlawful purposes cannot be properly separated. However, where the unlawful purposes can be properly separated, the court may make a finding that the trust is valid with respect to the lawful purpose or purposes which do not affect the validity of the trust to the extent and under the conditions as may be determined by it.[2] Where the trustee of an offshore trust is of the opinion that the trust is or may be, in whole or in part, invalid, he shall [*sic*] seek directives from the court as to the validity of the trust and as to any matter concerning the trust property and his obligations in relation to the trust.[3] A settlor or beneficiary of an offshore trust may also request such directives as to such matters.[4]

6.12.5 Registration

The provisions of the LOTA 1996 dealing with registration are optional and not compulsory. Section 12(1) merely provides that every offshore trust validly created in accordance with or as provided by the Act, whether in Labuan or abroad, 'may be registered' with the Labuan Offshore Financial Services Authority. If the offshore trust is registered, responsibility for its registration

---

1 Ibid, s 9(2). It is difficult to see what paras (b) and (c) add to the widely worded para (a).
2 Ibid, s 9(3).
3 Ibid, s 9(4).
4 Ibid, s 9(5).

and any subsequent changes in connection therewith rests with the trustee of the trust.[1] Registration is effected by filing with the Authority:

(a) a statement containing the name of the offshore trust, the date of its creation, the name and address of the trust company acting as trustee, the address of the registered office of the offshore trust, and the proper law of the offshore trust; and
(b) a declaration by the trust company acting as trustee of the offshore trust that the trust satisfies the conditions of the LOTA 1996 in order that it be an offshore trust.[2]

On being satisfied that all the requirements of the LOTA 1996 for the existence of an offshore trust have been complied with and upon payment of the prescribed fee, the Authority may register the trust and issue a certificate of registration accordingly.[3] Any subsequent change in the particulars of a registered offshore trust must be notified to, and registered with, the Authority in the prescribed form (within one month of the change) and shall not have effect until it is so registered.[4] The trustee of such a trust must also notify the Authority of the termination of the trust in the prescribed form within one month of the termination.[5] Moreover, the trustee of the registered offshore trust must notify the Authority in the prescribed form as to whether the trust is still in existence, and whether he is still the trustee thereof, not later than one month after every anniversary of the registration of the trust in Labuan.[6] Any trustee who fails to comply with these requirements shall be guilty of an offence and be liable to a fine of 10,000 ringgit.[7] In view of the fact registration is not compulsory, it is difficult to see why trustees would voluntarily subject themselves to such controls and potential penalties, unless public disclosure is specifically required.

The trustee of a registered offshore trust 'may furnish' the Authority with a copy of the trust instrument or any amendment thereto, which has been certified by the trustee, and the Authority shall register and file that copy as a true copy.[8] Every trust instrument must include the name by which the offshore trust is to be known and registered and such name shall remain unchanged until the termination of the trust, unless the Authority, having regard to the circumstances of the case, thinks it fit to authorise a change in the name.[9]

1 Ibid, s 12(2).
2 Ibid, s 12(3).
3 Ibid, s 12(4).
4 Ibid, s 12(5).
5 Ibid, s 12(6).
6 Ibid, s 12(7).
7 Ibid, s 12(8).
8 Ibid, s 13.
9 Ibid, s 14(1).

Chapter 7

ASSET PROTECTION TRUSTS

Geraint Thomas[*]

7.1 INTRODUCTION

The expression 'asset protection trust' is not a term of art. It does not describe or refer to a specific kind of trust or settlement. The expression is generally used to refer to any trust or arrangement which is designed and intended to protect assets from claims by creditors (and others). It is a means of organising one's affairs and assets in advance in order to safeguard against potential losses arising from some future calamity. In this sense, an asset protection trust ought to be, and usually is, regarded as an integral part of general estate planning, and, as such, many different considerations, extending well beyond the protection of assets from potential creditors, will be relevant and must be taken into account. Asset protection trusts are essentially symptoms of a changing economic and legal environment, in North America in particular. An explosion in litigation, and especially in professional malpractice suits and environmental claims, has occurred. The cost of professional indemnity insurance has increased dramatically as a result. Awards of damages are often punitive; and such awards are usually not protected by insurance in any event. In addition, the prospect of failure of a business enterprise or a trading firm due to an adverse economic climate, often after many years of successful endeavour, or the existence of unknown and almost open-ended liabilities, as in the case of some Lloyd's investors, have given an added impetus to the preservation of wealth. These factors, and many others, account for the appearance and growth of the asset protection trust. Nevertheless, the underlying purpose of an asset protection trust is to protect assets from and against potential claims which may be made by creditors who would otherwise have access, or be able to resort, to those assets in order to satisfy their claims.

[*] Barrister of 10 Old Square, Lincoln's Inn, and Professor of Equity and Property Law in the Queen Mary Law School, University of London.

To some extent, many of the above-mentioned concerns could be met by means of well-tried methods within the client's home jurisdiction, for example, by incorporation or transfer of assets to a spouse. However, in many countries – England and Wales and the United States among them – there are specific provisions which are designed to prevent a person from transferring or disposing of assets in order to defraud or defeat the claims of creditors, or, at least, to ensure that any transfer or disposition of assets which has been made and whose effect is to defraud or defeat the claims of creditors may be set aside. Indeed, the scope of such provisions, the readiness with which the courts have interpreted and applied them in favour of creditors, and the fact that many of them can operate even when the transferor has not been adjudicated bankrupt, pose serious obstacles to anyone who wishes to safeguard assets against potential creditors. In this sense, such jurisdictions can properly be characterised as 'pro-creditor' rather than 'pro-debtor'. Other jurisdictions (often referred to as 'offshore jurisdictions'), however, have introduced legislation which is designed to provide a substantial degree of asset protection for those whose home jurisdiction is 'pro-creditor'; and it is in such offshore jurisdictions that asset protection trusts (or the several components that may make up an asset protection trust) are generally created.[1] Thus, the essence of an asset protection trust (or similar arrangement) is that it is governed by a more sympathetic system of law than that applicable in the settlor's or transferor's home jurisdiction.

This chapter is divided into two sections. Section 1 examines the past and present law of England and Wales as it related or relates to the setting aside or defeating of transactions intended to defraud (or which have the effect of defrauding) creditors. One set of provisions applies only where the debtor has been adjudicated bankrupt; another set of provisions applies irrespective of bankruptcy. Although major changes were made in English law by the Insolvency Act 1986, pre-1986 law remains important not only in the interpretation of the 1986 Act itself, but also in any analysis of recent legislation in offshore centres (where the previous law was largely the same as pre-1986 law in England and Wales). Section 2 then describes and analyses the relevant legislation in the main offshore jurisdictions.

7.2 ENGLAND AND WALES

7.2.1 Statutory provisions

Prior to the enactment of the Insolvency Act 1985, the two main statutory provisions in English law preventing the use of trusts as a means of avoiding

---

1 An asset protection trust tends to be a combination of well-recognised methods traditionally employed in general estate planning, and, in particular, the use of companies and discretionary trusts.

liability to creditors were s 172 of the Law of Property Act 1925 and s 42 of the Bankruptcy Act 1914. Both of these provisions could be traced back to earlier statutes.

Section 172 of the Law of Property Act 1925 re-enacted the provisions of para 31 of Part II of Sch 3 to the Law of Property (Amendment) Act 1924 (which never came independently into operation). The provisions of para 31 replaced 'in very substantially different terms'[1] the provisions of the statute 13 Eliz I, c 5 (the 1571 Act).[2] Section 42(1) of the Bankruptcy Act 1914 reproduced s 47(1) of the Bankruptcy Act 1883, which in turn re-enacted the first part of s 91 of the Bankruptcy Act 1869 (save that the latter provision applied only to traders, and subject to other minor amendments). Both s 172 and s 42 have been repealed.[3] Nevertheless, they remain important because they are the basis of similar, if not identical, legislation in several overseas jurisdictions. There are provisions which are identical with (or broadly similar to) those in s 42 and/or s 172 (or even the provisions of the 1571 Act) still in force in each of the Australian States, in the British Virgin Islands, Gibraltar,[4] Hong Kong and New Zealand. Similar provisions were recently in force in The Bahamas, Bermuda, the Cayman Islands, and the Turks and Caicos Islands.

The decisions of English courts on the meaning, scope and operation of these early provisions are therefore relevant in the construction of similar overseas legislation. In addition, they are important in explaining the purpose, nature and form of recently introduced legislation (eg in Bermuda, the Cook Islands and Cyprus) which seeks to remove the obstacles to the creation of asset protection trusts in those jurisdictions. Indeed, it is increasingly becoming clear that much of the earlier case-law is relevant in the construction of the replacement provisions of the Insolvency Act 1986 itself.

7.2.2 The 1571 Act and the Law of Property Act 1925, s 172

In broad terms, the 1571 Act declared that all dispositions of real or personal property made with an intent to defraud, hinder or delay creditors were 'to be clearly and utterly void, frustrate, and of none effect'.[5] Similarly, s 172(1) of the Law of Property Act 1925 provided:

---

1 *Lloyds Bank Ltd v Marcan* [1973] 1 WLR 339 at 344, per Pennycuick V-C.

2 Entitled 'An Act Against Fraudulent Deeds, Gifts, Alienations, etc'.

3 Insolvency Act 1985, Sch 10.

4 See *Hess v Line Trust Corporation Ltd* (1998/99) 1 ITELR 249.

5 The Act declared void 'all and every feoffment, gift, grant, alienation, bargain and conveyance of lands, tenements, hereditaments, goods and chattels, or of any of them, or of any lease, rent, common, or other profit or charge, out of the same lands, tenements, hereditaments, goods and chattels, or any of them, by writing or otherwise, and all and every bond, suit, judgment and execution, at any time had or made ... to or for any intent or purpose before declared', namely those which 'have been and are devised and contrived of malice, fraud, covin, collusion, or guile, to the end, purpose, and intent to delay, hinder or defraud creditors and others of their just and lawful actions, suits, debts, accounts, damages, penalties'. The word 'void' was construed to mean 'voidable'.

> '(1) Save as otherwise provided in this section, every conveyance of property made, whether before or after the commencement of this Act, with intent to defraud creditors is voidable at the instance of any person thereby prejudiced.'

Although there are obvious differences in wording, the underlying purpose and overall effect of the two provisions were broadly similar, and authorities on the scope and interpretation of the 1571 Act were followed and applied in relation to s 172 of the 1925 Act.

Property within the statutes

Both the 1571 Act and s 172 extended to every kind of 'property' which could be regarded as assets for the payment of creditors.[1] Thus, the 1571 Act applied not only to land, tenements, hereditaments, goods and chattels,[2] and other types of property expressly referred to, but also to insurance policies and other choses in action,[3] reversionary interests,[4] the goodwill of a business,[5] and the proceeds of an action, when recovered.[6] For the purposes of the Law of Property Act 1925, s 205(1)(xx) declares expressly that '"property" includes any thing in action, and any interest in real or personal property'. In addition, property which was the subject matter of a general power of appointment was regarded as available property of the debtor for these purposes.[7]

Dispositions within the statutes

The 1571 Act extended to all 'feoffments, gifts, grants, alienations, conveyances, bonds, suits, judgments and executions' by which creditors might be delayed, hindered or defrauded. Thus, it applied to gifts to children or others;[8] to purchases in the name of a child or other third party,[9] or in the joint names of the debtor and a third party;[10] to sales in consideration of a payment

---

1 Only property which could be taken in execution came within the scope of both statutes (*Mathews v Feaver* (1786) 1 Cox Eq Cas 278), the relevant date for determining whether property could be so taken being the date of the relevant alienation (*Sims v Thomas* (1840) 12 Ad & El 536). See also *Hess v Line Trust Corporation Ltd* (1998/99) 1 ITELR 249.

2 See, eg, *Shears v Rogers* (1832) 3 B & Ad 363 (a lease); *Barton v Van Heythuysen* (1853) 11 Hare 126 (furniture).

3 *Barrack v M'Cullock* (1856) 3 K & J 110; *Stokoe v Cowan* (1861) 29 Beav 637; *Taylor v Coenen* (1876) 1 Ch D 636; *Re Mouat* [1899] 1 Ch 831; *Edmunds v Edmunds* [1904] P 362.

4 *Ideal Bedding Co v Holland* [1907] 2 Ch 157. See also *South Western Loan and Discount Co v Robertson* (1881) 8 QBD 17; *Bolland v Young* [1904] 2 KB 824.

5 *French v French* (1855) 6 De G M & G 95; *Neale v Day* (1858) 28 LJ (Ch) 45.

6 *Glegg v Bromley* [1912] 3 KB 474.

7 *Townshend (Lord) v Windham* (1750) 2 Ves Sen 1. This was not the case for the purposes of the Bankruptcy Act 1914, s 42, however: see *Re Mathieson* [1927] 1 Ch 283. Now see Insolvency Act 1986, s 283(4).

8 *Partridge v Gopp* (1758) Amb 596.

9 *Barrack v M'Cullock* (1856) 3 K & J 110.

10 *Stileman v Ashdown* (1742) 2 Atk 477; *Glaister v Hewer* (1802) 8 Ves 195.

to a third party;[1] to separation deeds (especially if voluntary);[2] to marriage settlements (especially if the marriage was part of the fraud and both husband and wife were parties to the fraudulent intent);[3] and to a judgment suffered.[4] The exercise of a general power of appointment could also be within the scope of the 1571 Act,[5] but not the exercise of a special power of appointment, unless the donee of the power was himself entitled in default of appointment.[6] A trust deed in favour of creditors, although *prima facie* not fraudulent, could be set aside if, in substance, it retained a benefit for the debtor at the expense of his creditors or if it sought to impose on the creditors obligations which were not required of them by law.[7] An assignment by an outgoing partner of his share in the partnership property to the sole continuing partner, in consideration of a covenant for the payment of partnership debts, could also be set aside as calculated to delay, hinder or defraud both the creditors of the firm and the separate creditors of the outgoing partner.[8] On the other hand, voluntary expenditure of money in the improvement of land belonging to another did not entitle the creditors of the person expending the money to a charge on that land, because the money had merged with the improved estate.[9]

Section 172 of the Law of Property Act 1925 applied to 'every conveyance' of property; and the expression 'conveyance' was defined widely to include a mortgage, charge, lease, assent, vesting declaration, vesting instrument, disclaimer, release and every other assurance of property[10] or of an interest therein by any instrument, except a will. The word 'convey' has a

---

1 *Neale v Day* (1858) 28 LJ (Ch) 45; *French v French* (1855) 6 De G M & G 95.

2 *Stephens v Olive* (1786) 2 Bro CC 90; *Hobbs v Hull* (1788) 1 Cox Eq Cas 445; *Nunn v Wilsomore* (1800) 8 Term Rep 521.

3 *Colombine v Penhall* (1853) 1 Sm & G 288; *Bulmer v Hunter* (1869) LR 8 Eq 46; *Re Pennington* (1888) 5 TLR 29.

4 *Imray v Magnay* (1843) 11 M & W 267; *Meux v Howell* (1803) 4 East 1.

5 *Townshend (Lord) v Windham* (1750) 2 Ves Sen 1 at 10; *Whittington v Jennings* (1834) 6 Sim 493.

6 A disentailing deed, executed by a debtor who was tenant in tail and by which the property was disentailed and resettled on the debtor for life, was not within the 1571 Act, for nothing was thereby taken out of the reach of creditors: *Clements v Eccles* (1847) 11 I Eq R 229. See also Law of Property Act 1925, s 172(2).

7 *Godfery v Poole* (1888) 13 App Cas 497; *Maskelyne and Cooke v Smith* [1903] 1 KB 671; *Spencer v Slater* (1878) 4 QBD 13; *Alton v Harrison* (1869) 4 Ch App 622; *Boldero v London and Westminster Discount Co* (1879) 5 Ex D 47; *Evans v Jones* (1864) 3 H & C 423; *Smith v Hurst* (1852) 10 Hare 30; *Pickstock v Lyster* (1815) 3 M & S 371; *Re Gillo* (1891) 8 Morr 157.

8 *Re Edwards-Wood* (1865) 4 De G J & Sm 664.

9 *Champion v Cotton* (1810) 17 Ves 263.

10 Law of Property Act 1925, s 172(2) itself declares that the section does not affect the operation of a disentailing assurance.

corresponding meaning.[1] Thus, the scope of the 1571 Act was preserved under s 172, and the case-law decided under the earlier statute continued to apply after 1925.

Fraudulent intent

It is clear that an intent to defraud creditors was a central requirement for both statutes: a disposition could not be set aside unless such an intent was established. However, neither statute defined the constituent elements of this pivotal concept. The 1571 Act did not confine itself to the defrauding of creditors, but referred in broad terms to 'the end, purpose and intent to delay hinder or defraud creditors and others'. Section 172(1) of the 1925 Act, in contrast, referred simply to an 'intent to defraud creditors'. It is doubtful whether this expression was any more than a contraction of that in the 1571 Act, but the point was never actually determined, it seems. In *Lloyds Bank Ltd v Marcan*,[2] Pennycuick V-C, having declared that the relevant provision in the Law of Property (Amendment) Act 1924[3] (which was replaced by s 172 of the 1925 Act) had 'substantially altered' the 1571 Act,[4] none the less concluded:

> 'I think it is fairly clear that the word "defraud" in this subsection is designed to reproduce the expression "hinder, delay or defraud" in the Statute of Elizabeth, and is not intended to be confined to cases of fraud in the ordinary modern sense of that word, ie, as involving actual deceit or dishonesty. It is quite inconceivable that if Parliament had intended to circumscribe the effect of the old provision it would not have done so in clear terms. The word "defraud" in the context of section 172, and having regard to the history of its statutory predecessor, must, I think, carry the meaning of depriving creditors of timely recourse to property which would otherwise be applicable for their benefit.'

Thus, a creditor could be 'defrauded' in this sense not only by an outright conveyance, but also by a lease, a charge, a contractual agreement, or in other ways. As for an 'intent' to defraud, Pennycuick V-C emphasised that this denoted a state of mind and that a man's intention was a question of fact.[5]

On appeal, Cairns LJ expressly disagreed with Pennycuick V-C's views and stated that, in his opinion, 'fraud involves dishonesty'; and that, in the context

---

1 Ibid, s 205(1)(ii). But for this extended definition, s 172 would extend only to a conveyance *stricto sensu* and not to a gift of personalty (as was held to be the case under the original legislation in Victoria, Australia (*Thomson v Nicholson* [1939] VLR 157) which resulted in the replacing of the word 'conveyance' with the word 'alienation'). In *Re Eichholz* [1959] Ch 708, Harman J considered that the word 'conveyance' in s 172 was not confined to a conveyance in writing, but extended to a parol direction by the debtor that his money should be applied in completing, by conveyance to his wife, the purchase of an estate which he had contracted to buy. This view was probably not maintainable in the light of *Gray v IRC* [1960] AC 1; *Beswick v Beswick* [1968] AC 58, especially at 73–77; and *Rye v Rye* [1962] AC 496.

2 [1973] 1 WLR 339 at 344.

3 Schedule 3, Part II, para 31.

4 He did not analyse in detail the ways in which the old law had been altered. One of the main changes was that the criminal sanctions of the 1571 Act were not reproduced.

5 [1973] 1 WLR 339 at 344.

of s 172, although deceit was not necessary, 'dishonest intention' was.[1] This was especially so in cases where the disposition had been made for consideration.[2] In the case of a voluntary disposition, it was easier to infer a dishonest intention. Nevertheless, it seems that Cairns LJ considered a dishonest intention to be essential even in such cases. However, he also seems to have conceded that, at least in some cases involving voluntary dispositions, 'no dishonest intention need then be established'.[3] In any event, it seems clear that Cairns LJ was not disputing Pennycuick V-C's view that a creditor could, in principle, be defrauded where he was merely being hindered or delayed,[4] but simply putting forward the qualification that, in many cases (such as those where consideration had been given) there had to be a *dishonest* intent and that, in such cases, 'perfectly honest hindrance or delay to a creditor'[5] would not suffice for the purposes of s 172. In the circumstances of the particular case, both Pennycuick V-C and the Court of Appeal concluded that the debtor's conduct was 'less than honest' and amounted to 'sharp practice'.[6]

Neither the 1571 Act nor s 172 prevented a debtor from preferring one creditor to another (unlike the bankruptcy laws). Therefore, a conveyance executed in favour of one or some only of the creditors of the grantor could, in principle, be *bona fide* and valid, notwithstanding that the grantor was aware at the time of the conveyance that execution was about to be issued against him, or that he was insolvent, or that the conveyance encompassed the entirety of the grantor's property.[7] Nor, indeed, was it necessarily fraudulent to have an intention to defeat an expected execution by a particular judgment creditor.[8] However, in such cases, the court would generally expect the alienation to have been made for full value and, as between the debtor and grantee, to have been a *bona fide* transaction.[9] Moreover, such an alienation could also be avoided if it was a mere cloak to secure a benefit for the debtor.[10]

---

1 [1973] 1 WLR 1387 at 1392.

2 He referred to *Copis v Middleton* (1818) 2 Madd 410; *Wood v Dixie* (1845) 7 QB 892; *Alton v Harrison* (1869) 4 Ch App 622; *Re Johnson* (1881) 20 Ch D 389; *Re David & Adlard* [1914] 2 KB 694.

3 He referred to *Freeman v Pope* (1870) 5 Ch App 538; *Ideal Bedding Co Ltd v Holland* [1907] 2 Ch 157; *Re Eichholz* [1959] 1 Ch 708.

4 See, eg, the reference to 'hindering creditors' at 1392D–E.

5 [1973] 1 WLR 1387 at 1390G, per Russell LJ. In fact, it is not at all clear that Pennycuick V-C expressed (or intended to express) views as wide as those attributed to him in argument in the Court of Appeal.

6 Ibid, at 1391B.

7 *Holbird v Anderson* (1793) 5 Term Rep 235; *Benton v Thornhill* (1816) 7 Taunt 149; *Alton v Harrison* (1869) 4 Ch App 622; *Middleton v Pollock* (1876) 2 Ch D 104; *Maskelyne and Cooke v Smith* [1902] 2 KB 158; *Glegg v Bromley* [1912] 3 KB 474; *Re Fasey* [1923] 2 Ch 1; *Re Lloyd's Furniture Palace* [1925] Ch 853.

8 *Wood v Dixie* (1845) 7 QB 892; *Hale v Saloon Omnibus Co* (1859) 4 Drew 492; *Darvill v Terry* (1861) 6 H & N 807. See also *Wolverhampton and Staffordshire Banking Co v Marston* (1861) 7 H & N 148.

9 *Coulston v Gardiner* (1861) 3 Swan 279n; *Alton v Harrison* (1869) 4 Ch App 622; *Middleton v Pollock* (1876) 2 Ch D 104; *Maskelyne and Cooke v Smith* [1902] 2 KB 158; *Glegg v Bromley* [1912] 3 KB 474; *Re Fasey* [1923] 2 Ch 1; *Re Lloyd's Furniture Palace* [1925] Ch 853.

10 *Alton v Harrison* (1869) 4 Ch App 622; *Maskelyne and Cooke v Smith* [1902] 2 KB 158; *Re Sinclair* (1884) 26 Ch D 319; *Allen v Bonnett* (1870) 5 Ch App 577.

Burden of proof

In broad terms, a distinction was drawn between those cases where the relevant conveyance or alienation was made for valuable consideration and those where it was voluntary. Where the alienation was for valuable consideration, the burden of proving an intent to defraud on the part of the debtor-grantor, and that the grantee was privy to the fraud, rested on the person claiming to set it aside.[1] However, where the alienation was voluntary, surrounding circumstances might be such as to establish a *prima facie* case of intent to defraud, in which case the burden of disproving such an intent would then be shifted to the person seeking to uphold the disposition.

Proving an intent to defraud

The question of intent to defraud was one of fact, one which the court had to decide in the circumstances of each particular case.[2] Pennycuick V-C was merely stating the obvious when he said, in *Lloyds Bank Ltd v Marcan*,[3] that 'a man's intention is a question of fact. Actual intent may unquestionably be proved by direct evidence or may be inferred from surrounding circumstances'. Thus, in *Re Fasey*,[4] for example, where the transferee was a company whose sole directors and shareholders were the bankrupt and his solicitor, the court had no difficulty in finding that the disposition could not be effective:

> 'this is a barefaced attempt to cheat the creditors of the bankrupt by a conveyance of the bankrupt's property to the bankrupt himself and to his solicitor.'[5]

According to Atkin LJ:[6]

> '... if a debtor, being sorely pressed by creditors, does in fact assign the whole of his property to a company of which he becomes the sole shareholder and all the shares are issued to him, an almost inevitable inference would arise that he did that with intent to delay and hinder his creditors. I think that they would in fact be hindered and delayed, because there is no doubt, that although they could seize the shares and although eventually they could ... by winding-up proceedings get the benefit of the assets, they would be delayed in their remedies against the assets of the debtor.'

---

1 *Re Johnson* (1881) 20 Ch D 389 at 394 (on appeal (1882) 51 LJ (Ch) 503); *Re Cranston* (1892) 9 Morr 160 at 166; *Re Tetley* (1896) 3 Mans 226; *Re Hirth* [1899] 1 QB 612; *Re Holland* [1902] 2 Ch 360; *Re Reis* [1904] 2 KB 769.

2 *Thompson v Webster* (1859) 4 Drew 628 at 632; *Godfrey v Poole* (1888) 13 App Cas 497; *Re Holland* [1902] 2 Ch 360; *Glegg v Bromley* [1912] 3 KB 474 at 492; *Pearce v Bulteel* [1916] 2 Ch 544; *Denny's Trustee v Denny and Warr* [1919] 1 KB 583.

3 [1973] 1 WLR 339 at 344.

4 [1923] 2 Ch 1.

5 Ibid at 9–10, per PO Lawrence J.

6 Ibid at 17.

Whether the disposition was made for consideration or was voluntary, the court would look at the whole of the surrounding circumstances in each case in order to establish whether it was *bona fide* or there was an intent to defraud, and also to determine upon whom the burden of proof would lie.[1] Thus, if the person claiming to set the disposition aside could prove that, at the date of its execution, one of the recognised 'badges of fraud'[2] was present in the circumstances under which it was made, or that the grantor was contemplating entering upon a hazardous business,[3] a *prima facie* case of intent to defraud would be established and the burden of upholding the alienation would then fall on those who sought to do so.

According to Pennycuick V-C,[4] the requisite 'intent may also be imputed on the basis that a man must be presumed to intend the natural consequences of his own act'. In some cases, such a presumption was indeed made. However, the extent to which it was regarded as a presumption of law or simply a rebuttable evidential presumption seems to have been a matter of debate and disagreement.[5] For instance, if the debtor created a voluntary settlement, and if it was the natural consequence of the alienation that his creditors were defrauded, would this inevitably lead to a finding of an intent to defraud or would it simply shift the burden of proof to those who sought to uphold the disposition? In such cases, the courts tended to favour the latter approach (ie that there was a rebuttable presumption of an intent to defraud) but the authorities are not entirely consistent. Each case was judged according to its own particular facts. Nevertheless, it is clear that there were certain recurring features to which special significance might be attached, eg whether, at the date of the disposition, the debtor was about to embark on a hazardous trade, whether he was already insolvent at that time, or whether the creditors who sought to have the disposition set aside became creditors after the time it was made, and so forth. These aspects will be dealt with in greater detail below.

The 'badges of fraud'

A number of circumstances weighed with the court in determining whether, in any particular case, there was an intent to defraud creditors. These circumstances – the so-called 'badges of fraud' – were first isolated in *Twyne's Case*[6] and they were relevant in cases where dispositions were made for consideration or voluntary (although obviously more so in the latter cases). The 'badges of fraud' were enumerated as follows.

1 *Thompson v Webster* (1859) 28 LJ Ch 700; *Harman v Richards* (1852) 10 Hare 81; *Re Holland* [1902] 2 Ch 360.

2 The 'badges of fraud' are dealt with more fully below.

3 *Mackay v Douglas* (1872) LR 14 Eq 106; *Re Butterworth* (1882) 19 Ch D 588.

4 *Lloyds Bank Ltd v Marcan* [1973] 1 WLR 339 at 344.

5 *Freeman v Pope* (1870) 5 Ch App 538; *Mackay v Douglas* (1872) LR 14 Eq 106; *Re Wise* (1886) 17 QBD 290; *Re Holland* [1902] 2 Ch 360; *Carruthers v Peake* (1911) 55 Sol Jo 291.

6 (1602) 3 Co Rep 80b; 76 ER 809.

(1) The fact that the alienation included all (or substantially the whole) of the grantor's property.[1]
(2) The fact that the grantor continued in possession of the property he had purported to alienate, when such continuance in possession was not in accordance with the tenor and object of the alienation.[2] The presumption of fraud would also be raised even though the grantee took possession jointly with the grantor.[3] Similarly, retention of the title deeds by the grantor was an indicator of fraudulent intent,[4] as was the reservation by the grantor of a power of revocation.[5] On the other hand, continuance in possession was not necessarily evidence of fraud where such possession was consistent with the nature and purpose of the grant, for example in the case of a mortgage.[6]
(3) The secrecy of the disposition.[7]
(4) The fact that the disposition was made when litigation was pending.[8]
(5) The fact that there was a trust between the grantor and grantee for the grantor's benefit.
(6) Unusual recitals or statements in the instrument of disposition declaring that it was made in good faith or without fraudulent intent.[9]

Any of these 'badges' could be relevant in any case where an intent to defraud had to be proved, although they were probably of greater assistance where the disposition was voluntary. The fact that a disposition was made for value did not prevent the statute applying, but it did make it more difficult to establish an intent to defraud.[10] Thus, if consideration had been given for a settlement, the fact that the settlor's extravagant habits made it probable that his future creditors would be defeated was not necessarily a ground for setting

---

1 *Stileman v Ashdown* (1742) 2 Atk 477; *Thompson v Webster* (1859) 4 Drew 628; *Oriental Banking Co v Coleman* (1861) 4 LT 9; *Ware v Gardner* (1869) LR 7 Eq 317; *Re Troughton* (1894) 71 LT 427; *Re Hirth* [1899] 1 QB 612 at 620.

2 *Barling v Bishopp* (1860) 29 Beav 417; *Reed v Blades* (1813) 5 Taunt 212; *Edwards v Harben* (1788) 2 Term Rep 587; *Paget v Perchard* (1794) 1 Esp 205; *Eastwood v Brown* (1825) Ry & M 312.

3 *Wordall v Smith* (1808) 1 Camp 332. It seems that the position was otherwise where the grantor and grantee were husband and wife and the property transferred consisted of furniture in a house occupied by both: *Ramsay v Margrett* [1894] 2 QB 18.

4 *Cracknall v Janson* (1879) 11 Ch D 1; *Perry-Herrick v Attwood* (1857) 27 LJ (Ch) 121; *Barling v Bishopp* (1860) 29 Beav 417.

5 *Holcroft's Case* (1596) Moore (KB) 486; *Tarback v Marbury* (1705) 2 Vern 510; *Middlecome v Marlow* (1742) 2 Atk 519; *Smith v Hurst* (1852) 10 Hare 30; *Acraman v Corbett* (1861) 1 John & H 410; *Jenkyn v Vaughan* (1856) Drew 419; *Re Lane-Fox* [1900] 2 QB 508.

6 *Reed v Wilmot* (1831) 7 Bing 577 at 583; *Martindale v Booth* (1832) 3 B & Ad 498.

7 *Ex parte Chaplin* (1884) 26 Ch D 319.

8 *Empringham v Short* (1844) 3 Hare 461; *Blenkinsopp v Blenkinsopp* (1852) 1 De GM & G 495; *Re Moroney* (1887) 21 LR Ir 27; *Barling v Bishopp* (1860) 29 Beav 417; *Bulmer v Hunter* (1869) LR 8 Eq 46. *Cf Re Wise* (1886) 17 QBD 290; *Alton v Harrison* (1869) 4 Ch App 622; *Re Fasey* [1923] 2 Ch 1. This particular 'badge' will be discussed further below.

9 *Penhall v Elwin* (1853) 1 Sm & G 258; *Kevan v Crawford* (1877) 6 Ch D 29.

10 *Holmes v Penney* (1856) 3 K & J 90.

aside the settlement.[1] However, even in relation to voluntary dispositions, the 'badges of fraud' were not conclusive. There is no reason to suppose that the 'badges of fraud' are any less relevant in the consideration and application of the provisions of the Insolvency Act 1986 (which have replaced s 172 of the 1925 Act) or the provisions of similar legislation in other jurisdictions. Indeed, in the United States they have been given statutory form: the Uniform Fraudulent Transfer Act 1984 (which is in force in certain States) lists 11 factors which may be considered in determining the existence of a fraudulent intent, many of them identical to the English 'badges of fraud'.

Future or subsequent creditors

There is no doubt that a future creditor – that is, a creditor whose debt had not been contracted at the date of the relevant disposition – who had been prejudiced by that disposition could seek to have it set aside and to share in the distribution of the property comprised therein. This proposition is supported by a large number of cases,[2] some of which will be considered in detail below. In *Stileman v Ashdown*,[3] Lord Hardwicke stated:

> 'It is not necessary that a man should actually be indebted at the time he enters into a voluntary settlement to make it fraudulent; for if a man does it with a view to his being indebted at a future time it is equally fraudulent.'

This was particularly relevant in cases where the disponor had disposed of property shortly before embarking on a trade or other hazardous venture. It was also relatively uncontentious where a future creditor could prove an actual intent to defraud on the part of the disponor. However, a future or subsequent creditor undoubtedly faced a more difficult task than a creditor whose debt was due at the date of the alienation in proving a fraudulent intent on the part of the disponor where such an intent had to be inferred from surrounding circumstances.

Mere indebtedness did not give rise to a presumption to defraud any creditors. On the other hand, it was not necessary to prove insolvency at the time the disposition was made. In *Holmes v Penney*,[4] Wood V-C stated that 'The settlor must have been at the time so largely indebted as to induce the court to believe that the intention of the settlement was to defraud the creditors of the settlor'. Moreover, the fact that, at the date of the alienation, the disponor was indebted to a considerable extent, though not insolvent, but, by the alienation, rendered himself unable to meet his then existing liabilities, furnished very

1 *Re Tetley* (1896) 75 LT 166; *Re Lane-Fox* [1900] 2 QB 508.

2 *Richardson v Smallwood* (1822) Jac 552; *Jenkyn v Vaughan* (1856) 3 Drew 419; *Ware v Gardner* (1869) LR 7 Eq 317; *Crossley v Elworthy* (1871) LR 12 Eq 158; *Mackay v Douglas* (1872) LR 14 Eq 106; *Taylor v Coenen* (1876) 1 Ch D 636; *Re Butterworth* (1882) 19 Ch D 588.

3 (1742) 2 Atk 477 at 481.

4 (1856) 3 K & J 90 at 99.

strong evidence of an intent to defraud creditors,[1] but such evidence was not necessarily conclusive.[2]

In *Townsend v Westacott*,[3] a voluntary settlement had been created by a person who was said to have been 'largely indebted' at the time (but there was no positive proof of his insolvency) and who became insolvent within three years thereafter. Lord Langdale, MR, stated:

> 'There has been a little exaggeration in the arguments on both sides as to the principle on which the Court acts in such cases as these: on one side it has been assumed that the existence of any debts at the time of the execution of the deed would be such evidence of a fraudulent intention as to induce the Court to set aside a voluntary conveyance, and oblige the Court to do so under the statute of Elizabeth. I cannot think the real and just construction of the statute warrants that proposition, because there is scarcely any man who can avoid being indebted to some amount: he may intend to pay every debt as soon as it is contracted, and constantly use his best endeavours, and have ample means to do so, and yet may be frequently, if not always, indebted in some small sum: there may be a withholding of claims, contrary to his intention, by which he is kept indebted in spite of himself; it would be idle to allege this as the least foundation for assuming fraud or any bad intention. On the other hand, it is said that something amounting to insolvency must be proved to set aside a voluntary conveyance: this too, is inconsistent with the principle of the Act, and with the judgments of the most eminent Judges.'

In *Crossley v Elworthy*,[4] Malins V-C 'adopted every word' of Lord Langdale's statement and stated that, 'though the mere fact of a man being indebted is not fatal to a settlement, it is not necessary to prove actual insolvency, but if insolvency takes place shortly after the execution of the settlement that is enough'. (He conceded that there may be an exception where the insolvency is caused by some exceptional loss or 'something which could not have been reasonably reckoned upon when the settlement was executed'.)

However, it was more difficult for future creditors to establish an intent to defraud. If, for instance, there were creditors in existence at the date of the disposition, it was said in *Jenkyn v Vaughan*[5] that it was established that it was 'not necessary for them to show from anything actually said or done by the [debtor] that he had the express design by the deed to defeat creditors'. If the debtor had included in the disposition property of such an amount that, having regard to the state of his assets and liabilities, its effect 'might probably be' to defraud creditors, then, if the court was 'satisfied' of that, the disposition fell within the scope of the 1571 Act. On the other hand, the Vice-Chancellor suggested that, if the disposition were to be challenged by a subsequent

---

1 *Townsend v Westacott* (1840) 2 Beav 340; *Jenkyn v Vaughan* (1856) 3 Drew 419; *Christy v Courtenay* (1858) 26 Beav 140; *Freeman v Pope* (1870) 5 Ch App 538; *Kent v Riley* (1872) LR 14 Eq 190; *Spirett v Willows* (1864–65) 3 De GJ & Sm 293; *Denison v Tattersall* (1868) 18 LT 303; *Re Holland* [1902] 2 Ch 360.

2 *Re Wise* (1886) 17 QBD 290; *Re Johnson* (1881) 20 Ch D 389; *Holmes v Penney* (1856) 3 K & J 90.

3 (1840) 2 Beav 340 at 344–345. See also *Skarf v Soulby* (1849) 1 Mac & G 364.

4 (1871) LR 12 Eq 158 at 167.

5 (1856) 3 Drew 419 at 424, per Kindersley V-C.

creditor, and if at the date of challenge the debts due at the date of the disposition had been discharged, the (subsequent) creditor would have to establish some ground other than the fact that the debtor was indebted at the date of the disposition in order to infer an intention to defraud creditors. He refrained from laying down such a rule. However, he stated:[1]

> 'if a subsequent creditor files a bill, and you can shew that the person who executed the deed, though indebted at the time he made it, had since paid every debt, it is very difficult to say that he executed the settlement with an intention to defeat or delay creditors, since his subsequent payment shews that he had not such intention.'

The broad principles on which the court acted were eventually summarised by Wright J in *Re Lane-Fox*.[2] In that case, A had executed a voluntary settlement on discretionary trusts to pay any of her then existing or future debts, and also to apply trust income during her lifetime for the benefit of herself or any husband or children of hers. The settlement included a power for A to revoke the settlement with the consent of the trustees. The few debts she had at the date of the settlement were paid out of cash in hand. A was subsequently declared bankrupt.

Wright J held that that the settlement was not fraudulent and void under the 1571 Act. He stated:[3]

> 'It seems to me that the law on the subject is this – that in a case like the present one, where there are no existing creditors at the date of the settlement for whom sufficient provision did not remain outside the settlement, it is necessary in order to avoid the settlement to shew that there was an actual intention to defeat, delay or hinder future creditors.'

Wright J then referred to the two propositions laid down by Lord Westbury in *Spirett v Willows*.[4] The first proposition concerned the position of a creditor whose debt already existed at the date of the relevant disposition.

> 'If the debt of the creditor by whom the voluntary settlement is impeached existed at the date of the settlement, and it is shewn that the remedy of the creditor is defeated or delayed by the existence of the settlement, it is immaterial whether the debtor was or was not solvent after making the settlement.'

This proposition had been thought too wide even by Lord Hatherley LC in *Freeman v Pope*,[5] who referred only to 'an amount without which the debts cannot be paid'. The second proposition concerned the position of a creditor whose debt did not exist at the date of the disposition.

---

1 Ibid at 425. See also *Re Kelleher* [1911] 2 IR 1.
2 [1900] 2 QB 508.
3 Ibid at 512.
4 (1864–65) 3 De GJ & S 293 at 367.
5 (1870) 5 Ch App 538 at 541.

> 'But if a voluntary settlement or deed of gift is impeached by subsequent creditors whose debts had not been contracted at the date of the settlement, then it is necessary to shew either that the settlor made the settlement with the express intent "to delay, hinder or defraud" creditors, or that after the settlement the settlor had no sufficient means or reasonable expectation of being able to pay his then existing debts, that is to say, was reduced to a state of insolvency, in which case the law infers that the settlement was made with the intent "to delay, hinder or defraud" creditors, and is therefore fraudulent and void.'

Wright J then concluded:[1]

> 'I think no decision can be found anywhere inconsistent with the proposition that an honest settlement, affirmatively proved to be honest, ought not to be set aside merely because some years afterwards it is proved to have the effect of defeating and delaying subsequent creditors. Here the case was one of an inexperienced and probably impulsive young woman, just come of age, possessed of considerable means … Everything was open, everything was in the ordinary form, and in perfect good faith, and to my mind it is affirmatively proved that this was a perfectly honest arrangement, and it is proved before me that there were no debts at the time beyond the amount of the moneys which were in hand to meet them. I think it would be outrageous if a settlement of such a description were to be set aside because afterwards the lady turns out to have become more extravagant than was supposed. Not merely were there no existing debts unprovided for at the time, but there was no reason to apprehend any future embarrassment … She had no intention of trading.'

Embarking on trade or other hazardous venture

The same broad principles applied in cases where the disposition was made by a person who was about to enter upon a trade or embark on some other hazardous venture. However, there clearly seems to have been a greater willingness to assist subsequent creditors in such cases, almost certainly because of the unavoidable risks inherent in such activities. In *Mackay v Douglas*,[2] it was held that a voluntary settlement, by means of which the settlor takes the bulk of his property out of the reach of his creditors shortly before engaging in a trade of a hazardous character, may be set aside by those who became creditors after the date of the settlement, despite the fact that there were no creditors whose debts arose before the date of the settlement or that it was doubtful, at that date, whether the arrangements under which the settlor was to engage in the intended business would take effect. In order to set aside the settlement, it was not necessary to show that the settlor contemplated becoming actually indebted: it was sufficient if he contemplated a state of things which might result in bankruptcy or insolvency. In such circumstances, there was a burden on the settlor to prove that he was in a position to make the settlement.

As Malins V-C stated:[3]

---

1 [1900] 2 QB 508 at 513–514.

2 (1872) LR 14 Eq 106.

3 Ibid at 118–119.

'Can a man who contemplates trade, or who, in point of fact, whether he contemplates it at the time or very shortly afterwards, enters into trade, and thereby incurs liabilities which end in a disastrous state of affairs, make a voluntary settlement which shall be good against the creditors who become so in the course of his trade? ... is the Statute of Elizabeth so very short in its effect that it will not cover a case where a man on the very eve of entering into trade takes the bulk of his property and puts it into a voluntary settlement and becomes insolvent a few months afterwards? Is it to be said that such a settlement cannot be reached by any principle of law? I think not.'

The Vice-Chancellor concluded that it was not necessary to show that there was an actual fraudulent intent. If the voluntary settlement had the necessary consequence that creditors would be disturbed, hindered, delayed or defrauded, the court would presume the intention to defraud and would attribute it to the settlor[1] In the present case, if the debtor:

'had neither gone into or contemplated going into trade at the time, but some years afterwards, by a totally new arrangement, made up his mind to do so, I should have had no hesitation in coming to the conclusion that his subsequent insolvency could have had no effect in producing invalidity of the settlement which he had made upon his wife and family.'[2]

He approved the statement of Lord Hardwicke in *Stileman v Ashdown*,[3] and then rejected an argument based on it to the effect that it meant that the debtor 'contemplated getting into debt':

'I read it thus: that if a man does it *with a view* of being indebted at a future time, that is, *with a view* to a state of things in which he may become indebted, that makes it fraudulent, just as if he were indebted at the time.'[4]

However, despite his preference for such a broad interpretation, it seems clear that Malins V-C intended to apply it only in the specific context of the speculative trader:

'The conclusion which I arrive at proceeds upon the broad ground that a man who contemplates going into trade cannot on the eve of doing so take the bulk of his property out of the reach of those who may become his creditors in his trading operations.'[5]

This approach reached its high-water mark in *Re Butterworth*,[6] where a trader, who had for many years carried on the business of a baker and had saved some money, being about to purchase a grocery business which he intended to carry on in addition to his bakery, created a voluntary settlement

---

1 (1872) LR 14 Eq 106 at 120.
2 Ibid at 121.
3 (1742) 2 Atk 477 at 481; see p 347 above .
4 (1872) LR 14 Eq 106 at 122 (emphasis added).
5 Ibid at 122.
6 (1882) 19 Ch D 588.

of the bulk of his property for the benefit of his wife and children. He afterwards bought the grocery business and carried it on for about six months, but lost money by it. He then sold it for as much money as he had given for it, and afterwards carried on the baker's business alone, until, about three years after the execution of the settlement, he filed a liquidation petition, his liabilities largely exceeding his assets. The debts which he owed at the date of the settlement had all been paid. The Court of Appeal held that, independently of the question whether he was solvent at the date of the settlement, the settlement was void as against the trustee in liquidation under the 1571 Act, on the ground that it was evidently executed with the view to putting the settlor's property out of the reach of his creditors in case he should fail in the speculation on which he was about to enter in carrying on a new business of which he knew nothing. It was also held that, in the circumstances, the settlement was void as against the trustee under s 91 of the Bankruptcy Act 1869.

Several observations can be made concerning *Re Butterworth*. First, several 'badges of fraud' were present. The debtor had settled not only some freehold houses bought with his 'savings' but also the furniture and other household goods in his own dwelling-house; and the settlement also recited that he was then 'in a solvent position and capable of paying his debts as they become due'. Secondly, it seems clear that the majority of the judges in the Court of Appeal preferred to base their decision on s 91 of the Bankruptcy Act 1869 rather than on the 1571 Act, for, without recourse to the settled assets, the debtor was not in fact in a position to pay all his debts. He had drawn up a statement of his assets (valued by him at £92) and debts (estimated by him at £58 15s), but he had included among his assets his working utensils and fixtures (valued by him at £60, but which were sold only three years later for only £12 9s 1d). In any event, as the Court of Appeal pointed out, if the debtor was intending to continue his business he could not take into account the value of the implements of his trade and of the goodwill of the business (or, at least, the value had to be such as would be realised on a forced sale). His debts amounted in reality to £111 and his assets to just £56.[1] Consequently, as a trader who was not 'at the time of making the settlement able to pay all his debts without the aid of the property comprised in such settlement', the debtor was caught squarely by s 91 of the Bankruptcy Act 1869. It was not strictly necessary, therefore, for the provisions of the 1571 Act to be resorted to. Indeed, Lord Jessel MR expressed the view that, because s 91 of the 1869 Act clearly applied, it was not necessary to decide whether the 1571 Act also applied; and Baggallay LJ expressly preferred to rest his decision on s 91.[2]

Thirdly, *Re Butterworth* involved a trader, a person who was embarking on a business of which he knew nothing and who deliberately attempted to

---

1 Ibid at 598 and 600.

2 Ibid at 599 and 601. Lindley LJ (at 601) also thought that s 91 applied.

safeguard his assets against the consequences of failure. The authorities show clearly that traders (and presumably others who embarked on hazardous ventures) were regarded as a special case. As Lord Jessel MR stated:[1]

> 'a man is not entitled to go into a hazardous business, and immediately before doing so settle all his property voluntarily, the object being this: "If I succeed in business, I make a fortune for myself. If I fail, I leave my creditors unpaid. They will bear the loss." ... The object of the settlor was to put his property out of the reach of his future creditors. He contemplated engaging in this new trade and he wanted to preserve his property from future creditors.'

Lindley LJ also concluded that the settlement was intended 'to screen and protect them (ie the wife and children) against the unknown risks of the new adventure'.[2] Thus, even as an authority on the 1571 Act, *Re Butterworth* was a typical decision on the position of traders and neither the reasoning nor the decision necessarily applied in any other context.

Certainly, the special position of traders was expressly recognised in *Re Wise*.[3] The facts of this case are simple and well known. The debtor, a master mariner, was married in Hong Kong on 31 May 1881. In August, an action for breach of promise of marriage was commenced against him in England; and the writ was served on him in Hong Kong on 8 October. Between 12 and 16 October, he learned that he had become entitled to a legacy of £500 on the death of his mother (who had died on 11 May). On 17 October, he settled £500 on himself, his wife and any children of their marriage. On 20 July 1882, judgment was obtained against him in the sum of £500. In November 1884, he was adjudicated bankrupt. He swore an affidavit from which it appeared that, when he executed the settlement, he was able to pay his debts without the aid of the property comprised in the settlement, and also that he was not influenced by the action which had been commenced against him. He was not cross-examined on his affidavit. It was held, by both the Divisional Court and the Court of Appeal, that there was insufficient evidence to warrant a finding that the settlement was intended to defraud creditors.

However, it was argued before the court that earlier authorities on the 1571 Act[4] showed that a man must be taken to have intended the natural and necessary consequences of his actions. In the words of Cave J:[5]

> 'It is said, however, that, although we may be of opinion that the bankrupt was acting perfectly bona fide, and that he had not the slightest intention of defeating or delaying his

---

1 Ibid at 598–599.

2 Ibid at 601.

3 (1886) 17 QBD 290; see especially at 293, per Cave J; at 295, per Grantham J; and at 298–299, per Lord Esher MR.

4 In particular, *Freeman v Pope* (1870) 5 Ch App 538; *Re Ridler* (1882) 22 Ch D 74; and *Three Towns Banking Co v Maddever* (1883) 27 Ch D 523.

5 (1886) 17 QBD 290 at 293.

creditors, yet, if it is the necessary result of what took place that his creditors will be defeated or delayed, we are bound to hold that he had that intention, though, in fact, we do not believe that he had.'

The question here concerns the extent to which an intent to defraud creditors would be presumed simply on the basis that it was the natural consequence of the relevant disposition that the disponor's creditors would be defrauded, defeated, hindered or delayed – or, in other words, the extent to which a person was presumed to intend the consequences of his own act. Clearly, the result of a voluntary disposition of property – or, indeed, any disposition for less than full consideration – was to leave the disponor with fewer assets with which to discharge his debts than he would have had but for that disposition, whether those debts existed at the date of the disposition or came into existence thereafter. To what extent could such a deliberate subtraction from the disponor's estate be construed as an intent to defraud his creditors? Indeed, did such an intent have to be found to exist in such circumstances?

In the event, Cave J rejected the argument and, in doing so, clearly considered that, if any such presumption could properly be made, it was confined to the 'trader cases'.

'In most of the cases which have been cited the settlor was a trader, and undoubtedly when a trader makes a settlement, more especially if he does so when he is just about to commence a course of trade which may turn out to be disastrous, it is difficult to come to any other conclusion than that he contemplates the possibility of his trade being unfortunate, and wishes to put his property out of the reach of his creditors. In the present case, however, it does not seem to be at all a necessary result of the settlement that his creditors would be defeated. … the settlor had no creditor whatever at the time when the settlement was made. He had no debt. I do not think that any of the decisions which have been referred to have ever been held to apply where there is nothing more than a liability of this nature. The bankrupt was not a trader, and he was not likely therefore to incur debts in the future.'

Grantham J took a similar, contextual approach:[1]

'When learned judges have said that, if the necessary result of a settlement is to hinder creditors, it must be taken to have been executed with that intent, this observation must be taken as applied to the character of the particular case in which it was made.'

In the Court of Appeal, Lord Esher MR was even more forthright in the rejection of such a presumption.[2]

'The argument was first put in this way – it is necessary to prove that the bankrupt, at the date of the voluntary settlement, intended to defeat and delay a creditor or his creditors

1 Ibid at 295.

2 Ibid at 298–299 (emphasis added).

> generally; the necessary consequence of what he did was to defeat and delay his creditors; and, therefore, *as a proposition of law*, the tribunal which had to consider whether he did intend to defeat and delay his creditors *was bound* to find that he did. In support of that proposition dicta of great and eminent judges were cited. I will venture to say as strongly as I can that to my mind that proposition is monstrous. It is said that it is a necessary inference that a man intends the natural and necessary result of his acts. If you want to find out the intention in a man's mind, of course you cannot look into his mind, but, if circumstances are proved from which you believe that he had that intention, you infer *as a matter of fact* that he had that intention. No doubt, in coming to a particular conclusion as to the intention in a man's mind, you should take into account the necessary result of the acts which he has done. I do not use the words "necessary result" metaphysically, but in their ordinary business sense, and of course, if there was nothing to the contrary, you would come to the conclusion that the man did intend the necessary result of his acts. But, if other circumstances make you believe that the man did not intend to do that which you are asked to find that he did intend, to say that, because that was the necessary result of what he did, you must find, contrary to the other evidence, that he did actually intend to do it, is to ask one to find that to be a fact which one really believes to be untrue in fact. ... That proposition or doctrine I entirely abjure.'

It seems clear that what was 'monstrous' in Lord Esher's mind was the proposition that, where a debtor had made a particular disposition which necessarily resulted in creditors being defrauded, he must be presumed, *as a matter of law*, to have intended to defraud creditors. On the contrary, the existence of such an intent was clearly a question of fact; and there is nothing in Lord Esher's judgment to suggest that, in appropriate circumstances, a presumption of intent to defraud might not properly be made *as a matter of fact or evidence.*

The same point was made by Lindley LJ:[1]

> 'the question is, whether we are driven (not by the statute of Elizabeth, but by a series of decisions upon it) to say that the settlement cannot stand. I do not think we are. It is true that voluntary settlements have been set aside under the statute, as it has been construed for a great number of years, in cases in which there was no actual intent to defraud. It has been held to be sufficient if, when the settlement is executed, the circumstances are such that it must have that effect. But the language which has been used in a great many cases, that a man must *in point of law* be held to have intended the necessary consequences of his own acts, is apt to mislead, by *confusing the boundary between law and fact, and by consequences which can be foreseen and those which cannot.*'

The debtor in *Re Wise* was not a trader; he was apparently not in debt at the date of the settlement; and the claimant was a 'subsequent' creditor. Consequently, the claimant could not rely on any presumption or inference based on indebtedness, but had to prove an actual intent to defraud creditors – something which she manifestly failed to do.

1 Ibid at 301 (emphasis added).

Contingent liabilities and unascertained creditors

As we have seen,[1] creditors whose debts came into existence after the date of the relevant disposition (subsequent creditors), as well as those whose debts already existed at that date, were persons who might have been prejudiced by that disposition and were therefore able, in principle, to seek to have it set aside. However, as we have also seen, subsequent creditors were in a more difficult position than existing creditors, because they had to show either that the disponor had made the disposition with the express intent to defraud creditors or that, after the disposition, the settlor had insufficient means or no reasonable expectation of being able to pay his then existing debts.[2] (Even in *Re Butterworth*[3] it is clear that, after creating the settlement, the settlor did not in fact have sufficient means to pay his then existing debts.) All this, however, left several crucial questions unanswered. What was an 'existing debt' for these purposes? To what extent would the disponor be liable for contingent or potential debts? Would such debts have to be in his contemplation at the date of the disposition (or, at least, ought they to have been)? Could any subsequent creditor seek to have the disposition set aside, or would he have to show that he was within the class of creditors whom the debtor intended to defraud? Such questions tended to arise in two classes of cases, namely those involving insolvent traders and those in which the plaintiff was seeking to enforce an award of damages obtained in litigation against the debtor-disponor. However, many of these questions were never explored satisfactorily in any of the cases.

Existing debts and contingent liabilities

In any assessment of the nature and extent of the disponor's assets and liabilities – which was clearly material not only on the question of his solvency but also on the issue of intent to defraud – debts which had actually accrued or been incurred before the date of the relevant disposition obviously had to be taken into account. In addition, an existing contingent liability, such as that under a guarantee of another's debts, had to be considered, notwithstanding that no attempt had as yet been made to enforce the guarantee.[4] In other cases, however, it was not clear that any contingent or potential liability actually existed or would ever come into existence, let alone what its extent might be. This was particularly relevant in those cases where an award of damages had been made against the debtor after the date of his disposition.

In *Barling v Bishopp*,[5] for instance, two writs had been issued against the debtor in an action of trespass. Some two weeks before the actions came on

---

1 See pp 347–350 above.

2 *Re Lane-Fox* [1900] 2 QB 508 at 513–514, per Wright J; and see pp 349–350 above.

3 (1882) 19 Ch D 588; and see pp 352–354 above.

4 *Re Ridler* (1882) 22 Ch D 74 (unless, perhaps, the liability of the guarantor was remote: here, the settlor's son, whose debts had been guaranteed, was already indebted in excess of the extent of the guarantee at the date of the settlement).

5 (1860) 29 Beav 417.

for trial, the defendant executed a voluntary conveyance of his real estate to his daughter. At that date, he possessed no other property apart from his clothes and a sum of cash which was insufficient to discharge his then existing debts. A verdict was obtained against the defendant in both actions. One of the successful plaintiffs brought an action against the daughter alleging that the conveyance was void under the 1571 Act, on the basis that it was intended to 'delay, hinder or defraud creditors and others of their lawful actions, suits, debts … to the let or hindrance of the due course and execution of law'. Sir John Romilly MR concluded[1] that there was such an intent. The debtor had remained in possession of the property and of the title deeds (two of the 'badges of fraud'); and neither he nor his daughter had given any explanation for the conveyance.

> 'I find two verdicts against him, and I must therefore assume that he was in the wrong. Every man knows that he cannot go to law without incurring some expense. This deed was to provide for the worst which might happen, by conveying away his property beforehand.'

In *Re Wise*,[2] Grantham J concluded that it was clear from the facts that no one could doubt that the debtor in *Barling v Bishopp* had a fraudulent intention.

In *Crossley v Elworthy*,[3] however, a settlement was set aside as against creditors generally in a suit by a person who had recovered judgment against the settlor in an action commenced after the date of the settlement for a tort committed before that date. The settlement in question had been created on 12 June 1866. An action for damages against the debtor was commenced in May 1867 (shortly before the debtor was adjudicated bankrupt, but by which time he was known to be insolvent). The plaintiff alleged that, in 1865, the debtor had made a false and fraudulent representation as to the value of a company, which representation had induced the plaintiff to take shares in that company. Judgment for the plaintiff was entered on 8 March 1868.

Malins V-C held that some debts which existed at the date of the settlement remained unpaid, and that it was therefore unnecessary to take into account the damages recovered by the plaintiff for fraudulent representation. However, he went on to state that such liability to the plaintiff could not be wholly disregarded. Knowledge of his erroneous and fraudulent statements must be attributed to the debtor and those erroneous statements made him liable for a debt as at the date of the settlement which he had not taken into account.[4]

---

1 Ibid at 421. Sir John Romilly gave some examples of cases in which creditors might be defrauded even though the grantor was not indebted at the time: a man might convey his property to his child and immediately after borrow a large sum of money, which he then spent; or a tenant might convey his property and then strip lead off the roof of the property which he occupied, leaving himself without assets out of which to pay damages recovered by his landlord.

2 (1886) 17 QBD 290 at 295–296.

3 (1871) LR 12 Eq 158.

4 Ibid at 168.

This unnecessary addendum would seem to suggest that, in principle, ascertaining whether a person was solvent or indebted at the date of a relevant disposition ought to take account of any liability which the disponor had incurred before that date, notwithstanding that no claim had then been made or no action had then been commenced in respect of that liability, or that the amount of damages remained unquantified.

In *Re Wise*,[1] as we have seen, an action for breach of promise of marriage was commenced in England in August 1881, against a master mariner in Hong Kong. The writ was served on him in Hong Kong on 8 October and he settled £500 on 17 October. Judgment was obtained against him on 20 July 1882. Despite the fact that the action had, to his knowledge, been commenced before he created the settlement, the Court of Appeal refused to set the settlement aside. According to Lindley LJ,[2] the action 'was in the highest degree speculative; he was not then indebted to the plaintiff but she had made a claim against him which might or might not result in damages.'

Similarly, Lopes LJ stated:

> 'The action might have failed for various reasons; the plaintiff might not have been willing to pursue it; it might have resulted in a verdict for the defendant, or in a verdict for the plaintiff with very small damages. There are many other ways in which the action might have terminated, without its resulting in a verdict for £500. It seems to me, therefore, that it cannot be said that the necessary effect of the settlement was to defeat or hinder the plaintiff.'

Similarly, Lord Esher MR stated:[3]

> 'Now with regard to the action, how could any one – how could his legal adviser – have told him what the amount of the verdict was likely to be? If the verdict had been for £50, and he had had £50 coming to him at the end of his voyage, he would have been able to pay it, and on another occasion he would have been able to pay the costs. It was entirely a matter of speculation what the amount of the verdict would be. Therefore he was not insolvent; it was not the necessary consequence of what he did to defeat or delay the plaintiff in the action, for, if the verdict had been for a small amount, she would not necessarily have been delayed for a week.'

These decisions undoubtedly left matters in an uncertain state. In both *Re Wise* and *Barling v Bishopp*, a writ had already been issued against the settlor at the date of the settlement (and to his knowledge) but judgment in those proceedings had not yet been delivered. In other words, it could be said that there then existed a potential, though not an actual, liability to an ascertained individual. However, it is clear from *Re Wise* that this alone was not enough. A contingent liability had to be taken into account, but only as one of the (probably several) surrounding circumstances: the weight to be attached to it

---

1 (1886) 17 QBD 290.
2 Ibid at 301.
3 Ibid at 300.

depended on a variety of other factors, such as the nature and seriousness (or perceived seriousness) of the claim and the likelihood of its success. Each case would turn on its own facts. There would obviously be a difference between a case where the settlor disposed of the property which was the subject matter of the claim against him, whilst retaining no other property of any value, and the case where the settlor genuinely considered the claim against him to be trivial or, at worst, one which would result in an award of minimal damages which he could easily satisfy out of retained assets. In *Re Holland*,[1] Vaughan Williams LJ cited *Re Wise* in support of the proposition that in each case the whole of the circumstances surrounding the execution of the conveyance must be looked at, and it must then be asked whether it was in fact executed with the intent to defeat or delay creditors.

However, the decision in *Crossley v Elworthy* clearly produced a potentially much more far-reaching principle. The events which constituted the actionable tort had occurred before the date of the relevant disposition, but no writ had then been issued. It was certainly possible to regard *Crossley* as an exceptional case: the debtor had clearly made a fraudulent representation – and he must have been aware not only of his deliberate falsehood but also of his victim. The debtor was speculating heavily on the stock exchange and 'he was by the settlement intentionally abstracting from his creditors, or those who were likely to become his creditors, the sum comprised in the settlement, which might otherwise have been made available to them'.[2] It could therefore be argued that there was no reason why *Crossley* should extend to a case where the settlor was not aware at the date of the disposition that he had committed a tort – and even less reason for it to apply (say) to the case of a professionally qualified (and probably licensed) individual who could probably be presumed, in the absence of evidence to the contrary, to have acted properly.

However, it was not clear whether the decision in *Crossley* could be limited in such a way. In any event, its relevance depended on the precise question being asked. Suppose, for example, that, at the date of the relevant disposition, no claim had been raised against the settlor, and that there was no reason why the settlor should anticipate any such claim. It is difficult to see why any claim made and pursued successfully thereafter should be regarded as a contingent liability of the settlor, and therefore material to the question of his solvency at the date of the disposition, even if the events or circumstances which founded that liability occurred before that date. On the other hand, if the issue was whether the settlor had an intent to remove assets out of the reach of those persons (ascertained or not) who might have a claim against him (in tort or otherwise), it would seem to be immaterial whether such a claim was founded

---

1 [1902] 2 Ch 360 at 372. In this case, the settled property had come to the husband in right of his wife and it was considered right and proper for him to make a settlement of some sort, provided that, at the relevant time, he was not unable to pay his creditors or contemplating entering upon or continuing in a business of such a speculative nature as to be likely to land him in financial embarrassment.

2 *Re Wise* (1886) 17 QBD 290 at 296, per Grantham J.

on events and circumstances which occurred before or after the date of the disposition, or whether the settlor knew of the existence of, or ought to have anticipated, any specific claim.

The position was similar in the 'trading' cases. Clearly, the settlor's solvency at the date of his disposition was a material issue and, again, his contingent as well as his actual liabilities would have to be taken into account. However, it is clear that, even where solvency at the date of the disposition could be established beyond any doubt, that disposition could still be set aside if the trader's intent was to remove assets out of the reach of those who might become his creditors in the future. The identity of such future creditor(s) need not be known at the outset: after all, a trader will require and depend on suppliers, many of whom will be unknown at the commencement of trading. However, even if the 'creditors' whom the debtor intended to defraud need not have been identifiable or specifically within his contemplation at the date of the disposition, it was not clear whether they had to be within a class or group of foreseeable potential creditors. Thus, for example, if a trader intended to defraud creditors, did any particular claimant have to be within a class of 'trade creditors' (as was the case even in *Re Butterworth*[1]); or would it be sufficient that he was simply a creditor, even of a kind not within the contemplation of the settlor? Similarly, it was never decided whether the words 'any person thereby prejudiced' included a person who could not properly be described as a creditor.[2]

Protection of bona fide purchasers

Both statutes expressly accorded a degree of protection for *bona fide* purchasers. A proviso in the 1571 Act declared that the Act did not extend to any estate or interest in any property 'upon good consideration and bona fide lawfully conveyed or assured to any person or persons ... not having at the time of such conveyance or assurance ... any manner of notice or knowledge of such covin, fraud or collusion as is aforesaid'. In this context, the words '*good consideration*' were always judicially construed to be the equivalent of 'valuable consideration'.[3] Thus, if a creditor was to succeed in impeaching an alienation of property by his debtor, he had to prove, in addition to a fraudulent intent on the part of the debtor, *either* that the alienation was not made for valuable consideration *or* that the grantee was privy to the fraud.[4] If

1 (1882) 19 Ch D 588.

2 *Cadogan v Cadogan* [1977] 3 All ER 831.

3 *Twyne's Case* (1602) 3 Co Rep 80b, 76 ER 809; *Mathews v Feaver* (1786) 1 Cox Eq Cas 278; *Myers v Leinster (Duke)* (1844) 7 I Eq R 146; *Re David and Adlard* [1914] 2 KB 694 at 699.

4 *Holmes v Penney* (1856) 3 K & J 90; *Graham v Furber* (1854) 14 CB 10; *Hale v Saloon Omnibus Co* (1859) 4 Drew 492; *Kevan v Crawford* (1877) 6 Ch D 29; *Re Johnson* (1881) 20 Ch D 389; *Re Tetley* (1896) 3 Mans 226 at 231; *Re Eyre* (1881) 44 LT 922; *Re Cranston* (1892) 9 Morr 160; *Re Reis* [1904] 2 KB 769, affd *sub nom Clough v Samuel* [1905] AC 442; *Re Gunsbourg* (1919) 88 LJ (KB) 562.

he could not do so, the grantee was protected by the proviso, notwithstanding that the creditor was in fact defeated by the grant.[1]

Section 172(3) of the 1925 Act similarly provided:

> 'This section does not extend to any estate or interest in property conveyed for valuable consideration and in good faith or upon good consideration and in good faith to any person not having, at the time of the conveyance, notice of the intent to defraud creditors.'

Valuable consideration

The requirement for 'valuable' consideration did not mean that the consideration given had to be the full value of the property,[2] especially, it seems, when the disposition or conveyance was made as part of a family arrangement.[3] However, it had to be more than nominal.[4] It was not sufficient, for instance, that the grantor had escaped from some liability attaching to the property, as in the case of an assignment of a lease or of shares in a company subject to unpaid calls.[5] On the other hand, a grant to secure the repayment of an existing debt was one for sufficient consideration;[6] and so, too, was a grant in consideration of the waiving of an equity to a settlement.[7] If, on the face of the instrument, there appeared to be no valuable consideration or only nominal consideration, evidence was admissible to prove the contrary.[8] Purchasers for value from the grantee were also protected if they had no notice of the fraud, the alienation by the debtor being good until avoided.[9]

Marriage was a sufficient consideration, even when the wife was aware that the husband was indebted at the time,[10] unless the wife knew of the acts of bankruptcy committed before the date of the settlement[11] or the marriage itself

---

1 *Holmes v Penney* (1856) 3 K & J 90; *Re Johnson* (1881) 20 Ch D 389.

2 *Stephens v Olive* (1786) 2 Bro CC 90; *Nunn v Wilsmore* (1800) 8 Term Rep 521; *Copis v Middleton* (1818) 2 Madd 410; *Thompson v Webster* (1859) 4 De G & J 600.

3 *Re Johnson* (1881) 20 Ch D 389; *Harman v Richards* (1852) 10 Hare 81; *Townend v Toker* (1866) 1 Ch App 446; *Arundell (Lady) v Phipps and Taunton* (1804) 10 Ves 139.

4 Law of Property Act 1925, s 205(1)(xxi).

5 *Re Ridler* (1882) 22 Ch D 74.

6 *Glegg v Bromley* [1912] 3 KB 474; *Re Bamford* (1879) 12 Ch D 314 at 323; *Alton v Harrison* (1869) 4 Ch App 622; *Martindale v Booth* (1832) 3 B & Ad 498.

7 *Re Home* (1885) 54 LT 301.

8 *Gale v Williamson* (1841) 8 M & W 405; *Pott v Todhunter* (1845) 2 Coll 76; *Leifchild's Case* (1865) LR 1 Eq 231; *Townend v Toper* (1866) 1 Ch App 446; *Bayspoole v Collins* (1871) 6 Ch App 228; *Re Holland* [1902] 2 Ch 360.

9 *George v Milbanke* (1803) 9 Ves 190; *Morewood v South Yorkshire Rail etc* (1858) 3 H & N 798; *Halifax Joint Stock Banking Co v Gledhill* [1891] 1 Ch 31; *Pearce v Bulteel* [1916] 2 Ch 544; *Noyes v Paterson* [1894] 3 Ch 267.

10 *Campion v Cotton* (1810) 17 Ves 263; *Russel v Hammond* (1738) 1 Atk 13; *Fraser v Thompson* (1859) 1 Giff 49 at 65 (reversed on a different point (1859) 4 De G & J 659). See also Law of Property Act 1925, s 205(1)(xxi).

11 *Fraser v Thompson* (1859) 4 De G & J 659.

was a contrivance to remove assets from the reach of creditors.[1] Post-nuptial settlements executed in pursuance of ante-nuptial agreements which could be specifically enforced were also made for valuable consideration (again in the absence of a fraudulent intent shared by both parties to the marriage consideration).[2] Separation deeds by which property was settled in consideration of no proceedings being taken against the grantor for divorce, or which contained a covenant by trustees to indemnify the husband against his wife's debts, were also made for sufficient consideration.[3]

In *Re Cole*,[4] it was held that a *bona fide* compromise of a *bona fide* action claiming rights against the defendant's property was valuable consideration for the purposes of s 42 of the Bankruptcy Act 1914; and it was stated that it was not the business of the Court of Bankruptcy, before which the settlement was subsequently impeached, to consider whether the action could possibly have succeeded if fought to a finish. There is no reason to assume that a different view would have been taken in relation to the same expression in s 172(3).

Good consideration

In view of the meaning accorded to the expression 'good consideration' in the 1571 Act, it would not be unreasonable to suppose, as a matter of statutory construction, that the use of both expressions – namely 'valuable consideration' and 'good consideration' – in s 172(3) was deliberately intended to change the pre-existing law, so that a person taking in good faith and for 'good consideration', such as natural love and affection, would also enjoy the protection of the statutory exception.[5] However, if this had been the case, s 172 would have provided little assistance to creditors: as was stated in *Twyne's Case*,[6] 'the statute would serve for little or nothing, and no creditor would be sure of his debt'. In *Re Eichholz*,[7] it was assumed (without argument) that 'good consideration' meant 'valuable consideration', as under the pre-1926 law. Nevertheless, the question was never tested directly and remained unanswered.

Good faith

In the absence of good faith on the part of the transferee, even a disposition for value was capable of being avoided under the 1571 Act. Absence of good

---

1 *Colombine v Penhall* (1853) 1 Sm & G 228; *Fraser v Thompson* (1859) 4 De G & J 659; *Re Pennington* (1888) 59 LT 774. See also *Smith v Cherrill* (1867) LR 4 Eq 390; *Re Cameron and Wells* (1887) 37 Ch D 32 at 36; and *Nairn v Prowse* (1802) 6 Ves 752. If the marriage was contracted in good faith it was immaterial that the settlement contained false recitals (*Campion v Cotton* (1810) 17 Ves 263a; *Kevan v Crawford* (1877) 6 Ch D 29) or a covenant to settle all after-acquired property of the husband (*Re Reis* [1904] 2 KB 769).

2 *Re Holland* [1902] 2 Ch 360. *Cf Warden v Jones* (1857) 2 De G & J 76.

3 *Hobbs v Hull* (1788) 1 Cox Eq Cas 445; *Stephens v Olive* (1786) 2 Bro CC 90.

4 [1931] 2 Ch 174.

5 See eg *Halsbury's Laws of England* (4th ed, 1973), Vol 18, para 372; DL McDonnell and JG Monroe (eds) *Kerr on Fraud and Mistake* (Sweet & Maxwell, 7th ed, 1952) p 341.

6 (1602) 3 Co Rep 80b at 81b.

7 [1959] Ch 708.

faith, in cases where the transferee had given value, was said to mean actual knowledge of the fraud. Thus, where there was a disposition for valuable consideration, the 1571 Act required only that the transferee had notice or knowledge of the fraudulent intent: he need not be actively engaged in the transferor's efforts to put property beyond the reach of his creditors.[1]

In *Kevan v Crawford*,[2] for instance, a marriage settlement which contained a false recital that the husband-settlor was indebted to his wife was not set aside on the application of the husband's creditors, on the grounds that valuable consideration had been given (marriage) and the wife was ignorant of the husband's fraud. On the other hand, in *Colombine v Penhall*,[3] the wife was aware of her husband's fraud and the marriage settlement was accordingly set aside.

7.2.3 Bankruptcy Act 1914, s 42

Section 42(1) of the Bankruptcy Act 1914 (which reproduced s 47(1) of the Bankruptcy Act 1883, which in turn re-enacted the first part of s 91 of the Bankruptcy Act 1869, save that the latter provision applied only to traders, and subject to other minor amendments) provided as follows:

> 'Any settlement of property, not being a settlement made before and in consideration of marriage, or made in favour of a purchaser or incumbrancer in good faith and for valuable consideration, or a settlement made on or for the wife or children of the settlor of property which has accrued to the settlor after marriage in right of his wife, shall, if the settlor becomes bankrupt within two years after the date of the settlement, be void against the trustee in the bankruptcy, and shall, if the settlor becomes bankrupt at any subsequent time within ten years after the date of the settlement, be void against the trustee in the bankruptcy, unless the parties claiming under the settlement can prove that the settlor was, at the time of making the settlement, able to pay all his debts without the aid of the property comprised in the settlement, and that the interest of the settlor in such property passed to the trustee of such settlement on the execution thereof.'

Thus, unlike the provisions of the 1571 Act and s 172 of the Law of Property Act 1925, s 42 of the Bankruptcy Act 1914 imposed fixed time-limits: a settlement of property was automatically void as against the trustee in bankruptcy if the settlor became bankrupt within two years of the date of the settlement; if the settlor became bankrupt after two years, but within 10 years of that date, the settlement was void unless the beneficiaries could establish one of the exceptions specified in the section; and if the settlor became bankrupt at any time after the expiry of 10 years from the date of the settlement, s 42 could not apply at all. Section 172 of the Law of Property Act 1925, in contrast, was subject to no time-limit. On the other hand, s 42 did not require an intent to defraud to be established.

---

1 *Re Fasey* [1923] 2 Ch 1, especially at 9 and 17.

2 (1877) 6 Ch D 29.

3 (1853) 1 Sm & Giff 228. There was an obvious difficulty in setting aside a marriage settlement, however, namely in establishing that the children of the marriage had knowledge of the fraud.

'Settlement'

Section 42(4) declared that, for the purposes of s 42, a 'settlement' included 'any conveyance or transfer of property'. In *Re Player*,[1] Cave J stated that, despite the width of this provision:

> 'a settlement in the ordinary sense of the word is intended. The transaction must be in the nature of a settlement, though it may be effected by a conveyance or transfer. The end and purpose of the thing must be a settlement, that is, a disposition of property to be held for the enjoyment of some other person …'

In *Re Plummer*,[2] the Court of Appeal laid down the principle that a settlement for the purposes of s 42 meant such a conveyance or transfer by the donor as contemplated the retention of the property by the donee, either in its original form or in such a form that it could be traced, and did not extend to a conveyance or transfer of property which could not be traced, such as, for instance, where there was a gift of money to be employed in a business or in the purchase of a business, and the money was so employed or spent, the business itself not being settled.[3]

Thus, the payment during the 10-year period of premiums on a life assurance policy, which was itself assigned outside that period, was held to be outside the scope of the section (the payment of an individual premium not being a settlement). A settlement by a husband of damages recovered in divorce proceedings, made with the consent of the court, was not within the section.[4] A settlement revocable by the settlor with the consent of the trustees of the settlement or of the court was also not void.[5] Nor was the exercise of a general power of appointment a settlement for these purposes[6] (nor, indeed, would the exercise of a special power have been[7]). In contrast, the purchase of a matrimonial home in a husband's name, but pursuant to an agreement with his wife that they should be tenants in common, and as a result of which the husband became a constructive trustee for the wife, was a settlement for the purposes of s 42.[8]

Property covered by the section

Section 167 of the 1914 Act provided that, for the purposes of the Act, 'property' included 'money, goods, things in action, land, and every description of property, whether real or personal, and whether situate in England or

---

1 (1885) 15 QBD 682 at 687. Cave J was commenting on the Bankruptcy Act 1883, s 47(3), which was identical to the Bankruptcy Act 1914, s 42(3). See also *Re Plummer* [1900] 2 QB 790; *Re Tankard* [1899] 2 QB 57.

2 [1900] 2 QB 790.

3 See also *Re Vansittart* [1893] 1 QB 181.

4 *Re Stephenson* [1897] 1 QB 638.

5 *Re Baker* [1936] Ch 61.

6 *Re Mathieson* [1927] 1 Ch 283.

7 *Re Harrison and Ingram* [1900] 2 QB 710.

8 *Re Densham* [1975] 1 WLR 1519.

elsewhere; also obligations, easements, and every description of estate, interest, and profit, present or future, vested or contingent, arising out of or incident to property as above defined'. Thus, s 42 applied, for example, to dealings with bills, bonds, notes and other securities, cheques, a transfer of shares, gifts of chattels and of money.[1]

Consideration

In general terms, the section was 'construed in a commercial sense'.[2] The 'consideration' given need not be equal to the assets acquired. Thus, in *Re Pope*,[3] an agreement by a wife to refrain from taking divorce proceedings against her husband was sufficient valuable consideration, and it was not necessary that money or physical property should be given. Similarly, in *Re Cole*,[4] a *bona fide* compromise of a *bona fide* action claiming rights against property was held to be 'valuable consideration' for a settlement of that property under that compromise.

Both cases were reviewed and confirmed in *Re Abbott*,[5] where it was held that the words 'purchaser ... for valuable consideration' were wide enough to cover a spouse whose claim to a property adjustment order under s 24 of the Matrimonial Causes Act 1973 had been compromised; and that the wife, by relinquishing her claim in return for the right to part of her husband's share of the proceeds of sale of the matrimonial home was a purchaser of that right for valuable consideration. Indeed, in *Re Charters*,[6] a covenant by the assignee of a reversionary share under a will to pay off a mortgage to which the share was subject and to keep the assignor indemnified was held to be sufficient consideration.

However, in *Re Windle*,[7] Goff J doubted the correctness of this decision and stated that, save only in cases where the equity of redemption was of no appreciable value, if a covenant of indemnity (express or implied) was of itself to be treated as valuable consideration for the purposes of s 42, no transfer of mortgaged land would ever not be for valuable consideration within the meaning of the section.

In *Re a Debtor ex parte the Official Receiver v Morrison*[8] it was said that the statute required 'a consideration moving to the debtor, which replaces the property extracted from his creditors'. However, in *Re Windle*,[9] Goff J

1 See, eg, *Ex parte Todd* (1887) 19 QBD 186; *Re Player (No 1)* (1885) 2 Mor 261; *Re Cole* [1964] Ch 175; *Re Tarlo* [1966] CLY 646.

2 *Ex parte Hillman* (1879) 10 Ch D 622 at 625, per Sir George Jesse, MR; *Re Charters* (1923) 8 B & CR 94 at 100, per Astbury J; *Re Densham* [1975] 1 WLR 1519 at 1527–1529, per Goff J.

3 [1908] 2 KB 169. *Cf Re Macdonald* [1920] 1 KB 205.

4 [1931] 2 Ch 174.

5 [1983] Ch 45.

6 (1923) 8 B & CR 94.

7 [1975] 1 WLR 1628 at 1637–1638.

8 [1965] 1 WLR 1498 at 1505, per Stamp J.

9 [1975] 1 WLR 1628 at 1637.

considered this definition too narrow: 'It is clear that the consideration does not have to replace anything in the debtor's estate for it may be something which he has bargained shall be provided for a third party, nor does it have to be equal to that which has been taken out.' According to Goff J,[1] the three relevant Court of Appeal decisions (*Hance v Harding*,[2] *Re Pope*,[3] and *Ex parte Hillman*[4]) established that 'for this purpose the expression "purchaser for valuable consideration" does not import a purchase in the strict sense of a contract of purchase and sale, but it does postulate a person who in a commercial sense provides a quid pro quo'.

The same view was adopted by Peter Gibson J and Megarry V-C in *Re Abbott*,[5] where the earlier authorities were again reviewed and where Peter Gibson J summarised their effect as follows:

> '(1) The word "purchaser" in section 42(1) means a buyer in the ordinary commercial sense, that is to say a person providing a quid pro quo …
> (2) The consideration moving from the purchaser need not replace in the hands of the debtor the consideration moving from the debtor …
> (3) The consideration given by the purchaser need not be equal in value to the consideration given by the debtor, though it must be valuable consideration in the commercial sense …'

The 'doctrine of replacement' suggested by Stamp J in *Morrison* was considered 'erroneous' and 'extinct'.[6]

Thus the word 'purchaser' was construed in the ordinary commercial sense and meant a person who had given value, not necessarily a purchaser in the legal sense of the word (ie not as a technical conveyancing term) and included, for example, a person who had given value in order to obtain property for a third party.[7] In addition, it had to be a purchaser 'in good faith'.

The words 'in good faith' appear to have had different meanings in different sections of the Bankruptcy Act 1914,[8] but it seems that, in the context of s 42, they meant the absence of dishonesty and of any conscious attempt to defraud any other person.[9] Thus, a purchaser who knew that the whole object of the transaction was to remove property from the reach of

---

1 Ibid at 1637.
2 (1888) 20 QBD 732.
3 [1908] 2 KB 169.
4 (1879) 10 Ch D 622.
5 [1983] Ch 45 at 54.
6 Ibid at 54 and 58.
7 *Hance v Harding* (1888) 20 QBD 732; *Ex parte Hillman* (1879) 10 Ch D 622; *Re a Debtor ex parte the Official Receiver v Morrison* [1965] 1 WLR 1498; *Re Densham* [1975] 1 WLR 1519.
8 See eg *Re Badham* (1893) 10 Mor 252, *Re Dunkley & Son* [1905] 2 KB 683, *Re Simms* [1930] 2 Ch 22 and *Re Seymour* [1937] Ch 668 in relation to s 45; *Re Dalton* [1963] Ch 336 at 402–403, in relation to s 46; and *Cohen v Mitchell* (1890) 25 QBD 262, in relation to s 47.
9 *Re a Debtor ex parte the Official Receiver v Morrison* [1965] 1 WLR 1498 at 1505, per Stamp J.

creditors was not one acting in 'good faith'.[1] However, in order to constitute a purchaser 'in good faith', it was sufficient if the purchaser himself acted in good faith and it was not necessary that both parties should so act.[2] The onus of proving lack of good faith, and also lack of consideration, lay upon the trustee in bankruptcy.[3]

Evidence was admissible to prove that a conveyance, expressed on its face to be voluntary, had in fact been made for valuable consideration, or, alternatively, that a conveyance expressed to have been made for value was in fact voluntary.[4]

There were certain additional exceptions. First, s 42(1) did not apply to a settlement made in consideration of marriage.[5] However, as in the case of s 172, it seems that an ante-nuptial settlement could be set aside if the object of both the marriage and the settlement was to defeat creditors. Secondly, it did not apply to a settlement made on or for the wife or children of the settlor of property which had accrued to the settlor after marriage 'in right of his wife'.

At first sight, this would seem to have been a merely historical anachronism. However, in *Re Bower Williams*,[6] it was held that, when a wife had died intestate and her husband, after taking out administration, had settled some of her former property on trust for the benefit of his daughters, the property had accrued to the husband after marriage 'in right of his wife'. These first two exceptions applied whenever the settlement had been created. The third exception applied where the settlor had become bankrupt within 10 years, but more than two years after the date of the settlement. In such a case, the settlement was not void if the parties claiming under the settlement could prove that the settlor was, at the time of making the settlement, able to pay all his debts without the aid of the settled property and that the interest of the settlor in such property passed to the trustee of such settlement on the execution thereof. In *Re Lowndes*,[7] Cave J stated that this provision was intended to prevent 'a settlement to operate in futuro, a covenant, for instance, to settle specific property which the trustees could have enforced against the trustee in the case of the settlor's bankruptcy'.

---

1 Ibid; *Re Windle* [1975] 1 WLR 1628. See also Muir Hunter and D Graham (eds) *Williams on Bankruptcy* (Stevens & Sons, 18th ed, 1968), p 375.

2 *Mackintosh v Pogose* [1895] 1 Ch 505; *Re Tetley* (1896) 3 Mans 321; *Re Windle* [1975] 1 WLR 1628 at 1632.

3 *Re Windle* [1975] 1 WLR 1628 at 1632; *Official Assignee of the Estate of Cheah Soo Tuan v Khoo Saw Cheow* [1931] AC 67.

4 *Walker v Burrows* (1745) 1 Atk 93; *Pott v Todhunter* (1845) 2 Coll CC 76; *Re Pope* [1908] 2 KB 169; *Re Charters* [1923] 8 B & CR 94.

5 See, eg, *Rennell v IRC* [1964] AC 173; *Re Densham* [1975] 1 WLR 1519.

6 [1927] 1 Ch 441.

7 (1887) 18 QBD 677 at 681 (in relation to the precursor of s 42 in the Bankruptcy Act 1883, s 47).

'Void'

Although s 42(1) declared that the settlement in question shall 'be void', this was 'against the trustee in bankruptcy' and not generally; and the word was therefore construed as 'voidable'. The settlement was not void against the settlor's trustee in bankruptcy from its date, but only from the date on which his title accrued. Consequently, if, before that date, the property comprised in the settlement had been sold in good faith to a purchaser for value, the title of that purchaser was good; and the vendor claiming under a voluntary settlement had a title which he could force on a purchaser.[1]

The consequences of the contrary conclusion were summarised by Lindley LJ in *Re Carter and Kenderdine's Contract*:[2]

> 'No conveyance or transfer of property which came within the definition of settlement in this … section could ever safely be made by anybody if that conveyance or transfer was what is called "voluntary", that is to say, without consideration. Just conceive what that means. Suppose a father gave his son a horse or some money in the funds. That father might of course become bankrupt within two years or within ten years, and, during those periods respectively, the son could not deal with that horse or give a good title to that money in the funds either for value or otherwise. … To my mind, good sense is shocked by such a startling construction as that.'

Indeed, the Court of Appeal held in *Re Hart*[3] that a purchaser for value from the donee under a voluntary settlement, without notice of an act of bankruptcy committed by the settlor, was entitled to retain the property as against the settlor's trustee in bankruptcy, even though the purchase was subsequent to the act of bankruptcy to which the trustee's title related back.

The extent to which a settlement could be valid *pro tanto* was unclear. One view was that a settlement could be partly voidable and partly valid.[4] However, in *Re Windle*,[5] Goff J concluded that the cases in which such a result had been reached[6] had been special cases; and he rejected the principle as one not having any general application. This 'all or nothing' approach would indeed seem to accord with earlier authority and practice. The avoidance of a settlement was a complete avoidance: it did not vest the property in the trustee in bankruptcy or enable him to stand in the place of the beneficiary so as to obtain priority over subsequent incumbrancers, such as mortgagees.[7]

Lindley LJ summarised the position in *Re Farnham*:[8]

---

1 *Re Carter and Kenderdine's Contract* [1897] 1 Ch 776; *Re Brall* [1893] 2 QB 381; *Re Vansittart* [1893] 2 QB 377; *Re Holden* (1887) 20 QBD 43.

2 [1897] 1 Ch 776 at 781.

3 [1912] 3 KB 6. *Cf Re Gunsbourg* [1920] 2 KB 426.

4 See eg *Halsbury's Laws of England*, Vol 3, n 5 on p 346, p 494, para 902.

5 [1975] 1 WLR 1628 at 1638–1639.

6 He referred only to *Re Naylor* (1893) 10 Morr 173 and *Sturmey's Trustee v Sturmey* (1912) 107 LT 718.

7 *Sanguinetti v Stuckey's Banking Co* [1895] 1 Ch 776; *Re Farnham* [1895] 2 Ch 799.

8 [1895] 2 Ch 799 at 808.

> 'If the settlement is void as against the trustee, it is void altogether. The section does not mean that the property, the subject of the settlement, vests in the trustee by a title which overrides both that of the donor and the donee. The settlement being void, the property reverts to the donor, and it is as the donor's property that it vests in the trustee and must be distributed correctly.'

If it were otherwise, the trustee would in effect be attempting to set up a settlement which he himself has set aside.[1]

This broad principle is not inconsistent, however, with the proposition that, in appropriate cases, where a person has acquired an interest under a settlement for consideration, the settlement will be set aside only to the extent of the property which was the subject matter of a voluntary disposition and will not affect the claim or title of that person who gave valuable consideration for that interest. Thus, where a wife was held to have a half share in the matrimonial home, but to have actually contributed only one-ninth of its purchase price, it was held that the husband had made a settlement in her favour of the difference between her half share and her 'purchased' one-ninth share; and such settlement was set aside under s 42, but without affecting her entitlement to her one-ninth share.[2] Also, where the estate of the bankrupt had had the benefit of the transaction, the settlement was said to have been made *pro tanto* for valuable consideration.[3] Moreover, a settlement was avoided only insofar as necessary to satisfy the debts and costs of the bankruptcy; and title to any surplus remained unaffected.[4]

Solvency of the settlor

If the settlor became bankrupt[5] within 10 years of, but more than two years from, the date of the settlement, it would not be void if the parties claiming under the settlement could prove *inter alia* that the settlor was, at the date of the settlement, able to pay all his debts without the property comprised in the settlement.[6] This was a question of fact. Thus, where a trader made a voluntary settlement of an estate subject to a mortgage and covenanted to pay interest on the mortgage and, when required, to pay off the principal, and when his assets exclusive of the mortgaged estate were not sufficient to pay his debts and the mortgage debt together, the settlement was held to be void.[7] In determining the solvency of a trader, the value of the implements of his trade and of the goodwill of his business, if he was intending to continue the

1 Ibid at 810, per Lopes LJ; and at 812, per Rigby LJ.

2 *Re Densham* [1975] 1 WLR 1519, esp at 1531.

3 *Re Naylor* (1893) 10 Morr 173; *Re Densham* [1975] 1 WLR 1519. It would seem that these are the types of cases which were referred to in *Halsbury's Laws of England* (4th ed, 1973), Vol 3, p 494, para 902, and to which Goff J referred (in *Re Windle* [1975] 1 WLR 1628 at 1638–1639) as 'special cases'.

4 *Re Sims* (1896) 3 Mans 340. *Cf Re Chiandetti* [1921] B & CR 82.

5 The expression 'becomes bankrupt' meant 'commits an available act of bankruptcy': *Fawcett v Fearne* (1844) 6 QB 20; *Ex parte Harris* (1875) LR 19 Eq 253; *Re Reis* [1904] 1 KB 451.

6 Bankruptcy Act 1914, s 42(1).

7 *Ex parte Huxtable* (1876) 2 Ch D 54.

business, could not be taken into account (or, at least, only their value on a forced sale).[1] On the other hand, a life interest reserved to the settlor under the settlement had to be taken into account.[2] It was apparently undecided whether evidence that, at some time after the date of the settlement, the settlor was solvent would, in the absence of any other evidence to the contrary, be *prima facie* evidence that he was solvent at the date of the settlement, without the aid of the property settled. Nevertheless, such evidence was probably admissible.[3]

7.2.4 The Insolvency Act 1986

The Insolvency Act 1986 (IA 1986) provides a comprehensive legislative framework for both individual and corporate insolvency. On bankruptcy, a bankrupt's[4] estate vests in the trustee in bankruptcy immediately on his appointment taking effect, and it so vests without any conveyance, assignment or transfer.[5] A bankrupt's 'estate' comprises all property belonging to or vested in the bankrupt at the commencement of the bankruptcy, subject to certain exceptions – in particular, property held by the bankrupt in trust for any other person.[6] As well as money, goods, things in action and land, 'property' includes every description of property, wherever situated, and also obligations and every description of interest, whether present or future or vested or contingent, arising out of or incidental to property.[7] Thus, an interest under a trust, such as a life interest or interest in remainder is included, but not a mere *spes* enjoyed by the bankrupt as an object of a discretionary trust, nor a special power of appointment exercisable by the bankrupt but of which he himself is not an object.

A bankruptcy petition may not be presented to the court unless the debtor:

(a) is domiciled in England and Wales,
(b) is personally present in England and Wales on the day on which the petition is presented, or
(c) at any time in the period of three years ending with that day has been ordinarily resident, or has had a place of residence, in England and Wales, or has carried on business in England and Wales.[8]

1 *Re Butterworth* (1882) 19 Ch D 588.
2 *Re Lowndes* (1887) 18 QBD 677.
3 See DL McDonnell and JG Monroe (eds), n 5 on p 362, pp 310–316.
4 Insolvency Act 1986, s 381(1).
5 Ibid, s 306.
6 Ibid, s 283; *Schuppan v Schuppan* [1997] 1 BCLC 258.
7 Insolvency Act 1986, s 436. See also *Morgan v Morris* (1998) Lawtel Document No C0004394 (1 April 1998); and *Re Landau* [1998] Ch 223. *Cf Re Scientific Investment Plan* [1998] PLR 141.
8 Insolvency Act 1986, s 265. In *Theophile v Solicitor-General* [1950] AC 186, the House of Lords held that a debtor continues to carry on business, as far as bankruptcy jurisdiction is concerned, until all trade debts and liabilities, including tax liabilities, arising out of the carrying on of the business have been paid.

The IA 1986 also includes several provisions dealing with transactions defrauding creditors; and, like their predecessors, they are not all dependent on bankruptcy. Section 42 of the Bankruptcy Act 1914 and s 172 of the Law of Property Act 1925 were both repealed by the Insolvency Act 1985[1] (the bulk of which was itself repealed by the IA 1986). They were replaced by new provisions which are broader in scope: settlements and prior transactions made by a person who is adjudicated bankrupt (which were formerly within the scope of s 42 of the Bankruptcy Act 1914) are now dealt with in ss 339–342 of the IA 1986;[2] and transactions defrauding creditors (which were formerly within s 172 of the Law of Property Act 1925) are now dealt with in ss 423–425 of the IA 1986.[3] In broad terms, the policy underlying these provisions – unlike that which underpins recent asset protection legislation in certain offshore jurisdictions – is an attempt to make life easier for the creditor by clarifying and simplifying, and indeed widening, the basis on which he may seek to set aside dispositions made by his debtor.

Transactions at an undervalue and preferences in the event of bankruptcy

Under s 339 of the IA 1986, where an individual is adjudged bankrupt and he has, at a relevant time, entered into 'a transaction with any person at an undervalue', the trustee of the bankrupt's estate may apply to the court; and, on such an application, the court may make such order as it thinks fit for restoring the position to what it would have been if that individual had not entered into that transaction. Section 339(3) then provides that, for these purposes, an individual enters into a 'transaction at an undervalue' if:

> '(a) he makes a gift to that person or he otherwise enters into a transaction with that person on terms that provide for him to receive no consideration,
> (b) he enters into a transaction with that person in consideration of marriage, or
> (c) he enters into a transaction with that person for a consideration the value of which, in money or money's worth, is significantly less than the value, in money or money's worth, of the consideration provided by the individual.'

Section 436 provides that a 'transaction' includes 'a gift, agreement or arrangement, and references to entering into a transaction shall be construed accordingly'. The meaning of the expression 'transaction at an undervalue' has

---

1 Schedule 10, Parts III and IV.

2 Under IA 1986, s 284(1), where any person is adjudged bankrupt, any disposition of property made by that person in the period to which the section applies, is void except to the extent that it is or was made with the consent of the court, or is or was subsequently ratified by the court. In *Re Flint* [1993] Ch 319, three weeks after a bankruptcy petition had been presented against the husband, an order was made in divorce proceedings, pursuant to the Matrimonial Causes Act 1973, s 24, ordering him to transfer his interest in the matrimonial home to the wife. A week later the husband was adjudicated bankrupt. The husband's trustee in bankruptcy obtained a declaration that the order was void as a disposition of property within IA 1986, s 284(1) and was void unless subsequently ratified by the court dealing with the bankruptcy.

3 G Miller [1998] 62 Conv 362.

been considered in several cases[1] in the context of ss 423–425 of the IA 1986, where the same expression is used. The observations made in those cases apply equally in relation to s 339 and ought to be referred to accordingly.[2] Moreover, in *Re Paramount Airways Ltd*,[3] the Court of Appeal held (in relation to the virtually identical provisions in s 238 of the IA 1986 relating to transactions at an undervalue made by a company) that the words 'any person' had to be given their literal meaning, unrestricted as to persons or territory, and an order could therefore be made against a foreigner resident abroad.

Similar provision is made in s 340 of the IA 1986 for the case where an individual is adjudged bankrupt and he has, at a relevant time, 'given a preference' to 'any person'. For these purposes, an individual has given a preference to a person if:

> '(a) that person is one of the individual's creditors or a surety or guarantor for any of his debts or other liabilities, and
> (b) the individual does anything or suffers anything to be done which (in either case) has the effect of putting that person into a position which, in the event of the individual's bankruptcy, will be better than the position he would have been in if that thing had not been done.'[4]

In relation to s 340 (but not s 339), the court is directed not to make an order in respect of a preference given to any person unless the individual who gave it was influenced, in deciding to give it, by a desire to produce in relation to that person the effect mentioned in para (b) above.[5] On the other hand, an individual who has given a preference to an 'associate of his (otherwise than by reason only of being his employed)' is presumed, unless the contrary is shown, to have been influenced by such a desire.[6]

A 'relevant time' for the purposes of both s 339 and s 340 is defined in s 341 as follows:

> '(a) in the case of a transaction at an undervalue, at a time in the period of 5 years ending with the day of the presentation of the bankruptcy petition on which the individual is adjudged bankrupt,
> (b) in the case of a preference which is not a transaction at an undervalue and is given to a person who is an associate of the individual … at a time in the period of 2 years ending with that day, and

---

1 See, eg, *Arbuthnot Leasing International Ltd v Havelet Leasing Ltd* [1990] BCC 636; *Chohan v Saggar* [1992] BCC 306; *Pinewood Joinery (a firm) v Starelm Properties Ltd* [1994] 2 BCLC 412; *National Bank of Kuwait v Menzies* [1994] 2 BCLC 306; *Agricultural Mortgage Corp plc v Woodward* [1995] 1 BCLC 1, [1994] BCC 688; *Royscot Spa Leasing v Lovett* [1995] BCC 502; *Schuppan v Schuppan* [1997] 1 BCLC 258; *Jyske Bank (Gibraltar) Ltd v Spjeldnaes (No 2)* [1999] BPIR 525. See also *Re MC Bacon Ltd* [1990] BCLC 324 (on the IA 1986, s 238(4)(b), which corresponds to s 423(1)(c)).

2 See pp 379–389 below.

3 [1993] Ch 223. See also *Jyske Bank (Gibraltar) Ltd v Spjeldnaes (No 2)* [1999] BPIR 525.

4 IA 1986, s 340(3).

5 Ibid, s 340(4).

6 Ibid, s 340(5). An 'associate' is defined in s 435.

(c) in any other case of a preference which is not a transaction at an undervalue, at a time in the period of 6 months ending with that day.'

It is further provided[1] that (subject to a 'two-year exception' mentioned below), none of the times specified above is 'a relevant time' unless the individual:

(a) is insolvent at that time; or
(b) becomes insolvent in consequence of the transaction or preference.

For these purposes, an individual is 'insolvent' if:

(a) he is unable to pay his debts as they fall due; or
(b) the value of his assets is less than the amount of his liabilities, taking into account his contingent and prospective liabilities.[2]

These requirements are presumed to be satisfied, unless the contrary is shown, where the individual has entered into a transaction at an undervalue with an 'associate' of his. Moreover, if the individual has made a transaction at an undervalue (as opposed to given a preference) at a time less than two years before the presentation of the bankruptcy petition, that time will be 'a relevant time' irrespective of his insolvency.[3]

An 'associate', for the purposes of the Act, is defined widely in s 435, which provides *inter alia* that a person is an associate of an individual if that person is the individual's husband or wife, or is a relative, or the husband or wife of a relative, of the individual or of the individual's husband or wife. A person is also an associate of any person with whom he is in partnership, and of the husband or wife or a relative of any individual with whom he is in partnership. He is also an associate of any person whom he employs or by whom he is employed. A person in his capacity as trustee of a trust (other than some specified exceptions) is an associate of another person if the beneficiaries of the trust include, or the terms of the trust confer, a power that may be exercised for the benefit of, that other person or an associate of that other person.[4]

The broad effect of these provisions is that, where an individual is adjudged bankrupt and he has entered into a transaction at an undervalue within two years of the presentation of the bankruptcy petition, then the court must make an order in respect thereof on the application of the individual's trustee in bankruptcy; and that, where he has entered into such a transaction within five

---

1 Ibid, s 341(2).
2 Ibid, s 341(3); *Schuppan v Schuppan* [1997] 1 BCLC 258.
3 Ibid, s 341(2).
4 Ibid, s 435(1), (2), (3), (4) and (5). Any provision that a person is an associate of another person is taken to mean that they are associates of each other: s 435(1).

years, but not within two years, of the presentation of the bankruptcy petition, similar consequences follow, but only if it is shown that the individual was insolvent at the time of the transaction or became so in consequence thereof (bearing in mind the presumption made against him if the transaction was made with an 'associate'). On the other hand, where the individual has given a preference to any person and such preference is not a transaction at an undervalue, a distinction is drawn between (a) a preference given to an 'associate' (where the relevant time-limit is within two years of the date of the presentation of the bankruptcy petition) and (b) one given to any other person (where the relevant time-limit is the period of six months ending with that date).

The court may make such order 'as it thinks fit' under s 339 or s 340, but s 342 lists various forms of order which the court may wish to make. For example, an order may:

(a) require any property transferred as part of the transaction, or in connection with the giving of the preference, to be vested in the trustee of the bankrupt's estate as part of that estate;
(b) require any property to be so vested if it represents in any person's hands the application either of the proceeds of sale of property so transferred or of money so transferred;
(c) release or discharge (in whole or in part) any security given by the individual;
(d) require any person to pay, in respect of benefits received by him from the individual, such sums to the trustee of his estate as the court may direct.[1]

An order under s 339 or s 340 may affect the property of, or impose any obligation on, any person whether or not he is the person with whom the individual in question entered into the transaction or, as the case may be, the person to whom the preference was given. However, such an order will not prejudice any interest in property which was acquired from a person other than that individual and was acquired in good faith and for value, or prejudice any interest deriving from such an interest; and it will not require a person who received a benefit from the transaction or preference in good faith, for value and without notice of the relevant circumstances, to pay a sum to the trustee of the bankrupt's estate, except where he was a party to the transaction or the

1 Ibid, s 342(a)–(d). See s 342 generally for the remaining forms of order and also for supplementary provisions.

payment is to be in respect of a preference given to that person at a time when he was a creditor of that individual.[1]

In addition, ss 335A,[2] 336 and 337 of the IA 1986 deal with the powers of the court in certain specific cases, namely cases where a trustee in bankruptcy applies (under s 14 of the Trusts of Land and Appointment of Trustees Act 1996) for an order for the sale of a dwelling-house of which the bankrupt and his spouse (or former spouse) are trustees for sale; cases where a spouse claims rights of occupation under Part IV of the Family Law Act 1996 and also cases where the bankrupt has rights of occupation by virtue of a beneficial interest and has infant children living with him.

A number of decisions – many of which show that some of the principles enunciated in the pre-1986 cases continue to be relevant – illustrate the operation of ss 339 and 340 of the IA 1986. In *Clarkson v Clarkson*,[3] A, B and C were directors and shareholders of a prosperous company. In 1989, they each took out a life insurance policy for £500,000 in order to provide cash for the other two to buy out the insured director's interest in the company when he died. C's policy was held on trust by A, B and C, who had a power to appoint the policy and its proceeds for the benefit of the insured director's spouse, children and grandchildren, and the other two directors; and, in default of appointment, on trust for A and B equally. In June 1991, the company went into administrative receivership. In June 1992, the trustees appointed the proceeds of the policy to C's wife. In January and February 1993, all three directors were adjudicated bankrupt. The trustees in bankruptcy of A and B claimed that the appointment (having been made within two years of the bankruptcies) was a transaction at an undervalue within s 339. The Court of Appeal rejected the claim, holding that the creation of the trust by C in 1989 had been a gift, but not the appointment made in 1992.

Hoffmann LJ stated:

> 'The appointment was merely the exercise of a fiduciary power to select the person to whom the gift should go. It has been for centuries a principle of the law of powers that an appointment under a special power takes effect as if it had been written into the instrument creating the power. The appointee takes the property of the settlor and not that of the donee of the power.'

The court was willing to give s 339 a purposive construction, holding that it was clearly intended to enable a trustee in bankruptcy to recover for the benefit of creditors any property which the bankrupt had given away or at an

---

1 Section 342(2), as amended by Insolvency (No 2) Act 1994, s 2. The purpose of the 1994 Act is to provide protection for an innocent purchaser from a donee who received property from a person subsequently declared bankrupt. See p 383 for a discussion of identical provisions in the Insolvency Act 1986, s 425 and of cases decided thereon.

2 Inserted by Trusts of Land and Appointment of Trustees Act 1996, Sch 3, para 23. See also *Re Raval* [1998] 2 FLR 718; *Judd v Brown* [1991] 1 FLR 1191.

3 [1994] BCC 921.

undervalue during the relevant period (as defined in s 341). What 'property' did A and B have at the relevant time? Under the settlement, each had a vested interest in the trust fund in default of appointment: however, such an interest was, in its nature, liable to defeasance. Each was a potential object of the power of appointment; but this was nothing more than a right to be considered as a potential appointee. Each was a trustee and donee of the power (along with C), but this clearly conferred no beneficial interest in the property[1] at all and the power had to be exercised jointly by all three trustees.

In *Re Kumar*,[2] a husband and wife were joint tenants of the matrimonial home, which was worth about £140,000 and was mortgaged to a bank. On 11 June 1990, the husband executed a transfer of his interest to the wife (to which the bank consented on condition that the mortgage was reduced). The wife thereupon became sole proprietor of the house and assumed sole liability for the mortgage. On 9 July, an action brought against the husband by former clients for negligence was compromised and a consent order made against him for payment of damages of £30,000 and costs by instalments or the immediate payment of £56,000 in default. On 24 July, the wife petitioned for divorce. On 20 December, the husband's former solicitors entered a default judgment against him for non-payment of their costs of some £22,500 and on 31 December the plaintiffs in the negligence action signed judgment for £56,000 and costs against him under the consent order, the terms of which he had been unable to satisfy. On 21 January 1991, a decree nisi was granted on the wife's petition. On 25 March, a bankruptcy petition was presented by the husband's former solicitors. On 19 April, under a consent order made in the divorce proceedings, the wife agreed to her claim for financial provision being dismissed in consideration of the husband's transfer of his interest in the matrimonial home to her and his agreement to make periodical payments. On 24 July, a bankruptcy order was made against the husband. The trustee in bankruptcy applied to the court for an order under s 339 of the Insolvency Act 1986 reversing the husband's transfer of the matrimonial home to the wife on 11 June 1990, on the ground that it was a transaction at an undervalue and was void as against his creditors.

Ferris J held that the compromise of a claim to financial provision in matrimonial proceedings was capable of being consideration in money or money's worth for the purposes of determining whether a transaction had been entered into at an undervalue for the purposes of s 339. However, whether it was relevant consideration depended on the value of the claim for relief which was compromised. Since the husband's interest in the matrimonial home had already been transferred to the wife by way of gift and there was no

---

1 The wide definition of a bankrupt's estate in IA 1986, s 283 clearly included a general power of appointment but not a power exercisable over property not for the time being comprised in the bankrupt's estate, and it did not extend to property held by the bankrupt on trust: s 283(3)(a) and (4).

2 [1993] 2 All ER 700.

evidence that the transfer had been executed in return for an agreement by the wife not to seek any further capital provision, and as she must have been aware that he had no other assets out of which to make any further capital provision, the purported compromise of the wife's claim did not amount to relevant consideration for the purposes of s 339. Furthermore, having regard to the difference in value between the equity of redemption and the amount of the mortgage, the wife's assumption of sole liability for the mortgage was significantly less than the consideration provided by the husband and was not sufficient to prevent the transaction being at an undervalue.

Ferris J referred[1] to the decision of Goff J in *Re Windle*,[2] to the effect that, where there is an equity of redemption of significant value, a mere covenant of indemnity against liability under the mortgage could not be regarded as valuable consideration for the purposes of s 42 of the Bankruptcy Act 1914. If the same reasoning were to be applied to s 339, it might lead to the conclusion that the assumption of sole liability under a subsisting mortgage did not, where the security by way of charge was more than adequate, prevent a transfer of a beneficial interest in the equity of redemption being a gift within s 339(3)(a). However, s 42 contained no provision for comparing the respective values of the consideration moving in each direction, of the kind now contained in s 339(3)(c). It was therefore arguable that the reasoning in *Re Windle* no longer compelled the conclusion that there was no valuable consideration in such a case.

Although *Re Abbott*[3] was an authority on s 42 of the Bankruptcy Act 1914, Ferris J concluded that it was also applicable to s 339 of the IA 1986 to the extent that it decided that a compromise of a claim to a provision in matrimonial proceedings is capable of being consideration in money or money's worth. However, there remained the question of the value of such consideration – a question which was required to be raised by s 339(3)(c). On the facts of this case, the only consideration given by the wife was the assumption of sole liability in respect of the reduced mortgage (of £30,000) and there was clearly an equity of redemption of very considerable value. Therefore, the value of such consideration was significantly less than the value of the consideration provided by the husband. The transfer of the husband's interest was therefore a transaction at an undervalue within s 339. (Even if there had been a compromise of the wife's prospective claim for capital provision – which the judge held was not the case – his conclusion would have been the same. The husband had made a disposal of his only remaining capital asset of any substance and it involved a substantial element of bounty on his part.)

---

1 Ibid at 710.

2 [1975] 1 WLR 1628. See p 365 above.

3 [1983] Ch 45.

In *Bishopsgate Investment Management Ltd v Maxwell*,[1] the defendant had created a charge (on 31 July 1992) over his interest in a flat in favour of his solicitors, to secure payment of unpaid costs and disbursements incurred and billed prior to that date. The plaintiff intended to allege that the charge was open to attack as a preference under s 340 or as a transaction at an undervalue within s 339 of the IA 1986. The plaintiff was allowed to present a bankruptcy petition immediately so as to bring himself within the six-month time-limit prescribed by the Act.

In contrast, in *Re Ledingham-Smith*,[2] A and B carried on a business in partnership. They employed the services of accountants whose fees were paid by monthly standing order for £1000. By the end of September 1989, A and B owed the accountants almost £8000 for services rendered. By the end of 1989, they owed around £24,000. In January 1990, the accountants declared that they would not continue to act for the partnership unless their outstanding fees were paid. The parties agreed that the partnership would pay £5000 a week, first to satisfy any fees incurred during that week and then to be used towards reducing the balance of outstanding fees. The partnership was declared bankrupt in April 1990, and the trustee in bankruptcy sought to recover, under s 40 of the IA 1986, sums which had been paid to the accountants pursuant to the agreement.

Morritt J held that there were three issues before the court.

(1) The first issue was whether A and B had put the accountants in a position which, in the event of their bankruptcy, would be better than if the thing had not been done (called a 'preference in fact').
(2) Secondly, if there was a preference in fact, whether A and B were influenced by a desire to confer a benefit (called 'the relevant influence').
(3) Thirdly, upon whom did the burden of proving the relevant influence rest?

As to the first issue, the judge held that there was no preference in fact. Section 340(3)(b) required that the recipient's position 'will be better' (not 'may be') in a bankruptcy after the doing of the thing in question. On the facts, the accountants could not be said to have been benefited: services were still being provided and expenses incurred. As to the second issue, it was not helpful to consider whether the words 'influenced … by a desire' in s 340(4) posed a greater or lesser test than the test under the former legislation of a dominant intention to prefer.[3] 'Intention', 'motive' and 'desire' were different concepts. The words 'desire' and 'influence' were not susceptible to any further

---

1 (1993) *The Times*, 11 February (hearing, 28 January 1993).

2 [1993] BCLC 635.

3 Millett J pointed out in *Re MC Bacon Ltd* [1990] BCLC 324 at 335 that the tests predicated by s 340 are completely different and consideration of the position under the old legislation cannot assist.

definition and the question was simply one of applying them to the facts of a given case. Here, it was not possible to infer from the facts a desire to prefer on the part of A and B. As to the third issue, it was clear from s 340(5) that the burden was on the trustee to show that a preference had been conferred.

Transactions defrauding creditors

Section 172 of the Law of Property Act 1925 was replaced by ss 423–425 of the IA 1986. Section 423 (unlike s 339 above) applies whether or not insolvency proceedings of any kind have been taken, and however long before the application to the court the transaction being impugned was entered into. However, (like s 339) it applies to a 'transaction at an undervalue', an expression which is defined in terms identical to those used in relation to s 339[1] and one which has been discussed in several recent cases. Section 423(1) provides that, apart from gifts and transactions made in consideration of marriage, a person enters into a 'transaction at an undervalue' with another person if he enters into a transaction with the other for a consideration the value of which, in money or money's worth, is significantly less than the value, in money or money's worth, of the consideration provided by himself. An almost identical provision (in s 238(4)(b) of the IA 1986) was considered in *Re MC Bacon Ltd*,[2] where the issue was whether the granting of a debenture by a company was a transaction at an undervalue, and in respect of which provision Millett J made the following observations:[3]

> 'To come within that paragraph the transaction must be (i) entered into by the company; (ii) for a consideration; (iii) the value of which measured in money or money's worth; (iv) is significantly less than the value; (v) also measured in money or money's worth; (vi) of the consideration provided by the company. It requires a comparison to be made between the value obtained by the company for the transaction and the value of the consideration provided by the company. Both values must be measurable in money or money's worth and both must be considered from the company's point of view. … The mere creation of a security over a company's assets does not deplete them and does not come within the paragraph. By charging its assets the company appropriates them to meet the liabilities due to the secured creditor and adversely affects the rights of other creditors in the event of insolvency. But it does not deplete its assets or diminish their value. It retains the right to redeem and the right to sell or remortgage the charged assets. All it loses is the ability to apply the proceeds otherwise than in satisfaction of the secured debt. That is not something capable of valuation in monetary terms and is not customarily disposed of for value.'

This passage in Millett J's judgment was approved by the Court of Appeal in *National Bank of Kuwait v Menzies*,[4] which held that the analysis applied equally to s 423(1)(c) of the IA 1986. It was also applied in *Agricultural Mortgage*

---

1 Section 423(1)(a)–(c); and see also IA 1986, s 339(2).

2 [1990] BCLC 324.

3 Ibid at 340–341.

4 [1994] 2 BCLC 306.

Corporation plc v Woodward,[1] where the Court of Appeal held that, in assessing the consideration moving between the parties to an impeached transaction, the court will look at the totality of the transaction, examine it realistically, and take into account the real value of the benefits and advantages accruing to either side, in the context of the purpose with which the transaction is found to have been carried out. In that case, the debtor had mortgaged his farm to the plaintiff (AMC) as security for a loan. He fell into arrears with the mortgage payments and AMC gave him a deadline to clear the arrears. Two days before the deadline, the debtor granted his wife a tenancy of the mortgaged property. The value of the mortgaged farm with vacant possession was over £1 million, whereas its value, subject to the tenancy, was less than £500,000. AMC sought to have the tenancy set aside. AMC conceded that the rent reserved under the tenancy agreement represented a full market value, but none the less argued that the consideration received by the debtor was less than the value of the consideration provided by him, on the basis that the value of his freehold interest was diminished by the grant of the tenancy and that this detriment was part of the consideration provided by him.

This argument was rejected at first instance and, even on appeal, the Court of Appeal preferred to leave this specific question open.[2] Nevertheless, the Court of Appeal allowed the appeal on the ground that the transaction had to be viewed as a whole and the tenancy gave the debtor's wife additional benefits, beyond the rights granted by the tenancy, for which she did not pay, namely the safeguarding of the family home, the acquisition of the farming business, and, in particular, the surrender value of the tenancy (ie the wife was placed in a 'ransom position' in that AMC would have to negotiate with her and pay her a high price in order to get vacant possession of the farm and sell it for the purpose of enforcing its security).

On the other hand, where a company transferred property worth £750,000, but encumbered with a mortgage for £2.65 million, to an associated company for £1, the transaction could not be said to be one at an undervalue.[3] Similarly, a letter of instructions from the debtor which did not create any security and simply gave effect to an agreement providing for the future allocation, as between two creditors, of sums to which they were already entitled as secured creditors, was not a transaction at an undervalue.[4]

---

1 [1995] 1 BCLC 1, [1994] BCC 688; *Barclays Bank v Eustice* [1995] 1 WLR 1238.

2 [1995] 1 BCLC 1 at 10 and 12, per Sir Christopher Slade and Neill LJ.

3 *Pinewood Joinery (A Firm) v Starelm Properties Ltd* [1994] 2 BCLC 412. The 'hope' value of property (ie any additional value arising from the hope or possibility that planning permission may be obtained) must obviously be taken into account in determining the value of the consideration given by the transferor. However, in this case, there was no evidence as to what the 'hope' value of the property might be: see 417.

4 *National Bank of Kuwait v Menzies* [1994] 2 BCLC 306. However, such an arrangement could well be open to attack as a preference. See also *National Westminster Bank plc v Jones* [2001] 1 BCLC 98. In *Knights v Seymour Pierce Ellis Ltd* (unreported decision of Robert Englehart QC, 13 June 2001: Lawtel Doc No C0101502) it was held that the mere transmission by a company of money from A to a third party B did

Those who may apply for an order under s 423

An application for an order under s 423 may not be made in relation to a transaction except:

(a) in a case where the debtor has been adjudged bankrupt (or is a body corporate which is being wound up or in relation to which an administration order is in force) by the Official Receiver, by the trustee of the bankrupt's estate (or by the liquidator or administrator of the body corporate) or, with the leave of the court, by a victim of the transaction;
(b) in a case where a victim of the transaction is bound by an approved[1] voluntary arrangement, by the supervisor of the voluntary arrangement or by any person who (whether or not so bound) is such a victim; or
(c) in any other case, by a victim of the transaction.[2]

An application made under any of paras (a)–(c) is to be treated as made on behalf of every victim of the transaction.[3] A 'victim' for these purposes means a person who is, or is capable of being, prejudiced by the transaction at an undervalue.[4]

Provision which may be made by order under s 423

Where a person (individual or corporate) has entered into a transaction at an undervalue with another person (individual or corporate), the court[5] may, if satisfied under s 423(3), make such order as it thinks fit for:

(a) restoring the position to what it would have been if the transaction had not been entered into, and
(b) protecting the interests of persons who are victims of the transaction.[6]

There is an element of discretion involved here (implicit in the word 'may'). Indeed, the Court of Appeal held, in *Re Paramount Airways Ltd*,[7] that this provision confers on the court an overall discretion, which is wide enough, if

---

not involve any kind of 'transaction' for the purposes of ss 238 and 423 of the IA 1986. And in *Treharne v Brabon* [2001] 1 BCLC 11, it was held that a sale effected by a bankrupt's wife as mortgagee was not 'entered into' by the bankrupt.

1 Ie approved under IA 1986, Part I or Part VIII.

2 Ibid, s 424(1).

3 Ibid, s 424(2).

4 Ibid, s 423(5). See also *Pinewood Joinery (A Firm) v Starelm Properties Ltd* [1994] 2 BCLC 412 at 417–418.

5 'The court' means the High Court or any other court which has jurisdiction in relation to a bankruptcy petition relating to the individual or to wind up the company: s 423(4). But *cf Moon v Franklin* [1996] BPIR 196; and *TSB Bank plc v Katz* [1997] BPIR 147.

6 IA 1986, s 423(2).

7 [1993] Ch 223, especially at 239–240. See also *Mackinnon v Donaldson* [1986] Ch 482; *Barclays Bank plc v Homan* [1993] BCLC 680 and *Hughes v Hannover Ruckversicherungs-Aktiengesellschaft* [1997] 1 BCLC 497.

justice so requires, to enable the court to make no order against the other party to the transaction or the person to whom the preference was given. In particular, if a foreign element is involved, the court will need to be satisfied that, in respect of the relief sought against him, the defendant is sufficiently connected with England for it to be just and proper to make the order against him despite the foreign element (which might be shown, for example, by his residence).

As Sir Donald Nicholls V-C stated:[1]

> 'This connection might be sufficiently shown by the residence of the defendant. If he is resident in England, or the defendant is an English company, the fact that the transaction concerned movable or even immovable property abroad would by itself be unlikely to carry much weight. Likewise if the defendant carries on business here and the transaction related to that business. Or the connection might be shown by the situation of the property, such as land, in this country. In such a case, the foreign nationality or residence of the defendant would not by itself normally be a weighty factor against the court exercising its jurisdiction under the sections. Conversely, the presence of the defendant in this country, either at the time of the transaction or when proceedings were initiated, will not necessarily mean that he has a sufficient connection with this country in respect of the relief sought against him. His presence might be coincidental and unrelated to the transaction. Or the defendant may be a multinational bank, carrying on business here, but all the dealings in question may have taken place at an overseas branch.
>
> …
>
> Thus in considering whether there is a sufficient connection with this country the court will look at all the circumstances, including the residence and place of business of the defendant, his connection with the insolvent, the nature and purpose of the transaction being impugned, the nature and locality of the property involved, the circumstances in which the defendant became involved in the transaction or received a benefit from it or acquired the property in question, whether the defendant acted in good faith, and whether under any relevant foreign law the defendant acquired an unimpeachable title free from any claims even if the insolvent had been adjudged bankrupt or wound up locally. The importance to be attached to these factors will vary from case to case.'

However, the discretion conferred by s 423(2) is not apparently an absolute and uncontrolled discretion: 'the courts must set their faces against transactions which are designed to prevent plaintiffs in proceedings, creditors with unimpeachable debts, from obtaining the remedies by way of execution that the law would normally allow them'.[2] An order shall be made only if the court is satisfied that the transaction was entered into:

> 'for the purpose –
>
> (a) of putting assets beyond the reach of a person who is making, or may at some time make, a claim against him, or

---

1 *Re Paramount Airways Ltd* [1993] Ch 223 at 240; *Jyske Bank (Gibraltar) Ltd v Spjeldnaes (No 2)* [1999] BPIR 525; *Polly Peck International Ltd v Citibank NA* (1993) *The Times*, October 20; *Polly Peck International plc v Nadir* [1993] BCC 886.

2 *Arbuthnot Leasing International Ltd v Havelet Leasing Ltd (No 2)* [1990] BCC 636 at 645, per Scott J.

(b) of otherwise prejudicing the interests of such a person in relation to the claim which he is making or may make.'[1]

The fact that the transaction was carried out pursuant to legal advice from solicitors or counsel and without dishonest intent does not by itself mean that the purpose of the transaction is not caught by s 423(3).[2]

Section 425 provides that, without prejudice to the generality of s 423 (and the discretion conferred on the court), an order made with respect to the transaction may:

(a) require any property transferred as part of the transaction to be vested in any person, either absolutely or for the benefit of all the persons on whose behalf the application for the order is treated as made;
(b) require any property to be so vested if it represents, in any person's hands, the application either of the proceeds of sale of property so transferred or of money so transferred;
(c) release or discharge (in whole or in part) any security given by the debtor;
(d) require any person to pay to any other person in respect of benefits received from the debtor such sums as the court may direct;
(e) provide for any surety or guarantor whose obligations to any person were released or discharged (in whole or in part) under the transaction to be under such new and revived obligations as the court thinks appropriate;
(f) provide for security to be provided for the discharge of any obligation imposed by or arising under the order, for such an obligation to be charged on any property and for such security or charge to have the same priority as a security or charge released or discharged (in whole or in part) under the transaction.

Section 425(2) then provides further that, although an order under s 423 may affect the property of, or impose any obligation on, any person whether or not he is the person with whom the debtor entered into the transaction, those exclusions which apply in relation to s 339 also apply in relation to s 423.[3] Thus, no order may be made which would prejudice the interests of a *bona fide* mortgagee.[4]

In any event, the court must attempt to provide for the restoration of the antecedent position 'as far as possible' and to protect the interests of the victims of the transaction so far as practicable. Thus, where the transaction is made up of more than one component, the court has power to set aside one

---

1 IA 1986, s 423(3).

2 *Arbuthnot Leasing International Ltd v Havelet Leasing Ltd (No 2)* [1990] BCC 636 at 644.

3 See IA 1986, s 342(2), and pp 374–375 above.

4 *Chohan v Saggar* [1994] 1 BCLC 706; *Judd v Brown* [1999] 1 FLR 1191.

component but not the other(s).[1] The court may also order the transferee under the impeached transaction to hold the property on trust for the transferor, but without prejudice to the claims of the creditors of the transferee himself, who may have become creditors after the date of the transfer.[2]

'For the purpose of'

One of the key requirements of s 423 is that the court must be satisfied that the transaction at an undervalue must have been entered into for one of the purposes specified in s 423(3).[3] This requirement replaces the all-important 'intent to defraud' in s 172 of the Law of Property Act 1925. It was a recommendation of the Cork Committee (whose work prepared the way for the IA 1986) that the law should be changed so as to make clear that:

> 'the necessary intent on the part of the debtor is an intent to defeat, hinder, delay or defraud creditors, or to put assets belonging to the debtor beyond their reach, and that such intent may be inferred whenever this is the natural and probable consequence of the debtor's actions, in the light of the financial circumstances of the debtor at the time, as known, or taken to have been known, to him'.[4]

It is not at all clear that s 423 has given full effect to this particular recommendation. In particular, the expression 'for the purpose of' is itself not free from ambiguity, and, in this respect at least, it is not at all obvious that the position of a person seeking to set aside a relevant transaction has been improved.

The meaning of the word 'purpose' in s 423 was considered in *Chohan v Saggar*,[5] where Edward Evans-Lombe QC (sitting as a deputy High Court judge) held that s 423(3) required a dominant purpose to remove assets from the reach of actual or potential claimants or creditors. The facts of the case were as follows. A transferred a house to B, subject to a legal charge in favour of a building society and apparently pursuant to a sale to B as a sitting tenant. B then executed a trust deed under which the property was held on trust for C, to whom A owed money. It was found that, at the date of the transfer, A was under great pressure from his creditors and was probably insolvent on an asset basis: certainly, he could not pay his debts as they fell due. (He was subject, for example, to two awards of damages for libel made against him.) It was also found that, in the circumstances of the case, the property had been disposed of

---

1 IA 1986, s 423(2)(a); *Chohan v Saggar* [1992] BCC 306, on appeal [1994] 1 BCLC 706; *Arbuthnot Leasing International Ltd v Havelet Leasing Ltd (No 2)* [1990] BCC 636.

2 Ibid at 645.

3 See pp 382–383 above.

4 *Report of the Review Committee on Insolvency Law and Practice* Cmnd 8558 (1982), p 277, para 1215(b) and p 291, para 1283(b).

5 [1992] BCC 306, on appeal [1994] 1 BCLC 706.

at a significant undervalue. However, it was argued that, even if A might have intended to put assets out of the reach of his creditors, this was not his sole purpose: he also intended to benefit B.

The judge considered that the word 'purpose' had to be construed 'bearing in mind the mischief against which the section in which that word appears is aimed'[1] – which, in the case of s 423, was the removal of assets by their owner, in anticipation of claims being made or contemplated, out of the reach of such claimants. He stated[2] that the words 'for the purposes of' in s 423 were 'equivalent to' the words 'with intent to' in s 172 of the Law of Property Act 1925, and he saw no reason to give s 423 a different meaning, or to approach it differently, from the way in which the Court of Appeal approached s 172 in *Lloyds Bank v Marcan.*[3]

> 'I propose to construe s 423(3) as requiring a plaintiff to demonstrate a dominant purpose to remove assets from the reach of actual or potential claimants or creditors, but as not excluding the possibility that there might also be other purposes behind the relevant transfer. To do otherwise would seem to me to remove s 423 from any practical use in restraining the mischief to which it was directed ...'[4]

In this case, A's dominant purpose had been to remove property from the reach of creditors, and the application of s 423 was not affected by the presence of another intention, namely one to benefit B and others. The transaction was therefore set aside. The Court of Appeal upheld this decision (subject to a slight variation in the form of order). Nothing was said in the judgments in the Court of Appeal regarding Evans-Lombe QC's views on the meaning of the expression 'for the purpose of' and it may therefore be assumed that his observations were thus approved by implication. The same approach seems clearly to have been adopted in *Arbuthnot Leasing International Ltd v Havelet Leasing Ltd (No 2)*,[5] *Agricultural Mortgage Corporation plc v Woodward*,[6] *Royscot Spa Leasing Ltd v Lovett*,[7] *Barclays Bank plc v Eustice*,[8] *Schuppan v Schuppan*[9] and *Jyske Bank (Gibraltar) Ltd v Spjeldnaes (No 2).*[10]

Thus, despite the fact that s 423(3) states that the transaction must have been entered into for 'the' purpose of putting assets beyond the reach of

---

1 Applying the remarks of Lord Oliver in *Brady v Brady* [1989] AC 755 at 779. The remarks of Edward Evans-Lombe QC were approved by the Court of Appeal in both *Royscot Spa Leasing Ltd v Lovett* [1995] BCC 502 and *Barclays Bank plc v Eustice* [1995] 1 WLR 1238 at 1247.

2 [1992] BCC 306 at 321, 323.

3 [1973] 1 WLR 1387; and see pp 342–345 above.

4 [1992] BCC 306 at 323.

5 [1990] BCC 636.

6 [1995] 1 BCLC 1.

7 [1995] BCC 502.

8 [1995] 1 WLR 1238 at 1247.

9 [1997] 1 BCLC 258.

10 [1999] BPIR 525. See also *DEFRA v Feakins* (unreported decision of Penry-Davey J 10 December 2001, Lawtel Doc No C01022527); *National Westminster Bank plc v Jones* [2001] 1 BCLC 98.

creditors or otherwise prejudicing them, the judge decided in *Chohan v Saggar* that a transaction might be set aside if this was just *one* of its purposes. Moreover, it seems that he decided that such a purpose need not even be *the* dominant purpose: the transaction might be set aside if such a purpose was simply *a* dominant purpose.[1] This, too, seems to be implicit in the decisions in both *Arbuthnot Leasing* and *Woodward*. Also, in *Jyske Bank (Gibraltar) Ltd, v Spjeldnaes (No 2)*,[2] Evans-Lombe J expressed the view that, where more than one reason was found for putting into effect a transaction which prejudiced creditors, the intention to defeat creditors must be a dominant purpose, even if it was to defeat creditors generally as opposed to the plaintiff in particular.

This approach was recently confirmed by the Court of Appeal in *IRC v Hashmi*.[3] The statutory purpose under s 423(3) does not have to be the sole, or even the predominant, purpose behind the impugned transaction; it is sufficient if it is a purpose and not merely a consequence of the transaction. The Court of Appeal pointed out that it will frequently be the case that a person's intention to move assets beyond the reach of creditors and, for example, his intention to provide for his family, will be so similar that he himself will not know which purpose was dominant. The crucial requirement is that a s 423(3) purpose is a purpose, rather than a by-product, of the transaction: if it is not of significance to the person or makes no contribution to his decision to effect the transaction, or if it is trivial, it can be excluded.

The question whether a particular purpose is a 'dominant' purpose is presumably a question of fact and will need to be decided on the particular circumstances of each case. It may involve difficult inquiries and give rise to distinctions of some nicety. Communications between the transferor and his legal advisers on how to structure the transaction at an undervalue in question are likely to be considered sufficiently iniquitous not to be subject to the protection of legal professional privilege and, therefore, for public policy to require that they be disclosed on discovery.[4] If it is sufficient that the defeat of creditors was but 'a' dominant purpose (as seems likely), one way of approaching the question may be to adopt a 'but for' test: would the transaction have been entered into but for the purpose of removing assets from the reach of creditors? Such a purpose may not have been the sole, or even the predominant, purpose of the transaction. However, if it were the case that the disponor would not have entered into that transaction unless he hoped and expected to achieve such a purpose, then it seems reasonable to conclude that that purpose was 'a' dominant one. If, on the other hand, he would have entered into the transaction in any event – and defeating his

1 In *Chohan v Saggar* [1992] BCC 306 at 323 the judge referred to both 'a' dominant purpose and 'the' dominant purpose.

2 [1999] BPIR 525.

3 [2002] All ER (D) 71, affirming the decision of Hart J at [2002] BPIR 271.

4 *Barclays Bank plc v Eustice* [1995] 1 WLR 1238; *Royscot Spa Leasing Ltd v Lovett* [1995] BCC 502. See also *Derby & Co v Weldon (No 10)* [1990] 1 WLR 660.

creditors was but an incidental purpose – it seems unreasonable to impeach the transaction under s 423.

Another difficulty is that the words 'intent', 'motive', 'desire' and 'purpose' may have different meanings, but they overlap and, in a particular context, can mean the same thing. As we have seen, in *Re Ledingham-Smith*,[1] Morritt J took the view that, in relation to the words 'influenced … by a desire' in s 340(4) of the 1986 Act, 'intention', 'motive' and 'desire' were different concepts. On the other hand, in *Arbuthnot Leasing International Ltd v Havelet Leasing Ltd (No 2)*[2] in relation to s 423 itself, Scott J referred to 'the intentions, the purpose, the motive – one may choose what word one will'; and Edward Evans-Lombe QC clearly adopted the same approach in *Chohan v Saggar*.

One difficulty is that the word 'purpose' itself does not have a clear meaning and has presented difficulty in other contexts. This is not a question that can be pursued here. However, a few examples may suffice. In *Chandler v DPP*,[3] for example, the House of Lords considered the word 'purpose' in relation to a charge of conspiracy to commit a breach of s 1 of the Official Secrets Act 1911 ('for a purpose prejudicial to the safety or interests of the state'). According to Lord Radcliffe:[4]

> 'All controversies about motives or intentions or purposes are apt to become involved through confusion of the meaning of the different terms and it is perhaps not difficult to show by analysis that the ideas conveyed by these respective words merge into each other without a clear line of differentiation. Nevertheless, a distinction between motive and purpose, for instance, is familiar enough in ordinary discussion …'

Should the word be given a subjective or an objective meaning? Lord Devlin had no doubt that it was subjective.

> 'A purpose must exist in the mind. It cannot exist anywhere else. The word can be used to designate either the main object which a man wants or hopes to achieve by the contemplated act, or it can be used to designate those objects which he knows will probably be achieved by the act, whether he wants them or not. … In the former sense, it cannot in practice be distinguished from motive which is normally irrelevant in criminal law. … a spy could secure an acquittal by satisfying the jury that his purpose was to make money for himself, a purpose not in itself prejudicial to the state, and that he was indifferent to all the other consequences of his acts. Accordingly, all the results which a man appreciates will probably flow from his acts are classifiable as "purposes" within the meaning of s. 1: and since the statute refers to "any purpose", the prosecution is entitled to rely on any of them.'[5]

Lord Pearce, on the other hand, thought that the word 'purpose', 'although it has some subjective content is used in an objective sense'. If the purpose was

---

1 [1993] BCLC 635: see pp 378–379 above.
2 [1990] BCC 636 at 643.
3 [1962] 3 All ER 142.
4 Ibid at 149.
5 Ibid at 155. See also at 146, per Lord Reid.

in fact prejudicial, the offence had been committed, no matter how benevolent the motive may have been.[1]

In *Sweet v Parsley*,[2] the House of Lords had to consider whether the appellant had permitted premises to be used 'for the purpose of smoking cannabis' (under s 5 of the Dangerous Drugs Act 1965). Lord Morris said[3] that the words denoted 'a purpose which is other than quite incidental or casual or fortuitous; they denote a purpose which is or has become either a significant one or a recognised one though certainly not necessarily an only one'. Lord Diplock[4] expressed the view that the word 'purpose' 'connotes an intention by some person to achieve a result desired by him'. He also stated that it is a general principle of construction of any enactment which creates a criminal offence that the words used are to be read as subject to the implication that a necessary element in the offence is the absence of a belief in the existence of facts which, if true, would make the act innocent.

In *Newton v Commissioner of Taxation of the Commonwealth of Australia*,[5] the provision under consideration (in the Privy Council) was s 260 of the Australian Income Tax and Social Services Contribution Assessment Act 1936–1951, which declared that any contract, agreement or arrangement entered into should be void as against the commissioner insofar as it had or purported to 'have the purpose or effect' of avoiding liability to taxation. It was held that 'purpose' meant not motive but the effect it was sought to achieve – the end in view. The statement of Williams J at first instance was adopted:[6]

> 'The purpose of a contract, agreement or arrangement must be what it is intended to effect and that intention must be ascertained from its terms. Those terms may be oral or written or may have to be inferred from the circumstances but, when they have been ascertained, their purpose must be what they effect.'

Or, in the words of Lord Denning:

> 'In order to bring the arrangement within the section you must be able to predicate – by looking at the overt acts by which it was implemented – that it was implemented in that particular way so as to avoid tax. If you cannot so predicate, but have to acknowledge that the transactions are capable of explanation by reference to ordinary business or family dealing, without necessarily being labelled as a means to avoid tax, then the arrangement does not come within the section.'

Where funds had been provided for a settlement, there was a strong inference that they had been provided 'for the purpose of the settlement'

---

1 Ibid at 160.
2 [1970] AC 132.
3 Ibid at 155.
4 Ibid at 165.
5 [1958] AC 450.
6 Ibid at 465.

(within s 454(3) of the Income and Corporation Taxes Act 1970) unless the purpose was shown to be for something else. It was not necessary that there should be a motivating intention to benefit those interested under the settlement.[1] In relation to s 108 of the New Zealand Land and Income Tax Act 1954 ('purpose ... of ... altering the incidence of income tax'), the 'purpose' of a particular transaction had to be determined by what the transaction had effected; and, where one purpose of an arrangement had the effect of altering the incidence of income tax, it did not matter what were the other purposes of the arrangement.[2]

How far (if at all) such cases are relevant to the interpretation of s 423 remains to be seen. There is no obvious reason why the meaning ascribed to a word when it constitutes an essential element of a criminal offence should also be adopted in the context of a civil claim, where the burden of proof is clearly different. In the recent case of *Pagemanor Ltd v Ryan*,[3] it seems to have been held that the wording of s 423 required a *subjective* test of the transferor's state of mind and intentions in making the relevant transfer. Whether this is indeed the case, without any qualification, is surely doubtful. Is the transferor free to set his own standards of honesty, for example? Must he also not be presumed to intend the natural consequences of his actions? In the classic type of case to which s 423 is intended to apply, the motive to defeat creditors and the motive to secure the transferor's family often co-exist, so that even the transferor would be unable to say which was uppermost in his mind;[4] and it seems unduly onerous for any defeated creditor to have to prove a subjective intention on the part of the transferor in such cases. As we have seen,[5] the word 'purpose' must be construed in its particular context which, in this case, is the mischief at which s 423 is aimed, namely:

> 'the removal of assets by their owner, in anticipation of claims being made or contemplated, out of the reach of such claimants if those claims ultimately prove to be successful. It would defeat that purpose if it were possible successfully to contend that if the owner was able to point to another purpose, such as the benefit of his family, friends or the advantage of business associates, the section could not be applied.'[6]

However, if it is indeed the case that the words 'for the purposes of' in s 423 are 'equivalent to' the words 'with intent to' in s 172 of the Law of Property Act 1925 (as was stated in *Chohan v Saggar*), then it seems to follow that the

---

1 *IRC v Mills* [1975] AC 38.

2 *Ashton v IRC* [1975] 1 WLR 1615.

3 Unreported decision of Sonia Proudman QC: 5 February 2002: Lawtel Doc No C0102643.

4 *Commissioners of Inland Revenue v Hashmi* [2002] BPIR 271.

5 See p 385 above.

6 *Chohan v Saggar* [1992] BCC 306 at 321, per Edward Evans-Lombe QC.

cases decided on s 172 (and on the provisions in the 1571 Act which preceded it) remain relevant.[1]

Quistclose trusts

The so-called *Quistclose* trust must also be mentioned briefly, because it could be said to be another kind of asset protection trust. In the case of the straightforward asset protection trust, the purpose of the settlor is to protect his (or its) own assets from creditors in the event of his (or its) own insolvency (actual or threatened). In the case of a *Quistclose* trust, however, the purpose of the settlor is to protect his (or its) assets against creditors in the event of the insolvency of another. The typical example of a true *Quistclose* trust is the case where A lends money to B for the specific purpose of paying that money to C.[2] The overriding interest of A in creating such a trust is not to protect his assets against creditors on his own insolvency, but to protect the loaned money against creditors in the event of B's insolvency; it is a form of security using the trust device. It is, of course, of the essence of both kinds of trust that property which is held by a bankrupt (or by a company in liquidation or receivership) as a trustee and in which he (or it) does not have a beneficial interest will not be available for distribution amongst creditors.[3] This is the case irrespective of the kind of trust upon which the property is held.[4] Nevertheless, a *Quistclose* trust – assuming that it is a distinct kind of trust at all – clearly has a different function and purpose from those of an ordinary asset protection trust. The *Quistclose* trust does not, therefore, warrant detailed examination and analysis in this chapter. However, a brief discussion of its nature and uses, and also of the difficult issues to which it has given rise, may be found in Chapter 6 'Purpose Trusts'.[5]

Public policy

In addition to the specific statutory provisions which have been outlined above, English law prohibits a settlor, on the grounds of public policy, from creating a settlement upon himself until bankruptcy. In such a case, although a

---

1 In *Chohan v Saggar* itself, the judge was clearly guided by the decision in *Lloyds Bank v Marcan* [1973] 1 WLR 1387.

2 It seems clear, however, that the *Quistclose* trust is not confined to cases where money is loaned for the purpose of onward transmission in the discharge of debts to creditors and it may apply wherever money (or another asset) is made available on the condition that it is to be used solely for a stipulated purpose: see, eg, *Re EVTR* [1987] BCLC 646; *Twinsectra Ltd v Yardley* [2002] 2 WLR 802 at 821–831; *General Communications Ltd v Development Finance Corp of New Zealand Ltd* [1990] 3 NZLR 406; *Anderson, Greene & Co Ltd v Kickley* [1934] 3 DLR 787; *Ferguson v City of Toronto* [1944] 3 DLR 317.

3 'It is trite law that only that part of the property of the bankrupt passes to his assignee in which he has both the legal and beneficial interest at the time of the bankruptcy': *Quistclose Investments Ltd v Rolls Razor Ltd* [1968] Ch 540 at 548, per Harman LJ. See also *Mogg v Baker* (1838) 3 M & W 195 at 197, per Parke B.

4 With the exception of 'illusory trusts', which are created by a debtor, for his own convenience, by settling property in favour of his own creditors, and which the court treats as revocable trusts.

5 See **6.2.5** above.

determinable interest has been created, the determining event is regarded as void as against the trustee in bankruptcy and the settlor's interest vests in that trustee.[1] This is so even in the case of an ante-nuptial settlement.[2] On the other hand, if a determining event other than bankruptcy is stipulated (and occurs), allowing the gift over to take effect prior to the bankruptcy of the settlor, the trustee in bankruptcy will be excluded.[3]

Domicile of a trust

The rules of private international law governing the domicile of a trust will clearly have a significant effect on the validity of an asset protection trust and on the jurisdiction of a particular court to set it aside. These rules are dealt with in detail elsewhere in this work, and the reader is referred to the relevant chapters.[4] In England the position is governed, in broad terms, by s 45(3) of the Civil Jurisdiction and Judgments Act 1982[5] which must be read and applied in conjunction with Arts 7 to 10 and 22 of the Hague Convention on the Law Applicable to Trusts and on their Recognition 1985[6] and Arts 5(6) and 60(3) of the Brussels Regulation 2002.[7] Even so, it is often not immediately obvious how the domicile of a trust is to be determined and the process of doing so involves numerous considerations, most of which are usually finely balanced.[8] In any event, the typical asset protection trust will almost certainly be created deliberately in order to take advantage of the laws of a specific jurisdiction and will expressly be made subject to those laws and that jurisdiction.

Reciprocal enforcement of insolvency laws and orders[9]

The effect of an English bankruptcy order is that all the bankrupt's property[10] (apart from specific exempted items) vests automatically in his trustee in bankruptcy, ie it purports to have worldwide effect. In practice, however, the

---

1 *Re Burroughs-Fowler* [1916] 2 Ch 360; *Re Wombwell* (1921) 125 LT 437; *Knight v Browne* (1861) 7 Jur NS 894; *Brooke v Pearson* (1859) 27 Beav 181.

2 *Higinbotham v Holme* (1812) 19 Ves 88; *Ex p Hodgson* (1812) 19 Ves 206 *Re Pearson* (1876) 3Ch D 807.

3 *Re Detmold* (1889) 40 Ch D 585.

4 See Chapters 1 and 3 above.

5 Now re-enacted in Sch 1, para 12 to the Civil Jurisdiction and Judgments Order 2001 (SI 2001/3929).

6 Enacted by the Recognition of Trusts Act 1987. See also J Harris *The Hague Trusts Convention* (Hart Publishing, Oxford, 2002).

7 Replacing the Brussels Convention on Jurisdiction and the Enforcement of Judgments in Civil and Commercial Matters 1968 (as from 1 March 2002). Article 5(6) applies only to express trusts and not to constructive trusts (on which see generally T Yeo 'Constructive Trustees and the Brussels Convention' (2001) 117 LQR 560). See also the Lugano Convention on Jurisdiction and the Enforcement of Judgments in Civil and Commercial Matters 1988 (between EC Member States and EFTA States), which is itself currently being revised in order to bring it into line with the Brussels Regulation 2002.

8 For a thorough survey and analysis of many of these considerations, and the applicable rules of law, as well as the relevant English procedural rules as to service, see the recent judgment of Lawrence Collins J in *Chellaram v Chellaram (No 2)* [2002] EWHC 632 (Ch).

9 See, generally, Chapter 1.

10 IA 1986, s 436 defines 'property' so as to include 'every description of property wherever situated'.

trustee's title to property situated outside the jurisdiction must be established in accordance with the local law. Similarly, it is a matter for the private international law of the *situs* to determine whether recognition will be accorded to the English adjudication, to the trustee's status, and to his title. The trustee's title to foreign assets is likely to be subject to any real rights in the property arising under the *lex situs*; and it is also likely that the courts of the *situs* will accord priority to certain personal rights arising in favour of local creditors.[1] The detailed principles and rules of private international law, as applied in England and Wales, are beyond the scope of this chapter.[2] In broad terms, however, foreign judgments may be enforced in England under the so-called 'doctrine of obligation', ie where a foreign court of competent jurisdiction has adjudicated a certain sum to be due from one person to another, the liability to pay that sum becomes a legal obligation that may be enforced in England by an action of debt.[3] Once the judgment is proved, the burden lies on the defendant to show why he should not perform the obligation.[4] A new right has been vested in the creditor and a new obligation imposed on the debtor at the instance of the foreign court. The liability arises upon an implied contract to pay the amount of the foreign judgment, ie for procedural purposes the debtor is regarded as having implicitly promised to pay.[5] This doctrine (which has effectively replaced the older doctrine of 'comity') thus eliminates any strict requirement of reciprocity.

Nevertheless, at common law, a foreign judgment, although creating an obligation that is actionable in England, cannot be enforced in England here without the institution of fresh legal proceedings.[6] Although a foreign court may have given a judgment which, according to its own system of law, is conclusively binding on the defendant, the circumstances must be such that, in the eyes of English law, the foreign court was justified in assuming jurisdiction. If they are not, the judgment does not create a cause of action that is actionable in England.[7] Thus, it will be highly material whether the defendant owed a duty to obey the command of the tribunal which has purported to create the obligation, for example whether he was/is present in the jurisdiction, or has/had a residence or place of business there, or whether he

---

1 I Fletcher *Cross-Border Insolvency* (JCB Mohr, 1992), pp 228–229. See also P St J Smart *Cross-border Insolvency* (Butterworths, 1998); *Re Roy Clifford Tucker* (unreported) 27 September 1988, Guernsey Court of Appeal.

2 See *Dicey and Morris on the Conflict of Laws* (Sweet & Maxwell, 13th ed, 2000), especially Vol I, Chs 14–16; Cheshire and North *Private International Law* (Butterworths, 13th ed, 1997), especially Ch 15.

3 *Russell v Smyth* (1842) 9 M & W 810; *Adams v Cape Industries plc* [1990] Ch 443 at 552–553; *Owens Bank Ltd v Bracco* [1991] 4 All ER 833 at 844.

4 *Schibsby v Westenholz* (1870) LR 6 QB 155 at 159.

5 *Grant v Easton* (1883) 13 QBD 302. The creditor's action is barred after six years, not after 12 years as in the case of an English judgment: *Re Flynn (No 2)* (1968) 112 Sol Jo 804.

6 Such an action is subject to the Rules of the Supreme Court in the normal manner, including summary judgment: *Grant v Easton* (1883) 13 QBD 302.

7 *Sirdar Gurdyal Singh v The Rajah of Faridkote* [1884] AC 670; *Pemberton v Hughes* [1899] 1 Ch 781; *Salvesen v Administrator of Austrian Property* [1927] AC 641.

submitted to that jurisdiction.[1] Other factors, such as the defendant's nationality, domicile, choice of governing law, and so forth, are more problematic.[2]

Moreover, there are several important limitations. No action is sustainable on a foreign judgment which is contrary to English principles of public policy.[3] Nor will an English court enforce foreign penal laws, either directly or through the recognition of a foreign judgment. (However, a civil judgment, though combined with a penal judgment, may be actionable in England as creating a separate and independent cause of action.)[4] In addition, the foreign judgment must be for a fixed sum: it cannot be a judgment for specific performance or the restitution of chattels, nor a judgment to pay an indefinite sum.[5] These principles of English common law were also generally applied and followed in countries and territories which were formerly British colonies – and in many of which they still continue to apply today.

English courts are also subject to specific statutory provisions. Under the Administration of Justice Act 1920, Part II, a judgment creditor who has obtained a judgment in a Superior Court in some part of the Commonwealth, under which a sum of money is made payable, may apply to the High Court at any time within 12 months (or such longer period as may be allowed by the court) after the date of the judgment, to have that judgment registered in the court; and, if the court thinks it just and convenient that the judgment should be enforced in the United Kingdom, it may order that the judgment be registered accordingly.[6] From the date of such registration, the judgment will have the same force and effect, and proceedings may be taken upon it, as if it were a judgment of the court in which it has been registered.[7] No registration is allowed if the original court acted without jurisdiction.[8]

Section 14 of the Administration of Justice Act 1920 should come into operation only by the issue of an Order in Council extending its provisions to some part of the Commonwealth in which reciprocal provision has been made for the recognition of judgments made in the Superior Courts of the United Kingdom. Part II of the Administration of Justice Act 1920 was, in fact, extended to almost the whole of the Commonwealth.[9] Under the Foreign Judgments (Reciprocal Enforcement) Act 1933, further provision was made

1 *Schibsby v Westenholz* (1870) LR 6 QB 155; *Adams v Cape Industries* [1990] Ch 443. See also Civil Jurisdiction and Judgments Act 1982, s 33(1).

2 See Cheshire and North, n 2 on p 392, pp 419–422.

3 *Re Macartney* [1921] 1 Ch 522; *Dalmia Dairy Industries v National Bank of Pakistan* [1978] 2 Lloyd's Rep 223 at 299–301.

4 See, eg, *Raulin v Fischer* [1911] 2 KB 93.

5 *Sadler v Robins* (1808) 1 Camp 253 at 256.

6 Administration of Justice Act 1920, s 9(1).

7 Ibid, s 9(3)(a).

8 Questions of jurisdiction will probably be determined in accordance with the common law principles outlined above: see pp 391–392.

9 SI 1985/1994.

for the registration of foreign judgments in England, in effect by extending existing provisions to any country which is prepared to afford substantial reciprocity of treatment to UK judgments.[1]

The United Kingdom also subscribed to the Brussels Convention 1968[2] (which was implemented by the Civil Jurisdiction and Judgments Act 1982 (CJJA 1982) and which, as from 1 March 2002, has been replaced for those EC States bound thereby by the Brussels Regulation).[3] Article 1 of the Brussels Convention specifically excluded from its scope 'bankruptcy, proceedings relating to the winding up of insolvent companies or other legal persons, judicial arrangements, compositions and analogous proceedings'. Article 1 of the new Brussels Regulation includes an exclusion in identical terms. This exclusion is wide enough to include proceedings under ss 339 and 238 of the IA 1986. Section 1(3) of the Civil Jurisdiction and Judgments Act 1991 (inserting Sch 3C into the CJJA 1982) also excludes the same matters.[4] Indeed, the European Court of Justice has held that Art 1 extends also to proceedings derived from and closely connected to such insolvency proceedings.[5] However, there are exceptions to this seemingly absolute exclusion.

First, s 25(1) of the CJJA 1982 (as amended) permits an English court to grant interim relief in aid of any foreign 'proceedings', even if the subject matter of those proceedings falls outside the scope of Art 1 (and thus extends to foreign insolvency proceedings).[6] Although this jurisdiction is useful, particularly to foreign representatives appointed in countries which have not been designated for the purposes of s 426 of the IA 1986 (as to which see pp 396–402), it is none the less limited in its scope. It does not affect the type of interim relief which may be granted by the court (eg it does not authorise the appointment of a provisional liquidator in respect of a foreign company).

---

1 Foreign Judgments (Reciprocal Enforcement) Act 1933, s 1. The foreign court must again have jurisdiction: s 4(1)(a)(ii). The relationship between the 1920 Act and the 1933 Act is somewhat complicated: see generally *Dicey and Morris*, n 2 on p 392, p 532 *et seq*; and Cheshire and North, n 2 on p 392, pp 462–473.

2 The Brussels Convention on Jurisdiction and the Enforcement of Judgments in Civil and Commercial Matters (27 September 1968). Article 1 is set out in Sch 1 to the CJJA 1982.

3 Introduced pursuant to Art 65 of the EC Treaty (inserted by the Treaty of Amsterdam). The UK reserved the right to opt out of Art 65, but opted back into this particular initiative. Denmark, which also has an opt-out, has decided not to adopt the Regulation and will continue to apply the Brussels Convention 1968. The basic principle of the Regulation (like the Convention) is that a defendant should be sued in the courts of his domicile. There is no definition of 'domicile' in relation to an individual, so each Member State must apply its own rules in that regard (in the UK, s 41 of the CJJA 1982). However, Art 60(1) defines the 'domicile' of a company (thereby replacing s 42 of the CJJA 1982 in the UK).

4 See the Civil Jurisdiction and Judgments Act 1991, Sch 1 (Title 1, Art 1(2) of the Lugano Convention, which forms the new Sch 3C to the CJJA 1982).

5 *Gourdain v Nadler* Case 133/78 [1979] ECR 733.

6 Civil Jurisdiction and Judgments Act 1982 (Interim Relief) Order 1997 (SI 1997/302). See also Rules of the Supreme Court (Amendment) 1997 (SI 1997/415); and IR Scott (1997) 16 CJQ 185, and P St J Smart (1998) 17 CJQ 149 and (1998) 114 LQR 46.

Moreover, 'proceedings' of some form must be on foot (or contemplated) in a foreign court before an English court can lend its assistance: it is not entirely clear whether the word 'proceedings' indicates that some form of civil litigation must be in progress (or contemplated) or whether it also extends to the foreign insolvency process itself, although the former is likely to be the case.[1]

Secondly, the fact that assets are located in England has often been regarded as a sufficient connection to the forum to make a winding-up order in relation to a foreign company.[2] Thus, where a foreign company is in liquidation abroad and has assets in England, an English court will entertain a winding-up petition coupled with an application for the appointment of a provisional liquidator.[3]

In accordance with the foregoing principles, English law has traditionally afforded assistance and co-operation to office holders in overseas insolvency proceedings, to enable them to act in relation to property located in England and Wales. Thus, foreign bankruptcy proceedings are recognised if they take place in the jurisdiction in which the debtor is domiciled in the eyes of English law, or if the debtor has submitted to the proceedings.[4] Where a foreign adjudication is recognised, English law will also recognise the person appointed under those proceedings as the equivalent of an English trustee in bankruptcy. In respect of the proprietary effects of a foreign adjudication, English law distinguishes between movable and immovable property. The bankrupt's movable property within the jurisdiction of the courts of England and Wales vests automatically in his trustee in bankruptcy (or equivalent) from the time of adjudication, subject, however, to any rights over, or claims to, the property which existed at the time when the trustee's title was acquired. In the case of English immovable property, the foreign adjudication is not capable of effecting a transfer of title, although, in practice, English courts have often been willing to assist the foreign trustee in procuring the vesting of title in himself, for example by compelling the bankrupt to execute a conveyance, or by appointing the foreign trustee as receiver of (and with power to sell) the bankrupt's property.

As from 31 May 2002, a new EU Council Regulation[5] on Insolvency Proceedings has come into force, which introduces provisions governing jurisdiction for opening insolvency proceedings (whether the debtor is a

---

1 See P St J Smart (1998) 17 CJQ 149 at 151; and also *Re International Power Industries NV* [1985] BCLC 128, especially at 137.

2 *Re Compania Merabello San Nicholas SA* [1973] Ch 75. Foreign companies are wound up under Part V of the IA 1986 (as 'unregistered companies').

3 See P St J Smart (1996) 112 LQR 397.

4 Fletcher, n 1 on p 392, pp 232–235. The same probably holds if the debtor is resident, or carried on business, in the country where he is adjudicated bankrupt, but there seems to be no clear authority in point.

5 Council Regulation (EC) No 1346/2000 of 29 May 2000: (2000) OJL 160/1. The UK and Ireland have adopted the Regulation, but not Denmark.

natural or a legal person, a trader or an individual); judgments delivered directly on the basis of insolvency proceedings and closely connected with such proceedings; and also the recognition of those judgments and the applicable law. The Regulation sets out, amongst other things, but only for the matters covered by it, uniform rules on conflict of laws which replace, within their scope of application, national rules of private international law. Broadly, the law of the Member State of the opening of the proceedings should be applicable, a rule that should be valid both for the main proceedings and for local proceedings, and should determine all the effects of the insolvency proceedings, both procedural and substantive, on the persons and legal relations concerned. The term 'insolvency proceedings' means the proceedings listed in Sch A of the Regulation, which, in relation to the United Kingdom, means winding up by or subject to the supervision of the court, creditors' voluntary winding up (with confirmation by the court) and administration.

In any event, proceedings to set aside an alleged transaction at an undervalue under s 423 of the IA 1986 (at least, in circumstances where there is no bankruptcy or winding up) were not excluded by Art 1 of the 1968 Convention,[1] and Art 1 of the new Brussels Regulation will be construed in the same way. Indeed, it is likely that a claim under s 423 brought by a liquidator or trustee in bankruptcy is also not excluded, for the cause of action is still independent of bankruptcy. Thus, reliance on s 423 will have obvious advantages (in comparison, say, with s 339) where the defendant has assets overseas, because questions of service and enforcement ought to be resolved in accordance with standard procedures. Moreover, s 423 almost certainly applies extra-territorially.[2] It will be recalled that s 425(1) of the IA 1986 authorises the court, when making an order under s 423, to require 'any property' transferred as part of the transaction to be vested in 'any person', or to require 'any person' to pay 'any other person' such sums as the court may direct. Section 436 declares that 'property' includes all types of property 'wherever situated'; and there seems to be no reason, in principle, why the words 'any person' should be confined to persons within the United Kingdom.[3]

However, s 426 of the IA 1986[4] now provides a legislative framework for inter-jurisdictional co-operation and reciprocal enforcement of insolvency

1 *Reichert v Dresdner Bank* (Case 115/88) [1990] ECR 1–27; *Reichert v Dresdner Bank (No 2)* (Case 261/90) [1992] ILPr 404; *Aiglon Ltd v Gau Shan Co Ltd* [1993] 1 Lloyd's Rep 164.

2 *Aiglon Ltd v Gan Shan Co Ltd* [1993] 1 Lloyd's Rep 164 (accepted that s 423 could apply to a transfer of money from an English company to a Swiss one). See also *Re Paramount Airways Ltd* [1993] Ch 223 (on s 238); *Re Mid-East Trading Ltd (No 2)* [1997] 3 All ER 481, affirmed [1998] 1 All ER 577 (on s 236); and *Rousou's Trustee v Rousou and Another* [1955] 2 All ER 169, [1955] 3 All ER 486 (transfer of money from one bank account in Cyprus to another attacked under the Law of Property Act 1925, s 172).

3 See *Re Paramount Airways Ltd* [1993] Ch 223, esp at 235–239.

4 Earlier provisions were found in the Bankruptcy Act 1869, s 74, the Bankruptcy Act 1883, s 118, and the Bankruptcy Act 1914, s 122. Cases on these earlier provisions include *Re Levy's Trusts* (1885) 30 Ch D 119; *Galbraith v Grimshaw* [1910] AC 508; *Re Osborn* (1931–32) B & CR 189; *Re Jackson* [1973] NI 67;

orders of all kinds (relating to both corporate and individual insolvencies). This framework is intended to apply not only in relation to England, Wales, Scotland and Northern Ireland, but also to 'any relevant country or territory'.[1] For these purposes, a 'relevant country or territory' means:

(a) any of the Channel Islands or the Isle of Man, or
(b) any country or territory designated for the purposes of s 426 by the Secretary of State by order made by statutory instrument.

The list of countries currently so designated includes: Anguilla, Australia, the Bahamas, Bermuda, Botswana, Brunei Darussalam, Canada, the Cayman Islands, the Falkland Islands, Gibraltar, Hong Kong, Republic of Ireland, Malaysia, Montserrat, New Zealand, St Helena, Republic of South Africa, the Turks and Caicos Islands, Tuvalu and the British Virgin Islands.[2] However, the operation of s 426 is confined to cases where a request for co-operation is made by *a court* in the overseas country or territory, and it is not competent for an office-holder to make a direct approach for assistance. Moreover, major trading partners such as the United States, France, Germany and Japan are not included in the list of designated countries.

Section 426 does not abolish or curtail the pre-existing common law rules dealing with international co-operation in insolvency matters: on the contrary, it now provides an additional basis for affording assistance to certain jurisdictions. One of the limiting factors under the common law rules was (and is) the requirement that the foreign adjudication was final and for a definite sum, and assistance is not directly available for restitution of assets. Section 426, however, is not so confined and thereby seems to extend the scope of remedies which may be granted. Section 426(4) declares that the courts having jurisdiction in relation to 'insolvency law' in any part of the United Kingdom 'shall assist' the courts having the corresponding jurisdiction[3] in any other part of the United Kingdom or any relevant country or territory. For the purposes of s 426 'insolvency law' means, in relation to any relevant country or territory, so much of the law of that country or territory as corresponds to provisions falling within paras (a)–(c) of s 426(10).[4] A request made to a court in any part of the United Kingdom by a court in a relevant country or territory is authority for the court to which the request is made to

and *Re a Debtor ex parte the Viscount of the Royal Court of Jersey* [1981] Ch 384. On s 426 generally, see *Re Woloniecki* (1986) 35 ICLQ 644.

1 IA 1986, s 426(4).

2 SI 1986/2123; SI 1996/253; SI 1998/2766.

3 As Lawrence Collins J pointed out in *Re Television Trade Rentals Ltd* [2002] EWHC 211 (Ch) (unreported), 19 February 2002, at [12], '*having a corresponding jurisdiction*' means that the foreign court must be the court with jurisdiction in insolvency matters, and not the court which would have jurisdiction in the foreign country to do what is asked in England. See also *Re Dallhold Estates (UK) Pty Ltd* [1992] BCLC 621 and *Re Bank of Credit and Commerce International SA (No 9)* [1994] 3 All ER 764.

4 IA 1986, s 426(10), (11).

apply, in relation to any matters specified in the request, the insolvency law which is applicable by either court in relation to comparable matters falling within its jurisdiction.

Thus, a foreign office-holder (acting through a request made by the relevant foreign court) could apparently enlist the assistance of an English court in impeaching a transaction made at an undervalue, or even in applying some remedy of foreign law. In exercising its discretion under subsection (5), a court is directed to have regard in particular to the rules of private international law.[1] It is not entirely clear how this restriction will be interpreted and applied. It has been suggested that the discretion being referred to is that of the *requesting* court,[2] but this has been rejected and, instead, it has been suggested that it means the discretion of the *requested* court to refuse assistance on the ground, for example, that the request infringes the rule that foreign tax claims will not be enforced.[3] In *Re Television Trade Rentals Ltd*,[4] Lawrence Collins J suggested (obiter) that this 'obscure and ill-thought out provision' meant that the court should take into account the foreign elements in deciding which law to apply, such as the connections of the parties with England and with the foreign country.[5] In any event, there seems to be no obvious reason why it should prevent an English court, in appropriate circumstances, from assisting a foreign court in the avoiding of voidable transactions. The underlying principle of s 426 is that a trustee in bankruptcy may obtain the assistance of the local court in gaining control of assets; and the international effect of a foreign (or an English) adjudication remains subject to the local rules of the private international law of each jurisdiction in which assets of the debtor are located.

The interpretation and scope, as well as the legislative history, of s 426 were considered by the Court of Appeal in *Hughes v Hannover Ruckversicherungs-Aktiengesellschaft*.[6] According to Morritt LJ, the reference to 'insolvency law' in s 426(4) serves to identify the courts in any part of the United Kingdom on which the obligation to assist is cast. There is nothing in s 426 to exclude the general jurisdiction and powers vested in those courts as such under the laws of England and Wales. The purpose of subsection (5) is not to reduce that jurisdiction or those powers, but to extend them for the purposes of subsection (4). Thus, a court in England, faced with a request from a relevant country, may, in respect of the matters specified in such request, apply either the insolvency law of the relevant country concerned or its own insolvency law. The concluding words of subsection (5) introduce the hypothesis that the

---

1 Ibid, s 426(5).

2 *Re Dallhold Estates (UK) Pty Ltd* [1992] BCLC 621 at 626.

3 *Re BCCI SA (No 9)* [1994] 3 All ER 764 at 785; *Re Television Trade Rentals Ltd* [2002] EWHC 211 (Ch), (unreported), 19 February 2002, at [**17**].

4 (Above) at [**17**].

5 In the case before him, this issue did not arise because there was no case for the application of Isle of Man law.

6 [1997] 1 BCLC 497.

matters specified in the request fall within the jurisdiction of the court applying the insolvency law under consideration insofar as 'comparable matters' do so. There is available to an English court, when asked for assistance by the court of a relevant country under s 426:

(a) its own general jurisdiction and powers;[1] and either
(b) the insolvency law of England and Wales as provided for in the Insolvency Act 1986, the specified sections of the Company Directors Disqualification Act 1986 and the subordinate legislation made under any of those provisions;[2] or
(c) so much of the law of the relevant country as corresponds to that comprised in (b).[3]

The request has a dual effect: it informs the English court what assistance is sought for the purposes of subsection (4); and it is the trigger to the enlarged jurisdiction for which subsection (5) provides.

Nevertheless, the obligation to assist is imposed on a court and not some executive agency. The function of the court under s 426 must be to consider whether, in accordance with the three sources of law identified earlier, the assistance may properly be granted. If it may, then it should be; if not, then it should be withheld. If the English court cannot do exactly what is sought, then it should consider whether it can properly assist in some other way in accordance with any of the available sources of law. Public policy may be one reason for refusing assistance, but it is not the only reason. The assistance is discretionary. The fact of the request is itself a weighty factor to be taken into account; and the English court may be expected to accept without further investigation the views of the requesting court. Moreover, the response of the English court will depend on the interaction of s 426 of the IA 1986 and the provisions of the CJJA 1982. Thus, if an English court has made an order at the suit of a creditor under s 423 of the 1986 Act, such an order must be enforced (if enforced at all) in Scotland or Northern Ireland under s 426(1), but it would be enforceable in (say) France or Germany under the Brussels Regulation 2002 (not being excluded by Art 1 of that Regulation and not being included within s 426 of the IA 1986). If a Scottish resident creditor enters a claim in an English insolvency, but has also attached the debtor's property in France, an injunction granted by the English court restraining the creditor from continuing with French proceedings cannot be enforced in France (being excluded by Art 1 of the Brussels Regulation 2002 and being outside the scope

---

1 The judges in *Re Osborn* (1931–32) B & CR 189, *Re Jackson* [1973] NI 67, and *Re a Debtor ex parte the Viscount of the Royal Court of Jersey* [1981] Ch 384, were said to have applied (a).

2 Chadwick J was said to have applied (b) in *Re Dallhold Estates (UK) Pty Ltd* [1992] BCLC 621.

3 Rattee J was said to have applied (b) and (c) in *Re Bank of Credit and Commerce International SA (No 9)* [1994] 2 BCLC 636. See also *Re JN Taylor Finance Property Ltd, England v Purves* [1999] BCC 197. See also *Re Television Trade Rentals Ltd* [2002] EWHC 211 (Ch), (unreported) 19 February 2002.

of s 426). However, it could be enforced in Scotland under s 18 of the CJJA 1982 (requiring reciprocal enforcement of judgments as between different parts of the United Kingdom) because, according to *Hughes v Hannover*, the jurisdiction to grant an extra-territorial injunction is derived from the court's general equitable jurisdiction and is not part of its 'insolvency law' jurisdiction under s 426.[1]

Nevertheless, the request itself can never be conclusive as to the manner in which the discretion of the court should be exercised. Thus, the approach of Richard Scott V-C in *Re Focus Insurance Company*[2] – summarising the views of Chadwick J in *Re Dallhold Estates (UK) Pty Ltd*[3] ('do what you are asked unless there is a compelling reason not to do so') and Rattee J in *Re Bank of Credit and Commerce International SA (No 9)*[4] ('do what you are asked unless there is some good reason for not doing so') – was approved. In *Hughes* itself, assistance in response to a letter of request from the Supreme Court of Bermuda was refused, on the basis that the property and the dispute in question was substantially in Massachusetts and there was no sufficient connection with England. Similarly, in *Re JN Taylor Finance Property Ltd, England v Purves*,[5] a request from the Supreme Court of South Australia for an order for the oral examination in England of certain parties to winding-up proceedings in South Australia was refused, on the basis that there was a divergence in the practice of English and Australian courts in the exercise of their discretion to order the examination of witnesses[6] and that a departure from the English practice was considered oppressive (although an order for production of documents was granted). However, s 426 of the IA 1986 was considered further in the more recent case of *Re Southern Equities Corp Ltd*,[7] where the Supreme Court of South Australia requested the English court to exercise its jurisdiction to assist it by making an order requiring the oral examination of the respondent (a partner in a firm of UK accountants) in accordance with Australian law and procedure. The respondent, who was a potential witness at a trial in South Australia, was not obliged, under Australian procedural rules, to provide a witness statement of his evidence to a liquidator in advance of the trial. Judge Weeks QC, at first instance, considered the decisions in *Hughes v Hannover*

---

1 See P St J Smart (1998) 17 CJQ 149 at 162.

2 [1996] BCC 659.

3 [1992] BCLC 621. It is not entirely clear, in fact, whether Chadwick J was prepared to concede any discretion to the court: see 626.

4 [1994] 2 BCLC 636.

5 [1999] BCC 197.

6 There was no reported Australian case where an order for examination under s 596B of the Australian Corporations Law had been refused on the ground that the corporation was currently being proceeded against by a liquidator in respect of a claim forming part of the subject matter, which it was the intention of the proposed examination to enquire into; whereas there was no reported English case where an examination had been allowed to proceed after a liquidator had commenced such proceedings against a proposed examinee.

7 [2000] 2 WLR 1141, [2000] 2 BCLC 21.

Ruckversicherungs-AG[1] and *Re JN Taylor Finance Pty Ltd*[2] and held that he had jurisdiction to make the order sought by the combined effect of s 596B of the Corporations Law (Aust) and s 426 of the IA 1986, and that, if the application had been made to a judge sitting in Australia, such an order would have been made; but he refused to make a similar order on the ground that a comparable application made by a liquidator of a company being wound up in England under s 236 of the IA 1986 (which was similar to s 596B) would be rejected as being oppressive of the witness.[3]

However, the Court of Appeal allowed the appeal of the liquidator. According to the Court of Appeal, when faced with such a request the court had a choice, afforded by s 426(5) of the IA 1986, of applying either s 236 of the IA 1986 or s 596B of the Australian Corporations Law. Once the court had chosen to apply s 596B, it had to direct itself by reference to the law of Australia, and s 236 of the IA 1986 ceased to have any relevance. Were it otherwise, s 426 of the IA 1986 would be deprived of much of its effect, since the choice of law of the requesting court would be circumscribed by limitations to be found in the corresponding provisions of the insolvency law of England. Furthermore, since one of the objects of s 426 was to provide for some form of reciprocal assistance for insolvencies with an international dimension,[4] it would be inconsistent with the need for comity evident in the framework provided for by the section to stigmatise either the substantive law or the exercise by the requesting court of the jurisdiction thereby conferred as oppressive. Moreover, in both jurisdictions the principles observed by the courts were directed to avoiding oppression of the witness, although the method by which that aim was to be achieved was different. Morritt LJ concluded[5] that both the decision of Evans-Lombe J in *Re JN Taylor Finance Pty Ltd*[6] and that of Judge Weeks QC in the present case involved:

> '(1) restricting the expression "insolvency law" so as to exclude the principles and practice in accordance with which the requesting court exercises its statutory jurisdiction, (2) ignoring the need for comity evident in the framework provided for by the section, and (3) giving no weight to the request.'

It followed that the judge had exercised his discretion on the wrong basis in refusing to make the order sought and had ignored the need for comity. Since

---

1 [1997] 1 BCLC 497.

2 [1999] 2 BCLC 256. It is clear from Morritt LJ's judgment in *Re Southern Equities* that he considered that Evans-Lombe J's judgment in *Re JN Taylor* (like Judge Weeks' decision in *Re Southern Equities* itself) was based on fallacious reasoning: see [2000] 2 BCLC 21 at 63.

3 See also *Cloverbay Ltd (joint administrators) v Bank of Credit anal Commerce International SA* [1991] Ch 90; and *British and Commonwealth Holdings plc (joint administrators) v Spicer & Oppenheim (a firm)* [1993] AC 426.

4 As Morritt LJ pointed out ([2000] 2 BCLC 21 at 64), this is confined, of course, to countries or territories with insolvency laws corresponding to the IA 1986, as designated by the Secretary of State.

5 Ibid at 64. Laws and Jonathan Parker LJJ agreed.

6 [1999] 2 BCLC 256. See also *Re Television Trade Rentals Ltd* [2002] EWHC 211 (Ch), (unreported) 19 February 2002, at [**13**].

there was no consideration of sufficient weight to justify not giving the assistance requested, the appeal was allowed and the relief sought by the liquidator was granted.

Recently, in *Re Television Trade Rentals Ltd*,[1] Lawrence Collins J considered applications by joint provisional liquidators of two Isle of Man companies for assistance to the High Court of Justice, Isle of Man: specifically, the request was for a declaration that the provisions of Part I of the IA 1986 (relating to company voluntary arrangements)[2] should apply to the two Isle of Man companies pursuant to the provisions of s 426 – this apparently being the first request made to extend Part I of the Act to overseas companies. Having pointed out that s 426 had been used to apply to foreign companies the provisions of the IA 1986 relating to administration orders, to transactions at an undervalue, to fraudulent and wrongful trading, and to the examination of officers, Lawrence Collins J concluded that the special features of company voluntary arrangements did not preclude s 426 orders applying to them for Isle of Man companies. It was true that court involvement in such arrangements was minimal, but reports and accounts had to be filed with the court, and the court had an important supervisory role. He did not consider that the court had the power to make such orders retrospectively but, in the circumstances of this case, he made the relevant orders with effect from the date of judgment.

Other considerations

There are other considerations which anyone involved in setting up, administering, or even advising upon, asset protection trusts must bear in mind. In particular, there are several grounds on which the adviser himself, and not just the debtor-client, may be pursued by, and perhaps held liable to, a creditor. In addition, there are specific sanctions in English criminal law of which an adviser must be aware. This is not the place to deal with such wide-ranging matters. However, the following specific considerations will be mentioned.

Constructive trusteeship

There is a risk that an adviser may become liable to a creditor as constructive trustee. The danger is illustrated by *Finers (A Firm) v Miro*,[3] for example, where a partner in a firm of solicitors had set up an intricate network of overseas companies and trusts to hold the client's assets. Subsequently, an investigation into the affairs of one of these companies gave rise to allegations of fraud against the client. The solicitors became concerned that some of the client's assets held by them may have been acquired from misappropriated funds.

---

1 [2002] EWHC 211 (Ch), (unreported) 19 February 2002.

2 Company voluntary arrangements are not known under the Isle of Man legislation. The application was made under s 426 of the IA 1986 because it was uncertain whether Part I of the Act was otherwise capable of being applied to overseas companies.

3 [1991] 1 All ER 182.

They froze the client's account and assets and applied to the court for directions as to how they should deal with these assets. The client applied to have the proceedings struck out.

The Court of Appeal held that, where a solicitor had strong evidence of suspected fraud on the part of a client, he was entitled, under the rule that fraud unravelled all obligations of confidence, to apply to the court (either under its inherent jurisdiction or under the Rules of the Supreme Court) for directions as to how to deal with the client's assets, notwithstanding the inevitable breach of the solicitor's duty of confidence to his client. Because the solicitor was potentially liable as constructive trustee at the suit of those entitled to assets misappropriated by the fraud, the court could direct the solicitor to notify interested persons of the existence of the proceedings.

There are, of course, several ways in which an adviser may become liable as constructive trustee. If he actually receives property which is subject to another's equitable interest (and assuming he is not a *bona fide* purchaser for value without notice), he will hold that property subject to such equitable interest. The beneficiary or true owner will then have a proprietary remedy against the transferee and will be able to recover the property itself (or other property representing it). If no such property (or insufficient property) remains in the transferee's hands, the beneficiaries or true owners may still have a personal remedy against the transferee, on the basis of his 'knowing receipt' of such property. In other cases, the adviser may never have received such property, but, because of his conduct, he may still be liable to account as a constructive trustee.[1] The law in this area has recently been considered extensively and clarified by the courts, although this chapter cannot deal with the relevant principles and authorities in any detail.[2] The following general observations may be made here, however.

A person who receives trust property (or property subject to a fiduciary obligation) with knowledge that it is trust property (or subject to such obligation) will hold that property (or its traceable proceeds) as constructive trustee, subject to the pre-existing equitable interests. If the recipient no longer holds the property (or its traceable proceeds) he may still be personally liable

---

1 *Barnes v Addy* (1874) 9 Ch App 244, especially at 251–252.

2 There is a large (and growing) body of literature on the subjects of 'knowing receipt' and 'knowing assistance'. See, eg, Goff and Jones *The Law of Restitution* (Butterworths, 5th ed, 1998), especially at pp 742–746; RP Austin and PD Finn (eds) *Essays in Equity* (Law Book Co Ltd, 1985), Ch 11; P Finn in D Waters (ed) *Equity, Fiduciaries and Trusts* (Carswell, 1993), Ch 10; PBH Birks (ed) *The Frontiers of Liability* (OUP, 1994); C Harpum (1986) 102 LQR 114 and 267; S Gardner (1996) 112 LQR 56; AJ Oakley 'The Liberalising Nature of Remedies for Breach of Trust' in Oakley (ed) *Trends in Contemporary Trust Law* (OUP, 1996), pp 239–247; C Harpum (1995) 111 LQR 545; M Halliwell [1995] Conv 339; R Nolan (1995) 54 CLJ 505; Berg (1997) 60 MLR 443; W Blair (2000) 30 Hong Kong LJ 74; J Chan (2001) 31 Hong Kong LJ 283; and A Stafford (2001) 17 PN 3. See also *Re Polly Peck (No 2)* [1998] 3 All ER 812, which has effectively rejected the possibility of a 'remedial' constructive trust in English law.

to account as a constructive trustee.[1] In either case, the knowledge of the recipient is critical.

In the *Baden* case,[2] Peter Gibson J identified five different categories of knowledge, namely:

> '(i) actual knowledge; (ii) wilfully shutting one's eyes to the obvious; (iii) wilfully and recklessly failing to make such inquiries as an honest and reasonable man would make; (iv) knowledge of circumstances which would indicate the facts to an honest and reasonable man; (v) knowledge of circumstances which would put an honest and reasonable man on inquiry.'

Categories (i)–(iii) inclusive clearly involve a higher degree of culpability; categories (iv) and (v) are commonly referred to as constituting the 'negligent standard' of notice. Until recently,[3] it was a matter of some uncertainty whether, in English law, a person could be made liable for 'knowing receipt' only if he had a degree of knowledge falling within categories (i)–(iii) above (or any one of them), or whether it would suffice if he was brought within category (iv) or (v). It was argued that some early authorities,[4] which were followed in *Baden*, took the view that knowledge of any one of the five kinds (including the 'negligent standard') would suffice. However, subsequent cases, referring to other pre-*Baden* decisions,[5] emphasised the need for dishonesty.[6] In the recent case of *Bank of Credit and Commerce International (Overseas) Ltd v Akindele*,[7] the Court of Appeal reviewed these earlier cases and clarified the law as to 'knowing receipt'.[8]

Similarly, where a stranger knowingly assists a trustee or fiduciary in a fraudulent and dishonest design, that stranger may be held to account as a constructive trustee. This liability – which is likely to be the more problematic for any adviser in the particular context of asset protection – is a personal

---

1 See, eg, *Re Montagu's Settlement Trusts* [1987] Ch 264; *Lipkin Gorman v Karpnale Ltd* [1992] 4 All ER 331; *Bank of Credit and Commerce International (Overseas) Ltd v Akindele* [2000] 4 All ER 221.

2 *Baden, Delvaux et Lecuit v Société Générale pour Favoriser le Développement du Commerce et de l'Industrie en France SA* [1983] BCLC 325 at 407. *Cf Eagle Trust plc v SBC Securities Ltd* [1992] 4 All ER 488.

3 *Bank of Credit and Commerce International (Overseas) Ltd v Akindele* [2000] 4 All ER 221.

4 See, eg, *Selangor United Rubber Estates v Cradock (No 3)* [1968] 1 WLR 1555; *Karak Rubber Co Ltd v Burden (No 2)* [1972] 1 All ER 1210; *Rowlandson v National Westminster Bank Ltd* [1978] 3 All ER 370; *Belmont Finance Corpn v Williams* [1979] 1 All ER 118. See also *Powell v Thompson* [1991] 1 NZLR 597; *Equitcorp Industries Group Ltd v Hawkins* [1991] 3 NZLR 700; *Marshall Futures Ltd v Marshall* [1992] 1 NZLR 316.

5 See, eg, *Carl-Zeiss Stiftung v Herbert Smith & Co (No 2)* [1969] 2 Ch 276; *Competitive Insurance Co Ltd v Davies Investments Ltd* [1975] 1 WLR 1240.

6 *Re Montagu's Settlement Trusts* [1987] Ch 264; *Lipkin Gorman v Karpnale Ltd* [1987] 1 WLR 987, [1989] 1 WLR 1340; *Cowan de Groot Properties Ltd v Eagle Trust plc* [1992] 4 All ER 700; *Agip (Africa) Ltd v Jackson* [1990] Ch 265; *Eagle Trust plc v SBC Securities Ltd* [1993] 1 WLR 484; *Polly Peck International plc v Nadir (No 2)* [1992] 4 All ER 769; *Royal Brunei Airlines Sdn Bhd v Tan* [1995] 2 AC 378; *Brown v Bennett* [1999] BCC 91. The two lines of authority are analysed in *Eagle Star v SBC Securities* [1996] BCLC 121 at 147–152, per Arden J; and *Citadel General Assurance Co v Lloyds Bank Canada* (1997) 152 DLR 411. See also *Grupo Torras SA v Sheikh Fahad Mohammed Al Sabah* [1999] CLC 1469.

7 [2000] 4 All ER 221.

8 See also pp 406–407 below.

liability and the stranger need not ever have received or held trust property in his own hands. As in the case of 'knowing receipt', with which cases of 'knowing assistance' are obviously closely related, the law in this area has recently experienced rapid development. It would seem, however, that the prevailing view, in relation to cases of 'knowing assistance' (as opposed to 'knowing receipt'), is that the degree of knowledge of the fraudulent and dishonest design required in order to render a stranger liable must be such that it falls within one of the *Baden* categories (i)–(iii), ie it must involve dishonesty of some kind, and satisfying the 'negligence standard' (ie categories (iv) and (v)) will not suffice.[1]

Indeed, both the Privy Council and the House of Lords have recently reviewed earlier authorities on 'knowing assistance' and concluded that *dishonesty* is an essential ingredient of accessory liability. In *Royal Brunei Airlines Sdn Bhd v Tan*,[2] in the Privy Council, Lord Nicholls pointed out that the word 'knowingly' was better avoided and the 'scale of knowledge' set out in *Baden* best forgotten. He also emphasised that dishonesty is an objective standard and means simply not acting as an honest person would act in the circumstances. It clearly has a subjective element (in that it is assessed partly according to what a person actually knows at the relevant time). Dishonesty is not the same as carelessness or imprudence, and it is generally equated with conscious impropriety. However, individuals are not free to set their own standards of honesty in particular circumstances.[3] Although this was a decision of the Privy Council, it has been applied in subsequent English cases. It was applied by the Court of Appeal in *Twinsectra Ltd v Yardley*,[4] for example; and in *Bank of America v Arnell*,[5] Aikens J, after referring to the five-fold classification of 'knowledge' in *Baden*, stated:[6]

> 'The case law has moved on since that decision. ... I think that it is clear from the judgment of Potter LJ in [*Twinsectra*] that the fundamental question that the court has to ask now is: was the recipient acting *honestly* when he received the funds? If he knows that the funds originated from a dishonest transaction or as a result of a breach of fiduciary duty, then no question arises. He is dishonest. Alternatively, the recipient may *wilfully* shut his eyes to the obvious facts ... Alternatively, it may be that the recipient, given his background knowledge and experience, would be *bound* to ask questions of the person who wished to pass on the funds and if he does not, either *wilfully or recklessly*, then he will be judged as having acted dishonestly. Potter LJ makes it clear that although the question of honesty must be viewed

1 See the cases cited in n 6 on p 385.

2 [1995] 2 AC 378.

3 *Royal Brunei Airlines Sdn Bhd v Tan* [1995] 2 AC 378, esp at 385–392. See also *Brink's Ltd v Abu-Saleh* [1996] CLC 133; *Dubai Aluminium Co Ltd v Salaam* [1999] 1 Lloyd's Rep 415; *Grupo Torras SA v Sheikh Fahad Mohammed Al Sabah* [1999] CLC 1469. On 'dishonesty' in the context of fraudulent trading by a company, see *Aktieselskabet Dansk Skibsfinansiering v Brothers* [2001] 2 BCLC 324.

4 [1999] Lloyd's Rep Bank 438.

5 [1999] Lloyd's Rep Bank 399.

6 Ibid at 406–407.

> objectively, the issue must be judged by reference to the character, background, profession and likely experience of the alleged "knowing recipient".'

The *Royal Brunei* test was also applied by Mance J in *Grupo Torras SA v Al-Sabah.*[1]

The question has finally been resolved by the House of Lords in the recent decision in *Twinsectra Ltd v Yardley*,[2] where the majority[3] adopted and applied the observations of Lord Nicholls in *Royal Brunei.* The first question facing the House of Lords was simply what Lord Nicholls had actually meant. The majority of the House understood him to have adopted a 'combined test' of dishonesty in *Royal Brunei* – one which combined an objective test and a subjective test.[4] In other words, in order to establish a defendant's liability for 'knowing assistance', more was required than knowledge of the facts which made the conduct wrongful: a dishonest state of mind – a 'consciousness that one is transgressing ordinary standards of honest behaviour'[5] – was also required. On the other hand, Lord Millett (dissenting) preferred the view that Lord Nicholls had adopted an objective standard of dishonesty by which the defendant was expected to attain the standard which would be observed by an honest person placed in similar circumstances. Account could be taken of subjective considerations such as the defendant's experience and intelligence and his actual state of knowledge at the relevant time, but it was not necessary that he should actually have appreciated that he was acting dishonestly: 'The question is whether an honest person would appreciate that what he was doing wrong or improper, not whether the defendant himself actually appreciated this'.[6] Whatever Lord Nicholls may have meant, as far as the House of Lords was concerned, the question was, of course, at large and the House could resolve it either way. In the event, however, the majority adopted the 'combined test' of *Royal Brunei* and held that, for a person to be liable as an accessory to a breach of trust, he had to have acted dishonestly by the ordinary standards of reasonable and honest people and have been himself aware that by those standards he was acting dishonestly.

Whether the same test should also apply to cases of 'knowing receipt' is, of course, a different matter – and one that was not decided in *Twinsectra* or *Royal Brunei.*

In the recent case of *Bank of Credit and Commerce International (Overseas) Ltd v Akindele*,[7] the Court of Appeal reviewed earlier authorities and considered the question whether the *Royal Brunei* test of 'dishonesty' in cases of 'knowing assistance' also applied to cases of 'knowing receipt'. The essence of the Court

---

1 [1999] CLC 1469.
2 [2002] 2 WLR 802.
3 Lord Slynn, Lord Steyn, Lord Hoffmann and Lord Hutton; Lord Millett dissented.
4 [2002] 2 WLR 802 at 809, per Lord Hutton.
5 Ibid at 807, per Lord Hoffmann. See also 812, per Lord Hutton.
6 Ibid at 836.
7 [2000] 4 All ER 221.

of Appeal's decision is that, just as there was a single test of dishonesty for 'knowing assistance', there should also be a single test of knowledge for 'knowing receipt'. Although a categorisation of different states of knowledge which might or might not result in a finding of dishonesty for the purposes of 'knowing assistance' was often helpful, its utility in cases of 'knowing receipt' was doubtful. All that was necessary was that the recipient's state of knowledge should be such as to make it unconscionable for him to retain the benefit of that receipt. The essential requirements of 'knowing receipt' were said to have been stated by Hoffmann LJ in *El Ajou v Dollar Land Holdings plc*:[1]

> 'For this purpose the plaintiff must show, first, a disposal of his assets in breach of fiduciary duty; secondly, the beneficial receipt by the defendant of assets which are traceable as representing the assets of the plaintiff; and thirdly, knowledge on the part of the defendant that the assets received are traceable to a breach of fiduciary duty.'

As *Belmont Finance Corporation v Williams Furniture*[2] had shown, a claim in 'knowing receipt' could succeed even though a claim in 'knowing assistance' might not; and it was clear authority for the proposition that dishonesty is not a necessary ingredient of liability in 'knowing receipt'. The same had been held in *Polly Peck International plc v Nadir (No 2)*,[3] *Agip (Africa) Ltd v Jacksons*[4] and *Eagle Trust plc v SBC Securities Ltd*.[5] The essential element was 'knowledge'. However, constructive knowledge (as under the doctrine of notice) was not sufficient, or even the same thing. As Megarry V-C had pointed out in *Re Montagu's Settlement Trusts*,[6] there was a fundamental distinction between notice and knowledge: the former was concerned with the question of whether a person took property subject to or free from some equity; the latter was concerned with whether or not a person was to have imposed upon him the personal burdens and obligations of trusteeship. The practical distinction manifested itself when the assets in question had been received and subsequently disposed of: unless the recipient had the requisite knowledge to constitute him a constructive trustee, there was no liability if the assets had gone and there were no traceable proceeds. The effect of this decision was that, in order to establish liability in 'knowing receipt', the recipient must have actual knowledge (or the equivalent) that the assets received are traceable to a breach of trust. There were decisions which seemed to suggest that constructive knowledge would suffice, but, on closer analysis, they were either cases in which actual knowledge was established or cases of 'knowing assistance' and not receipt.

---

1 [1994] 2 All ER 685 at 700.
2 [1980] 1 All ER 393.
3 [1992] 4 All ER 769 at 777.
4 [1992] 4 All ER 385 at 404.
5 [1992] 4 All ER 488 at 501.
6 [1992] 4 All ER 308 at 319.

Nourse LJ noted that, despite the observations of Lord Nicholls in *Royal Brunei* to the effect that the *Baden* classification was best forgotten, he himself thought that it is often helpful in identifying different states of knowledge, which may or may not result in a finding of dishonesty for the purposes of 'knowing assistance'. In any event, in the context of 'knowing receipt', the purpose to be served by a categorisation of knowledge was to enable the court to determine whether the recipient can 'conscientiously retain [the] funds' – or whether the recipient's 'conscience is sufficiently affected for it to be right to bind him by the obligations of a constructive trustee'. However, if that was the sole purpose, then there was no need for a categorisation. All that was necessary was that the recipient's state of knowledge must be such as to make it unconscionable for him to retain the benefit of the receipt. The Court of Appeal acknowledged that a test expressed in this form cannot avoid difficulties of application, but that it ought to avoid those of definition and allocation to which the previous categorisations had led. Moreover, it should enable the courts to give commonsense decisions in the commercial context, in which claims for 'knowing receipt' are now commonly made.

Criminal offences and criminal conspiracy[1]

Chapter VI of Part IX of the Insolvency Act 1986 contains a number of provisions prescribing offences which may be committed under the Act and the penalties for those offences. In particular, s 357(1) of the 1986 Act declares that a bankrupt is guilty of an offence if he makes, or causes to be made, or has in the period of five years ending with the commencement of the bankruptcy made or caused to be made, any gift or transfer of, or any charge on, his property. (This includes causing or conniving at the levying of any execution against the property.)[2] The bankrupt is also guilty of an offence if he conceals or removes, or has at any time before the commencement of the bankruptcy concealed or removed, any part of his property after, or within two months before, the date on which a judgment or order for the payment of money has been obtained against him, being a judgment or order which was not satisfied before the commencement of the bankruptcy.[3] (The 'commencement of bankruptcy' means the day on which a bankruptcy order is made.[4]) He is not guilty of an offence if he proves that, at the time of the conduct constituting the alleged offence, he had no intent to defraud or to conceal the state of his affairs.[5] If he is found guilty of an offence, the bankrupt is liable to imprisonment or a fine or both.[6]

1 See, generally, Smith and Hogan *Criminal Law* (Butterworths, 8th ed, 1996), pp 277–313.
2 Insolvency Act 1986, s 357(2).
3 Ibid, s 357(3).
4 Ibid, ss 278(a), 381(2).
5 Ibid, s 352.
6 Ibid, s 350(6).

Of more direct concern to those who advise a transferor on a course of action intended to defraud his creditors, or who assist him in such a course, is the possibility that they could themselves be guilty of the common law offence of conspiracy to defraud (preserved by s 5(2) of the Criminal Law Act 1977 (CLA 1977)) or of the offence of aiding and abetting the debtor to commit the statutory offence of conspiracy.

Section 1(1) of the CLA 1977 provides as follows:

> 'Subject to the following provisions of this Part of this Act, if a person agrees with any other person or persons that a course of conduct shall be pursued which will necessarily amount to or involve the commission of any offence or offences by one or more of the parties to the agreement if the agreement is carried out in accordance with their intentions, he is guilty of conspiracy to commit the offence or offences in question.'

Although the offence of conspiracy at common law was abolished by s 5(1) of the CLA 1977, this did not extend to the offence of conspiracy so far as it relates to conspiracy to defraud.[1]

According to Viscount Dilhorne, in *Scott v Metropolitan Police Commissioner*:[2]

> 'it is clearly the law that an agreement by two or more by dishonesty to deprive a person of something which is his or to which he is or would be or might be entitled and an agreement by two or more by dishonesty to injure some proprietary right of his, suffices to constitute the offence of conspiracy to defraud.'

Most agreements to defraud will be agreements to commit offences under the Theft Acts but it is clear that they need not be and, indeed, that there can be cases of fraud which are not substantive offences.[3] A person is defrauded when he is 'prejudiced', and conspirators have a sufficient *mens rea* if it is their purpose to cause that prejudice. However, in *Wai Yu-tsang v R*,[4] the Privy Council thought this was not necessarily required and that it is enough that the parties have agreed to cause the prejudice: if they have agreed to defraud, they intend to defraud, and it is immaterial that defrauding is not their purpose (their purpose usually being to benefit themselves, and not necessarily to cause loss to another).[5] 'Prejudice' includes putting at risk: if the conspirators know that the effect of carrying out the agreement will be to put the victim's property at risk, then they intend prejudice to him and, if they are dishonest, they are guilty of conspiracy to defraud him (and this is so if it turns out that the property is not impaired or even if the victim makes a profit).

---

1 Criminal Justice Act 1987, s 12 effectively provides that statutory conspiracy and conspiracy to defraud are not mutually exclusive.

2 [1975] AC 819 at 840.

3 Smith and Hogan, n 1 on p 408, p 294.

4 [1992] 1 AC 269.

5 *Cf Attorney-General's Reference (No 1 of 1982)* [1983] QB 751.

It is particularly difficult, in the case of conspiracy, to distinguish between *actus reus* and *mens rea.* The *actus reus* is the agreement, but agreement is a mental operation, although one manifested by acts of some kind. 'In the case of conspiracy as opposed to the substantive offence, it is what was agreed to be done and not what was in fact done which is all important.'[1] In *R v Seillon,*[2] A had been convicted of fraudulently inducing a bank to grant credit (in excess of £1 million) to one of his companies. He anticipated that he would be held personally liable to the bank and therefore, in conjunction with his solicitor and others, set about hiding away his assets (by purporting to give a fictitious person a charge and power of sale over certain properties). It was argued, at his trial, that, at the time of the conspiracy, the bank was not a creditor: it was only a potential creditor. It had a claim for damages against A, but it had no judgment. Consequently, there was no creditor who could be defrauded; and the count therefore alleged conspiracy to commit an impossible crime. (The events had occurred before the CLA 1977, and such a conspiracy was then unknown to the law.) The trial judge rejected the argument, and A appealed. The Court of Appeal rejected the appeal, stating that the offence of conspiracy is complete at the time of the agreement: the crime is usually in relation to a scheme to be carried out in the future. The crime is not impossible to commit because there is no creditor at that time, or because some anticipated event upon which the crime is to bite has not occurred at the time of the agreement. It would only be impossible if that event could not physically come about or if, in law, what was agreed could not amount to a crime.

The court also referred to *DPP v Alsford*[3] where Lord Scarman pointed out that conspiracy is a 'preliminary' or 'auxiliary' crime which is complete at the time of the agreement.[4]

An agreement in England to carry out a fraud abroad is not indictable as a conspiracy to defraud in England. However, it is often difficult to determine where the fraud has been committed.

In addition to the above, it is possible, in principle, for an adviser to be charged with other offences, for example money laundering, breaches of relevant exchange control regulations, breach of professional codes and regulations or of his duty to the court, and so forth. Similarly, he may find himself being sued for tortious conspiracy.[5] These and other matters are beyond the scope of this chapter.

---

1 *Bolton* (1991) 94 Cr App Rep 74 at 80, per Woolf LJ.

2 (Unreported) 14 May 1982, CA (Criminal Division).

3 [1978] CAR 116.

4 See also *McElhanon v Hing* (1985) 728 P 2d 256 (Ariz App); *Townsend v State Bar of California* (1948) 197 P 2d 326 (Cal).

5 See, eg, *Crofter Hand Woven Harris Tweed Co Ltd v Veitch* [1942] AC 435, especially at 439, per Viscount Simon; *Lonrho plc v Fayed* [1991] BCC 641; *Yukong Lines Ltd of Korea v Rendsburg Investments Corp* [1998] BCC 870; *Brown v Bennett* [1999] BCC 91.

7.3 FOREIGN JURISDICTIONS[1]

7.3.1 Introduction

Jurisdictions similar to England and Wales

Many foreign jurisdictions have legislation which is similar – and, indeed, is very often based on – the English 1571 Act (or s 172 of the Law of Property Act 1925) and s 42 of the English Bankruptcy Act 1914. Moreover, several such jurisdictions have also followed or applied English authorities in these matters.

Thus, in the context of bankruptcy, s 71 of the Bahamian Bankruptcy Act (1870) is similar to s 91 of the English Bankruptcy Act 1869 (and applies, as did the 1869 Act, only to 'traders'). Hong Kong follows English law: s 47 of the Bankruptcy Ordinance (c 6) is broadly similar to s 42 of the Bankruptcy Act 1914. Similarly, s 45(1) of the Bermudian Bankruptcy Act 1989 is similar to s 42, the main significant difference being that the period of 10 years specified in s 42(1) has been reduced to a period of only five years in Bermuda. Section 107 of the Bankruptcy Law (Revised) of the Cayman Islands is also identical to s 42 (with the same two-year and 10-year time-limits, and subject to the same exceptions). In Guernsey, the position is also similar to that in England. Bankrucptcy in Australia is governed by the Commonwealth Bankruptcy Act 1966, under which the position is broadly similar to that under English law when s 42 of the Bankruptcy Act 1914 was in force.[2] The period of 10 years specified in s 42(1) has been reduced to five years in Australia, but, in general, the statutory provisions are virtually identical and have been construed in the same way. However, as from 23 June 1993, a transaction by a company may be voidable if it is such that a reasonable person in the company's circumstances would not have entered into it having regard to the benefits and detriment to the company and benefits to other parties.[3]

Many foreign jurisdictions also have legislation similar to the provisions of the English 1571 Act (or s 172 of the English Law of Property Act 1925) in relation to the setting aside of transactions intended to defraud creditors

---

1 In recent years, 'offshore' jurisdictions have been subjected to a series of investigations and criticism: see, in particular, The Financial Stability Forum's *Report of the Working Group on Offshore Centres* (available at *www.fsforum.org.uk*); the Financial Action Task Force's *Review to Identify Non-Cooperative Countries or Territories* (available at *www.oecd.org/fatf*); the OECD's Reports entitled *Harmful Tax Competition* (1998) and *Towards Global Tax Cooperation* (2000) (both available at *www.oecd.org*); Andrew Edwards *Review of Financial Regulation in the Crown Dependencies* (Cmnd 4109); Powell (1999) 3 Jersey LR 22; Hay [1999] *Private Client Business* 345. Although these investigations focus, as their titles suggest, on financial stability and tax issues, their effect has been to make several offshore jurisdictions somewhat nervous about their activities and products; and this may well introduce a note of caution into their application of their legislation dealing with asset protection trusts.

2 Bankruptcy Act 1966, ss 120–121. See, generally, **7.2.3**. See also *Williams v Lloyd* (1933) 50 CLR 341; *Re Brown* (1950) 15 ABC 74; *Official Assignee of Braithwaite v B* [1923] NZLR 1186.

3 Corporations Law, s 588FB(1).

(irrespective of bankruptcy). Each of the Australian States has legislation based on the English 1571 Act,[1] and, in each case, an 'intent to defraud' creditors is central. English case-law on the 1571 Act and on s 172 of the Law of Property Act 1925 has been followed. Thus, as in England, a fraudulent intent will not be presumed from the mere fact that the settlor was in debt at the date of the settlement and it is not sufficient merely to show that the effect of the settlement was to defeat a creditor.[2] In Belize, s 149 of the Law of Property Act is identical to s 172, as indeed is s 81 of the Conveyancing and Law of Property Act in the British Virgin Islands. In Hong Kong, s 60 of the Conveyancing and Property Ordinance (c 219) is virtually identical to s 172. There are also similar provisions in Gibraltar.

In the United States, the Uniform Fraudulent Transfer Act, which has been adopted by over 30 States, also contains provisions which are broadly similar to those in the earlier English legislation (requiring an intent to hinder, delay or defraud creditors, and so forth).

Jurisdictions with asset protection legislation

Since 1989, several offshore jurisdictions have introduced legislation which is intended to enable settlors or transferors to create trusts which will, to varying degrees, put assets beyond the reach of creditors.[3] The precise terms of such legislation varies from jurisdiction to jurisdiction (sometimes substantially, sometimes only in respect of minor matters), but, in broad terms, the intention seems to be to provide a settlor with a degree of protection from or against claims by future unidentified creditors. In many offshore jurisdictions, such protection is afforded only to 'foreign' settlors or debtors, and, for their own domestic purposes, they may well have provisions which are similar to, if not identical with, those found in the English 1571 Act (or s 172 of the Law of Property Act 1925) or in the English Bankruptcy Act 1914 (see above).

7.3.2 Bahamas

As we have seen, s 71 of the Bahamian Bankruptcy Act is identical to s 42 of the English Bankruptcy Act 1914 (including the same two-year and 10-year periods, and subject to the same exceptions) but, unlike s 42, s 71 expressly applies only to 'traders' (as did s 91 of the English Bankruptcy Act 1869).

However, the Fraudulent Dispositions Act 1991 (FDA 1991) came into effect on 5 April 1991 ('the appointed date')[4] and replaced 'the law in effect

---

1 Conveyancing and Law of Property Act 1884 (Tas), s 40; Conveyancing Act 1919 (NSW), s 37A; Law of Property Act 1936 (SA), s 86; Property Law Act 1958 (Vic), s 172; Property Law Act 1969 (WA), s 89; Property Law Act 1974 (Qld), s 228.

2 See, generally, *Jacobs' Law of Trusts in Australia* (5th ed, 1986), pp 159–161, paras [960]–[964]. See also *Re Mackay* (1951) 16 ABC 18; *Brady v Stapleton* [1952] ALR 989.

3 For a useful survey of the difficulties that may arise (particularly from an ill-considered use of offshore legislation) see P Willoughby [1996] *Private Client Business* 226 and 302.

4 FDA 1991, ss 1(2), 2.

prior to the appointed date'.[1] The previous law was the same as English law – ie any disposition made with intent to defraud creditors was void – and English case-law was followed. The FDA 1991, however, seeks to strike a fairer balance between the protection of assets and the protection of creditors. Its main purpose is to avoid the situation where a person's assets are held subject to possible claims by creditors who are entirely unknown to him and whose identity cannot be seriously within his contemplation.[2]

The FDA 1991 applies, with effect from the appointed date, to every disposition of property made after the appointed date by any person, and whether or not the property which is the subject matter of the disposition is situate in The Bahamas or elsewhere.[3] Subject to the provisions of the FDA 1991, every disposition of property made 'with an intent to defraud and at an undervalue shall be voidable at the instance of a creditor thereby prejudiced'.[4]

A 'disposition', for these purposes, means 'any disposition or series thereof, however effected, and (without prejudice to the generality thereof) includes any transaction, gift, grant or transfer of property of any nature whatsoever'.[5] The word 'property' is not defined anywhere (not even by reference to another statute);[6] but it seems safe to assume that it encompasses every kind of property, including cash.[7] An 'intent to defraud' means 'an intention of a transferor *wilfully* to defeat an obligation owed to a creditor'.[8] An 'obligation' is defined as 'an obligation or liability (which shall include a contingent liability) which existed on or prior to the date of a relevant disposition and of which the transferor had actual notice'.[9] The disposition must also be made at an 'undervalue', which means either that no consideration was provided for it or that the value of such consideration as was provided for the disposition was 'significantly less' than the value of the property which was the subject matter of the disposition.[10] A 'creditor' means, quite simply, 'a person to whom an obligation is owed'.[11]

The burden of establishing an intent to defraud for the purposes of the FDA 1991 lies on the creditor seeking to set aside the disposition.[12] In any

---

1 FDA 1991, s 3(1).

2 In fact, neither the 1571 Act nor Law of Property Act 1925, s 172 were ever wide enough to assist a subsequent creditor who could not be seriously within the debtor's contemplation.

3 FDA 1991, s 3(1). In any action or proceedings commenced prior to the appointed date, or within six months of the appointed date but in respect of a disposition made prior to the appointed date, the FDA 1991 does not apply; the previous law continues to apply instead: ibid.

4 Ibid, s 4(1).

5 Ibid, s 2.

6 Such as, eg, the Trusts (Choice of Governing Law) Act 1989, s 2.

7 See pp 340 and 364–365.

8 FDA 1991, s 2 (emphasis added).

9 Ibid, s 2.

10 Ibid.

11 Ibid.

12 Ibid, s 4(2).

event, no action or proceedings can be commenced under the Act unless commenced within two years of the date of the relevant disposition.[1]

Thus, the FDA 1991 departs materially from (pre-and post-1986) English law in some crucial aspects. It is true that the obligation owed to the creditor may not only be an accrued liability (such as a debt the date for payment of which has already passed, or a final award of damages which has already been made but not yet satisfied) but it may also be a contingent liability – and, thus far, this accords with pre-1986 and existing English law. However, the relevant liability (contingent or otherwise) must be one which already exists on or prior to the date of the relevant disposition. In this respect, the FDA 1991 clearly seems to restrict the range of creditors who may seek to set aside that disposition. Moreover, the additional requirement that the transferor must also have had *actual* notice of the relevant obligation or liability restricts the scope of the Act even further.

Precisely what constitutes a 'contingent' liability is not made clear in the Act. However, it seems clear that it includes, for example, a debt (or liability) which has actually been incurred – and is known by the transferor to have been incurred – but which is not repayable (or to be discharged otherwise) until some future date. On the other hand, a transferor who makes a disposition of property immediately before entering upon a trading venture or other hazardous activity would seem not to be caught by the Act: although it may still be accurate to categorise his liabilities to his future creditors (say, suppliers of goods and services) as 'contingent' liabilities (as in *Re Butterworth* and associated cases),[2] such liabilities will not exist on or prior to the date of the disposition and, therefore, the transferor will not have actual knowledge of them unless and until they are actually incurred.

Similarly, if any obligations are owed at the date of the disposition, but they are all subsequently discharged, it is impossible for anyone who became a creditor thereafter to seek to have the disposition set aside under the FDA 1991. Indeed, it would also seem that, where a transferor may have committed a tort (say, some act of medical negligence) prior to the date of the relevant disposition, but in respect of which no writ had been issued and no notice of any impending claim had been given before that date, the victim who subsequently obtains judgment would encounter great difficulty in his attempt to have the disposition set aside: either the transferor was not under any liability – actual or contingent – to anyone at the relevant time or, alternatively, he did not have actual notice of any such liability.[3] Whether the same would be true of a transferor who had already been notified of an impending claim (although no proceedings had yet been commenced) – or even one who made the relevant disposition in circumstances in which it was obvious to him that

1 Ibid, s 4(3). A 'relevant disposition' means a disposition to which s 4(1) applies.

2 See pp 350–351, 356–360.

3 *Cf* the English cases of *Barling v Bishopp* (1860) 29 Beav 417; *Crossley v Elworthy* (1871) LR 12 Eq 158; and *Re Wise* (1886) 17 QBD 290, discussed at pp 353–355.

he had committed a tort or other actionable wrong and was clearly at risk of being sued – is less clear, but prudence would suggest that any disposition made in such circumstances should be assumed to be vulnerable under the terms of the Act.

There is no intent to defraud, for the purposes of the FDA 1991, unless the transferor 'wilfully' intended to defeat an obligation owed to a creditor. In other words, it appears that, even if a creditor can establish the existence of an obligation within the compass of the statute, this alone will not be sufficient: he must also establish that the transferor wilfully made the disposition which he seeks to set aside in order to defeat that obligation. In broad terms, the word 'wilfully' implies that a person 'knows what he is doing, and intends to do what he is doing, and is a free agent',[1] although, of course, the precise meaning can vary according to the particular context. In the context of the FDA 1991, it seems clear that the word implies that the transferor must *deliberately* and *knowingly*[2] intend to defeat an obligation to his creditor, and it would not be sufficient, for example, if he acted under an honest mistake, by accident or inadvertently.[3] Therefore, the word seems to connote dishonesty.[4] Mere indebtedness at the time of the disposition would not, by itself, be sufficient grounds on which it could be impeached. Nor could an intent to defraud be imputed or inferred on the basis that the transferor must be presumed to have intended the natural consequences of his own acts.[5] Such factors – presumably along with the traditional 'badges of fraud'[6] – may well still be relevant as items of evidence adduced in support of an allegation of wilful conduct on the part of the transferor, but they are clearly not sufficient or conclusive in themselves.

Thus, by way of summary, in order to set aside a disposition under the Act, a creditor must prove that:

(a) the transferor owed him an obligation (ie that he is a creditor);
(b) not only the obligation or liability existed on or before the date of the disposition but also the transferor then[7] had actual knowledge of it;
(c) the disposition was made at an undervalue; and

1 *Re Young and Harston's Contract* (1885) 31 Ch D 168 at 175, per Bowen LJ. See also *Lomas v Peck* [1947] 2 All ER 574 at 575, per Lord Goddard CJ: 'If a man permits a thing to be done, it means that he gives permission for it to be done, and if a man gives permission for a thing to be done, he knows what is to be done or is being done, and, if he knows that, it follows that it is wilful'.

2 *Cf* R *v Senior* [1899] 1 QB 283, especially at 290–291; *Hall v Jordan* [1947] 1 All ER 826; *R v Piche* (1967) 10 Cr LQ 107.

3 *Cf Smith v Barnham* (1876) 1 Ex D 419; *Graham v Belfast & Northern Counties Railway* [1901] 2 Ir R 19.

4 *Cf Lloyds Bank Ltd v Marcan* [1973] 1 WLR 1387 at 1392, per Cairns LJ. See p 344.

5 See pp 353–355.

6 See pp 345–347.

7 The word 'then' does not actually appear in the definition of 'obligation' but it seems clear that this is intended to be the time at which the transferor 'had' actual notice.

(d) the transferor made the disposition wilfully in order to defeat his obligation to the creditor.

The creditor must also bring proceedings within two years of the date of the disposition.

It will probably be very difficult for any creditor to satisfy all these requirements.[1] If he does succeed in doing so, the disposition shall be set aside under the FDA 1991, but only to the extent necessary to satisfy the obligation owed to that creditor (ie 'the creditor at whose instance the disposition had been set aside') together with such costs as the court may allow.[2] In other words, the entire disposition will not necessarily be set aside; and the success of one creditor will not enure for the benefit of any other.

Moreover, even in the event that a disposition is set aside under the FDA 1991, there is a measure of protection for the transferee (ie 'the person to whom a relevant disposition is made' and any successor in title).[3] Section 5(1) of the Act provides that, in that event, unless the court is satisfied that the transferee 'has acted in bad faith', the transferee shall have a first and paramount charge over the property which is the subject matter of the disposition, of an amount equal to the entire costs properly incurred by the transferee in the defence of the action or proceedings to set aside (and not merely such costs as might otherwise be allowed by the court); and the relevant disposition shall be set aside subject to the proper fees, costs, pre-existing rights, claims and interests of the transferee (and of any predecessor transferee which has not acted in bad faith).

Moreover, unless the court is satisfied that a beneficiary of a trust has acted in bad faith, the disposition shall only be set aside subject to the right of such beneficiary to retain any distribution made consequent upon the prior exercise of a trust, power or discretion vested in the trustee of such trust or any other person, and otherwise properly exercised. Thus, it appears that a distribution to a beneficiary by trustees who are themselves acting in bad faith could not be set aside or prejudiced, provided the beneficiary himself is not also acting in bad faith.

However, the trust, power or discretion must also be 'otherwise properly exercised'. Thus, a fraudulent exercise of a power by trustees (in the sense of a 'fraud on a power'), eg an appointment to a beneficiary on condition that he transfers the appointed property to a non-object, would not be validated under s 5(1)(b); and the property thus fraudulently appointed could be set aside by the court. The burden of proving that a transferee or beneficiary has acted in bad faith again lies on the person making the allegation.[4]

---

1 See, however, *The Private Trust Corporation v Grupo Torras SA* (1997/98) 1 OFLR 443 (the Court of Appeal of The Bahamas).

2 FDA 1991, s 6.

3 Ibid, s 2.

4 Ibid, s 5(2).

Precisely what constitutes 'bad faith' for these purposes is unclear. In some contexts, the words 'in good faith' have been construed to mean 'not only the absence of notice, but genuine and honest absence of notice'.[1] In other contexts, they have been construed as meaning 'honestly and with no ulterior motive'.[2] In either case, there seems to be a requirement of honesty; and it might therefore be argued that, in s 5 of the FDA 1991, the expression 'bad faith' requires the claiming creditor to prove that the transferee or beneficiary had acted 'dishonestly' and was not simply an 'honestly blundering and careless' individual. However, this does not necessarily require proof of actual conscious and deliberate dishonesty. As Lord Blackburn stated in *Jones v Gordon*:[3]

> 'if the facts and circumstances are such that the jury, or whoever has to try the question, came to the conclusion that he was not honestly blundering and careless, but that he must have had a suspicion that there was something wrong, and that he refrained from asking questions, not because he was an honest blunderer or a stupid man, but because he thought in his own secret mind – I suspect there is something wrong, and if I ask questions and make farther inquiry, it will no longer be my suspecting it, but my knowing it, and then I shall not be able to recover – I think that is dishonesty.'

Thus, actual knowledge on the part of a transferee or beneficiary may not be required; and wilfully closing one's eyes to the obvious, or even refraining from pursuing one's suspicions, may be sufficient to constitute 'bad faith'.

It seems clear from the definition of 'transferee', which includes not only the person to whom a relevant disposition is made but also any successor in title,[4] that any 'bad faith' on the part of a transferee need not be shown to relate to, or exist at the date of, the relevant disposition itself, but that it may be present at any subsequent time. Thus, for example, the transferee could lose the limited protection accorded by s 5(1)(a) not only in a case where, with full knowledge of the transferor's circumstances and obligations, he colluded with the transferor in making the relevant disposition which gave effect to the latter's intent to defraud creditors,[5] but also in the case where the transferee subsequently committed some act – such as the exercise of a power or discretion whereby property which was the subject matter of the disposition was distributed to a beneficiary – with a deliberate intent to defeat (or perhaps even unduly delay) a creditor seeking to have the disposition set aside.

However, it is not clear whether the court must be satisfied that the transferee or beneficiary has acted in 'bad faith' (whichever way it is construed,

---

1 See, eg, *Midland Bank Trust Co v Green* [1981] AC 513 at 528, per Lord Wilberforce.

2 See, eg, *Smith v Morrison* [1974] 1 WLR 659; *Central Estates (Belgravia) Ltd v Woolgar* [1972] 1 QB 48.

3 (1877) 2 App Cas 616 at 629. See also *Tatam v Haslar* (1889) 23 QBD 345, and the cases cited at pp 402–408.

4 FDA 1991, s 2.

5 And it must be remembered that the provisions of s 5 come into operation only when a disposition has been set aside, ie after the requisite intent to defraud has been established.

and irrespective of the time at which he may have so acted) in relation to the particular creditor who has succeeded in having the disposition set aside or whether it is sufficient that he has done so in relation to some other creditor (or anyone else). Suppose, for example, that a transferee-trustee knowingly and deliberately colluded with the transferor in defrauding Creditor A, but the disposition was subsequently set aside at the instance of Creditor B. Is the transferee deprived of the protection accorded by s 5 on the basis that he acted in bad faith towards Creditor A, or must the court be satisfied that he acted in bad faith towards Creditor B? The provisions of s 6 (which would limit the avoidance of the disposition only to the extent necessary to satisfy the obligation owed to Creditor B) might suggest that bad faith in relation to Creditor B must be established.

On the other hand, ss 5 and 6 are clearly aimed at different ends. Section 6 simply ensures that the benefit of setting aside the relevant disposition accrues only to Creditor B, but s 5 could affect the amount which Creditor B might be able to recover; and, in such circumstances, it might be said to be unreasonable that the transferee-trustee is protected by his bad faith towards Creditor A.

Section 7(a) of the FDA 1991 declares that nothing in the Act shall validate any disposition of property which is neither owned by the transferor nor the subject of a power in that behalf[1] vested in the transferor. This is self-evident and merely declaratory. Reliance on the FDA 1991 is clearly not required in order to impeach a purported disposition of property which does not belong to the transferor, or over which he has no lawful power of disposition. An 'intent to defraud' is defined by reference to the intent of a 'transferor'; and a 'transferor' is defined in terms of ownership of (or holding of a power over) property.[2] In *The Private Trust Corporation v Grupo Torras SA*,[3] the appellant (PTC) was the trustee of a Bahamian trust of which Sheikh Fahad Al Sabah was the 'primary beneficiary'. The respondents were alleging, in proceedings in England, that the Sheikh had defrauded them of approximately US$450 million while he was employed in their London office. The English court had granted a worldwide injunction against the Sheikh. In the course of the English proceedings, a connection was discovered between the Sheikh and the Bahamian trust. The respondents sought, and were granted, a *Mareva* injunction against the appellants in The Bahamas and an order for discovery. The Bahamian Court of Appeal, dismissing the appellant's appeal, held that the terms of the trust and the circumstances justified an assumption that the Sheikh had substantial and effective control over the trust funds. A *Mareva* injunction and an order for discovery were calculated to discover and immobilise the trust assets and would therefore be upheld.

1 Meaning, presumably, a power to dispose of property.

2 FDA 1991, s 2.

3 (1997/98) 1 OFLR 443. See also *Meespierson (Bahamas) Ltd v Grupo Torras SA*, Civil Appeal No 41 of 1998 (Court of Appeal decision, 16 April 1999): Bahamian courts have no jurisdiction to grant a free-standing *Mareva* injunction where there is no substantive claim against the defendants in the jurisdiction.

It is not at all clear why the court came to this conclusion. It may have been because it was clear, on the evidence, that the Sheikh had (or, at least, there was a very strong *prima facie* case that he had) purported to create a trust with someone else's money which he had acquired through fraud, ie he fell squarely within s 7(a) of the FDA 1991 (which was not in fact referred to). Consequently, the alleged trust would be void and the trustee, having notice of the alleged fraud, would hold the trust assets on constructive trust for the true owner. If this were the case, however, the specific provisions of the trust (including the flee clause) would have had no effect, and would not have required the detailed consideration which the court gave them. At one point, Gonsalves-Sabola P, delivering the judgment of the court, seems to have concluded that this was a sham trust,[1] but this view, also, seems misconceived: the notion of a sham trust applies to a purported disposition of property which the 'transferor' himself owns and not to an attempt to dispose of property fraudulently acquired from another. Much the greater part of the judgment is devoted to an examination of the specific terms of the trust. These included provisions to the effect that the trustee had a discretion to invest trust funds, but subject to the prior written consent of the Sheikh (or anyone whom he might designate) that the trustee had power in its sole discretion to apply either the trust capital or net income to or for the benefit of any one or more of the beneficiaries; that the trustee had power to add members to the class of beneficiaries, subject to the written consent of the protector; that the power to appoint the original protector was vested in the Sheikh (with each protector having power to appoint his successor); that proper law of the trust or its place of administration could be changed whenever the trustee determined that it would be in the best interests of the trust or its beneficiaries to do so; and that, upon the happening of certain specified events (including any action by or on behalf of any judicial authority prohibiting or restricting the transfer of trust property out of the jurisdiction) the trustee should automatically cease to be a trustee and be divested of title to the trust property. In the circumstances, these provisions were held to justify an assumption that the Sheikh 'had substantial and effective control over the trust funds'. However, such provisions are not in any way unusual for a discretionary trust under which the settlor is himself an object.[2] Moreover, under the terms of the trust, the crucial dispositive discretions were vested in the trustee, which clearly owed fiduciary obligations (to the Sheikh and to other beneficiaries) and which the court accepted had not been a party to the Sheikh's fraud. Consequently, it is difficult to see how the so-called 'trust fund' could be said to be property which effectively belonged to the Sheikh (or over which he had effective control). It would have made much more sense to say that the property had never belonged to the Sheikh in the first place.

---

1 (1997/98) 1 OFLR 443 at 453.

2 *Cf*, eg, the Cook Islands' International Trusts Act 1984, ss 13A and 13C; pp 436 and 441.

In any event, the court did not refer to or discuss any provision in the 1991 Act and for present purposes, therefore, it has limited significance. Indeed, Gonsalves-Sabola P gave the following warning:[1]

> 'The decision of this Court to uphold generally the Orders of Sawyer J turns on the view we take of the particular facts and issues in the case. It is in no way intended to give encouragement to a potential plaintiff to believe that injunctions and discovery against trustees in the Bahamas are to be had for the asking or that corporate veils may be pierced at the whim of a litigant who comes up against the prohibitory provisions of the Banks and Trust Companies Regulation Act.'

Nevertheless, despite such a disclaimer, the readiness with which the court seems to have reached its conclusion, as well as the lack of clarity and conviction in the reasoning underlying its judgment, might well be seen as seriously undermining the claims of The Bahamas to be an effective and reliable jurisdiction in which to base any asset protection strategy.[2]

Finally, s 8 of the FDA 1991 declares that nothing in the Act creates or enables any right, claim or interest on behalf of a creditor or person, which right, claim or interest would be avoided or defeated by the Trusts (Choice of Governing Law) Act 1989 (TCGLA 1989). The TCGLA 1989 provides *inter alia* that, in the creation of a trust, a settlor, whether or not he is resident in The Bahamas, may expressly declare in the trust instrument that the laws of The Bahamas shall be the governing law of the trust, and such an express declaration is valid, effective and conclusive regardless of any other circumstance.[3] Subject to certain exceptions, all questions arising in regard to a trust which is for the time being governed by the laws of The Bahamas, or in regard to any disposition of property upon the trusts thereof, will be determined in accordance with the laws of The Bahamas, without reference to the laws of any other jurisdictions with which the trust or disposition may be connected.[4] Section 7(2)(a) then declares that this general rule shall not validate *inter alia* any trust or disposition of immovable property situate in a jurisdiction other than The Bahamas in which such trust or disposition is invalid according to the laws of such jurisdiction.[5] In particular, s 8 of the TCGLA 1989 declares expressly that no trust governed by the laws of The Bahamas, and no disposition of property to be held on trust that is valid under the laws of The Bahamas, is void, voidable, liable to be set aside or defective in any manner by reference to a foreign law. There is no Bahamian statute similar to the English

1 (1997/98) 1 OFLR 443 at 453.

2 On the other hand, see *Meespierson (Bahamas) Ltd v Grupo Torras SA*, Civil Appeal No 41 of 1998 (Court of Appeal decision, 16 April 1999).

3 TCGLA 1989, s 4(1) and (2).

4 Ibid, s 7(1).

5 Section 7(2)(b) provides that s 7 shall take effect subject to any express term of a trust or disposition to the contrary. However, it is difficult to see how such an express term could override the provisions of s 7(2)(a).

Recognition of Trusts Act 1987 and The Bahamas have not adopted the Hague Convention on the Law Applicable to Trusts and on their Recognition 1985.

7.3.3 Belize

The legal system of Belize (formerly British Honduras) is based on that of England, together with local legislation. Prior to 1992, the principal trust legislation was the Trusts Act 1923, which was repealed by the Trusts Act 1992 (TA 1992). The TA 1992, which came into force on 18 May 1992,[1] provides a code dealing with the definition of a trust, the validity of trusts, the proper law of trusts, the creation and maximum duration of a trust, and so forth.

Under s 57 of the TA 1992, the court[2] has jurisdiction in respect of any matters where:

(a) the proper law of the trust is the law of Belize;
(b) a trustee of the trust is resident in Belize (and, presumably, only one of several trustees need be so resident);
(c) any property of the trust is situated in Belize; and
(d) any part of the administration of the trust is carried on in Belize.

On the application of a trustee, a beneficiary, a settlor or his personal representatives, a protector,[3] or, with the leave of the court, any other person, the court may *inter alia* make a declaration as to the validity or enforceability of a trust.[4] A trustee (but apparently not anyone else) may apply to the court for directions as to how he should or might act in any of the affairs of the trust and the court may make such order as it thinks fit.[5]

The TA 1992 also provides for the optional registration of trusts.[6] The settlor or trustee of a trust may, but (subject to the terms of the trust) shall not be obliged to, apply for registration of the trust on a register maintained by the Registrar of the court, upon payment of the specified registration fee and conforming with the procedures laid down. The register is not open for inspection except that the trustee of a trust (which, presumably, means all the trustees where there are several)[7] may in writing authorise a person to inspect the entry of that trust on the register.[8] This facility for secrecy is apparently

---

1 The day appointed by Order of the Attorney-General of Belize published in the *Belize Government Gazette*: see TA 1992, s 70.

2 Ie the Supreme Court or a Judge thereof: see TA 1992, s 68(1).

3 Section 16 deals with the appointment and powers of a protector and provides that, in the exercise of his office, he owes a fiduciary duty to the beneficiaries, but he is not to be accounted or regarded as a trustee.

4 TA 1992, s 58(1)(b).

5 Ibid, s 59. It is difficult to see what s 59 adds to s 58(1).

6 Ibid, s 63.

7 Ibid, s 29.

8 Ibid, s 63(7).

available to all trusts, irrespective of whether the proper law is the law of Belize.[1] In addition, if the trust is an 'exempt trust', it will not be subject to taxation in Belize[2] and will be regarded as not resident in Belize for the purposes of exchange control regulations.[3]

A trust is an 'exempt trust' in any year:

(a) if the settlor is not resident in Belize during that year;
(b) none of the beneficiaries is resident in Belize during that year; and
(c) the trust property does not include any land situated in Belize.[4]

For present purposes, the main provision of relevance is s 7 of the TA 1992. Section 7(2) provides that a trust will be 'invalid and unenforceable' *inter alia* to the extent that:

(a) it purports to do anything contrary to the law of Belize; or
(b) it purports to confer any right or power or impose any obligation the exercise of which or the carrying out of which is contrary to the law of Belize.

It will also be 'invalid and unenforceable' to the extent that:

(a) the court declares that the trust was established by duress, fraud, mistake, undue influence or misrepresentation; or
(b) the trust is immoral or contrary to public policy.

Where a trust is created for two or more purposes of which some are 'lawful' and others are not, or where some of the terms of the trust are 'invalid' and others are not, the consequences differ according to whether or not those purposes or terms can be separated. If they can not be separated, the trust is invalid. If they can be separated, the court may declare that the trust is valid as to the terms which are valid and the purposes which are lawful. Where a trust is partially invalid, the court may declare what property is to be held subject to the trust. Property provided by a settlor and as to which a trust is invalid shall be held by the trustee on trust for the settlor absolutely or, if he is dead, as if it had formed part of his estate at his death.[5]

Section 149 of the Law of Property Act 1925[6] is identical to s 172 of the English Law of Property Act 1925. Consequently, a transfer of property made with intent to defraud creditors is voidable in Belize, as it was in England, at

---

1 Ibid, s 66(3).
2 Ibid, s 64.
3 Ibid, s 65.
4 Ibid, s 64(1).
5 Ibid, s 7(3)–(5) inclusive.
6 Chapter 154 of the Revised Laws of Belize.

the instance of any person thereby prejudiced. Moreover, a trust created with such an intent could be said to fall within the first two limbs of s 7(1)(a) of the TA 1992 (being contrary to the law of Belize or conferring a right or power or imposing an obligation the exercise or carrying out of which is contrary to the law of Belize); and it may even fall within s 7(1)(b)(i) (being established by fraud). If so, such a trust would apparently be 'invalid and unenforceable', but it is not clear whether this means that it is void or simply voidable (as under s 149 of the Belize Law of Property Act and s 172 of the English Act). Nor is it clear how the 'purposes' of such a trust could be separated for the purposes of subsections (3)–(5).

Section 7(6) of the TA 1992 provides that where a trust is 'created' under the law of Belize, the court shall not vary it or set it aside or recognise the validity of any claim against the trust property pursuant to the law of another jurisdiction or the order of a court of another jurisdiction in respect of *inter alia* the claims of creditors in an insolvency. Thus, subsection (6) seems to apply only to a trust actually created under the law of Belize, and not to a trust the proper law of which was originally the law of a jurisdiction other than Belize but which has been changed to that of Belize.[1] Section 7(7) then declares that subsection (6) has effect notwithstanding the provisions of s 149 of the Law of Property Act, s 42 of the Bankruptcy Act and the provisions of the Reciprocal Enforcement of Judgments Act.

Section 3(1) of the latter Act[2] provides that, where a judgment[3] has been obtained in the High Court in England, the judgment creditor may apply to the Supreme Court in Belize at any time within 12 months after the date of judgment (or such longer period as may be allowed) to register the judgment; and it will be registered accordingly 'if in all the circumstances of the case [the Supreme Court] thinks it is just and convenient that the judgment should be enforced' in Belize. Section 3(2)(f) declares expressly, however, that no judgment shall be ordered to be registered if it was in respect of a cause of action which, for reasons of public policy or for some other similar reason, could not have been entertained by the registering court. Part II of the Act deals with reciprocal enforcement of judgments in relation to other foreign countries and a 'judgment' in this context is defined so as to include compensation or damages to an injured party as well as a payment of a sum of money.[4]

A judgment creditor within Part II may apply for registration of the judgment (within six years of the date of the judgment) 'subject to proof of … the other provisions' of the Act. Whether this latter requirement includes

1 But see TA 1992, s 66(3). Section 4 of the Act deals with the proper law of a trust and clearly recognises that the proper law may be changed to or from the law of Belize.

2 Chapter 133.

3 A 'judgment' refers to any judgment or order 'whereby any sum of money is made payable': Reciprocal Enforcement of Judgments Act, s 2.

4 Ibid, s 7.

s 3(2)(f) is unclear. The implication (especially in s 9(2)) is that the judgment must have been capable of being given originally in Belize. Thus, the precise manner in which the Reciprocal Enforcement of Judgments Act is intended to interact with the TA 1992 is not entirely free from doubt.

However, the effect of the provisions of the TA 1992 seems to be that s 7(6) clearly does not prevent a Belize court from varying or setting aside a Belize trust, or recognising a claim against property held in a Belize trust,[1] at the instance of a creditor pursuant to s 149 of the Law of Property Act 1925, provided that the creditor is not relying on the law of another jurisdiction or the order of a court in another jurisdiction. On the other hand, the enforcement of a law of a foreign jurisdiction or an order of a foreign court purporting to set aside a Belize trust in favour of creditors is not likely to be furthered or assisted in Belize if and insofar as it is contrary to Belize public policy or tends to undermine the provisions of the TA 1992.

Section 7(6)(c) refers only to the claims of creditors 'in an insolvency'. Section 68(1) of the Act provides that, unless the context otherwise requires, the word 'insolvency' includes the making of an administration order, the appointment of a receiver and the bankruptcy of any person. However, ss 423–425 of the English Insolvency Act 1986, under which an English court may set aside a transaction at an undervalue (eg a Belize trust created by a settlor domiciled in England), or make such order as it thinks fit to protect the victims of such a transaction, can operate entirely independently of insolvency. In such circumstances, it is not clear that s 7(6) of the TA 1992 would apply so as to prevent a Belize court from recognising the validity of the order of the English court setting aside the trust.

Section 12(4) of the TA 1992 declares that any rule of law or public policy which prevents a settlor from establishing a protective or spendthrift trust[2] of which he is a beneficiary is abolished. Thus, the so-called rule in *Re Burroughs Fowler*[3] no longer has any effect in Belize.

7.3.4 Bermuda

The trust laws of Bermuda are similar to those of England; and English case-law, though not binding, is of highly persuasive authority. The principal statutes of relevance here are the Trustee Act 1975, the Bankruptcy Act 1989, the Conveyancing Act 1983 (as amended by the Conveyancing Amendment Act 1994), the Trusts (Special Provisions) Act 1989 and the Trusts (Special Provisions) Amendment Act 1998. Bermuda is a party to the Hague

---

1 If the proper law of a trust is changed from the law of Belize to the law of another jurisdiction, no provision of the law of Belize (which must include s 149) shall operate so as to render the trust void, invalid or unlawful or to render void, invalid or unlawful any functions conferred on the trustee under the new law: TA 1992, s 4(6). *Cf* the jurisdiction conferred on the court by s 57 of the Act.

2 Section 12 deals generally with protective and spendthrift trusts.

3 [1916] 2 Ch 251. See also pp 390–391.

Convention on the Law Applicable to Trusts and on their Recognition 1985; and England's Recognition of Trusts Act 1987 has been extended to Bermuda.[1]

A settlement made by an individual who is declared bankrupt may be held void as against his trustee in bankruptcy under s 45(1) of the Bankruptcy Act 1989. Section 45 is similar to s 42 of the English Bankruptcy Act 1914, the main significant difference being that the period of 10 years specified in s 42(1) has been reduced in Bermuda to a period of only five years.

In addition, dispositions made with intent to defraud creditors are voidable, irrespective of bankruptcy, under Part IVA (ss 36A–36G) of the Conveyancing Act 1983 (CA 1983) (inserted therein by s 2 of the Conveyancing Amendment Act 1994 (CAA 1994)). Section 36C(1) provides that:

> 'every disposition of property made with the requisite intention and at an undervalue shall be voidable at the instance of an eligible creditor thereby prejudiced.'[2]

The key elements of this provision are defined in s 36A.

A 'disposition' means any disposition or series of dispositions of property of any nature whatsoever and however effected, and, without limiting the generality of the foregoing, includes any exercise of a power of appointment, any trust, gift, transfer, sale, exchange, demise, assignment, assurance, grant, lease, surrender, conveyance, reconveyance, release, reservation, any purchase or other acquisition, any covenant, contract or option and any compromise or other dealing or arrangement.[3] A 'relevant disposition' is a disposition to which s 36C applies. 'Property' includes money, goods, things in action, land and every description of property wherever situated and every description of interest, whether present or future or vested or contingent, arising out of, or incidental to, property.[4] The 'requisite intent' means an intention of a transferor (being a person who directly or indirectly makes a relevant disposition) to make a disposition 'the dominant purpose' of which is to put the property which is the subject matter of the disposition beyond the reach of a person, or a class of persons, who is making, or may at some time make, a claim against him.

An 'eligible creditor' means a person to whom:

---

1 Recognition of Trusts Act 1987 (Overseas Territory) Order 1989 (SI 1989/672) (operative on 1 June 1989).

2 The amendments made by the 1994 Act apply to every disposition of property made by any person, whether before or after the appointed day (the day on which the amendments came into operation), and whether or not the property which formed the subject matter of the disposition is situated in Bermuda or elsewhere: see s 36B(1); and see the exceptions specified in s 36B(2) and (3).

3 This is similar to, but broader than, the definition of 'disposition' in the Bahamian Fraudulent Dispositions Act 1991, s 2.

4 This is identical to the definition of 'property' in the English Insolvency Act 1986, s 436.

(a) on, or within two years after, the material date (being the date on which a relevant disposition is made) the transferor owed an obligation and on the date of action or proceeding to set aside the relevant disposition that obligation remains unsatisfied;
(b) on the material date the transferor owed a contingent liability and since that date the contingency giving rise to the obligation has occurred and on the date of the action or proceeding to set aside the relevant disposition that obligation remains unsatisfied; or
(c) on the date of the action or proceeding to set aside the relevant disposition, the transferor owes an obligation in consequence of a claim, made by that person against the transferor, arising from a cause of action which accrued prior to, or within two years after, the material date.

This does not mean, however, that any person who can show that he became a creditor of the transferor within two years of the material date (and would otherwise fall within categories (a) or (c)) can therefore seek to set aside the relevant disposition. Section 36C(2) provides that, where a person seeking to set aside a relevant disposition was not, on the material date, a person to whom an obligation was owed by the transferor, the court shall not set aside that disposition unless the court is satisfied that that person was, on the material date, reasonably foreseeable by the transferor as a person to whom an obligation might become owed by him. An 'obligation' means any obligation or liability, other than a contingent liability, to pay a sum of money or to transfer property. Finally, 'undervalue' in relation to a disposition of property means a disposition in respect of which (a) no consideration is given, or (b) the value of the consideration given is, in money or money's worth, significantly less than the value, in money or money's worth, of the property.[1]

In many respects, these provisions provide a greater degree of protection for a debtor than was the case under s 172 of the English Law of Property Act 1925 and are certainly far less favourable to a creditor than the provisions of the English Insolvency Act 1986. However, it is probably misleading to regard the Bermudian legislation as an 'asset protection code'. It is certainly more favourable to a creditor, and less favourable to a debtor, than recent legislation in some other jurisdictions, for example Belize and the Cook Islands. Indeed, the approach adopted by the 1994 Act seems to be rooted firmly in the provisions of the Elizabethan Statute of 1571 (and s 172 of the English Act which replaced it) and on the English case-law which construed and applied those provisions. The aim seems to have been to redress the balance slightly (and not overwhelmingly) in favour of the debtor and against the creditor; and the means by which it has been sought to achieve this end is by restricting the

---

[1] This is broadly similar to the definition of a 'transaction at an undervalue' in the English Insolvency Act 1986, s 423(1).

range of creditors who can seek to set aside a particular disposition, by imposing time-limits within which they must take action, and by according a degree of protection to both the transferee and the beneficiaries of such a disposition.

The definition of an 'eligible creditor', at whose instance a disposition shall be voidable, clearly identifies and separates categories of actual and potential creditors more specifically than English law does or ever did. Category (a) would clearly include those creditors to whom the transferor was already indebted at the date of the relevant disposition, as well as those to whom the transferor became indebted within two years thereafter (provided the latter were reasonably foreseeable).[1] Thus, where a transferor transferred property into a settlement and thereby rendered himself incapable of paying debts or meeting obligations which were reasonably foreseeable at the date of the transfer, and which were actually incurred and remained unpaid or unmet within two years of that date, the unpaid creditors would seem to fall squarely within category (a).

Similarly, in view of the reference, in the definition of 'requisite intention', to a 'class of persons who … may make a claim against him', it would also appear that, where an individual disposes of assets on the eve of embarking on a trade or other hazardous venture, those who supplied him with goods and services within two years of the date of the transfer, and who remained unpaid, would also seem to fall within category (a), provided they were 'reasonably foreseeable' creditors as at the date of the disposition.[2]

Category (b) includes, for example, those from whom the transferor had borrowed money before the date of the relevant disposition but where the debt was not due and payable until after that date, or those to whom he owed an obligation under a guarantee which existed at the date of the relevant disposition but the performance of which had arisen subsequently.[3]

Category (c) covers, for example, the case of the person who had a cause of action (say, in respect of some act of negligence) against the transferor, which cause of action had accrued before, or within two years of, the date of the relevant disposition,[4] and in respect of which, it seems, the transferor has actually been found liable (as opposed to being contingently liable)[5] on or

---

1 See CA 1993, s 36C(2).

2 Thus, it is not at all obvious that the result in *Re Butterworth* (1882) 19 Ch D 588 would not still be reached (subject to establishing the 'dominant purpose' of the disposition).

3 There is no two-year time-limit here. But see CA 1983, s 36C(3).

4 Thus, the plaintiffs in the English cases of *Barling v Bishopp* (1860) 29 Beav 417; *Crossley v Elworthy* (1871) LR 12 Eq 158; and *Re Wise* (1886) 17 QBD 290, would fall within category (c).

5 This seems to be implicit in the definition of 'obligation', which excludes a contingent liability. It is not clear, as a result, what the position might be if the transferor has been found liable at the relevant date, but the amount of damages has not then been determined. Is his liability still a contingent liability or not?

before the date on which that person commences his action to set aside the disposition.[1]

When a cause of action actually 'accrues' may well be problematic: for example, it might be the date when the act on the part of the defendant which gave the plaintiff his cause of complaint occurred, or the date on which damage results from that act. In addition, precisely how the latter part of this particular limb of the definition will operate in conjunction with s 36C(2) is not clear. Suppose, for example, that the transferor commits some act of negligence (eg negligent medical treatment or negligent advice) just before the expiry of two years from the date of the relevant disposition. Suppose, also, that the cause of action accrues at the date of that act of negligence.[2] In these circumstances, the victim could not have been a person to whom an obligation was owed at the date of the disposition. Is he none the less a person who was, at that date, reasonably foreseeable by the transferor as a person to whom an obligation might become owed by him (as required by s 36C(2))? Both s 36C(2) and the definition of 'eligible creditor' in s 36A refer only to 'a person' (and not to 'a class of persons' nor to 'one of a class of persons'). Only the definition of 'requisite intention' refers to 'a class of persons' and that, of course, is aimed at a different requirement. Even if it can be proved that the transferor intended to put his assets beyond the reach of a class of potential claimants, it does not follow that a particular individual – even one who might be within that class – can set aside the disposition: he must still be an 'eligible creditor'.

In the context of s 36C(2), such an individual must presumably still show that it was reasonably foreseeable, at the date of the disposition, that *his* cause of action might accrue, or that *he* might be a person to whom the transferor might owe an obligation, after the date of the disposition. It is difficult to see how, in any event, it could be said to be reasonably foreseeable by the transferor that he might commit a negligent act (or owe an obligation of the kind specified in the legislation) in the future, and even more difficult to see how this could be said to be the case in relation to someone who is (probably) an unknown and unascertained individual.

No disposition can be set aside unless it was made with 'the requisite intention'. This, in turn, requires an intention on the part of the transferor to make a disposition 'the dominant purpose' of which is to put property beyond the reach of a person or a class of persons who may make a claim against him. Although this requirement is similar to that in s 423(3) of the English Insolvency Act 1986,[3] there is a seemingly crucial difference in that s 423(3)

---

1 The 'date of the action or proceeding' seems to be the date on which the writ is issued or the relevant proceedings are otherwise formally commenced, although the Act does not make this clear.

2 Whether the cause of action accrues at the date of the act of negligence or when damage is suffered is immaterial for the purposes of this illustration. Clearly, if it accrues more than two years after the date of the disposition, the victim will not be an 'eligible creditor' within limb (b) in any event.

3 The possible meaning of the English provision has been discussed above, at pp 384–389.

refers only to 'the purpose' whereas the Bermudian counterpart refers to 'the dominant purpose'. It therefore seems clear that, in Bermuda, it is not sufficient for the transferor to have had as an incidental purpose, or even as just one of his purposes, the putting of assets beyond the reach of potential claimants. Such a purpose must have been his dominant purpose – indeed, it must apparently have been *the* dominant purpose and not just *a* dominant one. Thus, if, when a transferor transfers assets into a Bermudian settlement, he is primarily motivated by the desire to provide for the future benefit of his family, or by the desire to avoid taxation in another jurisdiction, or to take advantage of the Bermudian provisions permitting trusts for the benefit of non-charitable purposes, the fact that he might also intend, or hope, that those assets might thereby be protected from actual or potential creditors would not, in itself, be sufficient to establish the 'requisite intention'. Only if the desire to prejudice actual or potential claimants is the dominant purpose for which the disposition is made will that disposition be at risk.

In any event, it seems clear that not all future or subsequent creditors can invoke the provisions of the Act and, in this sense, the Bermudian provisions are narrower in scope (from the viewpoint of a creditor) than those in force in England before 1986. For example, a person who became a creditor of a trader more than two years after the date of the relevant disposition would not qualify as an 'eligible creditor' under limb (a), (b) or (c) of the definition of that expression.

In addition, s 36C(3) imposes an absolute time-limit for the bringing of proceedings. It provides that no action or proceeding to set aside a disposition shall be commenced pursuant to Part IVA of the CA 1983 unless such action or proceeding is commenced:

(i) in the case of an eligible creditor within category (a), within six years after the material date or after the date when the obligation became owed (whichever is the later date);
(ii) in the case of an eligible creditor within category (b), within six years after the material date; and
(iii) in the case of an eligible creditor within category (c), within six years after the material date or after the date when the cause of action accrued (whichever is the later).

Whether this absolute time-limit will benefit the creditor or the debtor will depend on the circumstances of the particular case. The effect of s 36C(3)(a) and (c), for example, is to provide a period of almost eight years during which some (but not all) eligible creditors within categories (a) and (c) can bring proceedings to set aside a relevant disposition (ie if the relevant obligation or cause of action, as the case may be, accrued shortly before the expiry of the period of two years after the material date). On the other hand, one effect of s 36C(3)(b) seems to be that a creditor, to whom a contingent liability was owed on the material date (for example, under a guarantee), cannot bring proceedings unless the contingency has occurred, and the obligation remains unsatisfied, within six years of the material date (and not within six years of the date on which the contingency giving rise to the obligation occurred).

In some respects, the Bermudian provisions are clearly more favourable to a creditor than the legislation in force in some other jurisdictions: for example, there is no requirement in Bermuda (unlike The Bahamas) that the transferor should have had actual notice of an obligation or liability which existed at the date of the relevant disposition. Nevertheless, their broad effect, as in the case of the Bahamian legislation, is to restrict the extent to which a person's assets may be subject to possible claims by creditors who are unknown to him, and who cannot seriously be within his contemplation, at the date of a relevant disposition, and also to specify a 'cut-off' point after which claims can no longer be brought, thus providing an element of clarity and certainty. In other respects, too, the Bermudian legislation provides greater clarity. For example, s 36C(5) declares that a disposition shall not be set aside by the court by reason only that it was made at an undervalue; and also that, for the purpose of setting aside a relevant disposition, the court shall determine, on a balance of probability, whether it was made with the requisite intent.

If a relevant disposition is set aside, and if the court is satisfied that the transferee (being the person to whom a relevant disposition has been made and also the successor in title of such person)[1] has acted in good faith, then:

(a) the transferee will have a first and paramount charge over the property, the subject of the relevant disposition, for an amount equal to all costs (and not only such costs as the court might otherwise allow) properly incurred by the transferee in the defence of the action or proceeding to set aside that disposition;
(b) the relevant disposition will be set aside subject to all fees and costs properly incurred and subject also to any pre-existing rights, claims and interests of the transferee and of any person through whom the transferee claims and who has acted in good faith; and
(c) in the case of a trust, the relevant disposition will only be set aside subject to the right of a beneficiary to retain any distribution made consequent upon the prior exercise of a trust, power or a discretion vested in the trustee of such trust or any other person, and otherwise properly exercised.[2]

These provisions are similar to those in s 5 of the Bahamian Fraudulent Dispositions Act 1991,[3] although there are some crucial differences. In The

1 CA 1983, s 36A.
2 Ibid, s 36D.
3 See pp 416–418.

Bahamas, the rights of the transferee and/or beneficiary are protected unless the court is satisfied that the transferee/beneficiary has acted in bad faith. In Bermuda, by contrast, such rights of the transferee are protected only if the court is satisfied that the transferee has acted in good faith. In both cases, the burden of proving bad faith or absence of good faith (as the case may be) lies upon the person making the allegation.[1] In both cases there is also a question as to what constitutes 'bad faith' or 'good faith' – in particular, whether presence or absence of dishonesty must be established, or whether the presence or absence of notice is sufficient.[2] Nevertheless, it is probable that it will be more difficult to establish that a transferee has actually acted in bad faith rather than that he has not acted in good faith.

In any event, as in the Bahamian legislation, there seems to be no requirement that the absence of good faith on the part of the transferee must have existed at the date of the relevant disposition. Subsequent lack of good faith will also deprive a transferee of the statutory protection – such as, for instance, where a trustee exercises a power so as to distribute property to a beneficiary at a time when the trustee had full knowledge that an eligible creditor was seeking to set aside the settlement and intended, by that exercise, to prejudice that creditor. The exercise of the power must not otherwise be excessive or fraudulent (in the sense of a 'fraud on the power').[3] On the other hand, s 36D(1)(c) (unlike its Bahamian counterpart) does not expressly impose a requirement of bad faith or good faith on the part of a beneficiary who has received a distribution from a trust, and it is difficult to see how one could be implied, given that such an express requirement is imposed in the same section in respect of a transferee. Thus, it would seem that, if a transferee/trustee had distributed property which had been settled by the relevant disposition to a beneficiary, by means of an exercise (say) of a power of appointment or of advancement, and if it could not be shown that the trustee had not acted in good faith – for example, by colluding with the transferor in his attempt to prejudice the eligible creditor – the trustee could claim the protection conferred by s 36D, and the absence of good faith (or the presence of blatant bad faith) on the part of the beneficiary would seem to be immaterial.

Section 36E of the 1983 Act declares that a relevant disposition may be set aside only to the extent necessary to satisfy the obligation owed to the eligible creditor at whose instance the disposition has been set aside. Thus, the success of one eligible creditor under the Act will not enure for the benefit of any other eligible creditor(s). Moreover, s 36G provides that nothing in these provisions shall be construed as creating or enabling any right, claim or interest on behalf of a creditor or person which right, claim or interest would be avoided by s 11 of the Trusts (Special Provisions) Act 1989 (TSPA 1989).

---

1 (Bahamian) Fraudulent Dispositions Act 1991, s 5(1); (Bermudian) CA 1983, s 36D(2).
2 As to which, see pp 416–418.
3 CA Act 1983, s 36D(1)(c).

Section 11 of the TSPA 1989 (which came into operation on 31 January 1990) provides that, where a trust is validly created under the law of Bermuda, the court shall not set it aside pursuant to the law of another jurisdiction in respect of *inter alia* the protection of creditors in matters of insolvency, unless the law of Bermuda has corresponding laws or public policy rules. The expression 'matters of insolvency' is not defined in the legislation and, as in the case of s 7(6) of the Trusts Act 1992 of Belize (which, apart from its closing words, s 11 closely resembles), it is not clear whether a Bermudian court will assist in giving effect (say) to the order of an English court setting aside a transaction at an undervalue under ss 423–425 of the Insolvency Act 1986 (which are not dependent on insolvency).

In addition, the word 'corresponding' seldom means 'identical' and usually requires only a degree of similarity. As we have seen, Bermuda has legislation which broadly corresponds to the provisions of s 172 of the English Law of Property Act 1925 and to substantial parts of the Insolvency Act 1986. It is therefore not obvious why s 11 of the TSPA 1989 should necessarily prevent a Bermudian court from giving effect to the order of an English court setting aside a Bermudian settlement created by an English domiciled settlor.

7.3.5 The British Virgin Islands

Section 81 of the Conveyancing and Law of Property Act (c 220) is identical to s 172 of the English Law of Property Act 1925.[1]

7.3.6 The Cayman Islands

On bankruptcy

Section 107 of the Bankruptcy Law (Revised) contains provisions which are identical to those in s 42 of the English Bankruptcy Act 1914 (with the same two-year and 10-year time-limits, and subject to the same exceptions).[2] Only 'debtors' may be declared bankrupt under the Law. 'Debtors' are defined to include any person, whether a British subject or not, who at the time when any act of bankruptcy was done or suffered by him:

(a) was personally present in the Islands; or
(b) ordinarily resided or had a place of residence in the Islands; or
(c) was carrying on business in the Islands, personally or by means of an agent or manager; or
(d) was a member of a firm or partnership which carried on business in the Islands.[3]

---

1 See **7.2.3**.

2 See **7.2.4**.

3 Bankruptcy Law (Revised), s 2.

A settlor with no relevant Cayman Islands connection at the date of the settlement may become subject to the Bankruptcy Law if he acquires a relevant connection at any time up until the tenth anniversary of the settlement. If property is added to an existing settlement, the 10-year period runs from the date of the addition and not the date of the original settlement.[1]

Irrespective of bankruptcy

Prior to the Fraudulent Dispositions Law 1989 (the 1989 Law), the position in the Cayman Islands was governed by the provisions of the English 1571 Act (which was generally accepted to apply).[2] However, s 3 of the 1989 Law provided that, with effect from 'the appointed date' (being 1 May 1990),[3] the 1989 Law shall apply in place of the law in effect prior to the appointed date to every disposition of property made before or after the appointed date by any person, and whether or not the property, the subject of the disposition, is situate in the Islands or elsewhere.[4]

The provisions of the 1989 Law are virtually identical with those of the Bahamian Fraudulent Dispositions Act 1991 (which seem to have been modelled on the 1989 Law and which have already been described above).[5] Thus, s 4(1) of the 1989 Law declares that, subject to the provisions of the Law, every disposition of property 'made with an intent to defraud and at an undervalue' shall be voidable at the instance of a creditor thereby prejudiced. The definitions of the key terms in s 2 are almost identical to the definitions of the same terms in the Bahamian legislation.[6] However, there are three differences, at least two of which (and probably all three) seem to render the Cayman Islands legislation more advantageous to a creditor than the Bahamian legislation which followed it.

First, although the definition of 'obligation' in the 1989 Law refers to an obligation or liability (including a contingent liability) which existed on or prior to the date of the relevant disposition, it must none the less be an obligation of which the transferor 'had notice'. This is virtually identical with the definition in the Bahamian Act, save that the latter expressly refers to such an obligation

---

1 Ibid, s 14.

2 The settlers who settled the Cayman Islands (between 1658 and 1734) were deemed to have brought with them English law in effect at the date of settlement. See now Interpretation Law 1963, s 40. The Cayman Islands' Special Trust (Alternative Regime) Law 1997, coupled with the Perpetuities (Amendment) Law 1997, provides the most sophisticated and flexible vehicle of all the offshore jurisdictions. These so-called STAR trusts may be used *inter alia* for the purpose of asset protection. However, STAR trusts are subject to the same rules and provisions as to 'fraudulent dispositions' as ordinary trusts and therefore do not require special treatment here.

3 Fraudulent Dispositions (Commencement) Law 1990, s 2.

4 Section 3 further provides a saving in respect of any action or proceeding commenced prior to the appointed date, or within six months thereof, in respect of a disposition made prior to the appointed date.

5 See **7.3.2**.

6 The word 'disposition' is defined by reference to Trusts (Foreign Element) Law 1987, s 2(1), where the word is given the same meaning as in the Bahamian legislation.

or liability of which the transferor 'had actual notice'. This suggests that, for the purposes of the 1989 Law, constructive (and even imputed notice) may be sufficient.

Secondly, s 4(3) of the 1989 Law declares that no action or proceeding shall be commenced pursuant to the 1989 Law unless commenced within six years of the date of the relevant disposition. The relevant period under s 4(3) of the Bahamian Fraudulent Dispositions Act 1991 is two years. (Thus, the Cayman Islands legislation is more favourable to a creditor than that in The Bahamas.)

Thirdly, s 5 of the 1989 Law (which accords a degree of protection to a transferee and a beneficiary of a trust to whom a distribution has been made) applies 'if the Court is satisfied that the transferee [or beneficiary] has not acted in bad faith', whereas its counterpart, in s 5 of the Bahamian Act, applies 'unless the court is satisfied that the transferee [or beneficiary] has acted in bad faith'. In addition, whereas the Bahamian legislation includes an additional provision (in s 5(2)) to the effect that the burden of proving that the transferee (or beneficiary) has acted in bad faith shall lie upon the person making the allegation, there is no such provision in the 1989 Law. This subtle difference therefore has the effect that, under the 1989 Law, the burden of proof on the question of protection for a transferee (or beneficiary) is effectively reversed: it is for the transferee (or beneficiary) to establish that he has *not* acted in bad faith, and not for the creditor to prove that the transferee (or beneficiary) has done so.

Finally, s 6 of the Trusts (Foreign Element) Law 1987 provides for the exclusion of foreign law in respect of a trust governed by the laws of the Cayman Islands, or a disposition of property to be held upon the trusts thereof.[1] However, it is difficult to see how this provision is relevant to the question of 'asset protection'. Section 6 declares that a Cayman Islands trust will not be void, voidable, liable to be set aside or defective in any fashion, by reason that the trust or disposition avoids or defeats rights, claims or interests conferred by foreign law, but this provision seems to be confined to such rights, claims or interests as are conferred by reason of personal relationship with the settlor, or by way of heirship rights. The rights and interests of creditors in an insolvency, for example, are not referred to and cannot, it seems, be included by implication.

Similarly, the alternative head under which a trust shall not be void, voidable, or liable to be set aside, namely that it contravenes any rule of foreign law or foreign judicial or administrative order or action, seems to be confined to such rules, orders or actions as are intended to recognise, protect, enforce or give effect to 'any such rights, claims or interests'. (In contrast, s 8

---

1 See *Re the Lemos Trust Settlement* (1992–93) CILR 26 and *Lemos v Coutts & Co (Cayman) Ltd* (1992–93) CILR 5.

of the Bahamian Trusts (Choice of Governing Law) Act 1989, provides generally that a Bahamian trust shall not be void, voidable or set aside 'by reference to a foreign law'.) Thus, there seems to be no obvious reason why an order of a foreign court (such as an order made by an English court under s 423 of the Insolvency Act 1986) should not be enforced in the Cayman Islands, even if it relates to the setting aside of a disposition to a Cayman Islands trust.

7.3.7 The Cook Islands

The Cook Islands have a separate legislative regime for offshore entities.[1] The governing legislation for international trusts is the International Trusts Act 1984 (ITA 1984) (as amended by a series of Amending Acts).[2]

An international trust is a trust which is registered under the ITA 1984 and in respect of which:

(a) at least one of the trustees, including a custodian trustee, or in the case of a disposition granting powers of appointment, maintenance or advancement, at least one of the donors or holders of the power of appointment or power of maintenance or power of advancement is either:
   (i) a registered foreign company; or
   (ii) an international company; or
   (iii) a trustee company;

   and shall include, where the context so permits, a trust which is established or settled under the laws of another jurisdiction but which, subject to paras (a) and (b) of this definition, is subsequently registered as an international trust under the ITA 1984; and
(b) the beneficiaries are at all times non-resident.[3]

---

1 Provided the requirements of the ITA 1984 are complied with (eg those relating to registration), an international trust enjoys many advantages, such as, eg, freedom from the rules against perpetuities, remoteness of vesting, and excessive accumulations: see ss 6 and 9 of the ITA 1984. The 1984 Act does not apply to a beneficiary who is domiciled or ordinarily resident in the Cook Islands: see s 22(1).

2 The International Trusts Amendment Act 1985, the International Trusts Amendment Act 1989, the International Trusts Amendment (No 2) Act 1989, the International Trusts Amendment Act 1991, the International Trusts Amendment Act 1995–96, the International Trusts Amendment (No 2) Act 1995–96 and the International Trusts Amendment Act 1999. References in this section are to the 1984 Act as amended.

3 ITA 1984, s 2. A 'non-resident' is defined (also in s 2) as: (a) an individual not domiciled in the Cook Islands; (b) an individual not ordinarily resident in the Cook Islands; (c) an international company; (d) a foreign company; (e) a trustee company; or (f) a subsidiary of a trustee company being either an international company or a foreign company.

A trust registered under the ITA 1984 is a valid trust notwithstanding that it may be invalid according to the law of the settlor's[1] domicile or residence or place of current incorporation.[2]

Section 13A deals specifically with bankruptcy and allied matters. It provides that, notwithstanding any provision of the law of the settlor's domicile or place of ordinary residence or the settlor's current place of incorporation, and notwithstanding further that an international trust is voluntary and without valuable consideration being given for the same, or is made on or for the benefit of the settlor, settlor's spouse or children of the settlor or any of them, an international trust and a disposition to an international trust shall not be void or voidable in the event of the settlor's bankruptcy, insolvency or liquidation (other than in the case of an international company registered pursuant to the International Companies Act 1981–82 that is in liquidation) or in any action or proceedings at the suit of creditors of the settlor, but shall remain valid and subsisting and take effect according to its tenor, subject to the provisions of s 13B.

Section 13B then deals with international trusts, and dispositions to international trusts, made or alleged to have been made with the intention of defrauding creditors. The provisions of s 13B (which have recently been heavily amended)[3] are declared to apply to all actions and proceedings brought in the High Court of the Cook Islands in which fraud, deceit, unconscionable conduct or any other inequitable conduct (however described) or any species of unjust enrichment is alleged, against any party (whether a party to the proceedings or not), with regard to the settlement or establishment of an international trust or the disposition of property to such a trust, or receipt of property by or for such a trust (or subsequent disposition of property from such a trust with the intention of prejudicing creditors of the settlor of such property or such trust); and the remedy conferred by s 13B(1) (see below) shall be the sole remedy available in such an action or proceedings, to the exclusion of any other relief or remedy against any party to the relevant action or proceeding.[4] It is also expressly provided that the provisions of s 13B operate to the exclusion of any other remedy, principle or rule of law, whether

---

1 A 'settlor' is defined in s 2 and in relation to an international trust means and includes an assignor of property to an international trust and each and every person who, directly or indirectly, on behalf of himself or any other(s), as owner, or as the holder of a power in that behalf, disposes of property to be held in such trust or declares or otherwise creates such trust. This definition, coupled with the definition of 'disposition', has the effect that the donee of a power of appointment could be a settlor for the purposes of the ITA 1984.

2 Ibid, s 5(2).

3 These amendments seem to have been prompted, at least in part, by the recent interlocutory decision of the Cook Islands Court of Appeal in *515 South Orange Grove Owners Association v Orange Grove Partners* (1995) No 208/94 (as to which see below). The amended s 13B(8), in particular, seems to apply only to every international trust settled or established on or after 8 September 1989, and to every disposition of property to such trust made on or after that date: see the International Trusts Amendment Act 1995–96, s 27(2) .

4 ITA 1984, s 13B(9).

provided for by statute or founded in equity or in common law, including (for the avoidance of doubt) the imposition of a constructive trust upon any interested party or the recognition and enforcement of any constructive trust imposed or recognised by the laws of any other jurisdiction.[1] Indeed, the provisions of s 13B apply not only to every international trust but also to every trust which, having been registered as an international trust, is no longer so registered (and in respect to all dispositions to such a trust).[2] Thus, the ITA 1984 provides a fairly comprehensive code for international trusts which may be – and is clearly intended to be – of considerable assistance to those who seek to avoid or defeat their creditors.[3]

Section 13B(1) provides that, where it is proven 'beyond reasonable doubt' by a creditor that an international trust settled or established, or property disposed to an international trust:

(a) was so settled, established or disposed by or on behalf of the settlor 'with principal intent' to defraud 'that creditor' of the settlor; and
(b) did at the time such settlement, establishment or disposition took place render the settlor insolvent or without property by which 'that creditor's' claim (if successful) could have been satisfied,

then such settlement, establishment or disposition shall not be void or voidable, but the international trust shall be liable to satisfy the creditor's claim out of the property which, but for the settlement, establishment or disposition, would have been available to satisfy the creditor's claim; and such liability shall only be to the extent of the interest that the settlor had in the property prior to settlement, establishment or disposition and any accumulation to the property (if any) subsequent thereto.

Thus, it is clear that a creditor who invokes the provisions of s 13B must establish that the settlor intended to defraud him, and not some other creditor. It is not clear, however, whether this burden can be discharged by showing that the settlor intended to defraud a class or category of creditors of which that particular creditor was a member, although it may be inferred from other parts of s 13B (for example, subsections (1)(b) and (2)) that a creditor who

1 Ibid, s 13B(10).

2 Ibid, s 13B(11). This is subject to s 16(6), dealing with deregistration and the consequences thereof.

3 The recent amendments to the 1984 Act have clearly strengthened the usefulness of the Cook Islands legislation for this purpose. However, any such legislation is seriously at risk unless it is interpreted and applied by a sympathetic judiciary, and the attitude of the Cook Islands judiciary to the legislation, as manifested in the *Orange Grove* case, seems to be anything but sympathetic. Although the Court of Appeal cannot be criticised for indicating that Cook Islands legislation was not intended to assist fraudsters, it does none the less appear to have favoured the interests of creditors rather than those of the settlers. On the other hand, on 11 August 1999, the High Court rejected an application by the US Federal Trade Commission (following the decision in *Federal Trade Commission (FTC) v Affordable Media LLC and Anderson* 179 F 2d 1228 (9 Cir 1999) (the *Anderson* case)) to have a Cook Islands trustee removed and its own appointee appointed as a new trustee and protector of a Cook Islands trust.

invokes s 13B must have been a creditor at the date of the settlement or disposition. A 'creditor' is not defined but is stated to include 'any person who alleges a cause of action'.[1] This must be read in the context of the other (somewhat convoluted) provisions of s 13B (which are dealt with below).

It is clear, however, that an intent to defraud a creditor must have been the settlor's 'principal intent'. Although it is not entirely beyond debate, this seems to require that such an intent must be *the* chief or paramount intention, and to indicate that it is not sufficient that it was an important consideration or motivation on the settlor's part, if it was not indeed his primary intent. It also appears that the creditor must establish both limbs of subsection (1) (which are joined by the word 'and'). In other words, proving a clear intent to defraud would not seem to suffice in itself if the settlor was not rendered insolvent or unable to satisfy the creditor's claim.[2] Similarly, proving that, as a direct result of the settlement or disposition, the settlor was rendered insolvent or unable to satisfy the creditor's claim would seem not to suffice if a principal intent to defraud could not be established.

In determining whether the creation of an international trust, or a disposition to an international trust, has rendered the settlor insolvent or without property by which a creditor's claim (if successful) may be satisfied, regard shall be had to the fair market value of the settlor's property (not being property of or relating to the trust) at the time immediately after the creation of the settlement or the disposition. In the event that the fair market value of such property exceeded the value of the creditor's claim at that time, then the trust or disposition shall, for *all* purposes (and not just for the purposes of the ITA 1984), be deemed not to have been created or made with intent to defraud the creditor.[3]

The ITA 1984 also imposes certain time-limits. The creation of, and a disposition to, an international trust shall for all purposes be deemed not to have been made with intent to defraud a creditor of a settlor:

(a) if it occurred *after* the expiration of two years from the date on which the creditor's cause of action accrued; or
(b) where it occurred *before* the expiration of two years from the date on which the creditor's cause of action accrued, *if* that creditor fails to commence, in a court of competent jurisdiction, proceedings in respect of that creditor's cause of action before the expiration of one

1 ITA 1984, s 13B(12).
2 See also the concluding words of s 13B(2) (although it is not clear that they add anything).
3 ITA 1984, s 13B(2).

year from the date on which the international trust was created or the relevant disposition made.[1]

In addition, the creation of, or a disposition to, an international trust shall not be fraudulent as against a creditor of a settlor if it occurred before that creditor's cause of action against the settlor accrued.[2] For these purposes (and also for the purposes of s 13K, dealing with the commencement of proceedings[3]) the date on which the cause of action accrued shall be determined in accordance with the recently amended provisions of s 13B(8). This provides, first, that it shall be the date of that act or omission which is relied upon to establish (wholly or partly) the cause of action. If there is more than one act, or the omission is a continuing one, then the date of the first act, or the date that the omission first occurred, as the case may be, shall be the date on which the cause of action accrued.

It is then provided further that the term 'cause of action' means the earliest cause of action capable of assertion by a creditor against the settlor of an international trust, by which that creditor has established (or may establish) an enforceable claim against that settlor.[4] Where a creditor has or asserts (or could have asserted) multiple or successive causes of action against a settlor (whether by virtue of the nature of the relevant circumstances of the case, or by reason of having attained the status of a judgment creditor in respect of one or more of such causes of action, or by reason of asserting or being able to assert an allegedly fraudulent settlement of or disposition to an international trust, or otherwise) the entitlement of such a creditor to relief under s 13B shall be determined, and the periods referred to in s 13B shall be calculated, by reference to one only of that creditor's causes of action, being that cause of

---

1 Ibid, s 13B(3). It is provided further that these latter provisions shall not have effect if (and subject also to subsection (5)) at the time of the creation of the international trust or of the relevant disposition, proceedings in respect of that creditor's cause of action against that settlor have already been commenced in a court of competent jurisdiction. It is difficult to see how this proviso fits in with subsection (3)(b). It also seems that the creditor has one year from the date of the relevant disposition to commence proceedings *in the Cook Islands*, and it is *not* the case that, provided he commences domestic proceedings within one year, he will have a further two years in which to commence proceedings in the Cook Islands: the second *Orange Grove* case (1996) 1 OFLR 3, CA.

2 Ibid, s 13B(4).

3 See below.

4 ITA 1984, s 13B(8)(b). Prior to the International Trusts Amendment Act 1995–96, s 13B(8)(b) of the 1984 Act declared that, in the case of an action upon a judgment, the date of the cause of action accruing should be the date of that act or omission (or, where there was more than one act or the omission was a continuing one, the date of the first act or the date that the omission first occurred, as the case may be) which gave rise to the judgment itself. In *515 South Orange Grove Association v Orange Grove Partners* (1995) No 208/94, where the issue was whether proceedings for a *Mareva* injunction taken in the Cook Islands to enforce a Californian judgment had been commenced in time, the Cook Islands Court of Appeal held that the effect of this provision, coupled with s 13B(3), was that the relevant time-limit before which a creditor had to bring proceedings under s 13B was the expiration of two years from the date of the finding of the Californian jury and not from the date when the original cause of action accrued. There were two *Orange Grove* cases, in fact (dealing with two identical trusts). It is believed that both cases were settled.

action which accrued first in time in accordance with subsection (8)(b).[1] However, nothing in subsection (8)(b) or (c) shall apply so as to affect the right (or requirement) of a creditor to commence separate proceedings under s 13B in relation to a cause of action where the court is satisfied (having regard to subsection (8)(c)) that both the circumstances out of which the cause of action arose and the subject matter of that cause of action are wholly unrelated to those of the other cause of action.[2]

A creditor seeking to enforce a claim under s 13B in reliance on a foreign judgment may not enforce such claim until such time as it (*sic*) can demonstrate to the reasonable satisfaction of the court that (a) it has exhausted all remedies available to it against the settlor's remaining property and (b) all rights of appeal against that foreign judgment have been exhausted.[3] For the purposes of assessing the liability of an international trust to a creditor under s 13B, where the amount of that creditor's claim against the settlor is wholly or partly in any way related to or evidenced by a foreign judgment, the court in making any award in favour of that creditor shall disregard and exclude any amount awarded in that foreign judgment to that creditor which comprises any form of exemplary, vindictive, retributory or punitive damages (by whatever name) or is an amount of damages arrived at by doubling, trebling or otherwise multiplying a sum assessed as compensation for the loss or damage (which types of damage are together called 'punitive damages').[4] The burden of proving that an amount awarded in a foreign judgment does not wholly or partly comprise punitive damages rests on the creditor.[5] However, the above-mentioned provisions of subsection (14) shall not apply if, at the time of the settlement, establishment or disposition (as the case may be), an award of punitive damages has already been made in a foreign judgment against the settlor.[6]

The burden of proving an intent to defraud on the part of the settlor lies on the creditor.[7] This burden is a heavy one, for the opening words of s 13B(1) make it clear that it must be proved 'beyond reasonable doubt' (and not just on a balance of probabilities) that an international trust was created, or a disposition to an international trust was made, not only with the principal intent to defraud but also that it resulted in the insolvency of the settlor or rendered him unable to satisfy the creditor's claim. In addition, a settlor shall not have imputed to him an intent to defraud a creditor, solely by reason that the settlor:

---

1 ITA 1984, s 13B(8)(c).
2 Ibid, s 13B(8)(d).
3 Ibid, s 13B(13).
4 Ibid, s 13B(14), inserted by the International Trusts Amendment Act 1999.
5 Ibid, s 13B(15), inserted by the International Trusts Amendment Act 1999.
6 Ibid, s 13B(16), inserted by the International Trusts Amendment Act 1999.
7 Ibid, s 13B(7).

(a) has settled or established a trust or has disposed of property to such trust within two years from the date of that creditor's cause of action accruing;
(b) has retained, possesses or acquires any of the powers or benefits referred to in s 13C(a)–(f);[1]
(c) is a beneficiary, trustee or protector;
(d) has settled or established a trust, or has disposed of property to such trust, at a time when proceedings in respect of that creditor's cause of action against that settlor have already been commenced in a court of competent jurisdiction.[2]

In the event that an international trust is liable to satisfy a creditor's claim in the manner provided for in s 13B(1), that creditor's rights to recovery shall be limited to that property referred to in subsection (1), or to the proceeds of that property, to the exclusion of any rights against the trustees of the international trust or any of them, against any other property of the international trust, or any of them; and, where the international trust is unable to satisfy the creditor's claim by reason of the fact that the property referred to in subsection (1) has been disposed of, other than to a *bona fide* purchaser for value, then any such disposition shall be void.[3] There are no special provisions in the ITA 1984 (unlike the legislation in force in The Bahamas and Bermuda, for example) giving protection (in respect of the costs of defending an action brought by a creditor or any other costs) to a transferee who has not given value but has acted in good faith (or not acted in bad faith) or to a beneficiary who has (in good faith or otherwise) received a distribution from an international trust.

Section 13C deals with the retention of control and benefits by a settlor. It provides that an international trust shall not be declared invalid, nor a disposition declared void or be affected in any way by reason of the fact that the settlor, and if more than one, any of them, retains, possesses or acquires:

(a) a power to revoke the trust;
(b) a power of disposition over property of the trust;
(c) a power to amend the trust;
(d) any benefit, interest or property from the trust;
(e) the power to remove or appoint a trustee or protector;
(f) the power to direct a trustee or protector on any matter;

or is a beneficiary of the trust, either solely or together with others.[4]

---

1 See next paragraph.
2 ITA 1984, s 13B(5).
3 Ibid, s 13B(6).
4 Ibid, s 13C(a)–(g). If the settlor retains such control, he is clearly at considerable risk of being compelled by the courts of his domestic jurisdiction to exercise his powers to repatriate the trust assets and of

Furthermore, s 13D deals specifically with the non-enforcement of foreign judgments. It is provided that, notwithstanding the provisions of any treaty or statute, or any rule of law or equity, to the contrary, no proceedings for or in relation to the enforcement or recognition of a judgment obtained in a jurisdiction other than the Cook Islands against any interested party shall be in any way entertained, recognised or enforced by any court in the Cook Islands to the extent that the judgment:

(a) is based upon the application of any law inconsistent with the provisions of the ITA 1984 (or of the Trustee Companies Act 1981–82) or;
(b) relates to a matter or particular aspect that is governed by the law of the Cook Islands.

In determining the governing law of an international trust, regard shall first be had to the terms of that trust and to any evidence therein as to the intention of the parties. The other circumstances of an international trust may be taken into account only if the terms of the trust fail to provide such evidence.[1] A term of an international trust expressly selecting the laws of the Cook Islands to govern the trust is valid, effective and conclusive regardless of any other circumstances.[2] Similarly, where a trust instrument[3] so provides, or where, in accordance with the powers contained in a trust instrument, the law of the Cook Islands is chosen to govern a particular aspect of an international trust, and law other than that of the Cook Islands is chosen to govern other aspects of that trust, then the choice of Cook Islands law and the choice of that other law as to their respective aspects shall be valid, effective and conclusive regardless of any other circumstances.[4]

Where a trust instrument contains a power to change the governing law of that trust, the law may be changed to or from the law of the Cook Islands in accordance with that power, and that change shall be valid, effective and conclusive according to the terms of such power; and such a change in governing law shall not affect the legality or validity of, or render any person

---

being penalised for contempt if he fails to do so: see, eg, *Ex parte Coffelt* 389 SW 2d 234 (7 Cir 1989); and especially *Federal Trade Commission (FTC) v Affordable Media LLC and Anderson* 179 F 3d 1228 (9 Cir 1999) (the *Anderson* case), where the settlors were protectors, co-trustees and beneficiaries of a Cook Islands trust. Following the decision in the latter case, the FTC brought proceedings in the Cook Islands to have the Cook Islands trustee removed, its own appointee appointed as trustee and protector, and the trust assets repatriated. The High Court of the Islands found in favour of the existing trustee and rejected the application (decision of 11 August 1999). See also *Re W Family Trust* (18 July 1999) HC of CI.

1 ITA 1984, s 13G(1).

2 Ibid, s 13G(2).

3 A 'trust instrument', 'instrument' or 'registered instrument' means the deed, trust agreement, will, codicil, settlement or instrument establishing or creating a trust and includes any variation or amendment to such deed, trust agreement, will, codicil, settlement or instrument: see ibid, s 2.

4 Ibid, s 13G(3).

liable for, any thing done before the change.[1] A change in the governing law of a trust shall not of itself interrupt the continuity of the relationships whether in equity or law established by the trust and, without limitation, will not constitute a resettlement of the trust.[2] The disposition of any property to or from a trust in accordance with the governing law of that trust at the time of the disposition shall not be affected or invalidated by a subsequent change from that governing law to some other law.[3] Where the donee of a power to change the governing law of a trust exercises that power in accordance with the terms of that power, then such exercise shall be deemed to have been proper.[4] The location of the interested parties, selection or imposition of jurisdiction, place of administration, or the situation of the property of the trust, will not affect the validity or effect of a choice of the governing law of a trust made in accordance with the trust instrument.[5]

Finally, where the governing law of a trust is changed to or from the law of the Cook Islands, the trustees are empowered to make all such consequential alterations or additions to the trust instrument as they consider necessary or desirable to ensure that the provisions, rights, liabilities, powers and obligations of and under the trust instrument shall be as valid and effective under the new governing law as they were under the previous governing law.[6]

All questions arising in regard to an international trust which is for the time being governed by the laws of the Cook Islands, or in regard to any disposition of property upon the trusts thereof – including *inter alia* any aspect of the validity of the trust or disposition or the interpretation or effect thereof and the existence and extent of powers conferred or retained – are to be determined (subject to certain specified exceptions) according to the laws of the Cook Islands, without reference to the laws of any other jurisdictions with which an international trust or disposition may be connected.[7] In addition, it is expressly declared that no international trust governed by the laws of the Cook Islands, and no disposition of property to be held upon the trusts thereof, is void, voidable, liable to be set aside or defective in any fashion, nor may relief be had under s 13B of the ITA 1984, nor is the capacity of any settlor to be questioned, by reason *inter alia* that:

(a) the international trust or disposition avoids or defeats rights, claims or interests conferred by the law of a foreign jurisdiction upon any person or contravenes any rules of foreign law or any foreign judicial

1 Ibid, s 13G(4), (5).
2 Ibid, s 13G(6).
3 Ibid, s 13G(8).
4 Ibid, s 13G(9).
5 Ibid, s 13G(10).
6 Ibid, s 13G(11).
7 Ibid, s 13H(1). The specified exceptions are set out in subsection (2).

or administrative order or action intended to recognise, protect, enforce or give effect to any such rights, claims or interests; or

(b) the laws of the Cook Islands or the provisions of the ITA 1984 are inconsistent with any foreign law.[1]

No action or proceedings, 'whether pursuant to this Act or at common law or in equity', to set aside the settlement of an international trust or to set aside any disposition to any international trust, or to seek relief or remedy under s 13B, shall be commenced, unless such action or proceedings is or are commenced (a) in the High Court of the Cook Islands and (b) before the expiration of 2 years from the date of the settlement of the international trust or the disposition to the international trust, as the case may be.[2] No action or proceedings, whether pursuant to the ITA 1984 or at common law or in equity, shall be commenced by any person:

(a) claiming to have had an interest in property before that property was settled upon or disposed to an international trust; and[3]
(b) seeking to derive a legal or equitable interest in property, unless such action or proceedings is or are commenced:
   (i) in the High Court of the Cook Islands; and
   (ii) before the expiration of two years from the date that such property was thus settled or disposed of.[4]

No action or proceeding (whether substantive or interlocutory in nature) to which either s 13K or s 13B applies shall be commenced, and no order shall be made or granted by the court in respect of or relating to such action or proceeding (including any injunction or order that would have the effect of preventing the exercise of, or the granting or restoring of any right, duty, obligation or power, or of preserving, granting custody of, detaining or inspecting any property, including for the avoidance of doubt any *Anton Piller* or any *Mareva* injunction) unless the court, having regard to the affidavit filed pursuant to subsection (4), shall first be satisfied, beyond reasonable doubt, that:

(a) commencement of the action or proceedings is not precluded by the provisions of subsections (1) and (2); and
(b) the remedy or relief sought is not precluded by the provisions of subsection (6);

and in any action or proceedings to which s 13B applies, that:

---

1 Ibid, s 13I.
2 Ibid, s 13K(1).
3 The 'and' actually seems to indicate 'or'.
4 ITA 1984, s 13K(2).

(c) the remedy or relief sought is not precluded by the provisions of s 13B; and
(d) the evidence as disclosed by the affidavit demonstrates the ability of the plaintiff to prove those matters necessary to establish a right to relief under s 13B(1).[1]

In every action or proceeding to which s 13K or s 13B applies, the plaintiff must, upon commencement of such proceedings, file an affidavit deposing as to the matters specified in subsection (4). These include:

(a) the facts and circumstances giving rise to the action or proceedings;
(b) whether an action or proceedings have been commenced in any other jurisdiction between any of the parties to the action or proceedings, or by any party against the settlor of any relevant trust or of property upon any relevant trust;
(c) such of the circumstances of the plaintiff as are or may be relevant to determine the quantum of security to be paid by the plaintiff;
(d) the date upon which the international trust or property, in respect of which the action or proceedings are brought, was settled or disposed of;

and, in any case to which s 13B applies:

(e) the facts and circumstances of the creditor's cause of action (and, in the case of multiple or successive causes of action, those of the first in time to accrue);
(f) the date on which that creditor's cause of action accrued; and
(g) whether an action or proceedings have been commenced in any jurisdiction in respect of that creditor's cause of action and the date of commencement of such action or proceedings.[2]

Notwithstanding any other provision of the ITA 1984, the provisions of ss 13A–13K inclusive shall apply to every international trust governed, or expressed to be wholly or partly governed, by the law of the Cook Islands. This includes a trust that formerly was not wholly or partly governed by the law of the Cook Islands, but in respect of which the governing law of the trust has been changed (whether before or after registration) so that the trust, or any aspect of it, is governed or expressed to be governed by the law of the Cook Islands; and, without limiting the generality of the foregoing and notwithstanding any other law to the contrary, after the date of registration:

(a) the settlement or establishment of such trust;

---

1 Ibid, s 13K(3).
2 Ibid, s 13K(4).

(b) every disposition to such trust, including any disposition occurring before the date of registration or change of law; and
(c) every proceeding commenced after the date of registration concerning such settlement, establishment or disposition,

shall be subject to the provisions of ss 13A–13K inclusive as if, upon the date that such settlement, establishment or disposition occurred, the trust was an international trust governed wholly and exclusively by the law of the Cook Islands.[1]

It is also provided that, in any action or proceedings (whether commenced pursuant to the ITA 1984 or at common law or in equity) wherein the usual or appropriate remedy (whether sought or not) would be either:

(a) the setting aside of the settlement of, or disposition to, an international trust; or
(b) the award of a legal or equitable interest in property settled upon or disposed of to an international trust,

but the grant of such a remedy is or would be precluded by s 13B or s 13K(1) or (2), then neither damages nor any other relief or remedy which is effectively an alternative to or consequential upon a precluded remedy shall be awarded.[2]

It is an offence for a person to divulge or communicate to any other person information relating to the establishment, constitution, business undertakings or affairs of an international trust. In addition, all judicial proceedings, other than criminal proceedings, relating to international trusts, must, unless ordered otherwise, be heard in camera and no details of the proceedings shall be published by any person without leave of the court or person presiding.[3] These provisions are subject to those of s 23(3) which provides that every decision of the court in respect of any proceedings concerning the application or interpretation of the ITA 1984 must be published or reported for the purposes of affording a record of those proceedings, provided that in every case:

(a) the written decision of the court shall be edited to such extent as shall be necessary to preserve secrecy in respect of the identity of the trust, of every interested party and of the subject matter of the proceedings; and
(b) no such report shall be reported or published unless or until a judge of the court shall have ascertained the views of the parties to the proceedings as to the adequacy of any editing undertaken, and

1 Ibid, s 13K(5), inserted in substitution for the original subsection (5) by the International Trusts Amendment Act 1999.
2 ITA 1984, s 13K(6).
3 Ibid, s 23(1), (2).

certified in writing to the Registrar of the Court that the decision as edited may be released for publication or reporting.[1]

Unless excluded by the terms of a trust instrument, a trustee or an officer or employee of a trustee company may divulge or make available information relating to the establishment, constitution, business undertakings or affairs of an international trust:

(a) to any person or class of persons as that trustee, officer or employee considers necessary from time to time, in its complete discretion, for carrying out the management and administration of the trust assets in the ordinary course of business; or
(b) to a legal practitioner:
    (i) for the purpose of obtaining legal advice relating to establishment, constitution, business undertakings or affairs of an international trust; or
    (ii) for the purpose of prosecuting or defending any litigation relating to the establishment, constitution, business undertakings or affairs of an international trust.

Although there is no legislation (other than those provisions in the ITA 1984 itself) providing specifically for the enforcement of a foreign judgment (other than New Zealand judgments) in the Cook Islands, there is a possibility that a foreign judgment which is registered in New Zealand will be moved to the High Court of the Cook Islands. Under the common law of the Cook Islands, a foreign judgment may be enforced in accordance with general principles of the conflict of laws – subject, of course, to the express provisions of the ITA 1984. However, in view of the express provisions of the ITA 1984 (and especially those in ss 13D and 13I), it seems most unlikely that a court in the Cook Islands would assist in the enforcement of a foreign court order which set aside, or purported to set aside, an international trust on the grounds that it defrauded creditors (unless, of course, the creditor could equally well have made out his case before a court in the Cook Islands).

There is no bankruptcy statute in the Cook Islands to govern individual bankruptcies.

7.3.8 Cyprus

Cyprus has also enacted legislation dealing specifically with 'international trusts'. The key provisions are to be found in the International Trusts Law

---

1 Ibid, s 23(3). This seems to be a response to the approach adopted by the Court of Appeal in *515 South Orange Grove Association v Orange Grove Partners* (1995) No 208/94, where an attempt to prevent publication of the judgment (under s 23(2)) was rejected and publication authorised both within and outside the Cook Islands.

1992 (the 1992 Law) which applies to all 'international trusts' created after 24 July 1992 (when the 1992 Law came into force).[1]

An 'international trust', for the purposes of the 1992 Law, is defined as a trust in respect of which:

(a) the settlor is not a permanent resident in the Republic of Cyprus (the Republic);
(b) at least one of the trustees for the time is, during the whole duration of the trust, a permanent resident in the Republic;
(c) no beneficiary (other than a charitable institution) is a permanent resident of the Republic;
(d) the trust property does not include any immovable property situated in the Republic.[2]

The expressions 'immovable property' and 'trust' have the meanings ascribed thereto in s 3 of the Trustee Law 1955.[3]

Section 3(2) of the 1992 Law provides that an international trust shall not be void or voidable in the event of the settlor's bankruptcy or liquidation of his property or in any action or proceedings against the settlor at the suit of his creditors, notwithstanding any provision of the law of the Republic or of the law of any other country and notwithstanding further that the trust is voluntary and without consideration having been given for the same, or is made for the benefit of the settlor, the spouse or children of the settlor or any of them, unless and to the extent that it is proven to the satisfaction of the court[4] that the international trust was made 'with the intent to defraud the creditors of the settlor at the time of the transfer of his assets to the trust'. The burden of establishing such an intent on the part of the settlor lies on such creditors.[5] Moreover, an action against a trustee of the international trust pursuant to the provisions of s 3(2) must be brought within two years from the date when the transfer or disposal of assets was made to the trust.[6]

The provisions of the 1992 Law are not as detailed as those in the Cook Islands legislation (or those of most other offshore jurisdictions, in fact) and may well be less advantageous to a creditor (an expression which is not defined). As we have seen, in the Cook Islands' International Trusts Act 1984, the creditor must be able to establish the grounds of his claim 'beyond reasonable doubt'. In contrast, no standard of proof is mentioned in the 1992 Law and it may therefore reasonably be assumed that the ordinary civil

1 Date of publication in the *Official Gazette*. See also s 13.
2 International Trusts Law 1992, s 2.
3 Ibid, s 2.
4 Meaning the President of a District Court or the Senior Judge of the district where the trustee(s) of the international trust (or any one of them who resides in the Republic) have their residence: ibid, s 2.
5 Ibid, s 3(2).
6 Ibid, s 3(3).

standard (on a balance of probabilities) applies. In Cyprus, the 1992 Law refers simply to an 'intent to defraud' (as did s 172 of the English Law of Property Act 1925), whereas the comparable Cook Islands legislation refers to 'the principal intent to defraud'. It may therefore not be necessary for the creditor to establish that the settlor had no other intention or purpose, provided that an intent to defraud was one of his intentions. Section 13B(1)(b) of the Cook Islands' ITA 1984 requires proof that the settlement or disposition rendered the settlor insolvent or without property by which the creditor's claim could have been satisfied. In Cyprus, such a result would probably be highly material in determining whether the settlor had the requisite intent to defraud, but it does not seem to be necessary to establish that the transfer of assets itself rendered him insolvent.

Indeed, in broad terms, the Cyprus legislation is very similar to s 172 of the English Law of Property Act 1925, save that there is an express time-limit (of two years) for bringing any claim to set aside the transfer of assets (whereas s 172 was subject to no time-limit at all). In the absence of a definition of a 'creditor' and also of some indication of the nature or extent of the obligations in respect of which a transferor might find himself liable to a creditor, it is difficult to see how far the 1992 Law will differ, in its effects, from either s 172 or the Cook Islands legislation. It is clear that, for the purposes of the 1992 Act, a creditor must have been a creditor of the settlor at the date of the transfer of assets. Thus, a transferor who settles his property on the eve of embarking on a trade or other hazardous venture would not be at risk from a person who became a creditor after that date – in other words, the settlement under challenge in *Re Butterworth*[1] would not have been set aside under the 1992 Law. Beyond this, however, many of the difficult questions which arose in relation to s 172 might still be pertinent in relation to the 1992 Law.

For example, in the English cases it was not entirely clear whether the 1571 Act or s 172 (as the case may be) could be of assistance to a person who had a cause of action against the transferor at the date of the relevant transfer of assets but who had not as yet obtained judgment. Was it sufficient that a cause of action had accrued by then? Did the cause of action have to have reasonable or realistic prospects of success? Would a person who had a cause of action against the settlor, but who was unknown to the settlor (for example because no claim had as yet been raised or made) be a creditor for these purposes?[2] The Cook Islands legislation makes express provision for such cases and clearly intends to include, within the class of potential claimants, those who had an accrued cause of action against the settlor (subject to the limitations specified). It is not clear, however, whether the 1992 Law has a similar intent or what its effect might actually be.

---

1 (1882) 19 Ch D 588.

2 See pp 356–360.

7.3.9 Gibraltar

In broad terms, the laws of Gibraltar are similar to, and indeed are derived from, those of England and Wales. Thus Gibraltar trust law is based almost entirely on English trust law. The same is also broadly true in matters of insolvency. Section 42 of the Bankruptcy Ordinance contains provisions similar to those of the English Bankruptcy Act 1914. A bankruptcy petition may not be presented in Gibraltar unless the debtor is domiciled in Gibraltar, or within a year before the presentation of the petition was ordinarily resident or had a dwelling-house or place of business in Gibraltar, or carried on a business in Gibraltar, either personally or by means of an agent or manager.[1] Moreover, the (English) 1571 Act still applies in Gibraltar.[2]

However, the provisions of both the Bankruptcy Ordinance and the 1571 Act are subject to important amendments, introduced in 1990, which are intended to provide a greater degree of protection for settled property against the claims of creditors. Section 42A(1) of the Bankruptcy Ordinance provides that, if:

(a) under or by virtue of any disposition made in respect of property the same becomes settled property; and
(b) the settlor is an individual; and
(c) the settlor is not insolvent at the date of the disposition;
(d) the settlor does not become insolvent in consequence thereof; and
(e) the disposition is registered in accordance with the requirements of any regulations,

such disposition shall not be voidable at the instance of or upon application by any creditor of the settlor.

A 'disposition' is defined in conventional terms as any disposition or series thereof, howsoever effected, and (without prejudice to the generality thereof) includes any transaction, gift, grant or transfer of property of any nature whatsoever.[3] 'Settled property' means any property held in or upon trust, other than any property held by any person as nominee for another person, or as trustee for any other person who is absolutely entitled to the beneficial interest in such property. 'The settlor', in relation to any settled property, includes the

---

1 In other words, this is similar to the English Bankruptcy Act 1914, s 4(d) (as applied to Gibraltar) and not entirely dissimilar from the English Insolvency Act 1986, s 265(1).

2 Incorporated into Gibraltar law by the English Law (Application) Ordinance. See *Hess v Line Trust Corporation Ltd* (1998/99) 1 ITELR 249 (Gibraltar Court of Appeal): claim under the 1571 Act struck out on the grounds that the settled property (shares in a Swiss company) were not amenable to execution by the Gibraltar court, and the claimant did not have an existing and quantifiable claim as creditor against the alleged fraudulent person.

3 In order to be effective, the particular disposition must, of course, comply with the rules of law applicable to dispositions of that kind: *Pehrsson's Trustee in Bankruptcy v Von Greyerz* [1999] 2 ITELR 230, PC.

maker of any disposition of property which in consequence thereof becomes settled property. A 'creditor' is not defined, but the word 'insolvent' means, in respect of a settlor, any settlor whose liabilities, both actual and contingent or prospective, exceed the value of his assets. It is further provided that no claim by creditors shall be deemed to be a contingent or prospective liability of a settlor who, at the time of making the disposition, does not have actual notice of such claim or of the facts or circumstances which may render him liable to such claim.[1]

In order that s 42A shall apply to a disposition, it must be registered in accordance with the requirements of the relevant regulations. Section 42A(4) empowers the Financial and Development Secretary to make regulations for the establishment of a register of dispositions and for all matters incidental to the maintenance of such register.[2] These regulations – the Bankruptcy (Register of Dispositions) Regulations 1990[3] – came into effect on 1 December 1990. The regulations established a register, set out what must be entered thereon, laid down registration requirements, stipulated the conditions that have to be met by trustees, and so forth.

The regulations also make provisions for the secrecy of registered dispositions. Every person having an official duty in the administration of the regulations must regard and deal with all documents, information and declarations relating to dispositions which have been registered, or in respect of which application for registration has been made, as secret and confidential. Any communication of, or attempt to communicate, such information or anything contained in such document or declaration is an offence in respect of which the guilty party is liable on summary conviction to a fine of £1000. It is also provided that no person employed in carrying out the provisions of the regulations shall be required to produce in any court or before any authority or person for any purpose whatsoever any document or declaration in his possession in pursuance of the regulations, or to divulge or communicate to any court any matter or thing coming to his notice in the performance of his duties under the regulations, except as may be necessary for the purpose of carrying into effect the provisions of the regulations or for the purposes of any criminal or civil proceedings in which such document, declaration, matter or thing is material.[4]

If s 42A applies to a disposition or settlement, then neither the (English) 1571 Act nor s 42 of the Bankruptcy Ordinance may do so.

---

1 All these terms are defined in the Bankruptcy Ordinance, s 42A(3).

2 Section 42A(4) provides further that, without prejudice to the foregoing, such regulations may include the matters specified in paras (a)–(g)

3 Legal Notice No 158 of 1990. See also the Registered Trust Ordinance 1999.

4 See Bankruptcy (Register of Dispositions) Regulations 1990, reg 9. The concluding words of reg 9(3) are very wide in their ambit and seem to contradict the restrictions laid down in the earlier parts of reg 9.

The interpretation of s 42A is not free from difficulty. Although it is clear that a relevant liability need not be an actual or accrued liability, it is not entirely clear whether a 'contingent' liability differs from a 'prospective' one.[1] The location of the words 'both', 'and' and 'or' in the phrase 'both actual and contingent or prospective' suggests that they are not intended to indicate different concepts. On the other hand, it seems likely that what is contemplated is a differentiation of actual, probable and possible liabilities. Suppose, for example, that, prior to the date of the disposition, the settlor has guaranteed another's liability. If performance of the guarantee has already been demanded, but not satisfied, the settlor is under an actual or accrued liability. If the question of performance has not yet arisen (or performance has not yet been demanded), the settlor is presumably under a contingent liability (ie his liability may become an actual liability if, but only if, the guaranteed person fails to meet his original liability). In addition, there may also be a liability which will probably (say, at a certain time in the future) become an actual liability.

The requirement that the settlor must have had *actual* knowledge at the time of making the disposition seems straightforward at first sight, but it, too, may be problematic. It does not apply, for example, to an actual or accrued liability. Consequently, it may be sufficient for a creditor to establish that a settlor had constructive (or even imputed) notice of such liability at the relevant time or, indeed, that no notice at all is required, ie the mere existence of the liability suffices. In addition, the requirement is not tied specifically to the contingent or prospective liability itself, but only to 'such claim' or to the facts or circumstances which 'may' render the settlor liable to 'such a claim'.

The word 'claim' is not defined, and it is not clear whether (and, if so, how) a 'liability' differs from, or is identical with, a 'claim' in this context, although it would seem that the intention is that a 'claim' indicates a state of affairs (of which the settlor had actual notice) which will or might lead to an actual liability. In other words, 'claim' seems to indicate both a cause of action and a claim that has actually been made (the writ having been served). Thus, a settlor who, at the date of the disposition, has actual notice of a claim against him (say, for some negligent act or omission, or for breach of some contract) – whether the writ has been issued or simply notice given that proceedings are about to be commenced – can reasonably be said to be under a contingent or prospective liability.

However, actual knowledge of 'facts or circumstances which may render him liable to such a claim' seems to be a very wide concept, and seems to suggest that the settlor need not necessarily have actual knowledge that a claim

---

1 It is also not obvious why the expression 'shall be deemed to be' has been used: the intention, it seems, is to ensure that a contingent or prospective liability of which the settlor does not have actual notice shall not actually be a contingent or prospective liability for these purposes (and not to identify and exclude a state of affairs which, by some deeming process, might otherwise be regarded as a contingent or prospective liability). See also pp 356–360.

will (or even may) be made on the basis of such known facts and circumstances. For instance, a settlor may create a settlement when he is about to embark on a trade or other hazardous venture – as in *Re Butterworth*.[1] He may subsequently become insolvent, leaving many of his suppliers unpaid. At the date of the disposition, he may not have had an intention of defrauding such creditors (as would have been required under s 172 of the English Law of Property Act 1925). Nevertheless, it still seems to be arguable that he then had actual knowledge of facts and circumstances which may render him liable to claims from such creditors. If this is correct, then there must be many cases in which s 42A of the Bankruptcy Ordinance will provide a settlor with no greater protection than did s 172 in England.

Such uncertainties would also seem to affect the question of the insolvency of the settlor. It is clear that the settlor must not be insolvent at the date of the disposition. However, it must also be the case that he has not become insolvent in consequence thereof. There is no time-limit during which such 'consequential' insolvency must be shown to have arisen. Indeed, in the case of a contingent or prospective liability, the question of 'consequential' insolvency must be determined *ex post facto* and may even be open-ended (subject to any limitation period applicable to the specific cause of action). If the settlor was under an actual liability at the time of the disposition, it should not be difficult to conclude whether or not, by and in consequence of that disposition, he was rendered incapable of discharging that liability, ie whether it rendered him insolvent or not. However, if, at the date of the disposition, the settlor simply had actual knowledge of facts or circumstances which may render him liable to a claim by a creditor, it is difficult to see how that liability can be quantified, in order to determine the effect of the disposition on his solvency, until the creditor has obtained final judgment. Thus, the absence of a time-limit for bringing an application to set aside a particular disposition could add to the uncertainty surrounding the insolvency of the settlor and the avoidability of the settlement.

In this sense, at least, the complete abandonment of any requirement of all intent to defraud (which, of course, never applied in bankruptcy cases, but which was – and presumably still is – central in relation to the 1571 Act), and its replacement by an almost mathematical requirement of insolvency, can be said to be detrimental, rather than helpful, to the debtor. For example, it would be quite possible, in appropriate circumstances, to find that a settlor or transferor did not have an intention to defraud his creditors, despite the fact that his disposition rendered him insolvent (especially in relation to future creditors) and, in consequence, for that disposition not to be set aside. However, where the criterion is the insolvency of the settlor or transferor (whether caused by or as a result of that disposition), all that is required is

1 (1882) 19 Ch D 588.

factual proof of such insolvency, and it becomes irrelevant whether or not he intended to defraud his creditors.

7.3.10 The Isle of Man

In broad terms, the law of the Isle of Man in relation to settlements by individuals who are adjudicated bankrupt is similar to that in s 42 of the English Bankruptcy Act 1914 (with the same two-year and 10-year limits). There are also similar preconditions (concerning domicile, residence and place of business) for the presentation of a bankruptcy petition in the Isle of Man; and it may be impossible to bankrupt in the Isle of Man a non-Manx settlor of a Manx trust.

A disposition to a Manx trust may be capable of being set aside (irrespective of bankruptcy) under the Statute of Fraudulent Assignments 1736, which provides that:

> 'all fraudulent assignments or transfers of the debtor's goods and effects shall be void and of no effect against his just creditors, any custom or practice to the contrary notwithstanding.'

Until recently, the scope of this provision was uncertain. Does it require some form of dishonesty on the part of the transferor of property, and does it apply to future debts as well as existing ones? It seems to have been assumed generally that its effect in Manx law was substantially the same as that of the 1571 Act on English law. Indeed, a statement to this effect seems to have been made by Kneen CR in *Re Corrin's Bankruptcy*,[1] but there is no report or transcript of the judgment in this case. In *Corlett v Radcliffe*,[2] the Judicial Committee of the Privy Council, on appeal from the Court of Chancery of the Isle of Man, considered the relationship between the (English) 1571 Act and the (Isle of Man) 1736 Statute, but in a somewhat inconclusive manner. Lord Chelmsford stated:[3]

> 'Each case must depend upon its own circumstances, and in all the question is one of fact, whether the transaction was bona fide, or was a contrivance to defraud creditors. It may, however, be stated generally that a deed is void against creditors when the debtor is in a state of insolvency, or when the effect of the deed is to leave the debtor without the means of paying his present debts. If this is the condition of the debtor, or the consequence of his act, it is not sufficient to render a deed valid that it should be made upon good consideration: for as is said in *Twyne's Case*,[4] "a good consideration does not suffice if it be not also bona fide".'

---

1 (1912) unreported: it is referred to, 'with caution', in *Re Heginbotham's Petition* [1999] 2 ITELR 95.

2 (1859) 14 Moo PCC 121.

3 Ibid at 135.

4 (1602) 3 Co Rep 80b.

Although the words 'whether the transaction was bona fide, or was a contrivance to defraud creditors' suggest that dishonesty was required if a transaction was to be caught by the 1736 Statute, this was by no means clear. Such a requirement would have distinguished Manx law from English law; and, indeed, the (Manx) 1736 Statute and the (English) 1571 Act are in very different terms. However, it is the 1571 Act that refers to an 'intent' to 'delay, hinder or defraud creditors', whereas the 1736 Statute makes no reference to any such 'intent'.

Some of these questions were resolved recently by the High Court of the Isle of Man (Common Law Division) in *Re Heginbotham's Petition.*[1] The petitioner had been awarded damages in default of defence to his counterclaim against a company; and his petition alleged that the company had transferred its assets (a property management portfolio, which generated a monthly income of £200, and a trading name)[2] to other companies, with 'no reasonable commercial ground or purpose', but solely to avoid the consequences of the litigation and of any judgment entered against it, and had therefore made a fraudulent transfer within the meaning of the 1736 Statute.

Deemster Cain held that, despite the absence of any reference to an 'intent' to defraud in the 1736 Statute, the expression 'fraudulent assignments or transfers' must impute an intent by the debtor to assign or transfer his goods or effects fraudulently, ie in the context of the relationship of debtor and creditor. This did not necessarily involve actual deceit, but there had to be dishonesty.[3] The next question was whether the intent to defraud applied only to existing creditors of the debtor at the date of the assignment or transfer or also to future creditors. In *Corlett v Radcliffe*, Lord Chelmsford referred to a debtor 'in a state of insolvency' and to the case 'when the effect of the deed is to leave the debtor without the means of paying his present debts'.[4] On this basis, Deemster Cain concluded:[5]

> 'A state of insolvency implies an inability to pay existing, or present, debts. A person is not in a "state of insolvency" merely because he may not be able to pay contingent or future

---

1 [1999] 2 ITELR 95. See also P Dougherty 'Asset Protection Trusts in the Isle of Man' (1999) 7 *Journal of International Trust and Corporate Planning* 177.

2 The 1736 Statute refers to the debtor's 'goods and effects'. It was conceded in *Corlett v Radcliffe* (1859) 14 Moo PCC 121 that lands liable to be taken for sale in execution for debt were considered by law goods, chattels or effects. In *Heginbotham* the property was intangible (business rights and goodwill) but there is no discussion in the case whether this constituted 'goods and effects' for the purposes of the Statute.

3 Adopting the observations of Cairns LJ in *Lloyds Bank Ltd v Marcan* [1973] 1 WLR 1387 at 1392: see pp 340–341.

4 See (1859) 14 Moo PC 121 at 135 (quoted above).

5 [1999] 2 ITELR 95 at 112. It is doubtful, in fact, whether Lord Chelmsford's observations were intended to have such wide application. *Corlett* decided that Manx and English law were the same only on the point that a deed is void against creditors when the debtor is in a state of insolvency or when the effect of the deed is to leave the debtor without the means of paying his present debts. It does not actually purport to decide anything on wider questions, such as similarities (if any) in the law relating to future creditors.

> debts, which may never materialise. … The expression "present debts" must have been a reference to the debts of the debtor at the date of the deed or other transaction. It cannot have been a reference to debts which that person might possibly incur at some future date. I would construe that term "present debts", however, to include known and ascertained debts which are to fall due on a date in the future. A transaction or contrivance designed to deprive known and ascertained future creditors of "timely recourse to property which would otherwise be applicable for their benefit"[[1]] would not be honest in the context of the relationship of debtor and creditor and would not therefore be bona fide.'

Thus, the (Manx) 1736 Statute has clearly not been construed as broadly as the (English) 1571 Act. The former does not assist future, unknown or unascertained creditors. Indeed, *Re Heginbotham* seems to suggest that only known or ascertained existing creditors are protected.

On the facts of *Re Heginbotham's Petition*[2] itself, it was held that the transfer of assets to other companies was a *bona fide* transaction and was not a contrivance to defraud the then present creditors or known and ascertained future creditors. At the time when the assets were transferred, the petition had served neither a defence in the action against him nor his counterclaim. Even if the existence of the counterclaim had been known, this would not have created a 'present' debt nor a 'known and ascertained future debt'. The petitioner was therefore not a creditor for the purposes of the 1736 Statute and the transactions were not void.

7.3.11 Jersey

Bankruptcy ('désastre') in Jersey is governed by the Bankruptcy (Désastre) (Jersey) Law 1990, the provisions of which are broadly similar to those of the English Insolvency Act 1986 as far as transactions at an undervalue are concerned. In Jersey, however, the definition of 'undervalue' depends largely on whether there has been a lack or insufficiency of 'cause' (which is broadly similar to, but not identical with, 'consideration' in English law).[3]

Until recently, Jersey law in relation to the setting aside of a disposition to defraud creditors was in a state of uncertainty, there being very little by way of authority on the matter. A Jersey court had held that a gratuitous transfer of assets by a person to a third party in order to defeat the claims of his creditors may be set aside,[4] and there seems to be no reason, in principle, why the same should not apply to a transfer of assets to trustees. Moreover, a disposition which defrauds creditors may be set aside in Jersey on the grounds that it is

---

1 As Pennycuick V-C said in *Lloyds Bank Ltd v Marcan* [1973] 1 WLR 1387.

2 [1999] 2 ITELR 95. See also P Dougherty, op cit, at 508d.

3 See Bankruptcy (Désastre) (Jersey) Law 1990, Art 17.

4 See, eg, *Golder v Société des Magasins Concorde Ltd* [1967] JJ 721. The disposition must not, of course, be a complete sham: *Rahman v Chase Bank (CI) Trust Company Ltd* (1991) JLR 103.

contrary to public policy,[1] although this will probably not be allowed where the action is essentially one to enforce the revenue laws of a foreign country.[2]

In addition, a Jersey court had shown itself willing to comply with a request from a foreign court (Florida) to direct trustees to exercise their discretion in a particular manner.[3] On this basis, it might have seemed somewhat imprudent to rely on the laws of Jersey for asset protection purposes. Recently, however, the Jersey courts have had to deal with complex litigation involving a series of claims made by a company, Grupo Torras SA, in an attempt to recover substantial sums of money lost as a result of the fraudulent activities of its chairman, one Sheikh Fahad. Two major judgments delivered recently in the course of this litigation have addressed and clarified many issues relevant to asset protection trusts and the way in which they may be dealt with under Jersey law.

The background to this litigation may be summarised as follows.[4] Grupo Torras SA ('GT') was a company owned by the Kuwait Investment Office. At all material times, Sheikh Fahad was its chairman. Between May 1988 and October 1990, the Sheikh conspired with others to defraud GT of some US$430 million, of which his personal share was $120 million. GT obtained judgment against the Sheikh in respect of the fraud in the English High Court for a total, with accrued interest, of some $800 million.[5] That judgment was registered in Jersey under the Judgments (Reciprocal Enforcement) (Jersey) Law 1960 and was therefore enforceable within the jurisdiction of the Jersey courts. Sheikh Fahad was hopelessly insolvent. He had been declared bankrupt in The Bahamas, where he now resided. GT was unable to recover its judgment debt from Sheikh Fahad's personal assets.

Between 1981 and 1994, the Sheikh set up a number of trusts in different jurisdictions. GT now sought to recover its judgment debt from those trusts. Two of them were situated in Jersey, in that the trustee was resident in the island and the trusts were governed by Jersey law. The first was the Esteem Settlement, established in 1981. At about the same time, Sheikh Fahad also acquired ownership of a Liechtenstein Anstalt called Ceyla Establishment

---

1 Trusts (Jersey) Law 1989, Art 10(2)(b)(ii).

2 *In the Matter of Tucker* (1987–88) JLR 473 (an application by an English trustee in bankruptcy for an order from the Royal Court to act in aid of and be an auxiliary to the English High Court (pursuant to the Bankruptcy Act 1914, s 122) was rejected on the grounds that the sole creditor was the UK Inland Revenue and the application was an indirect attempt to enforce a foreign revenue law). *Cf*, however, *Le Marquand and Backhurst v Chiltmead Ltd* (1987–88) JLR 86. See also *Re Roy Clifford Tucker* (unreported) 27 September 1988, Guernsey CA.

3 *Cadwell v Cadwell* (unreported) 8 August 1989. See also the Judgment (Reciprocal Enforcement) (Jersey) Law 1960 and *Le Marquand and Buckhurst v Chiltmead Ltd* (1987–88) JLR 86.

4 This summary of the facts is taken from the judgment of the Royal Court of Jersey of 17 January 2002: 2002/15A. For earlier proceedings in Jersey, see [2000] JLR N41; [2001] JLR 7; (2001) 3 ITELR 467.

5 *Grupo Torras SA v Sheikh Fahad Mohammed Ali Sabah* [1999] CLC 1469. For other proceedings in England arising from the 'Grupo Torras' litigation, see (2001) Lloyd's Rep Bank 36; [2001] CLC 221; [1999] CLC 885; [1997] 3 WLR 1143; (1997) *The Times*, 13 October; (1997) *The Times*, 17 April; [1995] CLC 1025; Lawtel Doc No C0100019 (11 October 2000); Lawtel Doc No C0006852 (13 May 1998).

('Ceyla'). In August 1992, Sheikh Fahad also established the Number 52 Trust. Prior to the commencement of the fraud, Sheikh Fahad contributed assets to the Esteem Settlement and to Ceyla from time to time. These transfers were not subject to attack. Between 1988 and 1992, after he had begun to defraud GT, he contributed further of his own funds to the Esteem Settlement and to Ceyla. In April 1992, he contributed £4.4 million of monies which he had stolen from GT. In August 1992, he contributed £4 million of his own funds to the Number 52 Trust. In 1999, the Royal Court gave directions on the procedure to be followed in order to resolve any questions as to the validity of the two trusts or of transfers of assets to those trusts in the light of the judgment of the English High Court. These proceedings were known as 'the 1999 Action'. In the 1999 Action, GT lay claim to all the assets in the two trusts on a number of grounds.

(1) It alleged that the general circumstances surrounding the use of the trusts by Sheikh Fahad enabled the trusts to be set aside in law on three grounds: namely, that they were contrary to public policy: that the 'veil' of the trusts should be lifted; or that a remedial constructive trust in favour of GT should be imposed on the assets of the trusts.
(2) It alleged that all transfers of assets to the trusts at any time after the fraud began in 1988 were made with the intention of defrauding creditors; such transfers were therefore liable to be set aside.
(3) It alleged a proprietary claim over certain of the trust assets in respect of £1,267,686.

In April 2000, before any of the above claims had been tried, the trustee of the trusts sought directions of the court ('the 2000 Proceedings') as to whether the assets of the two trusts should, pursuant to the discretionary powers conferred on the trustee by the trust deeds, be distributed wholly or partly to Sheikh Fahad, such distribution to be effected by way of payment to GT as his judgment creditor. (In so applying, the trustee surrendered its discretion to the court.) The Esteem Settlement was a discretionary trust for the benefit of the settlor (Sheikh Fahad), his children and remoter issue and those who married them. The Sheikh himself specifically objected to this course of action. The Jersey Court of Appeal ordered that the 2000 Proceedings should be heard before the 1999 Action. The Royal Court held that: (i) the trustee, and therefore the court,[1] could make a distribution for the benefit of a beneficiary against the objections of that beneficiary; (ii) on the facts of the case, a distribution by way of payment to Grupo Torras in reduction of the Sheikh's debt would not have been a payment for the benefit of the Sheikh; (iii) on the assumption (contrary to the court's conclusion) that such a payment would be

[1] It is not suggested, of course, that the court could exercise such a discretion or power where it had not been surrendered by the trustee to the court.

for the benefit of the Sheikh, any benefit to him would in reality be minimal[1] and it would be a wholly wrong exercise of discretion to pay out all or most of the trust fund so as to confer a very intangible benefit on him and cause a material disadvantage to the other beneficiaries. Grupo Torras, who had been joined as a party to the application, appealed.

The Court of Appeal upheld the decision.[2] It was held that where an inferior court had exercised a discretion on behalf of a trustee, an appeal court should not interfere with it and substitute its own discretion unless: (i) it could be shown that the inferior court had erred in law in relation to an issue that affected the exercise of its discretion or (put another way) had misdirected itself with regard to the principles in accordance with which its discretion had been exercised; or (ii) the court below had taken into account matters which it ought not to have taken into account or had failed to take into account matters which it ought to have done; or (iii) the decision of the inferior court was plainly wrong or (put another way) it appeared on other grounds that injustice would result from the manner in which the discretion had been exercised. The Court of Appeal concluded that the court below had been entitled to come to the conclusion that the payment of a small proportion of the beneficiary's indebtedness was of no material benefit. The fact that his debt arose out of fraud could not characterise a reduction in the debt as a benefit in circumstances where it would not be of benefit for a non-fraudulent beneficiary. Although there was no rigid rule that in no case would the reduction of a beneficiary's debts be of benefit to him, in the circumstances of this case the court had been justified in concluding that there was no sufficient benefit to justify the proposed distribution and that the interests of other beneficiaries would be prejudiced thereby.

Consequently, although the decision certainly does not preclude a creditor from applying to a Jersey court for an order that trust funds be distributed to him in payment of a beneficiary's debts – especially where a tangible and material 'benefit' to that beneficiary can be shown – the fact remains that it has severely restricted the chances of success of any such application. If the trustee, in the proper exercise of his discretion, decides not to make such a distribution, there is nothing that the creditor can do to challenge and overturn that decision. In these circumstances, the creditor would probably be better advised to seek the setting aside of the settlement.

In any event, following the failure of Grupo Torras in the 2000 Proceedings, the Royal Court ordered (on 12 February 2001) that the claims referred to in paragraphs (2) and (3) above be tried as separate issues prior to the trial of the remaining issues in the 1999 Action. By the time of the hearing,

---

1 Even if all the funds in all relevant settlements (of which the Esteem Settlement was but one) were distributed in payment of the Sheikh's debts, he would still have owed US$583 million.

2 *Abacus (CI) Ltd v Al Sabah* [2001] 4 ITELR 555, Gloster JA, Sumption and Rokison JJA.

following further amendment to its pleadings, GT's claims fell under three headings:

(i) a proprietary tracing claim in respect of £1.276 million (being the balance of the £4.4 million referred to above) and the tracing of this sum into the assets of the Esteem Settlement;
(ii) alternatively, a claim in restitution for the sum of £1.276 million against the Esteem Settlement;
(iii) a claim to set aside all transfers made into the Esteem Settlement, the Number 52 Trust and Ceyla at any time after the fraud began in May 1988, on the basis that these transfers were made in fraud of GT as a creditor of Sheikh Fahad. (This part of the claim is referred to as the 'Pauline action'.)

These claims raise a number of complex and novel issues of Jersey law, which the Royal Court identified as follows.

(I) Does Jersey law recognise the ability to trace assets and, if so, in what circumstances?
(II) Does Jersey law recognise a claim in restitution even where there is no fault on the part of an innocent recipient?
(III) Although the case of *Golder v Société des Magasins Concorde Limited*[1] establishes that Jersey law recognises a right of action to set aside gifts made in fraud of creditors, what are the limits of and principles underlying such an action?
(IV) What limitation period is applicable to the Pauline action?[2]

Each of these claims was then considered. A brief summary of the Royal Court's findings follows.

(I) Does Jersey law recognise the ability to trace assets and, if so, in what circumstances?[3]

The answer to this first question depended on the answers to a series of other, subsidiary questions. The first of these was: does the victim of fraud have an equitable proprietary interest in the proceeds of the fraud? It was acknowledged that, under English law and many other common law

---

1 (1973) JJ 721.

2 Claim (III) was referred to as 'the Pauline action', the title apparently being derived from the action of the same name in Roman Law. The Royal Court was anxious, however, to point out that it was not considering the exact nature of the action in Roman Law and how that would have applied to this particular case, but endeavouring to establish the parameters and principles of Jersey law: see 2002/15A, para 250.

3 2002/15A, paras 166–232. The court consisted of MC St J Birt (who delivered the judgment) and Jurats de Veulle and Georgelin.

jurisdictions, the position was clear:[1] a person in the position of Sheikh Fahad, who, as a director, defrauds the company of which he is a director, holds the proceeds on constructive trust for the company which has an equitable proprietary interest in the property in question. It was argued, however, that there was no justification for importing this concept into Jersey law. The Jersey law of property was very different and was essentially based on the civil law, which does not recognise differences between legal and equitable ownership. Even in the case of express trusts, the Trusts (Jersey) Law 1984 ('the 1984 Law') does not state clearly that beneficiaries have an equitable proprietary interest in the trust assets rather than a personal right against the trustee. Even if beneficiaries under an express trust do have such a proprietary interest, the same is not necessarily true in respect of a constructive trust. In the court's view, a beneficiary under an express Jersey trust has an equitable proprietary interest in the trust property. It was true that nowhere does the 1984 Law state specifically that a beneficiary under an express trust has an equitable proprietary interest in the trust fund. However, the 1984 Law is not a codification. Trusts were recognised and enforced by the Jersey courts well before the passing of the 1984 Law and, in doing so, they looked to English law for guidance on trust matters and, by and large, adopted English principles save where it was appropriate to differ. A Jersey trust is essentially the same animal as is found in English law subject to certain local modifications.[2]

It was then argued, relying in particular on Arts 29 and 50 of the 1984 Law, that, even if a beneficiary under an express trust has a proprietary interest, there was no reason to follow English law in holding that the position was the same outside the context of an express trust. If the notion of equitable property interests were current in Jersey, it was difficult to see why express provision had to be made for a constructive trust in the limited and simple case of a profit made by a trustee on trust property. Similarly, it would not have been necessary to have included Art 50(3) in a jurisdiction which already recognised the notion of an equitable proprietary interest arising in the event of an alienation or conversion of trust property. Thus there was no counterpart in the English Trustee Act 1925, no doubt because it was basic jurisprudence that trust beneficiaries can assert proprietary interests in the traceable proceeds of an unauthorised disposition. However, the court pointed out that the flaw in this argument was that the 1984 Law was not a codification, nor was it enacted in a vacuum. There was already a customary law of trusts in existence. Many of the provisions of the 1984 Law were simply reflections of the pre-existing law or of English principles. There was no implication that, because a provision was included in the 1984 Law, it was

---

1 The court referred to *Westdeutsche Landesbank Girozentrale v Islington London Borough Council* [1996] AC 669, at 716; *Black v S Freedman & Co* (1910) 12 CLR 105 at 110; *Lipkin Gorman v Karpnale Limited* [1991] 2 AC 548 at 565.

2 2002/15A, paras 167–170. The court approved the summary of the position expressed in Matthews and Sowden, *Jersey Law of Trusts* (3rd edn), at para 1.20.

something which did not exist beforehand. The court was, therefore, in no doubt that Jersey law was already to the effect that the making of a profit from a breach of trust gave rise to a constructive trust, but it was clearly reasonable and sensible to reflect that principle in the statute. A beneficiary under a constructive trust did have an equitable proprietary interest in the assets which are the subject of that trust.

The question then arose as to whether Jersey law should follow English law in holding that a constructive trust exists in circumstances such as the present. The constructive trust had been used by the courts of England and other jurisdictions as a mechanism to assist in fashioning appropriate remedies to deal with problems of commercial fraud. It accorded with the interests of justice. If the fraudster did not hold the property on constructive trust, the victim had to prove his claim alongside ordinary creditors of the fraudster, because the assets belonged to the fraudster and would be available for such creditors. The Royal Court had no doubt that Jersey law should draw on the experience of English law and other jurisdictions to impose a constructive trust in a case such as the present. Therefore, in Jersey too, when property is obtained by fraud, equity imposes a constructive trust on the fraudulent recipient so that the victim has a proprietary interest in such property.[1]

Does Jersey law permit tracing?[2] It was argued that Jersey law should be slow to adopt English rules in relation to tracing. It was clear[3] that, under English law, tracing was part of the law of property, not part of the law of unjust enrichment. However, the Jersey law of property had wholly different origins from that of England. It did not appear that countries based on the civil law have adopted the concept of tracing. There were only two previous Jersey cases dealing with the issue of tracing. The first was *Re the Viscount; In the matter of PKT Consultants (Jersey) Limited.*[4] This involved an insolvent company, PKT Consultants, which had undertaken trust and company administration. The records were unclear as to the source of funds for various assets held by PKT Consultants. A dispute arose as to whether the sale proceeds of a particular asset belonged to an intervening party in the désastre. Eventually there was an agreed order but the court carefully considered whether it was proper to make that order; and in doing so, Tomes DB[5] concluded that the Royal Court was a court of equity and had an inherent jurisdiction to do what is necessary to ensure that justice be done, not only between the parties, but between one of the parties, and applied English law. In *Royal Bank of Scotland*

---

1 2002/15A, paras 170–177. The court recognised that this conclusion raised questions concerning Art 10(2)(a)(iii) of the 1984 Law, but these were not sufficient to negate the conclusion.

2 The court adopted the meaning of 'tracing' (as opposed to 'following') now current in England and referred to L Smith *The Law of Tracing* (OUP, 1997), p 6; *Foskett v McKeown* [2000] 2 WLR 1299, at 1304, 1322.

3 From *Foskett v McKeown* (above), at 1322.

4 (Unreported) 1 August 1991.

5 Referring to *Re Halletts Estate* (1880) 13 Ch D 696; *Sinclair v Brougham* [1914] AC 398; *Re Diplock* [1948] Ch 465.

Limited v Khan,[1] the decision in *PKT Consultants* was approved and the court stated that it should allow tracing as part of its 'power in its equitable jurisdiction to remedy … fraud'. The upshot was that there was no Jersey authority which suggested that tracing should not be part of Jersey law; such authority as there was suggested that tracing did form part of Jersey law. Although accepting that Jersey law of property had very different roots from that of England, there appeared to be no practical difficulty or any objection of principle to recognising tracing of movable property. On the contrary, in the court's judgment, there were strong policy reasons for doing so. Tracing offered an effective method of vindicating and safeguarding proprietary rights, particularly in cases of fraud. It had proved a useful tool in English law.[2]

Although the rules of tracing that should be applied ought, as a starting point, to be the English rules, the court emphasised that it was not bound by them and, indeed, ought to depart from them if convinced that there was a better alternative. The court adverted to the debate in England as to whether the time has come for the common law tracing rules to be subsumed into the more flexible rules of equitable tracing. In particular, this would allow tracing through a mixed fund. Although it had not heard argument on this point, it expressed the preliminary view that the differences between the two systems of tracing in England had an historical origin which had no application in Jersey. On the face of it, there seemed to be little reason to incorporate such technical distinctions into Jersey law and some advantage in applying the more flexible rules of equitable tracing (as constituting the Jersey rules of tracing) to all tracing actions. In particular, in the case of a current account where trust monies had been mixed with monies belonging to an innocent third party, English law applied the 'first in, first out' (FIFO) basis (or the rule in *Clayton's case*.[3]) However, this rule worked in a haphazard manner and had been much criticised.[4] Consequently, the Royal Court concluded that it saw no advantage in adopting into Jersey law a rule which had been much criticised and which could clearly produce capricious and arbitrary results. The 'Apportionment Method' (as suggested in *Barlow Clowes*[5]) was more likely to produce a fair result and there was no reason not to adopt it. As a general rule, therefore, monies to be traced through a mixed bank account (whether current or deposit) should be dealt with under Jersey law by application of the Apportionment Method.[6]

Could tracing extend to improvements in pre-existing property? On the assumption that English law – and specifically *Re Diplock*[7] – prohibited tracing

1 1999/183: (unreported) 19 October 1999.

2 2002/15A, paras 178–189.

3 (1816) 1 Mer 572.

4 *Barlow Clowes International Limited (in liquidation) v Vaughan* [1992] BCLC 910; *Re Walter J Schmidt & Co ex parte Feuerbach* (1923) 298 F 314 at 316.

5 [1992] BCLC 910.

6 2002/15A, paras 190–196.

7 [1948] 2 All ER 318, especially at 360 (CA).

money into improvements in land already owned by a third party (and the Royal Court was not convinced that English law went this far), there was no reason why this principle should be applied in Jersey. If the English court held that, where funds being traced are mixed with an innocent recipient's funds and used to purchase real property, the funds can be traced into that property; but that where the funds being traced are used to improve an asset already owned, they cannot be traced, then it was hard to see the logic of this distinction. If the funds being traced had added value, why should the innocent volunteer benefit from that increase in value to which he had contributed nothing, but the beneficiaries whose funds have been used to add value not be entitled to anything? Fairness surely dictated that they should be able to recover that increased value. This would leave the innocent volunteer in no worse position than he was previously in the sense that he would be left with the value of the unimproved property. Consequently, the position in Jersey was held to be that, where funds being traced had been spent on improvements to property already owned by an innocent volunteer, the claimant could trace into the increased value of the property which was attributable to those funds. Clearly if, as envisaged in *Diplock*, there had been no increase in value attributable to the funds, there could be no tracing as the funds would have been lost.[1]

Finally, in relation to the tracing claim, the Royal Court held that:

(a) under Jersey law (as under English law) a plaintiff's equitable title is defeated and the right to trace is lost, either in whole or in part, in circumstances where it would be inequitable to allow the plaintiff to trace; and

(b) although the concept of the equitable charge (being the appropriate remedy for enforcing a tracing exercise through a mixed fund) was not known to Jersey law, the court did not foresee any insurmountable difficulty in the way of fashioning remedies which ensure that effect can be given to a tracing decision and was prepared to do so in an appropriate case. Indeed, it saw no reason why the court should not have such a power.[2]

(II) Does Jersey law recognise a claim in restitution even where there is no fault on the part of an innocent recipient?[3]

As an alternative to its proprietary tracing claim, GT brought a claim in restitution based upon unjust enrichment. It accepted that the claim arose only if it did not succeed in its tracing claim. In the light of the court's conclusions on the tracing claim, it was not strictly need to consider the restitutionary

1 2002/15A, paras 211–218.

2 Ibid, paras 219–223.

3 Ibid, paras 233–242. The court heard further argument on the question of change of position and delivered its conclusions on 11 March 2002. This part of the proceedings cannot be dealt with here.

claim. Nevertheless, the court thought it right therefore to express its conclusions. All parties agreed that, were this case being heard in England, a claim in restitution could not succeed. Under English law, where the property in question or its identified proceeds were still in the hands of the innocent recipient (applying the relevant tracing rules), the plaintiff was entitled to recover the property or those proceeds as a proprietary claim. But if the recipient did not still have the property or its identifiable proceeds, then no claim lay against the recipient unless he had been at fault in some way. If he was guilty of fault, equity treated him as a constructive trustee. The nature and degree of fault had been the subject of conflicting decisions in England,[1] but these did not bind the Royal Court and it declined to follow them. Instead, the court deliberately expressed its decision in terms that were no wider than was strictly necessary for the present case, without wishing to be taken to suggest that a remedy would not also be available in other analogous situations. It held that, under the law of Jersey, where property in respect of which a person (a beneficiary) has an equitable proprietary interest (because the property has been taken from the beneficiary by a person who is in a fiduciary position towards that beneficiary) is received by an innocent volunteer, the beneficiary has a personal claim in restitution against the recipient even where the recipient has not been guilty of any 'fault' in receiving the property. In other words, the state of mind required for a 'knowing receipt' claim under English law is not required in Jersey. It is a strict restitutionary liability. However, the claim is based upon unjust enrichment and, accordingly, the beneficiary can only succeed to the extent that the recipient remains unjustly enriched. A defence of change of position is therefore available. The court also emphasised that the liability is a personal one; the recipient is not a constructive trustee for the beneficiary.

(III) Although the Jersey law recognises a right of action to set aside gifts made in fraud of creditors, what are the limits of and principles underlying such an action?[2]

The third claim (referred to in the 1999 proceedings as 'the Pauline action') differed from the proprietary tracing claim and the claim in restitution, in that it was based on an acceptance by GT that Sheikh Fahad had transferred his own assets to the relevant settlements but it was alleged, instead, that he had done so in order to defraud GT as his creditor and that, in the circumstances, the transfers could be set aside.

It was clear that Jersey law recognised an ability, in certain circumstances, to set aside a transfer undertaken in fraud of creditors. There was judicial

---

1 Referring to *Re Montague's Settlement Trust* [1987] Ch 264 and *Belmont Finance Corporation v Williams Furniture Limited (No 2)* [1980] 2 All ER 393. For the current state of English law in this area, see pp 400–406 above.

2 2002/15A, paras 247–351. The court heard further argument on the question of entitlement to profits earned on an asset alienated in fraud of creditors, but subsequently recovered in a Pauline action, and delivered its conclusions on 12 March 2002. This part of the proceedings cannot be dealt with here.

authority to this effect, namely *Golder v Société des Magasins Concorde Limited*.[1] The facts in that case were clear-cut. The plaintiff, having been the managing director of the defendant company, brought an action for wrongful dismissal and conspiracy. Judgment on the issue of liability was given in his favour in February 1966. In June 1966, the defendant company sold its business to an associated Guernsey company partly for cash – sufficient to pay off the liquidated creditors of the company – and partly for shares. In July 1966, the Royal Court gave judgment on quantum. By then the defendant company had settled the claims of all its other creditors and had no assets left. It was unable to meet the liability to the plaintiff. The court held that the plaintiff was a creditor of the defendant company with effect from the date of the judgment on liability (February 1966) even though his claim was unquantified until the judgment on quantum. It further held that the sole purpose of the disposal by the defendant company to the Guernsey company had been to ensure that the defendant company had no assets with which to meet its liability to the plaintiff. The issue before the court in the 1999 proceedings was essentially whether Jersey law allowed recovery in circumstances that went beyond those which existed in *Golder*.

The first question that needed to be addressed was: *who is a creditor*? The defendants contended that only a person who is a creditor at the time of the transaction under attack could bring a Pauline action and that a person did not become a creditor until he has a certain claim. GT's claim did not arise out of contract, but out of tort. GT did not have a certain claim until the English court delivered judgment in its favour (June 1999). Any disposal made by Sheikh Fahad before that time could not be attacked by GT because GT was not then a creditor. This contention thus gave rise to two subsidiary questions:

(a) Does the claim of a creditor have to predate the transaction under attack? and
(b) When can the debt of a creditor be said to arise, particularly in cases of tort?

(a) Does the claim of a creditor have to predate the transaction under attack?

In dealing with this issue in the present case, the court considered a number of treatises by a variety of jurists – not only writers on Jersey law (such as Poingdestre and Le Geyt) but also French jurists (such as Pothier, Domat, Dalloz, Planiol and Ripert) writing both before and after the introduction of the Code Civil.[2] It was also referred to a number of cases decided under the English 1571 Act – decisions which the court did not find helpful. Having

---

1 (1973) JJ 721.

2 In the absence of judicial authority, considerable weight is attached to writers on the law of Jersey (in the present case, Poingdestre and Le Geyt), on the law of Normandy and also on French law.

surveyed such authorities, the court concluded that *Golder* had not specifically addressed this point but the court had gone to some trouble to show that, on the facts, the plaintiff had become a creditor of the defendant company before the disposal in question. It also held that it was quite clear that all the authorities before the introduction of the Code Civil in France required that the debt must predate the disposition. This was consistent with the underlying principle of the Pauline action, namely that a person contracts with a debtor on the strength of an implied undertaking that the whole of the debtor's patrimony was available to support his obligation and he would therefore not dispose of it to the prejudice of those contracting with him. In modern times (the earliest cases seem to date from the mid-nineteenth century) French law had changed the rule by providing that, in certain circumstances, future creditors might bring an action to set aside transactions effected before they became creditors.

In the court's judgment, this was one of those areas where it had to be wary of modern French Law. There was an authoritative statement from Poingdestre that Jersey Law required the debt to predate the transaction. The only Jersey judicial decision seemed to have proceeded on the same basis. It was not open to the court to say that, in the light of changes to the law of the Pauline action introduced by French judicial decisions since the Code Civil, it should depart from the existing law of Jersey as stated by Poingdestre, particularly when that was clearly consistent with the previous customary law of France. Even if it were open to the court, it did not think that it would be right to effect such a change by way of judicial development. Article 17 of the Bankruptcy (Désastre) (Jersey) Law 1990 provided for transactions at an undervalue to be set aside if they had occurred within a certain time before the bankruptcy. This was so regardless of whether the debts arose before or after the transaction in question. Any further development of the law to allow transactions undertaken before the facts giving rise to a debt occur should be a matter to be undertaken by the legislature. Just as it was right that creditors should be protected from fraudulent debtors, so was it important that security of receipt and an assumption of validity of transactions be considered. To set aside transactions at the instance of a person whose claim did not exist (even on the extended definition referred to below) at the time of the transaction was a major interference with the freedom for a person to deal with his assets freely and for persons who transact with him to be able to rely on what has been done. If to be undertaken at all, such a step should only be undertaken after widespread consultation and consideration of all the implications. Accordingly, the court held that the law of Jersey was as stated by Poingdestre, and, implicitly, by the Royal Court in *Golder*, namely that only a creditor whose debt preceded the transaction in question could bring a Pauline action.

(b) When does a person become a creditor?

The defendants argued that a person claiming in tort did not rely upon the debtor's creditworthiness and the implied undertaking that his patrimony was available to support his obligations. The Pauline action was therefore not available to a person claiming in tort until he becomes a judgment creditor (as in *Golder*). Moreover, they relied on the fact that, in the Bankruptcy (Désastre) (Jersey) Law 1990, Art 29 was drawn more narrowly than the equivalent provision in the Insolvency Act 1986 of the United Kingdom and only allowed proof in a désastre of:

> '... certain debts and liabilities, present or future, certain or contingent, to which the debtor is subject at the time of the declaration, or to which he becomes subject before payment of the final dividend by reason of any obligation incurred before the time of the declaration ...'

Thus a claim for liability in tort, particularly where the proceedings had not yet been brought, was not provable in a bankruptcy. The claimant could not, therefore, be classified as a creditor. It would be wholly illogical, said the defendants, for a person who could not claim in a bankruptcy to be treated as a creditor for setting aside a transaction in a Pauline action. In addition, the defendants relied upon the fact that the Pauline action originally envisaged a claim based in contract.

In the event, however, the court was clearly struck by the fact that the consequences of holding that a claimant had not become a creditor until the date of judgment in his favour were unreasonable and unacceptable. On this issue, therefore, it opted to have regard to modern French writers (Dalloz in particular) and held that, for the purposes of a Pauline action under Jersey law, a person was deemed to become a creditor when the facts giving rise to his cause of action occur, even if the validity of the cause of action was not established until later. All the facts necessary to give rise to the cause of action must have occurred before a person can be deemed to be a creditor. He cannot, in the court's judgment, be considered a creditor when only some of the facts which support his cause of action have occurred. However, once liability to the creditor is established, it relates back to the date of the facts which give rise to that liability.

Is insolvency on the part of a debtor required? If so at what stage?

It was clear that a Pauline action arises as a result of a disposal by the debtor to the prejudice of his creditors. All the texts agreed that it was necessary to show actual prejudice to the creditor. It was accepted by all parties that there must be insolvency at the date of the action; otherwise there were sufficient assets to meet the claim and therefore no prejudice. However, it was also argued that a creditor must also show that the debtor was insolvent at the time of the disposition or became insolvent as a result of it. Counsel for the plaintiff disagrees. In *Golder*, the court held that the principles stated in Dalloz on the requirement for insolvency accurately reflected the law of Jersey, namely that the creditor had to prove that insolvency existed at the time of the disposition or as a result of it. The court in the 1999 Proceedings similarly concluded that the weight of relevant authority was overwhelmingly in favour of such a requirement. In none of the texts cited was there anything to the contrary: indeed, almost all writers on modern French law maintained the requirement for insolvency at the time, or as a result of the disposition. The English cases, which turned on the terms of an English statute which had no application in Jersey, were not of assistance. The court could only disagree with *Golder* if it thought that it was plainly wrong. Far from so thinking, the court was satisfied that it was entirely right.

However, the court also added that it believed that the principles set out in Dalloz and approved in *Golder* had to be applied with common sense having regard to the modern world. At the time when *Golder* was decided, assets were comparatively few and readily identifiable. Nowadays, insolvency, particularly when the action was being heard many years after the disposition in question, cannot be measured with precision. Assets were more fluid. Furthermore, it was extremely unlikely that the creditor bringing the action would have access to all the information concerning the financial affairs of the debtor so many years ago. In addition, as the present case showed, the debtor's assets may be spread throughout the world and may be held through the medium of companies. Accordingly, the court held that, once the plaintiff had established insolvency on the part of the debtor at the time of the action, the burden then shifted to those seeking to uphold the disposition to prove that he was not also insolvent at the time of or as a result of the disposition. Furthermore, a broad commonsense approach had to be taken to the question of insolvency resulting from the disposition. Assets fluctuated greatly in value nowadays; much more so than when Dalloz was writing. This had to be taken into account. It was not a question of carrying out a meticulous balance sheet exercise the instant following the disposition. In most cases that was simply not practical and was an unfair and unrealistic burden on the creditor. It was more a question of seeing whether, within a reasonably short period following the disposition, the debtor became insolvent so that it could be said that the disposition contributed to or exacerbated the insolvency. The court must simply be satisfied that there was a close connection in time and effect between the disposition and the subsequent insolvency.

How was insolvency to be measured?

A claim which was contingent, but was later found to be due, should be brought into account when calculating insolvency at the time of the disposition. Once the liability is established by law, it relates back to the facts which give rise to the liability. Accordingly, the liability is to be taken into account from that time for the purpose of calculating solvency. Balance sheet solvency should be calculated as it always is, namely by calculating the value of all the debtor's assets and deducting his liabilities. There should not be excluded from the debtor's assets those items which are inalienable, difficult to distrain upon or concealed. On the other hand, if the court had been required to decide the issue, it would have held that assets in a revocable trust are not to be counted as assets of the debtor for these purposes: unless and until revoked, the assets are held by the trustees upon the trusts set out in the trust deed; and the trustees owe fiduciary duties to the beneficiaries, and the assets cannot properly be considered to be those of the debtor merely because he has a power of revocation.

The difference between transactions 'lucrative' and 'onéreuse'

In *Golder*, the Royal Court approved the statement of Poingdestre that there were two types of alienation to be considered in a Pauline action. The first was an alienation to a volunteer which Poingdestre called '*aliénations faites pour cause lucrative*'. The second was an alienation made for value which he calls '*aliénations faites pour cause onéreuse*'. In the first case, the alienation was voidable when the alienor alone was guilty of an intention to defeat his creditor but, for the alienation to be voidable in the second case, both the alienor and the alienee must be privy to the real nature of the transaction. An alienation did not become '*onéreuse*' simply because there was some 'cause' given. A transaction only becomes '*onéreuse*' if the 'cause' given by the recipient was commensurate and proportionate to the value of the thing alienated; if the price is not commensurate or proportionate in this way, it was a transaction '*lucrative*'.

What is the required state of mind on the part of the debtor?

GT argued that a debtor had the necessary intention for the purposes of a Pauline action if he was aware at the time he made the transfer that it would or could prejudice his creditors in the recovery of their debts. The defendants, on the other hand, argued that a plaintiff must show an intention on the part of the debtor to defeat his creditors. In *Golder*, the court had approved the following statement from Dalloz:

> '… the creditor in order to succeed had to prove the intention to defeat creditors and their actual defeat by showing that their debtor is insolvent and that his insolvency was due to the act which is challenged.'

The court in the present proceedings concluded that *Golder* correctly stated the law of Jersey on this point. It was clear that, at all times until well after the introduction of the Code Civil in France, the Pauline action required the two elements of prejudice to creditors and an intention on the part of the debtor to cause that prejudice. Dishonesty was required. It was accepted that, during the latter part of the nineteenth century and the twentieth century, French law had changed, and it was now enough that the debtor foresaw that prejudice would or might result from the transaction. This was very far removed from any normal meaning of 'intention'. On the contrary, a requirement merely to be aware that a particular result might follow was really a requirement of recklessness rather than intention. A debtor may indeed wish not to prejudice his creditors but may be prepared for other reasons (eg tax advantages) to go ahead and take the risk of it transpiring that they are in fact prejudiced.

In the court's judgment, GT's formulation – with its reference to the debtor making a transfer in the knowledge that it could prejudice his creditors – substituted a test which included recklessness for a test of intention. It was not open to this court to do that. Recklessness had never been sufficient until recent developments in French law. All the sources which carried weight in Jersey required intention. Accordingly, the court held that, in order to succeed in a Pauline action in Jersey, it must be shown that the transaction in question was undertaken by the debtor with the intention (object) of defeating his creditors. Of course, in order to ascertain the state of a person's mind the court had to consider all the evidence and draw inferences. The fact that the defeat of creditors was the natural result of a transaction was undoubtedly a material factor in assessing whether the necessary state of mind on the part of the debtor was established. The weight to be given to this factor will vary according to the circumstances, not least by reference to the degree of certainty that prejudice to the creditors will result from the transaction. The greater the certainty that prejudice will follow, the easier it will be for the court to conclude that the debtor intended that prejudice but this conclusion did not follow automatically.[1] Even if it were open to the court, it would not be right to change the law in this way. The underlying philosophy of the Pauline action had always been that it required an intention to cause prejudice to the creditors by defeating their ability to recover. The bankruptcy legislation of Jersey dealt with the position where there was no such intention by providing for transactions to be set aside in certain circumstances without regard to the debtor's intention. It would be going beyond the judicial function to change the customary law concerning the Pauline action in this way, when the legislature had already addressed this area and could do so further should the need arise.

Having held that a transaction may not be set aside unless carried out by the debtor with the intention of defrauding his creditors, what happened should the debtor have more than one purpose in relation to the transaction? Must the intention to defraud be the dominant purpose?[2] The court saw no reason for imposing a dominant purpose requirement. In reality, when there was more than one purpose, it would often be a very artificial exercise to try

---

1 The court referred here to *Re Mercer* (1886) 17 QBD 290.

2 Various English authorities were referred to, but these seem to have regarded as inconclusive on the point: *Lloyds Bank v Marcan* [1973] 1 WLR 1387; *Jyske Bank (Gibraltar) Limited v Spjeldnaes* [1999] 2 BCLC 101 at 120–121; and *Chohan v Saggar* [1992] BCC 306. The court had also been referred to the 'badges of fraud' but it was agreed that these were merely matters capable of giving rise to inferences that the debtor had the necessary intention; they were not presumptions of law.

and establish which purpose was dominant; furthermore, what if they were equal? The requirements of a Pauline action were satisfied under Jersey law if, where there was more than one purpose, a *substantial* purpose of the transaction was to defeat creditors.

The nature of the claim – possible defences[1]

According to the Royal Court, the Pauline action has always been a revocatory action. The creditor is not entitled to compensation from an innocent volunteer from whom the creditor has transferred property; he is entitled to reclaim the property. Where the original property is no longer in the hands of the recipient, it is clear that, in the case of innocent receipt, there is no liability beyond the enrichment (if any) which the recipient still enjoys. If, and to the extent, that the recipient no longer retains any benefit, then no recovery is permitted from him. Accordingly, it was held that, once a creditor has established that all the other conditions of a Pauline action are satisfied, the court must consider whether, in reliance upon the receipt, an innocent recipient has so changed his position that it would be inequitable to require him to make restitution or to make restitution in full. The underlying principle is that an order for restitution should not result in an innocent recipient being worse off as a result of the transactions in question than he would have been if those transactions had not occurred. The burden of showing that it would be inequitable to order restitution lies upon the recipient.

(IV) What is the limitation period?[2]

There was no judicial authority on the prescriptive period for a Pauline action. After considering a number of analogous authorities and relevant writers, the Royal Court concluded that a creditor has no title in the thing alienated. Indeed, he is not asserting any claim on his part to the thing itself. The creditor sues the defendant either to return the thing itself to the debtor's patrimony, if he still has it, or to return such value originating from the thing as may remain in the recipient's hands. In those circumstances, it is a claim for money. It went on to hold that a 10-year period (referred to by Le Geyt) should be a general period which should be taken to apply to all personal actions and all actions concerning movables save to the extent that they had already been held to be subject to a different period (eg tort, actions concerning estates, etc) or that some other period was, by analogy, clearly more applicable. The court also expressed the view (although the point did not have to be decided) that one prescriptive period should cover Pauline actions against innocent and fraudulent recipients (and that period in each case should be 10 years).

---

1 2002/15A, paras 313–321.

2 Ibid, paras 322–345.

Summary of the law on claim (III)

The judgment then provided a summary of the court's findings in relation to the Pauline action:

> '346. In briefest summary therefore we hold that a creditor, whose claim predates the disposition in question, may set aside a disposition made by his debtor where the debtor is insolvent at the time of the disposition or becomes insolvent in consequence thereof, provided that the disposition is made with an intention on the part of the debtor to prejudice his creditors and provided further that prejudice is indeed caused. For these purposes the claim of a creditor is deemed to arise upon the occurrence of the facts which give rise to the creditor's cause of action, regardless of the date upon which the creditor's claim is upheld by a court. The right of action against an innocent volunteer who was party to the disposition is restricted to the continuing enrichment in the hands of the recipient, who will therefore have available to him a change of position defence.
>
> 347. As can be seen, we have in general held the law to be as it has been stated by Jersey judicial decision, by writers on Jersey law and by writers on the law as it was in France before the introduction of the Code Civil. We have only applied more modern French authorities where they reflect the pre-existing position. We have in general declined GT's invitation to declare that the law of Jersey should follow the changes introduced in modern French law. For the reasons which we have given, we have not thought it open to us to accede to GT's invitation in this way.
>
> 348. But even had we considered that it was open to us to do so, we would have declined the invitation. Although we have considered each ingredient of the Pauline action separately, it is necessary to stand back and look at the overall nature of the Pauline action in the light of the individual ingredients. Each of them serves a purpose and they make up the whole. The effect of accepting GT's contentions in relation to each individual element would have been to transform the nature of a Pauline action as previously understood.
>
> 349. Thus the action would enable future creditors (ie persons who had not had any dealings with the debtor at the time of the disposition in question) successfully to attack a disposition made before their involvement with the debtor, merely because the natural consequence of the disposition *could* have been to prejudice such creditors even if the debtor had remained completely solvent as a result of the dispositions in question. The only requirement would have been that he must have been insolvent at the time that the creditor bought the action, which may have been many years later.
>
> 350. In our judgment, to widen the Pauline action to this extent would render security of receipt almost non-existent. Any gift (whether to a relative or to a trust) could prejudice creditors in the event of a subsequent insolvency on the part of the donor because the assets in question will no longer be owned by the donor. In effect, any creditor would be able to bring a Pauline action to set aside a gift to a relative or to a trust made at any time (within the prescriptive period) provided that the donor has at some stage subsequently become insolvent. All gifts to relatives and trusts would therefore be vulnerable to attack in the event of subsequent insolvency, even if wholly unrelated to the gift.
>
> 351. We appreciate that this is putting it at its highest, but it would lead to too much uncertainty. The law must be clear as to when gifts may be set aside and when they are valid. Furthermore the appropriate balance has to be struck between the need to protect creditors and the need to enable solvent individuals to dispose of their assets to their relatives, to charities or to trusts. In particular, gifts to trusts are a regular occurrence in Jersey and the law needs to be clear as to the circumstances in which a gift into trust may be set aside. In our judgment, the existing rules of Jersey law (under both customary law and the bankruptcy legislation) could be said to strike a reasonable balance but, should it be felt to be otherwise, we believe that this should be a matter for the legislature.'

The court then analysed the complex facts of the case and found that 'a substantial purpose' of Sheikh Fahad in making several of the transfers to the No 52 Trust, Ceyla and the Esteem Settlement was to defeat GT's claim against him. He therefore had the necessary intent to defraud. Indeed, the court added that, had it been necessary to do so, it would also have found this to have been his dominant purpose, with his tax planning purpose being of lower significance.

7.3.12 The Turks and Caicos Islands

English law was applied to and became part of the laws of the Turks and Caicos Islands (the Islands) in 1799. Thus, in general, English statutes (including the 1571 Act) applied in the Islands,[1] and English authorities also applied and continued to be recognised, except where they have been modified or supplemented by local legislation. The main legislation of relevance to trusts generally is the Trusts Ordinance 1990 (1990 Ordinance),[2] s 61 of which dealt with dispositions of insolvent settlors.[3] However, the Voluntary Dispositions Ordinance 1998 (1998 Ordinance)[4] has now amended, and makes new provision for, the law relating to dispositions to prejudice creditors and connected matters. With effect from the appointed day,[5] the 1998 Ordinance applies in place of the law in force prior to the appointed day to every relevant disposition[6] of property made before or after the appointed day and whether or not the property, which is the subject of the disposition, is situated in the Islands or elsewhere.[7] The 1998 Ordinance does not apply, however, to any action or proceedings commenced prior to the appointed day, or within six months of the appointed day, in respect of a disposition made prior to the appointed day, in which case the law in force prior to the appointed day shall still be applied.[8]

Dispositions subject to the 1998 Ordinance

The 1998 Ordinance applies to every disposition of property at an undervalue made by a transferor where, at the time of the transaction, the transferor is either insolvent or becomes insolvent in consequence of the transaction.[9] The key terms are defined in s 2 of the 1998 Ordinance.

---

1 The 1571 Act, and other related statutes, ceased to apply to dispositions to which the Voluntary Dispositions Ordinance 1998 apply, by virtue of the 1998 Ordinance, s 12 and Sch.

2 No 25 of 1990.

3 Section 61 of the 1990 Ordinance is repealed by the 1998 Ordinance, s 11.

4 No 14 of 1998. Assent was given on 17 December 1998.

5 As yet the 'appointed day' has not arrived. See the 1998 Ordinance, ss 1 and 2.

6 A 'relevant disposition' is a disposition to which the 1998 Ordinance, s 4(1) applies (as to which see below).

7 Ibid, s 3(1).

8 Ibid, s 3(2).

9 Ibid, s 4(1). On a literal reading of this provision, a disposition is caught only if the settlor is already insolvent when he made it or, alternatively, if the settlor immediately (ie at the time of the transaction)

(1) A 'disposition', in relation to property, means 'every form of conveyance, transfer, assignment, lease, mortgage, pledge or other transaction whereby any legal or equitable interest in property is created, transferred or extinguished'.

(2) 'Property' means 'property of any description, wherever situated, and, in relation to rights and interests, includes those rights and interests whether present or future, vested or contingent'.

(3) 'Undervalue', in relation to a disposition of property, means 'a disposition in respect of which: (a) no consideration is given; or (b) the value of the consideration given is, in money or money's worth, significantly less than the value, in money or money's worth, of the property the subject of the disposition'.[1]

(4) A 'transferor' is 'a person who directly or indirectly makes a relevant disposition or causes it to be made'.

(5) 'Insolvent', in respect of a transferor, means 'any transferor whose liabilities (actual or contingent) exceed the value of his assets'.

(6) The burden of establishing that the transferor was insolvent at the time of the disposition, or became insolvent in consequence of the disposition, rests upon the creditor.[2] A 'creditor' is a person to whom a liability (including a contingent liability) is owed by a transferor at the material date (meaning the date on which the relevant disposition is made), and which liability remains unsatisfied on the date of the action or proceedings brought under s 4(2); and it also includes the trustee in bankruptcy (wherever appointed) or the personal representative of such a person.[3]

(7) For these purposes, a 'contingent liability' does not include 'a contingent liability of which the transferor had no actual notice or in respect of which the transferor was not aware of the facts or circumstances giving rise to the liability'. Although it is clear that the transferor must have actual notice of any contingent liability and that constructive (and presumably imputed) notice will not suffice, it is not entirely clear what the second limb of the definition is directed at. Must the transferor's awareness of any facts and circumstances giving rise to a contingent liability also be an actual awareness? Or will it suffice if it can be said that he ought to have known that certain facts and circumstances have already given rise to a contingent liability, or that they will probably, or even might conceivably, do so? Suppose, for instance, that, in the exercise of his profession, a surgeon has

becomes insolvent in consequence of the transaction. It would seem that, if the settlor becomes insolvent a short time after making the disposition, then he is not caught, not even if his insolvency proves to be a consequence of the transaction. Whether or not this was intended must be doubtful.

1 This definition is broadly similar to that used in the English Insolvency Act 1986, ss 339 and 423.

2 Voluntary Dispositions Ordinance 1998, s 6.

3 Ibid, s 2.

carried out a surgical operation negligently. He will obviously know that he has carried out the operation and, in this sense, he will have actual knowledge of the facts and circumstances which may give rise to a claim against him and a contingent liability. However, does he also need to have actual awareness of the fact that he has been negligent? Is it sufficient if an allegation of negligence has been made (which he may or may not dispute)? Should a writ have been issued or be pending? There is simply no definition here of a 'contingent liability', or indeed of 'liability', but the definition of a 'creditor' (as to which, see above) as someone 'to whom a liability (including a contingent liability) is *owed* by a transferor at the material date' suggests that any such liability must then be an actual liability (albeit a contingent one), ie one which has already come into existence or has been established.

Who may apply to the court?

Section 4(2) of the 1998 Ordinance provides that, where a transferor has made a relevant disposition, the court (meaning the Supreme Court of the Islands) may, on the application of a creditor thereby prejudiced, make such order as it thinks fit for restoring the position to what it would have been if the disposition had not been made. However, despite the generality of s 4(2), it is provided that an application for a court order in respect of a relevant disposition shall not be made except:

(a) in a case where the transferor has been adjudged bankrupt, by the trustee in bankruptcy (wherever appointed),
(b) in a case where the transferor is a body corporate which is being wound up by the official liquidator or by the liquidator of the body corporate; or
(c) in any other case, by a creditor.[1]

An application made by a trustee in bankruptcy or a liquidator is to be treated as made on behalf of every creditor,[2] which, by implication, indicates that an application made by a creditor is made on his own behalf only and necessarily in respect of only his own loss.

Time-limit

No action or proceedings shall be commenced pursuant to s 4(2) unless it is commenced within three years of the material date.[3]

1 Ibid, s 4(3).
2 Ibid, s 4(4).
3 Ibid, s 4(5).

Powers of the court

Section 4(2) authorises the court to make such order as it thinks fit for restoring the position to what it would have been if the disposition had not been made. Section 5 then provides that, without prejudice to the generality of s 4(2), the court may:

(a) require any property transferred as part of the disposition to be vested in any person, whether absolutely or for the benefit of all the persons on whose behalf the application for the order is treated as made;
(b) require any property to be so vested if it represents, in any person's hands, the application either of the proceeds of sale of property so transferred or of money so transferred;
(c) release or discharge (in whole or in part) any security given by the transferor;
(d) require any person to pay to any other person in respect of benefits received from the transferor such sums as the court may direct;
(e) provide for any surety or guarantor whose obligations to any person where released or discharged (in whole or in part) under the disposition to be under such new or revived obligation as the court thinks appropriate;
(f) provide for security to be provided for the discharge of any obligation imposed by or arising under the order, for such an obligation to be charged on any property and for such security or charge to have the same priority as a security or charge released or discharged (in whole or in part) under the disposition.

An order made by the court under s 4(2) may affect the property of, or impose any obligation on, any person, whether or not he is the transferee.[1] This is subject, however, to the restrictions in s 5(3), to the effect that a court order shall not prejudice any interest in property which was acquired in good faith, for value and without notice of the relevant circumstances, or prejudice any interest deriving from such an interest.[2] Moreover, where the court is satisfied that a beneficiary under a trust has not acted in bad faith, an order shall not prejudice any interest in property which the beneficiary has acquired without notice of the relevant circumstances by virtue of a distribution made consequent upon the prior exercise of a power or discretion vested in the trustees of a trust or any other person and otherwise properly exercised.[3] Also, where the court is satisfied that a trustee of a Turks and Caicos trust has not acted in bad faith, negligently or with notice of the relevant circumstances, an order shall not prejudice the retention by the trustee of any money or other

1 Ibid, s 5(2).
2 Ibid, s 5(3)(a).
3 Ibid, s 5(3)(b).

property which it has received in payment of fees charged or in reimbursement of costs incurred in respect of the relevant disposition other than fees received or costs reimbursed in connection with proceedings brought under s 4(2).[1]

Where the court is satisfied that a transferee has not acted in bad faith, negligently or with notice of the relevant circumstances, the transferee shall have security to be given to the transferee by way of a charge over the property, the subject of the relevant disposition, for an amount equal to all costs properly incurred by the transferee in connection with proceedings brought under s 4(2) as would be allowed on taxation of costs on an indemnity basis.[2]

For the purposes of these provisions (in s 5), the relevant circumstances in relation to a disposition are the circumstances by virtue of which an order under s 4(2) may be made in respect of the relevant disposition;[3] and 'security' means any mortgage, charge, lien or any other security.[4]

Requirement of due diligence

It shall be the duty of every trustee or professional person who advises a transferor in connection with the making of a relevant disposition to carry out such due diligence procedures as may be prescribed in guidelines contained in regulations made from time to time by the Governor in Council. Different regulations may be prescribed for different cases or particular circumstances.[5]

Miscellaneous

Nothing in the 1998 Ordinance shall affect the recognition of a foreign law in determining whether the transferor is the owner of 'such property' or the holder of 'such power',[6] but it is not clear what the word 'such' refers to. Presumably, 'such property' is intended to refer to property which is the subject of a 'relevant disposition' for the purposes of s 4(1);[7] but there is nothing in the 1998 Ordinance to identify any 'such power' of the transferor.

Nothing in the 1998 Ordinance shall be construed as creating or enabling any right, claim or interest on behalf of a creditor or person which right, claim or interest would be avoided or defeated by the 1990 Ordinance.[8]

---

1 Ibid, s 5(3)(c).
2 Ibid, s 5(4).
3 Ibid, s 5(5).
4 Ibid, s 5(6).
5 Ibid, s 5(7)(1), (2).
6 Ibid, s 9.
7 See also ibid, ss 2 and 3(1).
8 Ibid, s 10. Section 61 of the Trusts Ordinance 1990 is repealed.

Chapter 8

TRADING TRUSTS

David Hayton[*]

8.1 WHAT IS A TRADING TRUST?

A trading trust exists where, under the terms of a trust, trust property held by trustees is used for the conduct of a business. In a private trust, it will normally be the trustees who carry out the trading activities but in a public trust (where the opportunity to become a beneficiary may lawfully be offered to the public) the trustees will be custodian trustees, having some extra monitoring duties imposed upon them in respect of a manager, like the manager of an authorised unit trust[1] who will conduct the business for the benefit of the 'investor-beneficiaries' who will have purchased the status of a beneficiary. In a private trust, beneficiaries will normally be 'donee-beneficiaries' as the objects of the settlor's bounty, although they can be investor-beneficiaries who have purchased their beneficial interests.

8.1.1 Partnership dangers

One has to be careful that the beneficiaries under a trading trust do not have powers sufficient to enable them as a practical matter to control the trustees' conduct of the business. If they do, then there may be a partnership between the beneficiaries using the trustees as their agents or between the trustees and the beneficiaries. 'Partnership is the relation which subsists between persons carrying on a business in common with a view of profit.'[2] It is generally accepted[3] that the relationship needs to be founded in a contract, for example the case of investor-beneficiaries. The parties will have a 'view of profit' where

---

* Barrister of 5 Stone Buildings, Lincoln's Inn, and Professor of Law, King's College, University of London.

1 See Financial Services and Markets Act 2000, Part X.

2 Partnership Act 1890, s l.

3 *Lindley and Banks on Partnership* (Sweet & Maxwell, 17th ed), p 16.

the trustee-manager is to receive remuneration out of the profits of the business and the beneficiaries are to receive distributions from such profits. It is not exactly clear[1] what degree of involvement in the activities of the trustee-manager will suffice as carrying on a business in common. However, it is clear that the fact that, under the rule in *Saunders v Vautier*,[2] the beneficiaries, if together absolutely entitled and *sui juris*, can terminate the trust and require the assets to be transferred to them does not mean that they are participants in the conduct of the business. Until they take advantage of the rule they have no right to give directions or be consulted[3] – unless given such right by the trust instrument.

If a trust is not a trading trust but an investment trust (as opposed to an investment trust company which is a company and not a trust) then the question of partnership cannot arise. Thus, trustees of unit trusts which invest in shares to provide dividends and capital growth for unit-holder beneficiaries are merely co-owners of the investments held on trust for the common benefit of the beneficiaries.[4] However, if a unit trust is to carry on trading activities, then to exclude any possibility of a partnership, the trust deed will contain a provision to the effect that the beneficial interest of a unit-holder shall not entitle the unit-holder to interfere with the rights or powers of the trustee or manager (save as otherwise provided in restrictive fashion in the deed). Unless such provision is a pretence or sham[5] it will oust any possibility of a partnership.

8.1.2 Trust has no legal personality

A trust is not a legal entity capable of owning property or of suing or being sued. It is a set of obligations owed by the trustees to the beneficiaries, in respect of the trust fund held by the trustees, who, as principals, personally enter into legal relationships with third parties and who can sue, or be sued by, such third parties. Strictly, it is thus the trustees who trade and not the trust, although as a matter of practical shorthand one commonly refers to a trust as a 'trading trust'. The personal liability of the trustees on their trading contracts (except as limited in such contracts[6]) has led to the practice of limiting such liability by having as trustee a limited liability company with nominal share capital. This has led Professor Ford to state:[7]

---

1 See Ford and Hardingham in PD Finn (ed) *Equity and Commercial Relationships* (Law Book Co Ltd, 1987), pp 75–79; Cullity in TG Youdan (ed) *Equity, Fiduciaries and Trusts* (1989), pp 201–203; Flannigan (1984) 6 Est & Tr Q 278, 287–292, (1986) 8 Est & Tr Q 37; Cullity (1985) 7 Est & Tr Q 35, (1986) 8 Est & Tr Q 130; *Waters' Law of Trusts in Canada* (Carswell, 2nd ed, 1984), p 445.

2 (1841) 4 Beav 115.

3 *Re Brockbank* [1948] Ch 206, except under Trusts of Land and Appointment of Trustees Act 1996, s 19.

4 *Smith v Anderson* (1880) 15 Ch D 247.

5 *Aslan v Murphy* [1989] 3 All ER 130 at 133; *Fitzwilliam v IRC* [1990] STC 65 at 118; *Hitch v Stone* [2001] EWCA Civ 63, [2001] STC 214.

6 See **8.4.1**.

7 (1981) 13 Melbourne ULR 1.

> 'The fruit of this union of the law of trust and the law of limited liability companies is a commercial monstrosity. The scope for frustrating creditors is considerable.'

8.2 TRADING TRUST STRUCTURES

Obviously, private trading trusts are structured to deal with the circumstances of each particular case, but we can assume there will be a corporate trustee, usually with only a nominal share capital. It will either hold the business on a discretionary trust for a specified class of persons or on a fixed trust for unit-holders who may themselves hold their units on a discretionary subtrust for members of their families. The discretionary trust model will be appropriate where former partners have created the trust for themselves, especially if it is possible that subsequently there may be additional quasi-partner beneficiaries. There will often be some equivalence between each unit-holder's beneficial interest and his interest in the corporate trustee.

A public unit trust will need to meet stringent statutory requirements.[1] It is crucial that the trust instrument contains the fullest possible powers to enable trading to be effectively carried out. There should not only be a wide trading power but also powers to borrow and raise other forms of finance, to give guarantees and indemnities and to give security whether fixed or floating.[2] Indeed, it is advisable to have a power to add or vary administrative powers so that any deficiency in such powers can be cured.

8.3 DOMINANT TAX CONSIDERATIONS

There are very few cases apart from tax considerations where it is sensible to use a trust rather than a company for the conduct of a business. After all, trust law, unlike company law, proceeds on the assumption that it is not normal and appropriate for a trust to carry on a business. A creditor will not receive payment out of a trading trust's assets if his transaction was *ultra vires* the trust,[3] even though the *ultra vires* doctrine has virtually been abolished for companies by s 35 of the Companies Act 1985. Moreover, a creditor will not receive payment out of the trust assets if the trustees have committed any breach of trust or are indebted to the trust,[4] so that he is affected by the internal affairs of the trust, even though an outsider dealing with a company's directors or

---

1 See n 1 on p 479. The detailed provisions concerning countries' public unit trusts are outside the scope of this chapter.

2 See **8.9**.

3 *Re Johnson* (1880) 15 Ch D 548 at 552.

4 *Re Evans* (1887) 34 Ch D 597; *Re Morris* (1889) 23 Ir 333; *Re British Power Traction and Lighting Co Ltd* [1910] 2 Ch 470.

officers or agents is to a large extent protected by the rule in *Royal British Bank v Turquand*,[1] by ss 35A and 35B of the Companies Act 1985 and by cases like *Freeman & Lockyer v Buckhurst Park Properties Ltd*[2] which developed principles about the apparent and ostensible authority of officers of companies. Trustees can find that under an order for general administration, which is obtainable by a single beneficiary unimpeded by the company law rule in *Foss v Harbottle*,[3] the trust's administration is very closely scrutinised indeed. Courts rarely interfere with company affairs due to the democratic control ultimately exercisable by the members. A special insolvency regime applies for companies, but not for trusts. Finally, where trustees do have power to carry on a business it is unclear whether the company law cases[4] dealing with the implied or incidental powers of a company have any application to trusts and it is unclear what standard of care is required of trading trustees as opposed to 'investing' trustees.

These problems require much skill in drafting trading trust deeds and can lead to difficulties in negotiating loans. Little English case-law subsists, except where executors have carried on a deceased's business, because English tax considerations favouring trading trusts have been of relatively minor significance. In Australia and, to a lesser extent, in Canada tax considerations at one time did significantly favour trading via the vehicle of a trust, so that recent case-law guidance is available in those jurisdictions.

Tax considerations fall outside the scope of this work: they can change swiftly so that up-to-date local specialist advice should always be sought.

8.4 TRUSTEE'S PERSONAL LIABILITY

Except to the extent that a trustee effectively restricts his personal liability under a contract, he is personally liable to the extent of his whole private patrimony (or fortune), and he remains so even if he retires as trustee,[5] unless by novation the creditor agrees for the new trustee to be substituted for the retiring trustee.

It is thus common practice for the trustee to be a limited liability company with nominal share capital or for the individual trustees to form a company to carry on the trading activities and simply hold[6] the shares in the company for the beneficiaries under the trust.

---

1 (1856) 6 E & B 327.

2 [1964] 2 QB 480.

3 (1843) 2 Hare 461.

4 Eg *Bateman v Mid-Wales Rly Co* (1866) LR 1 CP 499; *Peruvian Rys Co v Thames & Mersey Co* (1867) LR 2 Ch App 617; *Deuchar v Gas Light & Coke Co* [1925] AC 691.

5 It is just as if he had been carrying on business on his own account: *Wightman v Townroe* (1813) 1 M & S 412.

6 However, trustees with such shareholdings are under strict duties to monitor the activities of the company (unless qualified by the trust instrument): *Re Lucking's WT* [1968] 1 WLR 866; *Re Miller's Deed Trusts* [1978] LS Gaz 454; *Bartlett v Barclays Bank Trust Co* [1980] Ch 515.

8.4.1 Contractual restrictions upon liability

The onus lies on the trustee to displace the strong presumption of unlimited personal liability so that contracting descriptively 'as trustee' is not sufficient,[1] but contracting 'as trustee and not otherwise' will suffice because the phrase would be meaningless if not excluding personal liability beyond the value of the trust fund.[2]

However, particular problems arise if there are contracts with several creditors and the trust funds are insufficient to meet all claims. Let us assume that the trustee has contracted to limit his liability to the value of the trust fund from time to time so as not to be personally liable beyond the value of such fund. There appear to be two ways of construing the situation. The trustee may be regarded either as limiting the actual amount of each of the creditors' debts to whatever is rateably available in the trust fund to meet each debt when the debts fall to be paid or as providing that only whatever assets happen to be in the trust fund will be available to the creditors to satisfy their debts of certain amounts.

The former construction, arguably, could lead to the limitation being void for creating an obligation of uncertain indeterminate amount, assuming the creditors' claims are to abate rateably (rather than depend upon the order of creation or of enforcement of debts), so requiring valuation of the whole trust fund (with contingent liabilities). Such considerations support Lord Selborne's *dicta*:[3]

> 'A contract of the kind supposed would really be for limited liability, though of an anomalous nature; the limit being undefined as to amount, variable in different cases, and subject in many conceivable cases to various doubts and questions.'

The 'limited recourse' construction (which leaves the creditors unsecured[4]) avoids such problems because the amount of a creditor's debt does not vary, although the extent to which it is satisfied does vary. The courts should thus lean in favour of such construction if not explicit in the contractual terms.

What then is the position where the trustee is personally solvent and has contracted the trust debts on the basis that the creditors' recourse is expressly limited to the trust fund from time to time, so that there are no grounds for making the trustee personally bankrupt or, if a company, placing it in liquidation? Can a creditor acquire priority over another by suing the trustee and obtaining execution of the judgment against the trust fund before another

---

1 *Muir v City of Glasgow Bank* (1879) 4 App Cas 337. Legislation has reversed this in the Trusts (Jersey) Law 1984, Art 28 (as amended) and the Trusts (Guernsey) Law 1988, Art 37, but transactions in England by Jersey or Guernsey trustees will still be covered by *Muir*.

2 *Re Robinson's Settlement* [1912] 1 Ch 717; *Helvetica Insurance Co v Knight* [1982] 7 ACLR 225.

3 (1879) 4 App Cas 337 at 383–384.

4 *Swiss Bank Corporation v Lloyds Bank Ltd* [1980] 3 WLR 457, 469; *Re State Fire Insurance Co* (1863) 1 De GJ & S 634. An intention to create a charge is not lightly to be found.

creditor? Another existing creditor could presumably have the court consolidate the two actions, but what of a creditor with only a contingent or future obligation? Will the court require the trustee to disclose all obligations incurred on the trust's behalf and will the court afford other creditors the opportunity to interplead?

It would seem that the proper course for a solvent trustee of an insolvent trust should be to apply to the court for directions under RSC Ord 85 to fill the gap caused by the absence of any statutory framework for winding up insolvent trusts.[1] The court could then confirm or direct the cesser of trading activities and direct the trustee to compile a list of assets and of creditors and to pay the creditors rateably out of the assets. Although any creditor could sue and obtain judgment against the trustee it would seem equitable for the court to restrain execution of any such judgment pending the winding up of the trust's affairs pursuant to the court's directions.

In the United States it has been held[2] that a trustee who benefits himself by a limited recourse clause owes a duty of care in negligence to the creditor to safeguard the trust property out of which the creditor is to be paid. In England, it seems more likely that the creditor will be regarded as voluntarily incurring such risk if express contractual provision is not made against such risk.

So far, it has been assumed that the trustee is not to be personally liable beyond the value of the trust fund and will have a right to exhaust the trust fund if need be to satisfy creditors' claims. However, the trustee may not have such a right (for example, if indebted to the trust fund or if the relevant contract was improperly entered into) in which event he will be personally liable up to the relevant limit without any right of reimbursement.[3] Exceptionally, to provide the fullest protection for creditors and the trustee where the relevant contract was properly entered into, or otherwise the beneficiaries would be unjustly enriched, it seems that an express term of such contract can confer upon the creditor a primary (but unsecured) claim against the trust fund[4] irrespective of any indebtedness of the trustee to the trust and of whether or not the trustee has been replaced by new trustees.

---

1 On insolvent trusts, multiple creditors and the limitation of liability see I Lambert in (1992) *Tolley's Insolvency Law and Practice Journal* 121.

2 *James Stewart & Co v National Sharmut Bank* (1934) 69 F 2d 694, cert denied 294 US 722 noted 48 Harv LR 346, 20 Minn LR 574.

3 *Octavo Investments Pty Ltd v Knight* (1979) 144 CLR 360; *RWG Management Ltd v Commissioner for Corporate Affairs* [1985] VR 385.

4 See *De Vigier v IRC* [1964] 2 All ER 907 at 914–915; *Mathew v Blackmore* (1857) 1 H & N 762; and Trust Law Committee Consultation Paper 'Rights of Creditors against Trustees and Trust Funds' (Tolley Publishing Ltd, 1997), paras 2.55, 3.12, 4.1 and 4.2.

8.5 TRUSTEE'S RIGHT OF INDEMNITY

8.5.1 Proprietary right in the nature of a lien

Equity and statute[1] (since 1859) empower a trustee to reimburse himself for expenses paid by him *qua trustee* (a right of recoupment) and to pay directly out of the trust assets expenses incurred *qua trustee* (a right of exoneration): both rights amount to the right of indemnity. The trustee's right to retain trust assets until the right of indemnity is satisfied and, if need be, to sell the assets to obtain satisfaction is in the nature of an equitable charge or lien on the trust assets.[2]

8.5.2 Extent of right

As a necessary incident of the office of trustee, a trustee has a right of indemnity.[3] The nature of this becomes important once the trustee (T) no longer has the trust property, whether because of retirement in favour of new trustees or because of a transfer of the property to beneficiaries entitled under the terms of the trust or an appointment made thereunder. Former uncertainty as to the application of *dicta* indicating that T has an equitable lien in cases involving trustees still owning relevant trust property[4] to cases where trustees no longer own such property has led to the use of express indemnity covenants given to T by new trustees (empowered by the Trustee Act 1925, s 15) or by beneficiaries to whom trust property has been transferred absolutely beneficially.

In the absence of such express covenants it would seem likely that the court would order new trustees to reimburse T out of trust funds (by selling trust assets if need be), where T had properly incurred the relevant obligation and was not indebted to the trust fund,[5] irrespective of whether or not the new trustees were indebted to the trust fund. Thus, T should be regarded as having a beneficial proprietary interest in, and so a right of recourse against, the trust fund in the hands of the new trustees rather than having a derivative claim through the new trustees, requiring investigation of the state of accounts

---

1 Now the Trustee Act 1925, s 30(2).

2 *Jennings v Mather* [1902] 1 KB 1 at 6, 9; *Re Exhall Coal Co Ltd* (1866) 35 Beav 449 at 453; *Stott v Milne* (1884) 25 Ch D 710 at 715; *De Vigier v IRC* [1964] 2 All ER 907 at 915 per Lord Upjohn. It amounts to a proprietary interest (*Octavo Investments Pty Ltd v Knight* (1979) 144 CLR 360 at 370) but by *Chief Commissioner for Stamp Duties v Buckle* (1998) 72 ALJR 242 at 253 it is not a security interest that is an 'incumbrance' over the beneficiaries' interests, the trustee having 'a preferred beneficial interest in the trust fund'.

3 *Chief Commissioner of Stamp Duties v Buckle* (1998) 72 ALJR 243. Further, see Trust Law Committee Consultation Paper 'The Proper Protection by Liens Indemnities or Otherwise of Those who leave to be Trustees' (December 1999) at *www.kcl.ac.uk/depsta/law/tlc.*

4 See cases cited in n 2 and n 3 above.

5 See **8.5.3**, and for a former trustee's lien binding property owned by the new trustee, see *Collie v Merlaw Nominees* [2001] Victoria SC 39.

between the new trustees and the trust fund. However, where T had deliberately transferred trust property to beneficiaries, without taking any personal indemnity covenant or any proprietary security against his possible liabilities, it would seem likely that T will be regarded as accepting the risk of such liabilities so as to have no right of recourse against such trust property or its traceable product nor against the beneficiaries, his rights being regarded as rights concerning trust funds held by trustees and which automatically cease when the trust property is deliberately transferred to beneficiaries as absolute legal beneficial owners without reserving any indemnity rights. The trustee's indemnity rights are the price paid by the beneficiaries for the services of the trustee so that they are entitled to believe that they have paid the full price if the trustee transfers the trust property to them absolutely beneficially without reserving any rights.

8.5.3 Limitations on the right of indemnity

The right of indemnity is not available if excluded in the trust deed,[1] but this is very rare because a trustee could not then be relied upon to exercise discretions impartially and to the best effect if any expenses and liabilities had then to be paid for out of his own pocket, unless, perhaps, he had the benefit of a very favourable charging clause for his remuneration. The right of indemnity is also not available if the expenses are proved to have been improperly incurred[2] whether because there was no power or capacity to incur the liability in question, or because it was a breach of trust for the trustee to exercise the power in the relevant circumstances. Exceptionally, where T honestly but improperly incurred the expense in circumstances conferring a benefit upon the beneficiaries, then to prevent their unjust enrichment it is equitable for T to be entitled to an indemnity for the amount of the benefit conferred.[3] Finally, if the state of accounts between the trustee and the beneficiaries taking account of *any* losses caused by *any* breach of trust by the trustee is such that the trustee is in deficit, he has no right of indemnity,[4] for example if owing $105,000 in respect of some related or unrelated breach of trust, though having paid out or incurred a liability to pay out $100,000 for an unauthorised transaction.

---

1 Trustee Act 1925, s 69(2); *RWG Management Ltd v Commissioner of Corporate Affairs* [1985] VR 385; *Re German Mining Co* (1854) 4 De GM & G 19 at 52.

2 *Fraser v Murdoch* (1881) 6 App Cas 855 at 866, 873; *Strickland v Simmons* (1884) 26 Ch D 245 at 248; *Re Suco Gold Pty Ltd* (1983) 33 SASR 99, (1983) 7 ACLR 873. The *ultra vires* doctrine of voidness is restricted to companies and does not apply to trustees: *De Vigier v IRC* [1964] 2 All ER 907 at 913–914, per Lord Upjohn; *Rolled Steel Products (Holdings) Ltd v British Steel Corporation* [1985] 3 All ER 52 at 91.

3 *Vyse v Foster* (1872) 8 Ch App 309; *Re Leslie* (1883) 23 Ch D 552; *Re Smith's Estate* [1937] Ch 636.

4 *Re Johnson* (1880) 15 Ch D 548 at 552; *Re Frith* [1902] 1 Ch 342 at 345; *Re Evans* (1887) 34 Ch D 597 at 601; *RWG Management Ltd v Commissioner of Corporate Affairs* [1985] VR 385 (although contrast *Re Staff Benefits Pty Ltd* [1979] 1 NSWLR 207 where Needham J stated: 'It is not every breach of trust which will debar the trustee from indemnity – the breach must be shown to be related to the subject matter of the indemnity'.)

8.5.4 Personal right

If one or more persons of full capacity transfer burdensome assets to T to hold for them, then T has a personal right of indemnity against them solely or jointly and severally, as the case may be – or against transferees. Thus, the beneficial owner of unpaid shares is liable to indemnify his trustee-shareholder for calls under the *Hardoon v Belilios*[1] principle. However, the Privy Council has stated:[2]

> 'This principle by no means applies to all trusts and it cannot be applied to cases in which the nature of the transaction excludes it ... Clubs are associations of a peculiar nature ... They are not partnerships; they are not associations for gain; and the feature which distinguishes them is that no member as such becomes liable to pay any money beyond the subscriptions required by the rules of the club ... It is upon this fundamental condition, not usually expressed but understood by everyone that clubs are formed.'

If a club makes a profit this benefits the members and not the trustee, so if a trustee is to have a right of indemnity against beneficiaries personally in any circumstances other than in *Hardoon* principle cases, one would expect it to be found here, but the Privy Council rejected this. In the case of family trusts (*inter vivos* or testamentary) there seems less reason to make the beneficiaries personally liable. However, in *Balkin v Peck*[3] the New South Wales Court of Appeal held that where property is held on trust for B for life, remainder equally to C, D and E, and the English trustees have to pay overlooked inheritance tax on the death of the English resident B, then the trustees have a right of personal indemnity against C, D and E resident in Australia to whom the trustees had transferred the trust assets.

Of course any possible personal right to an indemnity can be expressly excluded. Indeed, it is not uncommon for a trust deed to exclude the personal right to an indemnity[4] where the beneficiaries are investing in a unit trust only on the basis that there can be no personal indemnity right in the trustee to which creditors of the trust might be subrogated.

8.6 CREDITOR'S RIGHTS OF SUBROGATION

8.6.1 Right in the nature of a lien

It is well established that creditors can be subrogated to a trustee's rights of indemnity out of the trust assets but that, because the right to stand in the

---

1 [1901] AC 118. For restrictions on this principle see KF Sin *The Legal Nature of the Unit Trust* (Clarendon Oxford, 1997) pp 179–185, criticising *Broomhead v Broomhead* [1985] VR 891.

2 *Wise v Perpetual Trustee Co* [1903] AC 139 at 149.

3 (1998/1999) 1 ITELR 717.

4 *McLean v Burns Philp Trustee Co* [1985] 2 NSWLR 623; *Hardoon v Belilos* [1901] AC 118 at 127.

trustee's shoes is wholly derivative, if the trustee has no claim to an indemnity, as where he improperly incurred the relevant liability or is indebted to the trust due to some wrongful conduct, then the creditors have no claim,[1] except to the extent that reliance can be had to developing unjust enrichment remedies where the beneficiaries would otherwise unjustly receive a benefit at the creditors' expense.[2] However, where there are two or more trustees and one trustee is indebted to the trust but another is not, the creditors can rely on the latter's right to an indemnity.[3]

Recourse will be made to the right of subrogation only where the personally liable trustee is insolvent or the circumstances are such as to lead to the reasonable conclusion that a judgment against the trustee would be fruitless.[4] To enforce the right of subrogation originally a trust creditor would seek a decree for administration or maintain a bill in equity against a trustee for equitable execution against the amount due to the trustee by way of indemnity but now he can proceed by way of originating summons. By 'lucky accident'[5] the trust creditor is in a better position than other unsecured creditors of the trustee because he is subrogated to the trustee's right of indemnity which is regarded in the nature of an equitable lien over the trust assets.[6] Of course, this lien is equally available to all trust creditors, although the consequence of allowing one particular creditor to enforce it may give him an advantage or preference over others. Significantly, direct payment out of the trust assets has been allowed only where the trust was subject to the administration of the court[7] or where the trustee acquiesced in an order for payment of what was the sole trust liability.[8]

8.6.2 Personal right

In principle and as a matter of policy it seems that trust creditors should also be subrogated to a trustee's personal rights of indemnity against the beneficiaries.[9] However, it may well be that a creditor seeking the benefit of

---

1 See cases in n 2 and n 4 on p 486, *ex parte Edmonds* (1862) 4 De GF & J 488 at 498; *Re Oxley* [1914] 1 Ch 604; 23rd Report of the Law Reform Committee, Cmnd 8733 (1982), para 2.17; and Trust Law Committee Consultation Paper 'Rights of Creditors against Trustees and Trust Funds' (Tolley Publishing Ltd, 1997), para 2.30, in respect of which a Report was published in June 1999, available at *www.kcl.ac.uk/depsta/law/tlc*.

2 *Devaynes v Robinson* (1857) 24 Beav 86; *Banque Financière v Parc (Battersea) Ltd* [1998] 1 All ER 737.

3 *Re Frith* [1902] 1 Ch 342 at 346.

4 *Owen v Delamere* (1872) LR 15 Eq 134; *Re Morris* (1889) 23 LRIr 333; *Fairland v Percy* [1875] LR 3 P & D 217.

5 *Re Johnson* (1880) 15 Ch D 548 at 552.

6 See n 2 on p 485.

7 *Re Evans* (1887) 34 Ch D 597; also see *Re Blundell* (1890) 44 Ch D 1; *Re London United Breweries* [1907] 2 Ch 511.

8 *Re Raybould* [1900] 1 Ch 199; see also *Re Pumfrey* (1882) 22 Ch D 255.

9 *Scott on Trusts* (Little Brown & Co, 4th ed, 1991), para 278; *Countryside (No 3) Pty Ltd v Bayside Brunswick Pty Ltd* (unreported) 20 April 1994, NSW Sup Ct, Brownie J; Ford and Hardingham in n 1 on p 480, p 82; *Marginson v Potter* (1976) 50 ALJR 735 at 740.

the trustee's right against a beneficiary personally will first have to make the trustee bankrupt[1] and have the liquidator or trustee in bankruptcy pursue the right of indemnity against the beneficiary for the benefit *pari passu* of all the unsecured trust creditors.

8.6.3 Exclusion of rights

The trust instrument may seek to exclude a trustee's lien or personal right of indemnity and so exclude creditors' derivative claims by way of subrogation. It seems clear that to the extent that the settlor himself is a beneficiary he will not be allowed to resist the subrogation claim.[2] In the case of other beneficiaries who are volunteers it may be that a court of equity will not permit the beneficiaries to invoke statutory sections[3] or general principle so as to defraud creditors: those who benefit should take subject to burdens.[4] However, in the case of investor beneficiaries a court may well find:[5]

> 'There is a perfectly proper reason for limiting the [personal] liability of investors in a unit trust, a reason which is not contaminated by fraud of creditors [and thus] there is no reason in public policy why the court should not give effect to it.'

If the beneficiaries have sufficient powers to enable them to control the trustee's trading activities then the creditors may be able to establish the personal liability of the beneficiaries as partners conducting a business, whether with the trustees or via the trustees as agents.[6]

8.7 BANKRUPTCY OR WINDING UP OF TRUSTEE

Neither bankruptcy nor winding up effects an automatic removal of the trustee unless so provided by the trust instrument, but it makes him or her or it liable to be removed from office.[7] Of course, trust assets are not generally divisible amongst creditors of the insolvent individual or corporate trustee, but trust

1 See Canadian cases, *Williams v Balfour* (1890) 18 SCR 472; *Creaser v Wall* (1983) OR (2d) 35 at 45–47 (reversed on other grounds 40 OR (2d) 644). In *Re Richardson* [1911] 2 KB 705 the trustee was bankrupt and the trust creditor prevailed over the private creditors of the bankrupt trustee.

2 *Re Johnson* (1880) 15 Ch D 548 at 550; *McLean v Burns Philp Trustee Co Pty Ltd* [1985] 2 NSWLR 623 at 641; *cf Re Burroughs-Fowler* [1916] 2 Ch 251.

3 Trustee Act 1925, s 69(2), allowing s 30(2) to be ousted.

4 *Re Johnson* (1880) 15 Ch D 548 at 550; *Re Burroughs-Fowler* [1916] 2 Ch 251; Ford and Hardingham in n 1 on p 480, p 83.

5 *McLean v Burns Philp Trustee Co Pty Ltd* (1985) 9 ACLR 926 at 940, [1985] 2 NSWLR 623 at 641.

6 See n 1 on p 480, and *Trident Holdings Ltd v Danand Investments Ltd* (1988) 49 DLR (4th) 1.

7 Trustee Act 1925, s 36.

creditors[1] may be able to take advantage of the trustee's right to indemnity out of trust assets in respect of unpaid liabilities, while to the extent that the trustee has already applied its own money to discharge liabilities of the trust, it can reimburse itself from, and so retain, trust assets which become available for division amongst its private creditors.[2] It seems, however, that the corporate trustee's right to an indemnity out of trust assets in respect of unpaid liabilities amounts to an asset out of which the expenses of the liquidation are payable.[3]

8.8 POSITION OF DIRECTORS OF CORPORATE TRUSTEE

If a corporate trustee is insolvent or only has a nominal paid-up capital the pursuit of personal remedies against it by beneficiaries will be pointless. Can they therefore proceed against the directors as the 'brains and hands' of the company? Generally, they cannot because it is the company that is the trustee not its directors or other officers.[4] The separate personality of the company means that the directors do not share the responsibilities of the company trustee to the beneficiaries, though the directors owe a fiduciary duty to the company. Exceptionally, the self-dealing rule applies to the company and to its directors so as to impose a direct obligation to the beneficiaries upon the directors.[5]

It is also possible to make a director (like anyone else) personally liable to account as a constructive trustee if he dishonestly assists in a breach of trust on the part of the company. Dishonesty involves[6] 'the taking of a risk to the prejudice of another's rights, which risk is known to be one which there is no right to take', such as a deliberate breach of trust or the objective standard of 'simply not acting as an honest person in the circumstances'.[7] Dishonest assistance involves actual knowledge of wrongdoing or a want of probity through deliberately shutting one's eyes to the obvious ('Nelsonian knowledge') or deliberately or recklessly refraining from making the enquiries

1 This lucky accident of being a trust creditor rather than a private creditor will thus afford an advantage to the trust creditor but he will not be entitled to receive a dividend from the private assets of the corporate trustee until the dividends paid to the private creditors equal those paid to the trust creditors out of the trust fund: *Re Oriental Island Steam Co* (1874) 30 LT 317, affd 9 Ch App 557.

2 *Re Suco Gold Pty Ltd* (1983) 7 ACLR 873 at 880–881. See further B McPherson 'The Insolvent Trading Trust' in P Finn (ed) *Essays in Equity* (Law Book Co Ltd, 1985).

3 *Re Barleycorn Enterprises Ltd* [1970] Ch 465; Insolvency Act 1986, s 156; and Insolvency Rules 1986, rr 4.218 and 4.220.

4 *Bath v Standard Land Co Ltd* [1911] 1 Ch 618; *HR v JAPT* [1997] Current Law YB 692; *Hurley v BCH Nominees Pty Ltd* (1982) 1 ACLC 387.

5 *Re James* [1949] SASR 143; *Boardman v Phipps* [1967] 2 AC 46.

6 *Baden Delvaux & Lecuit v Société Générale* [1983] BCLC 325 at 406, adopting a definition in *R v Sinclair* [1968] 1 WLR 1246.

7 Generally, see *Royal Brunei Airlines v Tan* [1995] 2 AC 378.

that an honest reasonable man should have made in the circumstances ('naughty knowledge').[1] With those directors who are the 'brains and hands' of the company there should be little difficulty in proving the requisite knowledge.

Where a breach of duty owed by a director to the trust company made the company liable for a breach of trust, the company has a right of action against the trustee, which right may be regarded as a traceable trust asset.[2] If the corporate trustee is insolvent and does not sue the director, then the beneficiaries should sue the director joining the corporate trustee as co-defendant.[3]

Creditors will be in a weak position especially if they deal with a company in ignorance that it holds property as a trustee. There is no implied warranty by the directors that the company property is owned by the company beneficially. However, if the company has gone into insolvent liquidation directors or shadow directors (persons in accordance with whose instructions the directors are accustomed to act) involved in the fraudulent or wrongful carrying on of a business by the company may be made personally liable for all or any part of the debts and liabilities as the court may direct.[4] Criminal charges relating to deception, fraud or conspiracy may also be brought against those involved.

8.9 GIVING SECURITY OVER TRUST ASSETS

Unsecured creditors of trading trusts will experience the problems discussed above, and so a creditor will prefer to be a secured creditor. If the requisite powers are in the trust instrument then it may be possible to create a fixed charge or a floating charge, although in practice only a corporate trustee will be able to create a floating charge over chattels because the Bills of Sale Acts create problems for individuals.[5]

There will be a power to create a floating charge[6] where the trust instrument empowers the trustee to charge the trust fund or the assets from time to time comprising the trust fund (as distinct from specific assets that are part of the trust fund at the relevant time) to secure obligations created by them for value or to make the creditor an equitable beneficiary in the trust fund in its state from time to time, the creditor's status as a beneficiary ceasing

---

1 *Agip (Africa) Ltd v Jackson* [1990] Ch 265, [1991] Ch 547; *Polly Peck International plc v Nadir* [1992] 4 All ER 769; *Brinks Ltd v Abu Saleh (No 3)* [1996] CLC 133.

2 *HR v JAPT* [1997] Current Law YB 692, (1998/1999) 2 OFLR 252; *Brink's Mat v Noye* [1991] 1 Bank LR 68.

3 *Parker-Tweedale v Dunbar Bank plc (No 1)* [1991] Ch 26.

4 IA 1986, ss 213 and 214. In Australia, the Corporations Law, s 233 makes directors of a trustee company personally liable in cases where the trustee (and so any trust creditor) is not entitled to be indemnified from the trust fund.

5 See Gower *Principles of Modern Company Law* (Sweet & Maxwell, 6th ed, 1997), pp 89–90.

6 See 23rd Report of the Law Reform Committee Cmnd 8733 (1982), paras 2.20–2.24.

when fully repaid.[1] However, the cautious view is that because the basis of such charge is contract law,[2] and because the burden of the first trustee's (T_1's) contract cannot, without a novation, be imposed on a subsequent trustee (T_2), a charge of future property created by T_1 will not operate upon property acquired after the appointment of T_2. A security document of this kind should therefore ensure that there will be no change of trustee without the chargee's consent (to enable a new arrangement to be entered into with the new trustee) and that the charge will automatically crystallise if a change does occur without consent. The document should also restrict the trustee's exercise of other powers that could detrimentally affect the chargee, for example distributive powers over capital.

The bolder view, which the courts should be prepared to accept, is that where £x has been borrowed by T_1 for the benefit of the beneficiaries in the exercise of a power to create a floating charge over the trust assets from time to time, neither T_2 nor the beneficiaries can challenge the validity of the charge, although T_2 cannot be personally contractually liable to the chargee unless entering into a fresh contract with him.

After all, why should equity not strive to give effect to the settlor's intention to allow T_1 to charge the assets that comprise the trust fund from time to time, especially if otherwise the beneficiaries might be unjustly enriched at the creditor's expense. If equity recognises T_1's gratuitous exercise of a power of appointment entitling X to obtain one-quarter of the assets comprised in the trust fund when X attains 25 years of age, should it not then recognise T_1's exercise for value of a power to create a floating charge in favour of creditor Y over the assets from time to time comprising in the trust fund?

8.10 PRECAUTIONS FOR CREDITORS ESPECIALLY LENDERS

In dealing with a company it is important to ascertain whether the company is or is not a trustee especially where assets are to be security for a loan. A *bona fide* purchaser of a legal interest (but not an equitable interest[3]) for value

---

1 On creation of charges see title reservation cases: *Clough Mill Ltd v Martin* [1985] 1 WLR 111; *Compaq Computer Ltd v Abercorn Group Ltd* [1991] BCC 484; *Re ILG Travel Ltd* [1995] 2 BCLC 128.

2 *Holroyd v Marshall* (1862) 10 HLC 191; *Tailby v Official Receiver* (1888) 73 App Cas 523; *Akron Tyre Co Pty Ltd v Kittson* (1951) 82 CLR 477.

3 As between competing equitable interests the first in time prevails unless the first person is estopped from claiming his priority by inequitable behaviour.

without notice of the trust will be protected but there are problems as to the ambit of constructive notice.[1]

It is crucial to ascertain that the trustee has power to enter into the relevant transaction and to assume that the scope of powers will be narrowly construed by the courts, for example a power to guarantee will not be construed as including a power to indemnify and a power to give security may be so closely linked to the power to borrow that it will not be construed as enabling security to be given in support of guarantees or indemnities.

It is also necessary to ensure that the power is not being improperly exercised for the furtherance of purposes other than those for which the trust was created. Thus, a power to give a guarantee and indemnity or security to a third party will not support the exercise of such a power in a way that does not confer any commercial benefit on the beneficiaries. Furthermore, the trustee's powers are fiduciary in nature so that there are problems where actual or potential conflicts of interest on the part of the directors of a corporate trustee arise, even though it is the company that is the trustee. It seems that if the directors are interested in a transaction into which the company enters as trustee the beneficiaries may avoid it unless they gave their fully informed consent or the directors are protected by a provision in the trust instrument. If the instrument provides for its own amendment by the trustee, then there is a problem if the directors of the trustee amend the instrument to protect themselves: such amendment is vitiated by their self-interest.

An unsecured creditor will want to ensure that the trustee's right of indemnity against the trust assets or the beneficiaries has not been excluded, but even if such right has not been excluded there is the risk that future misconduct of the trustee could make him indebted to the trust so as to exclude the right of indemnity. He may well therefore seek guarantees or indemnities from directors of a corporate trustee as well as seek indemnities from particular beneficiaries.

A secured lender where the trustee is not the first trustee of the trust should make inquiries to ensure that the assets have not been charged by any previous trustee. A floating chargee, where there is a power to vary the trust, will normally seek to have a deed of variation prohibiting, without the chargee's consent, any further amendment of the trust deed, any distribution of trust capital, any dispositions other than at arm's length in the ordinary course of business, any encumbering of the trust fund, any incurring of further borrowings or giving guarantees, or retiring as trustee. Where there is no power of variation, covenants from the trustee to like effect as those above should be sought.

---

1 A person has constructive notice of all matters which would have come to his knowledge if such inquiries and inspections had been made as ought reasonably to have been made by him in all the circumstances.

The over-protection of beneficiaries, while generally advantageous for such beneficiaries, may disadvantage them by deterring knowledgeable creditors from dealing with trustees other than well-respected 'deep-pocket' trustees. After all, as has been seen, a creditor (C) faces the following difficulties that flow logically from treating C's rights as derived from the rights of the trustee (T). He needs to check, if possible, that:

(a) T is empowered by the trust instrument or by law to enter into the transaction with C;
(b) T exercised such power in accordance with any internal procedures requisite to its exercise;
(c) T did not exercise such power in breach of T's equitable duties, for example to invest with the care of a professional trustee or a prudent businessman mindful that he is dealing with others' property, to diversify investments, to supervise agents, to take account of relevant considerations and to ignore irrelevant considerations.

After all, if T were in breach of (a), (b) or (c) he would have no right of indemnity against the trust fund, but C will have obvious problems in checking whether (c) and, perhaps, (b) were breached, and the time taken to try to resolve such problems may cause difficulties where deals need to be clinched promptly. It is also unsatisfactory, to say the least, that the better a bargain C makes for himself, the more likely it is that T has failed to exercise the standard of care expected of him.

Most unsatisfactory of all is that even if the deal between T and C satisfies (a), (b) and (c), but for some reason, involving T's conduct either before or even after the deal with C, T is otherwise indebted to the trust fund, then T has no right of indemnity against the trust fund and so neither has C. It is probable, however, that this grave disadvantage can be circumvented, where no breach of trust occurred within (a), (b) or (c) in the contract between T and C, if an express term of the contract gives C a primary direct unsecured claim against the trust fund independent of any money due to the trust fund from T at any time. After all, the authority of T to enter into the contract should implicitly extend to agreeing to such a term if negotiated as part of the 'price' of the contract. However, T can have no implicit authority to commit breaches of trust (a), (b) and (c), although a trust instrument can be drafted with an express provision to protect purchasers without actual knowledge of breaches (b) or (c) and to obviate the need for purchasers to make inquiries as to (b) or (c) type breaches. Such drafting will then produce the necessary reassurance for creditors if, exceptionally, the draftsman directed his attention to such matters: otherwise, creditors will need to see if they can rely upon developing uncertain unjust enrichment principles.

Chapter 9

PAYMENT BY TRUSTEES OF FOREIGN TAXES*

*Christopher Sly***
*John Glasson****

9.1 INTRODUCTION

The general rule of private international law that one country will not enforce the revenue laws of another has particular implications for trustees. If trustees provide trust funds for payment of a foreign tax where payment is not enforceable, the trustees may incur a liability for breach of trust. But the non-enforceability rule does not always operate and, even when it does, the trustees need to consider whether they nevertheless have a duty or power to pay the tax in question.

This chapter discusses the topic under the following headings:

(1) the nature of the non-enforceability rule;
(2) limitations on the scope of the rule;
(3) circumstances in which trustees might be permitted or required to provide funds to discharge a non-enforceable foreign tax;
(4) express powers to pay foreign taxes.

---

* The authors gratefully acknowledge the assistance of Scott Walters of Eversheds in the preparation of this chapter.
** Partner, Eversheds, Senator House, 85 Queen Victoria Street, London EC4 4LJ, tel 0207 919 4500, fax 0207 919 4919.
*** Consultant to Eversheds, Great Sutton Farm, Sutton, Stanton Lacy, Ludlow, Shropshire SY8 2AJ, tel 01584 861 536, fax 01584 861 699, email glasson@harvey.sonnet.co.uk.

9.2 THE NATURE OF THE NON-ENFORCEABILITY RULE[1]

Dicey and Morris[2] states the rule (in relation to English law) in the following terms:

> 'English courts have no jurisdiction to entertain an action … for the enforcement, either directly or indirectly, of a … revenue … law of a foreign State …'

The rule is recognised by most countries,[3] although there is relatively little judicial authority to support it. In England, for example, there were lingering doubts on the matter until 1955, when the House of Lords applied the rule in *Government of India v Taylor*.[4]

The theoretical basis for the non-enforceability doctrine has been much debated. The explanation favoured by *Dicey and Morris*[5] is that enforcement of foreign revenue claims would be an improper extension of sovereign power.

What counts, and what does not count, as a revenue law is decided by the courts of the jurisdiction in which enforcement is sought. The expression 'revenue law' has been held[6] to include income tax, capital gains tax, death duties and state insurance contributions, and a local government contribution towards the cost of improvement works, but not to include, for example, laws under which a state can recover social security payments or obtain legal aid contributions.

The doctrine of non-enforceability can be traced back to the statement by Lord Mansfield CJ in 1775[7] that 'no country ever takes notice of the revenue laws of another'. However, this statement expresses the principle too widely, since it is well established that courts will *recognise* foreign revenue laws and recognition, as will be seen below, may be enough to ensure that the foreign revenue authority gets paid,[8] or to permit a trustee who has paid foreign tax to reimburse himself from the trust fund.[9]

---

1 See also L Collins (ed) *Dicey and Morris on the Conflict of Laws* (Sweet & Maxwell, 13th ed, 2000), p 5-018R *et seq*; Cheshire and North *Private International Law* (Butterworths, 13th ed, 1999), p 107 *et seq*; Baker 'Transnational Enforcement of Tax Liability' in *Tolley's International Tax Planning* (Butterworths, 4th ed, 1999), p 34-1, and Lawrence *International Estate Planning*, p 765 *et seq*.

2 *Dicey and Morris*, n 1 above, p 5-018R (Rule 3).

3 See Baker, n 1 above, at the Appendix, for details of a number of jurisdictions that have recognised the rule.

4 [1955] AC 491.

5 Note 1 above, p 5-019. Adopting the view of Lord Keith of Avonholm in *Government of India v Taylor* [1955] AC 491 at 511, who goes on to state that 'an assertion of sovereign authority by one State within the territory of another, as distinct from a patrimonial claim by a foreign sovereign, is (treaty or convention apart) contrary to all concepts of independent sovereignties'.

6 See authorities cited in *Dicey and Morris*, n 1 above, p 5-028.

7 *Holman v Johnson* (1775) 1 Cowp 341 at 343.

8 As in *Re Lord Cable* [1977] 1 WLR 7 (discussed at **9.4.3**).

9 As in *Re Reid* (1970) 17 DLR (3d) 199 (discussed at **9.4.2**).

In Europe arrangements for enforcement of foreign judgments under the Brussels and Lugano Conventions, and under the Brussels Regulation 2000,[1] exclude revenue matters, although, as discussed below,[2] the European Union has adopted machinery for member states to assist one another in tax recovery. Currently, the worldwide Convention on Enforcement proposed by the Hague Conference excludes revenue matters.[3]

9.3 LIMITATIONS ON THE SCOPE OF THE RULE

Limitations fall under two headings, judicial and legislative.

9.3.1 Judicial limitations

Judicial narrowing-down of the rule has occurred in two types of situation:

(a) where country A has sought assistance in country B in relation to tax-related proceedings in country A; and
(b) where proceedings are brought in country B to enforce claims resulting from a tax-related insolvency in country A.

It might be thought that proceedings in either category (a) or (b), above, constitute indirect enforcement and therefore fall within the rule. However, the tendency has been for the courts to give the term 'indirect' a restricted sense and, for example, to permit assistance to be given to a foreign revenue authority even where they could not permit direct enforcement by that authority. This is illustrated by the English decision *Re State of Norway's Application (No 2)*.[4] The case involved a request by a Norwegian court, pursuant to the Evidence (Proceedings in Other Jurisdictions) Act 1975, for the oral examination of two witnesses in England for the purpose of obtaining information relevant to the assessment of tax in Norway. Referring to the non-enforceability rule, Lord Goff of Chieveley said:[5]

> 'It is of importance to observe that that rule is limited to cases of direct or indirect enforcement in this country of the revenue laws of a foreign state. It is plain that the present case is not concerned with the direct enforcement of the revenue laws of the State of Norway. Is it concerned with their indirect enforcement? I do not think so. It is stated in *Dicey and Morris*, at p 103, that indirect enforcement occurs (1) where the foreign state (or its

1 The Conventions and Regulation are discussed in Chapter 1, at **1.2**.

2 At **9.3.2***(C)*.

3 Hague Conference, Preliminary Draft Convention on Jurisdiction and Enforcement of Foreign Judgments, Art 1. For discussion of the Convention, see Chapter 1, at **1.2.8**.

4 [1990] 1 AC 723. See also, in the Isle of Man, *Re the Attorney-General of the Isle of Man* (1997/1998) 1 OFLR 419.

5 *Re State of Norway's Application (No 2)* [1990] 1 AC 723 at 809.

nominee) in form seeks a remedy which in substance is designed to give the foreign law extraterritorial effect, or (2) where a private party raises a defence based on the foreign law in order to vindicate or assert the right of the foreign state. I have been unable to discover any case of indirect enforcement which goes beyond these two propositions. Even so, since there is no authority directly in point to guide me, I have to consider whether a case such as the present should nevertheless be held to fall foul of the rule. For my part, I cannot see that it should. I cannot see any extraterritorial exercise of sovereign authority in seeking the assistance of the courts of this country in obtaining evidence which will be used for the enforcement of the revenue laws of Norway in Norway itself.'

There are a variety of examples of courts receiving applications in cross-border insolvencies where the sole or the major creditor has been the revenue authority of a foreign country.[1] In the Jersey decision *Le Marquand and Backhurst v Chilmead Ltd (in Liquidation)*[2] the liquidator of a UK company had obtained judgment in the United Kingdom against one of the directors, who had taken funds from the company to Jersey in breach of trust. The English judgment was then registered in the Jersey Royal Court under the statutory reciprocal judgments procedure. This was challenged in the Jersey court on the basis that the English judgment was very largely for the benefit of the UK Inland Revenue and it was, in effect, the enforcement of UK taxation by the Jersey courts. The challenge was unsuccessful, the Jersey court holding that the English liquidator was not acting as the Inland Revenue's agent. The fact there were other creditors apart from the Inland Revenue, even though only very minor by comparison, meant this was not indirect enforcement solely for the purpose of paying an Inland Revenue claim. A similar line has been taken by judges in Australia and South Africa.[3]

In contrast, in the Irish case *Buchanan v McVey*,[4] it seems the court did regard the liquidator as the Inland Revenue's 'puppet'. There was no other creditor, and the court refused to allow the liquidator to enforce his claims.

In the 1980s, the high profile bankruptcy of Roy Tucker, the former Rossminster director, gave rise to a number of tax-related insolvency applications in offshore jurisdictions – with mixed results. Each of these applications involved consideration of specific insolvency legislation: they are therefore discussed below at **9.3.2***(B)*.

In a 1999 decision,[5] the English Court of Appeal gave short shrift to an attempt by the liquidator of certain Danish companies to enforce claims against a UK resident individual. The liquidation occurred as a result of claims by the Danish tax authorities in respect of alleged tax fraud. Simon Brown LJ confirmed that the claim fell foul of the general principle of non-enforceability

---

1 See also discussion of this topic, in Baker, n 1 on p 496, pp 34-4–34-8.

2 [1987–88] *Jersey Law Reports* 86; *Butterworths Offshore Cases* Vol 1, p 507.

3 See *Ayres v Evans* (1981) 39 ALR 129; and *Priestly v Clegg* (1985) (3) SA 950. Both cases are discussed in Baker, n 1 on p 496, p 34-18.

4 [1954] IR 89; [1955] AC 516n.

5 *QRS v Frandsen* [1999] STC 616.

directly or indirectly of foreign tax laws. The Court of Appeal further decided that this rule was not affected by the Treaty of Rome, or the Brussels Convention 1968 on reciprocal enforcement of judgments.[1]

9.3.2 Limitations under domestic and international legislation

(A) Legislation relating to criminal proceedings[2]

The clear trend is for the operation of the non-enforceability rule to be excluded in legislation relating to mutual assistance in criminal matters. Thus, in *R v Chief Metropolitan Stipendiary Magistrate ex parte Secretary of State for the Home Department*[3] the court held that the doctrine did not prevent the extradition of a person for an offence arising from tax evasion, if the offence was an extradition crime under the Extradition Act 1870. The court commented:[4]

> '... the Extradition Acts and the extradition treaties are precisely the means by which in-roads into [the non-enforceability] ... principle are made.'

The specific issue of money laundering legislation is discussed at *(E)* below.

(B) Insolvency legislation

The issues arising in this area are exemplified by the *Tucker* bankruptcy litigation[5] (see **9.3.1**) which involved applications by a UK trustee in bankruptcy for assistance in Jersey, Guernsey, and the Isle of Man under s 122 of the Bankruptcy Act 1914. Although a provision of an English statute, s 122 applied, at the relevant times, in each of the jurisdictions in question. The section (now repealed) reads:

> 'The High Court, the county courts, the courts having jurisdiction in bankruptcy in Scotland and Ireland, and every British court elsewhere having jurisdiction in bankruptcy or insolvency, and the officers of those courts respectively, shall severally act in aid of and be auxiliary to each other in all matters of bankruptcy, and an order of the court seeking aid, with a request to another of the said courts, shall be deemed sufficient to enable the latter court to exercise, in regard to the matters directed by the order, such jurisdiction as either

---

1 Cf, however, *Bullen and Garner v Government of the UK* 553 SO 2d 1344 (Florida District Court of Appeal), a decision where the Florida court recognised a judgment in a UK criminal tax bankruptcy. The case is discussed in Baker, n 1 on p 496, p 34-27, who comments that 'the decision may best be regarded as per incuriam'.

2 For further detail of the legislative position in the United Kingdom, see Baker, n 1 on p 496, pp 34-19–34-20.

3 [1989] 1 All ER 151. See also, in Guernsey, *Century Holdings Ltd v HM Procureur General, Guernsey* (1997/1998) 1 OFLR 220, and, in the Isle of Man, *Re the Attorney-General of the Isle of Man* (1997/1998) 1 OFLR 419.

4 *R v Chief Metropolitan Stipendiary Magistrate ex parte Secretary of State for the Home Department* [1989] 1 All ER 151 at 162.

5 See also the earlier cases *Re Gibbons* [1960] Ir Jur Rep 60; *Ayres v Evans* (1981) 39 Aust LR 129.

the court which made the request, or the court to which the request is made, could exercise in regard to similar matters within their respective jurisdictions.'

In Guernsey,[1] the application succeeded. The Court of Appeal held that s 122 implicitly displaced any considerations of public policy relating to the enforcement of revenue debts. The Court went on to say that it did not intend to suggest that there were no circumstances in which the principle in *Government of India v Taylor*[2] can be relevant in the context of s 122:

> 'We have held that there is no place for the application of that principle in relation to the duty of the recipient court when considering how to give effect to a request for assistance under an order in aid made by the requesting court. But the question whether or not an order in aid should be made is one for the discretion of the requesting court; that is to say the court which is seized of the bankruptcy. We can envisage circumstances in which that court might take the view that it was not a proper exercise of that discretion to make an order which would lead to the recovery of assets in another jurisdiction solely for the purposes of satisfying the claims of the domestic revenue.'

In Jersey,[3] by contrast, the application was refused. Section 122 was held to be subject to the Jersey public policy rule that the courts will not enforce the revenue laws of a foreign state. The trustee in bankruptcy's application was regarded by the court as an attempt at indirect enforcement, the Inland Revenue being, by the time of the hearing, the sole claiming creditor.

In the Isle of Man,[4] where there was still one other creditor apart from the Inland Revenue, the Deemster granted an application by the trustee in bankruptcy to examine certain persons and obtain production of documents. His decision was upheld on appeal (the court stating that it would make no difference if the Revenue was the only creditor).[5] However, when, subsequently, the trustee in bankruptcy attempted to enforce his claim the action was struck out on the grounds that it was, by then, an attempt to enforce a foreign revenue debt (the UK Inland Revenue having become the only remaining creditor).

In the United Kingdom, s 122 is now replaced by s 426 of the Insolvency Act 1986 (discussed elsewhere in this work).[6] Subsection (5), which contains provisions relating to requests to a UK court for assistance by the courts of certain other jurisdictions, requires the court, in exercising its discretion under the subsection, to have regard in particular to the rules of private international

1 *In Re Tucker (A Bankrupt)* 23 (Civil) 1988; *Butterworths Offshore Cases* Vol 1, p 264.
2 [1955] AC 491.
3 *In the matter of Tucker* [1987–88] *Jersey Law Reports* 473; *Butterworths Offshore Cases* Vol 1, p 563.
4 The original Manx decision is reported at [1987–89] Manx LR 106, the appeal upholding the decision at [1987–89] Manx LR 220, and the final enforcement application at [1987–89] Manx LR 267.
5 Later, in *Re the Petition of John William McLean* (1997/1998) 1 OFLR 818, the Isle of Man court did in fact grant a petition seeking the court's assistance in examining three individuals to obtain evidence in a bankruptcy where the only creditor was the Inland Revenue.
6 See Chapter 7, p 396 *et seq*.

law. Although it is not yet clear how this provision will be applied, it has been suggested, in a first instance decision, that a valid reason for not giving assistance under the section might be that it infringed the non-enforceability rule.[1]

So far as countries in the European Union are concerned, the position changed again on 31 May 2002, when the EC Regulation on Insolvency Proceedings[2] came into force. The Regulation is designed to improve the efficiency and effectiveness of insolvency proceedings having cross-border effects. The preamble[3] states the intention as follows (emphasis added):

> 'Every creditor, who has his habitual residence, domicile or registered office in the Community, should have the right to lodge his claims in each of the insolvency proceedings pending in the Community relating to the debtor's assets. *This should also apply to tax authorities and social insurance institutions.*'

(C) The Mutual Assistance Directive and the Mutual Assistance Recovery Directive

Also in the context of the European Union, the Mutual Assistance Directive[4] lays down specific rules for collaboration between member states with regard to exchange of information and other assistance in relation to taxation matters.[5]

The application of the Mutual Assistance Directive was considered in *WN v Staatssecretaris van Financien*[6] in which judgment was given on 13 April 2000. This case held that the Dutch authorities were obliged to pass information to the Spanish authorities concerning maintenance payments made by a Dutch resident (for which he claimed a deduction in Holland) to his Spanish resident ex-wife. The grounds for this ruling were that the Dutch authorities had reason to suppose that an unjustified tax saving might otherwise exist in Spain. The amount of that tax saving was not relevant.

More significantly, probably, than the above Directive is the recent adoption in the European Union of a Directive enabling general cross-border tax recovery.[7] There was in place already a 1976 Directive[8] which related principally to VAT. This new Directive amends, and substantially broadens, the scope of the 1976 Directive. Under the amended 1976 Directive (known as the Mutual Assistance Recovery Directive), where recovery of a debt by a

---

1 *Re Bank of Credit and Commercial International SA (No 9)* [1994] 3 All ER 764 at 785, per Rattee J. The decision was varied on appeal ([1994] 1 WLR 708), but not on this point.

2 Regulation (EC) 1346/2000 (2000) OJ L 160/1.

3 Ibid, para (21). See also Art 39.

4 Directive 77/799/EEC (1977) OJ L 336/15.

5 Although probably not of great significance in a trust context, it should be noted that, in relation to VAT, there are current proposals for further strengthening co-operation between member states: COM (2001) final.

6 (Case C-20/98) [2000] ECR I-2847.

7 Directive 2001/44/EC (2001) OJ L 175/17.

8 Directive 76/308/EEC (1976) OJ L 73/18.

taxation authority in one member state is unsuccessful, that authority can request another member state to attempt recovery if the debtor resides or has assets there. Following the amendments, the arrangements now apply to both direct and indirect taxes, excise and customs duties, some agricultural levies, and also to penalties.

(D) OECD/EC Multilateral Convention on Mutual Assistance (1988)

A further Convention, the OECD/Council of Europe Multilateral Convention on Mutual Administrative Assistance in Tax Matters 1988, extends the powers of co-operation even further between those countries that ratify it. It has so far been ratified by only a few countries, including the Scandinavian states and the United States. It has also been signed by the Netherlands, Poland and Belgium. Article 11 of the Convention goes further than any other, as it empowers the requested state to take action to recover taxes owed by the applicant state as if it were a domestic law tax claim. Presumably, this will override any domestic law prohibiting the collection of tax by a foreign jurisdiction.

(E) Money laundering legislation

In the context of criminal law, one of the most significant developments of recent times has been the widespread promulgation of anti-money laundering legislation. Reference has been made earlier in this chapter to specific examples where country A has assisted country B in relation to alleged tax fraud in country B. Money laundering legislation can be seen as an extension of these principles and can have significant practical implications for trustees, particularly those in offshore jurisdictions.

So far as the United Kingdom is concerned, the Criminal Justice Act 1993 introduced 'all crimes' money laundering legislation for the first time, thus making it an offence to assist in the retention or disposal of the proceeds of criminal conduct. Initially, there was debate over the extent to which these provisions extended to the proceeds of foreign tax crime. Nowadays, however, it is generally accepted that tax evasion is covered. See also now the Proceeds of Crime Act 2002, which received Royal Assent on 24 July 2002.

'All crimes' money laundering legislation has also now been introduced in a large number of jurisdictions, including many offshore financial centres. In most of these jurisdictions, the legislation extends to foreign fiscal crime.

In consequence, trustees in the jurisdictions affected by such legislation will now need to take adequate precautions to protect themselves from criminal liability in that jurisdiction if they know or suspect (or, as in the UK under the Proceeds of Crime Act 2002 when the relevant provisions are brought into force, if they have reasonable grounds for knowing or suspecting) that they are assisting in foreign fiscal evasion. Consequently, they may be under a duty to report the circumstances to the authorities of their own jurisdiction.

(F) Double tax Conventions

Double tax Conventions between individual countries usually include provision for mutual assistance in relation to tax claims including, in some cases, tax recovery.[1]

(G) In the pipeline?

Currently, there is considerable international pressure, much of it coordinated by the OECD and the FATF, and affecting offshore centres in particular, for countries to offer greater assistance to one another in the tax area. This is a developing situation, and it is too early to forecast precisely what the outcome will be. Following the terrorist attacks in New York on 11 September 2001, the FATF expanded its mission to include isolating terrorist financing and the recommendations resulting from its meeting on 29–30 October 2001 are likely to spur co-operation between states and their taxation authorities.

9.4 CIRCUMSTANCES IN WHICH TRUSTEES CAN, OR SHOULD, PROVIDE FUNDS TO DISCHARGE A NON-ENFORCEABLE FOREIGN TAX

This section assumes that there is no specific power in the trust instrument to discharge foreign taxes[2].

The question of whether there is an obligation or power to discharge foreign taxes requires consideration in each of the following situations.

(1) Payment is required to achieve a fair and proper administration of the trust.
(2) The foreign state has a means of enforcing the liability against the trustee in its own jurisdiction.
(3) The tax in question is payable under legislation which forms part of the proper law of the trust.
(4) The tax is paid in exercise of a dispositive power for the benefit of a beneficiary.
(5) The trustees are called upon to indemnify the settlor against a tax liability imposed on him personally.
(6) Tax is paid for the benefit or protection of trust property.

---

1 For a fuller discussion, see Baker, n 1 on p 496, pp 34-66–34-68.

2 Although where there is such a power, the comments in this section may still be of relevance; see further **9.5** below.

9.4.1 Payment required to achieve a fair and proper administration

Judicial decisions suggest that, as a general rule,[1] the courts recognise as a general principle that executors (and by analogy trustees) have a duty to pay foreign taxes if unfairness to a beneficiary would otherwise result and if payment would be consistent with the intention or presumed intention of the testator (or settlor).

One example, from Scotland, is *Scottish National Orchestra Society Ltd v Thomson's Executor*,[2] which concerned the estate of a Mrs Thomson who was born in Scotland and who married a Canadian domiciled in Saskatchewan. She left her husband in 1934 and lived in Stockholm until her death in 1962. In 1951 she entered into a 'trust disposition' in Scotland. On her death the greater portion of her estate was in Scotland, but there were also assets in Canada and Sweden. Under Swedish law she was regarded as resident in Sweden and the Swedish court appointed an administrator of her estate. The executors obtained confirmation and probate of her estate in Britain and proceeded to administer it in terms of the trust disposition, which required payment of certain pecuniary legacies 'all free of Government duties' to legatees, three of whom were resident in Sweden. UK estate duty was paid on the property situated in Britain. In addition, the Scottish executors paid a sum of money to the Swedish administrator to enable him to meet Swedish estate duties. The residuary legatees under the trust disposition objected to this payment. The court held that if the only purpose which was required to be fulfilled by the Swedish administrator had been to pay the inheritance duty in Sweden, which was a proper charge under Swedish law, the executors could not properly have paid over the money to the Swedish administrator, but as the duty of the executors was *inter alia* to pay the legacies 'all free of Government duties' to the Swedish legatees, and as they could not receive these legacies while the Swedish inheritance tax was unpaid, the executors acted properly in remitting to Sweden the sum in question.

In Re Hollins[3] is a New York case. Here an English domiciled testatrix, the late Dowager Duchess of Manchester, had given, by her will, an annuity to a foreign legatee, the Countess Zichy. Other bequests had been made to English legatees by the testatrix. Under English law, legacy duty was imposed upon the annuity given to the Countess, but the English courts were unable to enforce payment of that duty by the Countess because of their lack of jurisdiction over her. American executors had been appointed to administer that part of the testatrix's estate located in the United States. It was clear that the English court would enforce payment of the legacy duty upon the Countess's annuity from

1 *Re Fudger* (1984) 18 ETR 12 (Ontario Supreme Court) is arguably an exception. The case is discussed at p 506 below.

2 1969 SLT 325.

3 79 Misc 200, 139 NYS 713 (Surr Ct NY Co 1913).

any property of the testatrix's estate located in England or forwarded to England by the American executors for the purpose of being applied to the payment of the other legacies. The New York County Surrogate described this prospect as an injustice to the English legatees and one which the US courts should not sanction. He added:[1]

> 'While it is doubtless true that this court will not aid a foreign country in the enforcement of its revenue laws, it will not refuse to direct a just and equitable administration of that part of an estate within its jurisdiction merely because such direction would result in the enforcement of such revenue laws. The court should favour such an administration of the estate here as will be in conformity with the intention of the testatrix.'

Hollins and other US decisions are discussed by Lawrence,[2] who concludes:[3]

> 'At least in New York, where the clear intention of the testator would be frustrated by non-payment of foreign taxes, it appears that the beneficiaries may compel the executors to pay foreign taxes that are legitimately due, even if foreign jurisdiction can be avoided. Conversely, beneficiaries have no automatic right to prevent executors from paying legitimate taxes even in instances where the taxing authority cannot obtain judicial enforcement of the levy.'

Compare these cases with the South African decision in *Jones v Borland*.[4] Here the testatrix had executed two wills in Scotland, where she was domiciled, one dealing with her assets in South Africa and the other with her assets in Scotland. The wills appointed South African executors for the former will and domiciliary executors for the latter. The assets for the non-South African estate having proved insufficient to pay all the estate duty levied in the United Kingdom, the South African executors applied for an order declaring whether or not part of the surplus of the South African estate should be transferred to the Scottish executors for payment of the remaining estate duty due overseas. It was held *inter alia* that as any claim by the overseas revenue authorities would be unenforceable in the South African courts, such claim could not be proved in the South African estate and, further, it was not the intention of the testatrix as expressed in her will that the surplus in South Africa should be transmitted to the executors in Scotland. Thus, the South African executors were held to be entitled to distribute direct to the heirs of the South African estate. As in *Hollins* the court infers an 'intention' on the part of the testatrix. Possibly a different intention might have been inferred if

---

1 Ibid at 208, 717.
2 Note 1 on p 496, pp 765 and 769.
3 Ibid, p 790.
4 1969 (4) SA 29.

any of the beneficiaries had claimed to be prejudiced,[1] although, as indicated in *Re Fudger*,[2] the mere fact of prejudice may not be enough.

In *Fudger*, the deceased had disposed of her Scottish property by deeds of settlement (referred to in the judgment as 'the Scottish will') in favour of a charity, and her Canadian property by will and codicil in favour of various friends and relatives. By reason of the deemed domicile of the testatrix in the United Kingdom, the UK Capital Taxes Office (CTO) claimed capital transfer tax on the deceased's worldwide estate. The amount of the tax claim greatly exceeded the value of the Scottish property. The court in Canada held that a general direction in the Canadian will for payment of duties or taxes did not, as a matter of construction, extend to UK capital transfer tax. Counsel for the Scottish executors had submitted that such a construction would frustrate the obvious intention of the testatrix to benefit the charity:

> 'If the taxes demanded by the CTO are not paid by the Canadian executors out of the Canadian estate and the CTO seizes (perhaps confiscates would be a more apt term) the Scottish estate as a consequence, then her intention to have benefited the Scottish charity would have been frustrated.'[3]

However, the judge, White J, took a different view on intention:

> '... the testatrix clearly demonstrated an intention that each set of assets and liabilities should be dealt with separately and distinctly. She made a will in Canada. She made a separate will in the United Kingdom. The assets disposed of in each will were limited to those which lay in each respective jurisdiction. Different executors were appointed for each. Different individuals or entities were benefited in each.
>
> The assets which pass under the Canadian will are not property passing under the Scottish will. Therefore, the testatrix intended, in my opinion, to restrict the direction in the will to pay estate, inheritance and succession duties or taxes in the Canadian will to property passing under the Canadian will. Such direction cannot be construed to include a direction to pay tax imposed under a foreign tax statute ... The testatrix clearly intended to divorce the testamentary administration of her Canadian assets from that of her Scottish assets.'[4]

Stopping here, *Fudger* is not inconsistent with either *Hollins* or *Scottish National Orchestra Society*, the difference in outcome being explained by the different intention presumed. However, White J gives an alternative ground for his decision:

> 'There is another reason to reject the position put forward on behalf of the Scottish executors: to do so would offend the well-settled rule of law that the Courts of Canada will not entertain an action for enforcement of the revenue laws of a foreign state [citing *USA v*

---

1 It appears from the report that no beneficiary of the Scottish will raised any objection to the refusal of payment of funds to the Scottish executors. The residuary beneficiaries under each will (after payment of certain unspecified legacies) were the same, but entitled in different proportions.

2 (1984) 18 ETR 12 (Ontario Supreme Court).

3 Ibid at 20.

4 Ibid at 21.

> *Harden* [1963] SCR 366]. Any claim made by the CTO for payment of tax against a Canadian executor is not provable or enforceable in Ontario. To construe the Canadian will in such a way as to require the Canadian executor to pay foreign taxes simply because a foreign beneficiary under a foreign will might otherwise be exposed to the payment of taxes imposed in the foreign jurisdiction, would be an indirect method of enforcing the revenue laws of the foreign jurisdiction.'[1]

In the foregoing extract, the critical word, perhaps, is 'simply'. The mere fact that a foreign beneficiary will be prejudiced is not enough, in White J's view, to justify payment of a foreign tax, but the judge was arguably not intending to rule out permitting payment of the foreign tax if the facts had demonstrated that it was the intention of the testatrix that the UK beneficiary should not be prejudiced. It should be noted that neither *Hollins* nor *Scottish National Orchestra Society* were considered in the *Fudger* case.

Two further cases, both from Jersey, are worth noting. In the first, *Re Marc Bolan Charitable Trust*,[2] the Jersey court authorised trustees to pay taxes owing in the United Kingdom. The court had regard to the fact that most of the beneficiaries lived in the United Kingdom and considered it in their interests for payment to be made. In the second, *Re Sidney Walmesley (decd)*,[3] the deceased died domiciled in Jersey owing unpaid UK income tax and capital gains tax. The Royal Court confirmed that an executor should not normally pay an unenforceable debt unless authorised by the court, and that authorisation would only be forthcoming in certain situations, for example where it was in the interests of the beneficiaries or where the executor might be exposed to penalties in the other country.[4] In this case, there were no exceptional reasons to authorise payment. Finally, it should be noted that, in the asbence of special circumstances, an application for a grant of probate or letters of administration is likely to fail if it is made in one jurisdiction for the purpose of remitting funds to pay tax in another jurisdiction.[5]

9.4.2 Payment where liability can be enforced in a foreign jurisdiction

A well-established principle of trust law is that a trustee is entitled to be indemnified from the trust fund for liabilities which he has properly incurred in the administration of the trust. The principle was described by Danckwerts J in *Re Grimthorpe*:[6]

---

1 Ibid at 21.

2 [1981] JJ 117. See also *Re X's Settlement* (1994) *Butterworth's Offshore Cases and Materials* 600, and n 3 to p 515.

3 [1983] JJ 35.

4 On the 'exposure' point, see also **9.4.2**.

5 *Bath v British and Malaysian Trustees Ltd and the Trustees Executors and Agency Company Ltd* (1969) 90 WN 9 NSW 44; *Clapham v Le Mesurier* (1991) *Jersey Law Reports* 5.

6 [1958] 1 All ER 765 at 769.

> 'It is a commonplace that trustees, who take the onerous and sometimes dangerous duty of being trustees, are not expected to do any of the work on their own expense; they are entitled to be indemnified against the costs and expenses which they incur in the course of their office; that necessarily means that such costs and expenses are properly incurred and not improperly incurred. The general rule is quite plain; they are, entitled to be paid back all that they have had to pay out.'

The question is whether, and if so in what circumstances, trustees can rely on this principle in order to pay from the trust fund a foreign tax which is unenforceable against them in their home jurisdiction, but which they none the less find themselves obliged to pay. There are no clearly established guidelines and in most cases the trustee will be best advised to seek the directions of the court. The court might be expected to look sympathetically at a trustee's plight if there is no fault on his part. However, what is the position if, in the court's view, enforcement has been triggered by the trustee's own conduct?

Consider some of the following examples.

(1) A trustee resident in country A pays a visit to country B which has a claim for unpaid tax. Shortly after the trustee's arrival in country B he is served with an order preventing him from leaving the country unless he gives proper security for the liability. It must be at least doubtful whether, in these circumstances, the trustee would be entitled to pay or reclaim any tax from the trust fund. Perhaps the outcome will depend on whether fault can be attributed to the trustee in putting himself in a vulnerable position. Relevant considerations might include his reason for visiting country B, the likelihood of enforcement action being taken when he got there, and whether such a visit might have been in the reasonable contemplation of the settlor.

(2) A trustee in country A makes a personal investment in country B where there is a tax liability. The authorities in country B impound the investment to meet the liability. The court in country A is unlikely to take a sympathetic view of any claim by the trustee for recovery of his loss out of the trust fund if he knowingly acquired assets in country B.

Where the administration of a trust ranges across two jurisdictions then, and in contrast to the above examples, a trustee faced with enforcement action in one jurisdiction might reasonably expect a sympathetic hearing in the other. Whether he will get it is uncertain. Case-law in Canada points both ways.

Re Reid[1] was an appeal to the British Columbia Court of Appeal. The respondent was an English company acting as executor of an estate situated mainly in British Columbia, but with some assets in England. The executor was accountable for English estate duty and was subject to the possibility of judgment for unpaid duty and the further possibility of being wound up. The

---

1 (1970) 17 DLR (3d) 199.

assets in England were insufficient to pay the duty and the executor was forced to meet the arrears of duty. The executor then sought to be reimbursed out of assets in British Columbia. The appellant (a beneficiary under the will) sought to rely on the non-enforceability doctrine but failed. The court's view was that the UK authorities were not seeking to enforce their tax claims in British Columbia. Rather, they were pressing the executor for payment of duty pursuant to English legislation. The executor company was therefore entitled to its indemnity.

In *Stringham v Dubois*[1] the Alberta Court of Appeal declined to follow *Re Reid*, and refused to allow a US executor to sell Canadian property in order to pay US estate taxes due in respect of the estate of a US domiciliary, even though the US executor could apparently be liable for the estate tax in any event.

The English case, *Re Lord Cable*,[2], which is considered below also bears on this issue.

9.4.3 Tax paid under legislation forming part of the proper law of the trust

It is arguable that a trustee is entitled to pay a particular state's taxes if the law of that state is also the law governing the trust. The decision in *Re Lord Cable*[3] supports the argument, albeit that an additional justification for permitting payment in this case was that non-payment would put the trustees at personal risk.

In this case, there were four trustees of the will of a testator who had died domiciled in India in 1927. One of the trustees was an Indian company, Standard Trust Co (Private) Ltd, and the other three were individuals who were domiciled and resident in the United Kingdom. The trustees held investments through an underlying company 'Union Trust Incorporated' in India. Under Indian exchange control regulations, there was a requirement that the proceeds of certain British government securities held by Union Trust should be remitted to India. Upon remission, the intention was for Union Trust to use the funds to reduce their indebtedness to the trustees, who would in turn have applied the money in part satisfaction of outstanding Indian estate duty. Certain beneficiaries of the trust resident outside India brought proceedings in England to prevent remission from the United Kingdom.

The action failed for the reasons set out in the extract below from the judgment of Slade J.[4]

1 [1993] 3 WWR 273.
2 [1977] 1 WLR 7. See also *Balkin v Peck* [1981] NSW SC 337.
3 [1977] 1 WLR 7.
4 Ibid at 22–26.

'It is a well-established principle that the court will not entertain an action for the direct or indirect enforcement of the revenue laws of a foreign state (see Dicey and Morris's *The Conflict of Laws*, 9th ed (1973), p 75 and the cases there cited). The House of Lords decision in *Kahler v Midland Bank Ltd* [1950] AC 24, however, demonstrates that exchange control legislation may for some purposes fall into a rather different category from other fiscal legislation of another country.

Nevertheless, for the purpose of applying the last-mentioned principles it would not, in my judgment be correct to say that the failure of the English court to intervene in regard to the redemption moneys amounted to an enforcement of the exchange control laws of India. It is one thing for the court to intervene by requiring trustees to a comply with foreign fiscal legislation; it is quite another thing for it to decline to prevent trustees of a foreign trust from complying with fiscal legislation of the country of the proper law, which under such foreign law they are entitled and indeed obliged to obey.

It appears on the evidence (in particular that of Union Trust's experts Mr Das and Mr Banerji) that if the court were to make an order of the nature contemplated, and the order were to achieve its purpose of preventing (through the intervention of the trustees) the remission of the redemption moneys by Union Trust to India, this would involve, inter alia, the following consequences:

(1) Union Trust would be in direct breach of its obligations under section 16 of the Foreign Exchange Regulation Act 1973.
(2) Under section 50 of that Act, Union Trust would be liable to a penalty of up to five times the value of the redemption moneys.
(3) By virtue of sections 68 and 50 of that Act, every director of Union Trust would be deemed to be guilty of the contravention and could be liable to the last-mentioned penalty accordingly, unless he could prove that "the contravention took place without his knowledge or that he exercised all due diligence to prevent such contravention", within the wording of the proviso to section 68(1) of that Act.
(4) Likewise every director of Union Trust would, under the combined effect of sections 68 and 56 of that Act, be liable to prosecution, with the possibility of imprisonment unless he could bring himself within the exemption to which I have just referred.
(5) The will trustees and each of them would be parties or privy to this contravention by Union Trust of that Act.

In my judgment no English court would at or after the trial make an order that entailed such potentially serious consequences both for the two corporate bodies and for the individuals concerned as the five which I have summarised, particularly in the light of the following points.

(a) The will trustees doubtless accepted their trusteeship in the belief, in my judgment justified, that Indian law was the proper law of the trust and in the knowledge that it had always been administered according to this law. In my judgment, save perhaps in the most exceptional circumstances, which are not present here, the court would not compel the will trustees to commit or be a party to a breach of the currency laws of India, being the country of the proper law. It is significant that the plaintiffs expressly disclaimed any suggestion that the will trustees would be acting in breach of trust in permitting the remittance of the redemption moneys to India. I think this concession was an entirely proper one, because it is difficult to see how the will trustees could possibly be in breach of trust in complying with the provisions of that system of law which the testator, by necessary implication, selected to regulate the rights of the parties under the trusts constituted by his will. The plaintiffs further disclaimed any suggestion that the will trustees would be exercising their powers improperly or in bad faith in allowing the remittance of the redemption moneys to India. Again, I think this concession was an entirely proper one; the will trustees have an obviously legitimate motive in allowing such remittance, namely their own protection. However, once it is accepted that the will trustees are not acting in breach of trust and not exercising their powers and discretions improperly or in bad faith in allowing the remittance of the redemption moneys to India, I cannot see what justification the English court would have to interfere. It was submitted on behalf of the plaintiffs that the justification would not be the disciplining of the will trustees, but the need to protect the beneficiaries, none of whom is resident in India. The beneficiaries, however, must in my judgment be regarded by the English court as having succeeded to their interests under this trust at least subject to the rights, even if not the obligations, of the will trustees, in administering the trust, to comply with the exchange control legislation of the country of the proper law of the trust. There is clear authority that the court will refuse to enforce a contract if its performance would be illegal under exchange control legislation enacted by the country of the proper law of the contract: see *Kahler v Midland Bank Ltd* [1950] AC 24; *Zivnostenska Banka National Corporation v Frankman* [1950] AC 57 and *Re Helbert Wagg & Co Ltd* [1956] Ch 323. Similar principles must in my judgment apply where beneficiaries under a will invite the English court to order trustees to act in violation of exchange control legislation enacted by the country of the proper law of the trust. This is not to say that the English court will intervene for the purpose of positively enforcing such legislation; it will, in my judgment, simply regard any equitable rights possessed by the beneficiaries to have their pecuniary interest protected by the English court as taking second place to the rights of the trustees to comply with such legislation if they think fit. Different considerations might conceivably apply if the particular exchange control legislation had been passed or was being used as an instrument of oppression or discrimination, but it has not been suggested that the Indian legislation relevant in the present case falls within this category.

(b) A fortiori, on the particular facts of the present case, the court would not in my judgment intervene for the purpose of compelling the will trustees to attempt to prevent the remittance of the redemption moneys to India, having regard to the close connection of so many of the individuals involved with India. Thus:

 (i) if the will trustees are to take effective steps to prevent Union Trust from effecting such remittance, Standard Trust Co (Private) Ltd will have to be party to such steps. For the evidence before me as to Indian law, as given in an affidavit sworn on behalf of the first, second and third defendants by their expert, Mr E C Meyer, is that under Indian law (section 48 of the Indian Trusts Act 1882) the will trustees must act unanimously in giving any directions or instructions. Standard, however, is a company situated in India and all its directors are resident in India. If, therefore, Standard and its directors are to join in taking action to prevent Union Trust from effecting the remittance, they will for practical purposes have to take such action in India. It is well established that the English courts will not compel the fulfilment of an obligation whose performance involves the doing in a foreign country of something which the supervenient law of the country has rendered it illegal to do (see *De Beeche v South American Stores (Gath and Chaves) Ltd* [1935] AC 148 at 156, per Viscount Sankey LC). Thus in my judgment the court would not compel Standard or its directors by action in India to be a party to a breach of Indian currency laws. A fortiori, in my judgment the court would not compel Standard and its three directors (all being Indian residents) to take action which inevitably involved Union Trust, an Indian company, and those same three individuals, who are also the three directors of Union Trust, in direct breaches of Indian currency laws.

(ii) Quite apart from the position of Standard and its directors, in the event of a failure to remit the redemption moneys to India, the defendants Mr Waters and Mr Vickers would be exposed to personal risks beyond those theoretical risks which must be run by any person who infringes the Indian exchange control legislation. The evidence shows that Mr Waters is a director of a company known as Inchcape & Co Ltd and as such he is required to make frequent visits to India, while Mr Vickers is a director of a number of companies carrying on business in India and he too has been making frequent visits to India in connection with the affairs of these companies.

It was, in effect, suggested that the apprehensions of the will trustees (and indeed of Union Trust itself) were somewhat exaggerated and, provided that they had used their best endeavours to secure the remittance of the redemption moneys to India, they would not, for practical purposes, be exposed to personal risk in India if they failed to achieve this result. I cannot, however, take this sanguine view, which is not, I think, supported by any evidence beyond the bare wording of the proviso to section 68 of the Foreign Exchange Regulation Act 1973 to which I have referred.

In discussing the position of the will trustees in relation to this motion, the only Indian legislation to which I have referred so far is the exchange control legislation. I have not hitherto referred to the estate duty position. As I have already said, the plaintiffs have accepted that, whether or not the trusts of the will are being executed by the court, the will trustees will have the right to be indemnified out of the trust assets for any Indian estate duty which they are obliged to pay under Indian law and do themselves pay; this would appear to be an entirely proper concession (compare *In Re Reid* (1970) 17 DLR (3d) 199). Nevertheless there remains an important area of dispute as to the relevant law between the plaintiffs and the will trustees. The plaintiffs contend that while, in the course of executing the will trusts, the English court would permit the will trustees to indemnify themselves for an Indian estate duty which they had actually had to pay, it would not give them leave to remit assets situated in the United Kingdom for the purpose of paying such duty. Some superficial support for this contention is to be found in a Scottish decision, *Scottish National Orchestra Society Ltd v Thomson's Executor*, 1969 SLT 325 at 330, in which Lord Robertson held that executors in Scotland could not properly have paid moneys over to a domiciliary administrator of a testatrix in Sweden if the only purpose had been to pay inheritance duty properly chargeable in Sweden, because it was a claim that could not have been enforced against the executors in Scotland. I think it clear on the authorities that the claim of the Indian revenue for estate duty similarly could not be enforced against the will trustees in any proceedings in this country. Lord Robertson, however, on the particular facts of that case held that the payment by the executors had been properly made, because the payment of Swedish duty had not been the only purpose of the payment, which had served the additional purpose of relieving those beneficially entitled to the assets in Sweden from having the value of their interests diminished by payment of the Swedish duty in respect of assets subject to the Swedish jurisdiction. Particularly bearing in mind that, if the Indian duty is not paid, the will trustees may be exposed to penalties in India of an amount representing double the amount of duty and that all the trust assets situated in England might not suffice to cover this amount, I strongly incline to the view that an English court in executing these foreign trusts, would regard the personal protection of the will trustees as affording sufficient justification for permitting a prompt remittance of trust assets to India, for the explicit purpose of paying Indian estate duty chargeable under the law of India, being the proper law governing the trusts of such assets. Correspondingly, I strongly incline to the view that, even if Indian exchange control legislation did not exist, it would not be appropriate for the court on this interlocutory motion to intervene for the purpose of preventing the will trustees from permitting or procuring the remittance to India of the redemption moneys, even though the sole or dominant purpose of such remittance was to enable the will trustees to pay Indian estate duty.

I do not, however, need to express any concluded view on this particular point. For the Indian exchange control legislation and the consequences flowing from that legislation to which I have referred already, are in my judgment by themselves conclusive reasons why the plaintiffs would not have any real hope of persuading the court, at or after the trial of these proceedings, to make an order against the will trustees of the only nature that would be any help to them; that is, an order compelling them to procure, or use their best endeavours to procure, that Union Trust should not remit the redemption moneys to India.'

9.4.4 Tax paid under a dispositive power to benefit a beneficiary

There are occasions when it would be appropriate to use a dispositive power either to pay a foreign tax or to enable a beneficiary so to do. Take, for example, a discretionary trust which is administered in the Isle of Man, but which has UK resident beneficiaries and a UK domiciled settlor. Distributions out of the trust are potentially subject to UK inheritance tax. If the trustees wish to make a distribution to a UK beneficiary of a sum net of tax, they can achieve this by fixing the distribution at such an amount as will leave the beneficiary with that sum after the tax has been paid (whether payment is made by the trustees or by the beneficiary). There can hardly be doubt, in the authors' view, that this is a proper exercise of a dispositive power in favour of that beneficiary notwithstanding that the UK Inland Revenue also benefits.

9.4.5 Payment by trustees to indemnify settlor

In the United Kingdom, at least, legislation exists in relation to both income tax and capital gains tax pursuant to which a settlor of a non-resident trust is personally liable to tax in respect of the income and gains of the non-resident trust, even though he is not a beneficiary and the trustees do not, therefore, have power to distribute funds to him. The relevant taxing legislation does, however, give the settlor a statutory right of reimbursement by the foreign trustees. The enforceability of this right and indemnity is unclear. The case of *Prestwich v Royal Bank of Canada Trust Company (Jersey) Limited*[1] concerned certain procedural issues. In that case, the UK High Court accepted jurisdiction in respect of a claim by a UK settlor against a Jersey trustee. However, assuming the English court gave judgment in favour of the settlor, it is uncertain whether that judgment would be enforceable against the trustee in Jersey. Conceivably, this may turn on the proper law of the settlement. If the proper law is English, the Jersey courts may accept the argument that the right of indemnity, being granted by an English statute, is enforceable notwithstanding

1 [1998] 1 ITELR 565.

that this might otherwise appear to be the indirect enforcement of a foreign revenue claim.[1]

The question of enforceability of the statutory right of reimbursement against Jersey trustees was expressly left open by the Jersey Royal Court in the case of *Re Colin Douglas 1990 Settlement*.[2]

9.4.6 Tax paid for the benefit or protection of trust property

If trustees properly acquire property in a particular jurisdiction by way of investment, or for use or occupation by a beneficiary, there is unlikely to be an objection to the payment of taxes and other fiscal liabilities relating to the property if payment is necessary to prevent enforcement action against the property.

9.5 EXPRESS POWERS TO PAY FOREIGN TAXES

In light of the problems that can arise for trustees faced with a foreign tax claim, it is not unusual these days to see in a trust instrument a widely drawn power to pay foreign taxes. A crucial question in relation to such a power is whether it is purely fiduciary, in the sense that it must be exercised solely for the benefit of some or all of the beneficiaries, or whether its purpose, or one of its purposes, is to protect the trustees from personal liability for fiscal claims. Naturally, the answer to this question in any particular case is a matter for construction of the trust instrument.[3] The following comments are of a general nature.

(1) It is rare to see the question of the power's fiduciary status expressly addressed in the trust instrument. One is therefore left to make inferences from the wording of the clause and the context in which it appears.
(2) Typically, the power is contained among the administrative powers of the trust instrument. This suggests a fiduciary intent, although (and to the contrary) the 'administrative' schedule to a trust instrument not infrequently extends to trustee protection provisions.

---

1 Another possible argument (not turning on the governing law) is that the settlor's reimbursement claim concerns not the direct or indirect enforcement of tax, but merely the incidence of tax already paid. See *Lewin on Trusts* (Sweet & Maxwell, 17th ed), para 21–12A.

2 [2000] 2 ITELR 682. In *Re T's Settlement* [2002] 41 ITELR 820, the Jersey court expressed 'some doubt' as to whether it could give effect to the statutory right of reimbursement.

3 Also to be considered, if the power is intended to be exercisable for the protection of the trustees, is whether a power of this nature is permissible under the governing law of the trust, and whether any necessary requirements of that law (eg as to obtaining the settlor's informed consent) have been complied with.

(3) The matter may be further complicated if, as is quite common, the power includes a provision permitting trustees to pay a foreign tax irrespective of whether payment will be to the disadvantage of any of the beneficiaries. At first glance this seems wide enough to entitle the trustees to use the power for their own protection. However, as it seems to the authors, this is not necessarily so. Such a provision is consistent with the purpose being merely to permit trustees to deal with the kind of situation arising in the *Hollins*[1] and *Scottish National Orchestra*[2] cases discussed above. That is to say, the power is to be exercised to ensure a fair and proper administration as between the beneficiaries, even though one or more beneficiaries might be disadvantaged. In both *Hollins* and *Scottish National Orchestra*, the executors were exercising a fiduciary responsibility rather than acting in their own interests.

(4) Support for the view that, as a matter of construction, a power to pay foreign taxes may be fiduciary in the sense mentioned above, or partly so, is to be found in the judgment of the Court of Appeal of Barbados in *Bank of Nova Scotia v Tremblay*.[3] The court was concerned with four deeds of settlements, clause 7 of each of which contained a fairly wide power to pay taxes in any part of the world. Clause 8 provided for the trustee company to be exonerated from any responsibility or liability to the beneficiary for loss or damage to the trust fund through a *bona fide* exercise by it of any power conferred on it by the deed. The court, in considering the question of a possible indemnity for the trustee on future termination of its trusteeship, commented as follows:[4]

> 'Although [the relevant subclauses of clause 7] give the trust company very wide authority to pay imposts which may be claimed in any part of the world, it appears to us that this authority must necessarily be subject to the provisions of clause 8, which are clearly of comprehensive application. On that footing, we find it difficult to envisage any circumstances in which the trustee can be said to be acting *bona fide* if the trustee satisfies any claims which, on the authority of *Government of India v Taylor*, they are not obligated by law to satisfy. Nevertheless, we would not go as far as to say that no such circumstances could arise which would permit the trust company to claim an indemnity. However that may be, we do not see any compelling reason to attach a lien to the trust fund or any part thereof in order to provide for an eventuality which may, but probably will not, occur at any time in the future.'

---

1 79 Misc 200; 139 NYS 713 (Surr Ct NY Co 1913).

2 1969 SLT 323.

3 [1998/99] 1 ITELR 673 at 690–692. Note also the Jersey decision *Re X's Settlement* (1994) *Butterworth's Offshore Cases and Materials* 600 where the exercise of an express power to pay foreign taxes had to comply with the requirement of Art 20(2) of the Trusts (Jersey) Law 1984 that trustees' powers be exercised only in the interests of the beneficiaries.

4 Ibid at 691–692.

(5) To the extent that, on a proper construction, the power is fiduciary, then the discussion at **9.4.1–9.4.3** above remains relevant.

Chapter 10

DISCLOSURE OF INFORMATION BY TRUSTEES

Emily Campbell[*]

10.1 INTRODUCTION

This topic is one of the most difficult facing advisers in the area of trusts. The reasoning in the relevant case-law is inadequate to provide a comprehensive description of when a trustee is under a duty to provide a beneficiary with information concerning the trust, or to provide an adequate explanation of the juridical basis for the existence of such a duty. Further, the distinction between factual situations where the duty has been found to exist and those where it has been found not to exist might, in some instances, be regarded as flimsy.

It is fair to say that the confusion in this area is attributable to the various principles at play. These include:

(a) the proprietary interest of a beneficiary in the trust property;
(b) the duty of a trustee to account to his beneficiaries for his stewardship;
(c) the absence of any duty owed by trustees to provide reasons for the exercise of their discretions;
(d) the need to protect confidentiality;
(e) the need for a party to litigation, in accordance with the procedural rules of the court, to disclose to the other parties documents relevant to the issues arising in those proceedings.

It is clearly appropriate to treat disclosure by trustees pursuant to the equitable rules quite separately from disclosure by a party to litigation pursuant to the procedural rules of the court (referred to in this chapter as 'procedural disclosure'). The majority of this chapter is concerned with the former type of disclosure, although see **10.6** for a discussion on procedural disclosure.

* Wilberforce Chambers, Lincoln's Inn, London.

The information which a beneficiary may ask his trustee to disclose will often be contained in existing documents. Examples of the types of documents are as follows:

(a) the trust deed, deeds of appointment and removal of trustees, deeds exercising the dispositive powers of the trustees;
(b) trust accounts and reports (such as actuarial reports and valuation reports) relating to the trust property;
(c) contracts and leases relating to the use and enjoyment of trust property;
(d) the agenda and minutes of meetings of the trustees;
(e) correspondence between the trustees and beneficiaries of the trust, or between trustees and other power holders (such as a protector);
(f) legal or other professional advice relating to the trust, including the instructions pursuant to which that advice was obtained.

However, it is important to appreciate that there will be numerous cases where a beneficiary might properly ask his trustee to provide him with information that is not set out in documents in existence. In such cases, the trustee may be obliged to produce a document containing the relevant information for the purposes of the disclosure of information.

The majority of the case-law in this area stems either from England or from Australia. In England, the leading authority is still *Re Londonderry's Settlement*.[1] There are a number of more recent authorities in Australia, which are referred to in the following paragraphs. Some cases from other jurisdictions can also be found. Although it is fair to assume for most purposes that the common law in this area is the same in all countries which have adopted an English legal system, this assumption should not be carried too far. There may be reasons of policy as to why the courts of another country might take a more liberal approach to disclosure than the English courts.[2]

10.2 JURIDICAL BASIS

Three main bases can be identified from the case-law:

(a) the proposition that a beneficiary is entitled to see the 'trust documents';
(b) the concept that a beneficiary has a proprietary interest in certain documents relating to the trust;

---

1 [1965] Ch 918, CA.

2 See eg the discussion in the dissenting judgment of Kirby P, sitting in the Court of Appeal of New South Wales in *Hartigan Nominees Pty Ltd v Rydge* (1992) 29 NSWLR 405 at 415 *et seq*.

(c) the trustee's duty to account to his beneficiaries.

As to basis (a) above, this proposition stems from old and well-settled case-law.[1] However, the proposition immediately begs the question 'what is meant by trust documents?' Whereas it might be obvious that the expression is capable of extending beyond the trust deed, it is equally clear that the expression cannot sensibly be used to refer to all documents in existence which relate in some way to the trust. The proposition is, therefore, of very limited assistance on the question of where to draw the dividing line between disclosable and non-disclosable documents. An insight into the ambit of the expression 'trust documents' was provided by Salmon LJ in *Re Londonderry*[2] as follows:

> 'The category of trust documents has never been comprehensively defined. Nor could it be – certainly not by me. Trust documents do, however, have these characteristics in common: (1) they are documents in the possession of the trustees as trustees; (2) they contain information about the trust which the beneficiaries are entitled to know; (3) the beneficiaries have a proprietary interest in the documents and, accordingly, are entitled to see them.'

As to basis (b), as will appear from the foregoing dictum of Salmon LJ, this basis is not entirely separate from basis (a). However, it is fair to say that the concept is sometimes treated by the courts as a separate juridical basis for the trustees' duty of disclosure.[3] The concept has shortcomings, which have been ventilated in a number of textbooks on the subject.[4] The basis for identifying the beneficiary's property interest in a document is often tenuous. Further, there are problems in applying this analysis where the person wishing to seek disclosure is the object of a discretionary trust or power, as that person has no identifiable proprietary interest in the trust property.

It is submitted that basis (c) is the most compelling juridical basis for disclosure of information by trustees. As explained below, it is settled that a beneficiary is entitled to documents concerning the state of the trust property, but not to the minutes of meetings at which the trustees take decisions. Basis (c) is adequate to explain this distinction. The provision of minutes of trustees' meetings is not a part of a trustees's duty to account to his beneficiaries. Nor does it flow from any other primary duty of the trustee, for example, the duty to give consideration to the exercise of a particular power or discretion.

---

1 *O'Rourke v Darbishire* [1920] AC 581; *Brookes v Prescott* [1948] 2 KB 133.

2 [1965] 1 Ch 918 at 938. For criticism of the circularity of this description, see *Hartigan Nominees Pty Ltd v Rydge* (1992) 29 NSWLR 405 at 413, 418 and 443.

3 See eg *Re Londonderry's Settlement Trust* [1965] 1 Ch 918 at 928; *Hartigan Nominees Pty Ltd v Rydge* (1992) 29 NSWLR 405 at 442–443, per Sheller JA.

4 See Ford and Lee *Principles of the Law of Trusts* (Law Book Co, 3rd ed, looseleaf), para 9000; Underhill and Hayton *Law of Trusts and Trustees* (Butterworths, 15th ed, 1995), p 660. See also *Morris v Morris* (1993) 9 WAR 150.

In reality, the trustees' duties to provide information dovetail with their primary duties. The trustee is not obliged to provide reasons for his dispositive decisions (unless required to do so by the trust instrument), because the object of a discretion has a mere right to be considered. The object usually[1] does not, to use a public law analogy, have a legitimate expectation that the particular discretion will be exercised in his favour. If he did, the giving of reasons for an unfavourable decision by the trustees might be a necessary part of a fair decision-making process.[2] As he has no such expectation, however, he correspondingly has no right to reasons. Further, the duty to account extends beyond a duty to provide documents in existence. A beneficiary is entitled to certain information, irrespective of whether a trustee has taken the care to record the information in documentary form.

This third approach is also the approach preferred by a number of textbook writers[3] and some case-law.[4] That is not, of course, to cast doubt upon the right of a beneficiary to disclosure of a document which is quite clearly a trust document (for example, the trust deed), or in which he can demonstrate a proprietary interest.

Finally, there is a growing body of case-law which suggests that the beneficiary does not have a right to disclosure at all, but rather the court has a discretion to order disclosure.[5] The approach preferred by the author is that a beneficiary does have certain *prima facie* rights to disclosure, but that the court has a discretion to allow the trustees to withhold disclosure in special circumstances.[6] This idea is discussed further at **10.5**.

---

1 See, however, *Scott v National Trust* [1998] 2 All ER 705 at 718, where Robert Walker J suggested that a beneficiary may in certain circumstances have a legitimate expectation that a discretion will be exercised in his favour (the example was given of an elderly, impoverished beneficiary, to whom regular discretionary payments had been made by the trustees), and that such a beneficiary may be entitled to reasons before the trustees denied him of that expectation. See, *per contra*, *Wilson v Law Debenture Trust Corp* [1995] 2 All ER 337.

2 *Cf* the public law case of *McInnes v Onslow-Fane* [1978] 1 WLR 1520, where Megarry V-C considered whether an applicant for a boxing licence had a right to reasons for refusal of the grant of the licence. The court held that a person already in receipt of a licence may have a legitimate expectation that the licence will continue, and therefore a right to reasons for refusal. A bare applicant will not have such a right.

3 See Ford and Lee, n 4 on p 519, p 423; Underhill and Hayton, n 4 on p 519, p 660.

4 See *Spellson v George* (1987) 11 NSWLR 300; *Chaine-Nicholson v Bank of Ireland* [1976] IR 393.

5 See eg *Re Cowin* (1886) 33 Ch 179; *Murphy v Murphy* [1998] 3 All ER 1; *Lemos v Coutts & Co* [1992–93] CILR 460.

6 For support for this proposition, see *Re the Rabaiotti 1989 Settlement* [2000] 2 ITELR 763, Royal Court of Jersey, where the court also held that it had jurisdiction to order disclosure of documents, which are not *prima facie* disclosable (in that case, a letter of wishes).

10.3 WHAT INFORMATION MUST THE TRUSTEES DISCLOSE?

Trustees are obliged to provide the following information:

(a) the trust deed, deeds of appointment, retirement and removal of trustees, and deeds exercising the trustees' dispositive powers (such as an overriding power of appointment);
(b) trust accounts;[1]
(c) details of trust investments, including details of persons in occupation of trust property;[2]
(d) formal documentation relating to trustee investments, for example, mortgage deeds;[3]
(e) details of dealings with the trust fund, for example, applications of trust capital to beneficiaries and changes of investment;[4]
(f) legal opinions and instructions to solicitors and counsel concerning the trustees' duties and the terms of the trust.[5] It is thought that this obligation does not extend to all legal advice provided to the trustees, for example, legal opinions provided to trustees for the purposes of hostile litigation with their beneficiaries.[6]

Trustees are not obliged to provide the following information:

(a) the agenda and minutes of meetings of the trustees;[7]
(b) reasons for dispositive and administrative decisions[8] of the trustees;
(c) correspondence passing between the trustees or other power holders;[9]
(d) correspondence passing between trustees (or other power holders) on the one hand, and the beneficiaries of the settlement on the other hand;[10]
(e) a letter of wishes produced by the settlor.[11]

---

1 *Re Tillott* [1892] 1 Ch 86; *Re Page* [1893] 1 Ch 304.

2 *Chaine-Nicholson v Bank of Ireland* [1976] IR 393.

3 *Re Tillott* [1892] 1 Ch 86.

4 *Chaine-Nicholson v Bank of Ireland* [1976] IR 393; *Spellson v George* (1987) 11 NSWLR 300.

5 *Re Londonderry's Settlement Trusts* [1965] 1 Ch 918.

6 See in this context, ibid at 938, per Salmon LJ.

7 Ibid.

8 The trustees of an occupational pension scheme in England are, however, required to provide a statement of investment principles: see Pensions Act 1995, s 35; and Occupational Pension Schemes (Disclosure of Information) Regulations 1996 (SI 1996/1655), reg 7. See *Wilson v Law Debenture Trust Corp* [1995] 2 All ER 337.

9 *Re Londonderry's Settlement Trusts* [1965] 1 Ch 918.

10 Ibid.

11 *Hartigan Nominees Pty Ltd v Rydge* (1992) 29 NSWLR 405. See, *per contra*, *Re the Rabaiotti 1989 Settlement* [2000] 2 ITELR 763, Royal Court of Jersey, where the court held that it had jurisdiction to order disclosure of a letter of wishes in the interests of the beneficiaries as a whole.

The above list is not intended to be comprehensive. Further, it is clear that there are classes of document where the question of disclosability is open to doubt, or will vary from case to case. For example, in *Tierney v King*,[1] the Supreme Court of Queensland held that the trustees of a pension scheme were not obliged to provide an actuarial report in their possession relating to the fund to a beneficiary. It might be argued in another case that the trustees have a duty to provide such a report pursuant to their duty to account.[2] A further example is the question of whether a beneficiary is entitled to see documents relating to the affairs of a company in which the trustees own shares. The answer will be governed by the size of the shareholding and the other circumstances of the case.[3]

The beneficiary must reimburse the trustee for the cost associated with the provision of the information.[4]

10.4 WHO IS ENTITLED TO INFORMATION CONCERNING THE TRUST?

It is clear that a beneficiary with a vested interest in the trust fund is entitled to disclosure of the documents referred to above. But what of a beneficiary with a contingent interest in the trust fund, or the object of a discretionary trust or power?

The New South Wales case of *Spellson v George*,[5] and the Irish case of *Chaine Nicholson v Bank of Ireland*,[6] each held that the trustees' duty to account,[7] and accordingly the duty to provide trust accounts and details of investments representing the trust fund, extends to objects of a discretion, and that such objects are entitled to copies of the trust accounts. In an English case, *Murphy v Murphy*,[8] Neuberger J held that the court had power, pursuant to its equitable jurisdiction, to order the provision of information to a member of a

---

1 [1983] 2 Qd R 580.

2 In fact, in England a disclosure obligation arises under statutory instrument: Occupational Pension Schemes (Disclosure of Information) Regulations 1996 (SI 1996/1655), reg 6.

3 *Butt v Kelson* [1952] 1 Ch 197.

4 *Re Bosworth* (1889) 58 LJCh 432; *Ottley v Gilby* (1845) 8 Beav 602.

5 (1987) 11 NSWLR 300. See also *Horan v James* (1982) 2 NSWLR 376; *Randall v Lubrano* (unreported) 31 October 1975, per Holland J.

6 [1976] IR 393.

7 See, generally, in relation to the duties of trustees to the objects of discretionary trusts and powers: *Gartside v IRC* [1968] AC 553; *McPhail v Doulton* [1971] AC 424; *Re Manisty's Settlement Trusts* [1974] Ch 17.

8 [1998] 3 All ER 1.

discretionary class. The question is still the subject of debate.[1] In *Rosewood Trust Limited v Schmidt*,[2] the High Court of the Isle of Man[3] sought to draw a distinction between objects of discretionary trusts (which trustees have a duty to exercise) and objects of fiduciary mere powers (which trustees need only consider exercising), and held that the latter type of object was not entitled to information concerning the trust, whereas the former type was.[4]

It should also be noted that, whereas a trustee is under a duty to inform a beneficiary when he becomes entitled to income or capital of the trust fund, the trustee is not obliged to inform mere objects of a discretionary trust or power that they are objects.[5]

The position of an assignee of an interest in a trust fund depends, in the author's view, upon the nature of the assignment. If, by reason of the assignment, the assignor retains nothing by a bare equitable interest under the trust, having no active duties to the assignee (and so falls out of the picture[6]), it is thought that the assignee should be in the position the assignor would have been in but for the assignment, and in particular he should be entitled to disclosure from the trustees of the information to which the assignor was previously entitled.[7] By contrast, some assignments do not purport to make the assignor 'fall out of the picture' under the terms of the trust. Furthermore, some rights under a trust are incapable of assignment in that way in any event, for example, a person's status as an object of a discretionary power. An assignment in such circumstances must operate (if at all) by subtrust or contract, and accordingly, the assignee will be able to claim disclosure only by forcing the assignor to sue the trustees.

10.5 DEFENCES TO DISCLOSURE

By 'defence', what is meant here is a ground upon which a trustee can justify withholding the disclosure of a document which he is *prima facie* liable to disclose. There is a growing amount of authority that the court may, in special circumstances, decline to order disclosure of documents which are *prima facie*

---

1 See DJ Hayton 'The irreducible core content of trusteeship' [1996] JTCP 3. See also *Hartigan Nominees Pty Ltd v Rydge* (1992) 29 NSWLR 405 at 432, per Mahoney JA. It appears to be settled in Jersey that the object of a discretion stands in the same position as a beneficiary for these purposes: see *West v Lazard Brothers & Co (Jersey) Limited* [1987–88] *Jersey Law Reports* 414; *Re the Rabaiotti 1989 Settlement* [2000] 2 ITELR 763, Royal Court of Jersey.

2 [2001] 3 ITELR 734. This case is under appeal to the Privy Council.

3 On appeal to the Court's of Staff of Government Division from an Order of Deemster Cain.

4 [*Editor's note:* See also the recent Guernsey appeal decision in *Stuart-Hutcheson v Spread Trustee Company Limited* (unreported) 15 July 2002, referred to below at **10.7.9**.]

5 *Re Manisty's Settlement Trusts* [1973] 2 All ER 1203, distinguishing *Hawkesley v May* [1956] 1 QB 304.

6 See *Oughtred v IRC* [1960] AC 206.

7 See, *per contra*, *Global Custodians Ltd v Mesh* [2000] ITELR 327, Supreme Court of New South Wales, a case concerning the assignment of a beneficial interest in a fighting fund trust.

disclosable.[1] Interestingly, it has also recently been suggested that the court may, in the interests of the beneficiaries as a whole, order disclosure of documents which are not *prima facie* disclosable.[2]

Confidentiality may be a defence to disclosure, although confidentiality has a wider relevance in this area. If a court were considering whether a trustee should disclose a particular document, the disclosure of which was not governed by existing authority, the fact that it was confidential would no doubt influence the court's decision on whether a trustee has any underlying duty to disclose such a document in the first place.[3]

The issue of confidentiality as a defence may arise where a settlor has inserted a clause into his settlement requiring the trustees to treat certain documents as confidential. It is thought that such a clause would be recognised by a court[4] within certain limits. A clause which sought to exclude the trustees' duty to account altogether would, it is thought, be void as being contrary to the fundamental nature of the trust. Similarly, a clause which sought to restrict the court's right to make appropriate orders for procedural disclosure would, it is thought, be void as being an attempt to oust the jurisdiction of the court. In England, the question of the validity of such a clause would no doubt now have to be judged in light of Art 6 (right to a fair trial) and Art 8 (right to respect for private and family life) of the European Convention for the Protection of Human Rights and Fundamental Freedoms 1950.[5]

Further defences to disclosure, which may be gleaned from the cases, are as follows: that the disclosure of the document concerned would not be in the general interest of the beneficiaries;[6] that the information sought to be disclosed is commercially sensitive;[7] that if disclosure were made, there would be an unjustified interference in the business of a partnership in which the trustee as such was a partner;[8] and that the documents sought were irrelevant or had limited probative worth compared with the prejudice to the other beneficiaries of the disclosure.[9]

---

1 See *Re Cowin* (1886) 33 Ch 179; *Murphy v Murphy* [1998] 3 All ER 1; *Rouse and Others v IOOF Australia Trustees Ltd* [1999] SASC 181; *Re Ojjeh Trust* [1992–93] CILR 348; *Lemos v Coutts & Co* [1992–93] CILR 460; *Re the Rabaiotti 1989 Settlement* [2000] 2 ITELR 763, Royal Court of Jersey; *Re Fairbairn* [1967] VR 633.

2 See *Re the Rabaiotti 1989 Settlement* (above).

3 See *Hartigan Nominees Pty Ltd v Rydge* (1992) 29 NSWLR 405.

4 See eg *Tierney v King* [1983] 2 Qd R 580, where the Full Court of the Supreme Court of Queensland appears to have given weight to a clause restricting the trustees to 'observe strict secrecy with regard to the affairs, accounts and transactions' of the occupational pension scheme with which the case was concerned. See also *Rouse and Others v IOOF Australia Trustees Ltd* [1999] SASC 181, per Doyle CJ.

5 See the Human Rights Act 1998.

6 *Rouse and Others v IOOF Australia Trustees Ltd* [1999] SASC 181, Supreme Court of South Australia. See also *Re the Rabaiotti 1989 Settlement* [2000] 2 ITELR 763, Royal Court of Jersey.

7 *Re Ojjeh Trust* [1992–93] CILR 348 (Cayman Islands).

8 *Morris v Morris* [1993] 9 WAR 150 (Australia).

9 *Lemos v Coutts & Co* [1992–93] CILR 460 (Cayman Islands).

10.6 DISCLOSURE PURSUANT TO PROCEDURAL RULES OF THE COURT

The procedural rules of the court, of course, vary from jurisdiction to jurisdiction. In England, procedural disclosure is now governed by Part 31 of the Civil Procedure Rules 1998 (CPR 1998).[1] Many jurisdictions may continue to have procedural rules like the old (English) Rules of the Supreme Court 1965,[2] Ord 24 which governed 'discovery', as it was formerly known.

If a trustee is a party to litigation against one or more beneficiaries, whether the court will order procedural disclosure of a particular class of documents will depend largely on the form of the litigation, and the issues arising. A court will usually order disclosure of documents relevant to the issues, and an English court will sometimes, under the CPR 1998, order disclosure of documents which are only arguably relevant, if the task of making the disclosure will not be unduly onerous to the trustee.

As is clear from *Re Londonderry's Settlement Trusts*,[3] if the beneficiary alleges fraud or wrongdoing in the making of a decision against the trustee, the court will usually order procedural disclosure of documents relating to the taking of the decision. Further, if a beneficiary brings proceedings against a trustee to have a decision declared void on the basis that in reaching it the trustee took into account irrelevant considerations, or failed to take into account relevant considerations,[4] the trustee will usually be ordered to disclose documents relevant to the decision-making process.

However, a beneficiary cannot obtain procedural disclosure simply by bringing proceedings requesting such disclosure. Further, a beneficiary could not properly be advised to bring proceedings to set aside a decision, alleging that the trustees in reaching the decision took into account irrelevant considerations or failed to take into account relevant decisions, unless he already has some evidence that the allegation was true. It has been said that 'a beneficiary may support a case by discovery, but may not use the process to ascertain whether a case exists'.[5]

If proceedings are brought by the trustees for a direction that they be at liberty to enter into a particular transaction, whether or not the application involves a surrender of the trustees' discretion to the court, the court will in all likelihood order procedural disclosure of the documents which show what factors the trustees took into account before deciding to promote the transaction.[6] This is because the court will need to be apprised of all relevant information in deciding whether or not to approve the transaction.

---

1 SI 1998/3132.

2 SI 1965/1776.

3 [1965] 1 Ch 918.

4 See *Re Hastings-Bass* [1975] Ch 25.

5 *Hartigan Nominees Pty Ltd v Rydge* (1992) 29 NSWLR 405 at 437, per Mahoney JA.

6 See *The Public Trustee and Another v Cooper and Others* [2001] WTLR 901, per Hart J.

Some documents ordered to be disclosed will, of course, be privileged from inspection. Privilege cannot be claimed by a trustee against a beneficiary in relation to documents to which he is entitled under the principles set out in *Re Londonderry*.[1] However, it is thought that privilege may be claimed in respect of documents which are not disclosable under *Re Londonderry*, but are ordered to be disclosed pursuant to the procedural discretion of the court.[2]

10.7 SPECIFIC STATUTORY PROVISIONS

A number of jurisdictions have enacted specific statutory provisions which are relevant to this topic.[3] The following list is not intended to be exhaustive.

10.7.1 Anguilla

The trustees' duty to keep accounts and their duty to supply information to beneficiaries is governed by ss 27(7) and 28 respectively of the Trusts Ordinance 1994.

10.7.2 Australia

Some individual states have produced legislation relevant to this area: see Trustee Act 1925 (NSW), s 102; Trustee Act 1898 (TAS), s 28; Public Trustee Act 1978 (QLD), ss 8(1), 60; Trustee Act 1936 (SA), ss 84A–84F; Trustee Act 1962 (WA), s 94.

10.7.3 The Bahamas

The Trustee Act 1998, s 83 contains a detailed statutory code setting out the nature and scope of the trustees' duties to provide information.

10.7.4 Belize

The trustees' duty to keep accounts and their duty to supply information to beneficiaries is governed by ss 27(7) and 28 respectively of the Trusts Act 1992.

---

1 *Re Mason* (1883) 22 Ch D 609; *Wynne v Humberston* (1858) 27 Beav 421; *Re Postlethwaite* (1887) 35 Ch D 722.

2 See *Re Londonderry's Settlement* [1965] 1 Ch 918 at 938. It is submitted that the statement in *Civil Procedure* (Sweet & Maxwell, 2nd ed, 1999), para 31.3.23 is formulated too widely.

3 The legislation referred to below is, in most cases, reproduced in J Glasson (ed) *International Trust Laws* (Jordans, looseleaf).

10.7.5 Bermuda

A statutory duty is imposed upon trust companies licensed under the Trust Companies Act 1991 to certify annually to the Bermuda Monetary Authority that proper trust accounts have been kept: see the Trust Companies Act 1991, s 12(2)(a) and Second Schedule.

10.7.6 The Cook Islands

Although the common law rules govern the trustees' duty to provide information, those rules must be read subject to the secrecy provisions of International Trusts Act 1984, s 23 whereby it is an offence to divulge information to any person relating to an international trust.

10.7.7 Cyprus

International Trusts Law 1992, s 11 contains comprehensive provisions relating to confidentiality in relation to international trusts.

10.7.8 England and Wales

Clearly, the common law rules are of paramount importance. However, advisers should be aware that trustees have a specific statutory duty of disclosure in relation to occupational pension schemes (for which, see the Occupational Pension Schemes (Disclosure of Information) Regulations 1996 (SI 1996/1655)) and in relation to notices of dealings with equitable interests (for which, see Law of Property Act 1925, s 137(8)).

10.7.9 Guernsey

The trustees' duty to keep accounts and their duty to supply information to beneficiaries are governed by ss 21 and 22 respectively of the Trusts (Guernsey) Law 1989 (as amended).[1] It is interesting to note that in Guernsey, a trust instrument can by its terms negative the trustees' duty to provide information to the beneficiaries.

10.7.10 Jersey

Certain statutory provisions are relevant: see Arts 17(5) and 25(d) of the Trusts (Jersey) Law 1984 (as amended).

---

1 The interpretation of s 22 was considered recently by the Royal Court of Guernsey in *Stuart-Hutcheson v Spread Trustee Company Ltd* [2001] 3 ITELR 683. [*Editor's note:* The court's decision was overturned on appeal on 15 July 2002, shortly after this chapter went to press. Briefly, the Appeal Court held that the Guernsey statute did not override pre-existing rights to information under Guernsey customary law, that these rights were similar to those under English law, and included rights for discretionary beneficiaries to receive significant information.]

10.7.11 Labuan

Statutory provisions have been enacted relevant to the trustees' duty to keep accounts and their duty to supply information to beneficiaries, including detailed provisions relating to confidentiality: see Labuan Offshore Trusts Act 1996, ss 30(4), (5), 41.

10.7.12 Liechtenstein

In broad terms, trustees have a statutory duty, subject to the terms of the trust instrument, to render annual accounts to the trusts' auditors or to the settlor: see Art 923 of the Personen-und Gesellschaftsrecht.

10.7.13 Mauritius

Statutory provisions set out the trustees' duties to keep accounts and to provide information to beneficiaries: see ss 30 and 32 of the Offshore Trusts Act 1992.

10.7.14 Nauru

Specific statutory provisions confer upon the Nauru Trustee Corporation a duty to provide audited accounts: see Nauru Trustee Corporation Act 1972, s 15(1).

10.7.15 New Zealand

The common law position is of primary importance, but certain statutory provisions are relevant: see Trustee Act 1956, ss 83A, 83B.

10.7.16 The Seychelles

Detailed statutory provisions govern the provision of information by trustees, and the rules as to confidentiality: see International Trusts Act 1994, ss 8, 9, 29, 31, 42.

10.7.17 South Africa

Certain specific statutory provisions are relevant: see ss 15–19 of the Trust Property Control Act 1998.

10.7.18 The Turks and Caicos Islands

The position is codified by statute: see Trusts Ordinance 1990, ss 20(5), 28.

10.7.19 United States of America

Some individual states have produced legislation relevant to this area, eg Florida and New York: see Fla Stat Ch 737.303 and NY Surr Ct Proc Act Ch 2308, 2309.

10.7.20 Other jurisdictions

The ordinary common law position still applies in many jurisdictions, for example, Barbados, the British Virgin Islands, the Cayman Islands, Gibraltar, Hong Kong, the Republic of Ireland, the Isle of Man and St Vincent and the Grenadines.

Chapter 11

RETENTION OF POWERS BY SETTLOR

Wolfe D Goodman QC[*]

11.1 INTRODUCTION

Where property has been settled on a trust, it may be possible to attack the settlement on the basis that the settlor lacked the ability to make the transfer. This can occur, for example, when the settlor is precluded under the law of his domicile or matrimonial domicile from making a gift which may impair his spouse's or his children's forced heirship rights or which consists of property which is subject to a community of property regime.[1] A number of jurisdictions specifically deny recognition by their courts of spousal rights and forced heirship rights arising under the laws of the settlor's domicile or other jurisdictions.[2] However, even those jurisdictions which decline to apply to trusts established under their law recognition of any foreign laws affecting such rights may still acknowledge specifically that this non-recognition does not apply to property not owned by the settlor at the time of its purported settlement.[3] Non-recognition may also occur when the settled property never

---

* Founding partner of Goodman and Carr LLP, a Toronto law firm. In addition to continuing to practise in the estate planning field, he is presently the General Editor of *Goodman on Estate Planning* (Federated Press, Montreal).

1 See J Goodwill 'Planning to Resist Hostile Litigation' [1999] JTCP 157 at 159–162.

2 Examples of this are the Labuan Offshore Trust Act 1996, s 10(1); Isle of Man Trusts Act 1995, s 5; Jersey Trusts (Amendment) (Jersey) Law 1989, Art 8A(2); Guernsey Trusts (Guernsey) Law 1989, s 11A; Cyprus International Trust Law 1992, s 3(1); Bahamas Trusts (Choice of Governing Law) Act 1989, ss 7–9; Anguilla Trusts Ordinance 1994, s 62; Turks and Caicos Islands Trust Ordinance 1990, s 14(2); Belize Trusts Act 1992, s 7(6); Bermuda Trusts (Special Provisions) Act 1989, s 11; British Virgin Islands Trustee Ordinance, s 83(1); Cayman Islands Trusts Law, ss 86–88; Cook Islands International Trusts Act, s 13; Mauritius Offshore Trusts Act 1992, s 11; Seychelles International Trusts Act, s 10(2); Barbados Trustee Act 1980, ss 16–18; Nevis International Trust Ordinance 1994, ss 28–29.

3 Anguilla Trusts Ordinance 1994, s 62; Bahamas (Choice of Governing Law) Act 1989, s 7; Turks and Caicos Islands Trust Ordinance 1990, s 13.

belonged to the settlor, but is the proceeds of theft or fraud or when the settlement itself constitutes a fraud on creditors.[1] Some offshore jurisdictions have attempted in their trust legislation to limit or even eliminate the application to trusts established there of claims of these types, although it is far from clear how such legislation would be interpreted in another jurisdiction, such as the jurisdiction of *situs* of some of the trust property.

The vulnerability of a trust to an attack on any of the foregoing grounds does not depend at all on the nature of the trust or the manner of its administration; rather, the mere fact that the settlor has deprived himself of the settled property is sufficient, of itself, to make it vulnerable. However, there are other situations in which the provisions of the trust instrument or the manner in which the trust is administered are themselves the basis for attack.

The latter kind of trust would appear to be vulnerable to possible attack on any or all of the following grounds:

(a) that the trust is merely a sham, which should be disregarded by a court;
(b) that it is essentially a testamentary disposition;
(c) that the rights which are reserved to the settlor preclude its recognition as a trust; or
(d) that certain provisions in the trust instrument which deny beneficiaries the right to an accounting deprive it of an essential element of a trust.

The following commentary discusses the first three of these grounds; the trustees' duties to account to beneficiaries are discussed in another chapter of this work.[2]

11.2 THE TRUST IS MERELY A SHAM

The classic definition of a sham is found in *Snook v London & West Riding Investments Ltd*,[3] per Lord Diplock at 528:

> '[I]t means acts done or documents executed by the parties to the "sham" which are intended by them to give to third parties or to the court the appearance of creating between the parties legal rights and obligations different from the actual legal rights and obligations (if any) which the parties intend to create. One thing I think, however, is clear in legal principle, morality and the authorities … that for acts or documents to be a "sham", with

1 In one of the interlocutory judgments in the Bahamian *Grupo Torras* litigation, dated 1 September 1995, Sawyer J stated that 'the pleadings allege that the fraud took place prior to the establishment of that Trust and that the corpus of the trust fund includes part of the proceeds of the fraud'; to that extent, the nature of the trust and the powers reserved to the settler were clearly irrelevant, since the question was merely one of tracing the proceeds.

2 See Chapter 10, 'Disclosure of Information by Trustees'.

3 [1967] 1 All ER 518, CA (England).

> whatever legal consequences follow from this, all the parties thereto must have a common intention that the acts or documents are not to create the legal rights and obligations which they give the appearance of creating …'

This definition was adopted by Estey J, of the Supreme Court of Canada, in *Stubart Investments Ltd v The Queen*,[1] in which, however, he expanded the elements required for a sham to include 'the element of deceit, which is the heart and core of a sham'.

Where a trust instrument is a sham, not intended to be acted upon, the purported settlor will still have real dispositive control over both the income and the capital; it can, therefore, be no more than a bare trust for the purported settlor.

The 1991 decision of the Royal Court of the States of Jersey in *Rahman v Chase Bank (CI) Trust Co*[2] involved the validity of a revocable *inter vivos* trust in which a Jersey trust company was named as trustee. A wealthy Lebanese had established the trust in order to defeat the claims, under Islamic *sharia* law, of his wife and certain of their children. After his death, his widow brought action against the trustee for a declaration that the trust was invalid. The court held that, under Jersey law, a revocable *inter vivos* trust was invalid, at least as regards a trust which had been established before the enactment of the Trusts (Jersey) Law in 1984. The first ground of the decision was that such a trust offended a principle of Jersey law which states, '*donner et retenir ne vaut*'.[3] The second ground was that the trust was a sham, never intended to be acted upon. In support of this ground, the evidence before the court showed that on numerous occasions during his lifetime the settlor had treated the trust property for all practical purposes as his own and that the trustee had acquiesced in this treatment. The court therefore concluded that the purported settlement on the trust was made to the trust company as agent or nominee:

> 'The trustee was never made the master of the assets. KAR [the alleged settlor] intended to and did retain control of the capital and income of the trust fund throughout his lifetime and used the trust and the deed of appointment made under the trust to make testamentary dispositions.'

The finding that the trust was a sham, in the strict legal sense of documentation that was never intended to be acted upon and which did not set out the true relationship between the parties, is one which could be made in any jurisdiction based on English law, as well as in Jersey, where local law also created another obstacle to the validity of this particular trust.

A distinction must always be made, at least in principle, between a trust document which was never intended to be acted upon, which is a sham,

---

1 84 DTC 6305 at 6321.

2 [1991] JLR 103.

3 This principle was abolished, in relation to transfers and dispositions to a trust, by the Trusts (Amendment) (Jersey) Law 1989, Art 1 (inserting a new Art 8A(1) into the Trusts (Jersey) Law 1984).

creating no rights whatever, and one which is regarded as having come into effective operation, but where the settlor, with the connivance of the trustee, appropriates the trust property and treats it as his own, in breach of the terms of the trust document. In the latter case, the beneficiaries named in the trust document have legal rights which they are entitled to protect, by bringing action against the settlor and the trustee for restitution to the trust of the appropriated property. This distinction could possibly have been important in *Rahman*, where the beneficiaries named in the trust document were different from those who benefited from the court's declaration of its entire invalidity, but it does not form part of the court's reasons for judgment.

In *Turner v Turner*,[1] the settlor established a trust, naming as trustees his father, his sister-in-law and her husband, none of whom had any experience with or understanding of trusts. At the settlor's behest, three purported appointments were made by the trustees in favour of his children, without really understanding what they were doing. The court held that these appointments were made in breach of their duty as trustees and they were therefore set aside.

In *OD-Bank in Liquidation v Bankrupt's Estate WKR*,[2] decided by the District Court of Zurich on 1 February 1994, the court examined the law of Guernsey, under which a trust had been formed and concluded that it had been validly established there. However, it then treated the trust as a sham, in accordance with the Jersey decision in *Rahman*, by reason of the manner in which the settlor, WKR, acted in respect of the property allegedly belonging to the trust.

In *Midland Bank plc v Wyatt*,[3] a matrimonial home was registered in the joint names of a husband and wife, who executed a legal charge to secure a mortgage loan to a bank. The husband then entered into a deed of arrangement giving his equity interest in the home to his wife and daughters. The bank was not aware of the trust deed, and the wife was not aware of its effect. The husband later negotiated further loans from the bank on the security of his interest in the home. When the bank brought an action against him, the husband sought to rely on the deed to resist the making absolute a charging order nisi obtained by the bank on his interest in the home. The court treated the deed as a sham and held that the bank did not have to prove a fraudulent motive nor to prove that both the husband and the wife intended the deed to have no effect. This latter aspect may represent a significant departure from the principle stated in *Snook*.

In a number of Australian Family Court decisions, the judges have required a husband to pay his wife sums out of a trust which the court held was under his control, where he could obtain the complete benefit of distributions from the trust. The court ignored the legal formalities and held that he had *de facto*

---

1 [1983] 2 All ER 745.
2 Case No FB920075 (unreported) 1 February 1994.
3 [1995] 1 FLR 696.

legal beneficial ownership of the trust property: see *In the Marriage of Ashton*;[1] *In the Marriage of Stein*;[2] and *In the Marriage of Goodman*.[3]

Some US courts have also treated trusts which they regarded as being under the settlor's effective control as the settlor's alter ego: see *Daryll W Pack v United States*[4] and *United States v Reinhard P Mueller*.[5]

11.3 THE TRUST IS A TESTAMENTARY DISPOSITION

If the document in question provides, in essence, that the property to which it refers can continue to be freely disposed of by the alleged settlor during his lifetime, in the same manner as before the alleged settlement, it is to be regarded as a testamentary disposition, which will be invalid unless the document has been executed in conformity with the special rules governing the execution of wills. The applicable principle was stated in *Cock v Cooke*,[6] to the effect that 'it is undoubted law that whatever may be the form of a duly executed instrument, if the person executing it intends that it shall not take effect until after his death, and it is dependent on his death for its vigour and effect, it is testamentary'.

In an early nineteenth-century English decision *Attorney-General v Jones and Bartlett*,[7] one Franklin executed a deed of trust, purporting to convey to the defendants, as trustees, his leasehold and personal property, for the use of himself for life, and of several named persons at his death, reserving a power of revocation. However, Franklin never parted with the deed nor with any part of the property during his lifetime and the trustees named in the deed were unaware of it until after his death. It was held that the trust was to be construed as a testamentary instrument, effective only at his death and rendering the property liable to legacy duty. Presumably, the deed had been executed like a will, so that it was effective to pass his property at his death. If this had not been the case, the document would have been entirely ineffective and the court would have held that his property passed by intestacy, possibly with much the same tax consequences.

In 1835 *Attorney-General v Jones and Bartlett* was distinguished in *Tompson v Browne*,[8] in which it was affirmed that a man could make a voluntary settlement by deed which reserved to himself a life-estate and a power of revocation, and avoided payment of legacy duty.

---

1 (1986) 11 Fam LR 457, Full Court of the Family Court of Australia.
2 (1986) 11 Fam LR 353.
3 (1989) Appeal No 172.
4 77 AFTR 2d Par 96–476, US District Court for Eastern District of California.
5 77 AFTR 2d Par 96–457, US Circuit Court of Appeal – 11th District.
6 (1866) 1 LR 1 P&D 241 at 248.
7 3 Price 369.
8 (1835) 3 My & K 32.

In *Re Pfrimmer's Estate*,[1] a document executed by Pfrimmer, entitled 'Declaration of Trust', was held to be a testamentary disposition, because it was concluded that it permitted the lands referred to in the document to be freely disposed of by him before the deaths of himself and his wife and merely provided for the distribution at death of whatever might not have been previously sold or distributed during their lifetimes. Not having been executed like a will, it was held to be invalid.

Pfrimmer can be contrasted with another Canadian decision, *Anderson v Patton*,[2] where a majority of the Alberta Court of Appeal upheld as a valid trust a document signed by B, acknowledging the receipt of $5000 from A, which B was to hold in trust for A and which B was to pay out to X and Y if anything should happen to B, but providing that the money would be returned to A on demand. The minority judges would have held the trust to be of both capital and income absolutely for the settlor, but if he did not demand the money for himself it was to pass to X and Y; they would have held that this was a testamentary disposition in favour of X and Y which was void for lack of will formalities.

11.4 THE RIGHTS RESERVED TO THE SETTLOR PRECLUDE ITS RECOGNITION AS A TRUST

An important decision in this area is the 1997 decision of the Bahamas Court of Appeal in *Private Trust Corporation v Grupo Torras*,[3] even though it dealt only with a preliminary skirmish in what developed into even more significant litigation. In that case, Sheikh Fahad Al Sabah provided the funds for a Bahamian trust, although he was not named as settlor. He was named as principal beneficiary, but with other family members also being named as possible beneficiaries of this discretionary trust. Some years after the settlement of this trust, Sheikh Fahad was accused of having defrauded the Kuwait Investment Office of a very large sum of money. As appears from the reasons for judgment of Sawyer J, dated 1 September 1995, it was alleged that some of the proceeds of the fraud were settled on various trusts, including the one which was the subject of this litigation. In addition, however, the allegedly defrauded parties brought action against the trustee on the basis that the rights over the trust and its property which the Sheikh had retained meant that he should be treated as the owner of the trust property, which could therefore be seized to satisfy a judgment which the defrauded parties expected to obtain against him. They therefore applied for a *Mareva* injunction, freezing the trust property and requiring it to be held until resolution of this litigation.

---

1 [1936] 2 DLR 460, Manitoba CA.

2 [1948] 2 DLR 302.

3 [1997/98] 1 OFLR 443.

This injunction was obtained from a single Bahamian judge, whose judgment was appealed to the Bahamian Court of Appeal, which dismissed the appeal and upheld the injunction.

The Court of Appeal took particular note of four specific provisions of the trust instrument.

(1) In exercising its investment powers, the trustee had to obtain the written consent of the principal beneficiary or his nominee. When it acted in accordance with this consent, it was indemnified against personal liability.
(2) Any beneficiary, including the principal beneficiary, had the right to request the trustee to make a distribution to himself.
(3) The trustee could be removed from office at any time by the protector, who had been appointed by the principal beneficiary. In addition, the trustee's remuneration was subject to agreement with the principal beneficiary.
(4) There was a 'flee clause' which provided *inter alia* that on the occurrence of certain events, including any action on behalf of any judicial authority to restrict, suspend or abrogate the trust or to prohibit, delay or restrict in any manner the free and immediate transfer of trust property into and out of the jurisdiction, the trustee's tenure would automatically terminate and it would automatically be divested of the trust property, in favour of a Turks and Caicos trustee.

It is noteworthy that each of these provisions, at least by itself, would appear to be compatible with the ordinary notion of a valid trust. For example:

(a) the first-mentioned provision does not seem to be substantially different from one which directs the trustee to engage a particular investment adviser selected by the settlor and indemnifying the trustee if it acts in accordance with the advice which is given. However, the fact that in *Grupo Torras* the investment adviser was, in effect, the principal beneficiary may be significant;
(b) while the Court of Appeal considered that the second provision indicated how accessible the trust fund was to the principal beneficiary, it is difficult to see how this provision added anything to the terms of the trust, since distributions were still entirely in the trustee's discretion;
(c) the right of the protector, appointed by the principal beneficiary, to remove and replace the trustee and the right of the principal beneficiary to determine the trustee's remuneration are fairly common provisions in offshore trusts, which, until *Grupo Torras*, few would have thought were significant;

(d) while the particular 'flee clause' in this trust instrument was perhaps more far-reaching than similar clauses in other offshore trusts, it was not very unusual, as a method of protecting such a trust from the vagaries of political and economic turmoil in the jurisdiction of its administration.

The Court of Appeal held that, if it was established that the principal beneficiary exercised substantial or effective control over the trust, the court could, in effect, lift the 'trust veil' and treat him as the beneficial owner of the trust assets, which would make them available to the defrauded parties, once they had obtained judgment against him. The court therefore upheld the *Mareva* injunction, freezing the trust assets and preventing them from being spirited away under the 'flee clause'.

Practitioners know that obtaining a *Mareva* injunction, although only a first step in asserting a claim, often results in settlement of the litigation. The subsequent developments of the *Grupo Torras* litigation are extraordinary. In June 1999 Manse J of the English High Court gave judgment in favour of Grupo Torras. Grupo Torras (GT) had previously obtained *Mareva* injunctions in a number of jurisdictions, including Jersey, freezing the assets in some discretionary trusts which the Sheikh had previously established. It therefore sought to enforce its claim against these trusts, on two alternative bases: first, that some of the proceeds of the fraud had found their way into these trusts, so that they could be traced and recovered by the plaintiff; and, secondly, that the terms of the trusts gave the Sheikh such control over the trust property that it had to be regarded as his property. The trustees resisted the plaintiffs' claim for immediate enforcement, arguing that until the validity of the trusts had been determined no judgment could be entered. However, the Jersey Court of Appeal refused to consider the objections of the trustees. It held that if the trusts had actually received the proceeds of fraud, the trust property could be recovered. While this aspect of the court's judgment could not be faulted, the court went much further, by holding that, even if the first question had not been determined, and notwithstanding the fact that there were other objects of the discretionary trusts, the Sheikh's wife and son, the court could disregard their legal positions and require the trustees to pay the plaintiffs' claims against the Sheikh out of the trust property. This second aspect of the court's decisions casts doubt on the legal efficacy of all asset protection trusts.

On 9 January 2001 the Jersey Court of Appeal then dealt with the 2000 action, deciding whether the trustee of the two discretionary Jersey trusts, with assets of about $18 million, frozen by a *Mareva* injunction, should pay them over to the plaintiff in partial satisfaction of its English judgment. The trustee had surrendered to the court its discretion in this matter.

This decision clearly states that the court is simply considering the exercise of the trustee's discretion because the trustee had surrendered it to the court. It says that:

> 'These powers must be exercised in the interests of the beneficiaries and on the basis of a valid trust containing untainted assets. The Court cannot have regard [in the current proceeding] to whether or not the assets in the trusts might have been stolen from GT or, even if not stolen, might have been contributed to the trusts in order to hide them from GT.'

It held that these were issues in a 1999 action in Jersey, which had not yet been determined. Not surprisingly, therefore, it held that a distribution of trust property to GT in reduction of Sheikh Fahad's debt would not be for his benefit and ought not to be made by the court. There were other objects of the trusts, including the Sheikh's wife and adult son, upon whom the court, acting in place of the trustee, ought not to impose its sense of morality. To do otherwise would be, in effect, a back-door method of satisfying creditors' claims against assets which were not in law available for creditors – it would set a dangerous precedent.[1]

In the end, GT's right to claim the trusts' assets will still have to be resolved in the 1999 action, in which it was alleged *inter alia* that there was a proprietary (tracing) claim against some of the assets, that the trusts were shams, not intended to be acted upon, and that the powers conferred on the Sheikh, the settlor of these trusts, were sufficient to treat him as the owner of the trusts' property.[2]

For other methods of attacking discretionary trusts, see the discussion of *Browne v Browne*,[3] in an article by John Mowbray, entitled 'Shams, Pretences, Blackmail and Illusion: Part 2'[4] and an article by Frank Hicks QC, 'Trusts under Attack'.[5]

The reasons given by the Bahamian Court of Appeal for upholding the injunction in the *Grupo Torras* case must be regarded as possibly breaking new ground, by establishing the principle that trust provisions such as those cited above may be sufficient, of themselves, to entitle a court to treat the person who provided funds to the trust as the real owner of the trust assets. Such a principle would come as a shock to many trust lawyers.

It would come as a shock especially to North American lawyers, who are accustomed to accept as a valid trust a revocable *inter vivos* trust, frequently referred to as a 'living trust', a very common part of US and Canadian estate planning practice. The typical revocable *inter vivos* trust involves the settlement of property on one or more trustees on terms that the income will be payable each year to the settlor and that the settlor will be entitled also to require the trustees to make capital distributions to him, at his request. The settlor will

---

1 [*Editor's note:* The court's decision was upheld on appeal: see *Abacus (CI) Ltd v Al Sabah* [2001] 4 ITELR 555, and the discussion in Chapter 7, at **7.3.11**.]

2 [*Editor's note:* For more recent developments in the litigation, see Chapter 7, at **7.3.11**.]

3 [1989] 1 FLR 291, CA (England).

4 (2000) *Private Client Business* 105; as well as an article in a US publication *Business Week* (26 July 1999), p 102.

5 (2001) *Trusts and Estates Law Journal* 9.

even be entitled to revoke the trust during his lifetime. Upon the settlor's death, the remaining capital will be dealt with by the trustees in much the same way as if the trust provisions were contained in a will. The settlor customarily retains the right to amend the terms of the trust, permitting him to change the beneficiaries who will receive the trust property after the settlor's death. When one adds to the list of retained powers the fact that the settlor is often, although certainly not invariably, the sole trustee during his lifetime, it is difficult to reconcile the prevalent North American view of the validity of a revocable *inter vivos* trust with the tenor of the views expressed by the Bahamian Court of Appeal in the *Grupo Torras* case.

Perhaps more disturbing, and of greater relevance to lawyers in other jurisdictions based on English law, were suggestions in the reasons for judgment in *Rahman v Chase Bank (CI) Trust Co*,[1] which may perhaps be *obiter*, that the retention of extensive powers by the settlor over the operations of the trust powers (which he not merely exercised, but on a number of occasions went well beyond) invalidated the trust.

In *Rahman* the settlor had transferred assets to a company on trust for himself for life, then for such of a specified class as he should appoint, but in default for certain beneficiaries. He had power in his lifetime, with the trustee's consent, to appoint capital as he saw fit to anyone including himself, and without the trustee's consent similarly to appoint in any 12-month period one-third of the then capital. The trustee had an independent dispositive power to transfer the capital to the settlor and in doing so had to have regard exclusively to the settlor's interests. All of the trustee's significant administrative powers, including powers of investment and of delegation, required his prior written consent for their exercise.

The court also referred particularly to a provision in the trust instrument dealing with the appointment by the settlor of an investment adviser and stating, 'if and so far as the Trustees follow the advice proffered by such investment adviser they shall not be responsible for the success or failure of the policy so pursued'. The court commented, 'The effect of [this clause] is that both trustee and investment adviser escaped all liability to the settlor and could safely accept his [the settlor's] instructions, which clearly they did'. This clause seems to be similar to those which are commonly employed when an investment adviser selected by the settlor is employed to advise the trustee, on the understanding that the trustee is not really intended to exercise any independent judgment concerning investments, so that the trustee is indemnified if loss results to the trust as a result of the trustee's reliance on such advice. It may therefore be less dangerous merely to state specifically that the trustee is free to reject any advice given by the adviser, but if the trustee chooses to accept such advice it should not be liable for any resulting loss.

---

1 [1991] JLR 103.

It is the view of Professor David Hayton that a trust in which the settlor reserves such extensive rights and interests over both the capital and the income that he has, in effect, not parted with any interest at all will be entirely ineffective, unless it is executed in accordance with the formalities of a will, in which case it will take effect only on the settlor's death.[1]

However, only a fine line distinguishes such a situation from one in which the settlor has actually, at the outset, conferred real interests, whether immediate or future, on other persons, even if such interests can be extinguished by the exercise of the settlor's reserved powers. It is on this latter basis that the revocable *inter vivos* trust, so common in the United States and, to a lesser extent, also in Canada, as a device for avoiding probate of a will, can be upheld. If it is clear that the trustee of such a trust has assumed possession of the settled property and has dealt with it strictly in accordance with the terms of the trust instrument, it should be recognised as legally effective. Where, as is common in the United States, the settlor is himself the sole trustee during his lifetime, it is essential that he clearly distinguish between the trust property and his own personal property, failing which the trust may fail.

The late Professor James A Casner, the pre-eminent estate planning authority in the United States, was a strong proponent of revocable *inter vivos* trusts as early as 1960.[2] Professor John R Price calls the trust 'one of the most important and flexible devices available to the estate planner'.[3]

The fourth edition of the leading US text *The Law of Trusts* by AW Scott and WF Fratcher, provides a categorical statement of the validity of the revocable *inter vivos* trust, in the following terms:[4]

> 'It is well settled that the reservation by the settlor of a power to revoke the trust does not of itself make the trust testamentary. It is also settled ... that the reservation by the settlor of a life interest does not make the trust testamentary. Does the reservation of a life interest together with a power of revocation have any greater effect? It is clear that it does not. If the owner of property transfers it in trust to pay the income to himself for life and on his death to pay the principal to others, reserving power to revoke the trust at any time as long as he lives, it is held that the trust is not testamentary. It is immaterial whether the settlor reserves simply a power to revoke the whole trust at one time or whether he reserves also a power to revoke the trust as to any part of the property from time to time. It is immaterial that the power to revoke includes a power to revoke by will as well as a power to revoke by a transaction inter vivos. It is immaterial that the settlor reserves not only a power to revoke the trust but in addition a power to alter or modify its terms.[5]

---

1 See 'When is a Trust not a Trust' [1992] 5 *Journal of International Planning* 3; Art 918 of the Liechtenstein Law of Persons and Companies provides that when a trustee must comply with the continuous instructions of the settlor, the relationship is treated as a simple mandate; presumably, in these circumstances the trust property is treated as being that of the settlor.

2 'Estate Planning – Avoidance of Probate' (1960) 60 *Columbia Law Review* 108.

3 In *Price on Contemporary Estate Planning*, a leading US text (Little, Brown & Co, 1992).

4 At para 57.1.

5 Interestingly, the authors cite *inter alia* in support of this statement a British Columbia decision *In re Evans* [1956] 7 DLR 445, which quoted from Scott the view here expressed.

> The reservation of a power of revocation and modification does not prevent the creation of a trust in the lifetime of the settlor, and the beneficiary at once acquires a future interest, although it is an interest subject to be divested by the exercise of the power. The death of the settlor is not a condition precedent to the vesting of the interest in the beneficiary. The distinction between a disposition to take effect only on the death of the donor and one to take effect immediately but subject to be revoked by the donor may seem to be formal rather than substantial, but it is an important one, and one which has a determinative effect on other problems than those here under consideration.'

The leading Canadian text, Professor Donovan WM Waters' *Law of Trusts in Canada*[1] discusses (at p 158) the degree of control which a settlor may retain without invalidating the trust, in the following terms:

> 'Suppose, then, that the settlor fully intends a trust, a trust is created, but in that trust a power of revocation is reserved to the settlor. Necessarily that power can only be exercised until the time of his death. Does this make the trust testamentary? The marked trend of the cases, reflected in the categorical statement of the Restatement [Restatement of Trusts, 2d, para 57] is to the effect that the power of revocation is not enough … If the modern cases are correct, and they constitute the overwhelming majority, then whether the settlor retains a limited or a general power of revocation, that power must be seen in the context of the entire settlement terms. On its own this power merely means that – though the settlor has fully set up the trust, conveying title to the trustees or clearly constituting himself trustee of the title – the power to bring the trust to a close does not constitute such a degree of control over the trust property that the inter vivos trust becomes in fact testamentary.'

In light of these impressive American and Canadian authorities, it would seem that the hesitancy of some English trust lawyers to make use of revocable *inter vivos* trusts is not indicative of the state of the law in the common law jurisdictions of North America. It is probably not even indicative of English law, having regard to the decision in *Tompson v Browne*.[2] This decision is the basis for the following comment by John Goodwill:

> 'It is very well settled as a matter of English law that an inter vivos settlement may reserve extensive interests and powers to the settlor, including a first life interest and an unfettered power of revocation, whilst still being entirely valid as an inter vivos disposition. There does, however, have to be some transfer of an equitable interest in the trust property [to someone other than the settlor] (even if it may be defeasible by the settlor exercising a reserved power of appointment or a power of revocation) for a valid inter vivos trust to be created.'[3]

It almost certainly follows that if the retention of massive powers by a settlor who establishes a revocable *inter vivos* trust does not result in its invalidity, the retention of lesser powers in an offshore trust, such as were involved in *Rahman* and *Grupo Torras*, would not, by itself, invalidate it.

---

1 2nd ed, 1984.

2 (1835) 3 My & K 32 at 35–36.

3 'Planning to Resist Hostile Legislation' [1999] JTCP 157, pp 159–162.

However, whether an English or other non-North American court would reach a similar conclusion is, as yet, unclear.

Bahamas Trustee Act 1998, s 3 specifically permits the retention by the settlor of an extensive list of powers, but it is unclear whether another jurisdiction would regard such retention as invalidating the trust. Similar provisions appear in Cook Islands International Trusts Act 1984, s 13C and Nevis International Exempt Trust Ordinance 1994, s 47.[1]

---

1 Although Cayman Islands legislation in the Trusts (Amendment) (Immediate Effect and Reserved Powers) Law 1998, is not as widely drawn as the other examples given it should also be referred to.

PART 3

The Civil Law Perspective

Editor's introduction to Part 3

In the planning stages of this book I intended to write for this Part an outline of the difficulties of reconciliation between civil law and common law. However, I abandoned this intention when Professor Donovan Waters' paper on the future of the trust became available – just in time for publication in this volume.[1] Professor Waters' contribution contains a graphic account of the difficulties which civil lawyers have with trust concepts, and includes discussion of a wide range of civil law and mixed jurisdictions.

The chapters in this Part deal with two civil law jurisdictions of particular interest in the context of trust recognition – namely Switzerland, which has not ratified the Hague Trusts Convention, and Italy, which has.

[1] It is reproduced, with some revision, as Chapter 14.

Chapter 12

SWITZERLAND

Alfred E von Overbeck[*]

12.1 INTRODUCTION[1]

There is no institution known as a 'trust', or any equivalent institution, in Swiss law. Practitioners tend to have recourse to trusts of other jurisdictions. This is mainly in the context of Swiss banks, notaries or attorneys acting for a foreign client. For persons domiciled in Switzerland, the possibilities for creating a trust are limited.

A Swiss banker, Ms Durr Gerber, has compared the advantages and disadvantages of trust companies in Switzerland or offshore.[2] She concluded that, at least as long as the Hague Convention on the Law Applicable to Trusts and on their Recognition 1985[3] has not been ratified by Switzerland, Switzerland is 'a very thorny environment for trust services' and that a fully

---

[*] Professor emeritus of the University of Fribourg (Switzerland) and former director of the Swiss Institute of Comparative Law, 15 Rue Forel, CH-1162 Saint-Prex.

[1] The following are cited only by name or abbreviation: C Reymond 'Le trust et le droit suisse' (1954) *Zeitschrift für schweizerisches Recht* (ZSR) 119a; FT Gubler 'Besteht in der Schweiz ein Bedürfnis nach Ein führung des Instituts der angelsächsischen Treuhand (trust)?' (1954) ZSR 215a, discussion, ibid, at 504a; Michel Jaccard (ed) *Droit et pratique des opérations fiduciaires en Suisse* CEDIDAC Vol 29 (Lausanne, 1994) (hereafter CEDIDAC 29); R Watter 'Die Treuhand im Schweizer Recht' (1995) ZSR II, 179; L Thévenoz 'La *fiducie*, cendrillon du droit suisse' (1995) ZSR 253; discussion, ibid, at 509; L Thévenoz and J-Ph Dunand 'La *fiducie*: droit des biens ou droit des obligations?' Swiss Reports Presented at the XVth International Congress of Comparative Law (Bristol, 1998), Publications of the Swiss Institute of Comparative Law, Vol 34 (Zurich, 1998), p 479; P Breitschmid *Trust and Nachlassplanung, Rechtskollisionen, Festschrift für Anton Heini* (Zurich, 1995), p 49; P Supino *Rechtsgestaltung mit Trust aus Schweizer Sicht* (St Gallen, 1994); DA Dreyer 'Le trust en droit suisse' *Etudes suisses de droit international*, Vol 21 (Geneva, 1981); A Necker *Fiduciary Institutions in Swiss Law, and Attorneys Acting as Trustees/Fiduciaries in The International Academy of Estate and Trust Law, Switzerland* (1991), p 4; (1996), p 12. See also recently, F Guillaume 'Incompatibilité du trust avec le droit Suisse? Un mythe s'effrite' (2000) 10 *Swiss Review of International and European Law* 1; DG Forbes-Jaeger and E Stormann 'The Trust in Switzerland – Revisited' [2000] JTCP 141.

[2] [1996] *Trust & Trustees* 38.

[3] For text, see Appendix and Report of the Hague Conference.

operative trust company in an offshore jurisdiction is preferable. This view is confirmed by other practitioners.[1]

There are no Swiss opinions on the basis of which trusts under a foreign law could be created in purely internal situations. Contrary to the opinions of some Italian writers,[2] the general view in Switzerland seems to be that this would remain the case even if the Hague Convention on Trusts were ratified.

This chapter first examines the private international law on trusts (**12.2**) and then the question of introducing trusts in Switzerland (**12.3**). Some Swiss institutions which fulfil functions comparable to those of trusts are then described (**12.4**), followed by some remarks on taxation (**12.5**).

12.2 FOREIGN TRUSTS IN SWITZERLAND

Swiss writers and some court decisions have generally held that foreign trusts, as regularly used by practitioners, are recognised in Switzerland. The most often quoted decision is the *Harrison Trust* case of 29 January 1970.[3] However, this case concerned a particular situation. The trustee of a 'settlement' (which had all the characteristics of a trust) was a Swiss bank, and by a supplementary arrangement the Canton of Zurich was chosen as forum. The Federal Court considered that in Swiss law there was no institution corresponding exactly to the 'settlement', stating in particular that the Swiss legal principles did not allow for the split ownership which it considered characteristic to a trust. The court tried to identify Swiss institutions which most resembled trusts in their legal consequences, and would thus enable the settlement to qualify *lege fori* as a mixed contract governed by Swiss law according to Swiss conflict-of-laws rules. In addition, the court considered that the choice of a Swiss forum constituted a presumption for the choice of Swiss substantial law. This reasoning is not convincing and the actual terms of the 'settlement' would have suggested rather an implied choice of the common law system of the settlor's domicile.[4]

Having decided on the application of Swiss law, the court then proceeded to implement the 'settlement' by utilising a number of Swiss institutions such

---

1 See also Watter, n 1 on p 547.

2 M Lupoi 'Effects of the Hague Convention in a Civil Law Country' in P Jackson and AC Wilde (eds) *The Reform of Property Law* (Dartmouth, 1997), p 22 and 'The Domestic Trust Theory Upheld in Italy' in (1988) *Trusts & Trustees* 24.

3 *Harrison v Schweiz Kreditanstalt, Arrêts du Tribunal fédéral suisse, Recueil officiel* (ATF) 96 II 79, *Journal des Tribunaux* (JT) 1971 I 329, note C Reymond, p 322; *Annuaire suisse de droit international*, 1971, Vol XXVII, p 223, note F Vischer, p 237; see also Thévenoz and Dunand, p 505; Supino, p 81; Dreyer, pp 118, 125; Necker, p 45 (all at n 1 on p 547).

4 Such an approach would have made the court's task much easier. It was followed by the Appellate Court of Paris in the case of *Courtois v Ganay* (10 January 1970), *Revue critique de droit international privé* 1971, p 518; note G Droz, p 525; *Journal du droit international*, 1973, p 207, note Y Loussouarn, ibid, p 214.

as power of attorney (*mandat*), fiduciary transfer of ownership, gift (*donation*) and stipulation for a third person (*stipulation pour autrui*) and finally, to a large extent, managed to realise the intentions of the 'settlor'.

The Swiss Statute on Private International Law, which came into force on 1 January 1989, does not contain any specific conflicts rule for trusts.[1] However, the contractual approach followed by the Federal Court in the *Harrison* case could no longer prevail. It is generally agreed that Arts 150–165 dealing with companies apply to most trusts, which would fall under the definition of Art 150:[2]

> 'As used in this Statute, the term companies means organized bodies of persons and organized units of assets.'

The *Einzelrichter im beschleunigten Verfahren am Bezirksgericht Zurich* applied Arts 150 *et seq* to a Guernsey trust in a decision of 1 February 1994, relating to bankruptcy proceedings against the infamous raider and swindler WKR.[3] The judge thoroughly discussed Guernsey and Jersey law, and the general principles of trusts. He considered that the trust was formally constituted according to Guernsey law, but that it was void because the settlor had no intention of creating a real trust and because he retained complete control over the trust assets.[4]

In a decision of 3 September 1999, the Swiss Federal Court abandoned the contractual approach of *Harrison Trust* and applied Jersey law to an express trust created in that jurisdiction.[5] The court held that the trust assets were sufficiently organised to fall under the provision of Art 150(1). It considered that Jersey had amended its statute in order to facilitate the introduction of the Hague Convention on Trusts and that conditions of the Convention set out in Art 2 were fulfilled. According to Art 154(1) of the statute, the court thus applied Jersey law under which the trust was organised.

In a decision of 19 November 2001, the Swiss Federal Court, confirming the judgments of the Geneva Courts, went a step further by declaring a constructive trust.[6] This case concerned the aftermath of 'Irangate'. To cover

---

1 Loi fédérale sur le droit international privé (LDIP) of 18 December 1987, *Recueil systématique du droit fédéral* (RS) 291, Art 90(2).

2 F Vischer *IPRG Kommentar* (Zurich, 1993), No 13 ad Art 150, p 1324; A Von Planta *Internationales Privatrecht, Kommentar* (Basel, 1996), Nos 12–15, p 1124; R Pease, 'The Tax Free Trinity: Switzerland, Liechtenstein and Monaco' in B McCutcheon and PC Soames (eds) *EURO-TRUSTS* (1993), p 239. Translation from PA Karrer and KW Arnold *Switzerland's Private International Law Statute 1987* (Deventer, 1989).

3 (1999) 52 *Blötter für zürcherische Rechtsprechung* 225 at 228. Summary and translation of substantial excerpts, Forbes-Jaeger and Stormann, n 1 on p 547, p 141.

4 See also Thomas A Wach 'Appraisal of a Guernsey Trust under Swiss law by the District Court of Zurich' (2000) *Trusts & Trustees* 28.

5 Tribunal fédéral Ie Cour civile *G v C Trust Co (Jersey) Ltd* (2000) *Semaine judiciare* I p 269, comment by Forbes-Jaeger and Stormann, n 1 on p 547, p 156.

6 Tribunal fédéral IIe Cour civile, No 5C.169/2001, *X v Etats-Unis d'Amérique* (not yet published).

his fees, a Geneva lawyer had seized (*séquestré*) about one million Swiss francs placed in several accounts in the name of H (an auxiliary of Colonel N who was in charge of the 'enterprise') at Swiss banks and financial societies. The United States claimed this amount. The court considered that H was an agent of the United States and, according to former Swiss case-law similar to the provisions of the statute, that the relationship between H and the United States was governed by US law. (The court did not designate a particular State of the United States, although it made reference to the American Law Institute's Restatement of the Conflict of Laws.) The court, after a thorough review of Swiss authors, decided that H had to be considered a 'constructive trustee' and that the United States could exercise a right *in rem* on the seized amounts. The court held that the distinction between legal ownership and equitable ownership is not incompatible with the Swiss principle of *numerus clausus* of real rights and that it is not contrary to Swiss *ordre public* that the United States as equitable owners are better protected that a Swiss *fiduciant* would be in a similar case.

Swiss banks, other financial institutions, and notaries have frequently to deal with foreign trusts. It should be noted that foreigners domiciled in Switzerland can choose in a will their national law instead of Swiss domiciliary law to govern their succession upon death.[1] A trust valid under that chosen law is thus effective in Switzerland. If a situation has sufficient connections with a foreign jurisdiction, there may be a Swiss trustee of a trust governed by foreign law.

AF Schnitzer sees as the greatest obstacle to trusts the difficulty which Swiss courts would have in exercising the supervision which English courts are accustomed to exercise.[2] Recently, however, a registrar of the Zurich *Obergericht* and lecturer, P Breitschmid, expressed the opinion that Swiss judges could quite well undertake such a function.[3] But what may be possible in Zurich might not be possible everywhere, as the organisation of the Swiss courts and civil procedure are mainly a matter for the law of each of the 26 Cantons.

Thévenoz considers it possible *de lege ferenda* to appoint a protector having powers, to a greater or lesser extent, over the fiduciary assets.[4] Watter recommends the establishment of a private system of supervision.[5] According to Necker, it is not uncommon for Swiss notaries or attorneys to serve as protectors to trusts created abroad for clients.[6]

One should keep in mind that the location of trust funds in Switzerland is subject to increasingly stringent measures against money laundering and other

---

1 LDIP, n 1 on p 549, Art 90(2).

2 'Trust und Stiftung' (1965) *Schweizerische Juristen-Zeitung* 197, 213 and 215; see also Gubler (1954) ZSR 420a.

3 Breitschmid, n 1 on p 547, p 65.

4 Thévenoz, n 1 on p 547, p 347.

5 Watter, n 1 on p 547, no 30, p 214.

6 Necker, n 1 on p 547, p 125.

criminal activities. According to a *Convention de diligence* between Swiss banks, the real owner of funds has to be identified. The obligations under this Convention are reinforced by provisions of criminal law.[1] In addition, since 1 April 1998 not only banks, but all financial institutions are under an obligation to inform the relevant authorities about any suspect transaction and to block the assets in question until an official decision is given.[2]

The ratification of the Hague Convention on Trusts[3] would, of course, facilitate trust activities in Switzerland. It determines the law applicable to trusts and provides for their recognition. Foreign trusts are subjected to the law chosen by the settlor or the law with which they have the closest connection, and are recognised with some restrictions. The Convention provides also for the recognition of institutions other than the typical common law trust. The present Swiss *fiducie* would not fulfil the criteria of the Convention, especially as far as separation of assets is concerned. However, the reinforced *fiducie* which, as we shall see, has been proposed by several Swiss writers, could be recognised under the Convention.[4] The same is true under recent Swiss banking law for the so-called 'Trust Agreement'. Professor Giovanoli has stressed this point and its importance for the Swiss financial environment at the Lausanne Colloquy.[5] Similar opinions were expressed at seminars organised by the Society of Trust and Estate Practitioners in Geneva and Zurich in May 1996 and at a meeting of Swiss private international law professors in Lausanne in March 1997. Banking circles, who used to be opposed to the Convention, seem to have become more favourably disposed to it.[6] It might be useful to follow the Dutch example and, in the context of ratification of the Convention, to introduce some statutory provisions on transfer of funds and separation of assets.[7]

---

1 Code pénal suisse, Arts 305 bis and 305 ter; Pease, n 2 on p 549, p 243; L Chan Keller 'Disclosure dilemma in Switzerland' in B McCutcheon and PC Soames (eds) *EURO-TRUSTS* (1993), p 225.

2 Loi fédérale concernant la lutte contre le blanchiment d'argent dans le secteur financier, RS 955.0.

3 See n 3 on p 547.

4 Thévenoz, p 350; Watter, No 217; Thévenoz and Dunand, p 506 (all n 1 on p 547).

5 CEDIDAC 29, p 216.

6 See A Fuchs *Soll die Schweiz die Haager Trust-Konvention ratifizieren?* (Publikation der Swiss Banking School, Zurich, no 188, 1998). The Swiss Ministry of Justice planned to organise a conference on the Convention in May 2002.

7 AE von Overbeck 'La ratification de la Convention de La Haye sur le trust par les Pays-Bas: un exemple pour la Suisse?' in *Collisio Legum Etudes de droit international privé pour Gerardo Broggini* (Milan, 1997), pp 367, 379. Thévenoz and Dunand, n 1 on p 547, p 507, think that the problem could be solved by case-law.

12.3 SHOULD TRUSTS BE INTRODUCED INTO SWISS SUBSTANTIVE LAW?

The question of whether trusts should be introduced into Swiss law has been raised from time to time. In particular it was discussed at the Swiss *Juristentag*, the meeting of the respected Swiss Lawyers Association (*Juristenverein*), in 1954. The reporters to the meeting were two practising lawyers of high standing, Dr FT Gubler and (later Professor) C Reymond.[1] Reymond drew attention to the comments made by an English author, FW Weiser,[2] according to whom in no country other than Switzerland is there such a contrast between the extensive use of the *fiducie* and an absence of efforts to introduce something similar to a trust.

Both reporters concluded that it was not possible to constitute a trust according to Swiss law, and that introduction of the institution would be contrary to the spirit of Swiss law and would meet dogmatic objections, especially in relation to the unity of property and the *numerus clausus* of real rights. They wished to improve the system of the *fiducie*, notably as far as protection of the assets are concerned, and possibly develop other institutions such as the testamentary executor and the family foundation.[3] In the discussion, Wyler, who had already published articles in favour of the trust in the 1930s, defended the possibility of introducing such an institution. However, especially in view of an investigation amongst interested circles, he accepted the idea that there was no need for a trust in Switzerland.[4]

The negative attitude of Swiss lawyers was criticised in 1955 by P Lepaulle, who submitted that the lack of the concepts of legal or equitable title in Swiss law should not prevent the introduction of a reasonable trust.[5]

A more positive attitude has also been taken by other authors, most notably by AF Schnitzer. He challenges the current conviction that real and obligatory rights are hermetically separated and that the principles on real rights of continental jurisdictions are inviolable.[6] According to Schnitzer, the *numerus clausus* theory in relation to real rights is only a scientific affirmation that is not laid down in any law. He demonstrates that trusts have been introduced in many mixed and civil law jurisdictions. Indeed, the split ownership which causes difficulties to civil lawyers is not an essential feature of trusts. In Scottish law, for instance, the only real rights are those of the trustee.[7]

---

1 (1954) ZSR 19a–476a and 504a–551a.

2 *Trust on the Continent of Europe* (1936), p 45.

3 See Supino, n 1 on p 547, p 143.

4 (1954) ZSR 519.

5 'Réflexions sur l'expansion des trusts' (1955) *Revue internationale de droit comparé* 318; cited by Supino, n 1 on p 547, p 144.

6 'Die Treuhand – Der Trust – und das Internationale Privatrecht' in *Gedächtnisschrift Ludwig Marxer* (1963), p 79. The recent decisions mentioned above confirm this view.

7 See KGC Reid, Scottish National Report, *Principles of European Trust Law* (1999), p 67.

As we shall see, current opinion in Switzerland does not favour the formal introduction of trusts, but prefers a reinforcement of the *fiducie*, especially in relation to the separation of assets.[1]

12.4 SOME SWISS INSTITUTIONS FULFILLING FUNCTIONS COMPARABLE TO THOSE OF TRUSTS

In Swiss law, various institutions can fulfil some of the purposes for which trusts are used. In fact, as Dr P Supino has convincingly demonstrated in his doctoral thesis, some parallels between Swiss institutions and the trust can be discovered, but none of the former can be assimilated with the latter.[2] For instance, the representative of a group of bondholders is not owner of the assets mortgaged in favour of the bondholders.[3] We shall discuss only two such institutions: the foundation and the *fiducie*.[4]

12.4.1 The foundation

The foundation (*fondation*, *Stiftung*) is governed by Arts 80 to 89 bis of the Swiss Civil Code.[5] To create a foundation, a patrimony has to be dedicated to a specific purpose by will or by a public deed. The foundation becomes a legal person by its registration in the *registre du commerce*.[6] This formality is not necessary for ecclesiastical and family foundations. The foundation is organised according to the act creating it and again, except for ecclesiastical and family foundations, placed under the supervision of the federal, cantonal or communal authority, depending on the scope of its activities.

Exceptionally, foundations may have a commercial purpose, but in principle they should pursue only philanthropical aims. They are very widely used for charitable, cultural and similar purposes. Foundations for social security of employees are very numerous, especially since the introduction of a compulsory pensions scheme in 1982.[7] It could be argued that the foundation

---

1 Things may change if Switzerland should ratify the Hague Convention on Trusts (see n 3 on p 547): this could promote a movement towards the introduction of domestic trusts, as the example of The Netherlands shows. See J Van Rijn van Alkamade 'Yes, the Dutch can tame the trust' WPNR 1998, no 6317, p 361, no 6318, p 379.

2 Supino, n 1 on p 547, p 112; see also Thévenoz, n 1 on p 547, p 296; Landolf and Graf, 'Der Trust im schweizerischen Steuerrecht' (1996/7) 63 *Archiv für schweizerisches Abgaberecht* 1.

3 Supino, n 1 on p 547, p 98; Code Civil Suisse (CCS), RS 210, Art 875; Code des Obligations (CO), RS 220, Arts 1157–1186.

4 One should also mention the *fonds de placement*, governed by a Federal Statute of 18 March 1994 (RS 951.31) which corresponds to mutual funds, investment trusts, and unit trusts: Thévenoz and Dunand, n 1 on p 547, pp 479, 483, 502.

5 See Tuor, Schnyder and Schmid *Das schweizerische Zivilgesetzbuch* (11th ed, 1995), p 143; H-M Riemer *Berner Kommentar zum schweizerischen Privatrecht, Bd I 3 Abt 3 Teilbd, Art 80–89 bis ZGB, Die Stiftungen.*

6 ATF 120 II 141.

7 Tuor, Schnyder and Schmid, n 5 above, p 145.

functions in the same way as charitable trusts in common law countries, even if it lacks the flexibility of a trust.[1]

The foundation can to a limited extent be used for beneficiaries in the sense of trust law. Swiss law has its own brand of rule against perpetuities. *Fidéicommis de famille* may not be constituted (Art 335(2) of the Swiss Civil Code)[2] and *substitution fidéicommissaire* is limited to one reversionary heir (Art 488 of the Swiss Civil Code).[3] A foundation cannot be constituted for the benefit of a specified person. Family foundations may be created by dedicating a patrimony to a certain family but a foundation cannot just provide income without qualification. Such a foundation can only cover the cost of carrying out specific purposes such as education, outfitting, or support in case of need, of the family members. The Federal Court has construed the statute narrowly.[4] It has been held by several writers that the scope of the family foundation should be broadened to allow trust-like arrangements. Objections on grounds of perpetuity could be met if the duration of such a foundation were limited.[5]

12.4.2 The *fiducie* in general

Present law

The institution with the closest resemblance to a trust is the *fiducie*, or *acte fiduciaire* (*Treuhand*), as developed by case-law.[6] It is used either as *fiducia cum creditore* for security, or as *fiducia cum amico* for purposes of administration or deposit of funds. This chapter will concentrate on the deposit of funds and also leave aside the special considerations applicable in the case of immovables.[7] Rapp gives the following definition of *fiducie*:[8]

> 'Contrat par lequel une personne, le fiduciant, transfère un droit à une autre, le fiduciaire, qui s'oblige à en user selon les indications du fiduciant, en général à le retransférer dans certaines conditions.'

---

1 Necker, n 1 on p 547, p 47.

2 Tuor, Schnyder and Schmid, n 5 on p 553, p 143.

3 A few ancient *Fidéicommis* still exist: see R Pahud de Mortanges 'Gegenwartslösungen für ein historisches Rechtsinstitut: Das Familienfideikommiss' in *Famille et Droit* (Mélanges Bernhard Schnyder, 1995), p 499.

4 ATF 73 II 86, 89 II 473. In 93 II 439 the Federal Court converted a family foundation which did not meet its criteria in an ordinary foundation. In 108 II 293 it decided that maintaining a vacation chalet could not be the purpose of a family foundation.

5 AF Schnitzer *Revue critique de droit international privé* (1965) 479; P Hefti (1954) ZSR 551a; Thévenoz, n 1 on p 547, p 300.

6 It was first recognised in 1905 by the Federal Court, ATF 31 II 105. See especially Thévenoz and Dunand, n 1 on p 547; see further G Reymond et J Revaclier 'Les opérations fiduciaires en droit suisse' in *Les opérations fiduciaires (pratiques, validite, regime juridique dans plusieurs pays européens et dans le commerce international)* (Colloque de Luxembourg des 20 et 21 septembre 1984, published under the direction of Clause Witz, 1985) (hereafter 'Opérations fiduciaires').

7 On the *fiducie-sûreté,* see Rapp, CEDIDAC 29, p 32.

8 CEDIDAC 29, p 27.

'A contract by which a person, the fiduciant, transfers a right to another person, the fiduciaire, who is obliged to use it according to the instructions of the fiduciant, in general to transfer it back under certain conditions.'

The differences from trusts are obvious. The *fiduciant* (*Treugeber*) is much less protected than the parties to a trust. None of the structures which under common law permit supervision of the trust exist (ie courts, protectors, enforcers). Thévenoz classifies the *fiducie* as *Cendrillon* (Cinderella); while Giovanoli classifies it as *Colosse au pieds d'argile* (an idol with feet of clay).

The Swiss *fiducie* derives from the rules on mandate (*mandat*, *Auftrag*). The *fiduciant* can give the *fiduciaire* any instructions at any time, while normally the settlor cannot dispose of the assets transferred to the trustee. Also, in principle, a *mandat* can be revoked at any time.[1] However, according to recent doctrine, the *mandat* may have only the power, but not the right, to revoke, if the contract provides to the contrary.[2] Some authors even contend that revocation can be altogether excluded by contract.[3] The Federal Court, in an unpublished decision of 26 March 1997, has rejected these opinions and maintained the obligatory character of the revocation.[4]

The *fiducie* is based on the *Vollrechtstheorie*, which means that the *fiduciaire* is full owner of the property.[5] He has more power than needed to fulfil his duties. On the death, incapacity or bankruptcy of the *fiduciaire* the fiduciary agreement ends (Art 405 of the Code of Obligations), unless it continues after the death of the *fiduciaire* according to the will of parties or because of special circumstances.[6] In that case, the fiduciary assets become part of the *fiduciaire*'s estate but his heirs are bound by his obligations. However, in 1992 the Federal Court decided that if one of several fiduciaries dies, the property of the assets accrues to the remaining fiduciaries.[7]

Under present Swiss law the *fiduciant* has few rights against third persons to whom assets may have been transferred: there is nothing comparable to the common law tracing rights of beneficiaries.[8] The acquisition by a third party to whom a *fiduciaire* has transferred assets cannot be challenged even if the third party was acting in bad faith: in the latter case such a third party may have to

---

1 Code des Obligations (CO), RS 220, Art 404.

2 Watter (1995) ZSR 79 *et seq*; Thévenoz, n 1 on p 547, p 339; F Werro *Le Mandat et ses effets* (1993), p 87, summary p 375 nos 1116–1123.

3 P Gauch *Art 404 OR – Sein Inhalt, seine Rechtfertigung and die Frage seines zwingenden Charakters Recht* (1992), p 17.

4 Ref 4C443/1996/zus.

5 Thévenoz, n 1 on p 547, p 274.

6 Watter, n 1 on p 547, Nos 87–88.

7 ATF 78 II 445, 452, JT 1953 I, p 523; see also ATF 91 II 442, 448, JT 1966 I 337; M Schwartz 'Essai d'analyse de la propriété en main commune de plusieurs *fiduciaires*' (1966) *Schweizerische Juristen-Zeitung* 319; Thévenoz, n 1 on p 547, p 276.

8 Thévenoz, n 1 on p 547, p 338, 274 note 77; HC Schulthess and AC Limburg 'Rechtsfragen der Ausüburg von Trustee Funktionen durch Schweizerische Trustees' *Der Schweizer Treuhänder* (1996), p 57, p 59; ATF 91 III 104 *obiter*.

pay damages.[1] If a bank, in breach of its obligation towards a client, has pledged the client's assets to a third party, the client has no right of separation in the bankruptcy of the bank, but can only claim damages against the estate in bankruptcy.[2]

The weakest point of the *fiducie* may be the situation in the case of the bankruptcy of the *fiduciaire*. The fundamental principle of Swiss bankruptcy law is that all the assets of the debtor have to be realised in favour of the creditors, thus including the fiduciary assets which are the full property of the fiduciary.[3]

However, there are some exceptions to this rule.

(i) *Compensation and retention* are restricted in some respects.[4]

(ii) *Article 401(3) of the Code of Obligations.* Article 401(3) of the Code of Obligations (CO) on undisclosed agency states:

> 'Le mandant peut, de même, revendiquer dans la faillite du mandataire les objets mobiliers acquis par ce dernier en son propre nom, mais pour le compte du mandant; sauf à la masse à exercer le droit de rétention qui appartiendrait au mandataire.'

> 'In the case of the agent's bankruptcy the principal may likewise claim the goods acquired by the agent in his own name but on account of the principal; the lien of the agent shall not be affected hereby.'

Should this provision be applicable in the case of *fiducie*? This has been answered in the negative.[5] The Federal Court applied Art 401(3) in a case which is considered the most favourable to *fiducie*.[6] This means that the *fiduciant* can withdraw any funds received by the *fiduciaire* on his behalf, on condition that they are separated from other assets. However, he cannot withdraw assets which he himself has transferred to the *fiduciaire*.

However, there are uncertainties as to the precise scope of this right. As Giovanoli shows, at different stages of a same operation, separation of assets may or may not be possible.[7] In a case decided in 1976 the Federal Court has emphasised the exceptional character of the *Vallugano* solution.[8] It refused separation, in favour of the owner of immovables, of an account in the name of a real estate agent (who became bankrupt) into which rents had been paid.

---

1 According to Watter, n 1 on p 547, Nos 140–143, contrary to the dominant opinion, a third party acting in bad faith does not acquire the property from the *fiduciaire*.

2 B Kleiner and B Lutz *Kommentar zum Bundesgesetz über die Banken und Sparkassen*, 9 Nachlieferung (1997), No 17 ad Art 37b.

3 ATF 117 II 430.

4 Thévenoz, n 1 on p 547, p 329; Watter, n 1 on p 547, Nos 75–76; in banking law, see Giovanoli, CEDIDAC 29, p 221.

5 Gubler (1954) ZSR 261a.

6 *Feras Anstalt e diversi contro Banca Vallugano* (13 July 1973), ATF 99 II 393, JT 1974 I, p 588, note C Reymond (referring also to former cases), p 596; Thévenoz, n 1 on p 547, p 277.

7 CEDIDAC 29, p 198; but see below on the changes resulting from the new provisions on banking law.

8 ATF 102 II 103, 108.

The main argument of the court was that there was a manoeuvre to give preference to a certain creditor. However, it also held that there could be no separation if the sums on the account could not be separately identified. Giovanoli has criticised this decision and considers that the impossibility of opening an *Anderkonto*, as recognised in Germany, constitutes a serious flaw. Giovanoli recommends that this problem should be dealt with by legislation.[1]

In a recent *obiter dictum*, the Federal Court raised the question of whether the application of Art 401(3) should be restricted to short-time *fiducies* where the only purpose is to procure as soon as possible the rights acquired by the *fiduciaire* to the *fiduciant*.[2] It has to be stressed that Art 401(3), even if interpreted broadly, does not apply to funds given by the *fiduciant* to the *fiduciaire*, but only to funds received by the latter from third parties. In the case cited above, the court recognised that the interests are the same in both cases, but felt unable to further enlarge the scope of Art 401(3) contrary to its clear wording.

Proposals for change

(i) The Lausanne Colloquy of 1994. In 1994 the *Centre du droit de l'entreprise* of the University of Lausanne (CEDIDAC) organised a colloquy on *Droit et pratique des opérations fiduciaires*.[3] A draft on *fiducie* along the lines of the new provisions of the Banking Statute was discussed and the hope was expressed that the courts could extend the solutions of that statute to the *fiducie* in general.

(ii) The Juristentag of 1995. In September 1995 the Swiss Lawyers Association discussed *fiducie*.[4] Both reporters spoke strongly in favour of a reinforced *fiducie* which would in fact have the main features of a trust. Thévenoz envisaged legislative action, while Watter would rather have relied on a new interpretation of existing law, without excluding legislation. He questioned the value of the dogmatic arguments founded on the theory of real rights.[5] In addition, why should what was possible for banks not be extended to other fiduciary relationships?[6]

The reporters at the *Juristentag* stated that:

(1) fiduciary assets should be segregated from the private patrimony of the *fiduciaire*;[7]

---

1 CEDIDAC 19, pp 193, 199, 222 and a proposed provision, p 227; see also Watter, n 1 on p 547, Nos 117–119 and note 219.

2 ATF 117 II 429.

3 The results are published in CEDIDAC 29.

4 (1995) ZSR II 179–363 and 509–535.

5 Note 1 on p 547, No 192.

6 Thévenoz, n 1 on p 547, p 283. On banking law see **12.4.3**.

7 Ibid, p 313; Watter, n 1 on p 547, Nos 210–211.

(2) contrary to Art 404 of the Civil Code, the *fiduciant* must have the possibility to stipulate a certain duration and to renounce, or restrict, his right to cancel the *fiducie*. However, a time-limit must be fixed in the case of death of the *fiduciant*;
(3) the *fiduciant* must be able to renounce to give instructions to the *fiduciaire*;
(4) the *fiduciant* must be able to confer rights on beneficiaries and to name a protector;[1]
(5) the *fiduciant* and possible beneficiaries must have a right of tracing against third parties acting in bad faith.[2]

The reporters were of the opinion that such a reinforced *fiducie* would render the formal introduction of trusts unnecessary.[3]

It should be noted that in these discussions the case in which a 'settlor' irrevocably transfers assets to a 'trustee' in favour of 'beneficiaries' was barely mentioned. In banking operations in particular, funds are lent to a third party and these funds eventually return, with interest, to the *fiduciant* who is thus, in terms of trust law, both the settlor and the beneficiary. However, the improved Swiss *fiducie* could well be used to the same purposes as the 'classical' settlor–trustee–beneficiary structure. Thévenoz describes what such a *fiducie-libéralité* could be.[4]

12.4.3 Banking law

By far the most important applications of *fiducie* in Switzerland are to be found in the field of banking. Recent legislation has brought important progress.[5]

The most important operations
The most important operations are as follows.

---

1 Thévenoz, n 1 on p 547, p 347; Watter, n 1 on p 547 No 30, p 214.

2 Thévenoz, op cit, p 338; Watter, op cit, No 141, p 211.

3 Thévenoz, op cit, p 348; Watter, op cit, Nos 217–218, after No 49 he gives a table showing various functions of trusts, their possible construction under present Swiss law and the perspectives of assuming these functions by means of a *fiducie* corresponding to his interpretation, and proposals for change.

4 Thévenoz, op cit, p 300; see also Reymond and Revaclier, 'Opérations fiduciaires', n 4 on p 554, p 440.

5 On fiduciary operations of banks in Switzerland, see G Ferrero, 'Les opérations *fiduciaires* dans la pratique bancaire', CEDIDAC 29, p 89; Necker, n 1 on p 547, p 124; statutory definition in CEDIDAC 29, p 121; M Giovanoli 'Les opérations *fiduciaires* dans la pratique bancaire suisse' in *La fiducie et ses applications dans plusieurs pays européens* (Colloque du 29 Novembre 1990) *Bulletin Jolly*, 1991, no 4 bis, p 31; Reymond and Revaclier, 'Opérations fiduciaires', n 4 on p 554, p 428; and C Reymond 'Aspects fiduciaires de quelques opérations bancaires, principalement dans l'Euromarché', ibid, p 13; Thévenoz and Dunand, n 1 on p 547, p 480. These authors mention also (at p 481) the fiduciary administration of estates, a solution which tends to disappear.

(1) The bank acts as *fiduciaire* in its name, but on behalf of a client (*fiduciant*) in the investment of funds in banks or companies abroad, in consideration for the payment of a fee (*placements fiduciaires*). This operation requires the conclusion of a written contract between the client and the bank. It is interesting to note that the model agreement drafted by the Swiss Bankers Association (*Treuhandvertrag, Contrat fiduciaire*) is called 'Trust Agreement' in English. The client bears the currency risk and the risk associated with the transfer to the foreign bank or company. The bank has the obligation to make the clients the beneficiaries of all income which arises from the investment. In 1992, the volume of these operations, which appear below the line in the balance sheets of the banks, was 320 billion Swiss francs, mostly placed by foreigners in foreign institutions.[1] An elaborate system of prescriptions by the Swiss Banking Commission and directives of the Swiss Bankers Association help to minimise risks for clients (especially compensation) and to prevent money laundering.[2] The contracts with clients generally provide that the *fiduciaire* is free to choose the foreign correspondent within the prescribed regulations.[3]

(2) Loans and fiduciary credits are made by the bank as *fiduciaire* for the benefit and at the risk of the client to third parties chosen by the latter (*prêts et crédits fiduciaires*).

(3) Acting as nominees in relation to foreign corporations (in particular US corporations): the Swiss banks act as shareholders of the corporation, but on behalf of their clients.[4]

(4) The fiduciary transfer for pledge purposes: this occurs, for instance, when the *fiduciant* transfers to the bank (the *fiduciaire*) shares, a mortgage, or assets for the guarantee of a debt to the bank, which the bank will transfer back when the client has paid his debts.

The new provisions of the Banking Statute

The most important recent developments in the matter are the new provisions of the Banking Statute introduced by the revised Bankruptcy Statute which came into force on 1 January 1997.[5] The text of these provisions is as follows:[6]

---

1 Ferrero, CEDIDAC 29, p 90.

2 See P-Y Despland 'Aspects prudentiels des opérations *fiduciaires*, surveillance des banques et des marchés financiers, diligence et vigilance', CEDIDAC 29, p 109.

3 Examples in CEDIDAC 29, p 99.

4 Thévenoz and Dunaud, n 1 on p 547, p 482; L Olgiati *Schweizerische Nominees im Aktienregister amerikanischer Publikumsgesellschaften* (1997).

5 Kleiner and Lutz, n 10 on p 555; U Bertschinger 'Zum neuen bankgesetzlichen Aussonderungsrecht' *Aktuelle juristische Praxis* (1995), p 426; D Zobl 'Kollisionen zwischen Sachen- und Zwangsvollstreckungsrecht' *Trust und Nachlassplanung, Rechtskollisionen, Festschrift für Anton Heini* (1995), pp 543, 547; Thévenoz, n 1 on p 547, p 282; Giovanoli, CEDIDAC 29, p 216.

6 Loi fédérale sur les banques et les caisses d'épargne, RS 952.0.

'Article 16 – Sont réputées valeurs déposées selon l'article 37b de la loi:

1. les choses mobilières et les titres déposés par les clients;
2. les choses mobilières, les titres et les créances que la banque détient à titre fiduciaire pour le compte des clients déposants;
3. les prétentions disponibles de la banque à des livraisons à l'encontre de tiers, résultant d'opérations au comptant, d'opérations à terme échoués, d'opérations de couverture ou d'émissions pour le compte des clients déposants.

Article 37b – En cas de faillite de la banque, les valeurs déposées, au sens de l'article 16, seront distraites de la masse en faillite au bénéfice du déposant, sous réserve des droits de la banque à l'encontre du déposant.

Si la banque en faillite est elle-même déposante auprès d'un tiers, les valeurs déposées seront présumées être celles de ses clients; elles seront dès lors distraites de la masse en faillite, conformément au premier alinéa.

L'administration de la faillite de la banque doit remplir à l'encontre d'un tiers dépositaire les obligations relatives au dépôt et les obligations résultant d'opérations prévues à l'article 16, chiffre 3.'

'Article 16 – Valuables in safekeeping accounts within the meaning of Article 37b of the Law are deemed to be:

1. movable goods and securities of the depositing customer;
2. movable goods, securities and claims which the bank holds on a fiduciary basis for the depositing customer;
3. freely available delivery claims of the bank from third parties from spot transactions, completed forward transactions, collateral transactions or issues for the account of the depositing customer.

Article 37b – Valuables in custody accounts as defined in Article 16 shall not be counted as part of the debtor's assets in the case of bankruptcy but shall be segregated subject to the total claims of the bank against the persons depositing the valuables in his/her favour.

Should the bankrupt bank have deposited itself valuables in custody accounts with a third party, the valuables in custody shall be assumed to be those of its own customers and segregated in accordance with paragraph 1.

The legal administrator of the bank must fulfil their custodian obligations vis-à-vis a third party custodian arising from transactions in accordance with Article 16 point 3.'

Article 16(1) confirms existing law. Article 16(2) contains the presumption that movables, shares and bonds (*titres*, *Effekten*), and claims held by the bank as fiduciary, are *valeurs déposées* (*Depotwerte*) or deposited funds. This is the most important provision because it covers not only funds held by the bank itself, but also the fiduciary operations described above, and shares and bonds not kept by the banks themselves but, as is mostly the case, deposited in central institutions (such as, for Switzerland, the SEGA, *Schweizerische Effekten-Giro AG*). The provision does only cover claims against third parties held by the bank as fiduciary, not debts of the bank itself, for example those represented by current accounts.[1] It applies to the *fiducie* for administration as well as to the *fiducie* for security. The essential difference with the current interpretation of

[1] See Kleiner and Lutz, n 10 on p 555, no 20 ad Art 16.

Art 401(3) of the Code of Obligations in matters of *fiducie* is that Art 16(2) applies to all funds including those remitted directly by the *fiduciant* to the *fiduciaire*.

Article 16(3) provides for the same presumption as far as liquid claims of banks against third persons on behalf of clients are concerned. This provision was drafted to cover the situation where the engagement to deliver bonds, which had been firmly subscribed by a bank, was considered to be not a mandate but a sales contract.[1] Consequently, separation in case of bankruptcy by the bank was not possible. The provision might cause some problems. Sometimes it will be difficult to establish which values due from a third party are to be allocated to which client. Further, what if the values do not cover the claims of all clients?[2]

Article 37b(1) provides for separation of assets in case of bankruptcy in favour of the depositor who has fulfilled all his obligations. Article 37b(2) extends this solution to funds deposited in a third bank and presumes that such deposits belong to the clients. Thus if the bank has deposited assets of clients as well as its own assets of the same type (eg shares in the same company) the client has first claim if the third party is not able to return all the assets.[3] Article 37b(3) preserves the rights of third parties.

Article 37b introduces a special procedure which, compared to the normal bankruptcy proceedings, facilitates the separation of assets. It is applicable both in bankruptcy and in the procedure called *concordat par abandon d'actif* where the assets are liquidated without a formal bankruptcy. In German terminology, the term *Absonderung* is used for this procedure, to distinguish it from the *Aussonderung (revendication)* in other bankruptcy proceedings. According to Art 37b, the liquidators have the duty to separate the values *ex officio*, while in normal bankruptcy proceedings assets must be claimed.

12.5 TAXATION

In Switzerland, each of the 26 Cantons has its own taxation system, and in addition, a federal system of taxation exists. Despite similarities between different laws, and a federal statute aimed at harmonising the systems,[4] Cantons have considerable freedom to legislate and to raise taxes and they can set the tax rates. With the exception of certain rules of the Geneva administration on inheritance tax in the case of trusts,[5] there are no written rules on taxation of trusts and judicial decisions are scarce. The writers who

---

1 ATF 112 II 444; Kleiner and Lutz, n 10 on p 555, no 22 ad Art 16.

2 Zobl, n 5 on p 559, p 553.

3 Kleiner and Lutz, n 10 on p 555, no 19 ad Art 37b.

4 Loi fédérale sur l'harmonisation des impôts directs des cantons et des communes, RS 642.14.

5 Instruction No 103 (May 1977); *Papers of the STEP-Seminar* reproduced and translated by P Sansonetti and K Stoyanov (6 May 1996).

have considered the subject deplore the fact that there is still a considerable uncertainty especially as far as taxation of discretionary trusts is concerned.[1]

Generally, trusts are not subject to tax in Switzerland, and trustees are not taxed.[2]

The following situations can be distinguished.

Neither settlor nor beneficiaries are Swiss residents, but trustees are Swiss residents

In this case, if the situation is clearly established, the income and capital of the trust fund are not taxed in Switzerland. There is a withholding tax of 35 per cent on Swiss shares, bonds and bank accounts which can be claimed back under the double taxation agreements.

Settlor resident in Switzerland

(i) Fixed interest irrevocable trusts. Upon creation of the trust, the settlor has to pay the Swiss cantonal and sometimes communal gift tax (in most Cantons this is similar to inheritance tax).

This tax is low or even non-existent if the donee is a spouse or a descendant of the settlor; in other cases it can be very heavy. The question is which rate should apply at creation of the trust. It can be argued that the degree of kinship between settlor and beneficiary should be taken into account, but apparently at least one Canton, Zurich, taxes at the maximum rate of 36 per cent if, after the creation of the trust, the income and the capital brought into the trust are no longer taxable.[3] Geneva authorities apply rules derived from the principles of taxation of *usufruits* to apportion the charge between life tenant and the remainderman.[4]

(ii) Irrevocable discretionary trusts. Here the solutions are uncertain. According to Pease, the Geneva authorities decide on a case-by-case basis. Landolf and Graf propose either to claim the gift tax only when the fund is delivered to the beneficiaries, or to tax at the moment of constitution of the trust at a mixed rate determined according to the kinship degree between the settlor and the several beneficiaries.

---

1 R Pease 'The Tax Free Trinity: Switzerland, Liechtenstein and Monaco', *EURO-TRUSTS* (1993) p 237; U Landolf and T Graf 'Der Trust im schweizerischen Steuerrecht' (1996/7) 63 *Archiv für schweizerisches Abgaberecht* 1; C Andina 'Die Besteuerung von in der Schweiz wohnhaften Empfängern von Leistungen seitens angelsächischer Trust Settlements' (1993) *Steuer Revue* 201, with indications on the practice of a few Cantons. See also Ph Maillard 'La régime fiscal et comptable des opérations fiduciaires' CEDIDAC 29, p 57, bibliography and table of cases, p 85; W Ryser 'Rapports de trust et impôts directs' (hereafter 'Rapports de trust') (1993) 61 *Archives de droit fiscal suisse* 748; 'Trust and double taxation treaties concluded by Switzerland' (1996/97) *Archives de droit fiscal suisse* 309.

2 However, according to Andina, n 1 above, p 206 the Canton of Zurich taxes resident trustees. We shall see that Landolf and Graf, n 1 above, p 18 propose to tax some discretionary trusts.

3 Landolf and Graf, n 1 above, p 11.

4 Pease, n 1 above, p 241.

(iii) Revocable trusts. In principle the settlor is still taxable for the capital and the income: however, the beneficiaries may be taxed for the income they receive.

(iv) Grantor trusts. The settlor has to pay income and wealth tax on the fund. The inheritance tax is due at the settlor's death, the capitalised value of his income being deducted from the capital.

Beneficiaries resident in Switzerland

(i) Fixed interest trust. The solution of this case is clear following a case decided in the Canton of Vaud and confirmed by the Federal Court.[1] The beneficiary is treated by analogy with an *usufruitier.* He has to pay income tax on the income of the trust fund, but not on capital gains or distribution of capital (which is a gift, so if the settlor is resident in Switzerland he is liable to gift tax).[2]

(ii) Discretionary trusts. Here again the solution is uncertain. According to Pease, the authorities follow a pragmatic approach. If the beneficiary has the 'effective economic enjoyment' of all or part of the income he will be assessed to tax. Otherwise he will not be taxable unless and until income is actually distributed to him.[3] Landolf and Graf seek a solution by taxing the trust as such by way of analogy with the *communauté héréditaire.*[4] Again, double taxation Conventions may have an influence, for example Swiss resident beneficiaries of a United Kingdom discretionary trust are not taxable in Switzerland.[5]

---

1 Commission cantonale de recours en matière d'impôt Vaud (7 June 1983) *Steuerentscheide* 1985 B52.1; Federal Court (5 September 1984) (1986) *Steuer Revue* 592.

2 Landolf and Graf, n 1 on p 562, p 16.

3 Pease, n 1 on p 562, p 242.

4 Landolf and Graf, n 1 on p 562, p 17.

5 Ryser, 'Rapports de trust', n 1 on p 562, p 753 note 8.

Chapter 13

ITALY

Ferdinando Albisinni[*]
Regina Gambino[**]

13.1 INTRODUCTION

In Italy, 10 years after the approval of the law of ratification of the Hague Convention on the Law Applicable to Trusts and on their Recognition 1985 (the Hague Convention),[1] the attitude among practitioners and academics has completely changed: the word 'trust' is no longer absent from the Italian legal vocabulary,[2] and the use of a trust is becoming one of a number of possible structures for holding property by private individuals or economic entrepreneurs, primarily in the areas of estate planning and closely held family businesses.

Even more relevant is the widespread consensus that trusts can be created (and are, in fact, created) by an Italian settlor, with an Italian beneficiary, in some cases with Italian trustees, to regulate assets located in Italy.

The discussion of issues related to trusts is no longer unusual to courts and public offices, and no longer limited to cases involving testamentary trusts of wealthy English people who retired in Italy. Limited in number, but significant in their implications, judicial decisions and the practice of some public offices are confirming the legitimate use of trusts in Italy.[3]

---

* Avvocato partner, Studio Legale Albisinni, Via Ciro Menotti 4 00186, Rome, Italy.
** Attorney admitted in the State of New York.

1 Ratified by Law No 364 of 16 October 1989.

2 For a traditional comparative analysis, under which the trust was deemed incompatible with fundamental principles of civil law systems, see David *I Grandi Sistemi Giuridici contemporanei* (Cedam, 2nd ed, 1973), p 316; for a forceful criticism of these positions from an historical perspective, see M Lupoi 'Il trust nell'ordinamento italiano dopo la Convenzione dell'Aja del 10 luglio 1985' (1992) *Vita notarile* 966; and a following series of significant studies, amongst which the exhaustive publication, *Trusts* (Giuffré, 2001).

3 See **13.5.2**.

Even politicians and legislators are considering the potential use of trusts as a means of resolving controversial issues, as those regarding the conflicts of interest of members of the government and of persons appointed to certain critical public offices, including regulatory agencies.[1]

The forecast made five years ago, in an earlier version of this chapter:

> 'notwithstanding the fact that the Hague Convention regulates private international law issues and is not intended to "introduce the trust concept into the domestic law of countries lacking the concept", it will inevitably have a significant impact on Italian domestic law'

has not only been realised, but in a much shorter time than anyone, including the authors, would have predicted.

In response to the ever-increasing interests in trusts, conferences on the possible use of trusts in Italy,[2] and publications on these themes,[3] have grown significantly in number. In addition to increased exposure with respect to the practical uses of trusts, distinguished legal scholars have published original comparative analyses, and Italian attorneys are, today, expected to have a general (even if not detailed) knowledge of common law trusts and the implications of the Hague Convention, in a situation significantly different from that which was common 10 years ago.[4]

The paradox is that the Italian legal system is still lacking definitions generally adopted in this sensitive area of law, tax regulations have not been revised to respond to the many issues raised by the introduction of trusts in day-to-day experience,[5] and even parliamentary discussions regarding the proposal to utilise 'blind trusts' to eliminate potential conflicts of interest[6]

---

1 See **13.7**.

2 See M Lupoi *Fiducia, Trust, Mandato ed Agency* (Giuffré, 1991), which is a collection of papers discussed at the Annual Meeting of the Association of Notaries, confirming the attention of a profession traditionally involved in all the themes related to the management of assets; more recently, see *I trusts in Italia oggi, a cura di Beneventi* (Giuffré, 1996), which contains the papers discussed in a conference organised in Milan by M Lupoi, during which many of the best-known legal scholars had been invited to discuss the nature, scope and uses of trusts in different perspectives. Other interesting conferences, *inter alia*, have been held in Milan 'Il trust anglosassone e l'attività fiduciaria italiana', Associazione di giuristi italo-britannica (7 April 1995); in Rome, 'Il trust anglosassone – Prospettive applicative in Italia', Centro di Studi e Proposte (23 May 1996); in Erice, 'Trust a fiducia' (5–8 December 1997); in Rome, 'Il trust. Un nuovo strumento giuridico', Associazione Italiana Giovani Avvocati (20 January 1998).

3 A non-exhaustive list of the books published after the ratification of the Hague Convention and dedicated to the theme of trusts includes: M Lupoi *Introduzione ai trusts* (Giuffré, 1995), *Trusts*, n 2 on p 565; Ponzanelli (a cura di) *Gli enti non profit in Italia – Associazioni – Fondazioni – Volontariato – Trust – Fondi pensione* (Cedam, 1994); Graziadei *Diritti nell'interesse altrui. Undisclosed agency a trust nell'esperienza giuridica inglese* (Trento, 1995); Calo' *Dal probate al family trust* (Giuffré, 1996); Salvatore *Il trust. Profili di diritto internazionale e comparato* (Cedam, 1996). Many articles have been published in legal periodicals from a comparative perspective, mainly with reference to tax and inheritance problems. There is also a legal periodical dedicated to *Trusts & Trustees* which is published in an Italian edition and a new legal periodical dedicated to *Trusts e attività fiducierie*.

4 When the mention of the word 'trust' to an Italian lawyer would more than likely have provoked discussions on monopolies rather than on common law trusts.

5 On the new legislation proposed, but still not adopted, see **13.7**.

6 Ibid.

found no other solution than the transfer of assets to a foreign trust created under foreign laws.

It remains true therefore that, despite a significantly changed attitude, the use of trusts in Italy must be approached with great caution, as long as such use is still based more on theoretical assumptions than on general rules officially adopted.

In any case, it must be stressed that trusts cannot be considered as a means to avoid obligations with respect to basic principles of Italian law (for example, the rights of heirs, or the liability against creditors or tax authorities).[1]

Therefore, even in a short review like this, it seems useful to examine the traditional approach of Italian law to the trust and similar structures.

13.2 TRADITIONAL APPROACHES

13.2.1 Rights of ownership

Two basic principles of Roman law retained in modern Italian law are that 'ownership is an absolute right'[2] establishing an exclusive right to the underlying property, and that 'there is a limited catalogue of property rights, known as the *numerus clausus*'.[3] Traditional analysis of the Italian legal system continues to assume that these principles are obstacles to the acceptance of the trust structure in a civil law jurisdiction, excluding the possibility of a split between legal title and beneficial ownership.[4]

In recent years, however, these principles have been viewed in a different light, partly due to influences arising from comparative studies and contacts with foreign experiences, and partly as a result of innovations introduced by legislation and judicial decisions, including the patrimonial fund,[5] the reform of laws regulating fiduciary management of assets,[6] and the judicial recognition of new protected interests on real properties.[7]

---

1 The *caveat* against 'false trusts', sometimes proposed by certain consultants as an easy way to avoid inconvenient laws to Italian clients not conscious of the consequences of such abuse, has been appropriately highlighted by M Lupoi 'Efficace risposta alla domanda proveniente da società a finanza' in *Il Sole – 24 Ore*, 8 March 1997, p 22.

2 See Italian Civil Code, Art 832 (hereinafter 'Civil Code').

3 See Chapter 3.

4 For a summary of traditional opinions see Busato 'La figura del trust negli ordinamenti di common law e di diritto continentale' Riv Dir Cav 1991, II/309. For a forceful criticism of these positions from an historical perspective, see M Lupoi, n 3 on p 566.

5 See **13.4**.

6 See **13.3.3**.

7 Separately from the developments surrounding the trust, property rights and *numerus clausus* have in recent years been the subject of significant debate. For example, with regard to parking areas in residential buildings, the Court of Cassation, after prior conflicting decisions, adopted a final holding establishing a distinction between ownership, freely transferable, and the destination of the property for the benefit of the owners of related apartments which cannot be altered. This means that the legal owner may freely transfer the property, but he must maintain the property for the sole benefit of the

Italian law also provides that while an asset can have more than one owner, each owner has distinct and separate rights to the portion of the property which is his and that it is not possible for more than one person to hold a valid claim in that same portion of the property interest. Even this 'absolute' rule has undergone some modification. Article 2659 of the Civil Code as originally drafted excluded the possibility that an unrecognised entity (an entity which does not enjoy legal status: Art 36 of the Civil Code) could be registered in the Land Registry as the owner of property. In 1985 this Article was modified to provide that a non-recognised association or a simple partnership may be registered as an owner of real property upon the disclosure of the identity of the individual who represents the association or simple partnership. In this case, two persons are recorded in the real property register; one who has the right of action (the individual representing the association) and the other who is the effective beneficiary (the unrecognised association or simple partnership). Thus, the relationship between the unrecognised association and its representative is no longer merely 'fiduciary' in the Italian sense of being merely a personal commitment from the fiduciary to the beneficiary.[1] Rather, it is valid and effective with respect to third parties who are now on notice of the relationship between the association or simple partnership and its representative.

13.2.2 Usufrutto

There are examples in civil law of the existence of more than one real right on the same property. Generally included under the heading of *diritti reali in re aliena* (rights in third party property) are the usufruct and the two minor figures of *uso* and *abitazione*. Commentators from other countries have often made comparisons between these structures and the common law trust. While there may be historical reasons for such comparisons, the concepts are fundamentally different. The *usufruttuario* (or beneficiary) not only benefits from the usufruct, but has the power to administer the property which is the subject of the usufruct and has a duty to maintain the property. The *usufruttuario* is therefore in a very different position from that of a trust beneficiary who usually has no right to control or administer the trust assets.

The *nudo proprietario* (owner of the bare property rights) has no right to the income or other fruits of the property, nor to be involved in its administration. The owner can only wait patiently (or impatiently) for the conclusion of the

---

owners of the related apartments, who are not necessarily the owners of the parking area. In fact, in the Land Registry, the name of the legal owner of the parking area appears, but not the name of the beneficiary of the use of the space. The Court has created a new legal concept in which there is a splitting between the legal title holder (with all the duties and burdens, including taxes) and the effective beneficiaries of the real property. This holding of the Supreme Court has been fiercely criticised by civil lawyers precisely because it does not respect traditional legal principles governing real property rights.

1 See **13.3**.

usufruct.[1] His position also differs substantively from that of either a beneficiary or a settlor of a trust.

Notwithstanding these clear differences, from a practical point of view, some of the goals of a trust (eg distribution and protection of family assets) may be achieved through the usufrutto. Although the usufrutto is less flexible than the trust, due to its nature and significant limitations imposed by law,[2] it does have the advantage of being a recognised and commonly used structure in Italy with its own clear tax regime.

13.2.3 Liabilities of ownership

Under Italian law, a person's entire estate, both present and future,[3] is available for attachment by creditors. Both civil[4] and penal laws[5] reflect this principle by punishing debtors who attempt to withhold or hide assets from creditors.[6]

According to this principle of Italian law, all assets held by a person belong to his indivisible estate. This principle is evident in the rules of the Civil Code of 1942 governing limited liability companies, which prohibit the creation of companies having only one shareholder.[7] If, at any time after its creation, all shares of a limited liability company came to be held by a sole shareholder, that shareholder would automatically become personally liable for the liabilities of the company.[8] This principle was subject to an important exception in 1993[9] when, in response to Directive 89/667/EEC of 21 December 1989, the Civil Code was modified so as to permit formation of companies with a single shareholder, without loss of limited liability status.

---

1 The *nudo proprietario* can, however, petition a court to take action if the *usufruttuario* does not respect the characteristics of the property and appears to be destroying it.

2 See eg Civil Code, Art 698 under which the testator may leave a right of usufruct to consecutive different nominees, but such transfer will be valid and effective only in favour of the first nominee still living at the time of the death.

3 See Civil Code, Art 2740.

4 See Civil Code, Art 1416 (simulated agreements), Art 2901 *et seq* (revocation of acts which prejudice creditors).

5 See Penal Code, Art 388 and Bankruptcy Law, RD 267, Art 216, of 16 March 1942 (removal of assets from creditors' reach).

6 This approach of non-divisibility of assets is interesting to compare with asset protection trusts which are being used, albeit cautiously, by professionals in some common law jurisdictions as a means of protecting assets from malpractice or creditors' claims.

7 See Civil Code, Art 2328 *et seq* for provisions relating to *società per azioni* (SpA) and Civil Code, Art 2474 *et seq* for provisions relating to *società a responsabilità limitata* (Srl).

8 Civil Code, Arts 2362 and 2497 (original text).

9 Article 17 of *Legge Comunitaria* No 142 of 19 February 1992; and Legislative Decree No 88 of 3 March 1993. For some comments, see Oppo 'Codice civile a diritto commerciale' (1993) Riv Dir Civ 221. See also Nazzicone *Le società unipersonali* (Giuffré, 1993).

13.2.4 Deceptive comparisons

While a number of devices exist in Italy which are often used to achieve some of the aims obtained through the trust in common law countries,[1] the similarity of the goals should not be confused with the profound differences of the means. The apparent affinity between the trust and instruments such as foundations, contracts of *mandato* and contracts with third parties are for the most part limited to single issues.[2] Specifically, with respect to foundations, no fiduciary relationship is established between the founder, the foundation's administrators and its beneficiaries.[3]

13.3 THE ROLE OF *FIDUCIA*

Attempts have been made to compare the trust and the fiduciary agreement (*negozio fiduciario*) by stressing the element of trust (*fiducia*).[4] Such comparisons neglect to consider, however, that the *fiducia* of the Italian fiduciary agreement is merely personal in nature with respect to the relationship between the 'beneficiary' and 'trustee' and does not confer any direct interest in the underlying property.[5]

13.3.1 Fiduciary agreements

Fiduciary relationships do exist in Italy as they do in common law systems and the problems arising from them must be addressed by the legal system.[6] The model traditionally adopted by legal scholars[7] and widely accepted by courts,[8] viewed the fiduciary agreement as the interaction of two agreements. The first agreement is external in nature: a voluntary act which is fully valid and actionable with respect to third parties. The transferred assets become a part of the estate of the transferee/*fiduciario* and, therefore, subject to attachment by creditors of the transferee. The second agreement is internal and personal: it

---

1 Gambaro 'Problemi in materia di riconoscimento degli effetti dei trusts nei paesi di civil law' (1984) I Riv Dir Civ 93 notes that 'in civil law countries where the common law trust is unknown, one uses an array of legal devices which on their own or, more often, combined can cover almost all of the functions of the common law trust'.

2 A relevant rule is set forth in Civil Code, Art 1707, establishing that the creditors of a person purchasing assets in the execution of a previous written mandate have no title against those assets. For a comparison between trust and mandate, see M Lupoi *Fiducia, Trust, Mandato ed Agency* (Giuffré, 1991).

3 For a more analytical comment on these comparisons, see Albisinni and Sinisi 'Trusts from the Italian Perspective' in *Trusts for Europe* (Legal Studies & Services Ltd, 1988), p 53.

4 See Franceschelli *Il trust nel diritto inglese* (Padova, 1935), p 450.

5 Galgano 'La Fiducia e il Trust' in *Atlante di Diritto Privato Comparato* (Zanichelli, 1992), p 179, emphasises that the analogy between the concept of *fiducia* or trust in civil law systems and 'trust' in common law is merely apparent.

6 See Lipari *Il negozio fiduciario* (Giuffré, 1969).

7 See Santoro-Passarelli *Dottrine generali del diritto civile* (Napoli, 1980), p 179.

8 See Cass 4438 of 7 August 1982.

modifies the 'external' agreement to the extent that it can compel the transferee to respect the obligations assumed with respect to the transferor.

The crucial limitation is that the transferor's remedies for breach of this second 'internal' agreement are limited to actions against the *fiduciario*. The transferor is not entitled to recover *in rem* or *in personam* against third parties, except in cases of bad faith. But this model is only adequate to encompass certain types of agreements where the element of *fiducia* is present and does not provide a general framework which can encompass all situations in which fiduciary-type arrangements are made such as 'testamentary *fiducia*' and 'fiduciary companies'. The consequence is that even today, the term *fiducia* does not have a widely understood or generally accepted definition in the Italian legal lexicon. According to one Italian legal scholar, 'where "*fiducia*" becomes legal, it is no longer "*fiducia*"',[1] a statement which reflects the frustration of Italian scholars when trying to categorise the fiduciary agreement and illustrates the fundamental difference between the civil law approach and that of common law where the element of 'trust' is actionable. The difficulties of categorising the fiduciary agreement within the structure of the Italian legal system, including its legitimacy as an agreement, its structure, and its relationship to indirect, simulated and fraudulent transactions, have caused some legal scholars to treat the fiduciary agreement as a metaphysical rather than legal concept.[2]

13.3.2 *Fiducia* in the Italian Civil Code

The difficulties inherent in comparing legal concepts between different systems are accentuated when the concept itself does not have an unequivocal term with which it is designated. In the Italian Civil Code, the term *fiducia* is found in two instances, and in both cases it occurs as an adjective ('fiduciary') and not as a noun, signifying that the term itself does not have a legislative definition.

Article 627 states that testamentary dispositions to a party named in a will are not subject to review on the grounds that the devisee is not the true beneficiary, even if there are indications in the will that the named devisee has only been appointed as a fiduciary. However, if the named devisee has in fact carried out the *disposizione fiduciaria* (fiduciary disposition) of the testator by transferring the testamentary assets to a third party beneficiary, the fiduciary cannot then petition to have the transfer voided.[3]

---

1 Grassetti 'Trust Anglosassone, proprietà fiduciaria e negozio fiduciario' (1936) I Riv Dir Comm 551.

2 Criscuoli 'Fiducia e fiducie in diritto privato: da inegozi fiduciari ai contratti uberrimae fidei' (1983) I Riv Dir Civ 136 emphasised that with respect to the fiduciary agreement 'all is open to discussion from its admissibility to its structure, from its borders to its relationship to indirect, simulated and fraudulent agreements'.

3 For a comment, see Gardani Contursi-Lisi *Dell'istituzione di erede e dei legati* (Zanichelli, 1983), p 75 *et seq*.

Articles 2357, 2358, 2359/bis and 2360 of the Civil Code, which govern the acquisition by a company of its own or affiliated company shares, provide that the same rules will govern acquisitions carried out by *società fiduciaria* (fiduciary companies) or by intermediaries. These Articles and the related references to fiduciary companies were added only in 1986[1] to meet EC requirements, while the reference to the *società fiduciaria* with respect to the purchase of a company's shares is designed to ensure the transparency of the relationship between the transferor and the fiduciary. In this manner, the legislation introduced a distinction between apparent title (to the *società fiduciaria*) and effective ownership, a distinction which already existed in the tax legislation and is now reflected in the company laws. But this distinction, originally developed in the fiscal laws to ensure that the effective beneficiary and not the fiduciary was taxed on the property, reduced the fiduciary to a mere façade which could be overlooked by Italian law, a stark contrast to the rigid distinction between a trust and its settlor or beneficiary under common law.

The two hypotheses present in the Civil Code are not congruous: the first is merely an application of the general principle prohibiting revocation of the payment of an amount made to fulfil an obligation (Art 2034 of the Civil Code), and the second expresses the criterion of transparency regarding the ownership of securities of a fiduciary company. A unified definition of *fiducia* is not, therefore, to be derived from the provisions of the Civil Code.

13.3.3 Management of assets

Another area where the element of *fiducia* is relevant in the Italian legal system is that of management of assets and securities. Different types of management are recognised among which are fiduciary companies (*società fiduciarie*), investment or mutual funds and securities brokerage companies (*società di intermediazione mobiliare* (SIM)).

Fiduciary companies

The management of an individual's portfolio is reserved to specially qualified companies. Fiduciary companies are regulated by Law No 1966 of 23 November 1939, which sets forth specific requirements for their creation and authorisation. Among the authorised functions of these companies are the provision of professional management of a client's assets, including real property and securities, and the representation of stock and bond holders. The most common reason for the assignment of assets to a fiduciary company is the maintenance of the true owner's privacy. Fiduciary companies, in fact, operate 'on behalf of third parties', but in their own name.

1 DPR No 30 of 10 February 1986.

The rules governing fiduciary companies[1] provide that fiduciary companies managing securities must be enrolled on a special register maintained by the National Commission for Companies and the Stock Exchange (CONSOB). Unauthorised fiduciary companies are subject to liquidation.

Investment and mutual funds, and securities brokerage companies (SIM)

The rules regarding investment and management of securities have been reformed by DLgs of 24 February 1998,[2] which abrogated many previous laws and introduced a unified text which, however, is not comprehensive but must be integrated by administrative decrees.

The law governs the creation of Italian investment or mutual funds, and the operation in Italy of foreign funds. Investment funds are required to have a minimum capitalisation, must obtain prior authorisation and are subject to the control of the Banca d'Italia and CONSOB. Investment fund directors and managers are required to demonstrate a significant level of professional expertise and there are strict provisions regarding investment policy which are designed to avoid undue concentration of the investments and conflicts of interest.

Securities brokerage companies (SIM) are a form of investment management vehicle introduced in 1991. These companies are regulated by CONSOB and by Banca d'Italia,[3] and must be incorporated as share companies or as partnerships limited by shares, with a minimum capital significantly higher than that normally required for a share company. These companies buy and sell securities, provide investment consulting and manage investments in securities. The purpose of the law is to provide the investor with certain guarantees regarding the professionalism and preparedness of investment advisers in securities transactions. In contrast to the fiduciary company, a SIM, when managing the assets of its clients, may do so only 'in the name of and on behalf of third parties'. The law expressly provides for the separation of the assets which are administered by the company from the assets actually owned by the company, thereby preventing creditors of the investment company from exercising their rights against the assets administered by the company.

This general principle has been reaffirmed by Art 22 ('Separazione patrimoniale') of the DLgs No 58 of 24 February 1998, according to which the assets of the clients remain separate from the assets of the managing company, and creditors of the managing company may not attach such assets.

---

1 See Law No 1 of 2 January 1991, abrogated by DLgs, 24 February 1998, No 58.

2 Approved on the basis of Law No 52 of 6 February 1996, implementing Directives 93/22/CEE (10 May 1993), and 93/6/CEE (15 March 1993).

3 For a comment on Law No 1 of 2 January 1991 and CONSOB regulations, see Clarizia and Magnoni *La Gestione Personalizzata di Patrimoni Mobiliari* (Giuffré, 1993).

An important case, involving the bankruptcy of a fiduciary company, was decided by the Court of Cassazione,[1] which overruled contrary decisions of the Tribunale and the Court of Appeal of Turin, and recognised the right of the clients to the securities deposited in the fiduciary company. The administrators of a fiduciary company, in violation of the rules, did not correctly maintain the registers listing the individual purchases on behalf of the clients and only some of the securities held by the company could be traced to specific clients. In this generally confused situation, the clients of the company, arguing that the securities belonged to the clients (even if the individual owners of the single stocks could not be identified), petitioned the court to exclude the securities from the fiduciary company's assets available for distribution to creditors. The 'curatore' (trustee in bankruptcy) moved to include these assets in the general assets available to satisfy creditors of the company. The main argument of the curatore and of the courts of first and second instance, was that only those assets which have been registered in conformity with the law should be removed from the reach of creditors of the company. The Supreme Court rejected this argument and, applying the rationale of the rules of the Civil Code related to deposit of goods (Art 1782) and of Art 17 of Law No 1 of 2 January 1991, and of DLgs No 415 of 23 July 1996, held that the securities given in administration by a client remain property of such client and are not part of the assets of the fiduciary company even if the company did not maintain proper records of each security. The Court of Cassazione therefore expressly recognised the 'separation' of assets, confirming the clients as 'effective owners' of the securities.

13.4 AN ILLUSTRATION OF SEPARATION OF ASSETS UNDER EXISTING LAW – THE PATRIMONIAL FUND

A structure which can be compared to the trust in certain of its aspects is the 'fondo patrimoniale', introduced in 1975 by the reform of the family law (which abolished the 'fondo matrimoniale' and dowry), and regulated by Arts 166–171 of the Civil Code. This type of fund may be created before or after a marriage, by either or both spouses or a third party, by *inter vivos* formal deed or by testamentary act. The fund is created by an allocation of assets to meet family needs. The critical element of this type of fund is that it is the beneficial use to which the assets are dedicated and not the ownership which is relevant. In the absence of dispositions to the contrary, ownership resides with both spouses (Civil Code, Art 168), but the law provides that a third party may retain ownership of the assets which form the basis of the fund or may

---

[1] Corte di Cassazione, sez I civile, 14 ottobre 1997 n 10031, Modiano c Soc Fundus in 1 ca, in *La rivista dei curatori fallimentari*, 1997, IV, 33, with a note by Macario 'Separazione dei patrimoni ed azioni ricuperatorie nelle procedure concorsuali relative alle società fiduciarie'.

transfer the ownership to only one of the spouses, to the children or even to a third party. Assets allocated to a patrimonial fund may include land, buildings, any assets registered in public offices such as cars, boats, or airplanes, and securities or credits. Public notice is required for all assets allocated to the fund through publication at the public register where the assets are registered. Normally, it is not possible to sell or place liens against such assets without the consent of both spouses, or, in the case of a minor, without court approval.[1] The patrimonial fund is not widely known and therefore rarely used, but merits attention especially with respect to Art 170 of the Civil Code, which prohibits creditors from attaching fund assets except for debts incurred to meet family necessities.

The separation of assets, the destination of assets to a specific goal, and the distinction between title and benefit are all characteristics in respect of which the patrimonial fund may well be compared to the trust.

13.5 CONTACTS BETWEEN THE TRUST AND THE ITALIAN LEGAL SYSTEM

Contacts between the trust and the Italian legal system prior to the ratification of the Hague Convention included a few noteworthy theoretical discussions by legal scholars, infrequent judicial encounters and, more recently, some international Conventions which indirectly introduced the concept of the trust to Italian law.

13.5.1 Scholarly interest

Scholarly interest in the trust structure dates to the 1930s, when during an active period of legal reform (the Italian Civil Code was enacted in 1942) Italian legal scholars exhibited great interest in foreign legal systems, primarily German and French, but also English systems. In 1935, Franceschelli wrote *The Trust in English Law*[2] followed the next year by Grassetti who wrote two articles for the *Rivista di Diritto Commerciale* (the *Commercial Law Journal*).[3] Since then Italian comparative law scholars have regularly used the trust structure as a point of departure in theoretical discussions concerning civil law and common law systems, but only very few scholars had written specifically on the issue, until the ratification of the Hague Convention.[4]

---

1 On the patrimonial fund, see T Auletta *Il fondo patrimoniale* (Giuffré, 1993).

2 Franceschelli *Il trust nel diritto inglese* (Padova, 1935).

3 Grassetti 'Trust Anglosassone, proprieta' fiduciaria e negozio fiduciario' (1936) I Riv Dir Comm 551; 'Del negozio fiduciario e della sua ammissibilità nel nostro ordinamento giuridico' (1936) I Riv Dir Comm 954; and successively, 'Trust and Trustee' (1940) XII Nuovo dig It 569.

4 For an in-depth comparative and historical analysis, see M Lupoi *Appunti sulla Real Property e sul Trusts nel Diritto Inglese* (Giuffré, 1971).

The years after the ratification of the Hague Convention have seen growing interest in the possible uses of trusts. Not only have numerous books and articles specifically on the subject been published, but it has become usual for legal publications concerning general topics (for example, estate law, property, finance, taxation) to include some reference to the trust. This interest encompasses not only the common law trust but developments in other countries such as France with respect to the *fiducie*.[1]

13.5.2 Judicial experiences

Although there are still few reported court judgments regarding the trust and the time-span between such judgments is notable, the first decisions appear much earlier than the scholarly articles noted above. However, even in the earliest cases, when courts declined to recognise the existence of the trust, they nevertheless had a tendency, indirectly and applying limited rules in each case, to carry out the trust purpose.

The two earliest decisions, dating back to 1899 and 1909, may have been the natural outcome of the increasing presence of foreign citizens, particularly British, with different methods of organising their affairs on Italian territory.

Cassation of Rome (1899)[2]

This case involved a testamentary trust 'for sale' for which the trustee was to sell rapidly the trust assets located in Italy for conversion into investment income in England for the use of the beneficiaries. The oldest son of the settlor had opposed the sale sustaining that the dispositions of the trust were void under Italian law. The High Court of Justice of London, in 1894,[3] rejected the son's petition and ordered the trustee to sell the assets. The Appeals Court of Cagliari in Sardinia, where the assets were located, refused to recognise the English Court's judgment on the grounds that it was contrary to Italian public order.[4] The Court of Cassation of Rome reversed the Cagliari Appeals Court's decision, holding that there was no conflict with Italian public order in that the trust for sale was not destined to have a long-term effect in Italy.[5]

Cassation of Naples (1909)[6]

In the second case, an English Duchess living in Naples had established a testamentary trust which, amongst other distributions, was to pay a legacy of two lire to her coachman. The coachman did not receive the two lire and brought suit. The question before the court was whether the action should be

---

1 See Munari 'Trust e "fiducie": un importante progetto di legge francese' (1993) Giur Comm 129.

2 Cassation of Rome (21 February 1899) Giur It, I-1, c 216.

3 *Re Piercy* [1895] 1 Ch 83.

4 Corte d'Appello di Cagliari (12 May 1898) Giur It, 1898, I/2, c 612.

5 For a comment on the case, see Tondo, in the papers presented by the Association of Notaries, n 2 on p 566, p 123.

6 Cassation of Naples (29 March 1909) Giur It, 1909, I/1, c 649.

brought against the executory trustee or the beneficiaries. The Court of Cassation of Naples held that the action should be brought against the beneficiaries and not the trustee, since the trustee could not be recognised as an heir.[1] Even while denying recognition to the trust, the court found that the protected interest in the property was that of the beneficiaries who were, therefore, found to be the effective owners.

These two cases seem to have remained long forgotten by both scholars and courts and have not been cited by any courts since the introduction of the Civil Code in 1942. Only in more recent discussions of the trust have these two holdings been 'resurrected'.

For a long time after the approval of the Civil Code, few published holdings were available which deal directly with the trust.

Tribunale di Oristano (1956)[2]

This case was brought by the beneficiaries of a testamentary trust created by an English citizen who sued to enjoin a public office from expropriating land held by the trust because they had not been notified of the expropriation. The Italian authorities had notified only the trustee (the settlor's wife) of the intended expropriation, presumably because she was the only owner registered in the Land Registry, but failed to notify the beneficiaries (the children of the settlor).

The court declined to recognise or enforce the trust on the grounds that it violated the basic principle of Italian law of *numerus clausus* of property rights.[3] None the less, the court found for the plaintiffs, holding that the intent of the testator must be respected. According to the law governing wills, and considering the intent of the testator which was to assign the benefits of the property to his children, they were to be considered the effective owners. The public office was therefore required to notify them of the expropriation.

Tribunale di Casale Monferrato (1984)[4]

It was only after 30 years that a second case was published, this one involving a testamentary disposition of an English citizen resident in the United Kingdom. The deceased had appointed an executory trustee to liquidate his property and hold the proceeds for the benefit of the deceased's daughter. Italian law provides that an executor must obtain judicial authorisation prior to disposing of testamentary assets.[5] Although appointed under English common law, the executory trustee equated his position with that of an Italian executor,

---

1 See Tondo, n 2 on p 566, p 124, and Lupoi, n 2 on p 566, p 102 for comments on this case.

2 Tribunale di Oristano (15 March 1956) *Piercy v Etfas* Foro It, 1956, I, c 1020.

3 See **13.2.1**.

4 Tribunale di Casale Monferrato (13 April 1984) *G Forbes, plaintiff* Giur It, 1985, II, c 760 *et seq*, with a note by Cassoni 'Il trust anglosassone quale istituzione sconosciuta nel nostro ordinamento'. In this context the use of the word 'sconosciuta' (unknown) is not surprising.

5 Civil Code, Arts 703 and 747 cpc.

and requested the Italian court to authorise the liquidation of the property located in Italy. Declaring itself incompetent to hear such a request, the court held that the trustee had become the owner of the property in his own name. According to the court, the trustee should not be compared to a testamentary executor, but rather to a fiduciary executor,[1] whose actions are not subject to judicial control. While the court focused on the trustee's position as owner and did not acknowledge a splitting of the title to the property, it nevertheless granted to the trustee a power to dispose of the property similar to that which he would have had under common law.

More recent cases, not directly involving trusts, provide insight into the changes occurring with respect to property ownership issues and to the issue of recognition of legal entities.

Corte di Cassazione (1986)[2]

A non-recognised committee (Art 36 of the Civil Code) purchased property to use in furtherance of its charitable activities. In accordance with the text of Art 2659 of the Civil Code then in force,[3] the registration of the property in the Land Registry was made in the name of only one member of the committee. After the committee was later recognised as a legal entity by the public administration, it requested that the property be transferred to it, which the unscrupulous 'fiduciary' refused to do. In holding for the plaintiff, the Court of Cassation established the principle that the registration by a physical person 'did not exclude the attribution of ownership to the committee'. The decision, which was issued prior to enactment of the revised text of Art 2659, was viewed by commentators as a recognition of dual ownership with respect to real property rights. This decision, regarded as innovative when it was issued, is now reflected in the revised version of Art 2659 of the Civil Code.

Tribunale di Roma (1989)[4]

A contribution by the Tribunale of Rome with respect to the 'splitting' of ownership rights involved property registered in the name of an Anstalt created in Liechtenstein. After brokering the sale of a villa in Tuscany, the real estate agency requested payment of its commission directly from the individual who appeared to be the owner of the property. The title of the property had been held in the name of 'Eldorado Trust Registered', an Anstalt which is in some respects comparable to a trust. The Tribunale of Rome rejected the theory of the defendant that the action should have been brought against the Anstalt and not him personally because he was only acting on its behalf. Instead the Tribunale found that the individual had presented himself as the effective owner, of the villa. In its holding, the court commented that the

---

1 Governed by Civil Code, Art 627.

2 Cass of 12 June 1986, No 3898, *Ravasio v Fondazione Unitas Catholica,* Foro It, 1986, I, c 2123.

3 See discussion at **13.2.1**.

4 Tribunale di Roma (6 December 1989) *Palla v Stewart e Vianelli* No 14153 in *Temi Romana* 1990, II, 531.

Anstalt is a form of 'personalised capital' and viewed as irrelevant the purpose for which it was created. According to the court, the Anstalt is like an empty container into which anything could be put. The court concluded that the formal title of the property being held by the Anstalt did not prohibit identification of an individual beneficiary as the effective owner. As the effective owner, the defendant was personally and directly responsible for the payment of the agent's commission.

Although the court in this case recognised the possibility of a split in formal and 'effective' title, including the consequences with respect to registration and the formalities of transferring property, the court refused to allow such recognition to be used in an unjust manner. While the decision may be subject to criticism according to a strict interpretation of Italian law, it does reflect a growing impatience with the traditional formal approach of Italian law toward real property and the greater attention which may be given to the substance of economic transactions. Significantly, this perspective is gaining ground in the rules governing tax matters.

Corte di Cassazione (1993)[1]

The orientation towards permitting new forms for the organisation of property rights and models 'imported' from other systems has gained significant support by a ruling issued by the Court of Cassation. The court held, in a case decided in 1993, that the public order is not violated by recognition of an Anstalt created by only one settlor, which thereby permits the creation of a type of separate patrimony.

The facts of this case are somewhat bizarre. An Anstalt brought a legal action against the person holding its power of attorney on the grounds that she had acted against the interests of the Anstalt. The defendant and holder of the power of attorney was the wife of the man who had created the Anstalt. This man and his wife countered the charges stating that the Anstalt could not be recognised as a legitimate subject in Italy and, in any case, that the husband was the 'real' owner of the Anstalt at the time the facts had occurred as the Anstalt was a mere façade.

The Court of Cassation rejected the arguments of the husband and wife, affirming the fundamental principle that each legal system has the power to determine which centres of interest can be considered as legal subjects and entitled to protection under the law. It may be assumed, therefore, that basic principles of protection to an Anstalt created by one person implies recognition of the operation of a trust, even without reference to the Hague Convention. The evolution of the court's judgments which reject the necessity of more than one founder for the creation of a legal entity is particularly significant in that it has developed parallel to the legislative reforms of 1993,

1 Cass of 15 February 1993, No 1853, *Clementi v Farfara Anstalt et al* Foro It, 1993, c 2535.

which allow the creation of limited liability companies with only one shareholder.[1]

Corte di Cassazione (1996)[2]

One of the difficulties encountered by the Italian legal scholar, dealing with problems related to the institution of a trust, is to establish whether the creation of a trust must be considered, or not, a gratuitous act. The consequences of the classification of an act under this category are relevant, with reference both to the form and the validity of the act (gifts must be made with a special notarial form and the presence of two witnesses), and this field of law is one of those with evident differences between common law and civil law systems.[3]

In this case of 1996, a commercial company had transferred some rights of credits to another commercial company of the same group against no declared price. After the bankruptcy of one of the interested companies, the transfer without apparent price was challenged on the basis it had to be considered a gift, and was therefore not valid in the absence of the special form required for gratuitous transfers.

The Court of Cassation, reversing the decisions of the courts of first and second instance, decided that the transfer of rights of credit among different companies being part of the same group, even when made without a declared price, and so gratuitous, is not a gift, because it is not made to enrich the transferee, but is attributable to an interest, albeit indirect, of the assignor.

This innovative principle, if applied to the transfer of assets from the settlor to the trustee, could lead to the conclusion that this is not a gift, as long as the transfer is attributable to an interest, albeit indirect, of the assignor (the settlor), with relevant consequences on the formal and substantive regime of those transfers.

Tribunale di Lucca (1997)[4]

An Italian citizen, resident in the United States, died in Italy. Under Italian private international law, his inheritance was regulated by Italian law, including rules establishing a forced heirship in favour of the issue. The deceased, a widower who had only one daughter, had made a testament in the English language, providing that all his assets should go in trust to a friend, who would

---

1 See **13.2.3**.

2 Cass of 11 March 1996, No 2001, *Soc Istituto per lo sviluppo immobiliare e mobiliare v Soc Borgosesia* Foro It 1996, I, c 1222.

3 G Gorla, one of the founders of Italian studies of comparative law, in his book, *Il contratto* (Giuffré, 1953), underlined that examination of different acts considered gratuitous in one legal system or the other is one of the best ways to isolate and understand similarities and differences between consideration in common law and causa in civil law.

4 Tribunale di Lucca (23 September 1997) *Casani v Mattei* (1998) I Foro It 2007, with a note by Brunetti 'Il testamento dello zio d'America – il "trust" testamentario', *ibid*, and by M Lupoi 'Aspetti gestori e dominicali, segregazione: "trust" e istituti civilistici' (1998) I Foro It 3391.

administer these assets during the entire life of the daughter of the deceased, distributing at intervals the income to the daughter and her son, and thereafter until the last of such grandchildren should reach the age of 25, at which time the capital was to be divided in equal parts among the grandchildren.

After the death, the will was published in Italy with deposit before a public notary of the original and of a translation, according to Italian laws. In the translation, the word 'trust' was translated, with an evident misunderstanding, as '*fedecommesso*'. The daughter contested the testament before the Tribunal, assuming that it was void, because it was in violation of Italian rules regarding *fedecommesso* (Art 692 of the Civil Code). During the trial it appeared clear to the parties that the act was not a *fedecommesso*, but a trust, and the lawyer of the daughter tried (belatedly) to contest the validity of the testament using a different argument, assuming that the use of the trust determined the nullity of the testament, due to the fact that the trust was to be deemed in palpable contrast with Italian substantive law *inter alia* because it violated the protected rights of the forced heirs.

The Tribunal, with a lucid analysis, rejected the petition of the daughter, and observed that, with the ratification of the Hague Convention, all the stipulating countries expressly agreed to consider the trust as not contrary to their own legal system.

Therefore, even for Italy, an act (in this case a will) cannot be considered void only because it creates a trust, and the trust so created must be considered as legitimately operating in the Italian legal system, under Art 11 of the Convention.

The Tribunal stressed that the legitimate use of a testamentary trust would not permit the violation of the rights of the legitimate heirs, but in this case the daughter brought her action only to assert the nullity of the testament, and did not move to enforce the different action intended to defend her rights to a quota of the inheritance.

To summarise, the conclusion of the Tribunal is the first and very clear judicial confirmation (even if still that of a court of first instance) of the thesis, proposed from the first edition of this chapter, according to which the Hague Convention, even if not intended to introduce the trust into domestic law of countries which did not have this institution, in fact eliminated the barriers to the entrance in Italian law, motivated in past times under general considerations.

Pretura di Roma and Tribunale di Roma (1999)

Two opposite decisions, adopted in April and July 1999, by the Pretore di Roma[1] and by the Tribunale di Roma[2] respectively, with reference to the same

---

1 Pretura di Roma (13 April 1999) *Zezza v Villa Gina spa e Nuova Clinica Latina spa* (2000) *Trusts e attività fiduciarie* 83.

2 Tribunale di Roma (2 July 1999) *Zezza v Villa Gina spa e Nuova Clinica Latina spa* (2000) *Trusts e attività fiduciarie* 85.

case, in the first instance and on appeal, have recently highlighted the difficult issues coming from the non-systematic introduction of the trust structure in the Italian legal system.

A physician, shareholder of two companies owning two private hospitals, was forced to dispose of his shares due to new Italian legislation on the national health system. He created a trust in Italy, instituted his wife as trustee, appointed his three minor children as beneficiaries, gave his mother the role and the powers of protector, and chose the law of Jersey as the law applicable to the trust. Therefore the trust was created in Italy, with reference to Italian assets, by an Italian settlor, with an Italian trustee and with Italian beneficiaries and an Italian protector, all resident in Italy. As such, it was a typical example of what has been called 'internal trust'.[1]

The trustee (the wife) deposited the shares in the offices of the two companies, in order to be admitted to participate in the annual meeting of shareholders, under the applicable Italian law.

After some time the husband/settlor and the wife/trustee quarrelled and went through judicial separation.

The trustee asked the two companies to give her back the shares, but the President of the two Boards of Directors (a relative of the husband/settlor) refused.

The trustee instituted a summary proceeding, assuming that she was entitled to the immediate return of the shares that she had previously deposited in the offices of the companies, and that the refusal of restitution was clearly illegal, being totally irrelevant to any dispute on the beneficial ownership of the shares.

In the meantime, the protector (the settlor's mother) revoked the trustee and instituted a new trustee. Therefore, during the proceeding before the Pretore, the legal representative of the two companies assumed that the wife, previously trustee, was at that moment no longer entitled to the restitution of the shares, having lost her position as trustee.

The Pretore rejected the arguments of the defendants, and ordered them to return the shares to the first trustee, assuming that any dispute regarding the modification of the position of the trustee was in that proceeding irrelevant, as long as any judicial dispute on possession must be intended primarily to re-establish the original situation (*spoliatus ante omnia restituendus*).

The defendants appealed to the Tribunale, and the Tribunale reversed the decision of the court of first instance, assuming that the first trustee was no longer entitled to the possession of the shares, under three concurrent reasons:

---

1 See Lupoi, n 2 on p 566.

(a) in the opinion of the court, the trust is a fiduciary relationship, comparable to the Italian mandate which can be revoked at any moment;[1]
(b) the first trustee had been revoked and replaced by another trustee, in accordance with the rules of the trust deed; and
(c) the substitution of the old trustee and the appointment of a new trustee did not involve issues of ownership, as long as – in the opinion of the court – the ownership remained vested in the trust, which, even if not giving rise to a legal entity, was in any case to be considered as a separate estate, holding legal rights; therefore the person who lost the position of trustee was no longer entitled to act for the protection of rights pertaining to the trust.

The deceptive comparison of the trust to the Italian mandate,[2] and the construction of the trustee as a sort of 'legal representative' of a separate estate, as proposed by the Tribunale di Roma, may be subject to criticism,[3] and legislative reform clarifying the most relevant issues posed by the use of the trust structure in Italy appears to be urgent.

It must be underlined that, irrespective of their opposite judgments on the case, the Courts of Rome had no hesitation in considering an internal trust, created in Italy by an Italian citizen and resident with regard to Italian assets, as a legal structure fully admitted to operate in the Italian legal system.

Even the decision of the Tribunale, which may be criticised from a technical point of view for the arguments adopted, may be considered – from a substantive perspective – as inspired by the underlying (even if not declared) aim of assuring protection to the beneficiaries, in a situation in which the first trustee was in a possible position of conflict of interest. The role of the protector appears crucial in the reasoning of the Tribunale, and the recognition of this role may be an answer to potential Italian settlors seeking reassurance.

To summarise, with regard to judicial decision-making, the issue nowadays appears no longer to be that of the recognition of the trust, as long as it is broadly admitted as an ordinary legal tool, but rather that of constructing an original complex of rules and reasonings, capable of integration with the institutes of civil law and able to give effective and adequate answers to the day-to-day problems which arise.

Italian courts are beginning to explore this difficult but original course.

---

1 See Civil Code, Art 1723.

2 See **13.2.4**.

3 See the critical comment of A Chizzini 'Revoca del trustee e legittimazione all'zione possessoria' (2000) *Trusts e attività fiduciarie* 47.

13.5.3 Prior international Conventions

The brief discussion above indicates that, notwithstanding the occasional examination of the trust by legal commentators and courts, it was not through scholarly writings or judicial holdings that the trust was admitted to the Italian legal system. Rather, the inclusion of the trust into the Italian legal lexicon came about through several international Conventions which addressed matters not directly related to the trust. Specifically, two Conventions made direct reference to the trust.

The Luxembourg Convention

The Luxembourg Convention of 9 October 1978,[1] which modified the Convention of Brussels of 27 September 1968 on jurisdiction and the execution of civil and commercial sentences, made reference to the trust in the context of setting forth criteria for choice of jurisdiction in legal actions between persons domiciled in different countries (see Arts 5 and 17).

The Convention between Italy and the United States for the avoidance of double taxation[2]

While not specifically covering trusts, the Convention for the avoidance of double taxation mentioned the trust in Art 4.[3] The Italian version of this article contains a notable example of the great difficulties existing even at the level of translation. Here, the word 'trust' was interpreted as *associazione commerciale*, a patently misleading translation.

13.6 THE HAGUE CONVENTION ON TRUSTS[4]

13.6.1 Ratification of the Convention

The Italian Parliament ratified the Hague Convention with Law No 364 of 16 October 1989 and the Convention entered into force on 1 January 1992 following its ratification by Australia. The ratification of the Convention by two common law countries, the United Kingdom and Australia, is unremarkable, but its ratification by Italy, second only to the United Kingdom, the 'home' of the trust, is noteworthy.

---

1 Approved by Law No 967 of 29 November 1980.

2 Approved by Law No 7663 of 11 December 1985.

3 'Article 4: Resident (1) For purposes of this Convention, the term "resident of a Contracting State" means any person who, under the laws of that State, is liable to tax therein by reason of his domicile, residence, place of management, place of incorporation, or any other criterion of a similar nature, provided, however, that: (a) ...; (b) in the case of income derived or paid by a partnership, estate, or *trust*, this term applies only to the extent that the income derived by such partnership, estate, or trust is subject to tax in that State, either in its hands or in the hands of its partners or beneficiaries.'

4 The full text of the Hague Convention is printed in the Appendix to this book.

Its relatively rapid approval may, in part, be attributed to the apparent lack of understanding of its potential impact and the absence of serious consideration of any provisions for its implementation with respect to tax laws.[1] This was not, however, the first time that in recent years legislation derived from foreign sources was passed without sufficient reflection on its impact on Italian domestic law. One conspicuous example was the passage of legislation regarding EEIGs which was approved, like the Hague Convention on Trusts, without adequate provision made for integration with existing domestic regulations.[2]

From a more general perspective, the rapid and uncontroversial approval by the Italian Parliament is a clear reflection of the process by which Italy's legal system is being exposed to and being changed by the influence of very different systems of law. Such exposure produces different results. New contractual forms derived from foreign models and imposed by commercial practices are absorbed into the Italian system, in many cases even maintaining their foreign terminology (eg leasing, factoring, engineering, franchising).[3] Another consequence is that legislative action becomes necessary to conform Italian laws to international agreements, especially with respect to EC Regulations.[4]

In the interval between Italy's approval (1989) of the law of ratification of the Hague Convention and the entering into force of the Convention (1992), there was remarkably little interest generated by the possibilities opened by the Convention, reinforcing the idea that the Convention's impact on Italian law was underestimated not only by the Parliament, but also by commentators.[5]

Recently, however, greater attention has been paid to this common law structure both on the part of legal scholars[6] and the general public.[7] For legal scholars, in particular, the approval of the Convention provided ample

---

1 See discussion below on the parliamentary report, from which emerges a striking underestimation of the impact of the approved legislation.

2 See Cottino, in *Le nuove leggi civile comm* (1992), p 1015, for a comment on Legislation Decree No 240 of 23 July 1991, which introduced the EEIG.

3 See Corapi 'Evoluzione economica e comparazione giuridica' in *Studi in Memoria di Pietro Gismondi* III (Giuffré, 1988), p 173 for an analysis of how commercial practices modify legal systems. See also Buonocore and Luminoso *Contratti d'impresa* (Giuffré, 1993).

4 In recent years, in response to the numerous criticisms directed at Italy for delays in implementing international agreements, especially by the European Community, the Italian Parliament has made efforts to conform its domestic laws with greater speed. Specifically, in 1990 the Parliament enacted the so-called 'Legge Comunitaria per il 1990' (Law No 428 of 29 December 1990), which introduced the principle of adopting, every year, with a single law, all conforming legislation. This procedure was repeated in 1991 with Law No 142 of 11 February 1992 and in the following years.

5 The interest remained limited above all to notaries. See the papers presented at the seminar organised by the Association of Notaries in Madonna di Campiglio, n 2 on p 566. In addition to these comments, see Malaguti 'Il futuro del trust in Italia' (1990) *Contratto ed Impresa* 983, and Corso 'Trust e diritto italiano' (1980) *Quadrimestre* 496.

6 See **13.1**.

7 A number of articles illustrating the possible uses of the trust by Italian citizens have appeared in financial newspapers.

opportunity to analyse the potential role which the trust will play in Italian jurisprudence.

The legislation for ratification was accompanied by a parliamentary report (the Report). The Report is an important document because it may be used by courts as an explanation of legislative intent. Although not binding, in the case of doubt regarding interpretation of the provisions of a law, a parliamentary report may be considered for assistance in the interpretation.[1]

13.6.2 Provisions of the Convention

Definition of trust

One of the most relevant consequences of the Convention is that through its very broad definition of 'trust' (see Art 2), it introduces a term to the Italian legal lexicon which provides both a general definition of the institution and a technical term of art. The Convention would appear thereby to eliminate the contradictions and uncertainties regarding the concept which had previously haunted the trust's forays in Italy.

Registration of trust assets

As clearly noted by the Italian legislators when introducing the law approving the Hague Convention, the separation of trust assets from the trustee's personal assets necessitates that the trustee be able to put third parties on notice of the dual rights on the trust assets. Only by putting third parties on notice does the trustee have a basis for opposing his or her personal creditors' claims against property held in trust. The Convention provides for such notice in Art 12 by permitting a trustee to register trust assets or their supporting documents in an appropriate public register.

This provision, at a minimum, complicates the activities of Italian notaries and public officials. All documents evidencing the transfer of real property, creation of mortgages and attachment of real assets (Art 2643 of the Civil Code) must be registered in the Land Registry on the principle of *prior in tempore, potior in jure*.[2] This registration is, however, permitted only for documents prepared according to specific formalities, ie notarised acts or judicial decrees.[3] Even contracts executed abroad but requiring performance in Italy must meet formal requirements for registration. These documents are deposited with a notary, legalised and accompanied by a translation in Italian, and the notary, in conformity with current practice, must review the document

1 Article 12 of the Preliminary Disposition of the Civil Code expressly provides the 'legislative intent' as a criteria of interpretation of the law. Although there is a tendency to emphasise that the 'intent' is determined foremost by a literal reading of the text, some relevance is also given to the preparatory work of the legislators. See Quadri *Dell'Applicazione Della Legge in Generale* (Zanichelli, 1974), p 194 *et seq.*

2 Civil Code, Art 2643.

3 Ibid, Art 2657.

to ensure that its provisions respect Italian law and are not contrary to public order.

In recent years, many legislative reforms have rendered ever more complicated the formalities required for the execution of real property agreements with non-compliance carrying the risk of void agreements. Notaries, *inter alia*, are required to verify compliance with zoning laws and to obtain declarations that building codes have been respected and applicable taxes have been paid. Notaries must also verify the power of the parties to enter into a contract. With respect to a trust, the notary would be required to verify the powers of the trustee and the validity of his or her nomination in circumstances involving a purchase or sale of trust property. These issues can be particularly complex and are not covered by the Convention nor by the Italian law ratifying the Convention.

Non-disclosure of beneficiary at time of registration

Apart from the possible difficulties which the implementation of the Convention has created and despite the protestations of the lawmakers who introduced it, the Convention's provisions have had a substantive impact. Article 12 provides that a trustee who desires to register assets, movable or immovable, or documents of title to them, shall be entitled, insofar as this is not prohibited by or inconsistent with the law of the state where registration is sought, to do so in his capacity as trustee or in such other way that the existence of the trust is disclosed.

It was not specified whether registration under this provision would also require disclosure of the identity of the beneficiary. In Italy, the registration of documents related to real property serves two purposes: that of recording the transfers and for taxation.[1] The dual functions of the registration requirement caused some commentators[2] to suggest that the law would require disclosure of the beneficiary's identity. In some respects this conclusion could be supported by general principles of Italian taxation which provide that tax liability is determined by 'effective' possession of income.[3] Requiring the identification of the beneficiary can be problematic if the beneficiary is not clearly ascertainable, as can be the case when the beneficiary is a class of persons or even an animal. Another issue to be addressed would be the loss of confidentiality which double registration would necessitate. In either case, whether such registration includes the trustee with legal title and the beneficiary with equitable title or just the trustee in his declared capacity, there would be a registration in the Land Registry of two types of protected interest. Thus, there will be a *de facto* splitting of title even at the time of registration

1 DPR No 635 of 26 October 1972, Art 15, para 2.

2 See Piccoli 'La Convenzione dell'Aja sulla legge applicabile ai trusts' (1990) Riv Not 91.

3 DPR No 917 of 1986, Art 1, and Constitution, Art 53. For a general survey on the Italian tax system, see Albisinni and Gambino's chapter on Italy in *Capital Taxes and Estate Planning in Europe* (Longman, 1993).

formalities, a result which is very distant from the *Oristano* case discussed at **13.5.2**, where the court insisted that such a splitting of property rights would violate a basic principle of Italian law and would be unenforceable.

Against the background of this highly controversial theoretical framework, actual experience suggests that it is admissible, even under the existing Italian law, for the registration of the transfer of real property in favour of a trust to disclose the name of the trustee acting in his declared role, and not the name of the beneficiary, overcoming the concerns of those who look at the trust without in-depth understanding of its nature.

This area has not yet been officially regulated and, in general, opinions are not uniform,[1] but the authors are pleased to share a significant professional experience: a trust constituted abroad with a trustee, which was a foreign company, purchased a villa in Italy and both the notary and the Land Register allowed the trustee to execute the contract of purchase in his declared position of trustee for a nominated trust, without disclosing the name of the beneficiaries, with a declaration in the formal contract of sale which made express reference to the Italian law of ratification of the Hague Convention as sufficient legal basis for such a purchase.

If the attitude demonstrated by the public notary and by the Land Register in the above-mentioned case becomes common, a significant step has been made, in Italy, toward full acceptance and effectiveness of the trust. It must, however, in all truthfulness, be noted that while this kind of registration of the transfer offers some relevant signals, it does not solve all issues, in particular those relating to the fiscal regime.

Italian citizens as beneficiaries or settlors of foreign trusts

As the parliamentary report emphasises, the Convention is not intended to allow the introduction of the trust into the Italian legal system as an autonomous private legal instrument. The declared purpose of the Convention is strictly limited to facilitating the operation in the Italian territory of trusts created abroad in conformity with the legal norms under which it was created. The Report states that the Convention is applicable to all trusts voluntarily created abroad in nations which recognise the trust, even if created by Italian citizens who have emigrated to that nation. The Report asserts that the Italian system:

> 'does not intend to create obstacles to impede Italian citizens who have emigrated to other nations in managing assets which are located in Italy *as long as Italian tax and exchange control regulations are respected.*' (emphasis added)

---

1 The Direction of the Land Register of Lombardia expressed, on 19 July 1994, an opinion contrary to the admissibility of the transcription in the Land Registry of acts related to trust, as illustrated by Piccoli 'Troppi timori in tema di trascrivibilità del "trust" in Italia', *Notariato* 6/1995, p 616; on the basis of information lately received, this position of the office has been mitigated. Piccoli, Corso and Dolzani 'La trascrizione degli atti riguardanti trusts' (1995) *Rivista del Notariato* 1389 agree to the possibility of transcribing real transfers with only the name of the trustee and not of the beneficiaries.

The Report refers to 'emigrants', but it appears more appropriate to interpret the language as applying to Italian citizens who are habitually resident abroad (more than six months according to Consolidated Text on Italian Income Taxes, Art 2) an interpretation supported by other indications in the Report suggesting that the controlling criteria is not citizenship, but residency.

However, in either case, the express parliamentary declarations contained in the Report confirm that Italian citizenship of the settlor or beneficiary would not, alone, constitute cause for denying recognition of a trust, nor would residence in Italy of a foreigner. Moreover, Italian public notaries in some cases have accepted the creation in Italy of trusts by Italian citizens residing in civil law countries.[1]

Public order considerations

On the basis of the experiences of the last years, it is possible to state unequivocally that a fundamental change has occurred with the approval of the Hague Convention. The trust per se can no longer be viewed, as it has been traditionally by the courts, as contrary to public order. Article 18 provides that the Convention's provisions will not be applicable when found to be contrary to principles of public order. But recognition of the admissibility of the trust structure with its split in legal and beneficial ownership under the general principles of the legal system of the signatory nation has effectively eliminated the fundamental controversy regarding the non-admissibility in Italy of forms of ownership different from the traditional, absolute property rights derived from Roman law.

The Convention does not, per se, allow the creation of a trust in Italy. However, if a trust is established in a jurisdiction which permits its creation it may operate in Italy with full powers limited only by the principles of public order which limit the activities of any Italian citizen (including protection of minors, matrimonial assets and forced heirship). Contrary to the assertions in the Report, therefore, the Convention does not merely establish rules governing conflicts of law, rather it will have an impact on substantive law.

The Italian legal system now permits the direct application of foreign laws governing trusts to determine the validity of transactions undertaken by the trustee. The Convention provides that a trust must be 'recognised' by the signatory nation. The Italian ratification law did not provide any procedures or authority which would be responsible for such recognition. But the lack of a 'recognition procedure' may be the natural result of the approach taken: it is not necessary for the signatory nation to 'recognise' the trust; it is only necessary for it to determine whether it is valid under the laws of the place chosen by the settlor at the time of creation and then apply those laws to it.

---

1 As was anticipated by Lupoi, n 2 on p 565, p 978.

This reasoning echoes the arguments adopted by the Court of Cassation in its decision of 1993 regarding the Anstalt[1] discussed above, and by the Tribunal of Lucca in its decision of 1997, regarding the testamentary trust of an Italian citizen: once a structure is validly created in its country of origin it should be accepted by Italian laws and allowed to operate. Domestic courts and international Conventions, moving from different starting points, seem to be travelling down common roads.

13.7 RECENTLY PROPOSED LEGISLATION

Three different legislative proposals, all discussed, but not finally approved by the Italian Parliament during the past legislature, involved, in various ways, the use of trusts in Italy.

13.7.1 Rules on the conflicts of interest of members of the government and persons appointed to critical public offices[2]

This proposal was developed during the first government presided over by Mr Berlusconi, in consideration of the fact that he is the owner, among other holdings, of three television networks. A commission of experts, consisting of three eminent legal scholars, concluded that one approach to the issues arising when very wealthy persons (defined as persons with at least 15 billion Italian lire in economic/financial entrepreneurial activities) directly participate in politics or have holdings in the area of mass communications could be found by separating those assets from the interested party for the entire period that the person held office.

The interested party, at the time of nomination to the relevant office, would be required to declare his assets and within a short period of time sell the property, or transfer it to a 'trust created in accordance with the provisions of the Hague Convention'. If the assets are not voluntarily transferred, the transfer to a trust will be undertaken by the anti-trust authority.[3]

According to this proposal, eligibility for nomination as trustee would be limited to only those professional management entities admitted to a special public role, which could include subjects residing in the European Union who are authorised to undertake such management activities.

---

1 See **13.5.2**.

2 The proposal was approved by the Chamber of Deputies in April 1998 (proposal C1236 of the Camera dei Deputati) but not by the Senate (proposal No 3236 del Senato).

3 Specific legislation against monopolies and an anti-trust authority have been introduced in Italy by Law No 287 of 10 October 1990, 'Rules for the Regulation of Competition and of the Market'. The first authoritative commentary on this law was by A Frignani, R Pardolesi, A Patroni Griffi and LC Ubertazzi and was interestingly called *Diritto Antitrust Italiano (Italian Anti-trust Law)* (Zanichelli, 1993).

It is interesting to note, for purposes of this discussion, that Art 10 of the proposed law guarantees the fiscal neutrality of the initial transfer and of the retransfer of the holdings to the office-holder at the end of his term, while for the duration of the trust it is the trustee who is subject to taxation on the income generated.

The discussions regarding this proposal included references to a 'blind trust' because the manager–trustee is prohibited from communicating with the interested party regarding the investments made, and the interested party may not request any information directly from the trustee. The office-holder may obtain an accounting of the overall financial results every 90 days from the anti-trust authority and may receive, every six months, income up to a maximum of one billion Italian lire (Art 8).

It has been observed by some commentators that this proposed legislation does not appear capable of dealing with the complex issues posed by possible conflicts of interest where the holdings of the interested party are so widespread, or of such a nature (eg holdings in the area of mass communication), as to render virtually impossible any attempts to limit information regarding their status.

In any case, this proposed legislation omitted the adoption of any rule regarding the problems of substantive law arising from the use of foreign trusts.

13.7.2 Proposal for reform of the law relating to fiduciary companies and to trusts[1]

This proposal has not been approved by either chamber of the Parliament, and has, in large part, been conceived in the knowledge that the eventual passage of the proposed legislation on conflicts of interest, discussed above, renders the need for clarity in these areas even more urgent. The role of the professional trustee is limited to fiduciary companies registered in a designated list and subject to control by relevant public offices. With respect to trusts, the proposal (Art 9) repeats only certain well-known principles, in addition to specifying the separation of property, but remains a victim of the ongoing confusion regarding the nature of fiduciary companies and trusts.

13.7.3 Proposed law regarding trusts in favour of disabled persons[2]

This is the most recent proposal and certainly the most interesting, due to the contribution of legal scholars who in the development of the legislation provided in-depth analysis of the issues relating to trust. The proposed legislation would provide for the creation of an Italian trust on the basis of a

---

1 Proposal C 5194 of the Camera dei Deputati, not voted upon by Parliament in the past legislature.

2 Proposal C 5494 of the Camera dei Deputati, not voted upon by Parliament in the past legislature.

document written in Italian with relevant formalities (including the authentication of the signatures by a notary). The proposed legislation foresees a 'guardian of the trust' or protector. The duration of the trust is related to the life of the disabled beneficiary. There are provisions limiting the right of the disabled beneficiary of the trust from exercising his forced heirship rights against the trustee and regarding the supervision of trustees' activities by the Tribunal.

A point of interest is that after only three rather scanty provisions regarding the substantive and procedural discipline of the trust, there follow five long provisions governing, in minute detail, various tax issues which arise, including the application of registration taxes, transfer taxes, mortgage taxes, property taxes and income taxes, calculations of capital gains and losses and requirements to obtain a fiscal code.

In a country where such paradoxes are not unusual, it is possible that the sympathetic attitude toward the disabled may result in the passage of legislation through which the trust will find a secondary, and somewhat hidden, entrance into the Italian legal system, but where the solutions proposed will eventually result in a much broader utilisation of the trust and for very different purposes.

Above all, this proposed legislation highlights the central role of the tax system. The problems related to the substantive law can probably find, and in part are already finding, coherent solutions within the general framework of the Italian legal system through a comparative analysis of the Hague Convention, but only the development of a comprehensive tax regime could contribute a decisive solution of outstanding issues.[1]

13.8 TRENDS

Certain trends can be identified as emerging from the historically difficult relations between the trust and the Italian legal system and the overcoming of the 'public order' obstacle. With the entering into force of the Hague Convention, foreign law governing trusts became directly applicable in Italy. Italian courts are required to apply these laws, including those protecting the beneficiary and settlor, and can no longer dismiss cases on the mere basis of preliminary considerations without entering into the merits of the trust itself.

On a more general level, once doubts are removed about the admissibility of splitting rights on the same assets at least for a trust created in a common law country or about the admissibility of the benefit of limited liability even in

---

1 Such a situation would, in fact, be analogous to that regarding leasing contracts, which was another foreign experience, introduced into Italy. Initially, there were many uncertainties regarding the use of this type of contract. However, notwithstanding the absence of civil law provisions, it was able to function satisfactorily through the introduction of specific tax regulations.

the absence of more than one shareholder, it is no longer possible to simply deny the admissibility in the Italian legal system of non-typical contracts (*licit ex* Art 1322 of the Civil Code) with which the parties may regulate their interests with respect to the use and benefit of assets with goals which are comparable to the trust.

The ongoing uncertainty of the tax regime on the relevant issues posed by the use of the trust structure (including the taxation applicable to transfer of assets, and to the allocation and distribution of benefits), and on the effects of general principles of the Italian tax system,[1] remain a relevant obstacle to a broader diffusion of the trust structure. But, notwithstanding this, the concurrent issues of fiduciary relationships, limited liability, and property designated for a specific purpose or for a specific beneficiary, appear more frequently and more significantly than in the past, and exemplify a growing interest in the themes that are the basis of the success of the trust in common law countries.

---

1 An issue largely discussed has been the applicability to trusts of the general rule of Art 37 of the DPR No 600 of 29 September 1973 (in the text, as modified by DL No 69 of 2 March 1989), under which the tax authorities can attribute to a person the income which he owns through an 'interposta persona' (in essence, a fictitious owner). The majority of commentators agree that such a rule is not applicable to trusts, due to the effective transfer of assets and rights of disposal deriving from the institution of the trust (unless – and it is clear – in case of abuse of the trust structure, or of creation of 'false trusts' – see n 1 on p 567); for a comprehensive comment, see Paparella 'Trust ed interposizione fittizia di persona nella disciplina delle imposte dirette' (1996) 19 *Il Fisco* 4182.

PART 4

Chapter 14

THE FUTURE OF THE TRUST FROM A WORLDWIDE PERSPECTIVE

Donovan Waters QC[*]

14.1 INTRODUCTION

In the days of Empire, the English trust got off the boat with the intending settlers and, regardless of local law, set up business in the high street, or the local equivalent, as if it were in any English county town. The new arrivals from the home counties, the shires, the west and north country, Ireland or Scotland made wills with trusts of residue and in due time, having got together some wealth and reflected upon mortality, they created *inter vivos* trusts. They very rarely imposed upon the local people their own succession law or family law. Those were sensitive areas, and it was better to have co-operation than resentful compliance. But again in due time, the trust would find its way into the lives of the local people through trading and a shared life experience. Trust theory was rarely known in detail to anyone on the local scene, but the arrivals had among them one or two who knew from 'the old country' how to draw a trust and roughly how it worked. And that was that. No more was needed, and the locals and the one-time settlers would absorb it into their shared law as they saw it fitting in. Ultimately, the law of the 'new country' would include this thing, the trust. Nobody wrote legal texts or instruction manuals about it all. It just happened and went unmarked.

What is more, the process continues. Within recent years a new creature has made its way from several small islands of what was once that Empire to the mainland common law jurisdictions. And it carries a name that is not

[*] Counsel, Bull Housser & Tupper, Barristers and Solicitors, Vancouver, British Columbia, Canada; Professor Emeritus, University of Victoria, British Columbia, Canada. This chapter is based upon a lecture delivered with the present requested title at the STEP Winter Conference in London, England, on 30 November 2001. The theme of the conference was global reform and the regulation of trusts.

unfamiliar even in civil law states, those, that is, that have never known the common law in their high streets or anywhere else. The new creature is 'the international trust'. No one appears to have defined it,[1] but practitioners and now writers are using the term with confidence. All of us have 'a fairly good idea', we think, of what it means, and we are prepared to leave it at that.

This chapter is concerned with the future of the trust idea in terms of what the word 'trust' means and the direction that idea may take in the coming years. My thesis is that, in the common law jurisdictions, we are fast approaching, if we have not already reached, a time of decision. We have to decide whether we want the trust that the last two hundred years has designed and left us, or we wish to be open to a range of possible conceptions about the nature of the trust. Certainly common law lawyers are constantly pushing further out the frontiers of the trust idea. The eventual outcome I see is that, if no decision is made or we throw up our hands about the situation, the common law trust will cease to have any real distinction from other legal 'ideas', and will disappear from usage where its factual elements cross borders between legal systems. My concern is with the trust idea in practice. Functionally, we will say, it is only usable in its common law homelands. That used not to be so.

14.2 THE TRUST IDEA IN THE COMMONWEALTH: TRANSITION AND CONTROVERSY

To have spent one's professional life during the last half century with the trust of the common law world has proved for the most part to be a prolonged experience of intermittent backwater stillness and sudden excitements. When I was a law undergraduate in England in the late 1940s and early 1950s, 'equity and trusts' seemed mostly concerned with English legal history and land holding. There was a bit of a lift with 'equity' when we received a visit from Denning J, as he then was, to talk once more about his decision in *High Trees House*.[2] We all learned from him how promissory estoppel would bring down the bastion of consideration in common law contract. But he was an enthusiastic speaker with a twinkle in his eye and an incredible ability to pitch to young university audiences. He could have sold coal to coal miners. For the most part, equity was instead a matter of imbibing time-honoured propositions, and trust law meant making one's way along a well-worn path of

1 In its International Trusts Act 1995, s 2(1), Barbados, for the purposes of the Act, sets out these requirements: a non-resident settlor and no resident beneficiary when the trust is funded, and no interest in assets with a situs in Barbados. On the other hand, a definition might be expected to point to a trust arising from the intent of the trust creator(s) where there is at least one factor, eg place of the intended administration of the trust, or the situs of the assets, that is located in a state other than the state (or unit within the state) that constitutes the applicable law.

2 *Central London Property Trust Ltd v High Trees House Ltd* [1947] KB 130.

express, implied, resulting and constructive trusts. It was almost a catechism; no one questioned that four-part analysis. Student wisdom was to the effect that trust law was 'dry stuff'. In those days the material was exclusively English, and the Trustee Act 1925,[1] its actual contents very rarely discussed, was put across, together with Westminster's property legislation of that year, as having been the dawn of a new epoch. 'Quite revolutionary', the lecturer would say, nodding his head gravely.

If you liked doctrine and had a taste for the inductive thinking of case-law, plus a pre-university attachment to English political and social history, the world of the late 1940s and the 1950s was made for you. Although this path of instruction would leave a glow of gentle and half-remembered things for those who graduated and went on to the Bar and chambers, or perhaps a solicitor's desk, trust law in practice was mostly a matter of drafting deeds or wills for the private client. It involved conveyancing law and regulation and, at the Bar, giving opinions on the construction of private clients' existing real estate and trust documents, themselves often of a remarkable antiquity. Indeed, well into the 1960s this sleepy, summer afternoon environment marked the subject of 'equity'. When a book of mine on the constructive trust was published in 1964, the first review to appear – in a solicitors' practice journal – declared that, although this work had 'nothing for the busy solicitor', there were one or two ideas in it that were of passing interest. Those ideas turned out to be from my introductory explanation of the existing law. My argument was that English constructive trust theory was going nowhere, and that the US restitutionary remedial approach was one that England could valuably adopt. Of this the reviewer made no mention. Evidently the constructive trust itself was academic enough.

Excitements there had been during the 50 or 60 years before the 1940s, but the argument, the sometimes passionate disagreement and the puzzled and puzzling case-law over the effect of the Judicature Act 1873,[2] which brought the administration of law and equity together in the one High Court, largely came to an end with the occurrence of the much more significant issues that arose out of the First World War. And in chambers and solicitors' offices, the 20 years between the wars were mostly spent trying to come to terms with the new social and economic order that the war had left in its wake. There was the statutory codification of 1925, as I have said, but that had been planned well before 1914. The trusts of the inter-war years were predominantly drawn for the private client, and were still of the fixed and successive interests model that had marked English trust practice since the seventeenth century.

However, the underlying social order of rural England that had produced these trusts and made them popular for over 300 years was now all but gone. To a significant extent this disappearance was hastened by the First World

---

1 15 & 16 Geo 5, c 19.

2 Supreme Court of Judicature Act, 36 & 37 Vict, c 66.

War, but the gradual decline of that world first became apparent with the agricultural depressions of the last quarter of the nineteenth century, and the rapid coincidental growth of huge urban centres focused on industry and trade. An unprecedented growth of mercantile wealth in the Victorian period and of a prosperous urban middle class had also occurred, and the successful merchants' trusts reflected much of the rural landed families' settlements. But John Galsworthy's Forsyte family, which epitomised that urban middle-class success, represented another world that was also savaged by the 1914–18 calamity. House of Lords decisions like *Sinclair v Brougham*[1] and *Nocton v Ashburton*[2] during the war period carried the seeds of many possible developments in the relief that equity might bring. But the opportunity for the exploitation of those seeds did not present itself until half a century later.

The Second World War put private client work very much on hold, and the men and women who returned were not interested in a judge-made equity when the occasion arose. A new world order had emerged, and it was the legislatures everywhere that were expected to put together significant new social and economic structures. Only in the late 1960s and the 1970s did a changed world of equity and trust usage begin to emerge, and only in part did this slow revival of interest in equity come to be reflected in the traditional case-law of trusts. Legislation and regulation and commercial practice led the change. Moreover, the change moved in the 1980s and 1990s at a rate, and in directions, that the pre-1939 age had never known or likely could have imagined.

Reading the future is always a hazardous business because one cannot know the social and economic occurrences that will call on the ingenuity of tomorrow's draftsmen and the response of the courts to litigated issues. With a concept so definitionally amorphous as the trust, there are likely also to be the doctrinal developments that are welcomed in one jurisdiction but rejected as unacceptable in others. Lord Denning's judicial life and the conceptual stimulation he provided are witness to this. Where he considered the merits between the parties called for it, he was ever fashioning new and controversial twists on doctrine. But in his home country surprisingly little has survived those years. It was not so elsewhere in the Commonwealth.

My own career took me to Canada in the mid-1960s, and at that time in Canada it was the plight of the wife on marriage breakdown that for both lawyers and the public was bringing the little-known doctrines of trusts law to the footlights. With the husband as the traditional head of the family, all the property associated with the married life of the average Canadian woman and her husband was held in title in the husband's name. The resulting and constructive trusts that had long ago come to Canada as part of the inheritance of English law became of central litigation importance. Now was the time to

1 [1914] AC 398, [1914–15] All ER Rep 622.
2 [1914] AC 932, [1914–15] All ER Rep 45.

put them to a new use. In the absence of legislation from undecided provincial governments and legislatures that would give the non-titled spouse at least some 'equity' when the marriage was dissolved, what relief – cried the populace – would the courts give? From the mid-1960s until the famous dissent of Laskin J in *Murdoch v Murdoch*[1] in 1973, lower courts, especially in Alberta and Saskatchewan as it happened, were leaning over backwards to produce that relief. The consistent fact-finding was of an intent by the married pair in happier times to acquire assets for both members of the marriage. So attention was riveted on the traditional resulting trust. Nevertheless, there was not much doctrinal development here, save for the wrongful supposition on the part of many courts of first instance that some kind of common intent had to be found. When controversy as to any such case arose, these cases proved to be controversial because of the hesitation of the appellate courts to reverse findings of fact.

So to the constructive trust, and the argument that, where the evidence undeniably showed no intent to create joint tenancy or tenancy in common, or enter into any sharing arrangement, the courts could impose a trust obligation upon the titled spouse to hold the house or other specific assets for the non-titled spouse. Western Canadian courts in particular were persuaded by this argument. Equity – of a kind – was the buzz even of television talk shows.

During this period, several friends in the United Kingdom wrote to me saying they had run into this situation in Canada. They asked what on earth was going on. And when in 1980 *Pettkus v Becker*[2] was decided by the Supreme Court of Canada confirming for common law Canada the validity of the so-called remedial constructive trust, and my name was associated with support for that decision, the number of letters increased from more than one part of the Commonwealth. It is common knowledge, I was reminded, that matrimonial breakdown is not one of the circumstances in which the courts have traditionally held the titled party to be a trustee. Those circumstances are few, and are essentially concerned with the fraudulent acquisition or retention of property. Because the constructive trust is concerned with substantive rights to property, the law possesses in effect a *numerus clausus* of such situations. To depart from that long-accepted approach in favour of bringing about a conceived equitable outcome for *any* perceived unjust enrichment – not merely for property division on marriage breakdown – one of my correspondents suggested, was destructive of the common law. Access to a proprietary remedy, awarding X's property to Y, should not be available on the discretionary say-so of the courts. Such discretion must be granted to the courts by statute. That was a parliamentary entitlement.

Canadians have now lived with unjust enrichment and discretionary remedies, including constructive trust, for over 20 years and, although the

1 [1975] 1 SCR 423, (1973) 41 DLR (3d) 367.

2 [1980] 2 SCR 834, 117 DLR (3d) 257.

flank of the English legal doctrine that previously prevailed in Canada has been turned, I know of no writing or opinion in Canada that has found fault with how the law has worked. There have been criticisms of this lower court decision or the other, but no denunciation along the lines of some of those who, following *Pettkus v Becker*, wrote to me or made a path to my door when I visited England.

Let me hasten to say, at a time when critical mainland voices are being heard about the last decade's offshore trust developments, that I do not consider my contrary opinion was necessarily correct. Whether there should be a discretionary proprietary remedy, applied as it was in the Supreme Court of Canada decision in *Lac Minerals Ltd v International Corona*[1] in 1989, may depend upon the attitude one has to the obligation/property dichotomy. That analysis holds that a right springs from obligation or from property, a source characterisation that remains with that right from its beginning to its end. In my view remedy supports right, and that right may be breached in a variety of ways. To associate a particular remedy with a particular right deprives remedy of the flexibility it should have in every instance of breach, whatever the nature of that breach. In my opinion the more recent decision of the same Supreme Court in *Soulos v Korkontzilas*[2] is a logical progression from *Pettkus v Becker*. It makes the remedial constructive trust available as remedy not only where unjust enrichment liability has been found, but where there has been a breach of 'good conscience' without any enrichment. However, as I admit, that Canadian view is, shall we say, not persuasive for everyone.

Certainly to this point the remedial constructive trust of US and Canadian law has not been adopted elsewhere. The courts of England and Wales are hostile, the New Zealand courts want to keep their options open, and the Australians have brought about quasi-marital property division with a constructive trust but on the basis of 'unconscionability'. US developments have gone their own way, most often oblivious to what is happening in the Commonwealth jurisdictions. The 1937 Restitution work of Warren Seavey and Austin Scott with 'Quasi-Contract' and Constructive Trust,[3] and the subsequent decision of Scott to exclude from his trusts treatise[4] any discussion of the constructive trust save so far as it gives relief in express trust situations, are now events of an epoch long ago. Among civil law practitioners the resulting and constructive trusts seem to be a totally unknown country. Even scholars are content to say, 'Well, of course, we have no need of that kind of thing'.

---

1 [1989] 2 SCR 574, 61 DLR (4th) 14.

2 [1997] 2 SCR 217, 146 DLR (4th) 214.

3 W Seavey and A Scott *Restatement of the Law, Restitution* (American Law Institute, 1937), Pt I 'Quasi-Contracts', Pt II 'Constructive Trusts'. The latter covers equitable proprietary remedies, ie, claims to a specific asset or fund, to have a lien imposed upon the asset or fund in favour of the claimant, or that the claimant be subrogated to the claim of another to that asset or fund.

4 WF Fratcher (ed) *Scott on Trusts* (Little Brown & Co, 4th ed), as it now is.

The constructive trust saga itself is now yesterday's news. Fairly firm positions have been taken, and it is unlikely that we shall see a significant *rapprochment* in the near future. Of course, it is perceived inadequacy in the response of the law to an also perceived need of action that causes these case-law developments. What happens in the long run is therefore difficult to predict. Have Canadians like Americans before them taken the trust beyond acceptable limits? There are certainly three types of constructive trust thinking. The *corpus* is made up of English thinking with the traditional analysis, Australian thinking turning to unconscionability as the theme of relief, and North American thinking with unjust enrichment in the United States and in Canada 'good conscience' as well as unjust enrichment. And there are those who conceive of unconscionability, unjust enrichment or 'good conscience' as being the basis of 'remedy', and those who mean by the constructive trust remedy proprietary relief to defend proprietary right. That difference of opinion exists both in the United States and in common law Canada. From time to time, not surprisingly, Commonwealth opponents of the remedy analysis deliver salvos on this difference.

So what is wrong here? Even allowing for a perfectly natural difference of opinion, which we can all understand, is it a terminological problem or one that is conceptual? I sometimes wonder whether, for all the impression of uncontroversial doctrine that law undergraduates were given at university in my time, the vital importance throughout common law history of the trust creator's intent has left instead a shifting sand of theory of what it is that constitutes a 'trust'. All the adjectives – express, implied, resulting, and constructive – merely had us chasing the peripheral. Today by contrast the charge of heterodoxy is hard to sustain when there is no undeniable conceptual orthodoxy.

The thought of equity principles themselves as a body of doctrine seems odd in a confidently inductive environment like the common law system. The instruments of equity are the measures of conscience and good faith. Except during Lord Eldon's Chancellorship, the desire of the most well-regarded equity judges has been that equitable doctrines be kept flexible and responsive, without the oppressiveness of procedure and rule as the containment technique and the contrivance of fictions wherewith to escape entrapment. As a result, applying principle to determine the merits on the facts as between the parties, and attempting to keep factual consideration within the realm of principle, equity doctrine has always been certainly more amorphous than that of law. If there have been unacceptable developments with the constructive trust in Canada, I am inclined to think – perhaps not to your surprise – that it is the type of development that remains within the corners of the broad canvas of established equity and trust law.

Indeed, whether case-law, or statute for that matter, is 'going too far' and should be rejected or severely narrowed in interpretation and construction may turn ultimately – if not earlier – on the perspective of the speaker, unless of course there is at least the germ of an idea upon which all can agree. My reader's interpretation of developments in the trust idea over the last thirty years – indeed, of what the trust is – may determine for him or her whether my conclusions at the close of this chapter are worth anything.

I intend to look first at the range of uses of the common law trust now existent, and in the light of that survey go on to examine what in common law jurisdictions at large is meant by a 'trust', conceptually and in practice. The latter leads me to the 'international trust', and to a short analysis of the offshore legislation that has been almost a non-stop occurrence within the last ten years. I intend to proceed to a study of 'fiduciary' relations in the civil law system, and continue with a glance at the common law trust. I then turn to think about the direction of the trust idea worldwide and the issues that confront us. At the close I take a look down the years ahead, and offer some thoughts as to what could be the fate of the common law trust in the next half century.

14.3 USES OF THE COMMON LAW TRUST CONCEPT

When in 1837 Thomas Lewin, Esquire, of Lincoln's Inn, London, wrote the first edition of his *Practical Treatise on the Law of Trusts and Trustees*[1] it was essentially a text for conveyancers. Like so many later writers of that century and the next, both in England and the United States, who followed in his footsteps he sought to elucidate for the reader the principles behind the trust idea. It was he who delineated the headings and subheadings by which for organisational and didactic purposes we still live today. The express trust, the implied trust, the resulting trust, and the constructive trust – which, as I say, were the basic fare of my law undergraduate training – were distilled by Lewin from a mass of undigested case-law, much of it historic. The trends of that case-law might have been read as pointing in more than one possible direction, as the organisational pattern of trusts law might have been different in other hands, but for the courts and the profession thereafter Lewin and his successors set the seal on doctrine.[2]

Lewin and later Underhill[3] were agreed, it is clear, that the trust is an equitable obligation whereby a person (a trustee) receives title to property (the trust property) from a transferee (a settlor or testator), which property the recipient is to hold, or to hold and administer, for the benefit of another, which may be the settlor or others, and of which he – the trustee – may be one. Alternatively, the settlor may declare himself a trustee for another or others of specific property he continues to own after the declaration.

---

1 Now J Mowbray and others (eds) *Lewin on Trusts* (Sweet & Maxwell, 17th ed, 2000).

2 See further DWM Waters 'The Role of the Trust Treatise in the 1990s' (1994) 59 Miss L Rev 121.

3 Now Underhill and Hayton *Law of Trusts and Trustees* (Butterworths, 15th ed, 1995).

The use of the trust for the holding and disposition of individual wealth within the family, both real estate and securities, cash, jewellery and art, furniture and other assets of value, was practically the sole use – certainly by far the predominant use – until the third quarter of the nineteenth century. The character of such a 'settlement' of land or trust of assets in general had remained much the same since the mediaeval origins of the trust concept. A settlor transferred title to property, a trustee received that legal title together with duties and powers, and the settlor was now out of it – as a settlor at least. The trustee accounted to persons, born and unborn, for the enjoyment yielded by that property. They or their guardians would bring court action against the trustee who did not strictly discharge the 'trusts' that he had undertaken to carry out disinterestedly and faithfully. It was the mid-nineteenth century draftsman who began to use the power of appointment, and court development of the doctrine of powers was in England to become a notable feature of that century's case-law. Although the deed making the appointment would be physically attached to the settlement indenture, the trust 'instrument' itself would not be definitive of those persons who were to enjoy or might enjoy the settlor-transferred property. Typically the power to appoint was retained by the settlor or it was granted to an adult beneficiary, and it was the authority to determine – sometimes long after the creation of the trust – those who should take successive interests in the trust 'fund' after the deaths of the first generation income beneficiaries. Later the trustee or trustees themselves were given powers of appointment, and so developed the science of mere powers and trust powers, and in the perpetuity context of general and 'fiduciary' powers.

However, the second half of the nineteenth century saw the trust for the first time applied outside the 'private client' field. Trusts of corporate supplied assets to secure the company's debenture holders, and public subscription unit investment trusts, were common in England as the nineteenth century turned into the twentieth, and the management of urban businesses by trustees following the death of the unincorporated successful entrepreneur was not unfamiliar. Most of these businesses would be small, and the presence of the new corporate limited liability would ultimately in England all but eliminate the business trust. But this mode of trust usage did exist and, although today the trust assets are more likely to be incorporated and the trustee-shareholders appoint themselves directors, it continues to exist.

In the present context, the point to be noted is that in each of these nineteenth-century instances the classic elements of the trust were present. A transfer of title by a settlor to trustees, a segregated trust asset or assets, a beneficiary or beneficiaries, and enforcement by way of a required accounting to the beneficiaries by the managing or holding trustees. So it has remained in mainland or onshore jurisdictions (as opposed to the offshore jurisdictions) to the present. Commercial usage of the trust has invariably recognised a clear distinction between agency and trust, as between a personified property management or holding vehicle like a corporation on the one hand and partnership and trust on the other. Unconcerned as is commerce with the successive beneficial interests that dominated for centuries the 'settlement' of land, the trust for sale, and the will trust of the private client, it might have been expected that this would not be so. Business concerns would surely wish to change the emphasis among the elements of the trust concept in order to better further commercial purposes. For instance, the *motive* for creating a trust would rank as more important than the persons who are to benefit as a consequence of the existence of its creation. The motive would then be stepped up to a trust object and appear as the main part of that object, persons being subsidiary. But this has not taken place on the mainland. There are other ways of doing the same thing, and these are ways more familiar to those who will ultimately work with the documentation.

While the trust as a more sketchy and adjustable case-law concept secures flexibility, the corporation created by statute is governed by precise statutory and regulatory rules. The two institutions work well employed together as complementary property holding and management devices. Indeed, the incorporation concept has its own potential flexibility. The corporate objects may constitute purposes of any kind, and different classes of shares, for example, voting and non-voting, participating and non-participating, for different persons and different family generations can reproduce much of the range of beneficial interests that we traditionally associate with the trust. The trust can add for the private client concerned with shareholding in the family corporation that peculiar ability of the trust concept to confer beneficial interests upon the unascertained and the unborn.

In fact the traditional trust elements have always worked advantageously even within the scope of the commercial deal itself. During the last half century it has been demonstrated that, where it is needed by commerce, the trust, as traditionally conceived, is capable of providing both self-contained solutions and also complementary support. Investment, security provision, lending, and property title holding are the areas in which the trust has been used. Throughout the common law jurisdictions this is uniformly so in my observation. Nevertheless, while manner of usage of the trust is bound to differ between jurisdictions because of differing commercial laws and practices, there has been no suggestion in writing of which I am aware that corporate or commercial counsel have found inadequacies in the long-accepted notion of assets administered by a titled and controlling trustee for the benefit of a person or persons who enforce the trustee obligations. My experience has been that, on those rare occasions where it is advantageous that the object of a transaction be stated as the attainment of a business purpose, incorporation of the property dedicated to that purpose is every North American lawyer's ready response. The trust can there play a complementary role with the holding, or holding and investment, of particular assets for a corporation or a nominee. One of its advantages is that, being a case-law creature, it is easier to create and certainly to terminate than a subsidiary incorporation.

The motto in practice is 'keep it simple'. If in doubt, the wisdom goes, use incorporation. Turn to the trust to secure informal, flexible, independent property holding but keep the central focus of your planning on the corporate *persona*. The more jurisdictions one is working across, the less one should be thinking of formulating new non-beneficiary trust objects. A closer look at the trust in commercial practice as an investment arrangement, as a means for the provision of security, and lastly as a holding device, may bear this out.

In Canada the investment trust in a public setting may take the form of unit (or mutual fund) trusts, including real estate investment trusts, and of trust corporation pooled funds. Investors in the oil and gas business may purchase units in royalty trusts. Corporations and public authorities will set up and operate employee benefit trusts, for the provision of pensions, sickness assistance, profit sharing, and savings schemes. Both for public investment and employment benefit plans, the trust is eminently adaptable to provision for a 'rolling' class of beneficiaries. Given a beneficiary class of 'investors' or 'employees', turnover of such persons as beneficiaries will be experienced in the nature of things. So far as the individual is concerned, where matters are simpler, the Canadian Government offers to the private person tax-sheltered saving schemes, for retirement and the education of family members, and in the past has offered the same facility for first-time home purchasers. Equipment trusts offer the individual the opportunity to take advantage for investment purposes of a fast 'write off' for industrial capital items such as railway box cars and highway trucks.

When the asset is to be held as security for a lender or is to be held by a neutral person for the purposes of a particular administration, the classic trust has proved ideal for the disinterested holding of title to such assets. The trust for debenture holders was mentioned previously as a security-providing vehicle, and another such instance is the mortgage trust where the title to the asset purchased by the borrower (or a registered interest in that asset) is in the trustee prior to completed repayment of the loan. A third instance is the trust proceeds clause. In this instance, where upon transfer of possession to the retailer the trustee holds title to goods, the proceeds clause gives the unpaid wholesaler an immediate absolute equitable interest in the proceeds upon authorised sale of the goods by the retailer. In this way the wholesaler retains his interest as against the floating charge of the retailer's lending bank, and against the retailer's bondholders. The property is never in the retailer. The statutory trust imposed on the head contractor in a substantial project commissioned by a land developer is a model of the classic trust. Legislation has been enacted in all common law provinces to protect the subcontractor as a supplier of labour or materials or both, from wrongful utilisation by the head contractor of moneys paid to him by the developer for work done, and from the claims of the head contractor's bridging loan grantor.

Mainland holding trusts are of particular interest in the present context since so many offshore non-charitable purpose trusts are employed for the holding of company shares. Again the absence of such purpose trusts in the mainland jurisdictions has not created any difficulty of which I am aware, and as an adviser to a law reform agency examining this subject it was once my task to seek out what consequent difficulties might have been experienced. If any whisper of possible difficulty were to occur, the incorporation alternative was regarded as always available. Canadian practice is fairly typical. Stakeholder trusts over assets in dispute pending resolution between the parties, and trusts of assets offered in settlement to meet class actions by plaintiffs, are familiar. Insurance policies are frequently held in trust, not only in private client estate planning, but in commerce. Buy-sell and stock purchase agreements are evidently in favour of ascertainable beneficiaries. The same is true of trusts of promoters' shares, and stock voting trusts. But in Canada custodian trusts holding the assets of corporate or institutional pension trusts are the most readily found examples of holding trusts. Usually the trust corporation custodian is relieved of all investment responsibilities; it is simply to assume title, hold the assets safe and to ensure that securities are available to the proper calls of the pension trustees' brokers. The beneficiaries of the custodian trust are the beneficiaries of the pension trust.[1]

14.4 EMERGENCE OF THE MAINLAND PRIVATE CLIENT TAX-PLANNED TRUST

However, if commercial and business uses of the trust have held to the classic elements of the trust, namely, trustee, trust property, and the enforcing beneficiary, the practice in connection with private client trusts may carry those elements to what would have been unimaginable for those now retired. And I underline that I am speaking of mainland private client practice. I am not suggesting either in what follows everyday practice. I am concerned only with what *can* be done in drafting a trust.

The trust of fixed successive beneficial interests that those practising until the early 1970s would have regarded as typical of all trusts – the number and complexity of the fixed interests would have been the only variant – has in some mainland jurisdictions almost completely disappeared. In those days the only dispositive trustee discretion of which almost all settlors or testators appeared to approve would have been that which arose if a 'protected' life tenant would otherwise have lost his income interest because he attempted to

---

1 For further reference see DWM Waters 'Learning the Law: Trusts in Business and Commerce' [1987] 14 *Malaysian and Comparative Law* 1 (a study of the usage in Canada); also JH Langbein 'The Secret Life of the Trust: The Trust as an Instrument of Commerce' (1997) 107 Yale LJ 165 (a study of the usage in the United States).

alienate it or it was about to be seized by a creditor or his trustee in bankruptcy. In such an event the 'protected' beneficiary with a determinable life interest, together with his or her spouse and children, then became the members of a discretionary trust class. The Trustee Acts of Commonwealth countries, save in Canada, carry provision for these trusts still.[1] Trustee powers of encroachment on capital in favour of income beneficiaries, and powers of maintenance or 'support' of minors out of income, were to be found in instruments, but, except for powers of appointment with gifts over in the event of non-exercise, that was it so far as dispositive powers were concerned. Indeed, older practitioners will recall that the conferment of extensive discretion upon trustees was thought inappropriate. It was considered that trustees should be given clear instructions as to the quantum of benefit each beneficiary was to receive – fixed interests – and each management power given should be carefully assessed as to whether the scope conferred was justifiable. Administrative powers also were carefully chosen for the trustee task in hand, and were limited to the performance of that task. Indeed, earlier generations kept trustees on a fairly tight rein.

The last 30 years have been dominated instead by the concern of high- and middle-income individuals with seemingly constant high levels of taxation. Gift tax, estate and inheritance taxes as capital transfer levies, as well as income tax and capital gains taxes, will differ moreover between jurisdictions. The primary desire of the settlor and the testator has been to ensure that, if tax cannot be avoided, every opportunity is taken by the manner of disposition chosen to minimise the amount due or to defer its payment. In every common law jurisdiction of my experience, the tax adviser is the first to have the ear of the client, and the immediate readiness of the client is for a dispositive vehicle that exploits the policy concessions and the exempt situations in the relevant jurisdiction's tax provisions. The consequence has been a total *volte-face* from the settlor values and the legal drafting of earlier times. The testator, as well as the settlor, now wants to create the most 'tax efficient' trust. He wishes to take full advantage of immediate tax saving or deferral opportunities, and to confer upon his trustees for the duration of the trust the maximum flexibility of movement. The trust creator often puts first – over spousal and family circumstances – the ability of the trustees to respond to changes in the state's tax provisions as occasion demands or opportunity offers. In fact the trust instrument that I frequently see is little more than a shell. It is clear that the meaningful content will be added at a later time, or that significant decisions as to what beneficial dispositions are to be made will never appear on the instrument at all. That is, the instrument does not contain the whole of the trust.

---

1 See HAJ Ford and WA Lee *Principles of the Law of Trusts* (3rd ed, looseleaf). This is an Australian text updated to the present. For New Zealand, a valuable text is D Breadon and others *Law of Trusts* (Butterworths, looseleaf, 2000).

Indeed, if we are to speak of the future it is worth examining further what can already be done for the private client, because I believe it has been the backcloth to much of what has been happening in recent years in the offshore jurisdictions. The classic elements of a trust – to flesh it out a little more – are a titled trustee, segregated trust assets, and a beneficiary who can enforce the trustee's obligation to hold the assets, or hold and administer them, for the sole benefit of the beneficiary. The trustee has control of the assets, and deals exclusively with third parties. The beneficiary or beneficiaries throughout the lifetime of the trust, ie until its objects are carried out, will require an accounting from the trustee. Although what is actually done will be dictated by the relevant tax structure – discretionary trusts were popular in the United Kingdom until a few years ago; now they are largely avoided because of serious adverse tax consequences – it is instructive to see not only what can be done, but what today's draftsman in any of our mainland common law jurisdictions can do with *those elements* of a trust.

The trustee may be made removable at the will of a beneficiary, usually someone like the trust creator's spouse who is a beneficiary. Alternatively, the removal and appointment power may be granted to a close non-beneficiary friend named in the instrument for this purpose. The question as to what effect this provision has upon a trustee, in particular one who undertakes trust services because of fees, is commonly met with the response that it has none. It is thought enough that, although the trustee can at any time be removed, albeit immediately under the terms of many instruments and without reason given, that fact is irrelevant to a fiduciary's conduct in the discharge of its duties and the discretionary exercise of its powers. Irrelevant it is, doctrinally.

As to the trust property, and I speak here of an *inter vivos* trust, this may consist of a nominal gold coin or ten dollars. The instrument will provide that further trust property may be added at any time by the settlor, or by another. Sometimes, for tax reasons, the consent of the trustee is required before further property is transferred to him by another. So it is evident that the actual trust property, as to the nature, amount and time of transfer to the trustee, will never be known to the trust instrument. There will be good reasons also for having only nominal property as the initial assets of a testamentary trust. The timing of the transfers of substantive assets to the trustee can be precisely planned. Then also the purpose of the trust may be to receive the fund of an existing trust that is to be coincidentally terminated or that comes to a close under its own terms as the testamentary trust takes effect. Another reason for the trust being in the will is that the executors may assign their choice of testamentary assets to it within a defined period of time after the death, and thus secure a tax advantage for the trust beneficiary. These are but three instances where nominal funding will be used, despite this being the final disposition of his means by the deceased.

Unless the jurisdiction has chosen to tax it heavily, the type of trust that for ten or fifteen years past has best demonstrated the possibilities for the contemporary draftsman, whether in the case of wills or *inter vivos* dispositions, is the discretionary trust. In my experience in Canada a few successive fixed interest trusts are still drawn, almost always in wills, and there is the occasional *inter vivos* or testamentary dynastic trust, usually created by the founder of a very successful trading or business corporation. The run-of-the-mill trust, however, is discretionary. It provides in the instrument a described list of persons, for example, spouse, children, and grandchildren who take by representation in the event of the parent child's death. According to Canadian practice, two or more named registered charities will usually be added to that list. These are the beneficiaries, and the trustee (or trustees) may dispose of income or capital or both among the beneficiaries as the trustees think fit without regard to whether any one person receives nothing or a much lesser amount than others. In fact the trustees will often make their periodic distribution decisions primarily with tax considerations in mind. No beneficiary is therefore entitled to any of the trust property; he or she is able to require only that the trustees consider his or her name and individual circumstances.

If the person included in the list of eligible persons wishes to assert that the trustees failed to consider his name or were prejudiced against him, he is told that he is fully entitled to make his case that the trustees did not act with good faith towards him. The beneficiary of course has the onus of proof, and he seeks to examine the trustees' papers or the trustees themselves in order to find evidence of his belief. However, he can be refused the papers and the opportunity to examine the trustees because it is the trustees' right not to reveal the reasons for their discretionary decisions. If he sues the trustees in order to obtain discovery of their files, but without *some* clear evidence of what he alleges, the trustees may successfully object that he is simply engaged in conducting 'a fishing trip'.

Nevertheless, as I say, a person in the list of beneficiaries has at least a right to be considered for distribution of trust property. If the draftsman has also conferred upon the trustees, or another named third party, the right, in furtherance of English case authority, to add further beneficiaries, those in the original list have their chances of being selected accordingly lessened. It is always possible that the appointor of further beneficiaries may have other distribution ends in mind. Most discretionary trust instruments that I have seen, unlike US instruments, give no stated reason for the creation of this kind of trust, either in the recitals or in the body of the provisions, and do not include criteria that the trustees are to have in mind in exercising their discretion. This happens because the settlor or testator, knowing only of the existing tax laws and regulations, wishes in no way to limit the scope of the discretionary authority. After all, especially if more than one taxing jurisdiction is concerned, who knows *what* tax changes may occur 'down the road'. The trustees must be fully armed for any contingency.

The tenuous position of the discretionary trust beneficiary receives the *coup de grâce* in the complementary power, again usually given to the trustees in a mainland trust instrument, that any beneficiary may be removed from the list. As persons may be added, so persons may be deleted. The usually cited authority is again English. And before we turn to the offshore contribution it should be observed that, with a power to add and delete, the settlor or testator on the mainland can bring about a situation where beneficiary status is in effect nothing. As practitioners of my father's generation understood the word, 'beneficiary', there are today in such circumstances no beneficiaries. Each beneficiary is such only so long as that is pleasing to the authorised remover of beneficiaries. This is grace and favour. Yet in trust theory, enforcement of the trustees' task is logically the peculiar right of the beneficiary.

A discretionary trust, being a trust power, allows the beneficiary not only to require he be considered, but to have access to trust documents and an accounting by the trustee. 'Mere' powers of appointment confer upon the stated object or objects of the power, as opposed to those who take in default of appointment, no right other than to be considered for appointment. Although the issue could be argued, the case authority is clear. Even if the appointors are trustees, such potential appointees have no right to information concerning the trust in which the power is contained. It is evident then that with mere powers existing mainland trust drafting practice can shift the whole emphasis of power and influence within the trust away from ascertained beneficiaries and towards the trustees, while the trustees themselves can be removed at will by one – the settlor or 'protector' – who may or may not *de facto* be accountable to anyone. It is a startling realisation.

To accompany this conception of the relationship of trustee, trust assets, and beneficiary, the settlor is free to employ dispositive and administrative powers of a far-reaching nature. The trustees will normally be given the power to vary any term of the trust instrument, including on occasion dispositive provisions, that in their view requires variation (commonly described as 'amendment'), and as an alternative to variation they will be empowered to terminate the trust at a moment of their choosing. Again this gives flexibility for tax purposes. The trust instrument here is essentially creating a neutral vehicle; it is to be used for later dispositive decisions regarding property and that property is itself to be alienated to the trustees at an opportune future moment. It is therefore also essential that the trustees be given the power to appoint the trust property to new trusts (sub-trusts) or other existing trusts. This is popularly known as a power to 'decant' the original trust. The trust into which the decanting takes place need not be in favour of the same beneficiaries, nor need the dispositive and administrative terms of the new trust be the same. The trust instrument of the original trust will expressly permit this departure from the provisions of the original trust. When the original trustees are creating new trusts, the art is in constituting the new trust with its own perpetuity period. If this cannot be achieved without creating other unwanted elements in the new trust, the opportunity may exist to have the governing law of a jurisdiction that has statutorily abolished the rules regulating perpetuity and accumulations.

The power to change the governing law is frequently seen in contemporary mainland discretionary trusts, and it is usually given to the trustees. That is certainly a feature of the last 10 to 15 years. Prior to that time there was little evidence that the average draftsman had given thought to the issue. The more sophisticated Canadian draftsman may bifurcate the governing law; one law to apply to the validity, construction and effect of the trust, and another to apply to the administration of the trust. The hostility to the severance of validity and administration issues that is seen in the English case of *Chellaram v Chellaram*[1] is not thought particularly persuasive in North America. Possibly because of US experience with 50 state jurisdictions, American jurisprudence to the contrary has long been more open to this *dépeçage* in appropriate factual circumstances, and Canadians are more drawn to this familiar state of affairs south of the border.

Although they frequently wish things were otherwise, settlors of mainland *inter vivos* trusts hesitate to reserve significant powers to themselves. The risk of attracting taxation to the settlor on the ground that he retains control over the title-transferred assets is too great. Increasingly a third party is being nominated to exercise these powers. Most often this person is a non-beneficiary, as we have seen, but he will likely be acquainted with the settlor and he is often intended to busy himself with the settlor's concerns. So-called 'advisers' can be found in trust instruments of the 1950s, and indeed there are occasional instances going back to the pre-1939 period. This date is interesting because here in North America are the seeds of the 'protector' in the offshore jurisdictions of the 1980s and the 1990s.

We have yet to see any court challenge of the increasing emulation in Canadian-drawn mainland trust instruments of the popular offshore 'protector'. And since for reasons I have noted the settlor avoids appointing himself as 'protector', an onshore challenge is not likely to succeed.

Exculpation is another interesting onshore development. The majority of instruments that I have had reason to see carry an express exculpation clause that makes the individual trustee (there may be two or more trustees) liable solely for the trustee's own acts or omissions, regardless of full delegation authority having been given. And the trustee is made liable for fraud and wilful wrongdoing only. Other instruments may refer to trustee negligence, but expressly state that liability is restricted to gross negligence. As we all know, whether or not the trustee in question is a professional, English case authority has approved the validity of such clauses.

---

1 [1985] Ch 409, [1985] 1 All ER 1043.

It is not my purpose to appear to criticise the contemporary primary concern with tax issues or accommodating modern drafting practices. Law and practice have always followed current economic and social concerns. They are doing so still. In high tax jurisdictions, the individual intent on conserving his wealth, and who wishes to transfer it to his family and the charitable and non-profit purposes he values, would be foolish not to be concerned first and foremost with the tax levies he must face. Subtlety in creating modes of appropriate provision for the family is of limited value if the public treasury is the *de facto* principal beneficiary of the available funds.

Rather it is my point that today, from the perspective of yesterday's understanding of the classic elements of a trust, some mainland trust practice, and to an extent the concept itself in the private client area, has taken on something of a hair-raising character. An earlier generation of practitioners was concerned with the prospective beneficiaries and the soundest provision that could be made for them. Today it seems we are more concerned with the creator of the trust, and the impact of tax upon that person or his or her estate. The professional trustee is concerned with liability in an increasingly litigious climate, and the trust instrument's exculpation and indemnity provisions recognise this.

Two thoughts arise out of these observations. First, that the classic elements of a trust, though formally the accepted thinking, may in fact be giving way in the mind of law professionals to something other. If so, we need to discover what is that other. What is it that draftsmen now consider to be the controlling legal criteria or, if you will, the limits that today fence the trust concept? What can be achieved conceptually and practically with the trust, or – to put the question another way – when should we be using the trust together with other property-management concepts, such as a corporation or a *fondation*, or not using it at all? Secondly, how much further can the limits be pressed without the trust concept, as hitherto it has been classically understood, crumbling instead into a jumble of ideas that has no convincing conceptual shape?

It is with this contemporary mainland experience and those two thoughts at the back of my mind that I turn to the innovations of the offshore jurisdictions.

14.5 TURBULENCE IN THE OFFSHORES

The work of the offshore jurisdictions around the world[1] is very different from the will drafting, marriage breakdown settlements, and protective and

---

1 For a full discussion of trust theory in these jurisdictions, see M Lupoi *Trusts: A Comparative Study* (Cambridge University Press, 2000), Ch 4 'The international trust model'. Reference should also be

discretionary trusts of mainland private client common law practice. Mainland lawyers serve an indigenous population with locally situated real estate and portfolio investments, with private companies and local business interests. These people have family members some of whom are living in other jurisdictions, but most of whom are likely to be domiciled with children and careers within the local nation state. Federal countries present jurisdictional problems within the nation state.

The 'offshores' can now in a non-literal sense be said to include Switzerland and New Zealand and other onshore jurisdictions engaged today in a not dissimilar practice. However, the offshores for the most part are small island territories with little land space and a comparatively minute indigenous population whose 'financial centres' constitute much the greater part of the economy. So far as the private client is concerned, these jurisdictions market estate planning to a foreign clientele with intended foreign beneficiaries. The offshore lawyer is engaged in a highly competitive business as between the 45 or more 'offshore financial centres', and this can encourage individual offshores to be anxious to accommodate client wishes. It is a marketing challenge.

Some of these jurisdictions have distinct specialisations in areas such as insurance, securitisation, and security transactions, as well as in institutional and public investment. For these jurisdictions, such commercial and business work is the greater part of their financial activity. But all of the offshores share in private client work. The mainland client who goes offshore has been advised of tax advantages that can be gained. The avoidance of probate and estate administration costs is another attraction. He may also be seeking asset protection, especially if he is a self-employed professional who is apprehensive of the possible size of any damages award that may be given against him in any future negligence action. A client may also wish to put business or personal assets beyond the reach of his spouse on a marriage breakdown, and the claims of family with mandatory succession rights to his estate on his death. He may prefer in the latter instance to leave his assets among his family members according to his own tailor-made plan, and avoid court awards or the pre-determined shares dictated in his country of domicile or nationality.

It is probable that the client would like to transfer the title to his assets to a trustee – transfer is usually the vital element in obtaining advantage for the client – but retain control of 'his' assets during his lifetime. His question then is whether, while creating a trust, he can reserve the power to veto any exercise by the trustees of their powers, administrative or dispositive, or better still to direct 'his' trustees in any such exercise. He will wish to add or remove beneficiaries as he thinks fit, and to dismiss and appoint trustees as he chooses. If there is no adverse tax consequence in his home jurisdiction, discretionary

made to the English journal, J Goldsworth (ed) *Trusts & Trustees* for articles, case notes, and commentary providing a rare coverage of offshore trust issues.

trusts will be attractive to him, or he may prefer 'mere' powers of appointment. In this latter case, any class of possible appointees, as we have seen, will have no access to trust information.

Over the past 20 years, the offshore jurisdictions in the Atlantic and the Caribbean, in the English Channel, the Irish Sea and the Pacific, by constantly adjusting their legislative provision have kept abreast of these market pressures. Asset protection trusts against future creditors and family claimants whose right of action accrues onshore are familiar. So are powers that secure to the settlor – or the protector he nominates – ultimate control over the investment and management of the trust assets. The technique with debtor protection is to exclude any creditor whose claim arose only after the moment of transfer of assets into the offshore trust, and to limit severely – some offshores allow only one year – the time during which, following transfer of assets to the trust, qualifying creditors may bring action in the offshore. In most offshores to this point, as in most mainland jurisdictions, there is no registration or public record of a trust of movables. Spousal claims to matrimonial property, whether foreign court awarded or community rights, and family mandatory succession rights under the foreign system, are simply not entertained in most – not all – offshores. In the case of retained control, or control given to a protector, control will extend to the power to add or delete beneficiaries as the power holder chooses. Initial nominal trust assets will, of course, voluntarily be added to by the settlor or others with the intended assets of substance, but only at a later stage.

Within the Caribbean, two popular features of this offshore legislation have been the asset protection trust, although this is now mirrored onshore in the legislation of Alaska and Delaware among other US states, and retained settlor (or protector) control over asset administration and distribution, especially highlighted in the legislation of the Bahamas and the Cayman Islands. Control implies the formal transfer of title, but the retention, whether partly or wholly, of the rights and powers that 'ownership' would involve. Again, US revocable trust theory permits the settlor during his lifetime to retain or grant considerable control, such as directing the trustees in the exercise of their powers and discretions. The offshores now market non-charitable purpose trusts, enforced by a settlor nominee, and the Cayman Islands have gone further to take right of enforcement from the human, capacitated beneficiary who now, being nominated a beneficiary in such a trust, has no right of action of his or her own against the trustee. The central element of the classic trust design – the legal relationship of trustee and beneficiary – in this instance is gone.

Whether the onshore courts will accept asset protection, wherever created, is likely frequently to be an academic issue because the settlor's assets will have been removed from the onshore forum's jurisdiction. Indeed, removal of all the settlor assets from the onshore jurisdiction and any other jurisdiction from which challenge is likely to come is clearly an advisable course for all aggressive asset protection trust creators. It is when this course has not been taken that claimants and nominated beneficiaries have a window of opportunity to press onshore conceptual and policy arguments against the validity of the offshore vehicle. Whether settlor or protector control of asset administration and eventual distribution can be contested offshore is an open issue. In circumstances of an extremely aggressive settlor provision, the attack may succeed if the creditor or family claimant is able to show that the provisions of the trust instrument do not represent the true intentions of the settlor. Although the instrument states that it is irrevocable, he is then shown to have left for himself the option to recover the enjoyment of the trust assets at any time. But these cases of 'sham', as of 'illusory trusts', are likely to be few. 'Sham' trusts do not include those instances where there is a patent demonstration in the instrument that there is an intended settlor (or protector) control of administration and distribution. The question then is whether the degree of retention of control from the trustee transferee in itself violates the trust concept.

The verdict from onshore courts on offshore non-charitable purpose trusts with onshore assets has yet to be heard. This is so whether this trust, including the Cayman STAR trust, seeks to come ashore under the umbrella of the Hague Convention on the Law Applicable to Trusts and on their Recognition 1985, or with the argument that inherently this is a conceptually sound trust provision. The *Restatement of the Law, Trusts, Third*,[1] is of the opinion that state legislation will likely be needed if this trust is to appear anywhere in the United States. In my opinion, because of the difficulty of determining what is a private *purpose* trust object, as opposed to a reason for creating a resulting trust, the same may be true also for the major Commonwealth common law jurisdictions. Together with the law reform agencies of Manitoba and British Columbia,[2] I do not see any insurmountable conceptual problem in the appointment, obligations and powers of an enforcer of such a trust. Indeed, with a Wyoming statutory trust and a certain modus of incorporation, the non-charitable purpose trust can in fact be simulated in the United States today. But that, one suspects, is another issue.

---

1 Reporters' Notes on para 47 (Council Draft No 2, Vol 1, 18 November 1998, at 401).

2 'Non-Charitable Purpose Trusts', Manitoba Law Reform Commission, September 1992, Report #77, British Columbia Law Reform Commission, November 1992, Report LRC 128.

14.6 THE CIVIL LAW AND THE TRUST IDEA[1]

The common law 'trust' became known to civilians during the latter half of the nineteenth century when it began to be more than an English conveyancing device and to be employed in business and commerce for investment and security holding purposes. This was the trust that took its name from the familiar conveyance, 'unto and to the use of [X] in trust for [Y]'. The use had been executed so that the feoffee to uses as 'trustee' held the common law estate and the 'beneficiary' the equitable estate. Civilians knew of the institution as the English or Anglo-Saxon 'trust'. The writing of civilian and common law scholars until the last quarter of the twentieth century very largely followed this usage and civilians spoke frequently of *le trust*. The Hague Conference that met between 1982 and 1984 to draft the Trusts Convention adopted the terms 'trust' and 'analogous institutions' very much in that manner.[2]

In the 1980s, however, civilians and some common law scholars were beginning to see the 'trust' from a structural point of view, and to apply the term to appropriate civil law structures as well as the common law institution. In 1988 Professor Johnston published in England his *Roman Law of Trusts*[3] which developed the thesis that Byzantine *fideicommissa* had both a structural and functional similarity to the common law trust. Comparative law scholars of the civil law tradition were commencing at the same time to see the trust in the same vein, and among these Professor Lupoi, a leading Italian comparativist, was to lecture and publish extensively in the 1990s, arguing that the trust is an older (and active) institution in the Roman-based civil system than is the form that that institution came to take in mediaeval England. He and other civilian scholars and practitioners continue to demonstrate the internationality of the trust idea.[4]

In this chapter I am primarily concerned with the future and fate of the common law trust, but I seek to assert no common law claim to the word 'trust'. I accept that when we turn from origins, symbols and the traditional usages of language to the analysis of structure, and also in my opinion to an examination of comparative functions, we enter a new era. Trust means simply placing confidence in and reliance upon another. Analysis and functional examination starts there.

---

1 For more extended discussion, see M Lupoi *Trusts: A Comparative Study*, n 1 on p 614, and DWM Waters *The Institution of the Trust in Civil and Common Law* (Academy of International Law, 1995) 'Recueil des cours', Vol 252. See also A Dyer and H van Loon *Report on Trusts and Analogous Institutions* Preliminary Document No 1, May 1982, Hague Conference of Private International Law, Proceedings of the Fifteenth Session, 1984, Book II, 'Trusts – applicable law and recognition'.

2 Book II, ibid, contains the text of the Convention, and the von Overbeck Report.

3 (Oxford University Press, 1988).

4 Note 1 on p 614.

The idea of A placing 'trust and confidence' in B that B will honestly and attentively manage property for the sole benefit of A or C is not of course peculiar to any one system of law. As can be seen in Muslim law and the *waqf*, the personal law systems also know the idea. Although the manager does not have ownership of the *waqf* property, the *waqf* provides for the independent administration of that property for both charitable purposes and personal benefit, and this may be for a considerable period of time. Of the two legal systems of Western civilisation, the civil law system is essentially to be found in mainland Europe, Central and South America, and a number of Pacific and African countries. Because of the Reception, which took place between the tenth and sixteenth centuries, it is of an older tradition than the common law system, and is largely a mixture of the received Roman private law and of local customary law, mostly in family and succession law. Obviously, in addition to the influence of local factors, the post-Renaissance nationalism and codification in every civil law jurisdiction have regionalised the laws of the system. Nevertheless, it is evident from the codes that the essential universality of Roman law in surprisingly large part remains.

The civil law therefore knows well the Roman concept of both *fiducia* and *fideicommissum*. Indeed, the Roman law inheritance from the first century BC to Byzantium in the sixth century AD was rich in the concept of *bona fides* (or 'good faith') in the performance of obligation.

The *fiducia* is different from the duty to act in good faith. It is an institution. The Romans knew it as a pact or agreement. It is full ownership with the obligation in described circumstances to restore the asset to the transferor. It was a very early concept in Roman law, and was employed principally to provide security for the repayment of loans. The lender on receiving ownership entered into an enforceable agreement to re-transfer the ownership as agreed, but meanwhile the lender was the full owner and his obligation to deal with the security and also to return it according to the agreement was a personal obligation only. The *fideicommissum*, as modern civil law knows it, was a Byzantine concept of the Corpus Iuris Civilis, and it suggests to a common law lawyer successive interests under a common law trust. In fact it was a fiduciary substitution, ie X owns subject to the condition that on the occurrence of a future date or event he is obligated by force of law to transfer ownership to Y. Such substitution was widely used in Europe after the Reception – it was the support of the *ancien régime* in France – but it was abolished by the 1804 Code Napoléon after the fall of that *régime*. Subsequent civil codes in Latin countries have followed that policy. However, *fideicommissum* survives to this date in the Civil Code of Quebec.[1] Quebec's law

[1] SQ 1991, c 64, as amended to 2000, c 53, s 67. Available through Wilson & LaFleur Limitée, Montreal, Quebec, looseleaf, with related statutes and regulations. For *fideicommissum*, see Book IV, Title 5, c 2 'Substitution', arts 1218–1255.

prior to its first codification in 1865 was the pre-Revolution customary law of Paris.[1]

Pure civil law jurisdictions, ie those that historically have never been subject to a common law ruler, seem invariably to conceive of the trust as contract or innominate personal obligation. Within civil law doctrine and code organisation it is both logical and sensible that the management of property by A for the exclusive benefit of B should be understood as a contractual joining of parties. Luxembourg's *fiducie* or 'fiduciary contract', adopted by decree in 1983, is part of this tradition, and the governmentally proposed ratification of the Hague Trusts Convention that is now before the Luxembourg legislature seeks to 'modify' this contract accordingly.[2] It does so in large part by introducing the conferment upon the fiduciary of ownership of the assets concerned, and in adopting the notion of the separation of the fiduciary's personal patrimony from the trust asset patrimony. Whatever their root in antiquity, these are the two prime features of the common law trust. The Luxembourg *fiducie* remains a banking, investment and insurance contract, but it now acquires these added features of fiduciary ownership and the segregation of fiduciary assets from the personal creditors of the fiduciary.

Contract in the civil law is either bilateral, ie agreement, or unilateral, ie gift. Agreement does not require reciprocal value, and a gift is only complete when the donee accepts the gift. What binds the parties to a contract is obligation; no *in rem* right is created. Remedy therefore is necessarily *in personam*; the successful plaintiff alleging breach obtains damages and, should the defendant be insolvent or bankrupt, takes his place among the unsecured creditors, unless of course as a contracting party he has bargained for the provision of security. The form of the civil law contract may well be that B receives a deposit of property that he is to manage exclusively for the benefit of A. B is now party to a nominate contract of *depositum* and to another of *mandatum* (or 'agency'). A has 'faith' in B that B will faithfully perform his obligations to keep the assets secure and to manage efficiently for A.

Where securities and monetary funds are concerned, persons in pure civil law jurisdictions who are entrusted with administering property for others may be in any one of several legal positions *vis-à-vis* the individual who made the property available for administration, whether for his own benefit or another's. The common law lawyer would be tempted to think of these as fiduciary positions each involving some degree of fiduciary obligation. Speaking generally, civilians would not use the term 'fiduciary'. There are also a number

1 The 1865 Code was named the Civil Code of Lower Canada. This was replaced by the Civil Code of Quebec, ibid, which continued to be rendered both in French and in English. The Civil Code of Quebec came into effect as a Code on 1 January 1994.

2 Introduced by Government into the Chamber of Deputies on 6 November 2000, as a *Projet de Loi* concerning the trust and its recognition in Luxembourg, fiduciary contracts, and associated statutory amendments and repeals. Accompanying the release by the Minister of Justice is an *Exposé* of the reasons for a change in the law, and the objects intended.

of possible relationships of the administrator with the trust assets. The relationship of the administrator with the funding party may be anything from that of nominee and principal, the nominee taking instructions on everything he does, to that of an investment manager making decisions of his own. The relationship with the property – the fund assets – may range from administering assets in the funding party's name to having title to the assets as well as comprehensive control powers. It appears that in this last situation the ability of the investor to recover his assets in the event of the manager's bankruptcy depends on whether the manager has invested and administered the individual client's assets separately or clients' assets have been mixed and individualised accounts alone been kept. Which course is taken may turn on business practice. Even if there is a contractual obligation upon the manager to keep separate the contracting party's assets and investment return, it would appear that this is only an obligation. That is, in the event of the manager's breach and bankruptcy only *in personam* remedies are available to the investor.[1]

The common law lawyer will insist that his version of the 'trust' requires a distinction to be drawn between the manner of creation of the trust, and the trust itself. The *trust*, says the Anglo-American, is the relationship expressed in obligation and rights between trustee and beneficiary. The civilian, however, will continue to see the trust only as obligation, and protest that the sole distinction between obligation and its manner of creation is that the creative act may be contractual, delictual, or restitutionary by way of compensation. There can be no other distinction, he will insist, however perceived.

The civil law jurisdictions differ among themselves as to whether there can be such a thing as fiduciary ownership. The scholar may say that ownership in civil law is indivisible; the rights of disposition, use and management are a totality and can only exist in the owner. There can be burdens on the ownership, such as the personal right of *usufruct* and the praedial right of mine to follow a path on land owned by another. But these are rights *over* another's asset, not rights *in* the other's asset. A 'fiduciary owner' would therefore be an owner, but subject to the use or enjoyment being *in* another. The civil law practitioner as opposed to the university scholar will often be less demanding. He will accept fiduciary ownership because he sees a parallel with the Roman fiduciary institute which is obligated to transfer, or condone the legal transference of ownership to the substitute. If an owner can be said to own although his ownership will be terminated as a matter of law by the occurrence of a contingency, namely, the occurrence of a date or an event, then ownership by one subject to use (or enjoyment) being enforceably in another is an acceptable proposition.

The core problem for the civilian with the common law trust is that it is a hybrid of undertaking (obligation) and of property. It is a concept that gives rise to both personal and proprietary remedies, according to how the trustee

---

1 B Vischer 'The Fiduciary in Continental Europe' *Trusts & Trustees*, June 1999, p 13.

has breached his trust. The Roman private law doctrine of the fundamental distinction between obligation and property is axiomatic in every civil law code, and statutory departures from it in civil law jurisdictions – when they exist at all – are often halting and ill thought through.

Conscious of the trading proximity of the United States and its common law trust, the Spanish speaking civil law jurisdictions of Central and South America since the first such innovation in 1925 have in a number of instances developed in their codes or in statute what is described as a *fideicomiso*.[1] Except in the case of Venezuela where there can be a trust over *legitime* interests, family law and succession law are untouched; this is a vehicle for commercial transactions only. However, the characteristics of this institution differ between the various national jurisdictions. Its essential form is contract. Sometimes the innovation contemplates a fiduciary ownership, and the most advanced jurisdiction today will have enacted a separation of patrimonies. This, however, represents changes made in the 1990s.

In most of the Spanish-speaking Americas, on the other hand, the effect of the insolvency or bankruptcy of the *fideicomisario* is a matter of silence (so that the remedies remain *in personam*). The alternative is often a rather muddled response. This may take the form of what can only be described as *in rem* recovery by the *beneficiario* from the third party when there has been an unlawful transfer by the *fideicomisario*, but no such recovery from the *fideicomisario* himself. The *beneficiario* must then establish actual fraud and, if successful, be content with compensation. The problem arises because the legislature has not thought of, or has thought fit not to embark upon the statutory creation of, a separate 'patrimony' in the name of the *fideicomisario*. Such a 'patrimony', of course, is a fund that is attachable only by creditors making claims that arose in the course of the *fideicomisario*'s discharge of *fideicomiso* duties, or for reimbursement of expenses (possibly also approved fees) incurred by the *fideicomisario* properly acting in carrying out those duties.

Since the received Roman law principle in every civil law jurisdiction is that there must be available to the owner's creditors all of his owned assets, and that he may do nothing to prevent that availability existing *vis-à-vis* any of those assets, the unseen doctrinal ramifications of introducing in any of the laws of the Americas the notion of a segregated fund of assets is obviously a concern not to be taken lightly. However, Venezuela was the earliest to recognize the trading advantages of adopting the segregated fund, and therefore the earliest to exclude the personal creditors of the *fideicomisario* from successfully claiming *fideicomiso* property.

A segregated fund is a crucial element in the common law concept, stemming from property administration, of the relationship between the trustee and the beneficiary. The fund is isolated. Such segregation is not expressed in the Dutch *bewind* (or the German *testamentvolstrecher*) where the

---

1 See further M Lupoi *Trusts: A Comparative Study*, n 1 on p 612.

property manager has the exclusive right to manage, but the title to the managed property is in the *bewind* beneficiary (or remains in the heirs in the case of the *volstrecher*). The title holder cannot deal with this property because he foregoes all his dispositional and management rights to the manager (the *bewindvoerder*). But in the event of the title holder's personal insolvency or bankruptcy his creditors can claim the managed property. This cannot occur with a common law trust if there was no initial fraud on the trust creator's creditors. Interestingly, the Dutch recognise the *bewind* as agency.

The influence of the common law trust in pure civil law jurisdictions that have a 'trust' is usually readily apparent. The Liechtenstein *treuhanderschaft*, which to some degree draws upon the Germanic *treuhand*, is legislation that was deliberately drafted to reflect the character of the common law trust. In 1926 this was one of the techniques used to attract business from English and American investors.[1] And earlier in 1922, having otherwise adopted in the last years of the nineteenth century the first draft of the German Civil Code, Japan introduced a Trust Law. This legislation was designed as part of a then move to regulate the trust and bank company industry, and was expressly based on the then trust law of California. It remains in force to this day. It has proved an excellent vehicle for transfers by A to T to invest for the benefit of A, but it creates succession law conflict problems of a daunting kind should A transfer to T for the benefit of B. The German Civil Code is simply incompatible with such a concept.

From outside the constant pressure upon the civilian is to give property characteristics to fiduciary contractual management. The ability of the common law beneficiary to trace assets under fiduciary management into the hands of the wrongdoing fiduciary, or of the culpable third party transferee, has not been successful in breaching the contractual ramparts, but, aided by the text of the Hague Trusts Convention, fiduciary ownership and the segregation of fiduciary property are beginning to make significant inroads. Whether the effects of this new approach have been totally calculated – indeed, whether departure from a strictly contractual approach to property management by A for the benefit of B has been justified – are subjects upon which voices from beyond the civil law precincts should probably remain silent.

The so-called mixed jurisdictions are those that at different times in their history have been ruled by Britain and one of Spain, France or Germany, each empire in its turn introducing its laws. These jurisdictions include the offshore islands of Mauritius in the Indian Ocean, Malta in the Mediterranean, and St Lucia in the Caribbean. Each has an adopted trust law, predominantly derivative from English law though it be. However, Scotland is probably the

---

1 See K Biedermann *The Trust in Liechtenstein Law* (English translation) (Alvescot Press, 1984). A short but valuable description of the Liechtenstein 'establishment', 'foundation', 'trust enterprise', and the 'trust' (*treuhanderschaft*) will be found in MG Kieber *Companies and Taxes in Liechtenstein* (Liechtenstein Verlag, 7th ed, 1992).

civil law jurisdiction whose private law has longest been intertwined with the common law. In operation and effect its trust so closely follows the classical common law model that the Scottish claim that it has a pre-eighteenth century origin within Scotland's unique civil law history will no doubt always be debatable. The Canadian province of Quebec is one of the best known of the mainland 'mixed' jurisdictions, and the state of Louisiana in the United States is another. Quebec has had a *fiducie* ('trust' in the English text of the Civil Code) since statute first introduced it into the province in 1879. The Louisiana Trust Code was enacted in 1964, its roots in large part going back into the nineteenth century. It inspiration is the Code Napoléon of 1804, but the draftsmen finally came to adopt the common law element of asset title being in the trustee. The likely costs of differing from the main elements of the trust law of the common law states of the Union were just too prohibitive.

However, perhaps one of the most intriguing mainland mixed jurisdictions is, and has long been, South Africa.[1] The old uncodified Roman–Dutch law was taken by Dutch farming immigrants, the Boers, into South Africa in the seventeenth century, and with the occupation of what is now South Africa by the British in the first years of the nineteenth century, Roman–Dutch law and English trust law came to be practised side by side. Intermingling was inevitable, and the trust concept that evolved is totally unique. It later travelled to then Rhodesia (now Zimbabwe), and in a weaker form to Ceylon (now Sri Lanka) also. The South African trust is a fascinating study in its own right. In 1988 that country introduced by statute a *bewind trust* as an alternative trust form.[2] The settlor retains ownership of the assets to be managed by the trustee, but assigns to the trustee all his rights of management and possibly of disposition. That assignment is irrevocable for the period of the trust's duration.[3] It is doubtful that the Netherlands will follow this innovation because for the Dutch, as previously mentioned, the *bewind* is agency. Nevertheless, the South African move reveals how close in some civilian thought is the *bewind* to the common law trust. Quebec's 1994 codification that introduced the *patrimoine d'affectation* of trust assets, and the acquisition by the trustee solely of *in personam* management and, where necessary, disposition rights, is not dissimilar thinking, though the South Africans would have had no part in 'unowned patrimony' theorising.

In some form or other, the influence of the common law has been a factor almost everywhere, so far as the trust idea is concerned. 'Analogous institutions' to the trust there may be, as the text of the Hague Convention would declare, but aside from the strong civil law traditions of contractual arrangement and property management through legal *personae* (incorporation for the common law lawyer) all have been touched by the common law trust.

---

1 T Honoré and E Cameron *Honoré's South African Law of Trusts* (Juta, 4th ed, 1992).

2 Trust Property Control Act, Act 57 of 1988.

3 Ibid, pp 3–6 and 222–226.

Wherever the British went, the trust went with them. Singapore trusts law remains the English law of the pre-European Union period, and in Malaysia it now is integrated with Muslim family law and succession law. The same intertwining of trust, family law and succession law has occurred in the one-time British territories of Nigeria, Kenya and Tanzania, and its contribution can be found in the laws of the Sudan. Egypt reflects both French and British influence. Clear traces remain from the post-1919 mandate period in modern Israeli trust law. In India in the Indian Trusts Act 1882, there was introduced by statute what is still recognised as one of the world's finest trust codes, and that code was largely copied in the Ceylonese (now Sri Lankan) trust code of 1917.[1]

The common law model always at the elbow, the trust idea is now being introduced into legal systems where the foot of the common law ruler has never trodden. Korea, Taiwan, and mainland China[2] (excepting Hong Kong) are principal instances of this. And in mainland Europe, where the civil law began, the ratification of the Hague Trusts Convention of 1985 by Italy and then by The Netherlands has raised the immediate question of what impact recognition of foreign trusts has had, will have, and can be permitted to have upon the domestic (or internal) law of each of these countries. This is not an academic issue; the answers are being urgently sought even as this page is written. The Convention is in force.

Over the last half century, the eclectic nature of the common law trust – its applicability as a property holding device in private client estate planning and in the business and commercial fields of law – has been one of its most distinguishing features, and this generalised character is of considerable value in the contemporary world of global corporate, commercial and investment activity. Everything from public unit or mutual fund investment and corporate pension plans, to the movement of assets off corporate books into holding arrangements, and the securitisation of debt, has occupied common law trust lawyers. The whirlwind of the offshore private client trust legislation is just another development of the last fifteen years. It seems not inexact to say that, while there is much that is conceptually absorbing in the new and original thinking of the mixed jurisdictions and in some of the pure civil law jurisdictions, the thrust of the trust as a worldwide and still developing concept belongs to the common law tradition.

---

1 On the Indian and Sri Lankan codes, see GW Keeton and LA Sheridan *The Comparative Law of Trusts in the Commonwealth and the Irish Republic*, (Barry Rose, 1972), Part Two, Chs III and IV respectively.

2 The Trust Law of the People's Republic of China was adopted on 28 April 2001, and came into effect on 1 October of that year. For a review of the law, see SM Nelson and DLF Chan 'New Trust Law in China' *Trusts & Trustees*, September 2001, Vol 7, issue 9, at p 12. However, whatever motivation the common law world may have provided, it will be recognised that the Trust Law has been heavily influenced by a contractual approach. Although the familiar hallmarks are present, this trust is very much as between trust creator and trustee.

14.7 THE COMMON LAW TRUST

The common law tradition that originated in tenth century England has today two clearly distinct modes of expression. The first is that of the Commonwealth. This is made up of England and Wales and one-time constituent parts of the former British Empire, later the British Commonwealth. These are jurisdictions originally settled or occupied by Britain, all of which at the time of settlement or occupation received then English law. The major jurisdictions, like Canada and Australia, became fully independent of the United Kingdom only in the twentieth century. New Zealand and most of the small island territories retain a final court appeal to the Judicial Committee of the Privy Council in London, and almost all the small territories also keep in place constitutional links with the United Kingdom. Although it has declined very considerably in common law Canada, and is beginning to decline in Australia, the influence and authority of English precedent is therefore elsewhere predominant.

The second mode of expression is that of the United States, all but one of whose fifty states received English common law early through settlement or later adopted. Trusts law everywhere is essentially a case-law supplemented in the Commonwealth by the Trustee Act facultative legislation largely reflecting a policy of settlor autonomy, and in the United States there is different state legislation on discrete matters within the law of trusts. Trust codification, an updated expression of the law, has been adopted in some states.[1] Nevertheless, although since the seventeenth century it has been independently developed and self-contained in the United States, the case-law of the two expressions remains doctrinally similar. This makes the differences of emphasis, where they occur, very evident and there are differences both as to the furtherance of settlor intent and permitted settlor control. The US states are markedly in favour of the first, so that for instance the English decision in *Saunders v Vautier* which overrules the trust creator's intent is followed in only one state. As to the second issue, particularly seen as to revocable living trusts, the latest comment[2] imposes today no limitations as to settlor retained control during his lifetime. US trusts law is also much more procedural in character. Marked and detailed differences in the taxation of trusts obviously impact upon trusts law practice, and very clear distinctions are evident here.

Frequently the doctrinal differences between these two expressions of trusts law are overlooked. Commonwealth writers retain an absorption with English appellate case-law to the exclusion of American authority, or else Commonwealth references to US law are slight and in the generalisations they make inclined sometimes to be misleading. With 49 states having separate jurisdiction in trusts law, US authorities hardly ever refer to English case-law.

---

1 See *Scott on Trusts*, n 4 on p 602, para 1.10, and annual Supplements.

2 *Restatement of the Law, Trusts, Third*, Tentative Draft No 1, 1996, para 25.

So it is a two-way street. Only the US law school journals will from time to time look across the Atlantic. Perhaps Canadian common law lawyers are particularly conscious of these two solitudes because as UK doctrinal thought – the one-time Canadian concern – is more and more involved with European law, and Canada given its continental position draws closer to US doctrinal emphases, the lack of in-depth awareness of each other, stemming from different world positions, social concerns and economic policies, is readily apparent. Today not only doctrinal material but trends of thought, even in trusts law, seem to go separate ways. I will return to this phenomenon in my close.

14.8 THE DIRECTION OF THE TRUST IDEA IN COMING YEARS

14.8.1 Civil law

Save for Italy and The Netherlands,[1] it is difficult to see the opportunities for much further development in the so-called 'analogous institutions' of the pure and mixed civil law jurisdictions. The mixed jurisdictions by and large are even less likely than the pure civil law jurisdictions to develop any generalised fiduciary property holding and management concept. Inevitably each such mixed jurisdiction is coming forward with its own peculiar historical, or otherwise locally explained, approach to the trust.

Apart from the civilian inclination to understand trust as contract, and to approximate it with the civil law's purely obligatory relationships, no two civil law jurisdictions can be described with confidence as possessing the same 'trust'. Even the *fideicomiso* of Latin America, a deliberate importation into these Latin codes, has a range of characteristics across Latin America from the entirely *in personam* to the functional (and in some cases theoretical) *in rem*. Nor could one expect otherwise. The trust as common law jurisdictions know it – a hybrid of undertaking and of property law – is simply not part of civil law thinking. It is largely irrelevant so far as the civilian is concerned; the Civil Codes respond to similar family and commercial circumstances in different ways, notably with the wide scope and applicability of a shared contract theory. Some states like Spain remain at best indifferent to the common lawyers' concept, and others like Germany are hostile to it as a potential cuckoo in the nest. Confronted with its employment, the tax authorities of jurisdictions with this reaction will often analogise at once with local conceptual thinking, however ill-fitting it is and whatever the incidental fall out in level of tax demanded. Caveat taxpayer!

---

1 To date these are the two civil law states, it will be recalled, that have ratified the Hague Trusts Convention.

However, there are positive changes on the horizon. First, Italy and The Netherlands are engaged on integrating the trust of the Hague Convention into their domestic laws. Italy is in the process of working out a domestic tax structure for trusts in Italy, and The Netherlands is studying how a segregated fund held by a titled owner can be woven into the Civil Code. Secondly, in its 1994 codification of private law Quebec, a mixed jurisdiction, sought seriously how to weave a trust (a *fiducie*) into the *Code Civil du Québec.* Both scholars and members of the Bar were involved with this issue for a number of years. It was not thought appropriate that the previous Code[1] left in doubt the position of a trustee with title to the trust assets, ie whether he is an owner subject to qualification, an administrator with some ownership powers, or some other type of manager. It was also not enough that the former Code restricted the *fiducie* to private client testamentary and *inter vivos* trusts. The change in the new Civil Code is extensive. Trusts can now be used in every business and commercial situation, and for non-charitable purposes as well as charitable purposes. However, the central conceptual change is to the adoption of a *patrimoine d'affectation.* The segregated trust fund under this Civil Code is owned by no one; the trustee for purposes of management, and the beneficiary for the purpose of acquiring his beneficial interest, have each rights *in personam* only.

The notion of a 'dedicated fund', as I will translate the French term, is not new. It was first coined by the French advocate of the trust, Pierre Lepaulle, whose writings were instrumental in 1932 in Mexico adopting the idea in its Code revision of that year. He saw the trust as an autonomous patrimony with a free destination. By free destination he meant the benefit of any person or persons, or the furtherance of any purpose. However, it was widely conceived in Mexico after the 1932 adoption that ownership of this 'dedicated fund' had to be in someone, and ultimately it was accepted by the Mexican courts that the trust property is owned by the trustee. This meant in effect that fiduciary ownership of a segregated fund was approved. The 'dedicated fund' also appeared in 1960 in Professor René David's drafting of a civil law code for Ethiopia. This first draft introduced a '*fidéicommis*' with a *patrimoine d'affectation.* Under the pre-1994 Code provisions on the subject of the *fiducie*, Quebec's courts, and the Supreme Court of Canada in appeals from Quebec, went through the same difficult patterns of thought as to where ownership lay and what kind of owner or agent the *fiduciaire* (the trustee) might be. In 1994[2] Quebec threw common law inspired convention to the winds, and described the *patrimoine d'affectation* in its new Code, as we have seen, as unowned property.

This difference of outcome between Quebec and Mexico (also Panama and Venezuela) suggests why the *patrimoine d'affectation*, however well thought through, will not necessarily be followed by other civil law jurisdictions

---

1 The Civil Code has possessed a *fiducie* (translated always as 'trust') since the nineteenth century.

2 See n 1 on p 618.

concerned with the trust. We have confronted a fault line in civil law theory. We have seen it before. Is fiduciary ownership a corrupt hypothesis which must be avoided by the civil law purist, or is it a logical deduction from the fiduciary substitution of the Byzantine sixth century AD? Roman law knew the *hereditas iacens* – the estate of the deceased that was unowned because the heir had not yet made an entry upon it – but it never conceived of a fund whose unowned status would endure over an indefinite period of administration. Despite the careful and informed thought that went into the Quebec Code's new *fiducie* formulation, it is difficult to believe that the unowned fund will be thought by other reformers to be a solution. The *hereditas iacens* itself has been described as 'an incomplete personification',[1] and this is the association one makes with the 'unowned' fund. Why not a *fondation* instead of an unowned fund? The lines are clearer and more understandable for client and practitioner. With Quebec's drafting personnel rejecting fiduciary ownership, was it the continued, if silent, pull of a common law North America that gave weight to the final adoption of the two patrimonies approach?

The contract analysis on the other hand, so fundamental to civil law thinking, will always dominate civilian thought. Moreover, since civil law jurisdictions do not need a trust, and recognition of the common law trust in their conflict-of-law rules has no particular attraction for most civil law jurisdictions, there is no point in their modifying this analysis. In any event without code or statute change modification can produce only the characteristics of a common law trust that are *in personam*, ie associated with the promisor's undertaking. Whatever particular Civil Code is under consideration, the civilian may think, why not simply leave the civil law contract for the benefit of the promisee, or of a third party, as it is? Why rename it? The trust problem, as it is seen from the international perspective, is not how to formulate in civil law jurisdictions a domestic trust, but the least damaging manner of recognition by these jurisdictions of the common law trust. In my opinion the Hague Conference in 1985 on the subject of trusts appreciated this. It is only those jurisdictions that are prepared to make a serious objective effort, either as a unilateral endeavour or through subscription to the international Convention, to fashion sensitive conflict-of-law rules that need to think of the impact of recognition on the recogniser's domestic law. From this point of view it is Italy and The Netherlands with their ratifications of the Hague Trusts Convention, and to some extent Switzerland with its unilateral efforts in recent years to come to terms with the common law trust, that mark the way of the future.[2]

A civil law jurisdiction that is considering whether to come to grips with recognition – and, as most European states have done, it may well choose not

1 WW Buckland *A Text-book of Roman Law* (Cambridge University Press, 1927), p 306. See also the later Peter Stein edition.

2 For an insight into Swiss thinking about the difficulties presented by the common law trust, see L Thévenoz *Trusts in Switzerland* (English translation) (Schulthess, 2001).

to do so – has to commence its task by accepting that the common law trustee/beneficiary relationship is obligatory, while the remedies for breach of that relationship, together with the beneficiary/third party relationship, are proprietary. It would perhaps be wise for that exercise to start with the Dutch publication, *Principles of European Trust Law*,[1] where it is underlined that at bottom there are two essential elements to a trust if it is to reflect both civil law and common law theory. They are: (1) a segregated fund that is not subject to the claims of personal creditors and the family members of the trustee, and that as a distinct fund can be recovered *in specie* from a wrongfully acting trustee or a knowing third party transferee from such a trustee; and (2) honest administration by the trustee. This approach dispenses with talk of relationships, and leaves the civilian, while content with obligatory standards of trustee conduct, also able to accept that the segregated fund takes him into proprietary considerations. I cannot help thinking that this initial conclusion helps to remove the misapprehensions right at the beginning of any civilian's inquiry.

14.8.2 Property management structures – a functional analysis

A legal arrangement for the management of property by one person for another, or for the accomplishment of a purpose, can be structured in a number of ways. The object of the administration is the benefit of the other person or of the purpose. Each arrangement reflects the conceptual and organisational fabric of the legal system of which it is part. There is a range or spectrum of possible devices. Obligation may be the *grundnorm* that generates management duties and enjoyment rights. Or the property under management may be the base that gives rise to duties and thus to rights. The duties and rights associated with the property management may be put upon the shoulders of the person undertaking the duties. Alternatively, those duties and rights, together with the property itself, may be personified. The property manager in the personification device is the *persona* itself. The directors of the *persona* will discharge the duties as, and in the name of, the *persona*.

At one end of the spectrum, the arrangement will take the form of personifying the duties of administration and the property (or assets) to be administered. This is the personification model. The objective the party or parties have in mind in creating the administration is a term in the constituting documents of the personification. The benefits emanating from the activities of the legal *persona* are an entitlement of the described person(s) or the purpose. Those persons or the purpose receive benefit in the form of units of value or right of action against the *persona*.

At the other end of the spectrum, the arrangement may be an agreement by the manager to administer according to initial, or continuing, instructions. This

---

1 DJ Hayton, SEJJ Kortmann and HLE Verhagen (eds) *Law of Business and Finance* (Kluwer, 1999), Vol 1.

is the contractual model. Title to the assets remains in the instructing party or, possibly together with bonding or other security provision, is transferred to the manager. The object intended to benefit is one of the contracting parties, a purpose that is to be furthered, or a third party. A designated person on behalf of the purpose, or the third party, will have right of action on the agreement.

In the middle of the spectrum, between personification and agreement, is an arrangement where the manager administers a segregated fund of assets. This is the property concept. Commonly, but not necessarily, the manager is a transferee of title to those assets, and administrative duties and powers, together with the distributive duties, are given to him coincidentally with the transfer. The person or purpose that is to be benefited is commonly said to acquire a proprietary interest in the fund, which he may assign on disposition or pledge. He may not only sue the manager for proper administration but also recover specific fund assets from wrongdoers and go ahead of the administrator's personal creditors.

Broadly therefore, looking across the spectrum from one side to the other, three possibilities exist. A personified structure, a proprietary structure, and an agreement structure. The first is monistic, the second is a relationship of manager and beneficiary each with property rights, and the third is purely obligation, ie *in personam*. The third may be expressed as an *in personam* relationship of manager and beneficiary (or enforcer of a purpose), but in the writer's opinion that relationship is a consequence. The primary feature is the obligatory undertaking of the manager. The relationship that is consequent may be between the creator of the device and the manager, or between the manager and the beneficiary (or enforcer). The ongoing relationship between creator and manager will readily pale at some point into contractual agency. Agency may be seen by some as a fourth property management device on the extreme of the agreement end of the spectrum.

The standard of conduct required of the manager is much the same as between all three (or four) structures. There is no conceptual reason for variation. Some management arrangements are seen to be more demanding of fidelity than others, but across the spectrum what is looked for is an honest (vigilant and objective) and careful discharge of duties and exercise of powers.

There are no variations on the first structure (personification); either there is a *persona* or there is not. Although the structuring problem may be approached conceptually from the two patrimonies angle, the *patrimoine d'affectation* – as the writer sees it – is a desperate effort to stay away from personification. But there can be variations on the second (the proprietary structure). These will lean towards the first, personification, such as in connection with the taxation of the structure or with the right of structure creditors to claim against the trust funds. Or they may lean the other way towards the third (the agreement structure). For example, the management creator does not drop out of the picture, but continues to play an active part in the management.

For the civilian there is a sharper line between the second (the property structure) and the third (the agreement structure), because a civil law right is classified distinctly as one or the other. Although Byzantine Roman law was undecided, the French jurist, Robert Pothier, in the eighteenth century and Latin codification in the nineteenth century[1] that adopted his theories, helped to confirm this dichotomy. The common law has never subscribed to that hard distinction. As a result, oscillation in the common law between the second and third structures is quite possible. Among the pure civil law jurisdictions, personification (the first option) is increasingly employed, but otherwise most management arrangements are contractual and carry no special features for the event of the manager's insolvency or bankruptcy. Leaving title in the creator of the structure, or insuring against management failure, is the usual response to the latter problem. These solutions essentially arise out of the fact that the agreement is contractual, and agency has an obvious appeal. So they are squarely in the third structure at one extreme of the spectrum.

Turning to see what the civil law jurisdictions have done with the three possible structures, we look first at the jurisdictions that belong to the pure civil law tradition. Personification at the other extreme from contract would be the natural civil law alternative to property and obligation. Familiar are the *fondation* of the Latin tradition, the *stiftung* of German origin, and the *stichting* of The Netherlands. From the latter two has developed the private purpose character of the *privatstiftung* of Liechtenstein and Austria. The *Stichting Particulier Fonds* of the Netherlands Antilles is another such legal entity serving private purpose ends. This is a very new introduction. Indeed, it seems that today, seeking simplicity, civil law clients are increasingly preferring the *persona* structure, and that common law estate planners, faced with a highly tax-regulated trust, are also looking at these civil law legal entities as bypassing devices. Panama has recently made a comparable move with a private *fondation*, and it appears that it is having an appeal among North American clients who feel that the common law trust is now tied hand and foot by state tax regulation.

Although it has not been extensively used, the Liechtenstein *treuhanderschaft* is the product of a 1926 statute assertively choosing the second (property) structure. However, the codes of Central and South America in introducing for commercial usage the *fideicomiso* are markedly conscious of the civil law's obligation/property dichotomy. From jurisdiction to jurisdiction, as this paper has stressed, one can see different responses to this phenomenon. Several have apparently decided to remain in silence with the third (obligation) structure, or when their *fideicomiso* is compared with the US institution they appear simply not to have seen – perhaps they have been content not to tackle – the insolvency and bankruptcy problem. Code drafting is often in remarkably generalised language, but others seem to align *in personam* remedies with

---

[1] The adoption was first made in the Code Napoléon in 1804.

specific restitution (or *in rem*) results. Only two jurisdictions appear now to have taken the firm step of introducing the two patrimonies of the *fideicomisario* (the fiduciary manager). Drawing one's conclusion from the periodic code revisions, it can be said that as a broad proposition the *fideicomiso* appears to move according to the jurisdiction between the third structure (obligation) and the second (property). It is again an oscillation, this time in the civil law system.

Mixed jurisdictions do not really make a choice between property and agreement structures, at least initially. Their present day codes and statutes effectively reflect the very singular conceptual intermixture with which their particular pasts have left them. It is when they codify, or respond statutorily to economic pressures, that choices are made as to what property management arrangements shall be permitted. Some are in the position of St Lucia in the Caribbean which looks as if it will continue to adhere to the property structure, while Louisiana somewhat reluctantly determined in the 1960s that it had no realistic choice within the US common law trust world but to do the same with its Trust Code. The Louisiana trustee holds title, whether that is legal, equitable or statutory, to the trust assets. On the other hand, as we have seen,[1] Quebec in 1994 chose to retain an existing *fiducie*[2] (translated as 'trust') that was introduced by statute in 1879 to accommodate the English of Montreal, but to change its whole character. Previously I posed this as a question, but I should go further and say that in my interpretation the 'dedicated fund', owned by no one, was a very deliberate effort to attempt to marry civil law theory with North American continental practicalities. It rationalises doctrinally the retention of the second (property) structure.

14.8.3 Common law

Although common law lawyers look back to Lord Nottingham LC, as the principal architect of the modern trust, and since the early nineteenth century this trust, as the traditional trust theory for the common law jurisdictions, has been firmly rooted in the second structure (property), the rationalisation of the Anglo-American trust is today more controversial than those who work with it daily appear to realise. In my opinion this controversy is not recognised as it ought to be, even in the literature.

The classic interpretation of the common law trust is that it is a property-based relationship between trustee and beneficiary. The settlor, having created the trust and transferred title in the trust assets to the trustee, has no more to do with the trust. If powers are retained, only a modicum of control remains with the settlor. The trustee may be in a contractual or tortious relationship with a third party as a result of properly carrying out his duties. The 'trust' is

1 Text to n 1 on p 619 and n 1 on p 620.

2 See nn 1 and 2 on p 619.

but a popular name for an institution that is a relationship, and not a legal person. The trustee holds title to the trust assets, and having such title either holds for another or controls the disposition and acquisition, and also the management, of the trust assets. The trust assets are not subject to the claims of the personal creditors of the trustee, nor the claims of his various family members under matrimonial property law or succession law. The beneficiary, or the Crown in supporting a charitable trust purpose, can recover *in rem* from a wrongfully appropriating trustee or a third party who took title with notice of such wrongdoing.

This classic interpretation is now called in question. In the United States there is a clearly discernible opinion that the 'trust' today should be designated a legal person. It is said that this change in the law would produce the protection for the trustee against personal liability that the limited liability corporation (and its directors) have long had. It is increasingly seen to be unfair (and unrealistic) that the trustee lacks this same protection. Corporation and trust are each property holding and administration devices. Why the difference? And these are widely heard complaints. Why should the properly acting trustee, faced with a third party claim and insufficient assets in the trust fund, be personally liable to the third party for the excess? It should not be a matter of an adequate exculpation clause, and negotiation by the trustee with the other contracting party on entering any contract, that the trustee be exposed to no personal liability. It should be clear in law, as it is with the corporation, that the third party looks to the trust fund as its recourse. The tort exposure in particular with jury-awarded damages can be horrendous. And why should the trustee not be able to borrow from the trust fund and give his own promissory note for repayment? He cannot be enabled to do this now because he cannot borrow from himself! The whole procedural process of the trustee wearing two hats, say the critics (one hat for his responsibility for the trust affairs, and the other for his personal affairs) is far too complex in today's fast pace economies.

Indeed, as Professor Edward Halbach, the Reporter to the *Restatement of the Law, Trusts, Third* fairly underlines,[1] tax law for many years has deemed the 'trust' a legal person; practitioners frequently refer to, and speak of, the 'trust' as if it were a legal person under existing law. Although he does not foresee the forthcoming Restatement departing from the classic expression of a trust, he does see the distinction made in 'an increasing number of states' between the trustee's personal capacity and his fiduciary or 'representative' capacity – note that adjective – as part of a subtle movement towards recognition of the trust as an entity. *Restatement, Trusts, Third* can be expected to depart from previous Restatements, he says, by 'providing that third parties' suits against trustees normally result in a judgment against the trustee in a representative capacity (that is, [a suit] "against the trust")'. In the writer's opinion, however,

[1] (2000) 88 Cal L Rev 1877 at 1882–83.

the notion of 'representation' can lead only to agency, which is not intended, or to personification. The fiduciary here 'represents' the *persona*.

Those who favour the personification (or 'entification') of the trust also see legal personification as producing very little change with regard to trust rules. In practical terms it would create little more, it is said, than a ripple. Here I would differ. The whole centre of the concept would change. The relationship between trustee and beneficiary goes. As an entity the trust must ultimately become another statutorily spelt out and regulated *persona*. If limitation of liability to the trust fund, save as to trustee wrongdoing, is indeed a desirable policy, and it may well be, I would much prefer to see trustee liability dealt with as an independent issue while the trust remains in the middle of the spectrum. It seems to me that personification of the trust will leave it indistinguishable in practical terms from any other entity. From it being essentially a relationship between manager and beneficiary as opposed to a *persona* comes in my opinion its uniqueness. From that relationship comes much of the flexibility which all shades of opinion associate with the trust concept. Moreover, if personification is the trust characterisation within the not so far future, I fear it will split North American trust law (including Canadian common law) from the law of the Commonwealth. I discern no enthusiasm for trust personification in the United Kingdom, Australia or New Zealand, nor have I found there any sense of its ultimate inevitability. On the other hand many Canadian practitioners and accountants, like their American counterparts, look upon the 'trust' as if it were already a person, and lawyers not infrequently draft in a manner which leaves this same impression.[1] The word 'trust' is creeping into Canadian legislation, replacing 'trustee', and this phenomenon is something, to be fair, which is observable even in England's Trustee Act 2000. The newly-adopted Uniform Trust Code, now commended to all the states of the United States, refers frequently to 'the trust', and this may be very significant in terms of what can be expected in the future. However, for the moment, as has been noted here, the *Restatement of the Law, Trusts, Third* is holding the line, and the saga of 'entification' is left to tomorrow in state legislation and state courts.

There is today another conception of the trust that also departs from the classic expression. While the *property-based* relationship in the classic interpretation of the trust emphasises the relationship of trustee and beneficiary to the exclusion of the settlor/trustee relationship, the view that the trust is an *agreement-based* relationship swings the emphasis away from trustee and beneficiary (and beneficiary and third party) to settlor and trustee. It has been pointed out to the present writer that in Canada old-timers drafted 'a Trust Indenture'; contemporary drafting lawyers draw 'a Trust Agreement'. But that is not quite the issue we are now considering. The trust instrument

1 The Income Tax Act (Canada), RSC 1985, c 1 (5th Supp), as amended, has for many years taxed the 'trust' as an individual.

does indeed represent an agreement by the trustee to act and to do so on the basis of the duties given to him with the powers conferred upon him. The common law concept does not require a trustee's formal consent to act and to be instructed by the trust terms. This is spelt out from the conduct of the trustee, as when the testamentary trustee comes forward to act on the winding up of the deceased's estate. Although formerly called an indenture, the trust instrument is a two-party instrument that is a convenient medium for setting out the trust terms, which the trustee takes away as its orders.

An agreement-based relationship on the other hand is one where the settlor/trustee agreement remains the nature of the concept throughout the entire duration of the trust. The agreement does not launch the trust – the trustee/beneficiary relationship *is* the trust. This is the third (agreement) structure on the spectrum. The trust is essentially a deal between a trust creator and a trustee, and its main characteristic is settlor autonomy. Although it is a hybrid of undertaking and property rules, the common law trust has in fact been explained as a contractual or agreement idea. Professor John Langbein's paper on 'The Contractarian Basis of the Law of Trusts'[1] is a forthright declaration of this position. He does not deny the property aspects of the common law trust, but he argues that the consequences of a tracing action can be simulated in contract law. Only historical accident prevented this from being said in the beginning. By way of contract, security for trustee performance can be supplied, and statute can provide – as it does in insurance legislation – that a fund shall be segregated from the manager's other assets. Because the trust is itself a deal between settlor and trustee, Professor Langbein contemplates enforcement by the settlor of the trustee's duties. And, if there is any contention that testamentary and personal *inter vivos* trusts are not contractual in character, he regards it as unquestionable that business, financial and commercial trusts are contractual in nature.

What is important to keep in mind in the evaluation of this thesis, however, is that the author has a limited purpose in mind. He does not deny that the trust is a hybrid, although he expresses that not as 'undertaking' but as *contract* and property. He sets out to contend that the development and future use of the trust would be easier if we saw things as they really are, namely, that the nature of the common law trust is in essence contract.

What brings the agreement-based relationship structure so much into focus today is the emergence of the private client tax-planned trust, which I discussed previously in this chapter, and in particular the development of the settlor/trustee relationship by the offshore jurisdictions. In this paper I have attempted to show how far the offshores have taken private client trust work into the realm of an ongoing relationship between settlor and trustee at the expense of the relationship between trustee and beneficiary. It is true that the beneficiary may have a discretionary trust interest (which is non-proprietary) or

---

1 (1995) 105 Yale LJ 625.

be the object of a 'mere power', and that either is a pretty slight interest. It is also true that this situation has long existed. However, the contemporary move to deny the requesting beneficiary information, in addition to adding names or deleting names from the trust object list without reason given, changes everything. Without information, a beneficiary in place cannot press grievances, and if he can be removed at discretion he is hardly in a position as a practical matter to press anything. That the enforcement right may be removed from him and given to another, as in the Cayman STAR trust, reinforces the picture of a beneficiary who has travelled from a position in Lord Nottingham's England at the centre of the trust to today's position of being a hopeful individual at the fringe of the structure.

Nor can one discount the fact that, although we speak of an agreement-based relationship between settlor and trustee as if they were parties with parity, it is more than likely that the settlor or protector will have a power to dismiss and hire trustees at discretion.

The other development offshore has been the conferment of retained control upon the settlor or his protector. No one argues, of whom I am aware, that all the powers that can be retained or given to a protector, listed as they are in the Bahamas and the Cayman trust legislation, could safely be conferred upon the same settlor or protector. These powers *in toto*, it will be recalled, enable the settlor or protector to control the exercise of all powers given to the trustees, or they confer upon the settlor or protector himself the power to make all the administrative and dispositive decisions. Nevertheless, no one knows how far those lists may be introduced in the one trust without causing a challenge. Several instruments that I have seen are breath-taking. And from whom is challenge realistically to come if the beneficiary is a cap in hand at the door?

Sham trust and illusory trust arguments show to some extent how far retained control can be carried, but essentially it is question of judgment for the draftsman and his client how far things can be taken before the property management arrangement passes to the extreme of the spectrum, namely, agency.

The legislation of the offshores is not the legislation that is to be found in the mainland common law jurisdictions and, save for the non-charitable purpose trust, the offshore legislation is concerned only with private wealth distribution trusts, not the range of investment, holding and security trusts that are employed in commerce and financial business. Nevertheless, I am beginning to wonder whether, without a clear and shared understanding of what is a trust, the common law world is in danger of seeing its use decline. At some point use of every concept turns into abuse. If, in the absence of authority no one is in a position to say with confidence what a common law trust is, those practising can have no clear picture in their minds of the character of this case-law creature. This poses obvious exposures. A code provides a clear picture to a civilian; common law lawyers in an environment of a shifting and spasmodic case-law read the law as they may. The only restraint upon 'pushing the envelope' yet further in response to client wishes is the sense of the practising lawyer – and who is to fault him – as to what he can 'get away with' or, to be more polite, achieve for the client.

14.9 CONCLUSION

In the circumstances that I have described, different people will draw different conclusions as to where the classic trust in common law jurisdictions is heading. As the horizons of the common law trust's usage and adaptability expand, some will excitedly say – and do say – that its limits seem endless. In my opinion, however, we are fast approaching, if we have not already overtaken, the practical limits. Should the trust be recognised in trusts law as a legal person? I think it will simply be another institution like the corporation, *fondation*, or *stiftung* and, as I have earlier suggested, be soon itself the subject-matter of statute and regulation. If registration as entity comes, can regulation be far behind? Much of the case-law provided flexibility will be gone. If it is taken the other way on the spectrum, to being explained in terms of an agreement between settlor and trustee as to how property shall be administered and distributed during the lifetime of the trust, and the settlor (or his nominated protector) plays a key role in those activities, I see it clearly being characterised as contract but on the edge if not over the edge into agency. At most the trustee is then a custodian.

My emphasis in making these remarks is upon the *practical* limits to what can realistically be done with the trust. I am thinking of the common law practitioner in any part of the common law world dealing with a client whose affairs involve foreign elements, and I particularly have in mind the notary, advocate or tax official in a civil jurisdiction called upon to understand and work with, rather than ride roughshod over, a common law trust.

I would suggest that the long success of the common law trust over the centuries is due to the fact that it stands midway between incorporated property management and property management by way of contract or agency. It remains largely a case-law creature, capable of being kept doctrinally abreast of the times by a judiciary trained in inductive law-making where policy and precedent go in measured step hand in hand. The classic property-based relationship of trustee and beneficiary is known. In my view it has stood the test of time. If we choose instead to push the apparent frontiers of the concept either to legal personality or to agency without any clear idea of what it is we are pushing the common law trust will not travel beyond common law borders. It will seem to other legal systems to be but a jumble of ideas without focus. Such a legal institution has no reliable utility. The question will always be – what is the neighbouring jurisdiction going to make of this thing? And there is little international conflict-of-law Conventions can do in a situation like this. Meanwhile, the foundation by contrast is conceptually simple to appreciate, and is reliable as to outcome. Who has problems of understanding with legal personification?

We have to face the fact that, much though we would like the common law trust to be an international property management vehicle, civilians have concluded they have no domestic need of this hybrid. That is the first strike against it. Their existing contractual and, as I say, personified management arrangements are enough. For the most part, therefore, the common law trust internationally presents an issue solely about recognition under conflict of law rules. But, if recognition is to be had in any state, that state must know what it is that is being recognised. Article 2 of the Hague Trusts Convention attempts to provide that. And for practical reasons, such as the possible movement of capital in the absence of some local 'trust' provision with the same advantages, the recognising state is ultimately likely to decide that it needs to have some domestic equivalent. This brings us back fully to the problem of the trust as a 'jumble of ideas'. How can the civilian effectively design that equivalent if there is uncertainty where the common law trust idea is to be found on the spectrum?

There is another difficulty. Because of what can be done with powers and changing the identity of intended trust beneficiaries, many civilians continue to think of the common law trust as a ready instrument for perpetrating fraud, both on others and, as civilians define it, on the law. In other words we have to be judicious as to how and when we employ the trust. We of the common law tradition have to accept that our policy decisions may not be those of others. Aggressive asset protection trusts already have a bad press, but although mandatory succession rights in civil law countries are a matter of *ordre publique* in only some such states, these rights have been indigenous to the civil law system since the eleventh century. It is a fact of life, as, since the demise of common law dower, testamentary freedom and a statutory right to judicial discretionary intervention constitute another set of values. Then there is matrimonial property. Is it to interfere in the neighbour's affairs for the 'friendly' foreign jurisdiction to offer the permanent resident of the civil law jurisdiction a sanctuary for assets comprising community property and so allow that resident to defeat spousal rights? With regard to matrimonial property rights, mainland common law jurisdictions, while otherwise supporting a much more considerable freedom of testation, may also share that sense of frustration.

On a recent occasion, a well-known member of STEP spoke to a conference audience on how in his view we should be handling the trust with our clients. He counselled that in order to forestall 'sham' and illusory trust attacks, the lawyer should explain carefully to the would-be settlor (not 'the client') what the trust can achieve and what it cannot. The settlor's plan of things for the future, said the speaker, should be carefully reviewed with him in a two-way discussion with mutual confidence. Where there are or should be concerns, the value of independent legal advice should be brought to the settlor's attention. The trust instrument when drafted should be read by the settlor, and the draftsman discuss the instrument with the settlor clause by clause. Evidence should be left in being of this process having taken place. And the following is of especial interest in the present context. Beneficiaries' rights should be respected, and the effect of exculpation clauses, the limitation of beneficiaries' rights to information, the power to add and remove beneficiaries, and the restriction of trustees' decisional powers over assets should be carefully considered before such clauses are introduced. Once the trust is in effect, the trustees in the speaker's view should discuss trust matters with the beneficiary family. This can create confidence and understanding, and often head off difficulties that left untended would lead to antagonism and *impasse*.

To that excellent advice, I can only add that the overall climate should be one of open, sensitive asset management between trustees and beneficiaries with a frank desire to meet the settlor's measured intentions, intentions that are as set out in the previously considered trust instrument.

By retaining the elements of the classic trust and ensuring that the particular trust is contemplated, planned, drafted, and carried out in this manner, I believe we will do much for the future of the trust concept. It will become a concept whose borders or practical limits are known, while civil law advocates and notaries will regard it as having a respect for the 'foreigner' both in theory and operation.

If on the other hand we of the common law world are prepared to let the trust drift on with its nature and conceptual direction the subject of debate among us, while many an onshore lawyer together with the marketing jurisdictions offshore are pushing its application to ever further limits, the concept will ultimately fold, I believe, into personification or contract or agency.

Common law codification along the lines of the Uniform Trust Code 2000 will provide some kind of focus for understanding. But that Trust Code is largely an assembly of default rules, and, save for which of those rules constitute the core elements of a trust, this is not the current worldwide problem. The Code does list core elements, and from my perspective that is good. However, we need to know very clearly how far the concept allows settlor autonomy to go, and we need to secure shape for the trust. There is no reason why we should not have in mind the contractarian view when revising trust law, but if we leave things untended so that the doctrinal uncertainties, the debate and the offshore trust continue we will probably end up having to take a route we have hitherto avoided. We will be faced, I sense, with codifying trust law. The code would likely have to be definitive, the only task being interpretation. Scope for the introduction of pre-existing case-law will exist, if at all, only when the code proves to have a *lacuna*. Is that an over-reaction?

And – putting aside for the moment the difficulties with multiple national codes, civil law style – how many governments, even advised of the need for action, are going to be prepared to allot cabinet and legislative time to vetting and seeing through a daunting trust code provision? Inevitably one is brought back to locating the common law trust firmly in a place on the spectrum, and that to my mind is at the centre with the property-based trustee/beneficiary relationship structure. However, the first step is to locate the trust on the spectrum, and that can be undertaken by the legal profession now and without government.

So for the future my fear is continued drift; my hope is for a clear concept and an enlightened manner of its application. My plea is that we realise what is happening before, as I see things, it is too late.

APPENDIX

Appendix

THE HAGUE CONVENTION ON THE LAW APPLICABLE TO TRUSTS AND ON THEIR RECOGNITION 1985

Chapter I

Scope

Article 1
This Convention specifies the law applicable to trusts and governs their recognition.

Article 2
For the purposes of this Convention, the term 'trust' refers to the legal relationship created – *inter vivos* or on death – by a person, the settlor, when assets have been placed under the control of a trustee for the benefit of a beneficiary or for a specified purpose.

A trust has the following characteristics –

(a) the assets constitute a separate fund and are not a part of the trustee's own estate;
(b) title to the trust assets stands in the name of the trustee or in the name of another person on behalf of the trustee;
(c) the trustee has the power and the duty, in respect of which he is accountable, to manage, employ or dispose of the assets in accordance with the terms of the trust and the special duties imposed upon him by law.

The reservation by the settlor of certain rights and powers, and the fact that the trustee may himself have rights as a beneficiary, are not necessarily inconsistent with the existence of a trust.

Article 3
The Convention applies only to trusts created voluntarily and evidenced in writing.

Article 4
The Convention does not apply to preliminary issues relating to the validity of wills or of other acts by virtue of which assets are transferred to the trustee.

Article 5
The Convention does not apply to the extent that the law specified by Chapter II does not provide for trusts or the category of trusts involved.

Chapter II

Applicable Law

Article 6
A trust shall be governed by the law chosen by the settlor. The choice must be express or be implied in the terms of the instrument creating or the writing evidencing the trust, interpreted, if necessary, in the light of the circumstances of the case.

Where the law chosen under the previous paragraph does not provide for trusts or the category of trust involved, the choice shall not be effective and the law specified in Article 7 shall apply.

Article 7
Where no applicable law has been chosen, a trust shall be governed by the law with which it is most closely connected.

In ascertaining the law with which a trust is most closely connected reference shall be made in particular to –

(a) the place of administration of the trust designated by the settlor;
(b) the situs of the assets of the trust;
(c) the place of residence or business of the trustee;
(d) the objects of the trust and the places where they are to be fulfilled.

Article 8
The law specified by Article 6 or 7 shall govern the validity of the trust, its construction, its effects and the administration of the trust.

In particular that law shall govern –

(a) the appointment, resignation and removal of trustees, and the devolution of the office of trustee;
(b) the rights and duties of trustees among themselves;

(c) the right of trustees to delegate in whole or in part the discharge of their duties or the exercise of their powers;
(d) the power of trustees to administer or to dispose of trust assets, to create security interests in the trust assets, or to acquire new assets;
(e) the powers of investment of trustees;
(f) restrictions upon the duration of the trust, and upon the power to accumulate the income of the trust;
(g) the relationships between the trustees and the beneficiaries including the personal liability of the trustees to the beneficiaries;
(h) the variation or termination of the trust;
(i) the distribution of the trust assets;
(j) the duty of trustees to account for their administration.

Article 9
In applying this Chapter a severable aspect of the trust, particularly matters of administration, may be governed by a different law.

Article 10
The law applicable to the validity of the trust shall determine whether that law or the law governing a severable aspect of the trust may be replaced by another law.

Chapter III

Recognition

Article 11
A trust created in accordance with the law specified by the preceding Chapter shall be recognised as a trust.

Such recognition shall imply, as a minimum, that the trust property constitutes a separate fund, that the trustee may sue and be sued in his capacity as trustee, and that he may appear or act in this capacity before a notary or any person acting in an official capacity.

In so far as the law applicable to the trust requires or provides, such recognition shall imply in particular –

(a) that personal creditors of the trustee shall have no recourse against the trust assets;
(b) that the trust assets shall not form part of the trustee's estate upon his insolvency or bankruptcy;
(c) that the trust assets shall not form part of the matrimonial property of the trustee or his spouse nor part of the trustee's estate upon his death;

(d) that the trust assets may be recovered when the trustee, in breach of trust, has mingled trust assets with his own property or has alienated trust assets. However, the rights and obligations of any third party holder of the assets shall remain subject to the law determined by the choice of law rules of the forum.

Article 12

Where the trustee desires to register assets, movable or immovable, or documents of title to them, he shall be entitled, in so far as this is not prohibited by or inconsistent with the law of the State where registration is sought, to do so in his capacity as trustee or in such other way that the existence of the trust is disclosed.

Article 13

No State shall be bound to recognise a trust the significant elements of which, except for the choice of the applicable law, the place of administration and the habitual residence of the trustee, are more closely connected with States which do not have the institution of the trust or the category of trust involved.

Article 14

The Convention shall not prevent the application of rules of law more favourable to the recognition of trusts.

Chapter IV

General Clauses

Article 15

The Convention does not prevent the application of provisions of the law designated by the conflicts rules of the forum, in so far as those provisions cannot be derogated from by voluntary act, relating in particular to the following matters –

(a) the protection of minors and incapable parties;
(b) the personal and proprietary effects of marriage;
(c) succession rights, testate and intestate, especially the indefeasible shares of spouses and relatives;
(d) the transfer of title to property and security interests in property;
(e) the protection of creditors in matters of insolvency;
(f) the protection, in other respects, of third parties acting in good faith.

If recognition of a trust is prevented by application of the preceding paragraph, the court shall try to give effect to the objects of the trust by other means.

Article 16

The Convention does not prevent the application of those provisions of the law of the forum which must be applied even to international situations, irrespective of rules of conflict of laws.

If another State has a sufficiently close connection with a case then, in exceptional circumstances, effect may also be given to rules of that State which have the same character as mentioned in the preceding paragraph.

Any Contracting State may, by way of reservation, declare that it will not apply the second paragraph of this article.

Article 17

In the Convention the word 'law' means the rules of law in force in a State other than its rules of conflict of laws.

Article 18

The provisions of the Convention may be disregarded when their application would be manifestly incompatible with public policy.

Article 19

Nothing in the Convention shall prejudice the powers of States in fiscal matters.

Article 20

Any Contracting State may, at any time, declare that the provisions of the Convention will be extended to trusts declared by judicial decisions.

This declaration shall be notified to the Ministry of Foreign Affairs of the Kingdom of the Netherlands and will come into effect on the day when this notification is received.

Article 31 is applicable to the withdrawal of this declaration in the same way as it applies to a denunciation of the Convention.

Article 21

Any Contracting State may reserve the right to apply the provisions of Chapter III only to trusts the validity of which is governed by the law of a Contracting State.

Article 22

The Convention applies to trusts regardless of the date on which they were created.

Article 23

For the purpose of identifying the law applicable under the Convention, where a State comprises several territorial units each of which has its own rules of law in respect of trusts, any reference to the law of that State is to be construed as referring to the law in force in the territorial unit in question.

Article 24
A State within which different territorial units have their own rules of law in respect of trusts is not bound to apply the Convention to conflicts solely between the laws of such units.

Article 25
The Convention shall not affect any other international instrument containing provisions on matters governed by this Convention to which a Contracting State is, or becomes, a Party.

Chapter V

Final Clauses

Article 26
Any State may, at the time of signature, ratification, acceptance, approval or accession, or at the time of making a declaration in terms of Article 29, make the reservations provided for in Articles 16, 21 and 22.

No other reservation shall be permitted.

Any Contracting State may at any time withdraw a reservation which it has made; the reservation shall cease to have effect on the first day of the third calendar month after notification of the withdrawal.

Article 27
The Convention shall be open for signature by the States which were Members of the Hague Conference on Private International Law at the time of its Fifteenth Session.

It shall be ratified, accepted or approved and the instruments of ratification, acceptance or approval shall be deposited with the Ministry of Foreign Affairs of the Kingdom of the Netherlands.

Article 28
Any other State may accede to the Convention after it has entered into force in accordance with Article 30, paragraph 1.

The instrument of accession shall be deposited with the Ministry of Foreign Affairs of the Kingdom of the Netherlands.

The accession shall have effect only as regards the relations between the acceding State and those Contracting States which have not raised an objection to its accession in the twelve months after the receipt of the notification referred to in Article 32. Such an objection may also be raised by Member States at the time when they ratify, accept or approve the Convention after an accession. Any such objection shall be notified to the Ministry of Foreign Affairs of the Kingdom of the Netherlands.

Article 29

If a State has two or more territorial units in which different systems of law are applicable, it may at the time of signature, ratification, acceptance, approval or accession declare that this Convention shall extend to all of its territorial units or only to one or more of them and may modify this declaration by submitting another declaration at any time.

Any such declaration shall be notified to the Ministry of Foreign Affairs of the Kingdom of the Netherlands and shall state expressly the territorial units to which the Convention applies.

If a State makes no declaration under this article, the Convention is to extend to all territorial units of that State.

Article 30

The Convention shall enter into force on the first day of the third calendar month after the deposit of the third instrument of ratification, acceptance or approval referred to in Article 27.

Thereafter the Convention shall enter into force –

(a) for each State ratifying, accepting or approving it subsequently, on the first day of the third calendar month after the deposit of its instrument of ratification, acceptance or approval;
(b) for each acceding State, on the first day of the third calendar month after the expiry of the period referred to in Article 28;
(c) for a territorial unit to which the Convention has been extended in conformity with Article 29, on the first day of the third calendar month after the notification referred to in that article.

Article 31

Any Contracting State may denounce this Convention by a formal notification in writing addressed to the Ministry of Foreign Affairs of the Kingdom of the Netherlands, depositary of the Convention.

The denunciation takes effect on the first day of the month following the expiration of six months after the notification is received by the depositary or on such later date as is specified in the notification.

Article 32

The Ministry of Foreign Affairs of the Kingdom of the Netherlands shall notify the States Members of the Conference, and the States which have acceded in accordance with Article 28, of the following –

(a) the signatures and ratifications, acceptances or approvals referred to in Article 27;
(b) the date on which the Convention enters into force in accordance with Article 30;
(c) the accessions and the objections raised to accessions referred to in Article 28;
(d) the extensions referred to in Article 29;
(e) the declarations referred to in Article 20;
(f) the reservations or withdrawals referred to in Article 26;
(g) the denunciations referred to in Article 31.

In witness whereof the undersigned, being duly authorised thereto, have signed this Convention.

Index

References are to paragraph numbers.